Law and Practice of the Common Commercial Policy

The First 10 years after the Treaty of Lisbon

Edited by

Michael Hahn and Guillaume Van der Loo

BRILL
NIJHOFF

LEIDEN | BOSTON

Cover illustration: "Charlemagne Building", Brussels, June 2020. Courtesy of Guillaume Van der Loo and Michael Hahn.

Library of Congress Cataloging-in-Publication Data

Names: Hahn, Michael J., editor. | Van der Loo, Guillaume, editor.
Title: Law and practice of the common commercial policy : the first 10 years after the Treaty of Lisbon / edited by Michael Hahn and Guillaume Van der Loo.
Description: Boston : Brill, 2020. | Series: Studies in EU external relations, 1875-0451 ; volume 18 | Includes bibliographical references and index. | Summary: Law and Practice of the Common Commercial Policy provides a critical analysis of the European Union (EU)'s trade law and policy since the Treaty of Lisbon. In particular, it analyses the salient changes brought by the Treaty of Lisbon to the Common Commercial Policy (CCP), focussing on the relevant case law of the Court of Justice of the European Union (ECJ), EU free trade agreements, investment protection, trade defence, institutional developments and the nexus between the CCP and other EU policies.
Identifiers: LCCN 2020037609 | ISBN 9789004393400 (hardback) | ISBN 9789004393417 (v. 18 ; ebook)
Subjects: LCSH: European Union countries–Common Commercial Policy. | Treaty on European Union (1992 February 7). Protocols, etc. (2007 December 13) | Treaty Establishing the European Economic Community (1957 March 25) | Court of Justice (Court of Justice of the European Union) | Constitutional law–European Union countries–Sources. | European Union countries–Economic integration.
Classification: LCC KJE2045 .L39 2020 | DDC 346.2407–dc23
LC record available at https://lccn.loc.gov/2020037609

Typeface for the Latin, Greek, and Cyrillic scripts: "Brill". See and download: brill.com/brill-typeface.

ISSN 1875-0451
ISBN 978-90-04-39340-0 (hardback)
ISBN 978-90-04-39341-7 (e-book)

Law and Practice of the Common Commercial Policy

Studies in EU External Relations

Edited by

Marc Maresceau (*Ghent University*)

VOLUME 18

The titles published in this series are listed at *brill.com/seur*

Contents

PART 1
The Scope of the CCP

PART 2
The EU's Investment Policies

Acknowledgements

The publication of this volume on the law and practice of the EU's Common Commercial Policy was made possible by the generosity, dedication and patience of all the contributing authors. Everything good about this book is the result of their enthusiasm, expertise, intellectual work and – as often the case with comprehensive volumes – patience: we are deeply grateful to all of them. Unless indicated otherwise, the chapters reflect the state of play as of January 2020.

Without the generous financial support of Van Bael & Bellis and VVGB Advocaten, the Brussels kick-off for this project, a workshop at which draft versions of most chapters included were presented and discussed, would not have been possible. The workshop also benefitted from the generous support from CEPS, the European Institute from Ghent University and the University of Bern's Institute for European and International Economic Law & World Trade Institute. We are also indebted to former Commissioner for Trade and WTO Director-General Pascal Lamy and Maria Åsenius, former Head of Cabinet of Commissioner Cecilia Malmström for their well-received keynote speeches on that occasion.

Chairman Bernd Lange and Director-General Sabine Weyand accepted our invitation to write forewords to this book. We are very grateful for their stimulating contribution and their kind words.

This book benefitted greatly from the editorial support by the Institute of European and International Economic Law team, consisting of Rachel Liechti, Laura Alper, Laurianne Junod, Andreas Gschwend and Dominik Reichle, as well as from Brill's SEUR team, in particular Anipa Baitakova, Ingeborg van der Laan and Marie Sheldon.

Both editors would like to thank their admired teacher Marc Maresceau for his continued support for this project. Last but by no means least, the editors would like to thank Jacques Bourgeois and Inge Govaere. With the benefit of hindsight, it seems clear that their kind invitation and hosting of Michael Hahn as Marcel-Storme-Visiting Professor and introduction to Guillaume Van der Loo in Ghent was the start of this project.

Michael Hahn
Guillaume Van der Loo

Forewords

Sabine Weyand
Director-General for Trade, European Commission

The Treaty of Lisbon represented a once in a generation reset of the EU's trade and investment policy. Effectively, it transformed trade into a truly European competence, providing the foundation for the EU to become the global trade and investment powerhouse it is today.

As the Common Commercial Policy (CCP) continues its transformation into a frontline European policy, highly important both in its own right and through its impact across the policy nexus, this book can serve as a "go-to" reference point for academics, researchers, policymakers and students of the European Union for years to come.

In a similar way to Opinion 1/94 on the WTO Agreement in the mid-1990s, the Treaty of Lisbon provided the basis for the EU to play its full role in the shaping of international trade and investment policy. It achieved this by completing the process – which had been taking place in fits and starts since 1957 – of transferring to EU level the competences which the EU's competitors wield.

Key in this has been the *Europeanisation* of trade competences regarding services, commercial aspects of intellectual property, and investment, which now join trade in goods as Union's exclusive competences. The EU now speaks with one voice on these matters at an international level, bringing its considerable heft to bear on crucial debates and acting decisively when legislative or treaty-making activity is required.

The second key stage of the post-Lisbon journey was Opinion 2/15, which joined the dots to create EU-only trade agreements. Whilst the Treaty of Lisbon was a significant step forward, it did not provide complete clarity in this regard.

It was, perhaps, inevitable that the agreement reached in the Constitutional Convention (which eventually led to the Treaty of Lisbon) would lead to debates on the precise extent of the transfer of competence.

This did indeed transpire to be the case, particularly in two fundamental areas of the EU's future trade and investment policy: trade and sustainable development (TSD) and investment. Between the entry into force of the Treaty of Lisbon and the rendering of Opinion 2/15 in May 2017, there was an ongoing tension between the Council and the Commission as to the exact contours of the Union's competence in these matters.

This manifested itself whenever the Commission made a proposal to the Council which touched on either one of these matters, leading the Commission to eventually request an Opinion from the Court as regards the Singapore FTA. The Court's Opinion confirmed the nature of the shift. Most importantly, it confirmed that the EU had exclusive competence for trade and sustainable development (TSD) matters and for foreign direct investment (albeit not for ISDS and portfolio investments).

This confirmation permits the Union to include TSD chapters in EU-level agreements and to ensure that these are ratified only at EU level, giving the EU a leading voice in developing a coherent approach to sustainability in its trade agreements.

Just as importantly, the Court confirmed that the Union had exclusive competence for investment market access and for investment protection rules (and shared competence for investment dispute settlement and portfolio investment).

This gives the Union a clear set of powers to act in the field of investment policy, an area which has received increased attention from policymakers in recent years.

Looking to the future, the European Union is taking steps to build on the foundations provided by Lisbon.

The Union's strength as a trading power is highlighted by the number of agreements it continues to sign and bring into force with partners around the world. Notable examples include the comprehensive deals with Japan and Canada.

The economic data is overwhelmingly positive in relation to the benefits of this trade agenda: estimates show that one in seven EU jobs is directly or indirectly supported by exports.

However, in the increasingly interconnected global economy, trade is by common consensus about much more than trade.

Recognising that "with great power comes great responsibility," European leaders are moving towards a view that the strength of the EU trade and investment policy should be leveraged for wider geopolitical goals, helping to defend European interests at home and abroad.

The Commission is notably reinforcing its implementation and enforcement agenda, both inside the Single Market and across the Union's worldwide network of trading relationships. This encompasses a mix of offensive and defensive tools, such as increased investment screening and measures to address the distortive effects of foreign subsidies within the Single Market, and internationally, stronger measures to help EU exporters gain more value from partner markets, and stronger enforcement of TSD commitments, notably on climate action and labour rights. With the clarifications brought by the Court in Opinion 2/15 regarding TSD this can advance on a solid base.

The CCP was already moving in an increasingly geostrategic direction before the Covid-19 pandemic struck. The unprecedented nature of the crisis – with its devastating health, social and economic impact – only served to boost the momentum and support behind this approach.

The coronavirus political environment accelerated changes and shifts that were already in evidence before the pandemic, including widespread calls for protectionism, stronger state intervention in the economy, economic nationalism and the rejection of global institutions.

The European Commission therefore adopted a twin-track approach to evolving the CCP, doubling down on its commitment to openness, global cooperation and rules-based multilateralism, while launching a root-and-branch review of the policy to assess where it could be reinvigorated to deal with the unique conflagration of new challenges.

The next evolution of the CCP, then, is centred around a bespoke EU trade policy approach for the post-coronavirus global economy, based on the concept of "Open Strategic Autonomy".

In essence, this means reaffirming the CCP's contribution to Europe's global leadership ambitions across a range of areas, in line with the aims of a more geopolitical European Commission;

"Open Strategic Autonomy" juxtaposes the need to build stronger alliances with like-minded partners and the need to shape a fairer and more sustainable globalisation based on strong and up-to-date multilateral rules, with a tougher, more assertive approach to protect European businesses and consumers, notably through stronger trade defence and enforcement, and through the diversification of supply chains to assure strategic independence.

With this latest evolution, the CCP continues to widen and deepen its significance and influence as a truly European policy, and this very welcome publication will provide a helpful compendium for the scholars and policymakers charged with its future development.

Bernd Lange
Chair of the Committee on International Trade, European Parliament

Trade Policy Since the Entry into Force of the Treaty of Lisbon

This book traces the development of the 'Common Commercial Policy' in the last 10 years, and editors and authors merit praise for their remarkable work: Indeed, the Treaty of Lisbon marks a fundamental shift in the evolution of the European Union's trade policy. It formalises the European nature of this policy field – for which the added value of a 'common' approach has been undeniable since 1957 – by subjecting the Common Commercial Policy to the full participation of the European Parliament. Europe is only strong when we speak with one voice on the global stage, and what better way to leverage the power of our common market than by representing it with a common stance when engaging with the rest of the world. Especially during times in which the global, rules-based order is under attack, the world needs a champion of values-based trade to defend the rule of law – an actor whose actions are based on a strong democratic mandate and whose executive is scrutinised by the directly elected Members of the European Parliament and the governments of EU Member states represented in the European Council.

Empowerment of the European Parliament

The Treaty of Lisbon turned the European Parliament into a fully-fledged co-legislator and thereby into a decisive actor on the trade policy stage. This marked a fundamental shift in how this institution and the Members of parliament engaged in this policy field. On the basis of Article 218 TFEU, the Parliament's approval of all trade agreements is now required. While this is primarily a change of internal EU institutional competence, granting Parliament competences where it used to have none, it meant *de facto* a substantial transfer of competence from the national level to the Union level. I remember very well how a Secretary of State of a Member state government called me after the Lisbon Treaty entered into force and asked me whether this transfer of competence was really to be understood in this way.

The European Parliament had to define its role, ambitions and positions and establish ways of engaging with other institutions, governments of EU Member states and those of third countries. This did not happen overnight.

Before the Lisbon Treaty, trade policy was, in the European Parliament, an appendix of industrial policy: During the 1990s, the Committee on Industry, External Trade, Research and Energy was in charge. The need to give trade policy a stronger weight was recognized by Parliament with the establishment of a separate committee and by engaging in a constant dialogue with those responsible in the Convention for a European Constitution, which then led to the Lisbon Treaty. Representative of the Parliament's commitment was Enrique Barón Crespo, who was also chairman of the new Committee on International Trade from 2004 to 2007.

Meanwhile, the European Parliament, led by the Committee on International Trade, has become a very active player in the world of trade and has ensured that the voices of citizens are not drowned out in this complex policy landscape.

Cooperation with other institutions, Member states, and third countries has become a regular feature of the day-to-day work of the INTA committee. The European Parliament has continuously fought for – and won – new rights in all phases of the common commercial policy. The main instrument for this was the inter-institutional framework agreement of 2010, which Parliament and the Commission concluded to fill their bilateral relations with substance. In it, the Commission committed itself to information and consultation routines vis-à-vis Parliament. For the phase prior to the Council's mandate to start negotiations of international trade agreements, a *de facto* informal right of consultation applies.

We have established an excellent working relationship with the European Commission's Directorate General for Trade based on the understanding that at the end of the day, we all work for the benefit of the citizens of the European Union but also because both the European Parliament and the Commission share the broad view that a European approach is the best way forward, in contrast to the Council which is often more oriented towards national interests. The Commission is fully aware of the fact that without a positive vote in the plenary of the European Parliament, no trade agreement or trade legislation will ever see the light of day.

This does not mean that we always see eye to eye, far from it. The Parliament has clashed with Commission and Member States on numerous occasions, most notably in 2012, when it proved that it would not shy away from voting down agreements that it considered lacking in substance or going against the interests of citizens. The most famous agreement which did not pass the test was the Anti-Counterfeiting Trade Agreement, also known by its acronym ACTA. For the first time, Parliament has made use of its right under the Lisbon Treaty to reject an international trade agreement. 478 MEPs voted against

ACTA, 39 in favour. 165 MEP s abstained. ACTA had become a symbol of pre-Lisbon intransparent backroom policies which parliamentarians clearly rejected. With this vote, the European Parliament had truly arrived on the trade stage.

Following up on the ACTA controversy, INTA pushed hard to increase transparency. Today, trade policy affects entirely new areas about which there is more need for public debate than was the case, when the crux of trade policy consisted in lowering tariffs. Transparency is therefore an absolute imperative; an intensive debate with civil society is equally so. In that context, I have secured acceptance for vital improvements: access to EU negotiating documents is markedly better, all MEP s have equal and full access to them, EU negotiating proposals are now published on the websites of the European Commission, minutes of negotiating meetings are made public, and a standing civil-society advisory group has been set up, among a host of other improvements.

The European Parliament has pushed for its own priorities on numerous other occasions. The current focus on trade and sustainable development would be unthinkable without the European Parliament championing this particular aspect of trade policy. The link between trade and labour and environmental standards is highlighted not only in the EU's trade agreements, but also in many regulations, most notably in the EU's Generalised System of Preferences, which requires the adherence to 27 international conventions in return for improved access to the European market.

The protection of investments through the use of Investor-State Dispute Settlement (ISDS) provisions marked a major clash at the beginning of the Juncker Commission's mandate. A majority of members of the European Parliament made clear that it rejected ISDS on grounds of far-reaching provisions protecting the rights of investors and their impact on the right of states to regulate, lack of transparency in proceedings and stipulations for the conducts and selection of arbitrators.

The vehicle used to deliver this message to the world was the European Parliament's resolution on the ill-fated Transatlantic Trade and Investment Partnership (TTIP) negotiations between the EU and the USA. In July 2015, the European Parliament adopted its recommendations to the European Commission for the negotiations with the USA on TTIP by 436 votes to 241 with 32 abstentions. As rapporteur and Chairman of the Committee on International Trade, I justified my position as follows:

> We are experiencing unprecedented globalisation and our citizens and businesses are in the midst of it. As MEP s, it is our democratic duty to play a leading role in this process. If this process is to benefit the whole population, we cannot allow the negotiators to act alone. That is why we

have [...] set out our guidelines for the type of trade agreement that the Commission should be advocating in the negotiations.

These guidelines led to an overhaul of the European Union's investment policy and a new approach to balance the rights of investors with the legitimate objective of states to regulate in the public interest. It was totally clear that a trade agreement with Canada (CETA) with an old style ISDS would not have had a chance of getting passed by the European Parliament. Working with other Social-Democrats, I have resolutely opposed private arbitration panels, which are not transparent, and, in the face of fierce resistance, I have secured acceptance for refocusing European investment policy. In the long term, we are committed to the establishment of a multilateral arbitration tribunal with an appeal chamber and independent judges. With my close personal involvement, we even managed to secure inclusion of those provisions in CETA, even after negotiations on the text had officially been concluded. The system that emerged, known as Investment Court System, has become the only acceptable dispute resolution mechanism for the EU's investment treaties from thereon and hopefully the foundation for a multilateral investment court.

As co-legislator, the European Parliament is also fully involved in the legislative process and has turned out to be a strong negotiator in its final phases, during the so-called trilogue, when Parliament's negotiating team, the Council presidency and Commission representatives meet to find a compromise that is acceptable to all institutions involved. Thanks to its years of experience in these settings, and faced with a rotating presidency which often has little experience dealing directly with the European Parliament, the Parliament's team enters these talks with a built-in advantage.

New Issues

Not only the actors have changed, so have the issues and the attention of the public, both having a strong effect on the way trade policy is shaped. We have moved away from a narrow approach to trade, with a focus on trade in goods and traditional barriers to their trade such as tariffs and quotas to a much broader approach. Today, every EU trade agreement features a trade and sustainable development chapter, with provisions on labour rights and environmental standards as well as corporate social responsibility. Services and intellectual property rights are covered extensively. We try and find ways to tackle 21st century challenges, such as data flows and look for answers to the question of how the challenge between the need to protect citizens' data and enabling companies to do business across borders can be resolved. Trade remains a slow-moving policy field, due to the ever-increasing number of actors, themes and stakeholders involved, but we are making steady progress.

The rise in public attention also has had a major effect on our trade policy. While trade traditionally was a rather niche policy field, public attention spiked during the early days of the TTIP negotiations. Tens of thousands of protestors took to the streets in my home country Germany, a protest movement unimaginable only a few months before. The ensuing public discussion saw the Commission being pushed into a corner, constantly having to defend itself against an ever-increasing list of accusations, some more true than others, ranging from conducting negotiations in secret, to undermining consumer standards and enabling 'fracking' inside the European Union. This development led to a substantial increase in transparency measures, long called for by the European Parliament and other actors. The European Commission, for the first time in its history, published EU negotiating positions on its website. I was personally involved in the push for transparency, having negotiated full access to all negotiating documents for Members of the European Parliament with then trade Commissioner *Cecilia Malmström*. This access was subsequently broadened and now applies to all EU trade negotiations.

Another remarkable development during the last years is the shift towards a values-based trade policy. If economic interests and European values diverge, the latter should prevail. While reality may still be lagging behind this ambitious goal, the European Commission's 2015 "trade for all" strategy nevertheless marked a clear departure from the approach of earlier Commissions.

This has also led to active enforcement of sustainable development provisions. For the very first time, the European Commission took action under an FTA to address non-compliance with TSD chapter provisions: The case launched against South Korea in 2019 is seen by many as a watershed moment in the Union's trade policy which may lead the way towards a trading block that enforces the entirety of its agreements with the same rigor. Proceedings on withdrawing preferential market access for Cambodia for non-compliance with the 27 core conventions which are part of the GSP regulation tell the same story.

Where Is Our Trade Policy Heading in the Next Decade?

In the face of global change, measures must be developed now to shape future trade. It seems clear that the consequences of the Corona pandemic will lead to a longer-term change of the role of the state and of the EU's positioning with regard to globalization. For the development of trade policy measures, the following four principles should offer guidance.

1. The best way to maintain economic, social and political stability is the further development of the multilateral system. It is therefore important to respect the rules of the WTO and, of course, to modernise them in order to adapt them to the requirements of these times. Unlimited subsidies for the relocation of production are not in line with the GATT agreements and Article 3 of the WTO Agreement on Subsidies and Countervailing Measures. As the WTO jurisprudence has shown, WTO rules are quite clear in this respect.

2. Values-based trade policy should always have the interest of the partners in mind, especially those of the less developed countries. This is particularly important given the current trend of nationalistic, selfish reflexes and brutal economic power structures.

3. Even if the current lockdown measures result in less CO_2 emissions, the climate crisis did not disappear with the corona pandemic. If no coordinated measures will be taken, more shocks for trade and value chains seem unavoidable. In this respect, the greening of trade policy must also rank high on the agenda of post-corona recovery trade policy

4. In all trade policy measures, it must also be clear who ultimately benefits from the measures. The retrospective analysis of the 2008/2009 global financial crisis management reveals that rescue operations benefited large companies more than ordinary people. In 2017, the OECD pointed out that this exacerbated pre-existing trends towards greater inequality of wealth and income. It will be crucial to ensure that the trade policy measures developed to fight the consequences of the Coronavirus pandemic benefit all stakeholders, including workers and SMEs and do not only benefit a few companies. Only if this is achieved, public acceptance of continued open trade will be possible.

Sustainability

Europe must ensure that trade policy supports green and sustainable policies across the board. There are many levers that we have already identified. Work on a carbon border mechanism is on-going, FTA provisions on trade and its impact on the environment are becoming more detailed and robust. As the largest economic bloc in the world, I believe we must also live up to the consequences of our consumption. We cannot tolerate human rights abuses and look the other way. That is why the European Parliament has pushed for a horizontal due diligence legislation. We have started work inside our house; I expect the Commission to come forward with a legislative proposal by next year. Very recently, the EU adopted a new strategy on a European green deal. A consensus is emerging that environmental provisions should be reinforced in the trade agreements in particular when it comes to enforcement.

Implementation

A key aspect for future work will be the implementation of concluded agreements and passed legislation. Insofar, we have our work cut out for us: the at times astonishingly low utilisation rates of our trade agreements by small operators needs to be analysed; no doubt, our agreements need to become more user-friendly. We need to be vigilant in applying the Union's trade defence instruments and investment screening policies to strike the right balance between a Europe that is open for business but not naïve. Compliance of our trading partners with the entirety of our trade agreements will also be high on our agenda. The creation of the post of a 'chief trade enforcement officer' suggests that the Commission has understood the task ahead and is willing to tackle it head-on. The European Parliament will keep close watch and will do its part in guiding the work of the enforcement officer.

Coherence

Trade policy is not conducted in a vacuum, a fact we at times forget. The most striking example of lacking coherence to me are the fisheries subsidies talks at the WTO, during which the EU was a staunch supporter of cutting subsidies to new fleets and the EU's very own fishery policy, in which it calls for the exact opposite. We need to ensure better coordination between policy fields, and trade policy, with its many cross-cutting issues, must pay special attention to this need

Resilient and Fair Supply Chains

At the time of writing, the Covid-19 crisis has the world in a tight grip. The crisis has spread from its Chinese origins with incredible speed and forced major economies into shut-downs, bringing production to a stand-still, disrupting global value chains and stifling demand. It also led to trade restrictions and export bans on medical products and even foodstuffs.

The most important lesson we need to learn from the current crisis is that value chains which rely exclusively on certain countries or regions are exposed to substantial vulnerabilities. In rebuilding more resilient supply chains, companies need to ensure that labour rights are guaranteed throughout the supply chain, that there is job stability to allow proper planning and that orders are paid on time. Outsourcing economic risks at any price is not compatible with global responsibility. There is a clear need for a level playing field. And the level playing field in the internal market also calls for a uniform EU approach. Europe needs a binding supply chain law that ensures the sustainability and crisis resistance of the value creation process. It should oblige companies to carefully examine their human rights' and environmental risks and their susceptibility to crises and to take appropriate measures to prevent and mitigate such risks.

It is abundantly clear that we live in a global village. Tackling global challenges will only be effective through international cooperation. Unilateral measures, going at it alone, will ultimately harm everyone in the interconnected global village. One result of the 2008/2009 global financial crisis was the G20's undertaking to abstain from protectionist measures and to maintain the rule-based trading system. However, the necessary steps remained very limited. In view of today's challenges, the need for a fair, rule-based multilateral trading system has increased significantly.

The Corona Pandemic will not end globalisation. We have the opportunity to make it better and fairer and the European Parliament has an important role to play.

Tables

Abbreviations

AA	Association Agreement
AAS	Advanced Authorization Scheme
AB	Appellate Body
ACAA	Agreement on Conformity Assessment and Acceptance of Industrial Products
ACP	African, Caribbean and Pacific (group of countries)
ACTA	Anti-Counterfeiting Trade Agreement
AD	Anti-Dumping
ADA	WTO Anti-Dumping Agreement ("Agreement on Implementation of Article VI of the General Agreement on Tariffs and Trade 1994")
ADD	AD duty
AfCFTA	African Continental Free Trade Area
AG	Advocate General
AIFM	Alternative investment fund managers
AoA	WTO Agreement on Agriculture
AS	Anti-Subsidy
ASEAN	Association of Southeast Asian Nations
ATAA	Air Transport Association of America
ATT	Arms Trade Treaty
AWG	Aussenwirtschaftsgesetz (German Foreign Trade and Payments Act)
AWV	Aussenwirtschaftsverordnung (German Foreign Trade and Payments Ordinance)
BCR	Binding Corporate Rule
BDI	Bundesverband der Deutschen Industrie (Federation of German Industries)
BIT	Bilateral Investment Treaty
BMWi	Bundesministerium für Wirtschaft und Energie (German Federal Ministry for Economic Affairs and Energy)
BRICS	Brazil, Russia, India, China, South Africa
CA	Cooperation Agreement
CAI	Comprehensive Agreement in Investment
CAP	Common Agricultural Policy
CAPD	Cooperation Agreement on Partnership and Development
CARIFORUM	Caribbean Forum; sub-group of the African, Caribbean and Pacific group of states
CBAM	Carbon Border Adjustment Mechanism
CCP	Common Commercial Policy
CEPA	Comprehensive and Enhanced Partnership Agreement

CETA	EU-Canada Comprehensive Economic and Trade Agreement
CFIUS	Committee on Foreign Investment in the United States
CFR	Charter of Fundamental Rights
CFSP	Common Foreign and Security Policy
CITES	Convention on International Trade in Endangered Species of Wild Fauna and Flora
CPTPP	Comprehensive and Progressive Agreement for Trans-Pacific Partnership
CSF	Civil Society Forum
CTSD	Committee on Trade and Sustainable Development
CVD	Countervailing Duty
DAG	Domestic Advisory Group
DCFTA	Deep and Comprehensive Free Trade Agreement
DCIT	Ductile cast iron tubes and pipes
DDA	Doha Development Agenda
DDS	Duty Drawback Scheme
DEPBS	Duty Entitlement Passbook Scheme
DG	Directorate General
DSB	Dispute Settlement Body
DSM	Dispute Settlement Mechanism
DSU	WTO Dispute Settlement Understanding
EaP	Eastern Partnership
EBA	Everything But Arms (scheme)
ECAA	European Common Aviation Area
ECHR	European Convention on the Protection of Human Rights and Fundamental Freedoms
ECJ	Court of Justice of the European Union
ECSC	European Coal and Steel Community
ECT	Energy Charter Treaty
ECtHR	European Court of Human Rights
ECOWAS	Economic Community of West African States
EDF	European Development Fund
EEA	European Economic Area
EEAS	European External Action Service
EFSA	European Food Safety Authority
EFTA	European Free Trade Area
EIB	European Investment Bank
EMAA	Euro-Mediterranean Association Agreement
EOU	Export oriented unit
EPA	Economic Partnership Agreement
ESMA	European Securities and Markets Authority
EU	European Union

EUSFTA	European Union – Singapore Free Trade Agreement
EUZBBG	Gesetz über die Zusammenarbeit von Bundesregierung und Deutschem Bundestag in Angelegenheiten der Europäischen Union (Law on the Co-operation between the Federal Government and the German Bundestag in European Affairs)
FA	Framework Agreement
FDI	Foreign Direct Investment
FET	Fair and Equitable Treatment
FIRRMA	Foreign Investment Risk Review Modernization Act
FMS	Focus Market Scheme
FPS	Focus Product Scheme
FTA	Free Trade Agreement
GATS	General Agreement on Trade in Services
GATT	General Agreement on Tariffs and Trade 1994
GDPR	General Data Protection Regulation
GE	General Electrics
GFC	Global Financial Crisis
GI	Geographical Indication
GMO	Genetically Modified Organism
GPA	WTO Agreement on Government Procurement
GRP	Good Regulatory Practices
GSP	Generalised System of Preferences
HRIA	Human Rights Impact Assessment
HS	Harmonized System (Harmonized Commodity Description and Coding System)
IBA	International Bar Association
ICAO	International Civil Aviation Organisation
ICH	International Council for Harmonisation of Technical Requirements for Pharmaceuticals for Human Use
ICS	Investment Court System
ICSID	International Centre for Settlement of Investment Disputes
IEC	International Electrotechnical Commission
ILC	International Law Commission
ILO	International Labour Convention
INSTEX	Instrument for Supporting Trade Exchanges
INTA	International Trade Committee
IP	Investigation period
IP	Intellectual Property
IPA	Investment Protection Agreement
IPI	International Procurement Instrument
IPR	Intellectual Property Rights

ISDS	Investor-State Dispute Settlement
ISO	International Organisation for Standardisation
ITU	International Telecommunication Union
JEFTA	Japan-EU Free Trade Agreement
JCPOA	Joint Comprehensive Plan of Action
KORUS	Korea-US Free Trade Agreement
LDC	Least Developed Country
LDR	Lesser-Duty Rule
LTAR	Less than adequate remuneration
MEA	Multilateral Environmental Agreement
MES	Market Economy Status
MFN	Most-Favoured-Nation
MIC	Multilateral Investment Court
MOFCOM	Ministry of Commerce (of China)
MRA	Mutual Recognition Agreement
NAFTA	North American Free Trade Agreement
NDRC	National Development and Reform Commission of China
OECD	Organisation for Economic Co-operation and Development
PA	Partnership Agreement
PARC	Partnership Agreement on Relations and Cooperation
PCA	Partnership and Cooperation Agreement
PDCA	Political Dialogue and Cooperation Agreement
PTA	Preferential Trade Agreement
QMV	Qualified Majority Voting
REACH	Regulation (EC) No 1907/2006 on Registration, Evaluation, Authorisation and Restriction of Chemicals
RTA	Regional Trade Agreement
SAA	Stabilisation and Association Agreement
SACU	Southern African Customs Union
SADC	Southern African Development Community
SCC	Standard contractual clauses
SCM	WTO Agreement on Subsidies and Countervailing Measures
SDGS	Sustainable Development Goals
SDoC	Supplier's Declaration of Conformity
SEM	Single European Market
SEZ	Special economic zone
SIA	Sustainability Impact Assessment
SME	Small and medium sized enterprises
SOE	State-owned enterprise
SPS	WTO Agreement on the Application of Sanitary and Phytosanitary Measures

SWIFT	Society for Worldwide Interbank Financial Telecommunication
TBT	WTO Agreement on Technical Barriers to Trade
TDI	Trade Defence Instruments
TEC	Treaty Establishing the European Community
TEU	Treaty on European Union
TFEU	Treaty on the Functioning of the European Union
TiSA	Trade in Services Agreement
TPC	Trade Policy Committee (of the Council of the European Union)
TPP	Trans-Pacific Partnership Agreement (now CPTPP, Comprehensive and Progressive Agreement for Trans-Pacific Partnership)
TRIPS	WTO Agreement on Trade-Related Aspects of Intellectual Property Rights
TSD	Trade and Sustainable Development
TSIA	Trade Sustainability Impact Assessment
TTIP	Transatlantic Trade and Investment Partnership
UN	United Nations
UNGA	United Nations General Assembly
UNCED	United Nations Conference on Environment and Development
UNCITRAL	United Nations Commission on International Trade Law
UNCTAD	United Nations Conference on Trade and Development
UNECE	United Nations Economic Commission for Europe
UNSCEGHS	United Nations Sub-Committee of Experts on the Globally Harmonized System of Classification and Labelling of Chemicals
USMCA	United States-Mexico-Canada Agreement
VAT	Value Added Tax
VCLT	Vienna Convention on the Law of Treaties
VCLTIO	Vienna Convention on the Law of Treaties between States and International Organizations or between International Organizations
WIPO	World Intellectual Property Organization
WTO	World Trade Organization
WTO GPA	World Trade Organization Agreement on Government Procurement
WTO SCM Agreement	World Trade Organization Agreement on Subsidies and Countervailing Measures
WTO TRIPS Agreement	World Trade Organization Agreement on Trade-Related Aspects of Intellectual Property Rights

Notes on Contributors

Andrej Auersperger Matić
is a member of the Legal Service of the European Parliament, with over fifteen years' experience as a lawyer working in and with European institutions. He specialises in European, human rights and trade law and holds degrees from the University of Ljubljana, Yale Law School and Maastricht University.

Fabian Blandfort
is a research assistant at the Chair for public law, European law and public international law of Professor Marc Bungenberg at Saarland University. He completed his law degree at Saarland University (First State Exam) at the top of his class, specialising in European Union and public international law as well as human rights protection law. His main fields of research are international investment law and European Union law.

Jacques Bourgeois
is senior legal adviser at Sidley Austin, guest professor at Ghent University (Jean Monnet Centre of Excellence) and professor at the College of Europe (Bruges). Prior to entering private practice, Jacques served for over 25 years as a senior official with the European Commission, joining its Legal Service in 1965. From 1987 to 1991, he was the principal legal adviser of the Commission in charge of foreign trade policy and, later, antitrust policy. Previously, he served for several years as head of the Trade Policy Instruments Division in the Directorate-General for External Relations, and was responsible for the implementation of the EU's regulations on anti-dumping and subsidies, as well as for safeguard measures and protection against illicit commercial practices.

Colin M. Brown
is an international trade and investment lawyer and since 2013 Deputy Head of Unit of Unit F.2 – Dispute Settlement and Legal Aspects of Trade Policy in the Directorate General for Trade of the European Commission. He leads the team of lawyers working on investor-state dispute settlement in the trade and investment policy of the European Union. He is the lead EU delegate to UN-CITRAL Working group III on ISDS reform. He also leads the teams providing legal advice on EU FTAs, including the EU-Japan Economic Partnership Agreement (EPA), the Comprehensive Economic and Trade Agreement (CETA) with Canada and the Transatlantic Trade and Partnership Agreement (TTIP). Before joining DG Trade in October 2006 he worked for 6 years for the Legal Service of

the European Commission, where he litigated WTO and EU law cases. He has been chair of the Legal Advisory Committee of the Energy Charter Treaty between 2004 and 2017. He is guest lecturer in EU External Economic Relations Law at the Law School of the University of Edinburgh and has taught EU and WTO law at IELPO, University of Barcelona and the Université catholique de Louvain.

Marc Bungenberg

is Director of the Europa-Institut and a professor of public law, European law and public international law at Saarland University in Germany, visiting professor at the University of Lausanne/Switzerland. Marc received his doctorate in law from the University of Hannover and wrote his habilitation treatise at the Friedrich-Schiller-University Jena. He holds an LL.M. from Lausanne University. His main fields of research are European (Common Commercial Policy, public procurement and state aid law) and international economic law, particularly international investment and WTO law.

Merijn Chamon

is Assistant Professor of EU Law at Maastricht University. Previously he was a postdoctoral Research Fellow of the Flemish Research Foundation (FWO) at the Ghent European Law Institute (Ghent University) where he also obtained his PhD. Merijn has a broad interest in EU law with a specific focus on EU constitutional law, EU institutional law and the law of EU external relations.

Barbara Cooreman

leads the sustainability and trade policy practices at Hanover Brussels, advising organizations across a variety of business sectors on the political and regulatory environments in order to develop and implement advocacy and reputation strategies and campaigns targeting both EU policymakers and stakeholder audiences. Before joining Hanover, Barbara worked at the Aerospace & Defence Industries Association of Europe (ASD) on EU and international environmental and energy policy. She started her career in academia as a researcher and lecturer in EU and WTO law. She holds a PhD in international trade law and EU environmental law.

Marise Cremona

is Professor Emeritus at the European University Institute, Florence. She was Professor of European Law and a co-Director of the Academy of European Law at the European University Institute (2006 – 2017). She was Head of the

Department of Law at the EUI (2009–2012) and President *ad interim* of the EUI (2012–2013). She is a member of the Editorial Board of the Common Market Law Review. Her research interests are in the external relations law of the European Union, in particular the constitutional basis for EU external relations law and the legal and institutional dimensions of EU foreign policy.

Philippe De Baere

is managing partner of Van Bael & Bellis' Brussels office. His practice focuses on EU and international trade law. He has been involved in most major EU trade defence proceedings since 1990 and has represented numerous clients before the European Commission, the Court of Justice of the European Union and the WTO Appellate Body. He frequently advises sovereign clients during their FTA negotiations with the EU or on Brexit-related matters. Philippe regularly lectures on EU Trade Law at the University Carlos III in Madrid and the Catholic University of Leuven (KUL).

Juhi Dion Sud

is a partner at VVGB Advocaten. Her practice focuses on EU and international trade law and WTO law. Ms. Sud obtained her LL.M. from Vrije Universiteit Brussel (summa cum laude) and LL.B. from the Faculty of Law, Delhi University. She holds a B.A. in History from St. Stephens College, Delhi. She has authored many articles.

Bart Driessen

reads law in Nijmegen and Budapest and received a Ph.D. in EU law from the University of Leuven (2006). Between 1994 and 2000 he worked as a trade lawyer in private practice, with a one-year interlude in DG TRADE. For the last two decades Dr Driessen has been a member of the Legal Service of the Council of the EU, dealing with institutional matters and external relations. Since 2016 Dr Driessen is the legal adviser to the Trade Policy Committee. He has been an agent for the Council in well over 200 cases before the Union courts, including in Opinion 2/15 (Singapore FTA) and the Opinion 1/17 (ICS).

Sophie Gappa

Sophie Gappa has been serving as a civil servant since 2014 in different functions in the German Federal Ministry for Economic Affairs and Energy. She has been working in the Ministry's division for trade policy for several years and – in this function – has been a member of the Trade Policy Committee (Deputies). She holds a PhD degree from the University of Münster.

Attila Gerhäuser

is Director at the German Tax Adviser Association in Berlin. Previously he worked in Brussels as Head of EU Office of the German Chemical Industry Association and as Policy Adviser in the Internal Market Committee of the European Parliament. Attila obtained his LL.M. from the Europa-Institut (University Saarland) with a special focus on EU trade law and internal market law.

Sieglinde Gstöhl

is Director of the Department of EU International Relations and Diplomacy Studies at the College of Europe in Bruges, where she has been Professor since 2005. From 1999–2005 she was Assistant Professor of International Relations at Humboldt University Berlin. She holds a PhD and an MA in International Relations from the Graduate Institute of International and Development Studies in Geneva as well as a degree in Public Affairs from the University of St. Gallen. Her recent books include The Proliferation of Privileged Partnerships between the European Union and its Neighbours (ed. with D. Phinnemore, Routledge, 2019); The European Union's Evolving External Engagement: Towards New Sectoral Diplomacies? (ed. with S. Schunz and C. Damro, Routledge, 2018); The Trade Policy of the European Union (with D. De Bièvre, Palgrave, 2018); and Theorizing the European Neighbourhood Policy (ed. with S. Schunz, Routledge, 2017).

Michael Hahn

is Professor of Law at the University of Bern, Managing Director of its Institute of European and International Economic Law and a Director at its World Trade Institute; he is also an Honorary Professor at the University of Waikato School of Law. He holds degrees from the University of Heidelberg and the University of Michigan Law School. Michael is on the list of arbitrators for CETA, CPTPP and the SADC-EU Economic Partnership Agreement and teaches, researches and consults on international trade law, Swiss-EU bilateral relations and EU external relations law.

Joni Heliskoski

is Acting Justice at the Supreme Administrative Court of Finland. From 2010 to 2019 he was Director of EU Litigation at the Ministry for Foreign Affairs and the Agent of the Government of Finland before the Court of Justice of the European Union. He has also worked as an expert on EU law at the Ministry of Justice, the Prime Minister's Office and the Permanent Representation of Finland to the European Union. Dr Heliskoski is also Adjunct Professor of International

Law at the University of Helisinki. He has published extensively on external relations law of the EU.

Frank Hoffmeister

studied law in Frankfurt, Geneva and Heidelberg (1989–1994) and received a PhD at the Max-Planck-Institute for Foreign Public Law and International Law (1998). Between 1998 and 2001 he researched and taught as University Assistant at the Walter Hallstein-Institute for European Constitutional Law at the Humboldt-University in Berlin. He then entered the European Commission, first as Cyprus desk at DG Enlargement and afterwards as a member of the Legal Service, where he specialised on international law and WTO issues. From 2010–2014, he served as the Deputy Head of Cabinet of EU Trade Commissioner De Gucht, and as of 2015 he is Head of Unit dealing with anti-dumping at DG Trade. Besides, Frank teaches international economic law at the Free University University of Brussels and has published numerous articles on European and international law topics. He also co-authored 'The Law of EU External Relations – Cases, Materials and Commentary on the EU as an International Legal Actor' (OUP 3rd edition 2020) together with J Wouters, G de Baere and T Ramopoulos.

David Kleimann

is a Post-Doctoral Fellow at the Foreign Policy Institute of Johns Hopkins School of Advanced International Studies in Washington DC and a member of the Executive Council of the Society for International Economic Law (SIEL). His research focuses on international trade law, EU external economic relations law, and trade policy. David has earned his PhD in European, International, and Comparative Laws at the European University Institute (EUI) in Florence, Italy, where he defended his thesis on 'The Transformation of EU External Economic Governance'. He holds a 1st of class Masters degree in International Law and Economics (MILE) from the World Trade Institute (WTI) in Berne, Switzerland, and an LL.M in International Law (with distinction) from Kent Law School in Brussels, Belgium. David has served as a policy advisor to the Chairman of the European Parliament's Committee for International Trade (INTA), Bernd Lange. He has taught WTO law at the law department of the University of Mannheim, Germany. He also acted as a consultant to the World Bank's International Trade Department and the EU – China Trade Project in 2014. In 2009/10 he coordinated the trade policy project of the German Marshall Fund of the United States (GMFUS) in Brussels.

Sam Koplewicz

is the Deputy Voter Protection Director for the Florida Democratic Party. He received a BA in Public Policy from Brown University and JD from Harvard Law School. Before law school, Koplewicz studied Croatia's change in money laundering law enforcement while the country was joining the EU as a Fulbright Scholar. Following law school, Koplewicz worked for Human Rights Watch in Beirut, Lebanon as Harvard Law Human Rights Satter Fellow. He returned to Croatia as a visiting professor at Zagreb University's faculty of law. Koplewicz also spent time in Amman, Jordan as the Policy and Advocacy Adviser for Oxfam's Syria Crisis Response. He has conducted research and taught on EU migration and foreign policy.

Pieter Jan Kuijper

is Professor emeritus of the Law of International (Economic) Organizations at the Faculty of Law of the University of Amsterdam (UvA), the Netherlands. Prior to his appointment at the UvA, he was principal Legal Advisor and Director of the 'External Relations and International Trade' team of the Legal Service of the European Commission (2002–2007) and Director of the Legal Affairs Division of the Secretariat of the World Trade Organization (1999–2002). Most recently he is one of the editors of and author of four chapters in *The Law of the European Union,* Kluwer Law International, Alphen a/d Rijn 2018.

Martin Lutz

German Federal Ministry for Economic Affairs and Energy, joined the Trade Policy Unit in 2011. He was the German representative in the Trade Policy Committee (Deputies) from 2011 to 2016. Since 2016 Co-Head of the Trade Policy Unit.

Bregt Natens

is an associate in Sidley's international trade group. He advises clients on EU and international trade issues, including in EU and WTO litigation and on trade remedies, customs rules, and market access and regulatory barriers. Prior to joining Sidley, Bregt gained experience in the Legal Affairs Division of the WTO, assisting a Panel in dispute settlement proceedings. He also was a researcher at the University of Leuven (Belgium), where his research and teaching activities focused on EU and WTO law, with a particular emphasis on trade in services. Bregt is a regular lecturer and speaker at international conferences. His research has been published in leading journals, and he published a monograph on international and EU trade in services with Edward Elgar.

Tamara Perišin

is Judge at the General Court of the European Union. Prior to this, she was Jean Monnet Professor of EU and WTO law at the University of Zagreb, and John Harvey Gregory Visiting Professor of Law and World Organization at Harvard Law School. Perišin graduated cum laude at Zagreb. As a Chevening scholar, she earned the degree of Magister Juris in European and Comparative Law at the Faculty of Law, University of Oxford, St. Edmund Hall and completed her PhD at the University of Zagreb, defending her thesis before an international committee. As part of her doctoral and postdoctoral research, Tamara Perišin studied: as a visiting researcher at the Asser College Europe, T.M.C. Asser Institute, The Hague; as a Fulbright scholar, at the Georgetown University, Washington D.C. and at the University of Michigan Law School, Ann Arbor, MI; as a Scholarship of Teaching and Learning Fellow at the Central European University, Budapest; as a research fellow at the Max Planck Institute for Comparative Public Law and International Law, Heidelberg; and as a postdoctoral visiting researcher at Harvard Law School, Cambridge, MA. Perišin was a member of the negotiating team for the accession of Croatia to the European Union. She has passed the Croatian bar exam and has been responsible for providing training on EU law to judges, practising lawyers, civil servants and diplomats. She served as Special Adviser to the Ministry of Science and Education and was editor-in-chief of a journal on EU law. She has authored and edited several books and numerous articles.

Reinhard Quick

is honorary professor for international economic law at Saarland University, Saarbrücken. Before his retirement he worked for more than thirty years as lobbyist for the European and German Chemical Industry Associations. Reinhard studied law at the Universities of Mannheim and Michigan.

Allan Rosas

Dr.Jur., Dr.Jur. h.c., Dr.Pol.Sc. h.c.; Visiting Professor at the College of Europe, University of Ghent (spring 2020) and the University of Helsinki; member of the Independent Ethical Committee of the European Commission. Former Judge at the European Court of Justice (January 2002–October 2019); Principal Legal Adviser and subsequently Deputy Director-General of the Legal Service of the European Commission (1995–2002); former Armfelt Professor of Law at the Åbo Akademi University (1981 – 1995) and Professor of Public Law at the University of Turku (1977–81). Before 1995 he was member of several Finnish governmental law commissions and advisory bodies; he represented the Finnish Government at a number of international conferences and expert meetings and had expert functions at the UN and UNESCO in particular. He has published extensively in areas such as EU law, international law and constitutional and administrative law; his most recent book: A Rosas and L Armati, EU Constitutional Law: An Introduction, 3rd rev edn (Hart Publishing 2018).

Pierre Sauvé

is a Senior Trade Specialist in the Macroeconomics, Trade and Investment Global Practice of the World Bank Group and an adjunct faculty member of the University of Bern's World Trade Institute. Previously, he served as Director of Studies and Director of External Programs and Academic Partnerships at the World Trade Institute. His research focuses on trade in services, the regulation of investment and the political economy of the multilateral trading system.

Marta Soprana

is Founder of TradePol Consulting. She is a trade policy advisor specialised in research and technical assistance on international trade policy issues. She has worked as a consultant for a number of international organizations – including FAO, ITC, UNCTAD, UNESCAP, World Bank and WTO – and national governments. She is currently pursuing a PhD in international law and economics at Bocconi University. Her research focuses on trade in service, artificial intelligence, digital trade, data governance, and international economic law. She also holds a Master in International law and Economics (MILE) from Bern's World Trade Institute (WTI), a Master in internationalization of SMEs from the Italian Trade Agency, and a MA in International Relations from the University of Bologna.

Geert Van Calster

is full professor at KU Leuven, visiting professor at King's College, London; Monash University, Melbourne; and the China-EU School of Law in Beijing. He is also adjunct professor at American University, Washington and a practising member of the Belgian Bar.

Isabelle Van Damme

is Counsel at Van Bael & Bellis and a Member of the Brussels Bar. Her practice focuses on WTO law, EU law, and public international law. Isabelle regularly advises governments and represents States and individuals before international courts and tribunals, including the WTO dispute settlement bodies and the Court of Justice of the European Union. Earlier in her career, Isabelle was a référendaire in the chambers of Advocate General Sharpston, at the Court of

Justice of the European Union, worked at a Geneva-based firm specialised in wto law and taught at the University of Cambridge, Clare College. She holds degrees from the University of Ghent (Bachelor of Law, Master of Laws), Georgetown University Law Center (LL.M.) and the University of Cambridge (Ph.D. in Law).

Guillaume Van der Loo

is a research fellow at the European Policy Centre (Brussels) and Egmont – the Royal Institute for International Relations and is Visiting Professor EU Trade Law at Ghent University. He obtained a PhD in Law (2014, Ghent University) on the EU's new generation of Deep and Comprehensive Free Trade Areas concluded with the EU's neighbouring countries. He was also a researcher at the Centre for European Policy Studies (ceps) and the Leuven Centre for Global Governance Studies. His research and publications focus on the law and policy of the EU's external relations and Common Commercial Policy, with a particular focus on the new generation of eu ftas, EU international agreements, EU external competences and EU neighbourhood relations. Guillaume has contributed to several international research projects funded by different EU institutions and member states. He also consults on EU trade and external relations law.

Peter Van Elsuwege

is professor of EU law and Jean Monnet Chair holder at Ghent University, where he is co-director of the Ghent European Law Institute (geli). He is also visiting professor at the College of Europe (Natolin Campus) and board member of the Centre for the Law of EU External Relations (cleer) at the Asser Institute in The Hague. His research activities essentially focus on the law of EU external relations and EU citizenship. Specific attention is devoted to the legal framework of the relations between the European Union and its East European neighbours. He published extensively in leading law journals such as Common Market Law Review, European Law Review, European Constitutional Law Review and others.

Edwin Vermulst

has practised international trade and EU law and policy since 1985 and is a founding partner of vvgb Advocaten. He is a member of the Brussels bar. Mr. Vermulst specialises in the representation of multinationals, governments, trade associations, exporters and importers in wto, trade remedy and customs cases, and he is, among others, the trade counsel of the World Federation of Sporting Goods Industry (wfsgi). He has co-authored nine books, including landmark comparative analyses of the anti-dumping systems and rules of origin of countries such as Australia, Canada, the EU and the United States and numerous articles. Mr. Vermulst is the Editor- in-Chief of the *Journal of World Trade* and a Faculty member of the World Trade Institute in Bern.

Geraldo Vidigal

is Assistant Professor at the University of Amsterdam, where he coordinates the LL.M. in International Trade and Investment Law, and Managing Editor of *Legal Issues of Economic Integration* (Kluwer). He has worked as a Dispute Settlement Lawyer at the World Trade Organization (Legal Affairs Division) and a Senior Research Fellow at the Department of International Law and Dispute Resolution of the Max Planck Institute in Luxembourg. He holds a PhD in Law from the University of Cambridge, a Master's in International Law from the Sorbonne Law School and a Bachelor's in Law from the University of São Paulo.

Stephen Woolcock

is an Associate Professor in International Relations at the London School of Economics where he teaches international political economy of trade and economic diplomacy. His main areas of research have been European Union trade policy and preferential trade and investment agreements as well as questions concerning the international trading system and trade frictions.

Claus D. Zimmermann

is a senior associate with Sidley Austin LLP in Brussels. He advises governments and private stakeholders on international and EU trade and investment matters, with a particular emphasis on litigation under the auspices of the WTO, the EU courts and at the member state level. Before entering private practice in 2011, Claus worked for, *inter alia*, the WTO Appellate Body Secretariat and the IMF Legal Department. Claus holds a DPhil in public international law from the University of Oxford and a PhD in economics from the University Paris 1 Panthéon-Sorbonne. Claus is a regular speaker at international conferences. His research on international economic law has been published in leading journals and his monograph "A Contemporary Concept of Monetary Sovereignty" was published by Oxford University Press.

Introduction

10 Years Common Commercial Policy Since the Treaty of Lisbon

Michael Hahn and Guillaume Van der Loo

> Does Europe not, now that is finally unified, have a leading role to
> play in a new world order, that of a power able both to play a sta-
> bilising role worldwide and to point the way ahead for many coun-
> tries and peoples?
>
> LAEKEN Declaration, 2001

∴

The Laeken Declaration – which ultimately led to the Treaty of Lisbon – is an
optimistic document: it anticipated for the European Union an important role
in the concert of nations, and proposed to enable the Union to carry out an effective and coherent foreign policy in order to address the challenges brought
by a "globalised; yet also fragmented world".[1] Many of these aspirations in the
field of foreign relations have not (yet) materialised: When the Treaty of Lisbon entered into force, Europe struggled with the *Global Financial Crisis* and
the ensuing Eurozone crisis, weakening its ability to speak to the rest of the
world with one voice. Also, the Union, created to ensure peace between its
Member states, had to deal with war and occupation at its Eastern border. The
satisfaction of contributing to China's re-integration into the multilateral trading system was soon overshadowed by what has been perceived as overly aggressive Chinese efforts to assert itself as global power. The European Union, in
contrast, has lost influence in many parts of the world, nowhere more visibly
than in the Middle East and Africa and has seen a permanent member of the
Security Council give up its Member state status.

Because of these developments, the intention of the Treaty of Lisbon to
"down-grade" the EU's trade and investment policy to be just one of several
foreign relations instruments at the disposal of decision-makers – whereas in

---

1   European Council, 'Laeken Declaration of 15 December 2001 on the future of the European
     Union', 15 December 2001.

the Treaty of Rome, the legal provisions dealing with foreign trade (the "Common Commercial Policy" (CCP)) was, by and large, the only explicit foreign relations power of the Union – has not quite materialized, despite the explicit submission of the CCP to the general external policy principles and objectives of the Union's external action (Article 21 TEU). However, the somewhat mixed success of establishing the EU as a *global actor* in all fields of international governance has not affected its influence as an economic power of the first order: when it comes to trade and investment, the Union – after all the world's largest trader – matters internationally.

But the Treaty of Lisbon did not only intend to reclassify the Common Commercial Policy. Rather it also significantly reformed both its scope and its procedures. The most important changes brought about insofar relate to the broadened scope of exclusive CCP competences under Article 207 TFEU (e.g. in relation to foreign direct investment) and the increased role of the European Parliament: without the latter's approval, the Council may not conclude trade agreements. Moreover, Parliament became a co-legislator for CCP legislation pursuant to the ordinary legislative procedure.

The EU had to roll out its reformed CCP in an increasingly challenging *internal* political environment. Mainly as a consequence of negotiations with the US on a Transatlantic Trade and Investment Partnership (TTIP) and due to those developments later with regard to the signature of the Comprehensive Economic and Trade Agreement with Canada (CETA), a heated debate emerged *within* the EU on the benefits and the consequences of the Union's embrace of trade-promoting FTAs. Several Member States governments, numerous Members of the European Parliament, national parliaments of EU Member States and civil society groups questioned the appropriateness of the Union's trade policy. Negative impact on the Union's environmental and labour standards and the sell-out of democratic choices of citizens ("right to regulate") were some of the concerns raised publicly. *Externally*, the Union was equally confronted with challenging developments: China's unique combination of one-party system and almost Macunian free market elements have affected the relevance of several WTO rules, leading to significant reforms in the Union's trade defence arsenal. Apart from some minor technical successes, the WTO's law-making facilities did not generate any of the reforms advanced by the Union; with the 45th US president taking office, US scepticism towards the multilateral trading system has given way to open hostility.

The tenth anniversary of the Treaty of Lisbon marks therefore a relevant moment to take stock of the EU's reformed CCP. Whereas the changes with regard to the CCP's objectives, competences and institutional dimension have already received ample attention,[2] this book focusses on how the EU actors, including its Member States, *implemented* its reformed CCP during the last decade. Thus: How did the Court of Justice of the European Union (ECJ) interpret the new competences in the area of trade? How did the institutional reforms brought by the Treaty of Lisbon impact the CCP? Which legislative and policy initiatives were taken in newly conferred areas such as investment, and how did the EU modify existing trade instruments in the area of, for example, trade defence and the General System of Preferences (GSP)? What is the scope and architecture of the new generation of EU FTAs since the Treaty of Lisbon? How did the CCP interact with other EU external policies such as human rights, sustainable development and the Common Foreign and Security Policy (CFSP)?

A group of distinguished authors, including former and current members of the ECJ, practitioners, officials from EU institutions and Member States and leading scholars in the area of EU trade and external relations law have accepted our invitation to address these questions and provide a comprehensive legal analysis of the law and practice of the CCP since the Treaty of Lisbon. The different chapters of this book do not stop at analysing the most important features of the CCP in the last decade, but draw lessons and indicate how the EU's trade and investment policy could and should develop in the future.

This introductory chapter gives first a brief overview of some of the most salient developments in the EU's CCP since the entry into force of the Treaty of Lisbon. Then, an overview of the different titles and chapters in this volume is provided, followed by a brief peak on the *von der Leyen* Commission's immediate plans for EU's future trade and investment policy.

---

2   See for example M. Krajewski, 'The reform of the Common Commercial Policy: Coherent and Democratic?', in A. Biondi, P. Eeckhout, S. Ripley (eds.), *EU Law after Lisbon* (Oxford, OUP, 2012), p. 292–311; M. Bungenberg, C. Herrman (eds.), *Common Commercial Policy After Lisbon* (European Yearbook of International Economic law) (Springer-Verlag, Berlin/Heidelberg, 2013); F. Hoffmeister, 'The European Union's Commercial Policy a year after Lisbon – Sea change or business as usual?' in P. Koutrakos (ed.), *The European Union's relations one years after Lisbon*, CLEER Working Paper 2011/3, pp. 83–96; M. Hahn, 'La Politique commerciale commune', in: J. Bourgeois (ed.), Commentaire J. Megret, Volume: Relations Extérieures (Brussels: Editions de l'Université de Bruxelles 2014), p. 9–86; M. Cremona, 'A Quiet Revolution: The CCP Six Years after the Treaty of Lisbon', *SIEPS Paper* 2017/2, 2017, p. 1–66; G. Villalta Puig, B. Al-Haddab, 'The Common Commercial Policy After Lisbon: An Analysis of the Reforms', *European Law Review* 36(2), 2011, p. 289–300; I. Bosse-Platière, C. Rapoport (eds.), *The Conclusion and Implementation of EU Free Trade Agreements* (Edward Elgar, 2019), 328 p. For an early contribution on the CCP, see M. Maresceau (ed.), *The European Community's Commercial Policy after 1992: The Legal Dimension* (Martinus Nijhoff Publishers, 1993), 472 p.

1   **A Bird's Eye Perspective on the EU's Trade and Investment Policies Since the Treaty of Lisbon**

The first decade of the Treaty of Lisbon overlapped almost squarely with two Commission terms, the *Barroso II Commission* (2009–2014) and the *Juncker Commission* (2014–2019).

The *Barroso II Commission's* trade and investment policy was guided by Trade Commissioner *Karel De Gucht*. Under his "Trade, Growth and World Affairs Strategy",[3] the EU's trade policy was supposed to become more assertive and to deliver the growth needed to emerge from the Global Financial Crisis (GFC). This strategy was largely a continuation of the 2006 "Global Europe Strategy"[4] which, in the context of the stalled WTO Doha Round, had prioritised the conclusion of a new generation of deep and comprehensive trade agreements (DCFTAs) with key trade partners. These FTAs were to be "comprehensive and ambitious in coverage, aiming at the highest degree of trade liberalisation including far-reaching liberalisation of services and investment".[5] In light of the growing integration of global supply chains and increased importance of 'behind-the-border' issues, the new generation FTAs cover, in addition to the liberalisation of trade in goods, *inter alia*, services and establishment, investment, competition policy, regulatory issues, intellectual property rights (IPR), trade-related energy, trade and sustainable development and public procurement. Starting with the first *new generation* EU FTA with South Korea in 2010, the Union concluded a number of FTAs with key trading partners, including Colombia and Peru (2012), and with Central America (2012). A specific type of DCFTA links the EU with Ukraine, Moldova and Georgia (2013); these agreements aim to gradually and partially integrate these countries into the EU Internal Market.[6] Negotiations with other partners of the first order were started, including the United States (TTIP), Canada (CETA), Japan, ASEAN member countries and China (Comprehensive Agreement in Investment, CAI). In this context the coming of age of the European Parliament in all trade matters under the reformed CCP should be mentioned. Under the

---

3   European Commission, 'Trade, Growth and World Affairs. Trade Policy as a Core Component of the EU's 2020 Strategy', COM (2010) 612, 9 November 2010.

4   European Commission, 'Global Europe: Competing in the World', COM (2006) 567 final, 4 October 2006.

5   *Ibid.*

6   On this issue, see G. Van der Loo, *The EU-Ukraine Association Agreement and Deep and Comprehensive Free Trade Area: A new legal instrument for EU integration without membership* (Brill Nijhoff, 2016), p. 1–416.

first post-Lisbon chairmanship of the Parliament's International Trade Committee (INTA), Professor Vital Moreira, Parliament established that its consent pursuant to Article 218 (6) TFEU had to be "informed consent"; in the Framework Agreement between the Commission and the European Parliament this demand was met.[7] While the Parliament's rejection of the Anti-Counterfeiting Trade Agreement (ACTA) on 2012 was controversial[8], the very act of voting down a Commission project ended any hope interested actors may have had that the Parliament would rubberstamp CCP initiatives supported by Commission and Council.

Despite the Barroso Commission's declared commitment to prioritize the multilateral trading system, the efforts to adapt the WTO to the changing environment had limited success: The Doha Development Agenda negotiations remained largely blocked, with the sole exception of the "Bali Package" concluded in December 2013, which consisted of Trade Facilitation Agreement and several Ministerial Decisions focussing on agricultural trade.[9]

Other noteworthy proposals by the Barroso Commission related to the EU's international investment policy (in the light of the EU's new competences in that area),[10] the International Procurement Instrument,[11] increased efforts to reform the Union's trade defence instruments,[12] and the EU's conflict mineral regulation.[13] Moreover, the EU reformed its General System of Preferences (GSP) in Regulation (EU) 978/2012:[14] it broadened the list of international

---

7   Framework Agreement on relations between the European Parliament and the European Commission, OJ 2010 L 304/47.
8   Summary and references to be consulted at https://www.europarl.europa.eu/sides/getDoc.do?type=IM-PRESS&reference=20120220FCS38611&format=XML&language=EN#title1.
9   Council of the EU, WTO: Council approves protocol on trade facilitation', press release 1 October 2015.
10   European Commission, 'Towards a comprehensive European international investment policy', COM (2010) 343 final.
11   European Commission, 'Proposal for a Regulation on the access of third-country goods and services to the Union's internal market in public procurement and procedures supporting negotiations on access of Union goods and services to the public procurement markets of third countries', COM (2012) 060 final.
12   European Commission, 'Communication on Modernisation of Trade Defence Instruments Adapting trade defence instruments to the current needs of the European economy', COM (2013) 191 final.
13   European Commission, 'Proposal for a Regulation setting up a Union system for supply chain due diligence self-certification of responsible importers of tin, tantalum and tungsten, their ores, and gold originating in conflict-affected and high-risk areas', COM (2014) 111 final.
14   Regulation (EU) No 978/2012 of the European Parliament and of the Council of 25 October 2012 applying a scheme of generalised tariff preferences and repealing Council Regulation (EC) No 732/2008 (OJ 2012, L 303).

conventions relevant for the GSP+-treatment, going beyond the core labour conventions and also covering sustainable development and human rights, and by developing stricter economic eligibility criteria, reflecting the changed focus on least-developed countries.

Leaving office with a bang, the Barroso Commission and its Trade Commissioner Karel De Gucht decided on their last day in office to bring a test case to clarify once and for all the scope of the reformed CCP by requesting an ECJ Opinion pursuant to Article 218 (11) TFEU. In its Opinion 2/15, the Court largely supported the Commission's expansive view of the scope of the Union's exclusive competence pursuant to Article 207 TFEU, with the notable exception of portfolio investment and investor-state dispute settlement mechanisms.

When the *Juncker Commission* took office, it was confronted with turbulent times for the EU's CCP: several elements of the EU's trade and investment policy were being contested both internally and from outside the EU, leading to several important legislative developments. In the 2015 "Trade for All" Strategy, Trade Commissioner *Cecilia Malmström* lay down the blueprint for strengthening the effectiveness, transparency and value-dimension of the EU's trade policy.[15] "Trade for All" also spelled out the objective to focus on new trade-related issues affecting the economy, such as services and digital trade. Particular attention was paid to ensuring that small and medium-sized enterprises (SMEs) benefit from more open markets, for example by including SME chapters in the new generation of EU trade agreements.

Also, the Juncker Commission undertook increased efforts to implement the mandate of Article 21 TEU to link the EU's trade policy with its values by, *inter alia*, strengthening the EU FTAs' commitments in the field of environmental, social and labour protection and human rights[16] and by using its GSP scheme. Negotiations on the new generation of EU FTAs, in particular those on CETA and TTIP, triggered a heated debate about the benefits and consequences of these far-reaching trade agreements that included maybe for the first time not just the usual participants. Rather, trade issues became a topic discussed on the front pages of popular newspapers, triggering some of the biggest demonstrations of the past decades in EU Member States. Important actors, including parliaments, governments, political parties and other civil society groups contested the new generation of EU FTAs, highlighting the danger of negative externalities for environmental and consumer protection, public

---

15   European Commission, 'Trade for all. Towards a more responsible trade and investment policy', COM(2015) 497 final, 14 October 2015.

16   See for example 'Non-paper of the Commission services -Trade and Sustainable Development (TSD) chapters in EU Free Trade Agreements (FTAs)', 11 July 2017.

services and labour standards. Another topic attracting wide attention was the claim that investors benefitted from positive discrimination and could stifle the democratic process ("right to regulate") by bringing claims to investment tribunals, targeting in particular the initial proposals for Investor-State Dispute Settlement (ISDS) mechanisms in TTIP and CETA.

The Commission responded by making trade negotiations more transparent, inviting the Council to disclose all FTA negotiating directives, publishing its own proposals during the negotiations, and reporting the preliminary results of each negotiation round and of the consolidated negotiation text.[17] In addition, the Commission proposed a fundamental reform of the ISDS and introduced its proposal for a new 'Investment Court System'. The Commission also ensured a voice for civil society within the EU's decision-making process, allowing, e.g., engagement in the context of the Sustainability Impact Assessments (SIAs) prepared for envisaged trade agreements.

Several FTAs with key trade partners were signed, among them notably Canada (2016), Japan (2018), Singapore (2018) and Vietnam (2019). Moreover, negotiations with Mexico and MERCOSUR were finalised and trade talks with Australia, New Zealand, Chile and Tunisia were intensified.[18] However, not all EU FTA negotiations launched in this period have been successful. Negotiations with the US on TTIP were suspended shortly after President Donald Trump took office in 2017. EU-US trade relations deteriorated following the unilateral trade measures imposed by the US administration: Invoking the national security clause of its Trade Act ('Section 232'), the US government imposed duties of 25% and 10% respectively on imports of steel and aluminium from the EU on 1 June 2018, thereby exceeding its bound tariffs pursuant to Article II GATT. The EU's response has been three-pronged, in line with a strategy outlined by the Commission in March 2018.[19] Firstly, the EU reacted by adopting rebalancing measures under the Safeguards Agreement that target a list of US products worth €2.8 billion, including steel and aluminium products, agricultural goods and various other products.[20] Second, the EU launched, together with several

17   For an overview, see A. Marx, G. Van der Loo, 'Transparency in EU Trade Policy: Achievements and Challenges', *RECONNECT Working Paper (forthcoming 2020)*.

18   For an overview of these negotiations, see: https://trade.ec.europa.eu/doclib/docs/2006/december/tradoc_118238.pdf.

19   European Commission, 'European Commission outlines EU plan to counter US trade restrictions on steel and aluminium', press release, 7 March 2018.

20   Commission Implementing Regulation (EU) 2018/886 of 20 June 2018 on certain commercial policy measures concerning certain products originating in the United States of America and amending Implementing Regulation (EU) 2018/724 (OJ 2018, L 158). The US has disputed the legality of these measures, European Union – Additional Duties

trade partners, legal proceedings against the US at the WTO by filing a request for consultations. Despite the current US administration's invocation of essential security interests (Art. XXI GATT), the EU considers these tariffs to be safeguard measures in disguise that are not compatible with US obligations under the WTO Agreement.[21] Third, the Commission imposed in February 2019 safeguard measures on imports of steel products,[22] exempting only the EEA countries, as imports of steel products into the EU had increased sharply due to the diversion of pertinent products to the EU market as a consequence of the US measures. President Juncker's visit to Washington in July 2018 led to the Trump administration's holding back on imposing additional tariffs of 20% on EU automobiles and auto parts.[23] The EU and the US agreed, *inter alia*, to work on "zero tariffs, zero non-tariff barriers, and zero subsidies on non-auto industrial goods" and tasked an Executive Working Group with finding common ground. As a consequence, the Commission adopted proposals in January 2019 for negotiating directives on conformity assessment and on the elimination of tariffs for industrial goods[24] which were adopted by the Council.[25] Negotiations are yet to begin: whereas the US aims at abolishing tariffs for both industrial and agricultural goods, the EU is not prepared to include agricultural goods in the discussions.

Lack of progress also characterized trade negotiations with several Asian countries, including Indonesia, the Philippines and Myanmar, for economic or political reasons. After the military takeover in Thailand, the EU suspended its negotiations with that country in 2014. After almost 6 years of negotiations, trade talks with India were brought to a *de facto* standstill in the summer of 2013 due to a mismatch in levels of ambition; despite a commitment of both sides at the 2017 EU-India Summit to re-engage actively towards a

---

on Certain Products from the United States, WT/DS559/2; for an early exploration of the undelying legal issues cf M. Hahn, 'Balancing or Bending? Unilateral Reactions to Safeguard Measures', in: JWT 39 (2006), p. 301 – 326.

21 WTO, 'United States – Certain Measures on Steel and Aluminium Products; Request for consultations by the European Union', WT/DS548/1, 1 June 2018.

22 Commission Implementing Regulation (EU) 2019/159 of 31 January 2019 imposing definitive safeguard measures against imports of certain steel products (OJ 2019, L 31/1).

23 'Joint U.S.-EU Statement following President Juncker's visit to the White House', 25 July 2018.

24 European Commission, 'Commission publishes proposal for agreement on conformity assessment with United States', press release, 22 November 2019.

25 Council of the EU, 'Trade with the United States: Council authorises negotiations on elimination of tariffs for industrial goods and on conformity assessment', press release, 15 April 2019.

relaunch of negotiations, no new progress has been made.[26] Due to the political situation in Turkey, the Council has yet to agree to launch negotiations on the modernisation of the EU-Turkey Customs Union. Negotiations on the EU-Morocco DCFTA have been hampered by several ECJ rulings on the application of the existing EU-Morocco trade agreements to the Western Sahara; in the Summer of 2019 both parties declared their willingness to relaunch negotiation.[27]

Progress with regard to signing and implementing the Economic Partnership Agreements (EPAs) with the African, Caribbean and Pacific (ACP) countries was also slow. Among the seven regional groups, only the CARIFORUM has so far concluded a full regional EPA. Some members of the Southern African Development Community (SADC), the Economic Community of West African States (ECOWAS), the East African Community and the other groups have concluded regional or bilateral interim EPAs restricted to trade in goods. However, many EPAs still await conclusion and implementation and the interim EPAs are supposed to be developed into full regional agreements.[28]

Since September 2018, the EU and the ACP countries are in the process of renegotiating their partnership for the time after the expiration of the Cotonou Agreement in 2020. In December 2017, the Commission proposed an umbrella agreement defining common values and interests ('common foundation') and three distinct tailor-made protocols ('regional partnerships') with, respectively, African, Caribbean and Pacific member states of the ACP group.[29] Pursuant to the Commission, EPAs are supposed to remain the central instruments for EU-ACP trade, but can be modified to include more countries or expand commitments. Negotiations at the level of the three regional components were officially launched in early 2019. With regard to African pillar of the new envisaged agreement, it is noteworthy the Member states of the African Union have established the African Continental Free Trade Area (AfCFTA); the EU

---

26   Council of the EU, 'EU-India summit: joint statement and joint declarations', press release, 6 October 2017.

27   On this issue, see G. Van der Loo, 'The Dilemma of the EU's Future Trade Relations with Western Sahara: Caught between strategic interests and international law?', *CEPS Policy Brief*, 20 April 2018.

28   For an overview of the state of pay of the EPAs, see: http://trade.ec.europa.eu/doclib/docs/2009/september/tradoc_144912.pdf.

29   European Commission, 'Recommendation for a Partnership Agreement between the European Union and countries of the African, Caribbean and Pacific Group of States', COM(2017) 763 final.

Commission is considering a continent-to-continent free trade area in the longer term.[30]

An important development took also place in relation to the *architecture* of EU trade and investment agreements. After the Walloon government temporarily blocked the EU's signature of CETA in 2016, a broader discussion ensued on whether in addition to the EU, all Member States need be involved in the conclusion and ratification of trade agreements (as so-called 'mixed agreements') or whether these FTAs should only be concluded by the EU (as so-called 'EU-only agreements'), thus avoiding the risk that one Member State can block the conclusion of an EU FTA for the entire EU.[31] This discussion took place with the landmark Opinion 2/15 as backdrop, in which the Court gave a broad reading to the EU's post-Lisbon trade competences and concluded that almost the entire EU-Singapore FTA fell within the exclusive competences of the EU, with the notable exceptions of portfolio investment and ISDS. In light of Opinion 2/15, the Commission proposed to separate (*"split"*) future trade and investment agreements into *EU-only* FTAs covering exclusive EU competence, on one hand, and a separate mixed investment agreement, on the other hand, in order to reduce as much as possible the need for (now) 28 ratification procedures by the Union and its 27 Member States.[32] In May 2018, the Council largely agreed with this proposal, but stressed that it would decide on a case-by-case basis on the 'splitting' of FTAs.[33] In the meantime, the Union signed its first 'split' FTAs and investment protection agreements with Singapore (2018) and Vietnam (2019).

In response to the contestation of the ISDS mechanism initially envisaged in TTIP and CETA, the Commission launched in 2014 a public consultation on the EU's approach to investment protection and investment dispute settlement.[34]

---

30   See for example, European Commission, 'State of the Union 2018: Towards a new 'Africa – Europe Alliance' to deepen economic relations and boost investment and jobs', press release 12 September 2018.

31   On this issue, see G. Van der Loo, 'The role of national parliaments in mixed trade agreements', *CLEER paper 2018/1*; G. Van der Loo, R. A. Wessel, 'The non-ratification of mixed agreements: Legal consequences and solutions', *Common Market Law Review* 54(3), 2017, p. 735–770.

32   European Commission, 'A Balanced and Progressive Trade Policy to Harness Globalisation', COM(2017) 492 final.

33   Council of the European Union, 'Conclusion on the negotiations of trade agreements', 8 May 2018.

34   European Commission, 'Online public consultation on investment protection and investor-to-state dispute settlement (ISDS) in the Transatlantic Trade and Investment Partnership Agreement (TTIP)', to consult at: https://trade.ec.europa.eu/consultations/index.cfm?consul_id=179.

This consultation led to a proposal for a new system in 2015 to resolve disputes between investors and states – the Investment Court System (ICS), now included in CETA and in the EU's IPAs with Vietnam, Singapore and the negotiated trade agreement with Mexico. These bilateral ICSs, composed of a Tribunal of first instance and an Appeal Tribunal, aim to address the main concerns about the traditional ISDS mechanism by, *inter alia*, limiting the grounds on which an investor can challenge a state through more precise investment protection standards; ensuring governments' right to regulate and to pursue legitimate public policy objectives; and by including specific rules on transparency and the qualification of the judges.

In parallel to the establishment of the ICS in its bilateral FTAs or IPAs, the Commission proposed in 2017 to establish a Multilateral Investment Court (MIC).[35] This MIC would be a permanent independent international court tasked to resolve investment disputes between investors and states having accepted its jurisdiction. Once established, the EU envisages to replace its recently concluded bilateral ICSs with the MIC. In March 2018, the Council authorised the Commission to open negotiations for a Convention establishing such an MIC.[36] In its landmark Opinion 1/17, delivered on 30 April 2019, the ECJ ruled that CETA's ICS is compatible with EU law, in particular with the autonomy of the EU legal order, with the general principle of equal treatment and the requirement of effectiveness, and with the right of access to an independent tribunal.[37] By concluding that CETA, and specifically the ICS included in the new generation of EU FTAs or IPAs, is compatible with EU law, the Court backed the Commission's efforts to pursue the establishment of a MIC which, however, have yet to attract the support of major investor countries such as China, Japan or the US.

In 2019, the EU adopted a screening framework for foreign direct investments. Regulation (EU) 2019/452 provides an EU framework for the screening of direct investments from non-EU countries on grounds of security or public order.[38] It establishes a possibility for Member States to have transparent, predictable and non-discriminatory mechanisms for examining incoming

35   European Commission, 'Recommendation for a Council Decision authorising the opening of negotiations for a Convention establishing a multilateral court for the settlement of investment disputes', COM (2017) 493 final.

36   Council of the EU, 'Negotiating directives for a Convention establishing a multilateral court for the settlement of investment disputes', 12981/17, 1 March 2018.

37   Opinion 1/17 (*CETA*), ECLI:EU:C:2019:341.

38   Regulation (EU) 2019/452 of the European Parliament and of the Council of 19 March 2019 establishing a framework for the screening of foreign direct investments into the Union (OJ 2019, L 79/1).

foreign direct investment on grounds of security or public order, and establishes cooperation procedures between the Member States and the European Commission.

The quest for WTO reform received added urgency under the Juncker Commission. Against a background of a stalling Doha Round, increasing trade tension due to what was perceived by many as Chinese circumventions of trade rules, and US protectionist trade policies, the EU tried, often jointly with like-minded countries, to prevent a complete demise of the multilateral trading system. Whereas the current crisis has been triggered by the US' complete blockade of Appellate Body appointments and the ensuing breakdown of the Appellate Body in December 2019 (when only one member was left whereas at least three members would be necessary to issue reports), a more comprehensive reform and modernisation of the WTO is called for: certain "old" disciplines enshrined in the multilateral trading system, such as those related to subsidies and state-owned enterprises, have not been adapted sufficiently to the new realities of international trade. Also, many of the "new" topics (such as data, climate change or competition) have received attention only in new FTAs concluded bilaterally, without having been addressed adequately in the WTO. In September 2018, the Commission published proposals for WTO reform, focussing on (i) rulemaking and development; (ii) regular work and transparency; and (iii) dispute settlement[39] and has advocated its approach in various fora, including the EU-China Working group on WTO reform, the Trilateral Ministerial Working group with Japan and the US and the G20. Several countries have already aligned with specific elements of the Union's proposals. For example, in November 2018 the Union submitted a concrete proposal for the reform of the WTO Appellate Body;[40] this has paved the way for the successful conclusion of a Multi-party interim appeal arbitration arrangement pursuant to Article 25 of the DSU, concluded by Australia, Brazil, Canada, China, Chile, Chinese Taipei, Colombia, Costa Rica, the European Union, Guatemala, Hong Kong, Mexico, New Zealand, Norway, Singapore, Switzerland, and Uruguay.[41] The agreement mirrors the WTO Dispute Settlement Understanding's appeal rules and can be used between any member of the WTO willing to join, as long as the WTO Appellate Body is not fully functional.[42] In addition, the EU continued its efforts

---

39   European Commission, 'EU Concept Paper on WTO Reform', 18 September 2018.

40   European Commission, 'WTO reform: EU proposes way forward on the functioning of the Appellate Body', Press Release, 26 November 2018.

41   Council of the European Union, 2 April 2020, Doc. No. 112/20, to be consulted at https://www.consilium.europa.eu/media/43334/st07112-en20.pdf.

42   European Commission, 'Trade: EU and 16 WTO members agree to work together on an interim appeal arbitration arrangement', press release, 24 January 2020.

to keep the WTO relevant with regard to substantive rules: thus, for example, plurilateral WTO negotiations on e-commerce were launched in Davos in January 2019 after a year of exploratory talks and some most tentative progress has been made on an agreement on fisheries subsidies.

Finally, it has to be noted that the Juncker Commission adopted or proposed several important pieces of CCP legislation. In the area of trade defence, the EU modernised its trade defence toolbox by adopting Regulation (EU) 2018/825 (i.e. the 'modernisation package'),[43] which, *inter alia*, enables the EU to impose higher duties in some cases by changing the *lesser duty rule*, shortens the investigation period to accelerate the procedure, and increases the relevance of social and environmental standards in anti-dumping investigations and the issue of "pre-disclosure". In December 2017 the EU had already adopted a new anti-dumping methodology in Regulation (EU) 2017/2321, introducing a new methodology for calculating dumping margins in case of "significant distortions" in the market of the exporting country.[44] Moreover, in order to overcome a legislative deadlock on its 2012 proposal, the Commission adopted in 2016 an amended version for an International Procurement Instrument that would enable it to open investigations into alleged discrimination against EU parties in foreign public procurement markets.[45] Also, it would allow the Commission to enter into consultations with the third country concerned to obtain reciprocal concessions on its procurement market; as a last resort, the proposal foresees the imposition of a price penalty on tenders originating in the third country concerned. However, Member States remain deeply divided over this issue. A last important legislative CCP act worthwhile mentioning is the Conflict Minerals Regulation (Regulation (EU) 2017/821), adopted in May

---

43   Regulation (EU) 2018/825 of the European Parliament and of the Council of 30 May 2018 amending Regulation (EU) 2016/1036 on protection against dumped imports from countries not members of the European Union and Regulation (EU) 2016/1037 on protection against subsidised imports from countries not members of the European Union (OJ 2018, L 143/1).

44   Regulation (EU) 2017/2321 of the European Parliament and of the Council of 12 December 2017 amending Regulation (EU) 2016/1036 on protection against dumped imports from countries not members of the European Union and Regulation (EU) 2016/1037 on protection against subsidised imports from countries not members of the European Union (OJ 2017, L 338).

45   European Commission, 'Amended proposal for a Regulation on the access of third-country goods and services to the Union's internal market in public procurement and procedures supporting negotiations on access of Union goods and services to the public procurement markets of third countries' COM (2016) 34 final.

2017.[46] This regulation aims to ensure that EU importers of tin, tungsten, tantalum and gold (3TG) meet international responsible sourcing standards set by the Organisation for Economic Co-operation and Development (OECD) and is supposed to break the link between conflict and the illegal exploitation of minerals by, *inter alia*, requiring EU companies in the supply chain to ensure they import these minerals and metals from responsible and conflict-free sources only.

2   Outline of the Book

The different contributions in this volume analyse in great detail the different institutional, legislative and FTA-related developments touched upon above, providing a comprehensive overview of the law and practice of the EU's trade and investment policy since the Treaty of Lisbon.

Part 1 of the volume explores the enlarged scope of the CCP following the amendments to Article 207 TFEU and the other reforms introduced by the Treaty of Lisbon, in the light of subsequent practice and case law of the ECJ, focusing in particular on Opinion 2/15. In Chapter 1, *Allan Rosas* provides first an overview of the different categories of Union external competence, as they follow from the relevant Treaty provisions and as interpreted by the ECJ. He analyses the situations in which it is either *necessary*, under the CCP or otherwise, or *possible* for the Union to conclude an agreement by the Union alone ('Union-only' agreement), focusing mainly on agreements falling within the CCP or otherwise being of economic or commercial relevance. In Chapter 2, *Marise Cremona* focuses on the identification of the field of action within which the EU's CCP competence may be deployed, on the degree to which the CCP may be used as a basis for exercising external regulatory power, and on the impact of broader EU external objectives on defining the scope of the CCP. She argues that the ECJ's *aim and effects* test has provided a flexible framework for determining the field of action of the CCP and is useful in its ability to be applied to a wide range of instruments and contexts. However, it may lead to a lack of predictability in defining the types of measure which may be adopted under CCP powers. She demonstrates that the general external objectives

---

46   Regulation (EU) 2017/821 of the European Parliament and of the Council of 17 May 2017 laying down supply chain due diligence obligations for Union importers of tin, tantalum and tungsten, their ores, and gold originating from conflict-affected and high-risk areas (OJ 2017, L 130).

introduced by the Lisbon Treaty have opened up the question of what a trade objective, and even a trade instrument, might be.

Part 2 analyses the Union's investment policies adopted since the Treaty of Lisbon, which expanded the scope of the CCP with the inclusion of FDI in Article 207 TFEU, and the relevant jurisprudence of the ECJ, focussing on Opinion 1/17. In Chapter 3 *Colin M. Brown* analyses how the EU is reshaping international investment protection policy. He first sets out how the framework created by the Treaty of Lisbon and the two key pieces of legislation (i.e. the Grandfathering Regulation and the Financial Responsibility Regulation) were instrumental in shaping EU investment policy, before turning to Opinion 2/15, which further defined this framework. The chapter then turns to examine the initial direction of the EU's investment dispute settlement policy before examining the significant changes that led to the creation of the ICS and then the MIC project. In Chapter 4 *Guillaume Van der Loo* analyses the landmark Opinion 1/17 of the ECJ on the compatibility of the ICS included in CETA with EU law. It focuses on two interrelated elements of the Opinion; firstly, the more lenient approach of the ECJ with regard to the principle of autonomy (in relation to international agreements establishing a dispute settlement mechanism (DSM) or a court) and secondly, the implications of the Opinion for future international agreements concluded by the EU, in particular for the MIC. He demonstrates that by conditioning CETA's conformity with EU law to several autonomy safeguards and by developing a new – but rather vague – criterion (i.e. that such courts or DSMs cannot call into question the level of protection of public interest established by the EU institutions in accordance with the EU constitutional framework), the Court raised considerably the bar for future agreements to comply with EU law. This chapter concludes by providing a brief outlook on the different investment agreements concluded or envisaged by the EU (including the intra and extra-EU BITs). In contrast, the following Chapter 5 by *Michael Hahn* focusses on the tension between the notion of "autonomy of the EU legal order" and the Union's ability to contribute to a rule-oriented international legal system by supporting strong and effective treaty-based dispute settlement mechanism. His analysis of the Court's pertinent jurisprudence reveals that the standard of review applied by the Court depends to a significant extent on whether the Court perceives the agreement with a third country (and its dispute settlement organs) as competition for the Union legal order and its High Court. In Chapter 6 *Marc Bungenberg* and *Fabian Blandfort* analyse the recently adopted investment screening framework (Regulation (EU) 2019/452) of the EU and compares it with existing national screening mechanisms of EU Member States. Particular attention is given to the Union competence for the CCP with regard to the access for foreign direct investments. The chapter assesses the different cooperation mechanisms and the competences of the EU Commission as well as the access to legal remedy for the foreign investor under the Regulation. Since the Regulation only states basic requirements and a cooperative framework to coordinate and harmonise the existing screening mechanisms without obliging Member States to adopt a national procedure, the authors argue that a circumvention of the EU screening framework is possible. Hence, to prevent such a circumvention, the authors hold that existing Member States' mechanisms are decisive, which therefore are analysed and compared as well, focussing on Germany, France, Austria and the Northern European Countries. Finally, an excursus provides a brief overview on the US screening mechanism and the recent reform of the Chinese Foreign Investment Law.

Part 3 of the volume explores the scope of the new generation of EU FTAS signed or concluded since the Treaty of Lisbon. It provides a comparative analysis of several of the most important chapters included in the new generation of EU FTAS. In Chapter 7, *Barbara Cooreman and Geert Van Calster* analyse the nexus between trade and sustainable development post-Lisbon. Their chapter takes a close look at the evolution of sustainable development provisions in post-Lisbon EU trade agreements and analyses how the Union actors addressed the challenges of developing and implementing effective trade and sustainable development policies. *Cooreman and Calster* show that the visible and formalized commitment to promoting environmental and social rights protection, reflected in recent trade and sustainable development chapters, do not automatically lead to a more effective pursuit of the Union's pertinent values. Chapter 8, authored by *Isabelle Van Damme*, addresses technical barriers to trade in the new generation of EU DCFTAS. Drawing on a comprehensive analysis of the chapters on technical barriers to trade in goods and related obligations in other chapters in the European Union's trade agreements, her analysis reveals a plurality of possible approaches to the regulation of technical barriers to trade, in particular with regard to reducing trade barriers resulting from conformity assessment procedures. In Chapter 9, *Stephen Woolcock* maps how the EU has used the vehicle of its recent DCFTAS to extend the coverage of procurement rules. His analysis reveals that pertinent efforts have had varying degrees of success; as a consequence, he explores whether the EU should partially retreat, and accept less commitments excluding procurement, or, rather, whether robust pertinent procurement provisions belong to the "bare essentials" of any ambitious new trade agreement. Turning to the topic of prudential carve-outs for financial services in EU FTAS, *Bregt Natens and Claus D. Zimmermann* provide in Chapter 10 an interpretation of the prudential carve-outs included in four recent EU trade agreements and one draft agreement (CETA, EUSFTA, EU-Vietnam FTA, EU-Korea FTA, TiSA), drawing on the GATS prudential carve-out in light of the Panel's findings in *Argentina – Financial Services*. Relying on the findings of the above comparative analyses, *Natens and Zimmermann* assess the legal relevance of the similarities and differences between the EU FTAs' prudential carve-outs, highlighting their importance for combining regulatory autonomy and legal predictability in trade in services commitments.

In Chapter 11 *Pierre Sauvé* and *Marta Soprana* analyse how, and to what extent, the new generation of EU FTAs incorporate provisions related to electronic commerce. The authors explore a representative sample of EU FTAs negotiated by the EU over the past decade. In so doing, the chapter explores how the nature, scope and depth of e-commerce provisions have evolved over this short time span. The chapter further takes up the EU's approach to data protection in discussing whether and how the experience of the EU's General Data Protection Regulation (GDPR) can inform and potentially shape digital trade norms at the regional and multilateral levels. The chapter concludes with conjectures on the likely direction of the EU's digital trade policy agenda.

Part 4 explores the EU's modernised trade defence toolbox. In Chapter 12, *Edwin Vermulst and Juhi Dion Sud*, address the increasingly aggressive application of the EU's anti-subsidy provision in the decade following the entry into force of the Treaty of Lisbon. It concludes that the European authorities have become increasingly aggressive in countervailing subsidies granted by third countries, notably China, and expresses concern that such approach may backfire *vis-à-vis* European exporting interests as the EU and its Member states may be have similar exposures as they would seem to not have 'clean hands'. Turning to the changes in the Union's anti-dumping legislation, *Frank Hoffmeister* provides, in Chapter 13, an overview about the main changes in the EU's anti-dumping legislation. On that basis, he analyses the legislative changes brought about by the new methodology (Regulation 2017/2321) and the modernisation package (Regulation 2018/825) and gives a first-hand guide on their possible interpretation and use in practice. He argues that the new rules keep the main political balance between the protection of producing interests and the respect for importing interests and downstream industry intact. However, the author points out that in many instances the "devil is in the detail" when it comes to the application of the new rules. Arguing from a practitioner's perspective, *Philippe De Baere* discusses in Chapter 14 the EU's amended Basic Anti-dumping Regulation. He describes the changes made to the EU's anti-dumping rules and examines its compatibility with the EU's WTO obligations. While expressing doubts as to full compatibility with the EU's international obligations, the author highlights the great care taken in drafting the new rules. In light of the stalemate at the WTO's Appellate Body, the author tentatively concludes that such a challenge is unlikely to succeed in the near future.

Part 5 analyses the nexus between the CCP and other EU external policies. In the light of the submission of the CCP to the general external policy principles and objectives of the Union's external action enshrined in Article 21 TFEU, introduced by the Treaty of Lisbon in Articles 205 and 207(1) TFEU, this title analyses how CCP objectives and instruments contribute to – or interact with – other external objectives and policies of the Union. In Chapter 15 *Sieglinde Gstöhl* analyses how and why the connection between the EU's CCP and its development policy has changed over the past decade. The author argues that the trade-development nexus has become more intertwined and more strategic as the EU draws on its economic power for leverage in the pursuit of trade liberalisation with developing countries beyond trade in goods, based on increased reciprocity and offensive interests as well as a more assertive promotion of its values. Two emblematic cases analysed in this chapter illustrate the tightening of the trade-development nexus: the EU's longstanding relations with the group ACP countries and with the beneficiaries of its GSP. Gstöhl argues that the reasons for the tightening of the trade-development nexus are both internal and external and generally linked to the EU's search for enhanced effectiveness: on the one hand, the reforms of the Lisbon Treaty recalibrated the goals and the competences in the field of EU external action for the sake of stronger coherence, while on the other hand the global power shift in favour of emerging economies and the policies of the WTO and the UN have also shaped the nexus. In Chapter 16 *Tamara Perišin* and *Sam Koplewicz* analyse the nexus between the CCP and the Common Foreign and Security Policy (CFSP). The authors demonstrate that these two fields are very distinct in terms of the distribution of competences between the Member State and the EU level, as well as regarding the division of power between the different EU institutions. The chapter illustrates that achieving consistency between the activities in these two fields is challenging by considering three sets of issues bordering between the CCP and CFSP: trade in dual-use items, arms trade, and restrictive measures. The authors illustrate this further with a case study on the EU's relations with Iran, focusing on the developments in 2018 related to the Joint Comprehensive Plan of Action, and highlighting how complex situations pose challenges in ensuring consistency between the EU's trade and security policies. In Chapter 17 *Peter Van Elsuwege* analyses the implications of the Treaty of Lisbon for the nexus between the CCP and the protection of human rights. He argues that the innovations of the Lisbon Treaty have significantly affected the law and practice of the CCP in the sense that human rights considerations have become an integral part of the EU's trade policy. This is reflected both at the procedural level, with the practice of human rights impact assessments as a clear example; at the judicial level, with the Charter of Fundamental Rights as a key point of reference for assessing the legality of the EU's external action; and at the practical level, with the introduction of new initiatives and mechanisms aiming at the promotion of respect for human rights in the framework of the CCP. In Chapter 18 *Pieter Jan Kuijper* and *Geraldo Vidigal* examine how the EU and the multilateral WTO regime interact with each other. In particular, this chapter examines the ways in which the EU has reacted to panel and Appellate Body Reports of the WTO. The rejection of direct effect of WTO law and jurisprudence by the ECJ left to the EU's political organs the task of determining the response to give to adverse WTO rulings. The authors find that reactions can be divided into three types. In some cases, the EU has gone beyond compliance, setting up an internal mechanism to ensure the dynamic adaptation of its measures to determinations made at the WTO level (retaliation) or becoming an enforcer of the ruling vis-à-vis other Members (zeroing). In other cases, adverse rulings were followed by *regular* compliance: the EU changed its own policies to adapt to the WTO's rulings. Finally, in a few cases the EU's response was to seek to change the global regulatory regime, either implementing the rulings and seeking to expand their scope, aiming to create a level-playing field for its economic agents (zeroing and agricultural subsidies) or seeking to establish, through bilateral understandings and agreements, a *de facto* parallel regime that allows it to keep its WTO-inconsistent measures.

Part 6 explores the implications of the new institutional and procedural architecture of the CCP for several EU trade and investment policies. In Chapter 19 *David Kleimann* reviews law, practice, and quality of institutional change in CCP treaty-making after the Treaty of Lisbon against the objectives set out by the 2001 Laeken Council, which committed the European Community to constitutional reform to enhance the legitimacy of EU governance through "more democracy, transparency, and efficiency", focusing on de jure legitimacy, output legitimacy, and input legitimacy. The author argues that putting an end to the tradition of *mixed* agreements in favour of *EU-only* economic treaty governance approximates the achievement of the Laeken Council objectives and renders EU external economic treaty-making more efficient and representative. However, he notes that legitimacy would benefit further from reinforced engagement of national parliaments. In Chapter 20 *Reinhard Quick* and *Attila Gerhäuser* analyse the internal and external challenges for the CCP. With regard to the former, the authors study the impact of Opinion 2/15 on the CETA ratification process. They explore whether CETA will be ratified by the Member States notwithstanding the outspoken opposition of several of them or if the

EU eventually will have to split CETA into two agreements as it did with the EU-Singapore Agreement. On the external dimension the authors discuss the EU's trade relations with the world's two largest economies, the US and China. In Chapter 21 *Jacques Bourgeois* and *Merijn Chamon* analyse the integration of EU trade defence in the horizontal comitology regime. This chapter finds that the Parliament has been instrumental in ensuring the subjugation of the implementation of the CCP to the default comitology regime. While initially there were fears that the integration of the CCP in the horizontal comitology framework would negatively affect the effectiveness of both regimes, the integration is found to have been successful. The authors demonstrate that in the EU's trade defence policy there are hardly any referrals to the Appeal Committee, illustrating how this policy is largely determined by the Commission. While there are still some transitional issues, the EU's trade defence policy is being implemented smoothly. The chapter argues that broadening the scope of the comitology regime to the EU's unilateral trade measures was the culmination point of an already ongoing evolution which has seen a progressive shift of power from the Member States in the committee to the Commission, in line with the Community Method. In Chapter 22, *Sophie Gappa and Martin Lutz* analyse the role of the Member States in the CCP. They recognize that as the Union's chief negotiator, the European Commission enjoys a pre-eminent position in the EU's trade policy, even in comparison with other areas of exclusive EU competence, despite the involvement of Council and European Parliament. However, Member states, indirectly through the Council and directly as contracting parties of mixed agreements remain important actors. In line with the German federal Constitutional Court they emphasize the importance of Member states involvement for democratic legitimacy. In Chapter 23 *Bart Driessen* investigates how the law and practice of the CCP since the entry into force of the Lisbon Treaty has affected the institutional balance. The author analyses the developments in the law and practice of the CCP, first in the relation between the Council and the Member States, then in the relationship between the Council and the Commission, and finally in the relationship between the Council and the Parliament. The chapter concludes that the first relationship has not moved very much. On the other hand, the Commission has gained much power at the expense of the Member States, and the Parliament's influence over commercial policy has increased. In Chapter 24 *Andrej Auersperger Matić* analyses the role of the European Parliament in the CCP since the Treaty of Lisbon. Article 207 TFEU introduced by the Treaty of Lisbon granted the European Parliament the power of legislating on an equal footing with the Council, as well as the power to give or deny consent to international trade agreements. This important institutional change brought about many uncertainties about the operation and substance of the Common Commercial Policy. However, the author argues that after a decade of experience under two legislatures, it is now clear that such concerns were unfounded. He argues that the European Parliament in fact adapted well to its new prerogatives without placing a substantial burden on the decisional process or disrupting the operation of the Common Commercial Policy formulated by its institutional counterparts. It has also improved the visibility of policy issues and political controversies about international trade while ensuring a heightened degree of transparency. In terms of substance, the chapter demonstrates that Parliament has not diverted the main policy orientations expressed by the Commission and Council. It has contributed to Union legislation and the shaping of trade agreements in a responsible fashion, by taking into account the lively public debate about the scope and possible effects of trade rules in the modern economy. However, the political disputes surrounding the negotiation of transatlantic trade agreements and the legal dispute over Union competences have demonstrated that there is, even after ten years of decision-making, still a lack of public acknowledgment of Parliament's role as the legitimising institution when it comes to trade policy in the EU. In Chapter 25 *Joni Heliskoski* provides an analysis of the law governing provisional application of FTAs concluded by the EU since the entry into force of the Treaty of Lisbon. The Chapter first addresses the questions concerning the legal basis of provisional application of international agreements under EU law as well as the status of agreements provisionally applied by the EU. The chapter then turns to the central issue of defining of the scope of provisional application of FTAs in relation to both the question of the various legal techniques applied for this purpose in practice and the choice of the substantive fields that are either included in – or left outside of – the scope of provisional application. There is also a discussion on the question of the termination of provisional application, notably in the light of a refusal by a Member State to ratify an agreement that the EU applies provisionally. The chapter concludes by way of an overall assessment of the practice of provisional application of FTAs, including in relation to the recent practice of *splitting* FTAs into a free trade agreement to be concluded only by the Union in its own right and an agreement on the protection of investment to be concluded as a mixed agreement.

3   Outlook: Priorities for the EU's CCP in the Next Decade

This introduction – and the volume at large – illustrate the fast pace that characterized the EU's foreign economic relations since the Treaty of Lisbon entered into force a decade ago. Without much phasing-in, the EU institutions had to apply their newly conferred competences (such as in the area of investment) within a new institutional set-up in order to address the various internal and external challenges sketched above. Several of the post-Treaty of Lisbon CCP legislative initiatives and reforms or trade agreements entered into force just before or after the tenth birthday of the CCP. It would seem therefore somewhat too early for a comprehensive ex-post implementation assessment of several key features of the post-Treaty of Lisbon CCP regime (e.g. the ICS included in bilateral FTAs or IPAs), although in this volume distinguished authors have offered preliminary evaluations of some legislative undertakings; also, for several elements an official interim-review has already taken place (e.g. for the GSP).[47] However, these trade instruments will play an important role in the next decade of the EU's CCP, together with legislative and treaty proposals that are already quite advanced (such as, e.g., in relation to the MIC, WTO reform and the International Procurement Instrument) – and others that will be prompted by future developments, such as the aftermath of COVID-19. In any case, a recent Eurobarometer on trade highlighted, *inter alia*, that a majority of citizens was in favour of international trade and believed that the EU is more effective in defending their respective countries' trade interests than if these countries were acting on their own.[48]

Of course, the EU's trade and investment policy will continue to be shaped by external challenges. This can already be discerned from the (trade-related) priorities of the new '*Geopolitical Commission*' (the *von der Leyen Commission* (2019–2024)), which aims to better align the EU's internal and external action and to create a Union which is more strategic, more assertive and more united in promoting its values and interests around the world.[49]

In the context of the US-China trade dispute, the various forms of foul play practised by several trading partners, a paralysed WTO Appellate Body and the success of identity politics and aggressive nationalism outside the Union and, unfortunately also internally, one of the key priorities for the new Commission will be to contribute to keeping and developing the public international law of international commerce. The obvious first endeavour will be to save, possibly even strengthen, the rules-based multilateral trading system, possibly

---

47   European Commission, 'Mid-Term Evaluation of the EU's Generalised Scheme of Preferences (GSP)', 8 October 2018.

48   European Commission, 'Eurobarometer survey: Majority of EU citizens positive about international trade', press release, 20 November 2019.

49   European Commission, 'Mission Letter from the President-elect of the European Commission to Commissioner-designate for Trade', 10 September 2019.

accepting second-best solutions (*"Reculer pour mieux sauter port en avant le cavalier"*). Thus, the EU will continue to lead efforts to reform the WTO, not only in relation to its dispute settlement mechanism, but also with regard to its rulebook, *inter alia*, in the area of services, subsidies, forced technology transfer and the *Special and Differential Treatment* for developing countries. In addition, the EU will aim to conclude the plurilateral negotiations on e-commerce and other crucial WTO negotiations on, for example, fisheries subsidies, investment facilitation and domestic regulation. In the area of investment protection, the EU may further pursue its MIC project: while its peers have so far been less than enthusiastic, perseverance may change that.

The more assertive approach of the new *Geopolitical* Commission is already now discernible from its increased efforts to establish a *level playing field* at the multilateral level and in its bilateral partnerships, with the focus on reciprocity and enforcement. For example, in order to protect the EU's trade interests in times of a potentially paralysed WTO DSM, the new Commission adopted in December 2019 a proposal to amend the Enforcement Regulation. The main focus and objective of updating the Enforcement Regulation is to cater "for situations where, after the Union has succeeded in obtaining a favourable ruling from a WTO dispute settlement panel, the process is blocked because the other party appeals a WTO panel report 'into the void' and has not agreed to interim appeal arbitration under Article 25 of the WTO DSU."[50] In addition, the EU aims to better protect its trade interests by using actively its recently adopted Investment Screening Framework, increasingly relying on the DSMs included in its bilateral FTAs, establishing an International Procurement Instrument and by appointing a *Chief Enforcement Officer* in the rank of a Deputy Director-General who is tasked to monitor and improve compliance with the EU's FTAs.

In addition, the EU aims to protect its role as leading trade power by developing balanced and mutually beneficial trading partnerships with trade partners that are also genuine superpowers: China and the US. Regarding the latter, the slow progress in the negotiations on the proposed agreement on industrial goods illustrate that stabilising or improving trade relations with the US will be very difficult at least until January 2021, and possibly for the longer term. This being said, the US remain, for the time being, the indispensable Western power in the WTO: the EU will need this ally in order to, *inter alia*, address constructively structural reforms of the WTO.

---

50   European Commission, 'Proposal for a Regulation amending Regulation (EU) No 654/2014 of the European Parliament and of the Council concerning the exercise of the Union's rights for the application and enforcement of international trade rules', COM (2019) 623 final.

In its bilateral relationship, the immediate task at hand is to come to a successful conclusion of the trade and investments agreements currently under negotiation, including with China (the Comprehensive Agreement on Investment), Australia, New Zealand, Tunisia and Mercosur; a continent-to-continent free trade area, bridging the EU Internal market and the AfCFTA will need time and effort. Finally, the EU will want to negotiate a mutually beneficial Agreement on a new partnership with the United Kingdom, its former Member State. The negotiating directives of the Council of 25 February 2020[51] and the Political Declaration between the EU and the UK of October 2019 establish first parameters for that future relationship.[52] It will be interesting to observe how the EU's position on the maintenance of a "level playing field" will be reconciled with the aspirations of the United Kingdom.[53]

Of course, climate change will, hopefully sooner than later, determine to a large extent the EU's trade policy. The EU and its actors will need to find ways to use trade as a tool to promote climate action. Currently, a Carbon Border Adjustment Mechanism (CBAM) is being developed, which the Commission intends to propose in the summer of 2021 as part of its Green Deal and the EU's efforts to achieve carbon neutrality by 2050.

During the last decade, the EU has developed or proposed the legal instruments that should allow the Common Commercial Policy to be fit for purpose in the years to come. However, as our look back *supra* has demonstrated, it is impossible to predict how the EU's trade and investment policy will look 10 years from now. Also, the Union's agenda-setting capability is limited, given that it is the only trade superpower that is *not* (yet) a Geopolitical Power. However, given the guidance of the Founding treaties and the Union's proven ability to react to unexpected internal and external challenges, a measured optimism would seem warranted.

---

51   Council of the EU, 'Council Decision authorising the opening of negotiations with the United Kingdom of Great Britain and Northern Ireland for a new partnership agreement', 5870/20, 25 February 2020.

52   'Political declaration setting out the framework for the future relationship between the European Union and the United Kingdom' (OJ 2019, C 384).

53   European Commission, 'Draft text of the Agreement on the New Partnership with the United Kingdom', 18 March 2020.

PART 1

The Scope of the CCP

∴

CHAPTER 1

Mixity and the Common Commercial Policy after Opinion 2/15

An Overview

Allan Rosas

1   Introduction

While provisions relating to a common commercial policy (CCP) were already to be found in Articles 110–116 of the original Treaty of Rome, and a common customs tariff was established during the 1960s,[1] it was only in an Opinion of 1975 that the European Court of Justice (ECJ) confirmed explicitly that the CCP belongs to the area of the *exclusive* competence of the Community.[2] The Court held that the field of export credits fell under the CCP, observing that a concurrent competence of the Member States would distort competition between undertakings of the various Member States. In subsequent case law, the Court, as far as the trade in *goods* was concerned, confirmed its fairly broad understanding of the concept of CCP, including various sorts of restrictions or regulations such as technical, sanitary and other barriers to trade and tariff preferences in favour of developing countries.[3]

Later developments, however, confirmed that the CCP fell short of covering the whole range of issues of relevance for international trade and that there continued to be areas falling under a *shared* competence, with the effect that international agreements could be concluded as *mixed* agreements, with the participation of both the Community and its Member States. Whilst in

---

1   P. Eeckhout, *EU External Relations Law* (OUP, 2011), p. 11–13. On the origins of the notion of the CCP as an exclusive competence see also M. Kaniel, *The Exclusive Treaty-Making Power of the European Community up to the Period of the Single European Act* (Brill, 1996), p. 67–79.

2   Opinion 1/75 (Understanding on a Local Cost Standard), EU:C:1975:145.

3   See, e.g. Opinion 1/78 (International Agreement on Natural Rubber), EU:C:1979:224 (which concluded, on the other hand, that Member States' participation in a financing scheme would imply a mixed agreement); Case C-45/86, *Commission v Council*, EU:C:1987:163; Case C-62/88, *Greece v Council* ('Chernobyl'), EU:C:1990:153. See also A. Rosas, 'Les relations internationales commerciales de l'Union européenne – Un aperçu juridique et développements actuels' in *Liber Amicorum Bengt Broms: Celebrating His 70th Birthday 16 October 1999* (Finnish Branch of the International Law Association 1999), p. 428.

Opinion 1/94,[4] the ECJ confirmed that all the multilateral agreements on trade in goods provided for in Annex 1A of the Marrakesh Agreement establishing the World Trade Organization (WTO) of 1994, fell under the CCP, some subsequent judgments were based on the idea that measures affecting international trade in goods may escape the realm of the CCP if the predominant objectives and components of the agreement could be located elsewhere, notably in the protection of the environment.[5]

As to *trade in services* and the *trade aspects of intellectual property rights*, the ECJ, in Opinion 1/94, ruled that matters dealt with in the WTO General Agreement on Trade in Services (GATS)[6] and the Agreement on Trade-Related Aspects of Intellectual Property Rights (TRIPS) fell, as a general rule, outside the realm of the CCP. As the formal distinction between exclusive (trade in goods) and shared competence (GATS and TRIPS) continued to be a source of uncertainty and concern,[7] various initiatives were taken to bring the latter under the umbrella of the CCP, with a view to strengthening the Community's hand as an international trade actor, speaking *with one voice.*

One such effort was made in the context of the Treaty of Nice of 2001, which amended, *inter alia*, the Treaty establishing the European Community (TEC), including its then Article 133 TEC relating to the CCP. While the new provision was intended to generally broaden the scope of the CCP, the text remained open to different interpretations and in the light of Opinion 1/08, it became clear that the GATS agreements could continue to fall under a shared competence, even if the non-exclusive part (concerning certain sensitive services) covered some provisions of the agreement only.[8]

---

4   Opinion 1/94 (WTO Agreement) 1994, EU:C:1994:384.

5   See, in particular Opinion 2/00 (Cartagena Protocol), EU:C:2001:664 and Case C-281/01, *Commission v Council* ('Energy Star'), EU:C:2002:761 (where the Court concluded in favour of the CCP) and Case C-94/03, *Commission v Council*, EU:C:2006:2 (where the Court acknowledged a CCP objective but that it had to be combined with another legal basis not providing for exclusivity).

6   See also Case C-360/93, *Parliament v Council*, EU:C:1996:84, where the Court, by referring to Opinion 1/94, observed that only services which are supplied across frontiers fell within the scope of the CCP (para. 29).

7   As TRIPS was considered to fall under a shared competence, the ECJ was in many cases confronted with the question of the division of competence between the Community and the Member States in order to ascertain which parts of the Agreement formed part of Community law. See, e.g. Case C-431/05, *Merck Genéricos – Produtos Farmacêuticos*, EU:C:2007:496.

8   Opinion 1/08, EU:C:2009:739, concerned the conclusion of agreements on the granting of compensation for modification and withdrawal of certain GATS commitments following the accession of new Member States to the EU.

The Treaty on the Functioning of the European Union (TFEU), as introduced by the Treaty of Lisbon, has brought important changes to the EU Treaty regime concerning external competence. The scope of the CCP has been broadened and the other areas which can give rise to a Union exclusive competence have been clarified, also through the case law of the ECJ. The central competence question of EU external relations continues nevertheless to be the distinction between exclusive and shared competence.[9] Whilst, as will be elaborated below, agreements which fall under a shared competence can, if the EU Council so decides, be concluded as Union-only agreements, Member States representatives in the Council in such situations usually insist on the conclusion of a mixed agreement. Although, as we shall also see below, the legal scope for mixity has been reduced, following the Lisbon Treaty and case law based upon it, it is still true that at least for the time being, "mixity is here to stay".[10]

The result may be that the conclusion and later application of agreements run into all sorts of legal and practical difficulties, including the possibility that the definitive conclusion of an agreement will be blocked by one single Member State.[11] Cases in point are the controversy surrounding the conclusion of an agreement on trade, development and cooperation with South Africa in 1999–2000, when the process was held up by an Italian refusal, at a very late hour, to ratify the agreement[12] and the more recent difficulties in obtaining Dutch participation in an Association Agreement with Ukraine[13] as well as Belgium's (to be more precise, the Walloon region's) consent to the signature

---

9   See, e.g. A. Rosas, 'The European Community and Mixed Agreements', in A. Dashwood, C. Hillion (eds.), *The General Law of E.C. External Relations* (Sweet & Maxwell, 2000) p. 200; J. Heliskoski, *Mixed Agreements as a Technique for Organizing the International Relations of the European Community and its Member States* (Kluwer Law International, 2001); C. Hillion, P. Koutrakos (eds.), *Mixed Agreements Revisited: The EU and Its Member States in the World* (Hart Publications, 2010).

10   The observation to this effect that I made some ten years ago is, at least to some extent, still relevant today, A. Rosas, 'The Future of Mixity', in C. Hillion, P. Koutrakos (n. 9), p. 367. See also A. Rosas (n. 9), p. 219–220.

11   See, e.g. A. Rosas, 'Exclusive, Shared and National Competence in the Context of EU External Relations: Do such Distinctions Matter?', in I. Govaere et al. (eds.), *The European Union in the World: Essays in Honour of Marc Mareseau* (Martinus Nijhoff Publishers, 2014), p. 17.

12   A. Rosas in C. Hillion, P. Koutrakos (n. 9), p. 368–369.

13   Association Agreement between the European Union and Its Member States, of the one part, and Ukraine, of the other part (OJ 2014, L 161/3). See also G. Van der Loo, Ramses Wessel, 'The Non-Ratification of Mixed Agreements: Legal Consequences and Solutions', *Common Market Law Review* 54 (2017), p. 735–736.

and provisional application of a trade agreement with Canada (the Comprehensive Economic and Trade Agreement (CETA)). The latter situation brought to the fore the risk that a veto power be held not by the federal Government or Parliament but by a sub-federal region of a Member State.[14]

In the following, I will provide, first, a brief overview of the different categories of Union external competence, as they follow principally from the relevant Treaty provisions, and then, following this structure, discuss the situations in which it becomes legally either necessary, under the CCP or otherwise, or possible to conclude an agreement by the Union alone (hereinafter 'Union-only' agreement). The main focus will be on agreements of relevance for international trade.

2   Union External Competence: a Categorisation

The main categories of Union external competence, taking also into account the competence which may remain with the Member States, can be structured as follows:

I.   Exclusive competence
II.   Shared competence (including parallel competence)
III. Supporting competence
IV. Common Foreign and Security Policy

The concept of exclusive competence can be divided into two parts: (I.1) the *a priori exclusivity* following from the explicit list contained in Article 3(1) TFEU and (I.2) the *implicit* or *supervening* exclusivity based on Article 3(2) TFEU.[15] The list contained in Article 3(1) includes "the common commercial policy". The scope of the CCP is defined in Article 207(1) TFEU, which refers, *inter alia*, to "trade in goods and services", "the commercial aspects of intellectual property" and "foreign direct investment". This provision does not repeat the reservations and exceptions to Article 133 of the EC Treaty (as modified by the Treaty of Nice), although it does provide for unanimity in the Council for the conclusion of certain agreements (paragraph 4) and confirms that agreements in the field of transport are not covered by the reference to services (paragraph 5).

---

14   On the discussions surrounding the CETA Agreement, see A. Rosas, 'The EU and International Dispute Settlement', *Europe and the World: A Law Review 1* (2017), p. 24–26; G. Van der Loo, R. Wessel (n. 13), p. 736.

15   On this terminology see A. Dashwood, 'Mixity in the Era of the Treaty of Lisbon', in C. Hillion, P. Koutrakos (n. 10), p. 356 and 360; A. Rosas (n. 11), p. 17–18.

Article 3(2) TFEU (category I.2) tells us that the Union "shall also have exclusive competence" for the conclusion of international agreements in three different situations: (I.2.a) "when its conclusion is provided for in a legislative act of the Union", (I.2.b) when its conclusion "is necessary to enable the Union to exercise its internal competence" and (I.2.c) "in so far as its conclusion may affect common rules or alter their scope". Of these three situations, the last point, based on the famous AETR/ERTA judgment of the ECJ[16] and ensuing case law, is in actual practice the most important ground for determining the existence of a supervening exclusive competence.

As to the areas of *shared* competence (category II), while Article 4(2) TFEU contains a non-exhaustive list, including environment, transport and energy, Article 4(1) provides that shared competence is the general rule: "[t]he Union shall share competence with the Member States where the Treaties confer on it a competence which does not relate to the areas referred to in Article 3 and 6". If an agreement, or a part of it sufficiently important to prevent an exclusive competence under Article 3(2) TFEU, belongs to the sphere of shared competence, the agreement, depending on the situation, may or must be concluded as mixed. Mixity in this case can thus be either *obligatory* or *facultative*.[17]

Mixity is facultative if there is a Union (potential) competence for the whole agreement (in this case the respective Union competence and Member States' competence can be said to be *concurrent*; this can be referred to as category II.1) and the EU Council decides to exercise this competence by concluding a Union-only agreement.[18] Likewise, a Union-only agreement is possible if there is a *parallel* competence (category II.2). This subcategory is referred to in Article 4(3) TFEU (listing the areas of "research, technological development and space") and Article 4(4) ("development cooperation and humanitarian aid") as a sphere where the exercise of the competence by the Union "shall not result in Member States being prevented from exercising theirs".[19] Finally, if some parts

---

16   Case 22/70, *Commission v Council* ('AETR/ERTA'), ECLI:EU:C:1971:32.

17   A. Rosas (n. 10), p. 203–207; M. Chamon, 'Implied Exclusive Powers in the ECJ's Post-Lisbon Jurisprudence: The continued Development of the ERTA Doctrine', *Common Market Law Review* 55 (2018), p. 1101–1102.

18   See Case C-600/14, *Germany v Council, EU:C:2017:935*, which confirms the possibility for the Council to decide to exercise a shared competence over the entire field of an agreement envisaged, thus resulting in a Union-only agreement. The question of when, and to what extent, the Council may be deemed to have exercised a (potential) Union competence will be further considered in section 6 below. On the notion of *concurrent* competence, see A. Rosas in A. Dashwood, C. Hillion (n. 9), p. 203–207.

19   This implies that the sentence of Art. 2(2) TFEU, stating that the Member States can only exercise their (shared) competence "to the extent that the Union has not exercised its competence", is not applicable.

of an agreement continue to belong to the exclusive competence of the Member States, mixity may become obligatory and the competene of the Union and the Member States, respectively, can be said to be *coexistent*[20]; category II.3).

The notion of *supporting* competence (category III), defined in Article 6 TFEU as a competence to carry out "actions to support, coordinate or supplement" actions of the Member States, which in Article 4(1) is excluded from the sphere of shared competence (see above), does not seem to be very relevant in the context of Union external relations, and in any case not for matters of international trade.[21]

The *Common Foreign and Security Policy* (CFSP), listed as category IV above, is obviously highly relevant for external relations. As contemporary trade agreements may contain a political part perceived as belonging to the CFSP, its relevance for the question of Union-only versus mixed agreements will be briefly considered below (section 5). Suffice it to note here that the place of the CFSP in the competence regime outlined above is far from clear. Although the CFSP is not mentioned in Article 4(1) as an area excluded from shared competence, it can be argued that the CFSP, because of the separate reference to it in Article 2(4) TFEU and the special provisions regulating it in the TEU (rather than the TFEU), should be viewed as a *sui generis* category.[22]

3   The Enlarged Scope of the CCP

Of the specific areas mentioned in Article 207(1) TFEU, trade in goods presents the most traditional and well-established area belonging to a Union exclusive competence. Also international trade in services is now an exclusive competence without reservations. The Court confirmed in Opinion 2/15 on the EU-Singapore FTA[23] that provisions of the draft agreement which contain commitments relating to market access of goods and services belong to the sphere of the CCP, with the exception of transport services.[24] In this context, it can also

---

20   A. Rosas in A. Dashwood, C. Hillion (n. 9), p. 203–207.

21   Article 6 mentions areas such as the protection and improvement of human health, industry, culture and education.

22   See, e.g. A. Rosas, L. Armati, *EU Constitutional Law: An Introduction* (Hart Publishing, 2018), p. 23–24. The specific provisions relating to the CFSP are contained in Title V, Chapter 2 (Arts. 23–46 TEU).

23   On this case, see also the contribution by M. Cremona in this volume.

24   Opinion 2/15, EU:C:2017:376, para. 40–77. In the draft agreement, the commitments relating to market access appear in chapters 2 to 8 and chapter 10. The exclusion of transport services stems from Art. 207(5) TFEU, according to which the negotiation and conclusion

be noted that all the commitments of the agreement relating to competition were considered by the Court to fall within the field of the CCP.[25] As to services more specifically, the Opinion confirms that Article 207(1) TFEU covers all four modes of services (that is, cross-border supply, supply in the Member State of the service provider, commercial presence (establishment) in another Member State and temporary presence in another Member State).[26]

There may nevertheless still be borderline cases relating notably to the question of whether an agreement regulates international trade and thus falls under the CCP or the internal market and thus falls under Article 114 TFEU.[27] This distinction came up in a case brought by the European Commission against the Council in 2012.[28] The Council had decided that the legal basis of the decision to sign a Council of Europe Convention relating to the legal protection of radio, television and information society services based on conditional access (access subject to prior individual authorisation) should be Article 114 TFEU relating to the internal market and that the Convention should accordingly be concluded as a mixed agreement.[29] The Court concluded, however, that the agreement was supposed to help extend the application of EU internal legislation beyond the borders of the EU in order to promote the supply of services to third countries, and that the aspects of the Convention which did not clearly relate to the international trade in services were of an incidental or ancillary nature.[30] The judgment confirms earlier case law relating to *ancillary* provisions, implying that it is sufficient for an act to fall under the CCP if its primary objective and content is to regulate trade with third countries.

As to the intellectual property rights, the case law requires that, in order for the commitments entered into by the Union to fall within the "commercial aspects" of such rights, within the meaning of Article 207(1) TFEU, they display "a specific link with international trade in that they are essentially intended

---

of international agreements "in the field of transport"shall be subject to the part of the TFEU dealing with transport (Arts. 90–100) rather than Article 207 itself.

25   *Ibid,* para. 131–138 (these commitments are contained in chapter 12 of the draft agreement).

26   *Ibid,* para. 54–55.

27   See the examples given above (n. 5).

28   Case C-137/12, *Commission v Council,* EU:C:2013:675. See also A. Rosas, 'EU External Relations: Exclusive Competence Revisited', *Fordham Journal of International Law* 38 (2015), p. 1082–1083.

29   Unlike the CCP, the internal market is in Art. 4(2) TFEU listed as an area of shared competence. See also Opinion 2/92 (Third Revised Decision of the OECD on National Treatment), EU:C:1995:83 (holding that the OECD rules in question were partly covered by the Unions internal market rules and not by the rules of the CCP).

30   Case C-137/12, *Commission v Council,* (n. 28), para. 76.

to promote, facilitate or govern such trade and have direct and immediate effects on it".[31] This requirement was highlighted in *Daiichi Sanko*.[32] The national judge wanted to know whether a provision of TRIPS (Article 27) setting out the framework for patent protection fell within an area for which the Member States continued to have primary competence – in which case they would have been free to decide on the possible direct effect of the provision in question.[33] The Court answered the question in the negative, concluding that Article 27 TRIPS falls within the field of the CCP.

This conclusion must be seen in the context of the arguments put before the Court by a number of Member States. They argued that the question should be approached in the context of the case law of the Court relating to mixed agreements, implying that there was an EU competence only to the extent that the European Union had exercised its powers and adopted provisions to implement the agreement. For these Member States, it was thus as if practically nothing had changed with the Treaty of Lisbon. Yet it had been the general understanding when the Lisbon Treaty was prepared that the Nice Treaty provision relating to the CCP did not go far enough and that the credibility, coherence and efficacy of the trade policy of the Union required a broader scope for the CCP.

The Court could not agree with this reductionist approach, observing, *inter alia,* that Article 207 TFEU differed noticeably from Article 133 of the Treaty establishing the European Community. In this new situation, Opinions 1/94 and 1/08 were no longer relevant. As to Article 27 of TRIPS, the entire agreement, being as it is an integral part of the WTO system, has a specific link with international trade. This can be seen, *inter alia,* from the fact that under this system, there may be *cross-suspension* of concessions between TRIPS and the other WTO multilateral agreements (GATT and GATS), meaning that a violation of, say, a rule in GATT relating to trade in goods may be met with sanctions, that is suspension of concessions, affecting the application of TRIPS, or vice versa.[34] The Court also observed that the terms used in Article 207(1) TFEU "correspond almost literally" to the very title of TRIPS.[35]

---

31   On the Court's use of this specific criterion in Opinion 2/15, see the contribution of
      M. Cremona in this volume.
32   Case C-414/11, *Daiichi Sanko,* EU:C:2013:520, para. 49–52. See also A. Rosas (n. 27),
      p. 1081–1082.
33   Case, C-414/11 *Daiichi Sankyo,* (n. 32).
34   *Ibid*, para 54.
35   *Ibid*, para. 55.

While this judgment should have settled the question of the status of TRIPS, it could still be argued that the situation was different with respect to the status of other international agreements relating to the protection of intellectual property rights such as those concluded under the auspices of the World Intellectual Property Organization (WIPO). This question came up in the fairly recent case of *Commission v Council*.[36] The Court annulled a decision of the Council which authorised the opening of negotiations on a revised Lisbon Agreement on Appellations of Origin and Geographical Indications as the Council decision was based on the premise that the draft revised agreement should be a mixed agreement. Also in this case, the Court concluded that the draft agreement was a trade agreement and that its negotiation thus belonged to the sphere of the CCP.

A similar conclusion was made in Opinion 2/15, where the Court found that all provisions of a trade agreement with Singapore relating to intellectual property rights belong to the sphere of the CCP. The Court pointed out, *inter alia,* that these commitments "enable entrepreneurs of the [EU] and Singapore to enjoy, in the territory of the other Party, standards of protection of intellectual property rights displaying a degree of homogeneity and thus contribute to their participation on an equal footing in the free trade of goods and services between the [EU] and the Republic of Singapore".[37] This reasoning also applied to the provisions relating to the implementation and enforcement of intellectual property rights. One specific point of this part of the Opinion still merits a comment: some Member States had argued that a reference in a provision of the draft agreement relating to copyrights and related rights to certain multilateral conventions which included a provision on "moral rights" rendered that particular provision "non-commercial" in nature. The Court observed that the reference in question was not enough to render that part of the draft agreement non-commercial in nature.[38]

Judging from *Daaichi Sanko, Commission v Council* and Opinion 2/15, the Court seems to give a fairly flexible meaning to the requirement of *specific link.* One could perhaps now argue that there is a presumption that all provisions on intellectual property rights contained in an international agreement which

---

36   Case C-389/15, *Commission v Council*, EU:C:2017:798.

37   Opinion 2/15 (n. 23), para. 122. The part of the Opinion dealing with intellectual property protection is to be found in para. 111 to 130. See also A. Rosas, 'The EU as a Global Trade Actor: The Scope of Its Common Commercial Policy' in *Challenges of Law in Life Reality: Liber Amicorum Marko Ilešič* (Univerza v Ljubljani, Pravna fakulteta, 2017), p. 443–444.

38   Opinion 2/15 (n. 24), para. 129.

provides protection for EU traders in the territory of a third country present a sufficient link with international trade to trigger the application of Article 207 TFEU.

That all international agreements touching upon intellectual property rights do not necessarily belong to the CCP, however, can be seen from Opinion 3/15, which concerned the Marrakesh Treaty to Facilitate Access to Published Works for Persons who are Blind, Visually Impaired or Otherwise Print Disabled.[39] The ECJ came to the conclusion that, whilst two of its provisions did indeed apply to the exports and imports of accessible format copies for the benefit of print disabled persons as beneficiaries, these provisions, which had a limited scope, served the overall purpose of the Treaty, which was not to promote, facilitate or govern international trade but to facilitate the access of beneficiary persons to published works, by providing for exceptions or limitations to certain copyrights. The facilitation of the cross-border exchange of accessible format copies thus appeared to be a "means of achieving the non-commercial objective of the Marrakesh Treaty"[40] and so this Treaty did not fall within the CCP.

As to the addition of *foreign direct investment* to the areas mentioned in Article 207(1) TFEU, the Court, in Opinion 2/15, concluded that non-direct (portfolio) investment falls outside Article 207 TFEU, pointing out that the use by the authors of the Treaty of the word *direct* "is an unequivocal expression of their intention not to include other foreign investment in the [CCP]". Even with respect to direct investment,[41] however, some Member States tried to argue that the CCP only relates to the admission of new investment and not to the protection of existing investment. The Court refuted this thesis, as well as the argument that certain provisions of the agreement enabling derogations with a view to safeguarding public order, public security and other public interests, or providing for guarantees that expropriations or criminal law, tax law or social security legislation be applied in a fair manner, would belong to an area of exclusive competence of the Member States.[42] It would appear that the Court adopted a holistic approach, based on the idea that the inclusion

---

39   Opinion 3/15, EU:C:2017:114. See also A. Rosas (n. 37), p. 438–439.

40   Opinion 3/15 (n. 39), para 90.

41   The Court, at para. 80 of the Opinion, recalled its case law relating to the notion of direct investment, which consists in investments "which serve to establish or maintain lasting and direct links between the persons providing the capital and the undertakings to which that capital is made available". With respect to companies limited by shares, the investment becomes of a direct nature "where the shares held by the shareholder enable him to participate effectively in the management of that company or in its control".

42   Ibid, para. 101–109.

of *foreign direct investment*, without any qualifications or limitations, in Article 207 TFEU must mean that in principle all provisions of a trade agreement relating to direct investment which aim at creating a level playing field for foreign investors (fair and equitable treatment, principle of non-discrimination, etc.) are integral parts of a contemporary trade policy.

This approach would apply to provisions relating to foreign direct investment of a substantive character. As to the institutional and procedural question of dispute settlement, Opinion 2/15 makes an important distinction between state-to-state and investor-to-state (hereinafter 'ISDS') dispute settlement.[43] While the former should follow the solution as regards the substantive commitments (in other words, dispute settlement between the EU and Singapore falls within the CCP as far as direct investment is concerned, whilst the settlement of disputes concerning portfolio investment would belong to the sphere of shared competence), the Court viewed the question of ISDS differently. It ruled that the ISDS provisions of the draft agreement, whether relating to direct or non-direct investment, fall within a competence shared between the EU and its Member States. The private investor, by submitting a dispute to ISDS, would create a situation which would remove the dispute from the jurisdiction of the courts of the Member State concerned. Such a system, according to the Court, "cannot [...] be established without the Member States' consent".[44] While no further explanation of this view is provided, it seems possible to argue that we have here a case of *obligatory* mixity, in other words that it would not be open to the Council to decide to conclude an agreement on the ISDS as a Union-only agreement.[45] The question is not entirely clear, however, as the Court concludes that ISDS falls within a competence shared with the Member States. Could the "consent" of the Member States be given in the Council, when it decides to conclude a Union-only agreement, rather than by becoming contracting parties in their own right?

In Opinion 2/15, the Court also dealt at length with the nature of the commitments concerning *sustainable development*.[46] These commitments relate to a certain number of provisions of the draft agreement having an economic, social and environmental dimension. In concluding that these provisions, too, fall within the CCP, the Court, *inter alia*, underlined that according to the

---

43   On these concepts see A. Rosas (n. 14), p. 23–26.

44   Opinion 2/15 (n. 24), para 292. The dispute settlement system of the draft agreement is discussed at para. 285 to 304.

45   L. Prete, 'Some thoughts on Facultative and Obligatory Mixity after Singapore and COTIF, and before CETA', *Verfassungsblog*, 13 October 2018.

46   Opinion 2/15 (n. 24), para. 139–167.

second sentence of Article 207(1) TFEU, "the [CCP] shall be conducted in the context of the principles and objectives of the Union's external action".[47] These principles and objectives, again, are stated above all in Article 21 TEU, which refers, *inter alia*, to sustainable development. The Court concluded that the relevant provisions of the agreement did not serve to harmonise the labour or environment standards of the parties but were intended to "govern trade [...] by making liberalisation of that trade subject to the condition that the Parties comply with their international obligations concerning social protection of workers and environmental protection".[48] The Court thus recognised that the aim of the negotiations had been "to reach agreement on a "new generation" of free trade agreement, that is to say, a trade agreement including – in addition to the classical elements in such agreements [...] other aspects that are relevant, or even essential, to such trade".[49] It can be surmised that in view of the reference in Article 207(1) TFEU to the principles and objectives of the Union's external action, trade agreements which contain, say, an environmental element, will more readily than in the past[50] be covered by Article 207 TFEU.

4   Exclusivity by Virtue of Article 3(2) TFEU

The *supervening* or *implicit* exclusive competence based on Article 3(2) TFEU is not limited to trade agreements but may arise in almost all areas of Union law. The main examples where the trade aspect is relevant concern transport (which is excluded from the remit of Article 207 TFEU), foreign non-direct (portfolio) investment and ISDS. These subjects were dealt with in Opinion 2/15 and they will be the main focus of the ensuing discussion. Of the three criteria mentioned in Article 3(2) TFEU, the AETR/ERTA principle (agreements which may affect common rules or alter their scope) is by far the most important one in practice.

While Opinion 1/94 relating to the WTO Agreements and some other decisions of the same period can be said to have adopted a rather restrictive view of the scope of the AETR/ERTA principle, Opinion 1/03 relating to the Lugano Convention set the ground for a more open approach to the application of AETR/ERTA.[51] Especially since 2014, that ground has been cultivated in a string

---

47   *Ibid*, para. 142.
48   *Ibid*, para. 152.
49   *Ibid*, para. 140.
50   Compare with Opinion 1/2000 (n. 5).
51   A. Rosas (n. 28), p. 1084–1086.

a cases, most of which resulted in the finding of an exclusive competence.[52] Case C-114/12 *Commission v Council* concerned the competence to negotiate a Council of Europe convention on the protection of neighbouring rights of broadcasting organisations.[53] Opinion 1/13 was about acceptance of the accession of a third State to the Hague Convention relating to child abduction[54] while Case C-66/13 *Green Network* was a request for a preliminary ruling concerning the competence of a Member State to maintain a provision of national law based on a bilateral agreement between that State and a third country relating to the import of green energy.[55]

Maybe the most important lessons to be drawn from these decisions is that, first of all, already a *risk* that common rules are affected can trigger the AETR/ERTA effect (which is in line with the wording of Article 3(2) TFEU, which uses the verb "may affect"), second, that the dicta in Opinions 2/91[56] and 1/03, according to which it is enough that EU legislation covers the draft agreement "to a large extent" for the AETR/ERTA effect to arise, has been confirmed, third, that the "area" to be taken into account when assessing whether there is coverage "to a large extent" should look at legal *regimes* rather than details of the relevant EU legislation and the draft agreement (which may imply that the entire agreement is considered as one regime, which would mean that EU legislation does not need to cover all the details of the agreement, as long as there is coverage of the whole regime "to a large extent")[57] and fourth, that also future foreseeable common rules may have to be taken into account in assessing whether they may be affected by the draft agreement.[58]

This case law relating to the application and interpretation of Article 3(2) TFEU has been completed by Opinions 3/15 and 2/15. With respect to the former, which was delivered first, it should be recalled that the ECJ did not find that the Marrakesh Treaty to Facilitate Access to Published Works for Persons who are Blind, Visually Impaired or Otherwise Print Disabled concerned international trade to such an extent that it fell under the CCP. Instead, the Court concluded that Directive 2001/29 on the harmonisation of certain aspects of

---

52   These judgements are analysed in greater detail by A. Rosas (n. 27), p. 1087–1094; M. Chamon (n. 17), p. 1123–1136.

53   Case C-114/12, *Commission v Council*, EU:C:2014:2151.

54   Opinion 1/13, EU:C:2014:2303.

55   Case C-66/13, *Green Network*, EU:C:2014:2399.

56   Opinion 2/91, (ILO Convention No 170), EU:C:1993:106.

57   This approach was taken in Case C-114/12, *Commission v Council*, (n. 55) (see in particular para. 78–84).

58   See Case C-66/13, *Green Network* (n. 57), para. 61.

copyright and related rights in the information society[59] did contain common rules which would be affected by the Marrakesh Treaty and that the Treaty fell under the exclusive competence of the Union, by virtue of Article 3(2) TFEU.[60] It should be noted, in particular, that the Court did not accept that the options given to Member States to implement certain exceptions and limitations to the application of the Directive implied that there was minimum harmonisation constituting a bar to an AETR/ERTA effect. The Court referred to "the body of obligations" laid down by the Marrakesh Treaty (thus in line with the reference in *Commission v Council* to a *regime* of rights and obligations) and concluded that this body of obligations was already covered to a large extent by common EU rules".[61]

The AETR/ERTA principle also became an important issue in the context of Opinion 2/15. The parts of the Opinion which deal with Article 3(2) TFEU present a mixed outcome. The Court ruled that all the provisions dealing with transport (international maritime transport, rail transport, road transport, internal waterways transport to services inherently linked to those transport services[62]) belong to the field of exclusive competence, as existing Union legislation would affect those common rules or alter their scope. The overall impression confirms what I have argued in the context of Opinion 1/13, namely that "the threshold for concluding an AETR/ERTA effect is not very high".[63]

As to portfolio investment, the Court concluded that exclusivity did not follow from the AETR/ERTA principle. The Court did not accept that the "common rules" referred to in Article 3(2) TFEU could include primary EU law (such as Article 63 TFEU relating to capital movement) and as there was no secondary EU legislation that could have been affected by the provisions of the Singapore agreement, the competence was deemed to be shared.[64] Nor did, as noted above, the ISDS dispute settlement provisions of the agreement fall under an exclusive competence.[65] The end result of Opinion 2/15 was thus that the free trade agreement with Singapore falls within the exclusive competence of the Union (on the basis of either Article 3(1) or 3(2) TFEU), with the exception of the substantive commitments relating to non-direct (portfolio)

---

59   Directive 2001/29/EC of the European Parliament and of the Council of 22 May 2001 on the harmonization of certain aspects of copyright and related rights in the information society (OJ 2001, L167/10).

60   Opinion 3/15 (n. 39).

61   *Ibid,* para. 129.

62   Opinion 2/15 (n. 24), para. 168–224.

63   Rosas (n. 28), p. 1091.

64   Opinion 2/15 (n. 24), para. 225–243.

65   See above (n. 44).

investment, some ancillary provisions of an institutional nature relating to portfolio investment as well as the ISDS provisions of the investment chapter of the agreement.

5   The CFSP

As was already noted in Section 2, the EU competence under the CFSP seems to be of a special nature. The CFSP does seem to present features similar to the *parallel* competence envisaged in Article 4(4),[66] which would mean that the exercise of a CFSP competence would not pre-empt Member States' activities covering the same field. It has been argued, however, that an exclusive Union competence could, in principle, follow from Article 3(2) TFEU, although such a situation would not be likely to arise in practice.[67]

Already well before the conclusion of the Lisbon Treaty, there was a tendency to include in trade and cooperation agreements clauses on political dialogue, which were then used as an argument in favour of a Member State competence and thus obligatory mixity.[68] Such clauses belonged, in principle, to the area of the CFSP, but before the Treaty of Amsterdam (entered into force in 1999), international CFSP agreements could not be concluded by the Union, while after Amsterdam, such EU agreements concerned specific CFSP missions or tasks[69] and clauses of a CFSP nature included in trade and cooperation agreements were not based on a CFSP legal basis.[70]

Even if after the Treaty of Lisbon, it has been considered possible to base such clauses on a CFSP legal basis (which implies that the Union exercises its CFSP competence), this has not become a common practice and such clauses have continued to trigger calls for mixity. Decisions on the provisional

---

66   F. Naert, 'The Use of the CFSP Legal Basis for EU International Agreements in Combination with Other Legal Basis', in J. Czuczai, F. Naert (eds.), *The EU as a Global Actor: Bridging Legal Theory and Practice* (Brill Nijhoff, 2017), p. 415–416.

67   M. Cremona, 'The Position of the CFSP/CSDP in the Constitutional Architecture of the EU', in S. Blockmans, P. Koutrakos (eds.) *Researach Handbook on the EU's Foreign and Security Policy* (Edward Elgar, 2018), p. 5–22.

68   A. Rosas (n. 9), p. 218.

69   See S. Marquardt, 'The Conclusion of International Agreements under Article 24 of the Treaty on European Union', in V. Kronenberger (ed.), *The European Union and the International Legal Order: Discord or Harmony?* (TMC Asser Press, 2001), p. 333; A., 'International Dispute Settlement: EU Practices and Procedures', German Yearbook of International Law 46 (2003), p. 285, 287–288, 307–308.

70   F. Naert (n. 68), p. 395–398, 409.

application of agreements with Ukraine, Georgia, Moldova and Kazakhstan, however, and the conclusion of a Union-only agreement with Kosovo include a CFSP legal basis (Articles 31 and 37 TEU).[71] It has been argued that "the reluctance of Member States to agree to the exercise by the EU of its CFSP competence in horizontal international agreements is mainly due to a preference by the Member States to emphasise their own presence in the framework of such agreements" and "may also be one of the ways in which some Member States try to help ensure that horizontal agreements remain mixed".[72]

A recent judgment of the ECJ relating to the application of the agreement with Kazakhstan, as signed and applied provisionally, may shed new light on the relevance of a CFSP component in such horizontal agreements dealing predominantly with trade and other matters of a non-CFSP nature.[73] The case concerned an EU Council decision on the position to be adopted on behalf of the EU within the Cooperation Council established under the agreement. The Commission proposal referred, as a procedural legal basis, to Article 218(9) TFEU, which concerns positions to be adopted on the Union's behalf in bodies set up by agreements, in conjunction with Article 37 TEU, which enables the conclusion of CFSP agreements. The Commission argued that decisions based on Article 218(9) TFEU, read in conjunction with the first sentence of Article 218(8) TFEU, should always be taken by qualified majority. The Court disagreed, stating that in order to determine whether a decision adopted within the framework defined in Article 218(9) covers a field for which unanimity is required, "it is necessary to refer to its substantive legal basis".[74] If the substance of the agreement concerns (also) the CFSP, and the position to be adopted under Article 218(9) "concerns exclusively the CFSP",[75] the decision must, in principle, be adopted unanimously.

---

71   *Ibid*, p. 410–417. Naert refers to the provisional application of the association agreements with Ukraine, Georgia and Moldova and of an Enhanced Partnership and Cooperation Agreement with Kazakhstan. For the Stabilisation and Association Agreement with Kosovo, see Council Decision (EU) 2016/342 of 12 February 2016 (OJ 2016, L 71/1).

72   *Ibid*, p. 416.

73   Case C-244/17, *Commission v Council*, EU:C:2018:662. See P. Van Elsuwege and G. Van der Loo, 'Legal Basis Litigation in Relation to International Agreements: *Commission v. Council* (Enhanced Partnership and Cooperation Agreement with Kazakhstan', *Common Market Law Review* 56 (2019), p. 1333–1354. See also Council Decision (EU) 2016/123 on signing, on behalf of the European Union, and provisional application of the Enhanced Partnership and Cooperation Agreement between the European Union and its Member States, of the one part, and the Republic of Kazakhstan, of the other part (OJ 2016, L 29/1).

74   Case C-244/17, *Commission v Council* (n. 75), para 35.

75   *Ibid*, para. 38.

With the regard to the substantive legal basis, the Commission had proposed Articles 207 (CCP) and 209 TFEU (development cooperation). The Court embarked on a discussion on the status of the CFSP-related clauses in the Kazakhstan agreement and concluded that these clauses were, first, few in number as compared to the overall content of the agreement and, second, were limited to declarations on the aims that joint cooperation should pursue and the subjects to be discussed and did "not determine in concrete terms the manner in which the cooperation will be implemented".[76] They were accordingly not of a scope "enabling them to be regarded as a distinct component of the agreement" but were, on the contrary, "incidental to that agreement's two components constituted by the [CCP] and development cooperation".[77] The Court, in fact, held *expressis verbis* that the links between the agreement and CFSP were "not sufficient" for it to be held that the legal basis for the signing of that agreement and its provisional application should include Article 37 TEU.

It seems obvious that the Court in its discussion on the relation between CFSP and TFEU legal bases followed the same approach as with regard to the choice of legal bases in general. If the *predominant purpose or* content concerned non-CFSP matters, the latter became incidental and did not allow for a separate CFSP legal basis. As a result, agreements such as the one concluded with Kazakhstan, could in the future be based on Article 207 TFEU, and as the case may be, also Article 209 TFEU, and thus be adopted by qualified majority, even if they contained a limited number of CFSP-related clauses of a general nature. It remains to be seen, on the other hand, whether this result will trigger further requests, at the level of the EU Council, to consider such CFSP clauses as relating to a national competence and thus to require mixity, once again. This brings us to the question of the scope left for mixity in general, or in other words, the question as to when Union-only agreements are legally necessary or possible.

6   Conclusion: When Are Union-only Agreements Legally Necessary or Legally Possible?

It remains to gather the different threads from the preceding discussion together to expose the situations where Union-only trade agreements become

---

76   *Ibid*, para. 44.

77   *Ibid*, para. 46.

legally necessary, or where they may be concluded by the Union alone (mixity, in other words, would be facultative). In this context, it will also be asked whether the conclusion of international agreements rather than the enacting of EU-internal legislation may constitute "common rules" under Article 3(2) TFEU, rendering an AETR/ERTA effect possible. Some words will also be said about agreements which are formally concluded as mixed, but in respect of which the Union act concluding the agreement must be deemed to cover the whole agreement, rendering Member State adherence largely symbolic.

As to the CCP, it is obvious that with the new wording of the Treaty of Lisbon, in combination with the case law of the ECJ, a broad range of measures related to international trade have the potential of falling under this provision, including flanking measures of an environmental or social character, or concerning the CFSP. The main limitations relate to portfolio investment and investor-to-state dispute settlement (ISDS). Moreover, as confirmed by Opinion 3/15,[78] if the overall aim of an agreement has little or nothing to do with international trade, it may be held to be of a non-commercial nature and thus outside the scope of Articles 3(1) and 207 TFEU. If, again as demonstrated by Opinion 3/15, the agreement is not covered by the CCP, it has to be asked whether there would be an AETR/ERTA effect, by virtue of Article 3(2) TFEU.

It is in this respect obvious that in the light of the wording of this provision ("may" affect, in French "susceptible d'affecter"), the ever broadened range of Union secondary law (legislative and other legal acts) which may be "affected" and the current state of case law,[79] Article 3(2) TFEU has the potential of rendering the competence to conclude a wide range of international agreements exclusive. To take an example, while transport is a shared competence, the extensive reach of EU legislation in this field, and taking into account that the whole transport sector of the Singapore agreement was ruled by the ECJ to fall under an exclusive competence, could arguably mean a similar result for most international transport agreements. It could be asked to what extent the requirement that "a large extent" of the agreement is covered by existing Union rules in order for the agreement to fall within an exclusive AETR/ERTA competence (the requirement might be fulfilled if, say, 70–80 per cent of the agreement is covered), is applicable also if there is an exclusive Member State competence, or a CFSP competence, involved. At least if the exclusive Member

---

78   Opinion 3/15 (n. 39).
79   The reader is referred to section 4 of this contribution.

State, or the CFSP part, of the agreement is "ancillary" or "incidental", a Union-only agreement would seem to be called for.[80]

Opinion 2/15, on the other hand, makes it clear that primary law (such as the TEU and the TFEU) cannot constitute such "common rules" to trigger the AETR/ERTA effect.[81] A question which still does not seem to have been addressed head-on in case law is whether, and to what extent, international agreements previously concluded by the EU may constitute "common rules" as envisaged in Article 3(2) TFEU.[82] It is difficult to see why they would not, considering also that by such agreements, the EU has assumed obligations vis-à-vis third States and a new agreement affecting such older agreements could raise issues of the international responsibility of the Union under public international law. The fact that Member States often insist on the mixed character of a given agreement may suggest that they do not exclude the potential of an AETR/ERTA effect of the agreement and that they wish to avoid such a preemptive effect.[83] That said, not all international agreements binding on the EU would have such an AETR/ERTA effect on new agreements to be concluded by the EU.[84]

In the above discussion on Article 3(2) TFEU, everything has centered around the AETR/ERTA principle, as it is this criteria which almost exclusively has led to agreements belonging in principle to a shared competence falling under an exclusive competence. What about the so-called 1/76 criteria,[85] which, to cite Article 3(2) TFEU, implies that an agreement may fall under an exclusive competence when its conclusion "is necessary to enable the Union to exercise its internal competence". That such a situation may be an independent ground for exclusivity has been open to debate[86] but the question has been settled by its inclusion in Article 3(2) TFEU. One may ask whether the 1/76 principle could have the potential of becoming more relevant in the future (*sleeping beauty?*).

---

80   On "ancillary" provisions of agreements see A. Rosas in A. Dashwood and C. Hillion (n. 9) p.204–205. On Case C-244/17 *Commission v Council* relating to the relationship between "incidental" CFSP and other provisions see at n. 76 above.

81   See at n. 66. For a critical comment to the exclusion of primary law, see M. Chamon (n. 17), p. 1128–1130.

82   See M. Chamon (n. 17), p. 1111–1112, with references to literature.

83   See also M. Chamon (n. 17), p. 1112.

84   For instance, it would seem to be possible to *isolate* the effects of bilateral readmission agreements, that is agreements by which two parties commit themselves to take back their nationals whose presence in the other party is irregular, from future such agreements, as it is difficult to see why such a bilateral agreement would be affected by the conclusion of other corresponding agreements. That said, in practice EU readmission agreements are concluded as EU-only agreements, A. Rosas (n. 11), p. 34–35.

85   See Opinion 1/76, EU:C:1977:63.

86   A. Rosas (n. 11), p. 23–24.

As was already noted earlier, recent case law has confirmed that agreements which do not fall under Article 3(1) or Article 3(2) TFEU may still be concluded as Union-only agreements, namely if the Council has decided that the EU will exercise its (shared) competence over the entire agreement.[87] Moreover, there is one category of agreements which are concluded as mixed agreements but may nevertheless come close to Union-only agreements. I am thinking above all of mixed agreements which have not been concluded by all Member States (*incomplete* mixity).[88] In actual practice, *incomplete* mixity seems to be limited to multilateral rather than bilateral agreements. It is arguable that in the case of concurrent competence (shared competence across the board), the entire agreement becomes Union law, as the Council must be deemed to have exercised the Union's (shared) competence over the whole agreement. If that were not the case, there would be a serious problem with respect to the reach of the Union's obligations internally and its responsibility externally. This is because the Union, if there was a *Member States' part* of the agreement over which the Union had not exercised its competence would not be able to fulfil the obligations stemming from that part, while the territory of some Member States (those who have decided to stay outside the agreement) would not be covered by the agreement either. Such a situation could in fact amount to an unlawful reservation, assuming that reservations would be excluded or limited under the agreement or the gap identified above would be so broad that it would run counter to the object and purpose of the agreement.[89] *Incomplete* mixity certainly does not help to dispel the legal uncertainties surrounding mixed agreements but rather tends to constitute one more illustration of those uncertainties.

Finally, it should be noted that various theories have been espoused as to the possibility of constitutional limits to the right of the Council to opt for mixity, in situations which are not covered by the grounds of exclusivity in Article 3. The reader is here referred to the existing literature on the subject.[90]

---

87   Readmission agreements being an example, see n. 85.
88   On the notion see A. Rosas (n. 9), p. 206. On such mixed agreements not concluded by all Member States more generally see G. Van der Loo, R. Wessel (n. 13).
89   See Arts. 19–23 of the Vienna Convention on the Law of Treaties and A. Aust, *Modern Treaty Law and Practice* (Cambridge University Press, 2000), p. 108 et seq.
90   For a recent and comprehensive contribution to this discussion, with references to existing literature, see M. Chamon, 'Constitutional Limits to the Political Choice of Mixity', in E. Neframi, M. Gatti (eds.), *Constitutional Issues of EU External Relations Law* (Nomos, 2018), p. 137.

CHAPTER 2

Defining the Scope of the Common Commercial Policy

Marise Cremona

1 Introduction

This chapter will examine the scope of the common commercial policy (CCP) following the amendments to Article 207 TFEU and the other reforms introduced by the Treaty of Lisbon, in the light of subsequent practice and case law, including Opinion 2/15.[1] It will in particular focus on the identification of the field of action within which the EU's CCP competence may be deployed, on the degree to which the CCP may be used as a basis for exercising external regulatory power, and on the impact of broader EU external objectives on defining the scope of the CCP. Each of these questions are ultimately concerned with the boundary between the CCP and other policy competences. With the changes to CCP decision-making procedures introduced by the Treaty of Lisbon, in particular the introduction of the ordinary legislative procedure, this boundary is less sensitive than it was. Nevertheless, it does mark the boundary between an *a priori* exclusive external competence under Article 3(1) TFEU and shared competence that might become exclusive based on Article 3(2) TFEU, and Opinion 2/15 illustrates the implications of this distinction. The debate over the boundaries of trade policy also reflects the increasing political contention over how trade policy is determined (and by whom), the purposes for which it is used, and its links to the principles and objectives which underpin the EU's external action.

Defining the scope of the CCP gives rise to three interlinked questions.

The first is to define the field of action of the CCP: this policy, according to Article 207 TFEU, concerns "trade in goods", "trade in services", the "commercial aspects of intellectual property" (IPR), and "foreign direct investment" (FDI). How should these concepts be defined? To what extent should we map them against the scope of EU internal competences over (e.g.) services or

---

1 Opinion 2/15, EU:C:2017:376.

direct investment so that the CCP becomes an external face of the internal market? To what extent, alternatively or complementarily, should they be defined in terms of existing international economic law practice in the WTO or in standard investment agreements?

The second question concerns the type of measure which may be adopted under CCP powers. It is certainly not limited (as argued in the early years) to measures which directly impact the volume or flow of goods, and now services, across borders (such as tariffs or quotas), and may cover behind-the-border restrictions on trade resulting from domestic regulation such as product standards, as well as market regulation at an international level.[2] It has also been clear for many years that although trade liberalisation is a policy goal of the CCP, it is not the only goal; CCP powers may also be used in ways which regulate markets and protect consumers. But to what extent may regulatory measures concerning goods, services, FDI or IPR, whether contained in legislation or international agreements, be adopted on the basis of CCP powers? How are we to establish the boundary between the EU's general internal market-based regulatory competence and the CCP, and is there a danger that the CCP may be used to outflank or avoid the normal legislative procedural balance of power?

And these questions lead to a third: to what extent is the scope of trade policy (the CCP) linked to trade objectives? The questions that have arisen in an internal context on the boundary between the internal market and other policy fields, such as public health or environment, arise also in this external context. And if it is clear both that trade liberalisation is not the only goal, and that trade instruments may be used to achieve other purposes – including development, environmental, social and foreign policy objectives – to what extent (if at all) do the Treaties define the goals of EU trade policy?

In approaching the scope of the post-Lisbon CCP the Court of Justice, while stressing the changes made by the Lisbon Treaty, has used as a starting point a test developed in earlier cases where the boundary between the CCP and the EU's regulatory competence was at issue, especially cases on trade and environment or IPR.[3] As now expressed in Opinion 2/15:

---

2   On the former see e.g. Decision 80/45/EEC laying down provisions on the introduction and implementation of technical regulations and standards (OJ 1980, L 14/36); on the latter see e.g. Opinion 1/78, EU:C:1979:224.

3   See e.g. Opinion 2/00, EU:C:2001:664; case C-281/01 *Commission v Council*, EU:C:2002:761, para. 40–41; case C-347/03, *Regione autonoma Friuli-Venezia Giulia and ERSA*, EU:C:2005:285, para. 75; case C-411/06, *Commission v Parliament and Council*, EU:C:2009:518, para. 71.

> It is settled case-law that the mere fact that an EU act, such as an agreement concluded by it, is liable to have implications for trade with one or more third States is not enough for it to be concluded that the act must be classified as falling within the common commercial policy. On the other hand, an EU act falls within that policy if it relates specifically to such trade in that it is essentially intended to promote, facilitate or govern such trade and has direct and immediate effects on it [...].[4]

A CCP measure therefore concerns international trade (trade with third States), and in order to "relate specifically" to (as opposed to merely *having implications* for) international trade it must (i) be essentially intended to promote, facilitate or govern international trade, and (ii) have direct and immediate effects on such trade. These two factors logically reflect the traditional legal basis tests of the aim and content of a measure.

This approach has allowed the Court to draw on both external (e.g. the WTO TRIPS agreement in *Daiichi Sankyo*[5]) and internal (e.g. deriving the meaning of direct investment from internal market case law in Opinion 2/15[6]) sources to define the field of action of the CCP. It is an approach which, rather than seeking to establish a conceptual or abstract definition of the external dimension of trade in services, "commercial aspects of intellectual property" or direct investment, offers a focus on the predominant purpose and immediate effects of a measure, which appears practical. Its common sense is attractive, but its obviousness (an international trade measure is one which is intended to, and will, affect international trade) contains an element of tautology, as well as more than a little of *I know it when I see it*, which suggest an attempt to avoid being tied by definition. And does it offer sufficient traction to enable us to answer predictably the trickier boundary questions just posed? Certainly, when one tries to tease out the extent to which the CCP may cover regulatory measures on the basis of how this seemingly straightforward test has been applied by the Court (in Opinion 2/15 and elsewhere) and in the light of Article 217(6) TFEU, the result is complex and by no means obvious. It is, for example, not clear whether a different approach is warranted where an autonomous regulatory measure is adopted, as opposed to the conclusion of an international agreement which will need to be implemented via internal legislation.

---

4   Opinion 2/15 (n. 1), para. 36.
5   C-414/11 *Daiichi Sankyo Co. Ltd*, EU:C:2013:520, para. 53–60.
6   Opinion 2/15 (n. 1), para. 80.

2   Defining the Field of Action

The approach just outlined, based on a measure's trade-related aims and effects, has meant that each contested measure should be examined individually, without the need to create specific conceptual definitions of *trade in goods
or services*, the *commercial aspects of intellectual property*, or *foreign direct investment* for the purposes of defining the scope of the CCP. Instead of attempting to define the *external dimension* of services, IPR or direct investment either
based on, or distinguished from, that applicable internally the Court of Justice
has focused on the essential idea that the CCP is concerned with international
trade, looking for the presence (or absence) of effects on trade.

Thus, "trade in goods" covers types of goods that were or still are, elsewhere
in the Treaties, subject to specific regimes such as agricultural and fisheries
products, Euratom products, and even coal and steel products where they
formed part of a general agreement on trade in goods (agreements specifically relating to coal or steel were concluded under ECSC powers while that
Treaty was in force). Despite the "significant development of primary law" on
the scope of the CCP brought about by the Lisbon Treaty,[7] this approach has
not fundamentally altered. The emphasis is on the effects and purpose of the
measure in question, and the Court draws both on international trade and on
internal definitions, without prioritising one over the other.

Trade in services maps onto international instruments, in particular the
WTO agreements, in terms of both sectors and modes of supply. It is capable of
covering all four of the GATS modes of supply.[8] Thus "services" in the context
of the CCP is not given the residual meaning attached to Article 56 TFEU, and
may include "establishment" in the sense that the latter term is used in the
internal market. There is one significant exception to this approach: according to Article 207(5) TFEU international agreements "in the field of transport"
are excluded from the CCP, falling rather within the Treaty title on transport
policy. Here the Lisbon Treaty does not alter the pre-Lisbon position, and in
Opinion 2/15 the Court referred to Opinion 1/08 in holding that the aim of
this rule is that external powers in the field of transport should be governed
in parallel to the EU's internal competence, "remaining anchored" in the Title
on the common transport policy.[9] The transport exclusion covers all modes of

---

7   C-414/11, *Daichii Sankyo* (n. 5), para. 48.
8   That is, cross-border supply (mode 1), supply in the territory of one Member to the consumer
    of another Member (mode 2), supply through commercial presence (mode 3) and supply
    through presence of natural persons (mode 4); Opinion 2/15 (n.1), para. 54.
9   Opinion 1/08, EU:C:2009:739, para. 164.

services supply, and applies not only to transport services themselves, but also to other services that are "inherently linked to a physical act of moving persons or goods from one place to another by a means of transport".[10] The Court here explicitly followed case law on the (internal) Services Directive which excludes "services in the field of transport", an exclusion which also extends to services "inherently linked" to transport services.[11] Although in Opinion 2/15 the Court largely followed the Singapore FTA's own categorisation as to which services were linked to transport and which were not, it also followed the internal case law approach by deriving support from the legal basis of relevant internal legislation. In *Grupo Itevelesa* vehicle road testing was the subject of legislation based on the transport, rather than the services, title of the Treaty, and was excluded from the Services Directive. In Opinion 2/15 the Court relied on the fact that internal EU legislation on the sale and marketing of air transport services is based on a services (not a transport) legal basis, to conclude that this particular matter was not inherently linked to transport and so fell within the scope of Article 207(1) TFEU.[12] Thus although the overall approach to the scope of trade in services is based on the WTO / GATS, the scope of the exclusion – which places international transport services within the common transport policy – is based on the boundary between services and transport established internally.

In *Daichii Sankyo,* the Court found that the TRIPS agreement as a whole falls within the scope of "the commercial aspects of intellectual property" and thus within the CCP: TRIPS is "an integral part of the WTO system" and thus has "a specific link with international trade". Where measures in the field of IPR are not "commercial", however, they are excluded from the CCP. The reasoning in Opinion 3/15 is important: it is not the *type of IPR* which is categorised as non-commercial, it is *the purpose of the measure* – which, the Court found, was not "intended to promote, facilitate or govern" international trade:

> the purpose of the Marrakesh Treaty is to improve the position of beneficiary persons by facilitating, through various means, the access of such persons to published works; it is not to promote, facilitate or govern international trade in accessible format copies.[13]

---

10   Opinion 2/15 (n. 1), para. 61.

11   C-168/14 *Grupo Itevelesa and Others,* EU:C:2015:685.

12   Opinion 2/15 (n. 1), para. 67–68.

13   Opinion 3/15, EU:C:2017:114, para. 82.

Indeed, even the measures in the Marrakesh Treaty governing export and import of accessible format copies, which clearly would have an effect on international trade (the second limb of the test), were found to fall outside the CCP on the basis of their purpose: "the facilitation of the cross-border exchange of accessible format copies appears to be a means of achieving the non-commercial objective of the Marrakesh Treaty rather than an independent aim of the treaty".[14] We will return to the question raised here of the relevance of non-commercial objectives.

Article 207 TFEU covers measures relating to foreign direct investment (FDI), thereby creating a distinction between different types of foreign investment (direct and non-direct) which does not reflect current international investment agreement practice. Nor does the definition of FDI map neatly onto the internal Treaty provisions, although it is based on a categorisation developed internally. The Treaty provisions on capital movements cover both direct and non-direct (foreign) investment, and direct investment may fall within the scope of both capital movements and establishment.

FDI for the purposes of Article 207 TFEU is based on the definition of direct investment developed in the context of capital movements, as investment which "serves to establish or maintain lasting and direct links" between the investor and the undertaking and which enables the investor's participation in the management or control of the company. In Opinion 2/15, the Court made it clear that this definition satisfies the CCP's "specific link to international trade" criteria:

> any EU act promoting, facilitating or governing participation – by a natural or legal person of a third State in the European Union and vice versa – in the management or control of a company carrying out an economic activity is such as to have direct and immediate effects on trade between that third State and the European Union, whereas there is no specific link of that kind with trade in the case of investments which do not result in such participation.[15]

Foreign investments "which do not result in such participation", such as portfolio investments, therefore fall outside the scope of the CCP; instead they are governed by the Treaty provisions on capital movements, which also cover movements between the EU and third countries.[16]

14　Opinion 3/15 (n. 13), para. 90.
15　Opinion 2/15 (n. 1), para. 84.
16　Opinion 2/15 (n. 1), para. 227.

Where the investor's holding is sufficient to enable him or her "to exert a definite influence on the company's decisions and to determine its activities", then direct investment may fall within internal EU law rules on establishment.[17] Since freedom of establishment only applies within the EU, preserving a distinction between internal and external action, the application of the CCP to foreign direct investment which meets this threshold is not put into question.

On the other hand, given that the freedom of movement of capital applies also to movements to and from third States, there is a potential overlap between FDI as covered by the CCP and FDI as covered by the free movement of capital, and their legal implications are very different. The free movement of capital is a matter of shared competence; and the Treaty establishes a specific relationship, as regards movements of capital between the EU and third countries, between EU and Member State competence and between the principle of liberalisation and permissible restrictions (which are cast as exceptions).[18] Article 207 TFEU, in contrast, is an exclusive EU competence and the Treaty does not dictate the degree of liberalisation to be achieved, nor establish conditions for the imposition of restrictions.

To sum up: in defining the CCP's field of operation the Court has drawn both from international (especially WTO) practice and internal market rules. It bases its approach on the aim and effects of the measure in question, in line with the traditional method for determining the legal basis of a measure. It is workable, despite operating more as an *ex post* rationalisation than having any great predictive effect. Its results are inclusive and its limits are largely the result of legislative choice, such as the exclusion of portfolio investment, services in the field of transport, and the non-commercial aspects of IPR.

3 Regulatory Measures and the CCP

Our second question concerns the type of measure that may be adopted under CCP powers. Article 207(1) TFEU refers to tariff and trade agreements, achievement of uniformity in measures of liberalisation, export policy and trade protection measures. It is an open-ended list and from an early stage it was accepted that the CCP was not limited to measures directly affecting

17   See e.g. C-326/07, *Commission v Italy*, EU:C:2009:193, para. 34.
18   See e.g. Art. 64(1) TFEU and its interpretation in a case such as C-464/14 *SECIL – Companhia Geral de Cal e Cimento SA*, EU:C:2016:896.

trade flows such as tariffs and quotas. Although there was no explicit provision for the adoption of regulatory measures affecting external trade, GATT Tokyo Round commitments on regulation were implemented using CCP powers,[19] and since Opinion 1/78 it has been recognised that an external regulatory competence needs to accompany liberalisation if the Union is to carry on an effective commercial policy.[20] As the CCP has broadened to include services, IPR and FDI, the importance of its application to regulatory measures has grown, as has the potential overlap between internal regulatory legislation and CCP instruments. We cannot simply say that internal powers are concerned with internal measures and the CCP with international agreements: internal market powers can be used not only for adopting legislation but also for concluding international agreements; and the CCP is not confined to international agreements but also includes the adoption of unilateral measures.[21]

To define the type of measure that falls within the CCP the Court uses the same test as it uses to define the sectoral field of action: the measure must relate specifically to international trade in the sense that it is "essentially intended to promote, facilitate or govern international trade" and has "direct and immediate effects" on trade. Here, however, the open-endedness of the test makes it difficult to identify a precise boundary between Article 207 TFEU and other legal bases for regulatory measures. While establishing a regulatory framework for activities within the internal market would normally be seen as an internal competence, regulatory measures will often cover both internal and external trade. More particularly, we have to bear in mind Article 207(6) TFEU;[22] the CCP should not operate to distort the balance of power between EU and Member States or between the institutions, nor circumvent internal decision-making procedures. The result is a complex picture, depending on the type of regulatory measure envisaged.

---

19   See n. 23.

20   Opinion 1/78, EU:C:1979:224. See also Opinion 1/94, EU:C:1994:384.

21   As expressed by the Court as early as Opinion 1/75, EU:C:1975:145, "A commercial policy is in fact made up by the combination and interaction of internal and external measures, without priority being taken by one over the others. Sometimes agreements are concluded in execution of a policy fixed in advance, sometimes that policy is defined by the agreements themselves".

22   Art. 207(6) TFEU reads "The exercise of the competences conferred by this Article in the field of the common commercial policy shall not affect the delimitation of competences between the Union and the Member States, and shall not lead to harmonisation of legislative or regulatory provisions of the Member States in so far as the Treaties exclude such harmonisation".

3.1   Governing the Adoption and Implementation of Regulatory Measures

The CCP may be used as the legal basis for rules, in international trade relations, which (while not themselves establishing substantive standards) govern the adoption or application of EU regulations or standards in third country trade, or which impose conditions on the application of Member State rules.

In relation to trade in goods, legislation implementing the GATT Tokyo Round on the application of technical regulations and standards to third country goods was adopted in 1980 on the basis of CCP powers. This provides that standards harmonised at EU level apply equally to goods of non-EU origin, and where standards have not been harmonised the Member States are to apply national standards on a national treatment basis to third country imports.[23] The WTO agreements on sanitary and technical standards and regulations (SPS and TBT) were concluded under CCP powers, the Court finding that the SPS was intended to establish rules and disciplines to "guide the development, adoption and enforcement" of measures so as to "minimise their negative effects on trade", and the TBT was designed "merely" to ensure that technical regulations and standards do not create unnecessary obstacles to trade.[24] Neither of these agreements actually establish harmonised standards; they establish a framework of rules guiding their adoption and application.

Thus, clauses in agreements (or legislation) which are concerned not with establishing or harmonising regulation, but with its operation via mutual recognition, conformity assessment, regulatory cooperation or non-discrimination requirements, can be based upon CCP powers, whether the regulations in question have already been harmonised at EU level or derive from Member State powers. This is the principle underlying the passages in Opinion 2/15 dealing with investment protection, intellectual property, renewable energy, and sustainable development. In relation to renewable energy, for example, the Court said that the relevant chapter of the EU-Singapore FTA "does not establish any environmental standard" but rather imposes an obligation of non-discrimination and removes some barriers to market access by requiring acceptance of conformity assessments.[25]

---

23   Decision 80/45/EEC laying down provisions on the introduction and implementation of technical regulations and standards (OJ 1980, L 14/36). The Decision is still in force. Where the EU establishes only minimum harmonisation, direct imports from third countries will be subject to the relevant national regulations, which may exceed the minimum; the right of market access on the basis of the EU minimum standards is applicable only to third country goods already in free circulation.

24   Opinion 1/94 (n. 20), para. 30–33.

25   Opinion 2/15 (n. 1), para. 73–74.

The Court also applied this reasoning to the investment protection chapter of the EU-Singapore FTA. It rejected an argument that the CCP is limited to market access commitments on FDI, holding that the CCP may also cover investment protection, since these provisions on national treatment and the prohibition of arbitrary treatment "contribute to the legal certainty of investors" and "concern the treatment of the participation of entrepreneurs of one Party in the management or control of companies carrying out economic activities in the territory of the other Party".[26] Thus, for example, it found that the fair and equitable treatment obligation "does not contain any commitment for the Member States relating to their criminal law, tax law or social security", but rather provides that "relevant legislation must in each case be applied to an investor of the other Party "in an equitable and non-discriminatory manner"".[27] Similarly, the investment protection measures (like Article 65 TFEU) envisaged derogations on grounds of public order or public security. Although these were argued to fall within Member State powers, the Court held that the agreement "does not establish any international commitment concerning public order, public security or other public interests",[28] but deals rather with *how those powers are exercised* in relation to third country direct investment. The provision in question, therefore "does not encroach upon the competences of the Member States regarding public order, public security and other public interests, but obliges the Member States to exercise those competences in a manner which does not render the trade commitments entered into by the European Union [...] redundant".[29]

In the case of intellectual property it is harder to maintain a distinction between the creation or harmonisation of rights and the adoption of "homogeneous standards of protection" which are not, according to the Court, an end in themselves but "a means to the end of developing trade between the contracting parties in a fair manner".[30] However in the discussion of intellectual property protection in the post-Lisbon case law (which we will not explore further here)[31] the Court does try to walk this tightrope.[32]

---

26   *Ibid,* para. 94–95.

27   *Ibid,* para. 108.

28   *Ibid,* para. 101.

29   *Ibid,* para. 103.

30   C-389/15, *Commission v Council*, EU:C:2017:798, para. 60.

31   On this issue, see the contribution by Inge Govaere in this volume.

32   See e.g. Opinion 2/15 (n. 1), para. 122–126; C-389/15, *Commission v Council* (n. 30), para. 49–62; see also C-414/11, *Daiichi Sankyo Co. Ltd* (n. 5), para. 58–60.

We may conclude that the EU has the power on the basis of Article 207 TFEU to enter into agreements with third countries which commit the EU and its Member States as to how its regulations (whether national or EU in origin) will be applied to third country nationals and undertakings, as long as such commitments will facilitate international trade.

Closely connected to this is the principle that the CCP may encompass clauses in an agreement which refer to existing standards established in other international agreements binding the EU – including environmental and social standards – and which are designed to ensure that trade with third countries complies with those standards. Where an EU trade agreement does not create new regulatory norms but instead commits the parties, in giving effect to the trade liberalisation envisaged in the agreement, to respect those contained in other international agreements already binding on the EU, no additional legal basis is required. Such clauses, according to the Court, do not create new obligations but simply preserve the right of the parties to set their own standards in conformity with their existing international obligations, and in accordance with their own internal legislative procedures.[33] We should note here the Court's care to ensure that the EU's *internal legislative procedures* are not compromised. This is the principle behind the Court's treatment of the trade and sustainable development (TSD) chapter of the EU-Singapore FTA in Opinion 2/15. The parties, it held, "undertake, essentially, to ensure that trade between them takes place in compliance with the obligations that stem from the international agreements concerning social protection of workers and environmental protection to which they are party".[34] The FTA, in its view, does not create new commitments and therefore a separate legal basis is not required. A couple of points may be made briefly here.

First, in using this form of reasoning on sustainable development, the Court categorises the TSD chapter as an integral part of the trade provisions, not a separate (if subsidiary) element of the agreement. In reaching this conclusion, the Court applied its standard CCP criteria. The TSD provisions are intended to "govern" trade in that they are designed to ensure that the trade provisions are implemented in a way that ensures compliance with other international norms. They have a direct effect on international trade, since (i) the parties agree not to seek to encourage trade by lowering their environmental and social standards; (ii) the parties agree not to apply the international standards "in a protectionist manner"; (iii) the international commitments level the trade

---

33 Opinion 2/15 (n. 1), para. 165; C-414/11 *Daiichi Sankyo Co. Ltd* (n. 5), para. 59–60.
34 Opinion 2/15 (n. 1), para. 152.

playing field between the parties; and (iv) the parties will introduce verification and certification schemes for trade in some products (timber and fisheries). In this way, the concept of a *trade instrument* is broadened to encompass new kinds of sustainable development flanking disciplines, akin to procurement or competition rules. This approach contrasts with that of Advocate General Sharpston in the same case, who argued that general external objectives such as those found in Articles 3(5) and 21 TEU do not affect the scope of the CCP, and that references to fundamental labour rights in the FTA were relevant to the substantive compatibility of the agreement with EU primary law but not to the scope of EU competence.[35] We will return in section 4 to this question of the relevance of non-commercial objectives in defining the scope of the CCP.

Second, the Court supported its argument that the TSD chapter may directly affect trade by arguing that a material breach of the sustainable development commitments could lead to a suspension of the trade liberalisation provisions.[36] This argument was based on general treaty law, citing Article 60(1) of the Vienna Convention on the Law of Treaties, rather than any explicit provision to this effect in the FTA under consideration. The TSD chapter is thereby turned into a form of sustainable development conditionality, potentially strengthening its effect. Although the weak enforcement of the sustainable development dimension of trade agreements has been a source of criticism of EU trade policy, this line of argument gives rise to several questions. First, this possibility of suspension sits uneasily with the exemption of the TSD chapter from the FTA's normal dispute settlement procedures.[37] And second, if the possibility of suspension is taken seriously then this would appear to undermine the Court's contention that the TSD chapter does not impose new obligations on the parties.[38]

We may conclude at this stage that the CCP encompasses regulatory provisions that are concerned with minimising trade barriers caused by the application of domestic standards, or with ensuring that trade liberalisation does not undermine mutual commitments to internationally-agreed standards. But

---

35   Opinion of AG Sharpston in Opinion 2/15, EU:C:2016:992, para. 495.

36   Opinion 2/15 (n. 1), para. 161.

37   Art. 13.16(1) EUSFTA. L. Ankersmit, 'Opinion 2/15: Adding Some Spice to the Trade & Environment Debate', EuropeanlawBlog, 15 June 2017.

38   In contrast to the Court, the Advocate General concluded that while the TSD chapter did not represent a form of trade conditionality, "its effect is to incorporate those [existing multilateral] commitments into the EUSFTA and therefore make them applicable between the European Union and Singapore *on the basis of the EUSFTA*", thereby creating a new obligation for the Parties (Opinion of AG Sharpston in Opinion 2/15 (n. 35), para. 490–498, emphasis in original).

what of the conclusion of international agreements (or the adoption of legislation) designed to establish new harmonised standards or regulatory controls, going beyond mutual recognition, regulatory cooperation and ensuring non-discriminatory application of domestic standards?

3.2 *Establishing Regulatory Standards*

In principle, the choice of legal basis should be governed by the primary or predominant purpose of the legislation, or agreement. The fact that third country enterprises or imported goods are included within the scope of an EU regulatory measure does not necessarily require the use of Article 207 TFEU. A regulatory measure which impacts external trade (imports or exports of goods from or to third countries, services offered by external providers, or non-EU enterprises) should nonetheless be adopted on an internal market legal basis if the regulation of external trade is ancillary or incidental to the main internal market objective. So for example, although Directive 2001/37 on the production, marketing and labelling of tobacco products was adopted on the joint basis of internal market and CCP powers,[39] the Court held that the CCP legal basis was unnecessary and should not have been used. The prohibition on manufacture of non-compliant products did affect products designed for the export market but its main objective was the protection of the internal market from illegal re-imports and Article 95 EC (now Article 114 TFEU) was the appropriate legal basis.[40] Likewise, Regulation 1007/2009 on trade in seal products was based on Article 95 EC only, and was framed as essentially an internal market measure, applying to seal products imported from third countries "[i]n order to ensure that the harmonised rules provided for in this Regulation are fully effective".[41]

In the field of services, we find a similar approach in legislation adopted since the Lisbon Treaty. The current directive on the authorisation and supervision

---

39   Directive 2001/37/EC on the approximation of the laws, regulations and administrative provisions of the Member States concerning the manufacture, presentation and sale of tobacco products (OJ 2001, L 194/26), was adopted on a joint legal basis of Art. 95 and 113 TEC. Its predecessors had been based on an internal market legal basis alone but since Directive 2001/37 also covered tobacco products to be exported from the EU the CCP legal basis was added: see recital 11, and Art. 3 which sets maximum tar, carbon monoxide and nicotine yields for all cigarettes manufactured in the EU whatever their destination.

40   C-491/01, *The Queen v Secretary of State for Health, ex parte: British American Tobacco (Investments) Ltd and Imperial Tobacco Ltd*, EU:C:2002:741, para. 81–91. The Court went on to find, however, that since the co-decision procedure required by Art. 95 TEC had in fact been used, the addition of Article 133 TEC as a legal basis did not invalidate the directive.

41   Regulation 1007/2009/EC on trade in seal products (OJ 2009, L 286/3), recital 13. For a discussion see T. Perišin, 'Is the EU Seal Products Regulation a Sealed Deal? EU and WTO Challenges', *International and Comparative Law Quarterly* 62 (2013), p. 381–387.

of credit institutions, based on Article 53 TFEU (an internal market legal basis), contains a title on relations with third countries, including the establishment of third country banks in the EU, and envisaging the possibility of agreements with third countries on both authorisation and consolidated supervision of credit institutions.[42] Other recent legislation regulating the financial services sector, and covering institutions established in third countries and offering services in the EU, has likewise been adopted on an internal market legal basis. For example, the regulation on the supervision of credit rating agencies, based on Article 114 TFEU, contains provisions on the activities in the EU of credit rating agencies established in third countries, as well as regulatory cooperation between the EU's supervisory body (ESMA) and the supervisory authorities of third countries.[43] The directive on the authorisation and supervision of alternative investment fund managers (AIFMs), based on Article 53 TFEU, covers both those that have their registered office in a Member State (EU AIFMs) and those that have their registered office in a third country (non-EU AIFMs).[44]

In the nature of things, for both practical and legal reasons, including compliance with WTO and bilateral treaty obligations, regulation will generally be designed to apply equally to domestic goods and imports, and to domestic and foreign investors or service providers; the use of an internal legal basis – as in the examples above – will reflect its predominant purpose. Where, on the other hand, a measure is designed to regulate international trade as well as trade within the internal market, a dual legal basis may be appropriate. The EU's conclusion of the WHO Convention on tobacco control, for example, which establishes harmonised rules on the packaging and labelling of tobacco as well as containing provisions on trade in tobacco products, was based on Articles 95 and 133 EC (now Articles 114 and 207 TFEU).[45] The dual legal basis, which was not challenged, could be justified on the ground that the Convention is equally concerned with trade and with product regulation for purposes of public health.[46]

---

42 Directive 2013/36/EU on access to the activity of credit institutions and the prudential supervision of credit institutions and investment firms (OJ 2013, L 176/338); for the provisions on relations with third countries see Title VI, Articles 47–48.

43 Regulation 513/2011/EU (OJ 2011, L 145/30).

44 Directive 2011/61/EU (OJ 2011, L 174/1).

45 Council Decision 2004/513/EC of 2 June 2004 concerning the conclusion of the WHO Framework Convention on Tobacco Control(OJ 2004, L 213/8).

46 C.f. case C-94/03, *Commission v Council*, EU:C:2006:2, holding that a dual legal basis (environment and trade) should have been used to conclude the Rotterdam Convention on the Prior Informed Consent Procedure for certain hazardous chemicals and pesticides in international trade.

What of regulatory measures that have a *primarily external* focus? For the reasons just given, this is a less common scenario, but nonetheless examples do exist. To mention one, in *Commission v Council (Energy Star)* a bilateral agreement between the EU and the USA on an energy-efficiency labelling programme for office equipment (establishing common specifications and a common logo) was held to fall within the scope of the CCP.[47] The Court found that the main purpose of the agreement was the facilitation of trade, the promotion of energy conservation being only "an indirect and distant effect", whereas the effect on trade in office equipment would be "direct and immediate".[48] Importantly for our purposes, the Court stressed that the agreement would not introduce new energy-efficiency requirements. While this is strictly true, as the Court also states, it "renders the specifications initially adopted by the EPA [the US environmental protection agency] applicable on both the American market and the European market".[49] Thus, as far as the EU was concerned, a new, albeit voluntary, labelling system was introduced.

In the *Energy Star* case the EU was adopting an existing system and agreeing on its future joint management with a third country. Where an international agreement does not create new regulation for the EU, but seeks to extend existing internal market regulation to third countries, then again the CCP may be the appropriate legal basis. In *Commission v Council (conditional access services)* the CCP was held to be the correct legal basis for the signature of a Convention which would "extend beyond the European Union the legal protection introduced by Directive 98/84".[50] The internal EU rules had already been adopted under internal market powers and the Court held that the aim of the projected agreement was not to harmonise internal EU rules; rather, it was to extend them to third countries in order to promote trade:

> since the approximation of the legislation of Member States in the field concerned has already been largely achieved by Directive 98/84, the primary objective of the Convention is not to improve the functioning of the internal market, but to extend legal protection of the relevant services beyond the territory of the European Union and thereby to promote international trade in those services.[51]

---

47   C-281/01, *Commission v Council* (n. 3).
48   *Ibid,* para. 41.
49   *Ibid,* para. 42.
50   *Ibid,* para. 61.
51   C-137/12, *Commission v Council*, EU:C:2013:675, para. 67.

Thus, CCP powers can be used to extend to third countries existing regulatory measures adopted within the internal market. On the other hand, were a trade agreement to include provisions establishing new harmonised standards or post-establishment regulatory controls, should these also be regarded as falling within the scope of the CCP? Or should they be seen rather as the external dimension of the internal regulatory competence, requiring an internal market legal basis?

Article 207(6) TFEU provides that the exercise of the competence conferred by Article 207 "shall not lead to harmonisation of legislative or regulatory provisions of the Member States insofar as the Treaties exclude such harmonisation". Harmonisation is excluded, for example, in relation to public health.[52] *A contrario*, it would appear that insofar as the Treaties do *not* exclude harmonisation, Article 207 could be used as a basis for external measures involving harmonisation of Member State regulation. But Article 207(6) TFEU may help to set limits to the CCP in a slightly different way. To recall, its first clause provides:

> The exercise of the competences conferred by this Article in the field of the common commercial policy shall not affect the delimitation of competences between the Union and the Member States.

This provision is not drafted so as to restrict the scope of application of Article 207 TFEU, but rather to restrict the legal effects of the exercise of CCP competence.[53] It ensures that the exercise of the EU's *external* powers under Article 207 TFEU in fields such as intellectual property and FDI, and the exercise of its regulatory competence in relation to goods or services in an external context, does not in itself imply exclusivity in those fields when the EU acts *internally.* External (exclusive) action does not result in the displacement of Member State competence internally through pre-emption (sometimes referred to as a 'reverse-AETR effect'[54]). Article 207(6) TFEU thus confirms that although exclusive *external* competence (via the CCP) extends into fields which are not

---

52   Art. 168(5) TFEU.

53   M. Cremona, 'A Quiet Revolution: The Changing Nature of the EU's Common Commercial Policy', in M. Bungenberg, et al. (eds.), *European Yearbook of International Economic Law,* 2017, Vol 8, p. 3.

54   A. Dashwood, J. Heliskoski, 'The Classic Authorities Revisited' in A. Dashwood, C. Hillion (eds.), *The General Law of EC External Relations* (Sweet & Maxwell, 2000), p. 13. P. Strik, *Shaping the Single European Market in the Field of Foreign Direct Investment* (Hart Publishing, 2014), p. 80–81. For an account of the genesis of Article 207(6) TFEU, see J-F. Brakeland 'Politique commerciale commune, coopération avec les pays tiers et aide humanitaire' in G. Amato, H. Bribosia, B. de Witte (eds.), *Genèse et Destinée de la*

yet covered by internal EU rules (e.g. IPR, but also non-harmonised product standards), this does not mean that the Member States are automatically completely excluded from adopting internal rules over such fields, nor that internal rules adopted at EU level should necessarily be based on Article 207 TFEU.[55] An agreement concluded under Article 207 TFEU, and thus within exclusive EU competence, may contain commitments which will be implemented internally by the EU under shared powers, or even by the Member States. Such an approach is consistent with the Court's statements in Opinion 2/15 and allows us to reconcile the grant of exclusive competence in Article 207(1) TFEU with the proviso as to the delimitation of competence between Union and Member States found in Article 207(6) TFEU. Following this line of argument, Article 207(6) TFEU simply provides that the exercise of CCP powers does not interfere with internal competence allocation (nor the express exclusion of harmonisation competence in specific sectors). It does not, in itself, help us to set the boundary between the CCP and other regulatory power-conferring provisions in the context of external action.

Further, the "aim and effects" test[56] is likely to be satisfied, given that regulatory action which has a primarily external focus will generally be designed to impact international trade.[57] However, it is possible to argue that measures that are essentially aimed at regulatory harmonisation, or at establishing new regulatory systems, fall outside the scope of Article 207 TFEU. In pointing out that the TBT and SPS agreements were "confined to" rules on the adoption and application of regulations, Opinion 1/94 could be read as suggesting that agreements which go beyond this to include substantive harmonisation should not be based on CCP powers alone.[58] In deciding in favour of a CCP legal basis in the *Energy Star* case, the Court denied that the agreement contained new energy efficiency requirements.[59] Opinion 2/15 also seems to take this position. The Court went to some lengths to argue that the FTA provisions on IPR, sustainable development and investor protection did not create new regulatory standards. In holding that the TSD chapter in the EU-Singapore agreement fell

Constitution Européenne: Commentaire du traité établissant une Constitution pour l'Europe à la lumière des travaux préparatoires et perspectives d' avenir (Bruylant, 2007), p. 849.

55 A. Dimopoulos, 'The Effects of the Lisbon Treaty on the Principles and Objectives of the Common Commercial Policy', *European Foreign Affairs Rev* 15 (2010), p. 159. See also C-414/11 *Daiichi Sankyo Co. Ltd* (n. 5), para. 59, and AG Sharpston in Opinion 2/15 (n. 35), para. 107–109.

56 Opinion 2/15 (n. 1), para. 36, cited at note 4.

57 See e.g. C-281/01, *Commission v Council*, (n. 3), discussed above.

58 See text above at n. 24.

59 See text above at n. 48.

within the scope of the CCP the Court stressed that it was "intended not to regulate the levels of social and environmental protection in the Parties' respective territory" but rather to make liberalisation of trade subject to a condition of compliance with pre-existing international obligations in these fields.[60] It also found that the provisions on intellectual property "in no way [fall] within the scope of harmonisation of the laws of the Member States of the European Union".[61]

In using this form of argumentation the Court was setting boundaries to the reach of Article 207 TFEU which operate alongside the *aims and effects* test; in its view the CCP does not provide a basis for adopting measures which themselves address the harmonisation of IPR, or the regulation of social, environmental or labour standards. Such matters would fall within the relevant competences on intellectual property, or social or environmental protection, which are matter of shared competence.[62] In making this argument, the Court cites Article 207(6) TFEU in support of its identification of some limits to the scope of Article 207 TFEU, given its expansive approach to the ways in which regulation may have direct and immediate effects on trade.

4   The CCP and Non-commercial Purposes

Finally, let us turn to the purposes of the CCP and how they relate to its scope.

It might appear paradoxical that on the one hand, the test for whether a measure falls within the scope of the CCP is defined in terms of its aims as well as its effects (it must be "essentially intended" to promote, facilitate or govern international trade), while on the other hand, the Treaties allow great latitude to the institutions in defining the purpose of trade policy. Certainly, trade liberalisation is a Treaty-mandated objective of EU trade policy,[63] but as long ago

---

60   Opinion 2/15 (n. 1), para. 166; see section 3(i) above.

61   Opinion 2/15 (n.1), para. 126.

62   "[...] the exclusive competence of the European Union referred to in Article 3(1)(e) TFEU cannot be exercised in order to regulate the levels of social and environmental protection in the Parties' respective territory. The adoption of such rules would fall within the division of competences between the European Union and the Member States that is laid down, in particular, in Article 3(1)(d) and (2) and Article 4(2)(b) and (e) TFEU" (Opinion 2/15 (n.1), para. 164). Art. 3(1)(d) TFEU covers fisheries conservation (exclusive competence), Art. 4(2)(b) and (e) TFEU refer to social policy and the environment respectively, both shared competence subject to the possibility of exclusivity under Art. 3(2) TFEU.

63   Art. 206 TFEU.

as 1979 it was made clear that it is not the sole or overriding objective.[64] Trade policy has long been used for other purposes,[65] including development,[66] foreign policy,[67] environmental protection,[68] or the protection of human rights.[69] There are cases – such as the *Energy Star* case already mentioned – where the non-trade objective, while recognised, is regarded as ancillary or incidental. In the classic pre-Lisbon cases we can see trade instruments being used for non-trade purposes, but it is always clear that these are standard trade instruments (a preferential tariff, an export or an import ban, certification schemes). The non-trade purpose is ulterior, incidental or ancillary, but there is also a trade purpose: the instrument is designed to facilitate or govern trade. So the measures meet the Court's standard aims and effect test.

It is not always easy to distinguish means and ends, to draw the line between an ulterior or ancillary non-trade objective for a trade measure (as in *Energy Star*[70]), and the use of a trade instrument to pursue a predominant non-trade objective (as in the *Waste Shipments* case[71]). In Opinion 3/15 it was held that a measure which certainly aimed to facilitate the cross border movement of goods was not a trade measure because it was "not specifically intended to promote, facilitate or govern international trade in accessible format copies"; it was "a means of achieving the non-commercial objective of the Marrakesh Treaty" rather than "an independent aim of the treaty".[72] The predominant purpose (facilitating access) took the measure outside the scope of the CCP. In contrast, in *Geographical Indications*, the trade objective was dominant: "the specific protection of appellations of origin that is provided for by the Lisbon

---

64   "Although it may be thought that at the time when the Treaty was drafted liberalization of trade was the dominant idea, the Treaty nevertheless does not form a barrier to the possibility of the Community's developing a commercial policy aiming at a regulation of the world market for certain products rather than at a mere liberalization of trade" (Opinion 1/78 (n. 20), para. 44.

65   On the nexus between the CCP and (i) development cooperation, (ii) the CFSP and (iii) human rights, see, respectively, the chapters by Sieglinde Gstöhl; Tamara Perišin and Sam Koplewicz; and Peter Van Elsuwege in this volume.

66   E.g. the Generalised System of Preferences: Case 45/86, *Commission v Council*, EU:C:1987:163.

67   E.g. economic sanctions: Case, C-124/95 *Centro-Com*, EU:C:1997:8.

68   C-281/01 *Commission v Council* (Energy Star Agreement), note 3.

69   Council Regulation 1236/2005/EC concerning trade in certain goods which could be used for capital punishment, torture or other cruel, inhuman or degrading treatment or punishment (OJ 2005, L 200/1).

70   C-281/01, *Commission v Council*, (Energy Star Agreement) (n. 3).

71   C-411/06, *Commission v European Parliament and Council*, EU:C:2009:518.

72   Opinion 3/15 (n. 13), para. 89–90.

Agreement is not an end in itself, but a means to the end of developing trade between the contracting parties in a fair manner".[73]

While these latter cases demonstrate continuity with earlier case law, as well as the occasional difficulty of determining the predominant purpose of a measure, there are signs of a shift in this classic approach to non-trade objectives, although the full implications are not yet clear. We now have widely-drawn general external objectives in Articles 3(5) and 21 TEU, which include sustainable development, support for human rights and safeguarding the fundamental values and interests of the Union. Trade policy is to pursue these objectives and we can see from Opinion 2/15 their practical importance.[74] But how exactly do they form the *context* in which trade policy is conducted? Do they do more than confirm what we already knew, that trade policy may be used to serve broader political aims?

In Opinion 2/15, in discussing the sustainable development chapter, the Court concludes that "the objective of sustainable development henceforth forms an integral part of the common commercial policy".[75] Instead of using a trade instrument to achieve other objectives, we have here non-trade instruments (international agreements on social and environmental protection) being used to govern, and facilitate, trade liberalisation. This development is possible because the sustainable development purpose of those instruments is found to be (also) a purpose of trade policy. This is not a case of sustainable development as an ulterior purpose of trade policy (as in the case of the Generalised System of Preferences or economic sanctions); nor is it a case of an ancillary or indirect objective which can be disregarded for the purposes of legal basis (as in the case of the environmental objective in the *Energy Star* case). Here, the objective of sustainable development is treated *as an integral part* of trade policy – as a trade objective. And the broadening of the objectives of trade policy is a basis for broadening the concept of a trade instrument, or what may be included in a trade instrument. This is why the Court needed to take care to spell out that the commitments in the FTA were not new but were to existing agreements – this ruling does not establish the possibility of using the CCP as a basis for adopting new international environmental protection standards for the purposes of sustainable development. It

---

73   C-389/15, *Commission v Council* (n. 30), para. 60.

74   Art. 21(3) TEU and Art. 205 and 207(1) TFEU.

75   Opinion 2/15 (n.1), para. 147. Contrast the Advocate General, who took the view that "neither fundamental rights at work nor standards of environmental protection form an integral part of the common commercial policy"(Opinion of AG Sharpston in Opinion 2/15 (n. 34), para. 496.

is rather that sustainable development instruments may be used to further trade policy.

A similar development may be observed in *Commission v Council (Kazakhstan)*, although concealed behind predominant / ancillary purpose reasoning.[76] The case concerned the substantive legal basis for the adoption of a Council decision establishing the Union position in the Cooperation Council established under the Enhanced Partnership and Cooperation Agreement between the EU and Kazakhstan, and more specifically whether a Common Foreign and Security Policy legal basis was required alongside the CCP and development cooperation legal bases.[77] The Court concluded that although the agreement contained CFSP-related provisions, these were too limited in scope to amount to a distinct component of the agreement: they were "incidental to that agreement's two components constituted by the common commercial policy and development cooperation".[78] In coming to that conclusion, the Court argued that the CFSP-related provisions "fall fully within the objective of the Partnership Agreement [...] of contributing to international and regional peace and stability and to economic development".[79] This is a somewhat puzzling step in the argument, since indeed one would assume that an agreement's provisions fall within its own objectives. In fact, the significant question in determining whether a broad legal basis such as development cooperation or the CCP can also cover an agreement's ancillary provisions, is whether the ancillary provisions serve the objectives of the main legal basis and do not impose such extensive obligations as to constitute objectives distinct from that legal basis.[80] In other words, are the different substantive components of the agreement adequately reflected in the legal basis (or bases) chosen? Thus, in order for the CFSP-related provisions of the agreement with Kazakhstan to be covered by the CCP and development cooperation legal bases it must be shown that they fall within the policy objectives of (one of) these policy fields.

---

76 C-244/17, *Commission v Council (Kazakhstan)*, EU:C:2018:662.

77 The addition of a CFSP legal basis would have necessitated a unanimous vote in the Council, under the terms of Art. 218(8) TFEU: C-244/17, *Commission v Council (Kazakhstan)* (n. 76), para. 20–30. See further P. Van Elsuwege, G. Van der Loo, 'Legal Basis Litigation in Relation to International Agreements: *Commission v. Council* (Enhanced Partnership and Cooperation Agreement with Kazakhstan', *Common Market Law Review* 56 (2019), p.1333.

78 C-244/17, *Commission v Council (Kazakhstan)* (n. 76), para. 46.

79 *Ibid.*

80 See e.g. C-377/12, *Commission v Council (Philippines)*, EU:C:2014:1903, para. 35–39, cited by the Court in C-244/17, *Commission v Council* (n. 76) at para. 45. In case C-377/12 the ancillary provisions were found to fall within the scope of development cooperation objectives, and were not sufficiently substantial to require their own separate legal basis.

As mentioned by the Court, one of the agreement's key objectives, which the CFSP-related provisions were designed to promote, was "contributing to international and regional peace and stability". The finding that these provisions did not require a separate legal basis is therefore not only a function of their limited content, but also implies that this objective (one of the EU's general external objectives[81]) may be regarded as an objective of the EU's trade and / or development policies. So just as Article 21(2) TEU may justify the use of sustainable development instruments to further EU trade policy (as in Opinion 2/15), CFSP instruments (as contained in the agreement with Kazakhstan) may be used to further EU trade and development policies.

As this discussion demonstrates, it is not always straightforward to ascertain whether (i) the non-commercial objective of a measure is an ulterior objective which does not detract from the direct trade purpose; or (ii) the non-commercial objective may be treated as part of the trade objective (e.g. sustainable development); or (iii) the non-commercial objective is in fact the primary objective and thus the measure does not fall within the CCP at all.

5   Some Concluding Observations

This chapter has assessed the scope of the EU's trade policy, or CCP, from three perspectives: defining the field of action; defining the types of measure that may be adopted, and in particular the extent to which the CCP may be used to exercise a regulatory competence; and the relevance of objectives to the scope of the CCP. It is of course selective in this choice of issues.[82] It has been argued that the Court of Justice has used a flexible test for defining the scope of the CCP, based on ascertaining first, whether the measure is essentially intended to promote, facilitate or govern trade with third countries, and second, whether it has direct and immediate effects on such trade. This *aim and effects* test, which reflects a standard legal basis approach, has provided a flexible framework for determining the field of action of the CCP, drawing on both international practice and internal EU law, and generally avoiding conceptual distinctions between types of services, IPR or FDI. These distinctions have been

---

81   Art. 21(2)(c) TFEU.

82   Many other aspects which deserve attention, such as the degree to which CCP competence may cover dispute settlement, or the relevance of human rights compliance to the exercise of trade policy powers, have been omitted for reasons of space or because they are dealt with elsewhere in this volume, such as in the chapters by Peter Van Elsuwege.

addressed only where necessitated by the wording of the Treaty itself, such as to determine the exclusion of agreements in the field of transport, or the scope of "direct" foreign investment.

The flexibility of the *aims and effects* test, while useful in its ability to be applied to a wide range of instruments and contexts, also leads to a lack of predictability in defining the types of measure which may be adopted under CCP powers, and the boundary between the CCP and other competences. This question arose in the CCP's earliest years and is now more important than ever, given both the expanded field of action within which the CCP operates and the increasing focus on the regulatory dimension of trade agreements. The new generations of trade agreements contain more extensive regulatory commitments across wider sectoral fields, and these agreements have become politically more contentious. The scope of (exclusive) trade competence and its relation to other regulatory competences has become a significant issue with both legal and political salience, and which the *aim and effects* test does not fully answer. Opinion 2/15 demonstrates both the potential breadth of the test and the Court's attempt to draw a line – without, however, providing a clear boundary to CCP powers with real predictive traction.

Although the Court's test includes the need for a CCP measure to have a trade-related aim, and although it has long been accepted that such an aim may be supplemented by non-commercial ulterior or ancillary objectives, the general external objectives introduced by the Lisbon Treaty have opened up the question of what a *trade objective* might be. At least one of these general objectives (sustainable development) has been defined as an integral part of trade policy, raising the question whether sustainable development is somehow a special case,[83] or whether other general external objectives might also be so defined.

The potential significance of these developments lies in the possibility that the general external objectives in the context of which the EU's CCP is to be conducted may have the effect of expanding the types of instrument which may be used as an integral part of trade policy. Not only are trade instruments used, as they have long been used, for ulterior political or environmental objectives; we now see environmental and social (and perhaps also CFSP) instruments used to further trade objectives, without necessarily requiring a separate legal basis. It is for this reason that, when defining the scope of the CCP, we

---

83   Based both on Art. 9 and 11 TFEU and on the commitment to "free and fair trade" in Art. 3(5) TEU: see Opinion 2/15 (n.1), para. 146.

are likely to see increasing focus on the extent to which the CCP can be used as a legal basis for establishing new regulatory commitments, under what conditions a sustainable development or political commitment in a trade agreement is sufficiently substantial to represent a distinct objective requiring a separate legal basis, and on the uses to which trade policy is put.

PART 2

The EU's Investment Policies

∴

The First 10 Years of the European Union's Policy on Investment Dispute Settlement

From Initial Reforms to the Multilateral Investment Court

Colin M. Brown

1   Introduction

When the European Union (EU) acquired competence for investment protection on the entry into force of the Treaty of Lisbon in 2009 little presaged the profound impact it would have on international investment policy making. Nowhere has that impact been more significant than in the field of investment dispute settlement policy. The first decade after the Treaty of Lisbon has seen the EU move at first quietly and then latterly more dramatically to reshape international investment policy. At the tenth anniversary of the Treaty of Lisbon the direction is clear but many obstacles remain.

This contribution seeks to set out the trajectory that has led the EU to potentially dramatically reshape international investment dispute settlement policy. It is submitted that both the shape of that reform and the potential political vulnerabilities stem from a combination of the framework established by the Treaty of Lisbon and the EU's experience of – and approach to – dispute settlement in general.

This contribution first sets out how the framework created by the Treaty of Lisbon and the two key pieces of legislation (i.e. the Grandfathering Regulation and particularly the Financial Responsibility Regulation) were instrumental in shaping the basics of EU investment policy. Following this, Opinion 2/15, which further shaped and defined this framework, is discussed. The chapter then turns to examine the initial shape and direction of the EU's investment dispute settlement policy before examining the significant changes that led to the creation of the investment court system and then the multilateral investment court project. It concludes with some final thoughts on the next 10 years of EU investment policy.

© KONINKLIJKE BRILL NV, LEIDEN, 2021 | DOI:10.1163/9789004393417_005

2   Setting the Scene: the Framework Created by the Treaty of Lisbon
       and the EU's Framework Legislation

2.1   *The Initial Understanding of the Treaty framework*

There were a number of different views on the nature of the EU's competence
in the period after the entry into force of the Treaty of Lisbon.

The Commission had a more traditional understanding of the nature of
EU competence for investment. This had three elements. First, there was an
express exclusive competence for foreign direct investment, which is mentioned directly in Article 207 TFEU. Second, there was an exercised implied
competence for portfolio investment. This came through the treaty rules on
free movement of capital with third countries (Article 63 TFEU). Third, dispute settlement, both state-to-state dispute settlement and investor-to-state
dispute settlement was considered to be ancillary, following what had been a
well-established approach of the Court of Justice in previous rulings.[1]

The Member States had different views.[2] Some argued that foreign direct investment only covered market access, i.e. liberalisation of investment and not
investment protection. Others claimed that the Member States had retained
competence for portfolio investment. On dispute settlement, there were various different ideas, with some Member States arguing that the Member States
were entitled to defend their measures. This was, of course, in contrast to the
accepted approach in the WTO, where the Union consistently defends Member
State measures.

This debate was at the same time both academic and intense. It was academic, in the sense that the standard international policy approach in respect
of investment protection is not to distinguish between foreign direct investment and portfolio investment. Hence, if the EU was to develop a policy on
investment protection it would have to, at least if it followed the standard
approach, cover also portfolio investment. Therefore, the idea of splitting by
competence was largely academic. Indeed, this was required in the sense that
for the EU to replace the bilateral investment treaties (BITs) concluded by the
Member States it needed to have the agreements negotiated by the EU having the same scope as the Member States' agreements. Furthermore, dispute
settlement applies indistinctly to both foreign direct investment and portfolio
investment. So there was no effective option for the EU to seek to conclude

---

1   Opinion 1/91 (*EEA*), EU:C:1991:490.
2   These are noted in the Council's Conclusions on European Investment Policy 'Conclusions
    on a Comprehensive European International Investment Policy' from 25 October 2010 and in
    the submissions of the Member States to the Court in Opinion 1/17 (*CETA*), ECLI:EU:C:2019:72.

agreements which only covered one area where the EU could have been considered competent. This in turn led to fierce clashes over competence, and the understanding of the structures of the instruments being adopted to manage the EU's emerging investment policy.

Nevertheless, as illustrated below, the legislation actually adopted and the policies adopted tended not to make distinctions on the basis of competence in terms of their operation.

2.2   *The Grandfathering Regulation (Regulation EU No. 1219/2012)*

This Regulation was adopted in 2012 and sets out the treatment of existing Member States investment treaties and sets up a process for permitting Member States to negotiate new treaties or amend their existing bilateral investment treaties.[3] For existing treaties, it operates to clarify and ensure their status under EU law, guaranteeing that, as regards the fact that they impinge on EU competence matters, they can be maintained in place. Where a Member State wants to amend an existing treaty or enter into new treaty obligations, the regulation sets down a number of procedures whereby the Member State concerned is required to seek the authorisation of the Commission to initiate or to conclude negotiations.

In this regard, the regulation treats Member State investment treaties as a whole and without distinction as to competence. So they are *grandfathered* as a whole and Member States are given authorisation to negotiate new agreements as a whole. The Commission makes requests of the Member States in terms of what they should be pursuing in their negotiations and does so without distinguishing matters of competence. In practice there is no distinction based on competence.

This means that the EU can require that the investment treaty which the Member State wishes to negotiate conforms in its entirety to EU policy. For example, the Commission requires that the Member States include transparency provisions for dispute settlement or a clause seeking to apply the multilateral investment court, despite the fact that according to Opinion 2/15 these matters fall under the shared competence of the Member States.[4] This is of course logical, given that the Member States' agreements fully cover these areas.

Article 13 of the Regulation deals with disputes which may arise. It states:

---

3   Regulation (EU) No 1219/2012 of the European Parliament and the Council of 12 December 2012 establishing transitional arrangements for bilateral investment agreements between Member States and third countries (OJ 2012, L 351/40).

4   Opinion 2/15 (*Singapore FTA*), EU:C:2017:376.

Where a bilateral investment agreement falls within the scope of this Regulation, the Member State concerned shall:

(a) inform the Commission without undue delay of all meetings which will take place under the provisions of the agreement. The Commission shall be provided with the agenda and all relevant information permitting an understanding of the topics to be discussed at those meetings. The Commission may request further information from the Member State concerned. Where an issue to be discussed might affect the implementation of the Union's policies relating to investment, including in particular the common commercial policy, the Commission may require the Member State concerned to take a particular position;

(b) inform the Commission without undue delay of any representations made to it that a particular measure is inconsistent with the agreement. The Member State shall also immediately inform the Commission of any request for dispute settlement lodged under the auspices of the bilateral investment agreement as soon as the Member State becomes aware of such a request. The Member State and the Commission shall fully cooperate and take all necessary measures to ensure an effective defence which may include, where appropriate, the participation in the procedure by the Commission;

(c) seek the agreement of the Commission before activating any relevant mechanisms for dispute settlement against a third country included in the bilateral investment agreement and shall, where requested by the Commission, activate such mechanisms. Those mechanisms shall include consultations with the other party to a bilateral investment agreement and dispute settlement where provided for in the agreement. The Member State and the Commission shall fully cooperate in the conduct of procedures within the relevant mechanisms, which may include, where appropriate, the participation in the relevant procedures by the Commission.

The Commission has been increasingly active under paragraph (b) of Article 13. It has required Member States to provide notification to it of disputes which have arisen. In contemplating action, it has particularly focussed on disputes where EU law elements have arisen. Thus, it has submitted an amicus curiae brief in the *Safa vs Greece* case where EU state aid law issues may be at issue.[5]

---

5   *Iskandar Safa and Akram Safa v. Hellenic Republic* (ICSID Case No. ARB/16/20). Commission Decision on intervention as a non-disputing party in the ICSID arbitration proceedings (Case No. ARB/16/20) brought against Greece by Mr Akram Safa and Mr Iskandar Safa on the

Paragraph (c) of Article 13 concerns state-to-state dispute settlement under investment agreements. This mechanism is rarely used in general but has some potential for greater use. This paragraph has in fact been triggered once when one EU Member State was contemplating dispute settlement under a BIT. In that case the Commission provided authorisation to the Member State concerned although the case was never in fact initiated.

As noted, the part of the regulation dealing with the interaction with disputes under the Member States BITs applies to any disputes under the BIT, irrespective of whether the matter concerns FDI or portfolio investment.

2.3   The Financial Responsibility Regulation (Regulation EU No. 912/2014) and the Respondent Mechanism

The Regulation on Financial Responsibility was one of the earliest elements of the EU's policy to develop. Reference to the idea can be found in the Commission's 2010 Communication and in the Council Conclusions of September 2010 where the Council requested the Commission to bring forward legislation[6].

The central concern behind the Regulation is to determine who pays in the event of an investment dispute being brought against the EU. Should the Union budget be held responsible for internationally illegal acts adopted by an individual Member State? In the WTO or in bilateral FTAs, the Union as a whole is responsible for illegal acts of an individual Member State and exports from all Member States can be subject to any suspension of concessions or retaliation under those agreements. With the significant amounts of money potentially involved in investment litigation, it was considered necessary to decide this matter in a definitive manner. As a result, the main concept in the Regulation is that the entity which caused the damage (either the Union or the Member State) should be financially responsible. It is then for the Union or the Member State concerned to identify and decide within their own structures where the financial consequences should lie.[7]

---

basis of the Bilateral Investment Treaty between Greece and Lebanon C(2018)1916/F1 of 4 April 2018.

6   European Commission 'Towards a comprehensive European international investment policy', COM (2010) 343 final, 7 July 2010 and Council of the European Union, 'Conclusions on a Comprehensive European International Investment Policy', 25 October 2010.

7   Several Member States have legislation in place allowing them to allocate the financial consequences of international and European litigation. See the Explanatory Memorandum to the Commission's proposal for further analysis (European Commission, 'Proposal for a Regulation of the European Parliament and of the Council establishing a framework for managing financial responsibility linked to investor-state dispute settlement tribunals established by international agreements to which the European Union is party', COM (2012) 335 final – 2012/0163 (COD)).

This led naturally to the question of representation i.e. which entity should be the respondent. In the Commission's view, the legally correct approach would have been for the Union to have been the respondent, represented by the Commission, because the Union was responsible for the external representation (including in legal proceedings) for matters where the Union has exclusive competence.[8] The ability to engage in dispute settlement was understood to be ancillary to the substantive disciplines, following the Court's pronouncements on a consistent basis since Opinion 1/91.[9] This would have meant that the Union would have been the respondent in all cases, but would have used the Regulation in the event that the financial responsibility lay with one or other Member State.

However, this was reconsidered for two reasons. First, it was considered advantageous for the Member State to defend when there was no risk of the EU's budget being affected since that would imply that the EU's institutional machinery would simply not have to be involved. Second, it was considered that Member States would prefer – and indeed this was a strong demand – that they be in a position to defend cases when they would bear the financial consequences arguing that this was preferable in terms of responsibility. This led the Commission to propose a combination of the Member States being able to act as respondents in international agreements (the "respondent mechanism" based on the EU's Statement for the Energy Charter Treaty[10]) together with establishing the mechanisms for how that would be decided and operational rules for ensuring effective co-ordination in the Regulation on Financial Responsibility. In EU law terms, permitting the Member States to act as respondents was conceived as a delegation of power back to them, in the terms of Article 2 TEU.[11]

---

8   Confirmed by the CJEU in the itlos case. See Case C-73/14, Council of the European Union v European Commission, EU:C:2015:663, para. 58.

9   *Ibid.*

10   See 'Statement submitted by the European Communities to the Secretariat of the Energy Charter pursuant to Article 26(3)(b)(ii) of the Energy Charter Treaty (ECT)', (OJ 1998, L69) revised in the Statement submitted to the ECT Secretariat pursuant to Article 26(3)(b)(ii) of the ECT replacing the statement made on 17 November 1997 on behalf of the European Community (OJ 2019, L 115).

11   In the Explanatory Memorandum it is stated "[..] while for the reasons mentioned above, the Union should, in principle, act as respondent in any dispute concerning an alleged violation of a provision of an international agreement falling within the Union's exclusive competence, even if such violation arises from a Member State's action, it may be possible, as provided expressly in Article 2(1) TFEU, to empower a Member State to act as respondent in appropriate circumstances given the potential for significant demands (even temporary) on the Union budget and on Union resources were the Union to act as respondent in all cases" (COM (2012) 163).

Importantly, the respondent mechanism included in the recent EU FTAS or investment agreements provides that the EU (and not the investment tribunal) decides and links to the Regulation in terms of making the determination of the respondent. The respondent mechanism is found in Article 8.21 of CETA, Article 3.5 of the EU-Singapore Investment Protection Agreement (IPA) and Article 3.32 of the EU-Vietnam IPA. The determination made on the basis of the Regulation is notified and then is binding on the tribunals. This structure is deliberately designed to avoid that the investment tribunal would have a say on the division of competence between the EU and its Member States. Giving it the possibility to decide on the division of competence would have run counter to the exclusive jurisdiction of the Court of Justice to decide on matters of competence. This was indeed confirmed by the Court in Opinion 1/17 which distinguished this approach from that for the EU's Protocol of Accession to the European Convention on Human Rights (ECHR) which was found inconsistent with EU Law.[12]

One of the features of the Member States acting as respondent is that it is necessary that their consent is provided for in the agreement. This is because in order for awards to qualify under the ICSID Convention or the New York Convention and hence to be enforceable it is necessary for the consent of the respondent (as one of the parties to the dispute) to be given. The drafting of this provision has been carefully constructed, to be in the passive, designed to make it clear that it was in fact the European Union which was giving consent on behalf of the Member State. Despite this drafting, and the fact that the action of the Member State was set up as a delegation of power from the Union to the Member State, this element turned out to be key in the reasoning of the Court of Justice when it came to examine the division of competence in Opinion 2/15.

Finally it should be noted that this Regulation, like the Grandfathering Regulation, is indistinct in its application to foreign direct investment and portfolio investment and it is an EU act by which respondent status is decided, irrespective of the underlying competence.

3   Opinion 2/15 on the Singapore FTA

The TTIP and CETA debate on competence for investment, which fed into the broader debate concerning these trade agreements and which took

---

place before and in the shadow of the Court's Opinion 2/15, was illustrative of the ongoing division of views on competence between the Commission and Member States. In that debate, and indeed in the initial discussions on competence which had foreshadowed that debate, the Member States insisted, with varying theories, that Member States retained competence for some or all elements of investment policy. Whilst the difference of views on the division of competence remained, the insistence on subjecting these agreements to ratification at Member State level can be contrasted with the practical steps taken in the management of the policy in the two regulations discussed above. The pragmatic outcomes of the processes leading to the Grandfathering and Financial Responsibility Regulations nevertheless showed that the core of the issue was the power to be able to ratify international agreements and the resulting control that ultimately gave Member States over the process, arguably at the expense of the true effectiveness of EU policy-making.[13]

In some concrete cases the EU has been reduced to the lowest common denominator. An example is the Mauritius Convention on Transparency in ISDS. This Convention was submitted for ratification by the European Commission in January 2015 but at the time of writing has still not been approved by the Council.[14] This is striking, because it deals with the issue of transparency for ISDS. That matter is largely uncontroversial in ISDS policy making, being already an integral part of the EU's investment treaties. However, ratification is being held up by resistance from one Member State.

Opinion 2/15 was sought to clarify this overall situation of disagreement over competence in relation to trade and investment, and to give all players an idea of where the competence lies. On investment, as is well known, the Court found that there remains shared competence for portfolio investment and that there is shared competence for ISDS.[15] This analysis, together with the approach taken for the other parts of the FTA, has provided the basis for a new architectural approach for EU trade agreements.[16] However, it has not entirely clarified matters for investment.

As regards portfolio investment the Court has since clarified that the shared competence for portfolio investment can be exercised by the European

---

13   On this issue, see the contribution by D. Kleimann in this volume.
14   European Commission, 'Proposal for a Council Decision on the signing, on behalf of the European Union, of the United Nations Convention on transparency in treaty-based investor-State arbitration', COM (2015) 21 final, 29 January 2015.
15   On Opinion 2/15, see also the contributions by A. Rosas and M. Cremona in this volume.
16   On this issue, see the contribution by D. Kleimann in this volume.

Union.[17] This useful clarification was nevertheless not surprising since there are only three categories of external competence relevant to trade and investment policy (exclusive EU, shared and exclusive Member State competence).[18] Nevertheless, whilst the Court's concerns about implied exclusive external competence being derived from Treaty obligations are understandable, it is not clear how the Member States can act externally as regards portfolio investment given the free movement of capital with third countries is enshrined in the TFEU. There is no scope for the Member States to act as a practical matter in negotiating agreements with third countries regulating only portfolio investment and no particular EU policy spheres to be protected.

As noted, the Court also found a shared competence for ISDS. It considered, in a departure from its previous case-law (which as previously noted had underpinned the approach to the Financial Responsibility Regulation) that the dispute settlement provisions for investment were not ancillary. This is a key finding, because the Court had not had occasion before to discuss the question of whether dispute settlement provisions could not be ancillary and in what circumstances this might not be the case. Indeed, the Court's previous reasoning on institutional provisions, including dispute settlement, appears to be that they are, by nature, ancillary.[19] There was no discussion in either the written proceedings or the oral stages of the Opinion as to whether the ISDS provisions in the EU-Singapore FTA were in fact ancillary.

The Court reasoned that the ISDS provisions were not ancillary because the ISDS regime "removes disputes from the jurisdiction of the courts of the Member States". This reasoning, unfortunately, raises practical problems. With respect, ISDS does not function to remove jurisdiction from Member State courts. Jurisdiction in Member States is based on Member State law (including EU law). The jurisdiction of ISDS Tribunals, as the Court later noted in Opinion 1/17, is based on the international agreements which establish or give jurisdiction to the tribunals and hence they can only rule on international law and not domestic law.[20] ISDS does not therefore structurally remove jurisdiction from the courts of Member States.

The references to domestic courts in EU agreements (like other international investment agreements) are rather intended to avoid that multiple

---

17   Case C-600/14, *Federal Republic of Germany v Council of the European* Union (COTIF), EU:C:2017:935, para. 68.

18   On this issue, see the contribution by A. Rosas in this volume.

19   The Court summarises that case-law in para. 276 of Opinion 2/15 where it states that institutional provisions "are of an ancillary nature".

20   See Opinion 1/17, para. 120–135.

proceedings are ongoing regarding the same situation, hence avoiding the risk of over-compensation and avoiding, or at least minimising, the number of cases which a respondent government needs to deal with at the same moment in time. Multiple proceedings are possible because domestic law (at least in EU Member States) often contains similar protections to those found in substantive investment rules (as regards protection from uncompensated expropriation and general principles of fair and equitable treatment – but not non-discrimination) which may be available to foreign owned operators. Investors may therefore well seek to pursue remedies in domestic legal systems rather than pursue (what will typically be more expensive and potentially time-consuming) international adjudication. Hence, the provision is designed not to impact the ability of a Member State or other court to handle a particular dispute but rather to ensure co-ordination between different proceedings.

This led the Court to say that the Member States' consent was required to set in place such a regime and that as a consequence competence was shared between the Union and the Member States (without however making reference to Article 4 TFEU which provides for shared competence in certain areas). As previously noted, however, the notion of the consent being required of Member States in agreements was conceptualised, because of the assumption of ancilliarity, as a delegation of power (from the EU's competence to regulate foreign direct investment) to the Member States.

This leads to a number of problems. First, what is the basis for the EU's competence if the ability to enter into agreements with ISDS is not ancillary (i.e. not part of) the EU's competence for the common commercial policy? The Court has confirmed that there is EU competence in Opinion 2/15, had confirmed that such provisions can be included in a manner consistent with EU law in Opinion 1/17 and indeed, the Council has adopted both the Singapore and Vietnam Investment Protection Agreements.

Second, what is the basis for the competence of the Member States? This is puzzling, because the Member States do not have competence for the substantive rules when they affect foreign direct investment (i.e. the application of the rules on non-discrimination, protection against uncompensated compensation and fair and equitable treatment) given these are exclusive EU competence (and for portfolio investment such rules can be exercised by the Union given they are matters of shared competence). Hence, their courts cannot have jurisdiction over such matters, and there is no way to identify which Member States powers are to be exercised in approving agreements including ISDS.

This is particularly complicated for situations in which the Union and its Member States are seeking to address a discrete problem in the field of ISDS policy rather than the more binary question of whether or not to agree to ISDS in a particular case. Transparency and the Mauritius Convention provide a good example of this. There is a wide consensus that there should be transparency for ISDS proceedings i.e. that documents should be publicly available and hearings should be open to the public. The Commission was granted an authorisation to negotiate an international convention providing for transparency rules to be applied to existing bilateral investment treaties. The EU interest is focussed on the Energy Charter Treaty, the only existing treaty containing ISDS which the EU is party to. For Member States, the interest is evidently in the stock of investment treaties. This resulted in the Mauritius Convention on Transparency in Investor State Dispute Settlement, which permits countries to decide to apply transparency rules to their existing treaties on the basis of who would be the respondent.

The question arises, then, how to apply the Court's rulings on competence for ISDS to the EU's decision to apply the Mauritius Convention? The decision to be taken at EU level concerns only the question whether the EU itself should accede to the Mauritius Convention. It does not impact the question of whether Member States should accede. Should the consent of all Member States be required? There is nothing in the Mauritius Convention which treats the question of withdrawing litigation from domestic courts. So should it be the case that all Member States be required to separately consent as a matter of Member State exclusive competence to the exercise by the EU of its competence? This has been the position of the Council, with the result that it has proven impossible to approve the Council decision authorising the Union to sign the Convention because one Member States refuses to give its authorisation. This also implies that the EU cannot definitively ratify the Convention until all Member States have approved, although it is unclear what they should approve. Similar problems may arise in the future if further instruments, dealing with specific problems of ISDS but not creating the possibility to actually initiate claims should be contemplated. The ICSID reforms are an example of this and indeed a future statute establishing a Multilateral Investment Court could also be subject to the same approach.

The EU is thus left, for investment policy, with a complicated division:
- overall competence is shared with the EU having the exclusive competence for the core matters (substantive rules of investment protection applying to FDI) but not for portfolio investment or for ISDS.
- functionally the Grandfathering Regulation and the Financial Responsibility Regulation operate without distinction to the division of competence. That makes sense from a practical and policy perspective.

4   Initial Policy Approaches: the 2010 Communication and the Initial Treaties with 3rd Countries

4.1   *The 2010 Communication on Investment Policy*

It was in 2010 that the Commission first started to develop its international investment policy with the adoption of a Communication.[21] This document accompanied the adoption of the Commission's proposal for the Grandfathering Regulation. This document has the first sketches of the EU's approach on ISDS, including references to transparency and the possible creation of an appellate mechanism. With the benefit of hindsight it could be considered a timorous effort, which shows little of the ambitious approach which was later to characterise EU ISDS policy. However, it has to be recalled that in 2009 and 2010 the vast majority of EU Member States were against any reform of investment policy and in particular ISDS. It was, for example, in part the scepticism of EU Member States which meant that efforts in ICSID in the 2000s to establish an appellate mechanism did not bear fruit.

The Communication received reactions from the Council and the Parliament. The resolution of the Parliament (2011) takes a very progressive approach to investment policy, also referring to the possible creation of an appeal mechanism.[22] The Commission's Communication and the Parliament's Resolution can be contrasted to the Council conclusions on investment policy, which are much less innovative in policy terms, and sketches a direction much closer to traditional ISDS policy.[23] This was largely driven by the Member State insistence on Member State competence for investment. Therefore, the Council conclusions contained various references to the best practices already established by the Member States.

Given the prevailing uncertainty on competence the substantive content of the policy was therefore finely balanced between different visions. However, from this moment, the knowledge that the consent of the Parliament was required for an international agreement dealing with investment policy and ISDS started to have an impact on the shape of the EU's investment policy.

---

21   European Commission, 'Towards a comprehensive European international investment policy', COM (2010) 343 final, p. 9 and 10.

22   European Parliament resolution of 6 April 2011 on the future European international investment policy (2010/2203(INI)).

23   Council, 'Conclusions on a comprehensive European international investment policy', 3041st Foreign Affairs Meeting, 25 October 2010.

4.2   The Initial Approach in CETA and the Agreements with Singapore and India

The first test of the EU's incipient ISDS policy came with the negotiating directives for the EU's negotiations then underway with Canada, Singapore and India. The Commission pushed in the negotiating directives for a more progressive approach in investment dispute settlement. This was finally resolved by including references to the notion that the EU's approach to ISDS should reflect "state of the art" policy.[24]

This was translated into fairly progressive dispute settlement texts, for example providing for a rendez-vous clause creating the possibility to establish an appeal mechanism (but not an actual appeal mechanism). These texts were prepared for the negotiations with the three countries which took place as of 2011. The Commission argued that this needed to be done to satisfy the European Parliament and as a necessary reform of the policy. However, the Member States in the Council pushed back, able to argue, against a background of uncertainty, that their agreement was needed because the envisaged agreements were mixed. These texts form the basis for the initial agreements with Canada and Singapore (negotiations with India stalled with the overall lack of momentum in these negotiations) before these were adjusted to include the Investment Court System.

4.3   The UNCITRAL Transparency Rules and the Mauritius Convention

At the same time as the negotiations of CETA and the agreements with Singapore and India were progressing discussion and work started on the development of the UNCITRAL Transparency Rules and thereafter the Mauritius Convention. The objective behind these discussions was to establish international rules for transparency for ISDS. These dealt with issues such as the publication of submissions, open hearings and the possibility for amicus curiae submissions. Eventually, agreement was reached on the UNCITRAL Transparency Rules in 2013. The United Nations Convention on Transparency in Investor-State Dispute Settlement (the Mauritius Convention) was then negotiated in order to apply these transparency rules to the stock of existing treaties. That Convention contains a mechanism which provides that a respondent state can subscribe to the Transparency Rules and then apply it in investment treaty

---

24   See Decision of 15 December 2015 from the Council declassifying the investment protection negotiating directives for CETA ((OR. en) (12838/11 EXT 2)). The directives for Singapore and India are identical to those for CETA as regards investment dispute settlement.

proceedings where another state party to the same treaty has also signed up to the Mauritius Convention.

The negotiations took place in the United Nations Commission for International Trade Law (UNCITRAL). This is a UN body, so all Member States could be present, and many were. The Member States also asserted their competence in this forum. Whilst there were difficult discussions as the EU gradually shaped and asserted a policy, the EU eventually became one of the main actors pushing first the UNCITRAL Transparency Rules and then the Mauritius Convention. The initial efforts were somewhat limited by the fact that the UNCITRAL Transparency Rules were voluntary rules, which would be applicable to investment treaties after 1 April 2014 where they were included by reference to the UNCITRAL Arbitration rules or specifically to the UNCITRAL Transparency Rules. This meant that there was no need legally for the Commission to seek and the Council to adopt negotiating authorisation. This was not the case for what was to become the Mauritius Convention, where authorisation and negotiating directives were required (granted in 2014).[25] This, as is legally required, led to the requirement that the Member States active in UNCITRAL seek to achieve the objectives set out in the directives and led to a greater degree of cohesion and co-operation in UNCITRAL.

As previously noted, the division of competence plays an important part in ratification. The Commission proposed Council decisions on the signature and then conclusion of the Mauritius Convention in 2015[26]. Since then, the Council has failed to act. In the first place, this was because Member States were waiting to see the outcome of Opinion 2/15 on the Singapore FTA. Once that Opinion has come out, as already noted, the Council has taken the view that the agreement of all Member States is required in order for the ratification at Union level to go ahead. This has led to blockage, essentially by one Member State, who has some concerns on transparency as regards situations where the European Union would be a respondent under the Energy Charter Treaty. Despite the existence of exclusive competence, several Member States have gone ahead and signed the Mauritius Convention but have thus far refrained from ratifying the agreement.

Transparency is now regarded as a standard part of EU policy, with all four of the EU investment agreements which have been negotiated (with Canada,

---

25   The authorisation and negotiating directives have not been published.

26   European Commission, 'Proposal for a Council Decision on the signing, on behalf of the European Union, of the United Nations Convention on transparency in treaty-based investor-State arbitration', COM (2015) 21 final, 29 January 2015.

Singapore, Vietnam and Mexico) containing the UNCITRAL Transparency Rules or equivalent transparency rules. Indeed, it has become the lesser of the reforms which the EU is pursuing. Nevertheless, the division of competence, flowing from Opinion 2/15 as understood by the Council, means that one Member State can hold up ratification of policy choices made and agreed at EU level.

5 The Policy Shift to the Investment Court System

5.1 *The Initial Traces in the 2010 Communication on Investment Policy*
As noted, the traces of the idea of the investment court system can be found in the 2010 Communication and the Parliament's resolution. The 2010 Communication refers to the following as a "main challenge":

> The atomisation of disputes and interpretations [:] Consistency and predictability are key issues and the use of quasi-permanent arbitrators (as in the EU's FTA practice) and/or appellate mechanisms, where there is a likelihood of many claims under a particular agreement, should be considered.[27]

The text of the first EU proposals (for the agreements with Canada, Singapore and India) did not, however, go as far as proposing the creation of standing bodies or of an appeal mechanism. Rather they foresaw using the mechanism of rosters where the disputing parties were unable to agree on adjudicators (based on the EU's state-to-state dispute settlement practice) and included a clause which could lead, via a further decision, to the establishment of an appeal mechanism. The more significant changes came from the changes that were initiated as part of the reforms flowing from the TTIP negotiations.

The TTIP negotiations started in 2013 and it quickly became clear that ISDS was one of the focal points for criticism despite being included in the negotiating directives by the Council with the unanimous support of the Member States. Indeed, there was already an awareness of the possibility that ISDS would be controversial because the TTIP negotiating directives provided for a number of specific provisions on ISDS. First, the negotiating directives stated that:

---

27 European Commission, 'Towards a comprehensive European international investment policy', COM (2010) 343 final, p. 10.

After prior consultation with Member States and in accordance with the EU Treaties the inclusion of investment protection and investor-to-state dispute settlement (ISDS) will depend on whether a satisfactory solution, meeting the EU interests […], is achieved. The matter shall also be considered in view of the final balance of the Agreement.[28]

Second, the standard language on ISDS in the negotiating directives was augmented with additional language stressing that:

[t]he investor-to-state dispute settlement mechanism should contain safeguards against manifestly unjustified or frivolous claims. Consideration should be given to the possibility of creating an appellate mechanism applicable to investor-to-state dispute settlement under the Agreement, and to the appropriate relationship between ISDS and domestic remedies.[29]

These are the first EU negotiating directives which have a reference to the possibility of creating a standing mechanism. The issue of the relationship with domestic remedies was also brought up.

Despite this language in the directives it quickly became clear that the issue of inclusion of ISDS in the agreements raised significant political concerns. This led the Commission to pause the negotiations on investment protection and ISDS in late 2013 and conduct a public consultation on the appropriate path forward. The public consultation was based on the negotiated text for CETA and garnered 150,000 responses.[30]

5.2   The 2015 Concept Paper/TTIP Proposal

The Commission assessed the outcome of the public consultation during 2014 and into early 2015. As the outcome of the consultation was being digested there was significant discussion and reflection also in the Member States on the path forward.

The German Government came forward at that time with the idea of setting up a court to apply in investment disputes between developed

---

28   See para. 22 of the Council's Decision of 9 October 2014 ((OR. en) (11103/13 DCL 1)) declassifying the negotiating directives for the Transatlantic Trade and Investment Partnership between the European Union and the United States of America.

29   *Ibid*, para. 23.

30   European Commission, 'Consultation on investment protection in EU-US trade talks', 13 January 2015, to consult at: http://trade.ec.europa.eu/doclib/press/index.cfm?id=1234.

countries.[31] That did not provide, however, for enforcement via either the ICSID Convention or the New York Convention. At the same time, the French Government came forward with an idea to create a permanent appeal mechanism which would fit in with the ICSID Convention and the New York Convention and hence ensure enforcement.[32]

The Commission's May 2015 Concept Paper "Investment in TTIP and beyond – the path for reform, Enhancing the right to regulate and moving from current ad hoc arbitration towards an Investment Court" was the policy document by which the Commission responded to the outcome of the public consultation. It did not however, envisage the establishment of a two-tier court on a bilateral basis. Rather, it envisaged the creation of an appeal mechanism and a roster from which adjudicators could be chosen by the disputing parties (earlier EU texts had provided a roster in case the parties failed to agree).

In July 2015 the European Parliament adopted a resolution on TTIP. In that resolution the Parliament stated that the negotiation should:

> [...] ensure that foreign investors are treated in a non-discriminatory fashion, while benefiting from no greater rights than domestic investors, and to replace the ISDS system with a new system for resolving disputes between investors and states which is subject to democratic principles and scrutiny, where potential cases are treated in a transparent manner by publicly appointed, independent professional judges in public hearings and which includes an appellate mechanism, where consistency of judicial decisions is ensured, the jurisdiction of courts of the EU and of the Member States is respected, and where private interests cannot undermine public policy objectives.[33]

The Concept Paper had foreseen the creation of a permanent court but as a development of the initial ideas and on a multilateral basis. It stated that:

---

31   The text was prepared at the request of the German Ministry of Economic Affairs by Prof. Dr. Markus Krajewski of University of Erlangen-Nürnberg, to consult at: https://www.rph1.rw.fau.de/files/2016/02/150429-muster-bit-fr-industriestaaten-krajewski-englische-bersetzung.pdf.

32   The French paper 'Vers un nouveau moyen de régler les différends entre États et investisseurs' of May 2015 is available (in French) at : https://www.diplomatie.gouv.fr/IMG/pdf/20150530_isds_papier_fr_vf_cle432fca.pdf.

33   See Point (d)(xv) of European Parliament resolution of 8 July 2015 containing the European Parliament's recommendations to the European Commission on the negotiations for the Transatlantic Trade and Investment Partnership (TTIP) (2014/2228(INI)).

[...] the creation of a fixed list of arbitrators will already move ISDS procedures closer to a permanent court. A development that would institutionalise ISDS even further is to establish an actual permanent investment court with tenured judges. Pursuing such an investment court for each individual EU agreement that includes ISDS presents obvious, technical and organizational challenges. [...] Therefore, the EU should pursue the creation of one permanent court. This court would apply to multiple agreements and between different trading partners, also on the basis of an opt-in system. The objective would be to multilateralise the court either as a self-standing international body or by embedding it into an existing multilateral organization. Work has already begun on how to start this process, in particular on aspects such as architecture, organisation, costs and participation of other partners.[34]

The Commission drew on these elements to develop the key ideas which were included in the TTIP proposal. The Commission's central idea was to combine the notions in the French and German papers by creating a two-tier level court and at the same time ensure enforcement via the ICSID Convention and the New York Convention. These are the key features of the draft TTIP text which was made public on 12 November 2015 in what came to be known as the Investment Court System.[35] It can be seen that these elements flow collectively from the positions of France, Germany, the European Parliament and the Commission itself. That text already foresaw the movement towards a Multilateral Investment Court. Article 12 of the text provided that:

> Upon the entry into force between the Parties of an international agreement providing for a multilateral investment tribunal and/or a multilateral appellate mechanism applicable to disputes under this Agreement, the relevant parts of this section shall cease to apply. The [...] Committee may adopt a decision specifying any necessary transitional arrangements.

Central to this move was the knowledge that TTIP would have to be approved by all Member States. Hence the significant reform process that the EU has

---

34   European Commission, 'Investment in ttip and beyond – the path for reform, Enhancing the right to regulate and moving from current ad hoc arbitration towards an Investment Court', May 2015, p.11.

35   The EU's proposal in the context of TTIP of 12 November 2015 is available at: https://trade.ec.europa.eu/doclib/docs/2015/november/tradoc_153955.pdf .

embarked on is bolstered by the impetus coming from the Member States and the European Parliament.

The EU then of course had to decide how to handle the negotiations with Canada. These had at that moment been closed and the agreement was undergoing legal scrubbing. However, the public consultation had taken place on the basis of the ISDS provisions in CETA as they had stood at that moment in time before the scrub had started. It was clear that politically, these provisions would be in danger if they were not addressed in order to bring them in line with the TTIP proposal. CETA was viewed politically as being very closely related to TTIP. This led to the inclusion of the Investment Court System in CETA.

It was the inclusion of the Investment Court System in CETA which created the dynamic for the work towards the creation of the Multilateral Investment Court. The idea is also mentioned in the Commission's 2015 Communication "Trade for All" which sets out the Commission's trade and investment policy for the mandate of the previous Commission (2014–2019).[36] More significantly, it features in the Joint Interpretative Instrument which was adopted by the EU and Canada at the same time as CETA was signed. It states:

> [...] CETA represents an important and radical change in investment rules and dispute resolution. It lays the basis for a multilateral effort to develop further this new approach to investment dispute resolution into a Multilateral Investment Court. The EU and Canada will work expeditiously towards the creation of the Multilateral Investment Court. It should be set up once a minimum critical mass of participants is established, and immediately replace bilateral systems such as the one in CETA, and be fully open to accession by any country that subscribes to the principles underlying the Court.[37]

The following reference is also made in a declaration of the Council associated with CETA:

> [...] the Council supports the European Commission's efforts to work towards the establishment of a multilateral investment court, which will

---

36   European Commission, 'Trade for all – Towards a more responsible trade and investment policy', October 2015, p. 20.

37   Joint Interpretative Instrument on the Comprehensive Economic and Trade Agreement (ceta) between Canada and the European Union and its Member States (OJ, 2017 L 11/3).

replace the bilateral system established by CETA, once established, and according to the procedure foreseen in CETA.[38]

These elements became firmly anchored the Investment Court System and the Multilateral Investment Court project in the EU's trade and investment policy.

5.3   *CETA and the Agreements with Singapore, Vietnam and Mexico*
The Investment Court System has now been included in the EU's agreements with Canada, Singapore, Vietnam and Mexico.

The main innovation of the Investment Court System is to establish a permanent two-tier system for the resolution of disputes, with a tribunal of first instance and an appeal mechanism.[39] Adjudicators are subject to strict ethics rules so that they are unable to act as counsel at the same time as acting as adjudicators. Equal numbers of adjudicators have to appointed from either party and non-nationals have to be appointed to act as chairs of the tribunals. Part of the logic of this set-up is that because the adjudicators would be permanent they would act, in formal and informal ways, in order to ensure the consistency and predictability of rulings under the mechanism. An appeal procedure would ensure both correctness and consistency. Importantly, the system is designed in such a way as to ensure enforceability under the New York and ICSID Conventions. There is enforceability under the New York Convention because the New York Convention can apply to permanent bodies where the disputing parties do not choose their adjudicators (such as the Iran-US Claims Tribunal) provided that both parties express their consent to be bound by the adjudication. There is enforceability under the ICSID Convention because the initial award is treated as a preliminary award, subject to an appeal. The Appellate tribunal sends the matter back to the first instance tribunal to complete and issue the award. This ensures compliance with the Article 53 rule against appeals in the ICSID Convention. In any event, it is accepted in Article 42 of the Vienna Convention on the Law of Treaties that two states may bilaterally modify multilateral treaties under certain conditions. These conditions are clearly met here.

The Commission is currently preparing a mechanism for the appointment of adjudicators to sit on the tribunal established by these agreements. This

---

38   Declaration no 36 'Statement by the Commission and the Council on investment protection and the Investment Court System ('ICS')' (OJ 2017, L 11/9).

39   See, for more details, M. L. Andrisani, A. von Walter, 'Resolution of Disputes', in M. Mbengue, S. Schacherer (eds.) *Foreign Investment Under the Comprehensive Economic and Trade Agreement (CETA)*, (Springer 2019), p. 207–238.

would be modelled on the procedure established under Article 255 TFEU for the appointment of judges to the Court of Justice of the EU.[40]

As noted previously, these agreements have different architectural set-ups. CETA is part of an integrated FTA. Whilst the bulk of CETA is provisionally applied, the investment protection and Investment Court System is not being provisionally applied.[41] It will only be applied once the agreement has been ratified by all Member State parliaments. With the trade agreements negotiated with Singapore and Vietnam, following Opinion 2/15, the institutions have agreed to split the agreements into an FTA which will be concluded only by the EU and a mixed Investment Protection Agreement (IPA), which will include the investment protection provisions and the Investment Court System.[42] The agreement with Mexico forms parts of a larger Association Agreement which will in any event be ratified by all the Member States before entering into force.

The EU has included the Investment Court System in its ongoing negotiations with Chile, China and Indonesia and has been clear that it will be a necessary component of any future investment protection agreement, until such time as a Multilateral Investment Court is in place.

6 The Multilateral Investment Court

6.1 *The 2015 Concept Paper and CETA*

When developing the ideas that led to the creation of the Investment Court System the EU institutions had to wrestle with the fact that it is relatively expensive to set up a court with permanent members for each bilateral investment treaty negotiations which the EU is undertaking. This prompted discussion of the idea of establishing a multilateral investment court (MIC). Fundamentally, this would serve to rationalise the approach in EU-level agreements, by creating a single permanent mechanism which would adjudicate disputes under multiple agreements. It could also, importantly, apply to the existing agreements of EU Member States, which number around 1400 of the 3000 existing treaties.

This idea was already mentioned in the TTIP Concept Paper and the Trade for All Communication and the fundamental idea was that work on the MIC would move in parallel to the establishment of the investment court systems in the bilateral agreements. This approach is reflected in the EU's agreements

---

40   At the time of writing, this text was not publicly available.

41   On provisional application, see the contribution by J. Heliskoski in this volume.

42   On this issue, see the contribution by D. Kleimann in this volume.

including the investment court system. These agreements foresee that the re-formed bilateral system is to be replaced by a multilateral reformed system. For example, Article 8.29 of CETA states:

> The Parties shall pursue with other trading partners the establishment of a multilateral investment tribunal and appellate mechanism for the resolution of investment disputes. Upon establishment of such a mul-tilateral mechanism, the CETA Joint Committee shall adopt a decision providing that investment disputes under this Section will be decided pursuant to the multilateral mechanism and make appropriate transi-tional arrangements.

The EU initiated the first steps in the creation of the MIC in 2016.

6.2   The EU's Negotiating Directives (March 2018)

The Commission launched work on an impact assessment with regard to a MIC in 2016. In September 2017 the Commission made public the impact as-sessment and issued a Recommendation to the Council to open negotiations on the establishment of a MIC.[43] The authorisation and negotiating directives were adopted by the Council and the Member States (on account of the shared competence) in March 2018.[44]

The negotiating directives foresee a court structure with an appeal mech-anism, staffed by full-time and highly qualified adjudicators. The logic is that this addresses a significant part of the concerns as regards legitimacy and eth-ics with the adjudicators in the present system. It also foresees an opt-in sys-tem based on the Mauritius Convention which would allow application to the stock of 3000 existing treaties.[45]

Importantly, because the EU Member States are members of UNCITRAL, the negotiating directives foresee very close co-ordination between the Union, rep-resented by the Commission, and the Member States including the possibility

---

43   European Commission, 'Recommendation for a Council Decision authorising the open-ing of negotiations for a Convention establishing a multilateral court for the settlement of investment disputes', COM (2017) 493 final, 13 September 2017; European Commission, ' Impact Assessment – Multilateral reform of investment dispute resolution, SWD (2017) 302 final, 13 September 2017.

44   Council, 'Negotiating directives for a Convention establishing a multilateral court for the settlement of investment disputes', Document 12981/17 of 20 March 2018.

45   See C. M. Brown, 'A Multilateral Mechanism for the Settlement of Investment Disputes. Some Preliminary Sketches', *ICSID Review* 32(3), 2017, p. 673–690.

that the Member States, as voting Members of UNCITRAL, vote on the basis of the negotiating directives and further positions as defined by the EU.

6.3   *UNCITRAL Discussions*

The United Nations Commission on International Trade Law (UNCITRAL) decided to initiate work on the multilateral reform of investment dispute resolution in July 2017. This came after various informal discussions between a number of actors (in particular the EU) and various elements arose in establishing a mandate for an UNCITRAL Working Group (later Working Group III). One was that many countries did not want it to be a foregone conclusion that work would be on a multilateral investment court. This meant that the mandate had to be open. Another important element, of major concern to the EU, was that delegations should be government-led, to ensure that the positions expressed were true government positions and not those of individuals (whether they be practitioners or academics with a stake in the existing system). It was also important to ensure the involvement of other international organisations. The mandate is worth setting out in full:

> [...] the Commission [the United Nations Commission for International Trade Law] entrusted Working Group III with a broad mandate to work on the possible reform of investor-State dispute settlement (ISDS). In line with the UNCITRAL process, Working Group III would, in discharging that mandate, ensure that the deliberations, while benefiting from the widest possible breadth of available expertise from all stakeholders, would be government-led with high-level input from all governments, consensus-based and be fully transparent. The Working Group would proceed to: (i) first, identify and consider concerns regarding ISDS; (ii) second, consider whether reform was desirable in light of any identified concerns; and (iii) third, if the Working Group were to conclude that reform was desirable, develop any relevant solutions to be recommended to the Commission. The Commission agreed that broad discretion should be left to the Working Group in discharging its mandate, and that any solutions devised would be designed taking into account the ongoing work of relevant international organizations and with a view of allowing each State the choice of whether and to what extent it wishes to adopt the relevant solution(s).[46]

---

46   Official Records of the General Assembly, Seventy-second Session, Supplement No. 17 (A/72/17), para. 264.

The UNCITRAL process was preferred because of its transparency, inclusiveness and accessibility. Meeting reports and audio recordings of all Working Group sessions are published on the UNCITRAL website and participation is open to all UN members and to interested parties.[47] International organisations are fully involved and can bring their expertise to bear. There is an Academic Forum and a Practitioner's Group both of which are intended to assist the Working Group.

The first two rounds of discussions of Working Group III took place in Vienna (Austria) from 27 November to 1 December 2017 and in New York (US) from 23 to 27 April 2018. After its second meeting, the Working Group had finalised discussions on step 1 and had concluded that there were significant concerns relating to ISDS. In its meeting of 29 October to 2 November 2018 it concluded that those concerns merited reforms. Since April 2019 the Working Group has been starting its work on developing reforms. Delegations were invited to make submissions on possible reforms by July 2019 and 19 submissions have been made (including one from the EU and its Member States).

The Union has submitted a paper setting out its views of the concerns associated with the ISDS regime, essentially arguing that it is not fit for dealing with matters of public law which come up in the investment treaty regime.[48] The Union and its Member States also submitted a paper setting out, in conceptual terms, how a Multilateral Investment Court would operate.[49]

Negotiations and discussions will continue. Any solutions developed by the Working Group will go the United Nations General Assembly for approval. They will then be subject to ratification by parties interested in utilising them.

7   Conclusion: the Next 10 Years?

This contribution has sought to survey the development of the EU's investment dispute settlement policy over the 10 years since the entry into force of the Treaty of Lisbon.

It has, it is submitted, been a remarkable 10 years, where the Union has transformed the shape of international investment dispute settlement policy.

---

47   To consult at: https://uncitral.un.org/en/working_groups/3/investor-state.
48   UNCITRAL, European Union – 'The identification and consideration of concerns as regards investor to state dispute settlement', 20 November 2017 (A/CN.9/WG.III/WP.145).
49   UNCITRAL, European Union and its Member States – 'Establishing a standing mechanism for the settlement of international investment disputes', 18 January 2019 (A/CN.9/WG.III/WP.159/Add.1).

If it is successful in taking its reforms to the multilateral level through the UN-CITRAL process it will amount to the most significant reform of the investment regime since the system was created in the 1950s and 1960s. This arises when other countries are also adapting their approach to investment dispute settlement (for example Brazil), so one challenge will be how to find a coherent multilateral set-up which can take into account these different reform efforts.

In making this progress, whilst it might have seem bedevilled by the disputes over competence, there has gradually come to be a unity of purpose and views between the three EU institutions and the Member States. This has translated into the construction of an effective policy both in putting in place the internal workings necessary for the external policy and in projecting it externally. Opinion 2/15 has created challenges in ratification which will test the extent of this unity of purpose. Opinion 1/17 on CETA has given a green light for the work on the Multilateral Investment Court and will frame the nature of what the Union can agree to. In particular, in the negotiations the Commission will need to ensure that the MIC complies with the conditions set out by the Court in Opinion 1/17 (for example in relation to autonomy).[50]

In addition to the external projection of the policy, the next 10 years are likely to see the internal framework tested in practice. Given the continued sustained level of litigation, the Commission will continue to be active in disputes under Member State's agreements under the Grandfathering Regulation. The Commission is also likely to be active in defending disputes against the EU with the first one (Nord Stream 2) in its initial stages at the time of writing.

The Union is likely, therefore, to continue to be a major policy player on investment dispute settlement. It is transforming international investment policy. However, the tension between action at EU level and the need for Member State ratification is likely to continue to play out.

Acknowledgement

The views expressed herein are not to be attributed to the European Commission but only to the author.

50   On this issue, see the contribution by G. Van der Loo in this volume.

CHAPTER 4

Opinion 1/17

Legitimising the EU's Investment Court System but Raising the Bar for Compliance with EU Law

Guillaume Van der Loo

1 Introduction

On 30 April 2019, the Court of Justice of the European Union (ECJ) decided in Opinion 1/17[1] that the Investment Court System (ICS) included in the EU-Canada Comprehensive Economic Trade Agreement (CETA)[2] is compatible with EU law. It will be recalled that in one of the many statements adopted on the occasion of CETA's signature in October 2016, Belgium had committed itself to "ask the European Court of Justice for an opinion on the compatibility of the ICS with the European treaties" in order to persuade Wallonia to drop its blockage of the signature of this landmark trade agreement.[3]

The Opinion follows largely the structure of the Belgian request, analysing firstly whether the envisaged mechanism for the resolution of disputes between investors and States (hereinafter: "ISDS") is compatible with the autonomy of the EU legal order; secondly, whether CETA's ISDS mechanism is compatible with the principle of equal treatment and of effectiveness of EU law and; thirdly, whether CETA's ISDS mechanism sufficiently ensures the right of access to an independent tribunal pursuant to Article 47 of the Charter of Fundamental Rights of the European Union (hereinafter: "the Charter").

Opinion 1/17 is for several reasons a landmark case in EU external relations law. *Firstly*, the Opinion is – so far – the climax in the discussion about

---

1   Opinion 1/17 (*CETA*), ECLI:EU:C:2019:341.
2   Comprehensive Economic and Trade Agreement (CETA) between Canada, of the one part, and the European Union and its Member States, of the other part (OJ 2017, L 11/23).
3   Statement 37 by the Kingdom of Belgium on the conditions attached to full powers, on the part of the Federal State and the federated entities, for the signing of CETA (OJ 2017, L 11/9), 27 October 2016. On these Statements, see G. Van der Loo, 'CETA's signature: 38 statements, a joint interpretative instrument and an uncertain future', *CEPS Commentary*, 2016.

the stance of the ECJ towards international dispute settlement mechanisms (DSMs) or courts established by international agreements concluded by the EU. The ECJ has been very critical of the EU subjecting itself to an international dispute settlement mechanism as the Court has applied *autonomy* as a constitutional principle in an expansive way with a view to safeguarding its exclusive jurisdiction to interpret and apply EU law from interference by other international courts.[4] Not only did the Court block the EU's accession to the European Economic Area, the Unified Patent Court and the European Convention on the protection of Human Rights and Fundamental Freedoms (ECHR),[5] it also ruled that ISDS mechanisms in intra-EU Bilateral Investment Treaties (BITs) are incompatible with EU law.[6] This negative stance of the Court has been criticised in the literature and even been labelled as "selfish" and "fearful".[7] However, it will be demonstrated in this chapter that the Court applied in Opinion 1/17 a more pragmatic approach, while at the same time also developing new *autonomy criteria* that may complicate the EU's accession to future international agreements.

Secondly, by giving a green light to CETA, the Court sanctified in Opinion 1/17 one of the most controversial and debated trade instruments developed in the first decade after the Treaty of Lisbon, i.e. the Investment Court System. This implies that the EU can proceed with the ratification process of CETA and the other free trade agreements (FTAs) or Investment Protection Agreements (IPAs) that include a similar ICS (e.g. with Singapore, Vietnam and Mexico).[8]

---

4   B. De Witte, 'The Relative Autonomy of the European Union's Fundamental Rights Regime', *Nordic Journal of International Law* 65 (2019), p. 72–73.

5   Opinion 2/13, *Accession of the Union to the ECHR*, EU:C:2014:2454; Opinion 1/91, *EEA Agreement*, EU:C:1991:490; Opinion 1/09, *Agreement on the creation of a unified patent litigation system*, EU:C:2011:123.

6   Case C-284/16, *Slowakische Republik v Achmea BV*, ECLI:EU:C:2018:158.

7   C. Riffel, 'The CETA Opinion of the European Court of Justice and its Implications – Not that Selfish After All', *Journal of International Economic* Law 22 (2019), p. 503–521; J. Odermatt, 'The Principle of Autonomy: An Adolescent Disease of EU External Relations Law?', in M. Cremona (ed.), *Structural Principles in EU External Relations Law* (Hart, 2018), p. 316; G. De Búrca, 'After the EU Charter of Fundamental Rights: The Court of Justice as a Human Rights Adjudicator?' *Maastricht Journal of European Comparative Law* 168 (2013); B. de Witte, 'A Selfish Court? The Court of Justice and the Design of International Dispute Settlement Beyond the European Union', in M. Cremona, A. Thies (eds.), *The European Court of Justice and External Relations Law: Constitutional Challenges* (Oxford: Hart, 2014), p. 39; E. Spaventa, 'A Very Fearful Court? The Protection of Fundamental Rights in the European Union after Opinion 2/13', *Maastricht Journal of European and Comparative Law* 35 (2015), p. 47.

8   On this issue, see the contribution by C. Brown in this volume.

Moreover, the Opinion seems to support the European Commission in its pursuit to establish a Multilateral Investment Court (MIC) within Working Group III of the United Nations Commission on International Trade Law (UNCITRAL), although several of the Court's newly developed autonomy criteria may complicate this project.

And *finally*, Opinion 1/17 is a remarkable case in EU external relations law as the Commission, the Council and all the intervening Member States (12 in total)[9] pleaded strongly – and often in close coordination, as evidenced during the hearing of the Opinion – in favour of the ICS' compatibility with EU law. Somewhat surprisingly, the European Parliament chose not to submit observations, although it previously backed the conclusion of CETA.[10]

This chapter will first analyse Opinion 1/17 by following the structure of Belgium's request and the Opinion itself, i.e. the compatibility of CETA's ICS with the autonomy of the EU legal order (2.1); the compatibility of the ICS with the general principle of equal treatment and with the requirement of effectiveness (2.2) and the compatibility of the ICS with the right of access to an independent tribunal (2.3). The chapter then proceeds by commenting on several key features of the Opinion, focussing on the Court's pragmatic approach *in casu* concerning the principle of autonomy and the jurisdiction of the ICS (3.1) and the implications of Opinion 1/17 for future agreements concluded by the EU such as the envisaged MIC (3.2). This chapter concludes by providing a brief outlook on the different investment agreements concluded or envisaged by the EU and its Member States (including the intra and extra-EU BITs) (4). The EU's competences in the area of investment (protection) and ISDS and the conceptualisation and functioning of the ICS and the MIC are discussed elsewhere in this volume.[11] Moreover, the following chapter in this volume by M. Hahn analyses in detail how the Court's interpretation of the autonomy principle developed in its case law and discusses the broader implications of the Opinion for EU treaty-making.

---

9   With the notable exception of Slovenia.
10   European Parliament legislative resolution of 15 February 2017 on the draft Council decision on the conclusion of the Comprehensive Economic and Trade Agreement (CETA) between Canada, of the one part, and the European Union and its Member States, of the other part (OJ 2018, C 252/348).
11   For an analysis of the EU's competences in the area of, *inter alia*, investment (protection), see the contributions by M. Cremona and A. Rosas in this volume. On the ICS and the MIC, see the contribution by C. Brown in this volume.

2   Opinion 1/17: a Legal Analysis

2.1   *The Compatibility of CETA's ICS with the Autonomy of the EU Legal Order*

2.1.1   The ECJ's Autonomy Criteria and Belgium's Doubts about the ICS

In Opinion 1/17 the Court took off by first recalling its well-established case law that holds that:

> [An] international agreement providing for the creation of a court responsible for the interpretation of its provisions and whose decisions are binding on the European Union, is, *in principle*, compatible with EU law. Indeed, the competence of the European Union in the field of international relations and its capacity to conclude international agreements necessarily entail the power to submit to the decisions of a court that is created or designated by such agreements as regards the interpretation and application of their provisions.[12]

The Court has emphasised that this is especially true "where the conclusion of an agreement is provided for by the Treaties themselves", such as in the case of trade agreements covering investment protection. In Opinion 2/15 the Court emphasised that this competence "entails the power to submit to the decisions of a body which, whilst not formally a court, essentially performs judicial functions, such as the Dispute Settlement Body created within the framework of the WTO Agreement".[13] This reasoning also applies to the ICS in CETA, which the Court considers to be "hybrid in nature", in that it contains, in addition to characteristics of judicial bodies, a number of features of traditional arbitration mechanisms.[14]

Although this seems to indicate that the Court has a rather internationalist and open attitude towards dispute settlement mechanisms included in international agreements concluded by the EU, it has developed through landmark Opinion procedures (i.a. Opinion 1/91 (EEA), Opinion 1/00 (ECAA), Opinion 1/09 (Patent Court), Opinion 2/13 (Accession to the ECHR)) several strict – but sometimes also rather vague – criteria to which international agreements and their dispute settlement mechanisms have to comply with in order not to adversely affect the autonomy of the EU legal order.[15] The Court has stressed that

---

12   Opinion 1/17, para. 106. Emphasis added.
13   Opinion 2/15, *Singapore FTA*, ECLI:EU:C:2017:934, para. 299.
14   Opinion 1/17, para. 193.
15   For a detailed analysis of these cases, see the contribution by M. Hahn in this volume.

"an international agreement entered into by the Union may affect the powers of the EU institutions". However, conditions for safeguarding the essential character of those powers are indispensable to ensure that "there is no adverse effect on the autonomy of the EU legal order".[16] The Court's pre-Opinion 1/17 case law establishes that in order to comply with the autonomy of the EU legal order an international agreement and its dispute settlement mechanism (DSM):

(*i*)   cannot alter the distribution of powers between the EU and the Member States;[17]

(*ii*) may not have the jurisdiction to examine the validity of an act of EU law;[18]

(*iii*) cannot adversely affect the Court's exclusive jurisdiction over the interpretation of EU law by having the possibility to interpret and apply, beyond the provisions of the agreement itself, primary and secondary EU law (and thus binding the EU and its institutions to a particular interpretation of EU law);[19]

(*iv*) cannot rule on disputes between Member States concerning interpretation and application of EU law;[20]

(*iv*) cannot deprive Member State Courts from their competences to interpret and apply EU law as this would adversely impact the Court of its powers to reply to preliminary rulings of these national Courts pursuant to Article 267 TFEU[21]

The drafters of CETA went to great lengths to take these criteria on board when finalising the wording, clearly aiming to pre-empt any possibility of a red light from the Court. As further discussed below, the ICS includes several *autonomy safeguard provisions* related to, inter alia, the "applicable law and interpretation",[22] the determination of the respondent[23] and the parties' right to regulate.

Despite these efforts, Belgium still voiced several concerns regarding the compatibility of the ICS with the *autonomy of EU law* as developed by the ECJ. In particular, Belgium argued that CETA's provision concerning the "applicable law and interpretation" before the ICS was insufficient to safeguard

---

16   Opinion 1/00, *Agreement on the establishment of a European Common Aviation Area*, EU:C:2002:231, para. 20 and 21; Opinion 2/13, para. 183.

17   Opinion 1/91, para. 31–35; Opinion 1/00, para. 16; Opinion 2/13, para. 215–235.

18   Opinion 1/00, para. 14; Opinion 1/09, para. 78.

19   Opinion 1/09, para. 123; Opinion 2/13, para. 184; Opinion 1/91, para. 30–35; Opinion 1/00, para. 13.

20   Case C 249/81, *Commission v. Ireland*, ECLI:EU:C:1982:402; Opinion 2/13, para. 213.

21   Opinion 1/09, para. 89.

22   Art. 8.31 CETA.

23   Art. 8.21 CETA.

the required autonomy of the Union legal order. This provision (Article 8.31) provides that the applicable law for the purposes of an ICS dispute is CETA itself, supplemented by other rules and principles of international law applicable between the Parties.[24] Moreover, the CETA Tribunal does not have jurisdiction to determine the legality of a measure, alleged to constitute a breach of this agreement, under the domestic law of a Party.[25] The Tribunal may only consider the domestic law of a Party "as a matter of fact" and has to follow the prevailing interpretation of said given to that law by the courts or authorities of that party.[26] In addition, any meaning attributed to domestic law by the Tribunal shall not be binding upon the courts or the authorities of that Party.[27]

Belgium argued that this provision does not alter the fact that, where the Tribunal will have to examine whether a measure adopted by the EU is contrary to one of the investment standards enshrined in CETA, it will be compelled to "interpret the effect of that measure" and thus usurp a competence essentially reserved for Union courts.[28] Moreover, Belgium claimed that there is no guarantee that an interpretation of the relevant EU law by the Court will be available in all instances. Considering that the ICS does not provide an obligation for the Tribunal to refer to the Court a question for a preliminary ruling on the interpretation of EU law, Belgium was concerned that – in the absence of pertinent ECJ case law – this could lead to situations in which the ICS Tribunal would be in a position to interpret EU rules for the first time in order to establish the relevant facts in the dispute at hand.[29]

2.1.2   Constitutional Principles

In Opinion 1/17 the Court broadens the constitutional fundament of the notion of *autonomy of the Union legal order* and refines some of its previous autonomy criteria. The Court starts by recalling that autonomy resides in the fact that "the Union possesses a constitutional framework that is unique to it".[30] This framework encompasses the founding values set out in Article 2 TEU, the general principles of EU law, the provisions of the Charter, and the provisions of the TEU and TFEU, which include, *inter alia*, rules on the conferral and division of powers, rules governing how the EU institutions and its judicial system are

---

24   Art. 8.31(1) CETA.
25   Art. 8.31 (2) CETA.
26   *Ibid.*
27   *Ibid.*
28   Para. 48.
29   Opinion 1/17, para. 48–50.
30   *Ibid*, para. 110.

to operate, and fundamental rules in specific areas. The Court then continues by underlining that, in order to preserve those specific constitutional characteristics, the Treaties have established a judicial system intended to ensure consistency and uniformity in the interpretation of EU law. In this system, it is for both the national and EU courts to ensure the full application of EU law in all the Member States, with the Court as authoritative interpreter of that law.[31]

Linking these rather broad considerations with the case at hand, the Court observed that CETA's ICS "stands outside the EU judicial system".[32] The Court argues that this in itself does not mean that this mechanism adversely affects the autonomy of the EU legal order. Because of the reciprocal nature of international agreements and the need to maintain the powers of the Union in international relations the Union can enter into an agreement that establishes a court with the competence to interpret that agreement.[33] Consequently, the Court argues that it has in principle no objections to the ICS in CETA and, "subsequently, a multilateral investment Tribunal".[34] However, very much in line with its earlier Opinions, the Court immediately adds two conditions to be met by CETA, or any international agreement establishing a court or tribunal, in order to comply with the autonomy of the EU legal order:

1.   CETA may not confer on its ICS "any power to interpret or apply EU law other than the power to interpret and apply the provisions of that agreement having regard to the rules and principles of international law applicable between the Parties", and;

2.   The ICS' Tribunals decisions may not have the effect of preventing the EU institutions from operating in accordance with the EU constitutional framework.[35]

2.1.3   No Jurisdiction to Interpret and Apply Rules of EU Law Other than the Provisions of CETA

According to the first condition, which was already established by the Court in its previous case law (cf. *supra*), CETA cannot confer on the ICS Tribunal "any power to interpret or apply EU law other than the power to interpret and apply the provisions of that agreement".[36] Not the least due to its various *autonomy safeguard clauses*, CETA passed this test without great difficulty. According to

---

31   *Ibid,* para. 11.
32   *Ibid,* para. 113.
33   *Ibid,* para. 117 and 106 and cited case law.
34   *Ibid,* para. 118.
35   Opinion 1/17, para. 119.
36   *Ibid.*

the Court, Article 8.31 of CETA on "applicable law and interpretation" ensures that the ICS Tribunal can only apply CETA itself and has no jurisdiction "to determine the legality of a measure, alleged to constitute a breach of this Agreement, under the domestic law of a Party".[37] In other words, the ICS cannot apply the municipal law of a party, as made plain in Article 8.31 CETA that reads as follows:

> For greater certainty, in determining the consistency of a measure with this Agreement, the Tribunal may consider, as appropriate, the domestic law of a Party *as a matter of fact.* In doing so, the Tribunal shall follow the *prevailing interpretation given to the domestic law by the courts or authorities of that Party* and *any meaning given to domestic law by the Tribunal shall not be binding upon the courts* or the authorities of that Party.[38]

This provision reassured the Court that CETA's ICS Tribunal can under no circumstances give an interpretation to EU law which would be binding on the Court or the Union institutions or Member States. The Court recognises that when checking compliance with CETA, the CETA Tribunal will inevitably have to undertake an examination of the "effect" of the contested measure adopted by the EU or Member State.[39] While this examination by the CETA Tribunal may require that EU law has to be taken into account; this examination can, pursuant to Article 8.31.2, not be classified as equivalent to an interpretation of EU law. When taking into account EU law as a matter of fact, the ICS Tribunal is obliged to follow the relevant case law of the ECJ; *e contrario*, this mechanism confirms that the ECJ is not bound by the meaning given to EU law by that Tribunal.

The Court distinguishes CETA from the agreement examined in Opinion 1/09, which envisaged conferring upon a (patent) court positioned *outside* the EU judicial system the competence to interpret and apply future EU secondary law (relating to, *inter alia*, Community patents).[40] The Court also distinguished CETA from *Achmea,* where the BIT in question overlapped with Internal Market law, creating the possibility that the BIT adjudicative body may interfere with the interpretation and application of EU law vested in the Court.[41] By doing so, the Court went out of its way to limit *Achmea's* relevance to the facts of

---

37   *Ibid,* para. 121 referring to Art. 8.31.2 CETA.
38   Emphasis added.
39   Opinion 1/17, para. 131.
40   *Ibid,* para. 123–125.
41   *Ibid,* para. 126 referring to Case C-284/16, *Achmea,* para. 42, 55 and 56.

the case, stressing that the BIT in question had not been concluded by the EU but by its Member States. The Court stressed that within the EU the principle of mutual trust applies between Member States, which entails that Member States must consider that all the other Member States comply with EU law, including the right to an effective remedy before an independent tribunal as laid down in Article 47 of the Charter.[42] The Court ruled that this principle does not apply between the Union and non-Member States, and therefore not to EU investment agreements concluded with a third country such as Canada.

The Court also gave its green light to the mechanism that determines the respondent for disputes with the EU or its Member States included in Article 8.21. It seems that the Commission had sufficiently taken note of the irritation of the Court with regard to the attack of its monopoly of interpreting EU law in the accession agreement to the ECHR; it will be recalled that, in the Court's reading in Opinion 2/13, it would have been up to the ECtHR to determine the apportionment of responsibility between the EU and its Member States for violations of the ECHR.[43] The respondent mechanism in CETA avoids a similar understanding as it provides that the EU (and not the ICS Tribunal) will determine whether the EU or a Member State will be the respondent, preventing the ICS Tribunal from having a say on the division of competence between the EU and its Member States.[44]

The absence of a prior involvement procedure, which would permit or oblige the ICS Tribunal to make a reference for a preliminary ruling to the Court, is not viewed as problematic given that the Tribunal's jurisdiction is confined to the provisions of CETA. Such a prior involvement procedure is for example included in the State-to-State DSM s established by the DCFTA s with Ukraine, Moldova and Georgia to avoid that the arbitration panel would rule *de facto* on provisions of EU law (which are abundantly included in these agreements).[45] Other international agreements including explicit references to EU secondary law allow national courts, joint bodies established by those agreements or even the contracting Parties themselves to refer a preliminary ruling to the Court;[46] interestingly, these procedures have so far never been used.

---

42   *Ibid*, para. 128.

43   *Ibid,* para. 132.

44   The EU has already adopted a legal mechanism in Regulation 912/2014 to deal with such a division of competence and liability. On this regulation, see the contribution by C. Brown in this volume.

45   On this issue, see G. Van der Loo, '*The EU-Ukraine association agreement and deep and comprehensive free trade area: a new legal instrument for EU integration without membership?*' (Brill, 2016), p. 296.

46   The arbitration panels established by the State-to-State DSM s in the Association Agreements (AA s) concluded with Ukraine, Georgia and Moldova are obliged to ask the

2.1.4   No Effect on the Operation of the EU Institutions in Accordance with
        the EU Constitutional Framework – Protection of the Level of the
        Public Interest

The second autonomy criterion of the Court, i.e. the requirement that the ICS Tribunal's decisions may not have the *effect* of preventing the EU institutions from operating in accordance with the EU constitutional framework, is the most fundamental addition to the Court's prior case law. The Court already held in Opinion 1/00 concerning the ECAA that an international agreement cannot "alter the essential character of the powers of each of the Union institutions".[47] Significantly, the Court also used in *Pringle* this test to analyse to what extent the Member States can entrust tasks to the institutions outside the framework of the Union.[48] Opinion 1/17 specifies that test in relation to international agreements.[49]

Belgium and some governments observed that CETA's Tribunal might in the course of its examination of the relevant facts, which may include the basis of which the contested measure was adopted, weigh the interest protected by CETA's freedom to conduct business (and relied on by an investor) against public interests, set out in the TEU and TFEU and in the Charter (and relied on by the Union).[50] CETA's investment court would accordingly have jurisdiction to determine whether a given EU measure violates one of the investment protection standards in CETA (e.g. FET[51] or indirect expropriation).[52] Belgium claimed

---

ECJ for a preliminary ruling for disputes relating to the interpretation of the EU *acquis* referred to in the agreements (e.g. Art. 322 Ukraine AA, OJ 2014, L 161/3). The ECAA, inspired by the EEA model, foresees the possibility for national courts or tribunals of the ECAA partners to ask the ECJ for a preliminary ruling when a question of interpretation of the agreement, of the *acquis* in its annexes or acts adopted in pursuance thereof, arises in a case pending before that court or tribunal. On this issue, see Opinion 1/00. The EEA Agreement provides, on the one hand, the possibility for the contracting parties to request the ECJ to give a ruling on disputes concerning the interpretation of the incorporated EU *acquis* (Art. 111(3)), and, on the other hand, Art. 107 and Protocol 34 EEA foresee that EFTA countries may allow their national courts or tribunals to ask the ECJ to decide by way of a binding preliminary ruling on the interpretation of an EEA provision which is identical in substance to a provision of the EU *acquis*. It has to be noted that under the EU-Turkey Ankara Agreement from 1963 the Association Council can submit a dispute to the ECJ or to any other existing court or tribunal (Art. 25, OJ 1964, L 217).

47   Opinion 1/00, para. 21.
48   Case C-370/12, *Thomas Pringle v Government of Ireland*, ECLI:EU:C:2012:756, para. 158.
49   K. Lenaerts, 'Modernising trade whilst safeguarding the EU constitutional framework: an insight into the balanced approach of Opinion 1/17', Speech – Belgian Ministry of Foreign Affairs – Seminar on Opinion 1/17, 6 September 2019. To consult at: https://diplomatie.belgium.be/sites/default/files/downloads/presentation_lenaerts_opinion_1_17.pdf.
50   Opinion 1/17, para. 137.
51   Art. 8.10 CETA.
52   Art. 8.12 CETA.

that such findings would therefore be of the same nature as those of the Court when it reviews the validity of secondary law and would likely adversely affect the exclusive jurisdiction of the Court. Moreover, CETA defines "investment" broadly[53], permitting the envisaged tribunals to hear a wide range of disputes, and confers upon the ICS the competence to award monetary compensation.

Against this background the Court comes to the crux of Opinion 1/17 as it established the following limit:

> If the CETA Tribunal and Appellate Tribunal were to have jurisdiction to issue awards finding that the treatment of a Canadian investor is incompatible with the CETA because of the level of protection of a public interest established by the EU institutions, this could create a situation where, in order to avoid being repeatedly compelled by the CETA Tribunal to pay damages to the claimant investor, the achievement of that level of protection needs to be abandoned by the Union.[54]

That the ICS may not call into question the level of protection of any public interest reflected in measures limiting a Canadian investor's freedom to conduct business is, according to the Court, a necessary built-in limitation, without which CETA could create a risk that EU institutions amend or withdraw legislation because of assessments made by the Tribunal regarding the level of protection of public interests established by the EU institutions in accordance with the EU constitutional framework.[55] In the Court's view, this would be incompatible with the autonomy of the EU legal order, as the interference of another adjudicative body would infringe on the ECJ's exclusive competence to review the compatibility of the level of protection of public interest established by EU legislation with, i.a., the TEU and TFEU, the Charter and the general principles of EU law.[56]

On the basis of this far-reaching premise, the Court analyses whether CETA contains sufficient guarantees in this regard. Significantly, the drafters of CETA included numerous provisions and safeguards guaranteeing the Parties' right to regulate.[57] It will be recalled that this was one of the main concerns advanced

---

53   Opinion 1/17, para. 139 referring to Art. 8.1.

54   *Ibid*, para. 149.

55   *Ibid,* para. 150.

56   *Ibid,* para. 151.

57   On the right to regulate in CETA, see C. Titi, 'Right to Regulate', in M. M. Mbengue, S. Schacherer (eds.) *Foreign Investment under the Comprehensive Economic and Trade Agreement* (CETA) (Springer, 2019), p. 159–183.

by the critics of ISDS in the heated TTIP debate that led to the EU/Canada reform efforts to move from an ISDS-mechanism to the ICS model. This point is reinforced by both Parties in the Joint interpretative instrument (cf. *infra*).

The Court took note of CETA's General Exception clause (Article 28.3), modelled on Article XX GATT, which states that the agreement cannot be interpreted in such a way as to prevent a Party from adopting and applying measures necessary to protect public security or public morals or to maintain public order or to protect human, animal or plant life or health, subject only to the requirement that such measures are not applied in a manner that would constitute a means of arbitrary or unjustifiable discrimination between the Parties where like conditions prevail, or a disguised restriction on trade between the Parties.[58] In addition, Article 8.9.1 CETA concerning investment protection rules states explicitly that the Parties have the right to regulate "within their territories to achieve legitimate policy objectives, such as the protection of public health, safety, the environment or public morals, social or consumer protection or the promotion and protection of cultural diversity". Further, Article 8.9.2 CETA provides that "for greater certainty, the mere fact that a Party regulates, including through a modification to its laws, in a manner which negatively affects an investment or interferes with an investor's expectations, including its expectations of profits, does not amount to a breach of an obligation under this Section".

Significantly, the Court also relied on the Joint Interpretative Instrument, adopted jointly by the EU and Canada in the context of CETA's signature.[59] This document aimed to convince the Walloon region to reconsider and to sign, after several weeks of rejecting CETA, the mixed agreement. This document, which is considered as part of the context for the purpose of the interpretation of CETA pursuant to Article 31(2)(b) VCLT,[60] was designed to accommodate some of the concerns of the Walloon government (and other critics) of CETA by clarifying the right to regulate enshrined in CETA. Point 1(d) and Point 2 of the Joint Interpretative Instrument provide that CETA will "not lower [the standards and regulations of each Party] related to food safety, product safety, consumer protection, health, environment or labour protection", that "imported goods, service suppliers and investors must continue to respect domestic requirements, including rules and regulations", and that CETA "preserves the ability of the European Union and its Member States and Canada to adopt and

58   Opinion 1/17, para. 152.
59   On this Joint Interpretative Instrument, see G. Van der Loo (n. 3).
60   Statement (38) by the Council Legal Service on the legal nature of the Joint Interpretative Instrument (OJ 2017, L 11/9).

apply their own laws and regulations that regulate economic activity in the public interest".

Reading these provisions together with other additional direct or indirect references to the right to regulate,[61] the Court concludes that the Parties have sufficiently ensured that the discretionary power of the CETA Tribunals "does not extend to permitting them to call into question the level of protection of public interest determined by the Union following a democratic process",[62] and therefore does not adversely affect the autonomy of the EU legal order.[63]

2.2   Compatibility of CETA with the General Principle of Equal Treatment and with the Requirement of Effectiveness

The Court then returned to the compatibility of the ICS with the general principle of equality and the requirement of effectiveness. Belgium had expressed doubts whether the ICS complies with Article 20 of the Charter, which enshrines the guarantee of "equality before the law", and with Article 21(2) of the Charter, which prohibits discrimination on grounds of nationality.

Significantly, the Court first clarified the legal status and applicability of the Charter in relation to international agreements concluded by the EU, thereby addressing the claims of several Member States and the Council that there was no requirement for the ICS to be compatible with those provisions of the Charter.[64] It recalled that international agreements concluded by the EU must be entirely compatible with the Treaties and with the constitutional principles stemming therefrom.[65] A judgement of the Court on the compatibility of an envisaged agreement with "the Treaties", pursuant to Article 218(11) TFEU, must also cover points of substantive law, including the guarantees enshrined in the Charter "since the Charter has the same legal status as the Treaties".[66]

As regards to Article 21(2), the Court however concluded that this provision has a limited personal scope of application. This provision, which explicitly provides the prohibition of discrimination on grounds of nationality, shall apply "within the scope of application of the Treaties". As can be derived from the Explanations relating to the Charter, this corresponds to the first paragraph of

---

61   These are, for example, Point 3 of Annex 8-A CETA on Expropriation and the exhaustive list of types of treatment that constitute "fair and equitable treatment" (Art. 8.10.2 CETA).

62   Opinion 1/17, para. 156.

63   *Ibid,* para. 161.

64   *Ibid,* para. 163 – 175.

65   *Ibid,* para. 165 referring to Opinion 1/15 (*EU-Canada PNR Agreement*), EU:C:2017:592, para. 67, and Case C-266/16, *Western Sahara Campaign UK*, EU:C:2018:118, para. 46.

66   *Ibid,* para. 167.

Article 18 TFEU and is, therefore, limited to situations involving EU Member State nationals.[67] As a result, Article 21(2) of the Charter is not intended to apply to cases where there is a possible difference in treatment between nationals of Members States and nationals of non-Member States (like Canadian investors).[68]

On the other hand, Article 20 of the Charter, which provides that "everyone is equal before the law", does not contain any express limitation on its scope and is therefore applicable to all situations governed by EU law, including those falling within the scope of an international agreement entered into by the Union.[69] Consequently, the Court held that investments made within the Union by Canadian enterprises fall within the scope of EU law and, therefore, within the scope of the equality before the law guaranteed in Article 20 of the Charter.[70] However, the Court clarified that "equality before the law", as laid down in Article 20 of the Charter, "requires that comparable situations must not be treated differently and different situations must not be treated in the same way".[71] Belgium's question related to the fact that EU Member States' nationals having invested in another EU Member State will not have access to CETA's ICS while Canadian investors will. However, the Court concluded that the situation of a Canadian investor in the EU is not the same as that of EU Member State investors investing in another EU Member State.[72] This is exactly the reason why Canadian investors in the EU have the possibility of relying on CETA's investment protection standards before the ICS, in particular considering that they cannot directly invoke CETA's investment protection standards before the courts of EU Member States and the ECJ.[73]

In this context the Court also rejected Belgium's claim that awards by the ICS would undermine the effectiveness of competition law since the ICS might issue awards that cancel out the effect of a competition law fine imposed by the Commission or national competition authorities. Considering the grounds on which the ICS may award damages (e.g. CETA's FET standard or the fundamental right of property), as well as the Parties' recognition of the importance

---

67   *Ibid,* para. 168.
68   Opinion 1/17, para. 169 referring to Case C-22/08 and C-23/08, *Vatsouras and Koupatantze,* EU:C:2009:344, para. 52.
69   *Ibid,* para. 171.
70   *Ibid,* para. 172.
71   *Ibid,* para. 176.
72   *Ibid,* para. 180.
73   Art. 30.6.1 CETA.

of free and undistorted competition, the Court ought such an award "unimaginable" where the Commission or national competition authority has applied the competition rules correctly.[74] Because an EU investor could resort to EU remedies for obtaining the annulment of the fine, both the EU investor and the Canadian investor have remedies available to challenge such fines so that there is no situation of unequal treatment.[75] The Court also argues that the effectiveness of EU competition law would not be jeopardised by such an award as described by Belgium, as EU law itself permits annulment of a fine when that fine is vitiated by a defect corresponding to that which could be identified by the ICS.[76]

2.3   The Compatibility of the Envisaged ISDS Mechanism with the Right of Access to an Independent Tribunal

In the last part of the Opinion the Court had to consider whether the ICS is compatible with the right to an "independent and impartial tribunal previously established by law", as laid down in the second paragraph of Article 47 of the Charter and to "effective access to justice", as enshrined in the third paragraph of Article 47.

The Court first confirmed that, in accordance with its case law concerning the binding effect of the Charter (see above), Article 47 is binding on the EU and that the Union must ensure that each court established by an international agreement "has the characteristics of an accessible and independent tribunal".[77] This reasoning is not invalidated by the fact that the third State with which the EU concluded the agreement is not bound by the safeguards provided under EU law, nor that the ICS is considered "hybrid" in nature, in that it contains, in addition to characteristics of judicial bodies, a number of elements that continue to be based on traditional arbitration mechanisms in relation to investments.[78] The Court indeed considered that several features of the ICS, such as those related to the composition of the tribunals, are clearly distinct from the rules in relation to arbitration and give expression to the intention of the parties that "CETA moves decisively away from the traditional approach of investment dispute resolution and establishes independent, impartial and permanent investment Tribunals, inspired by the principles of public judicial systems", codified in Point 6 of the Joint Interpretative Instrument. The Court

---

74   Opinion 1/17, para. 185.
75   *Ibid*, para. 186.
76   *Ibid*, para. 187.
77   *Ibid*, para. 191.
78   *Ibid*, para. 193.

therefore concludes that the Tribunals established by the ICS will, "in essence exercise judicial functions".[79]

With regard to the guarantee of *accessibility*, the Court accepted that access to the ICS could be limited provided that any restrictions are proportionate, pursue a legitimate aim and do not adversely affect the very essence of the right of access.[80] The Court's assessment of whether the ICS is accessible focused primarily on the financial burden for investors, in particular for natural persons and SMEs. The Court recognised that the ICS is open to any EU enterprise and any natural person that invests in Canada (and vice versa) and recognises the agreement's objectives and efforts to structure the ICS in such a way that investors with limited resources (e.g. natural persons or SMEs) have effective access to the ICS.[81] However, despite several mechanisms in the ICS that aim to reduce the financial burden of using the ICS (such as the cost of legal representation and the cost of the proceedings),[82] the Court concluded that in the absence of rules designed to ensure that the CETA Tribunal and Appellate Tribunal are financially accessible to natural persons and SMEs, the ISDS mechanism may, in practice, be accessible only to investors who have available to them significant financial resources.[83] The Court therefore analysed whether CETA offered guarantees that a body of rules ensuring the level of accessibility required by EU law would be put into place as soon as the Tribunals are established. The Court was reassured by Statement No 36 of the Council and the Commission[84] which states that the EU will rapidly and adequately implement Article 8.39.6 CETA.[85] This provision provides that the CETA Joint Committee shall "consider supplemental rules aimed at reducing the financial burden on claimants who are natural persons or small and medium-sized enterprises". Significantly, the Court stressed that the conclusion of CETA by the Council (which in practice will only occur after the ratification of all Member States) is subject to the premise that the financial accessibility of the ICS for all EU investors will be ensured.[86] Compatibility with Article 47 is thus conditional

---

79   *Ibid*, para. 197.
80   *Ibid*, para. 201 referring to Case C-205/15, *Toma and Biroul Executorului Judecătoresc Horaţiu-Vasile Cruduleci*, EU:C:2016:499, para. 44 and the case law cited.
81   *Ibid*, para. 206.
82   For example, Article 8.27 CETA provides for the possibility of having cases heard by a sole Member of the Tribunal, reducing the costs of the procedure. However, this is only possible if the respondent agrees.
83   Opinion 1/17, para. 213.
84   Statement (36) by the Commission and the Council on investment protection and the Investment Court System ('ICS') (OJ 2017, L 11/9).
85   Opinion 1/17, para. 217.
86   *Ibid*, para. 221.

upon the actual adoption of effective rules ensuring financial accessibility to the CETA Tribunals.[87]

With regard to the requirement of *independence* the Court examines two aspects: *Firstly*, whether the Tribunal can exercise its functions wholly autonomously. The Court recognises that Members of the ICS Tribunal will be appointed for a fixed term, that they need to possess a specific expertise, will receive a remuneration commensurate with the importance of their duties and includes protection against the removal of members.[88] The fact that the CETA Joint Committee has certain powers in relation to the appointment and removal of members, their remuneration and the adjustment of the number of members is not incompatible with the requirement from external independence.[89] Also the fact that this Committee may adopt an interpretation of the agreement that will be binding on the CETA Tribunal does not, in the Court's assessment, affect the capacity of that Tribunal to exercise its functions wholly autonomously, in particular as such interpretations are to be considered as "subsequent agreement" as provided for in Article 31(3) VCLT.[90] However, the Court underscores that such an interpretative decision of the Joint Committee needs to respect EU primary law and may not have retroactive effect neither direct effect on pending cases.[91]

The *second* aspect analysed by the Court in the context of judicial independence, which is internal in nature, concerns impartiality and seeks to ensure that an equal distance is maintained from the parties to the proceedings.[92] The Court is satisfied that CETA contains sufficient guarantees to ensure that necessary requirement. In particular, the Court points to Article 8.27 which provides that cases will be decided by a division composed randomly and by the reference to the International Bar Association (IBA) Guidelines on Conflicts of Interest in International Arbitration.[93] In addition, CETA contains ethical rules that require sitting members of the Tribunal to be impartial and independent both at the time when a claim is brought and throughout the proceedings. The Court therefore concludes that the agreement includes sufficient provisions with regard to the prohibition of conflict of interest, which can even be supplemented by the Committee on Services an Investment.[94]

---

87   *Ibid*, para. 222.
88   *Ibid*, para. 223–226.
89   *Ibid*, para. 227–230.
90   *Ibid*, para. 232–234.
91   *Ibid*, para. 235–236.
92   *Ibid*, para. 202–203.
93   *Ibid*, para. 238.
94   *Ibid*, para. 240–243.

Consequently, the Court concludes that CETA is compatible with the requirement of independence.

3 Comments

3.1 *A Pragmatic Approach by the Court?*

By concluding that CETA is compatible with EU law, the Court did not only remove a significant obstacle to one of the most important and debated initiatives in the EU's trade and investment policy since the Treaty of Lisbon, i.e. the ICS, but also paved the way towards the EU's proposed multilateral investment court (MIC). A negative outcome would have caused a major blow to the EU's international investment (protection) policies, as this would have torpedoed the conclusion of the new EU FTAs including an ICS (with Canada and Mexico) or IPAs (with Singapore and Vietnam). Moreover, it would have casted dark clouds over the more than 1000 Member State BITs with third countries.

It appears that the Court was in Opinion 1/17 sympathetic to these policy objectives – and to the EU's capacity to act on the international stage – and therefore loosened its strict approach regarding the jurisdiction of international courts to interpret international treaties concluded by the EU. The Court confirmed its previous position that the EU may, in principle, become a party to an international agreement providing for the creation of a court responsible for the interpretation of its provisions and whose decisions are binding on the European Union.[95] This approach is essential to allow the EU to fulfil its constitutional duty, enshrined in Article 21 TEU, to "develop relations and build partnerships with third countries, and international, regional or global organisations". The Court's attitude flows from the recognition of "the reciprocal nature of international agreements and the need to maintain the powers of the Union in international relations that it is open to the Union".[96]

The Court's "pragmatic"[97] or "lenient"[98] approach in Opinion 1/17 regarding the compatibility of an international agreement establishing its own court with EU law seemingly departs from its previous narrow and strict understanding of the notion of autonomy, developed in, *inter alia*, Opinion 2/13. In fact,

---

95   Opinion 1/17, para. 106.
96   *Ibid*, para. 117.
97   P. Koutrakos, 'More in Autonomy – Opinion 1/17', *European Law Review* (2019), p. 293–294.
98   S. Gáspár-Szilágyi, Between Fiction and Reality. The External Autonomy of EU law as a 'shapeshifter' after Opinion 1/17', *European Papers* (forthcoming): To consult at: https://papers.ssrn.com/sol3/papers.cfm?abstract_id=3527563.

the Court had to apply its own pre-Opinion 1/17 criteria in a flexible and creative fashion to allow for this shift. Moreover, the Court's new criteria seem to raise new questions. This can be illustrated with a few examples.

First, the Court was easily convinced that the Appellate Tribunal cannot interpret or apply EU law other than the provisions of CETA. Article 8.28(2) CETA contains a broad list of grounds of appeal, including "manifest errors in the appreciation of the facts, including the appreciation of relevant domestic law". Domestic law includes necessarily EU law as far as the EU and its Member States are concerned, implying that the Appellate Tribunal has jurisdiction to interpret or apply EU law – albeit only within the context of the appreciation of facts, which nonetheless can be decisively important in specific cases.[99] However, the Court swept away these concerns by simply stating that "it is nonetheless clear from the preceding provisions that it was in *no way the intention of the Parties to confer* on the Appellate Tribunal jurisdiction to interpret domestic law".[100] The fact that the Court was reassured by the Parties' intentions is in sharp contrast with the distrust that permeated Opinion 2/13, considering that in this case even any potential threat to autonomy was sufficient for the Court to render the accession agreement to the ECHR incompatible with EU law.

Second, the Court concluded that the Appellate Tribunal is compatible with EU law, even though the Court could have no knowledge of how the Tribunal will function in practice, as the detailed provisions on its actual administrative and organisational functioning (e.g. appointment of its Members and their remuneration, procedures for the initiation and the conduct of appeals and "any other elements it determines to be necessary for the effective functioning of the Appellate Tribunal") still had to be adopted by the Joint Committee.[101] Remarkably, the Court was convinced that the decisions of the Joint Committee would be compatible with the autonomy criteria developed in Opinion 1/17. Moreover, the Court did not deem it necessary to develop or suggest guidelines or benchmarks for such a decision. The Commission has however not let the Court down: its proposal on the position to be taken on behalf of the EU in the Joint Committee as regards to adoption of this decision, which includes rules on the composition of the Appellate Tribunal and on the "Conduct of Appeals", seems to be in line with the criteria developed by the Court in Opinion 1/17,

---

99   N. Lavranos, 'CJEU Opinion 1/17: Keeping International Investment Law and EU Law Strictly Apart', *European Investment Law and Arbitration Review* 4 (2019), p. 247.

100   Opinion 1/17, para. 133. Emphasis added.

101   Art. 8.28(7) CETA.

although no explicit reference to Opinion 1/17 has been included in the text (for example in the recitals).[102]

Third, as noted above, the Court was not convinced by CETA's provisions which aim to improve the financial accessibility of the ICS for natural persons and SMEs – in essence because these are not binding.[103] Nevertheless, the Court concluded that the ICS is compatible with the requirement of accessibility, as enshrined in Article 47 of the Charter, as it was reassured by the commitment from the Commission and the Council in Statement 36. There, the two institutions pledge to adopt additional rules to reduce the financial burden imposed on natural persons and SMEs for ICS proceedings, as foreseen in Article 8.39.6 CETA, and that "irrespective of the outcome of the discussions within the Joint Committee, the Commission will propose appropriate measures of (co)-financing of actions of small and medium-sized enterprises before that Court". Again, the Court seems to put a lot of trust in that Joint Committee: despite the fact that the compatibility of the ICS with the requirement of accessibility depends on future decisions of that Committee, the Court abstains from establishing pertinent guidelines or conditions for the Committee. However, it underscores that the conclusion of CETA by the Council is subject to the premise that the financial accessibility of the ICS for all EU investors will be ensured.[104] At the moment of writing this chapter, the Commission still has to adopt such a proposal.

Fourth, the Court concludes that the autonomy safeguard in Article 8.31 of CETA on "applicable law and interpretation" leaves no doubt that the ICS Tribunal can only apply CETA itself and international law applicable between the Parties. In particular, the Court was reassured by the fact that the ICS Tribunal can only interpret EU law "as a matter of fact" and that any meaning given to domestic law by the Tribunal is not binding upon the Court or EU institutions. It is noteworthy that by excluding domestic law from the applicable law the

---

102   European Commission, 'Proposal for a Council Decision on the position to be taken on behalf of the European Union in the CETA Joint Committee established under the Comprehensive Economic and Trade Agreement (CETA) between Canada, of the one part, and the European Union and its Member States, of the other part as regards the adoption of a decision setting out the administrative and organisational matters regarding the functioning of the Appellate Tribunal (COM (2019) 457 final). The Commission also adopted proposals for such Council Decisions with regard to a code of conduct for member of the ICS (COM (2019) 259); rules for mediation (COM (2019) 460); and rules for binding interpretations to be adopted by the CETA Joint Committee (COM (2019) 458). The Council adopted these decisions on 18 May 2020 (OJ 2020, L 161).

103   Opinion 1/17, para. 216.

104   *Ibid*, para. 221–222.

drafters of the Treaty broke with the practice of investment treaties that often provide that domestic law is part of the applicable law, as for example illustrated by the intra-EU BIT at issue in *Achmea*.[105] The ICSID Convention indeed provides that, if the Parties do not agree on the applicable law, the tribunal shall apply the law of the host state.[106] However, it has been argued that the dividing line between taking into account an issue as a matter of "fact" or "law" is not always crystal clear,[107] or can even be considered as "a legal fiction".[108] Indeed, Article 8.31 does not exclude the possibility that the ICS Tribunal may have to interpret or apply EU law – albeit as a matter of fact – to some extent in order to determine whether an investment rule in CETA is breached. It has been demonstrated that international investment tribunals routinely discuss or interpret EU law, in either the jurisdictional or the merits phase, regardless of whether EU law applies to the dispute as applicable law or relevant fact.[109] Or, in the context of the WTO, WTO dispute settlement panels often discuss and interpret EU law (for example in the case of anti-dumping matters) in order to properly determine whether WTO obligations are being violated.[110] However, as confirmed by the ECJ, WTO panels (or the appellate Body) cannot, in principle, rule on the validity of an EU measure or bind the Court.[111] International courts that assess the conformity of EU measures with an international treaty need to interpret EU law to fulfil their functions, but they cannot invalidate it.[112]

Fifth, the Court's second autonomy criterion in Opinion 1/17, i.e. that the ICS must allow the EU institutions to function in accordance with the EU constitutional framework, in particular with respect to determining the level of protection of public interest, raises several questions. The Court holds that when ascertaining whether an EU measure violates one of CETA's investment

---

105   Case C-284/16, *Slowakische Republik v Achmea BV*, ECLI:EU:C:2018:158.

106   Art. 42(1) ICSID Convention.

107   N. Lavranos (n. 99), p. 245.

108   C. Titi, 'Opinion 1/17 and the Future of Investment Dispute Settlement: Implications for the Design of a Multilateral Investment Court', in L. Sachs, L. Johnson and J. Coleman (eds.), *Yearbook on International Investment Law & Policy* 2019 (Oxford University Press, forthcoming-2020).

109   S. Gáspár-Szilágyi, M. Usynin, 'The Uneasy Relationship between Intra-EU Investment Tribunals and the Court of Justice's Achmea Judgment', *European Investment Law and Arbitration Review*, (2019), p. 29.

110   *European Union – Anti-Dumping Measures on Certain Footwear from China*, DS405, para. 7.63 et seq.; *European Union – Anti-Dumping Measures on Biodiesel from Argentina*, DS473, para. 7.146 et seq.

111   Joined cases C-659/13 and C-34/14, *Clarck and Puma*, EU:C:2016:74

112   S. Gáspár-Szilágyi (n. 98).

protection rules, the ICS Tribunal cannot "call into question" the level of protection of any public interest which that measure pursues.[113] It is, however, not entirely clear when exactly, or under which conditions, the ICS would prevent (or "call into question") the EU institutions from determining the level of protection of public interests. As the ICS Tribunal cannot oblige the EU to withdraw or amend legislation but can only award monetary damages or restitution of property,[114] the Tribunal can only *indirectly* have an adverse impact on the level of protection of public interest. The Court gave actually only one example of such a situation: i.e. when, "in order to avoid being *repeatedly* compelled by the CETA Tribunal to pay damages to the claimant investor"[115], the EU would abandon the level of protection that led to the introduction of the challenged EU measure.[116] Although such concerns are not unfounded, this scenario can hardly be considered as a clear guideline or benchmark for this crucial new autonomy criterion. In any case, as illustrated above, the Court concluded that the right to regulate, enshrined in several provisions in CETA, ensures sufficiently that the discretionary power of the CETA Tribunals "do not extend to permitting them to call into question the level of protection of public interest determined by the Union following a democratic process". But this line of reasoning leaves several important questions (deliberately?) unanswered. For example, the Court does not explicitly rule out (or confirm) that the ICS Tribunal has jurisdiction to decide whether an EU measure challenged by an investor is effective and proportionate to achieve certain public interests (or falls under CETA's right to regulate) when determining if this measure violates investment protection rules in CETA. If this would not be the case, the host state could easily invoke for each measure contested by the investor the right to regulate, challenging the jurisdiction of the ICT Tribunal. Moreover, it is not entirely clear what would happen if the ICS Tribunal would uphold jurisdiction in such a scenario and would find that such a measure violates one of CETA's investment protection standards, although this measure was taken to pursue a public interest falling under CETA's right to regulate.[117] The President of the ECJ, Judge Koen Lenaerts, has noted in this regard that the Court is here not attempting to protect measures of general application as nothing in CETA suggests that that such measures are "immune" from review for the ICS Tribunal.[118] He argues

---

113   Opinion 1/17, para. 148.
114   Art. 8.39 CETA.
115   Emphasis added.
116   Opinion 1/17, para. 149.
117   On this issue, see C. Titi (n. 108).
118   K. Lenaerts (n. 49).

that what the Court is protecting instead is "the essence of the democratic process leading to the adoption of EU norms protecting public interests, a process which forms part of the EU constitutional framework".[119] These constitutional considerations do however not address the questions raised above.

3.2   *Implications for Future Agreements and the MIC*

The aforementioned examples and arguments illustrate that the Court was rather flexible in applying its own autonomy criteria to the ICS in CETA, revealing a more lenient approach of the Court vis-à-vis DSM s included in international agreements concluded by the EU – in particular compared to its previous strict approach in, for example, Opinion 2/13. However, by relying heavily on the different autonomy safeguards included in CETA in order to give green light to the ICS, the Court raised considerably the bar for compliance with the principle of autonomy – and with EU law as such (including the Charter) – for future international agreements concluded by the EU.

The Court considered that the different autonomy safeguards included in CETA were sufficient – but at the same time also essential – for compliance with EU law. In particular, Article 8.31 on "applicable law and interpretation" was for the Court essential to ensure that under no circumstances the ICS Tribunal can give an interpretation to EU law which would be binding on the Court or EU institutions; the respondent mechanism provided for in Article 8.21 was crucial for the Court to conclude that the ICS Tribunal cannot have a say on the division of competences between the EU and the Member States; the different provisions ensuring the right to regulate included in CETA and the Joint Interpretative Instrument were deemed essential to ensure that the ICS Tribunal cannot call into question the level of protection of any public interest determined by the EU; and the commitment from the Commission and the Council adopted in Statement 36 were vital to persuade the Court that the ICS will be financially accessible to natural persons and SME s – and therefore complies with the accessibility criteria enshrined in Article 47 of the Charter.

Therefore, it appears that future agreements will need to include similar autonomy safeguards on, inter alia, applicable law, the determination of the respondent, the right to regulate and financial accessibility for natural persons and SME s (although this last safeguard would not be required in relation to State-to-State DSM s (e.g. the WTO DSM and State-to-State arbitration panels in FTA s)). However, including such autonomy safeguard clauses can face legal

---

119   *Ibid.*

and political challenges, as for example illustrated in the context of the EU's proposal for a MIC.

At first sight Opinion 1/17 seems to legitimise the Commission's efforts to develop a MIC within UNCITRAL Working Group III, provided that the MIC is based on the autonomy safeguards included in CETA's ICS and the criteria laid down in this Opinion.[120] The Court even explicitly mentioned that it has, in principle, no objections against a multilateral Investment Tribunal modelled upon the ICS.[121]

However, it is not a given that all of CETA's autonomy safeguards and other provisions aiming to ensure compliance with EU law (sanctified by the Court in Opinion 1/17) can be included in the Convention establishing the MIC. Although the mandate of UNCITRAL Working Group III is broad, it is essentially confined to the procedural dimension of ISDS reform and does not cover substantive provisions such as, for example, the right to regulate or investment protection standards (e.g. FET and expropriation).[122] The Convention establishing the MIC would therefore not include such substantive provisions, as these are – or will be – included in the existing (or future) investment agreements concluded between the Parties to the Convention. Moreover, the MIC would only have jurisdiction over disputes in such agreements if these Parties have notified ("opt-in") that their agreement would be subject to the jurisdiction of the MIC. This may explain why the Council's negotiating directives for a Convention establishing a MIC[123] and the EU's submission to UNCITRAL Working Group III[124] do not envisage provisions on, for example, the right to regulate or applicable law.[125] The EU's submission even explicitly recognises that "the precise scope of jurisdiction of the [MIC] and the substantive rules that it would apply are determined by the underlying treaties" and that, therefore, "the substantive rules that the [MIC] would apply may evolve with the underlying treaty rules".[126]

---

120   On this issue, see the contribution by Colin Brown in this volume.

121   Opinion 1/17, para. 118.

122   On this issue, see the contribution by Colin Brown in this volume.

123   Council of the EU, 'Negotiating directives for a Convention establishing a multilateral court for the settlement of investment disputes', 12981/17 ADD 1 DCL 1, 20 March 2018.

124   European Union, 'Possible reform of investor-state dispute settlement (ISDS), Submission from the European Union and its Member States, A/CN.9/WG.III/WP.159/ADD.1, 24 January 2019.

125   The EU's submission to UNCITRAL does however state that: "In a multilateral standing mechanism covering multiple bilateral agreements it would be necessary to ensure that the parties to a bilateral agreement would retain control over the interpretation of their agreement by being able to adopt binding interpretations" (para. 26) (*Ibid*).

126   *Ibid*, para. 37.

Nevertheless, in order to ensure compliance with the EU law – as set out in Opinion 1/17 – several sovereignty safeguards, mirroring those included in CETA, need to be included in the Convention setting up the MIC. For example, the Convention should include a provision stipulating that, to the extent that the EU or a Member State is party to the dispute, the applicable law for the MIC Tribunal is only international law – including the underlying investment agreements – and that the multilateral Tribunal cannot (i) determine the legality of a measure under the domestic law of a Party or (ii) interpret the municipal law of a party (only as a matter of fact). In addition, for such disputes the Tribunal will (iii) need to follow the prevailing interpretation given to the domestic law by the courts or authorities of that Party and (iv) it has to made clear that any meaning given to domestic law by the MIC will not be binding upon the courts or the authorities of that Party. Such a provision would not conflict with the recently negotiated EU FTAS or IPAS as these all include a provision on *applicable law* similar to Article 8.31 CETA.[127]

It is also not entirely clear if, or how, such a Convention would be able to ensure that the MIC Tribunal cannot "call into question" the level of protection of any public interest established by the Parties. Substantive provisions on the right to regulate do not seem to fall within the mandate of UNCITRAL Working Group III and are not mentioned in the EU's proposals. In any case, a requirement in such a Convention that the MIC would need to take into account the level of protection of a public interest or the right to regulate would not conflict with the underlying EU FTAS or IPAS, as these include strong language on the Parties' right to regulate. Such a requirement in the Convention would also fill the gap in extra-EU BITs that lack provisions guaranteeing the Parties' right to regulate.

Considering the Court's arguments in relation to accessibility of the ICS (in the light of compatibility with Article 47 of the Charter), the MIC Convention should make serious efforts to ensure that the MIC would be financially accessible to natural persons and SMEs. The Council's negotiating directives indeed mention that the Convention should ensure the access of all SMEs and natural persons by reducing costs.[128] For example, the Convention could include provisions on cost reduction, access to legal aid through an advisory centre, the

---

127 See for example Art. 3.42 IPA with Vietnam; footnote 29 to the IPA with Singapore, Art. 15 draft Chapter on Resolution for investment disputes EU-Mexico FTA (to consult at: https://trade.ec.europa.eu/doclib/docs/2018/april/tradoc_156814.pdf).

128 Council of the EU, 'Negotiating directives for a Convention establishing a multilateral court for the settlement of investment disputes', 12981/17 ADD 1 DCL 1, 20 March 2018, para. 17.

acceleration of proceedings and class actions by SMEs and individual investors with respect to identical claims.[129]

The requirement of *independence,* as enshrined in Article 47 of the Chapter, seems less problematic for the envisaged MIC as the EU's proposals and the Council's negotiating directives envisage detailed provisions that aim to ensure both the internal and external dimension of the MIC's independence, mirroring the ICS in CETA (e.g. concerning the composition of the Tribunal, ethical requirements, remuneration and qualifications adjudicators and the appointment process).

4   Conclusion and Outlook

By concluding that CETA is compatible with EU law, the Court legitimised one of the most important and debated initiatives in the EU's trade and investment policy since the Treaty of Lisbon, i.e. the ICS included in the new generation of EU FTAs or IPAs. This contribution highlighted two interrelated elements of Opinion 1/17: firstly, the more lenient approach of the ECJ with regard to the principle of autonomy (in relation to international agreements establishing a DSM or court) and secondly, the implications of the Opinion for future international agreements concluded by the EU, in particular the MIC.

With regard to the former, it has been demonstrated that the Court departed from its previous narrow and strict understanding of the notion of autonomy and its distrust towards DSMs or courts established by international agreements concluded by the EU. It seems that the Court was in particular concerned about the EU's capacity to act on the international stage and to allow the EU to fulfil its constitutional duty to "develop relations and build partnerships with third countries, and international, regional or global organisations".[130] Therefore, the Court had to apply its own pre-Opinion 1/17 criteria in a flexible and creative fashion to allow for this move. The Court also developed a new crucial autonomy criterion, i.e. DSMs or courts established by international agreements concluded by the EU must allow the EU institutions to function in accordance with the EU constitutional framework, in particular with respect to determining the level of protection of public interest. However, this new criterion also raises several new questions. For example, it is not

---

129   M. Bungenberg, A. Reinisch,' From Bilateral Arbitral Tribunals and Investment Courts to a Multilateral Investment Court', *European Yearbook of International Economic Law* (Springer, 2020), p. 21.

130   Art. 21 TEU.

entirely clear when exactly, or under which conditions, a DSM or court would prevent (or "call into question") the EU institutions from determining the level of protection of public interests. Moreover, the Court leaves the question unanswered whether such a court or DSM would have jurisdiction to decide if an EU measure challenged by an investor in ICS proceedings is effective and proportionate to achieve certain public interests developed within the EU's constitutional framework (or falls under the agreement's right to regulate). If the answer would be in the negative, the ICS Tribunal will not be able to perform one of its *raisons d'être*.

With regard to the implications of the Opinion for future agreements concluded by the EU, it was observed that the Court relied heavily on the different carefully-worded *autonomy safeguard provisions* enshrined in CETA, including the Joint Interpretative Instrument and Statement No. 36 of the Commission and the Council. The Court considered that these clauses were sufficient – but at the same time also essential – for compliance with EU law. Therefore, the Court raised considerably the bar for compliance with the principle of autonomy – and with EU law as such (including the Charter) – for future international agreements concluded by the EU. Future agreements setting up a DSM or a court will need to include similar autonomy safeguards on, inter alia, applicable law, the determination of the respondent, the right to regulate and financial accessibility for natural persons and SMEs (although this last safeguard will not be required in relation to State-to-State DSMs). This will not be a problem for the other recent EU FTAs or IPAs that include an ICS (e.g. those recently negotiated or signed with Vietnam, Singapore and Mexico) because these agreements include similar autonomy safeguard clauses. However, this contribution demonstrated that these conditions significantly tie the hands of the Commission in its pursuit to set up a Convention establishing a MIC in the framework of UNCITRAL Working Group III. In the case that the EU cannot include (several of) these autonomy safeguard clauses in a Convention setting up a MIC, the Court could find in a possible future Opinion on such a Convention that the MIC is only compatible with EU law under the condition that the missing autonomy safeguards in the Convention are included in the underlying investment agreements concluded by the EU (or its Member States) over which the MIC has jurisdiction.

Also in the area of investment protection, the impact of Opinion 1/17 on existing and future intra and extra-EU BITS will need to be considered and addressed. With regard to extra-EU BITS, it has to be noted that several of such agreements contain clauses that expressly designate each party's national law (and hence EU law) as part of the applicable law or do not include CETA-like provisions ensuring that the investment tribunal cannot call into question the level of protection of public interests established by the EU institutions (e.g. the right to regulate). It could be argued that the extra-EU BITs do not bind the EU and, therefore, cannot affect the powers of the EU institutions in a manner contrary to the principle of autonomy. However, even if the EU is not a party to the extra-EU BITs, the measure challenged by the claimant under those agreements may well be an EU measure and/or a measure taken by a Member State in order to implement EU law.[131] This implies that decisions of arbitration tribunals under extra-EU BITs may well have the effect, in practice, of forcing the EU to abandon its chosen level of protection in order to avoid Member States being repeatedly compelled to pay damages for complying with EU law.[132] Therefore, the Member States should take the necessary steps to align their extra-EU BITs with Opinion 1/17 by including CETA-like autonomy safeguard clauses. Significantly, the Council's negotiating directives for a Convention setting up a MIC state that the Convention should allow the Member States to bring their extra-EU BITs under the jurisdiction of the MIC (intra-EU BITs would not be covered).[133]

The future of the existing intra-EU BITs is already in limbo since the Court's ruling in *Achmea*. Following Declarations of the Member States on 15 and 16 January 2019 on the legal consequences of *Achmea*,[134] EU Member States finally reached an agreement on 24 October 2019 on a plurilateral treaty for the termination of intra-EU BITs. On 5 May 2020 23 Member States signed the agreement.[135] However, the Member States could not agree on the implications of

---

131 Y. Mersch, *et al.*, 'The new challenges raised by investment arbitration for the EU legal order', *European Central Bank Legal Working Paper Series* 19 (2019), p. 24.

132 *Ibid.*

133 Council of the EU, 'Negotiating directives for a Convention establishing a multilateral court for the settlement of investment disputes', 12981/17 ADD 1 DCL 1, 20 March 2018, para. 17.

134 'Declaration of the Member States of 15 and 16 January 2019 on the legal consequences of the *Achmea* judgment and on investment protection', to consult at: https://ec.europa.eu/info/publications/190117-bilateral-investment-treaties_en.

135 The agreement can be consulted at: https://ec.europa.eu/info/files/200505-bilateral-investment-treaties-agreement_en. It has to be noted that several Member States did not sign the agreement. The Commission has announced to initiate infringement procedures against EU Member States that do not terminate their intra-EU bilateral investment treaties (European Commission, 'EU Member States agree on a plurilateral treaty to terminate bilateral investment treaties', Statement, 24 October 2019). For example, the European Commission has sent in May 2020 letters of formal notice to Finland and the United Kingdom for failing to effectively remove intra-EU BITs from their legal orders (See European Commission May 2020 infringement package, to consult at: https://ec.europa.eu/commission/presscorner/detail/en/inf_20_859). On this issue, see N. Lavarnos, 'The EU Plurilateral Draft Termination Agreement for All Intra-EU BITs: An End of

Achmea for the Energy Charter Treaty (ECT).[136] Although it is not entirely clear whether Opinion 1/17 is applicable to the ECT,[137] several steps have been taken to bring the ECT in line with Opinion 1/17 and the autonomy safeguard clauses in CETA. Not only did the EU and the Member States submitted a Statement to the ECT Secretariat to replace the procedure for the determination of the respondent by the procedure foreseen in Regulation (EU) No 912/2014,[138] the Council's negotiating Directives for the Modernisation of the Energy Charter Treaty also state that the EU should strive to ensure that the treaty's dispute settlement mechanism is in line with the EU's new approach with regard to investment protection and that a future MIC should apply to the ECT.[139] Significantly, the Council's negotiating directives include references to the right to regulate but not to the financial accessibility of natural persons and SMEs.

Finally, it should be stressed that CETA's autonomy safeguard clauses should not only be included in future FTAs or IPAs, but in any agreement concluded by the EU establishing a court or DSM responsible for the interpretation of its provisions and whose decisions are binding on the EU. Moreover, international agreements that make explicit reference to provisions of EU law – or where the applicable law includes EU law – will need to include a prior involvement

---

the Post-Achmea Saga and the Beginning of a New One', *Kluwer Arbitration Blog*, 1 December 2019.

136   22 Member States extended the effect of *Achmea* also to intra-EU disputes within the context of the Energy Charter Treaty (ECT), while several Member States refrained from taking a position and argued that it would be more appropriate to wait until the ECJ has explicitly ruled on the compatibility of the ECT arbitration clause with EU law (See the Declaration by Finland, Luxembourg, Malta, Slovenia and Sweden from 16 January 2019, to consult at https://www.regeringen.se/48ee19/contentassets/d759689c0c804a9ea7af6b2de7320128/achmea-declaration.pdf). In a separate Declaration, Hungary rejected the application of the *Achmea* judgment to the ECT altogether (to consult at: https://www.kormany.hu/download/5/1b/81000/Hungarys%20Declaration%20on%20Achmea.pdf).   The Commission is of the view that the investor-state arbitration clause of the ECT, "if interpreted correctly", is not applicable between EU Member States (European Commission, 'Protection of intra-EU investment', COM(2018) 547). On this issue, see M. Beham, 'Intra-EU Investment Reform: What Options for the Energy Charter Treaty?' *Kluwer Arbitration Blog*, 7 January 2020, to consult at: http://arbitrationblog.kluwerarbitration.com/2020/01/07/intra-eu-investment-reform-what-options-for-the-energy-charter-treaty/.

137   N. Lavranos (n. 99), p. 257.

138   'Statement to be submitted by the European Union, the European Atomic Energy Community (Euratom) and those Member States that are party to the Energy Charter Treaty (ECT) to the ECT Secretariat pursuant to Article 26(3)(b)(ii) of the ECT replacing the statement made on 17 November 1997 on behalf of the European Communities', ST/7830/2019, 4 April 2019.

139   Council, 'Negotiating Directives for the Modernisation of the Energy Charter Treaty', 10745/19, 2 July 2019.

procedure obliging such a Court or DSM to make a reference for a preliminary ruling to the ECJ. The Commission's proposal for the Agreement on the New Partnership with the United Kingdom and the draft text of the Interinstitutional Agreement between the EU and Switzerland indeed oblige the respective arbitration tribunals to request the ECJ for a preliminary ruling if a dispute would raise a question of interpretation or application of EU law.[140] Similar procedures were already included in the Association Agreements with Ukraine, Moldova and Georgia.[141] The Court did not find such a procedure necessary in CETA given that the ICS' jurisdiction is confined to the provisions of CETA.[142]

In sum, in Opinion 1/17 the Court sanctified one of the most contested trade policy instruments developed since the Treaty of Lisbon, i.e. the ICS. For pragmatic reasons the Court applied *in casu* a more lenient approach with regard to the principle of autonomy and the jurisdiction of international courts or DSMs to interpret international treaties concluded by the EU. However, by conditioning CETA's conformity with EU law to several autonomy safeguards and by developing a new – but rather vague – criterion (i.e. that such courts or DSMs cannot call into question the level of protection of public interest established by the EU institutions in accordance with the EU constitutional framework), the Court raised considerably the bar for future agreements to comply with EU law.

Acknowledgements

The author would like to thank M. Hahn and M. Chamon for their useful comments on earlier drafts of this chapter.

---

140   Art. 16, 'Disputes raising questions of Union law', Draft text of the Agreement on the New Partnership with the United Kingdom (UKTF (2020) 14, 18 March 2020); Article 10 Draft 'Accord Facilitant Les Relations Bilatérales entre L'Union Européenne et la Confédération Suisse dans les Parties du Marché Intérieur auxquelles la Suisse participe', to consult at: https://www.eda.admin.ch/dam/dea/fr/documents/abkommen/Acccord-inst-Projet-de-texte_fr.pdf.
141   On this issue, see (text to) footnote 44.
142   Opinion 1/17, para. 134.

Never Get High on Your Own Supply – 'Autonomy of the EU Legal Order' and Effective Treaty-Based Dispute Settlement Mechanisms

Michael Hahn

1   Introduction

Opinion 1/17,[1] delivered by the Full Court on 30 April 2019, is for many reasons a seminal decision of the Court of Justice of the European Union (ECJ): For one, it was the preliminary happy ending (on the EU side) of the CETA-saga: After the well-known *querelles belges* of 2016[2] almost derailed the conclusion of CETA, it is now clear that as a matter of Union law the deep and comprehensive free trade agreement with one of the European Union's closest allies and partners is on solid ground; this is not to say that CETA may not still have to face problems in certain Member states.[3] But even more important than this

---

1   Opinion 1/17 (*CETA*), ECLI:EU:C:2019:341.

2   Cf. *Wallonia is adamantly blocking the EU's trade deal with Canada* – A tiny region of Belgium opposes trade for reasons that are hard to understand, https://www.economist.com/europe/2016/10/22/wallonia-is-adamantly-blocking-the-eus-trade-deal-with-canada; see also I. Laird, F. Petillion, 'Comprehensive Economic and Trade Agreement, ISDS and the Belgian Veto: A Warning of Failure for Future Trade Agreements with the EU?', *Global Trade and Customs Journal* 12 (2017), p. 167–174, at 171; this situation is reflected in Statement 37 to the Council minutes on 27 October 2016: "Belgium wishes to make clear that, in accordance with its constitutional law, the result of the consent procedures undertaken both in the Federal Parliament and in each of the parliamentary assemblies of the Belgian Regions and Communities may be that the process of ratifying CETA has permanently and definitively failed in the sense of the Council statement of 18 October 2016. ... In the event that one of the federated entities should inform the Federal Government of its permanent and definitive decision not to ratify CETA, the Federal Government will notify the Council, no later than one year from the notification by the entity concerned, that Belgium is permanently and definitively unable to ratify CETA. The necessary steps will be taken in accordance with EU procedures (to be consulted at https://data.consilium.europa.eu/doc/document/ST-13463-2016-REV-1/en/pdf).

3   Cf., e.g., regarding the situation in Cyprus and Germany: Cyprus mail of 4 August 2020, "Talks to begin with parties after rejection of CETA" (https://cyprus-mail.com/2020/08/04/talks-to-begin-with-parties-after-rejection-of-ceta/); the pertinent procedures before the Bundesverfassungsgericht are pending: cf. https://www.bundesverfassungsgericht.de/EN/Verfahren/Jahresvorausschau/vs_2018/vorausschau_2018.htm; only the applications for a preliminary

concrete result is the message the Court sends with Opinion 1/17: the Court will grant the Union's political institutions leeway to structure the Union's foreign relations as they deem fit (and the Court will abstain from tackling the pertinent efforts by Union institutions and the Member states), provided the substantive law of the agreement is compatible with the EU and FEU Treaties[4], *and* does not infringe the "autonomy of the Union legal order". Contrary to some expectations based in particular on the Court's recent case-law on *autonomy*,[5] the latter requires only that the agreement and its dispute settlement mechanism do not interfere with the ability of the EU institutions to discharge their function pursuant to the roles conferred to them, in particular, the overall integrity of the decision-making regime established by the Treaties and hence, the homogeneity of the Union legal order.

Opinion 1/17 confirms the Court's jurisprudence that the autonomy of the Union legal order is not affected by the possibility of a (temporary) divergence between the jurisprudence of a treaty-based dispute settlement mechanism (DSM) and its own case-law, provided that, firstly, the agreement in question is not in essence an expansion or a subset of the Union legal order[6] and, secondly, the agreement ensures through judicial or political mechanisms that the role of the Court as ultimate interpreter of EU law is ensured. Therefore, despite the Court's leap of faith (see 4.2 or 4.3), it needs to be underscored that the acceptance of some temporary divergence is far from unqualified, as the previous chapter by *Van der Loo* and the following discussion will show.

As an immediate consequence, the political institutions of the Union may continue their pertinent efforts to pursue, initially amongst a closer circle of friends,[7] and ultimately with a broader constituency, the Investment Court

---

injunction in the "CETA" proceedings have so far been unsuccessful; cf. Press Release of the Federal Constitutional Court No. 71/2016 of 13 October 2016 regarding the judgment of 13 October 2016 to be consulted at https://www.bundesverfassungsgericht.de/SharedDocs/Pressemitteilungen/EN/2016/bvg16-071.html; cf. also M. Nettesheim, 'Umfassende Freihandelsabkommen und Grundgesetz. Verfassungsrechtliche Grundlagen der Zustimmung zu CETA', Berlin: Duncker & Humblot, 2017. As of March 2020, only 13 of the 27 Member States had completed their ratification processes; cf. https://www.consilium.europa.eu/ en/documents-publications/treaties-agreements/agreement/?id=2016017.

4 Including, in particular, the Charter of Fundamental Rights (CFR).
5 Cf. e.g. S. Schill, 'The European Union's Foreign Direct Investment Screening Paradox: Tightening Inward Investment Control to Further External Investment Liberalization', *Legal Issues of Economic Integration* 46 (2019), p. 105–128, 127.
6 The ECJ's strong reaction to perceived "contamination" is also underscored by P. J. Kuijper and G. Vidigal in their contribution in this volume.
7 For example, Vietnam, New Zealand, Australia, Singapore, Mexico and Canada. For details see: https://ec.europa.eu/trade/policy/countries-and-regions/negotiations-and-agreements/

.

System.[8] More importantly, a significant impediment for political imagination and creativity to find, in the future, mutually acceptable treaty-based solutions with third countries on all sorts of subject-matter areas has, one hopes, been neutralised: given the diversity of partners (from countries like Canada that share values, principles of government and political affiliations to countries with completely different values which march to a very different tune than Western democracies) and given the range of topics (from access to raw materials to privacy, from climate change to international cooperation on tax matters, from trade to outer space), this is not an easy exercise and does not lend itself to a one-size-fits all approach. Political judgments calls will be unavoidable. They need to abide by the EU's "constitutional charter", but should not be hampered by an expansive application of the notion of autonomy which puts the Union's separation of powers in Foreign relations into question.[9]

The reason for the successful conclusion of CETA and the success for the Union as an international actor is the restrained and "pragmatic" application of the principle of *autonomy of the Union legal order* in Opinion 1/17.[10] The assertive use of this notion in some recent instances, even against the treaty-mandated accession to the ECHR,[11] had raised concerns that the effort of the Union and its Member states to pursue a policy of creating (or reinforcing) a safety net for a stagnating (and, as has become painfully clear, endangered[12])

---

8   M. Bungenberg, A. Reinisch (ed.), 'The Anatomy of the (Invisible) EU Model BIT', *Journal of World Investment & Trade*, Special Issue 15 (3–4) (2014).

9   Cf. Article 13 (2) TEU, Articles 218, 207 TFEU.

10   Developed in Opinion 1/91, *EEA Agreement*, EU:C:1991:490.

11   Opinion 2/13, *Accession of the Union to the ECHR*, EU:C:2014:2454; Opinion 1/09, *Agreement on the creation of a unified patent litigation system*, EU:C:2011:123; Case C-284/16, *Slowakische Republik v Achmea BV*, ECLI:EU:C:2018:158. The literature is too vast to cite comprehensively: see, with further references, C. Riffel, 'The CETA Opinion of the European Court of Justice and its Implications – Not that Selfish After All', *Journal of International Economic Law* 22 (2019), p. 503–521; J. Odermatt, 'The Principle of Autonomy: An Adolescent Disease of EU External Relations Law?', in M. Cremona (ed.), *Structural Principles in EU External Relations Law* (Hart, 2018), p. 316; B. de Witte, 'A Selfish Court? The Court of Justice and the Design of International Dispute Settlement Beyond the European Union', in M. Cremona, A. Thies (eds.), *The European Court of Justice and External Relations Law: Constitutional Challenges* (Hart, 2014), p. 39; and the contribution by G. Van der Loo in this volume.

12   The Crisis of the WTO is well documented. See M. Hahn, 'For Whom The Bell Tolls,' in M. Elsig, M. Hahn, G. Spilker (ed.), *The Shifting Landscape of Global Trade Governance* (CUP, 2019), p. 121 with further references; see for the recent effort to reduce the impact of the US policy the Multi-party interim appeal arbitration arrangement pursuant to Article 25 of the DSU, concluded by Australia, Brazil, Canada, China, Chile, Chinese Taipei, Colombia, Costa Rica, the European Union, Guatemala, Hong Kong, Mexico, New Zealand, Norway, Singapore, Switzerland, and Uruguay; cf.

multilateral trading system by concluding deep and comprehensive free trade agreements (DCFTAs) was being critically hampered. Particular danger seemed to exist for the EU's push for a "relaunch" of investment arbitration by establishing an adjudicative mechanism that aims to preserve the advantages of current investment arbitration while being receptive to the ever-increasing criticism voiced not only in left-of-centre political families.

Not surprisingly, therefore, the doctrinal reactions to Opinion 1/17 tend to be positive: points highlighted are its pragmatism and its responsiveness to the needs of the times. While this chapter joins the praise as to the outcome of the case,[13] it takes the view that the (highly desirable) result of Opinion 1/17 could only be achieved by differentiating the applied standard of review on the basis of the degree of interworkings between the agreement examined and the EU legal order. The standard applied in Opinion 1/17 is reminiscent of the pragmatic and separation-of-power-conscious approach taken with regard to the EEA.[14] This is welcome news: the sharpening of the Court's "external autonomy jurisprudence" occurred in the context of veiled or direct attacks on the autonomy and position of the Court of Justice, endangering its role as ultimate arbiter of Union law. DSMs of "normal" treaties, the structure and design of which do not threaten regulatory competition may benefit from a more lenient approach, free from the suspicion present in decisions such as ECHR.[15]

The structure of this paper will be as follows: In a first step, the case that introduced "autonomy of the Union legal order" as a benchmark for the lawfulness of international treaties concluded by the Union will be recalled and analysed. Not just because it was the *first* instance in which the concept of autonomy as a benchmark for an international agreement and its dispute settlement mechanism was developed and applied by the Court, but mainly because in contrast to much of the subsequent "external-autonomy-case-law", it is *directly* dealing with the subject matter area this volume deals with – the EU's external trade relations – a short recapitulation of what was at stake then seems warranted.

Council of the European Union, 2 April 2020, Doc. No. 112/20, to be consulted at https://www.consilium.europa.eu/media/43334/sto7112-en20.pdf.

13   See for example the contribution by G. Van der Loo in this volume.

14   Opinion 1/91, *EEA Agreement I* (*EEA I*), EU:C:1991:490; Opinion 1/92, *European Economic Area II* (*EEA II*), EU:C:1992:189.

15   Opinion 2/13, *Accession of the European Union to the European Convention for the Protection of Human Rights and Fundamental Freedoms* (*ECHR*), EU:C:2014:2454.

Afterwards, this paper will, standing on the shoulders of a by now significant body of literature on the autonomy of the Union legal order,[16] look at the non-trade-relations-centred use of the concept of autonomy and examine to what extent Opinion 1/17 internalises, to paraphrase *Keck*, "in law and in fact" the further development of the concept of autonomy in the application of the legal standard to the facts of the case. Therefore, in a second step, this paper will explore the argument that the development of the concept of autonomy in the post-Opinion-1/91-jurisprudence needs to be understood as being prompted by measures that put in question the institutional integrity of the Union legal order, and in particular of its most important characteristics, the Court of Justice's unique role as guardian and engine of EU law.

In a third step, it will be examined how Opinion 1/17 applies the ECJ's case-law to the facts before the Court in *CETA*. This will show that Opinion 1/17 while claiming to base its analysis on the consolidated case-law on "autonomy" does so in a different way than in previous decisions, giving CETA not only the benefit of the doubt, but actually engages in remarkable assumptions in order to reconcile the legal standard it puts forward and the result it clearly wanted. By doing so, it *de facto* applies the standard that rendered the current judicial architecture of the EEA possible.

On this basis, the argument is put forward that the "autonomy of the Union legal order" should be applied in a manner commensurate with the threat the agreement represents for the independent functioning of the EU's institutional apparatus. Applied without such differentiation, the principle would be hardly compatible with the separation of competences within the institutional matrix of the Union, but also not sufficiently internalise the aspiration of the Union to actively engage at the world scene and contribute to world peace through law,[17] as expressed in Article 3 (5) TEU[18] and Article 21 (2)

---

16   See, *inter alia*, C. Contartese, 'The Autonomy of the EU Legal Order in the ECJ's External
       Relations Case Law: From the 'Essential' to the 'Specific' Characteristics of the Union
       and Back Again', *Common Market Law Review* 54 (2017), *p. 1627– 1672;* P. Koutrakos, 'The
       Autonomy of EU Law and International Investment Arbitration', *Nordic Journal of
       International Law* (2019), p. 41–64; B. De Witte, 'The Relative Autonomy of the European
       Union's Fundamental Rights Regime', *Nordic Journal of International Law* (2019), p. 65–85;
       N. Nic Shuibhne, 'What is the Autonomy of EU Law, and Why Does that Matter?', *Nordic
       Journal of International Law* (2019), p. 9–40.
17   G. Clark; L.B. Sohn, *World Peace Through Law* (2nd ed.) (Harvard University Press, 1962).
18   "[T]he Union shall [...] contribute to peace, security, the sustainable development of the
       Earth, solidarity and mutual respect among peoples, free and fair trade, eradication of
       poverty and the protection of human rights, in particular the rights of the child, as well as
       to the strict observance and the development of international law, including respect for
       the principles of the United Nations Charter."

TFEU.[19] Opinion 1/17 shows that it is possible to protect the integrity of the Union legal order from overreach of a treaty-based DSM without endangering pertinent efforts to render the Union's international relations more certain and predictable. In particular, the application of the CFR to international agreements, by now a fixture of ECJ jurisprudence, facilitates a differentiated approach.[20]

The chapter concludes that already now, the notion of "autonomy of the Union legal order" is a tale of two different concepts: One that applies to direct (if possibly unintended) attacks on the role of the Court, in particular by setting up a form of parallel European structure creating normative and regulatory competition. The other applies to such international (economic) treaties that establish an effective treaty-based DSM which, however, must not be allowed overreach of that treaty DSM into the autonomy of the Union legal order.

2   The ECJ's *EEA* Opinions: Autonomy of the Union Legal Order and Treaty-Based Dispute Settlement Mechanisms in International Economic Law

2.1   *Overview of Opinion 1/91*
Some 30 years after *Van Gend & Loos'* foundational claim that the Treaties had established "a new legal order of international law",[21] the Court used for the first time the "integrity" of that (by then well-established) legal regime as a

---

19   "2. The Union [...] shall work for a high degree of cooperation in all fields of international relations, in order to: (a) safeguard its values, fundamental interests, security, independence and integrity; (b) consolidate and support democracy, the rule of law, human rights and the principles of international law; (c) preserve peace, prevent conflicts and strengthen international security, in accordance with the purposes and principles of the United Nations Charter, with the principles of the Helsinki Final Act and with the aims of the Charter of Paris, including those relating to external borders; (d) foster the sustainable economic, social and environmental development of developing countries [...]; (h) promote an international system based on stronger multilateral cooperation and good global governance."

20   For example, in Opinion 1/15 the Court based for the first time, the disapproval of an international agreement exclusively on an incompatibility with the Charter of Fundamental Rights (CFR); cf. C. Kuner, 'International agreements, data protection, and EU fundamental rights on the international stage: Opinion 1/15, EU-Canada PNR', *Common Market Law Review* 55 (2018), p- 857–882; H. Hijmans, 'PNR Agreement EU-Canada scrutinised: ECJ gives very precise guidance to negotiators', *European Data Protection Law Review* 3 (2017), p. 406–412.

21   Case 26/62, *NV Algemene Transport- en Expeditie Onderneming van Gend & Loos v. Netherlands Inland Revenue Administration*, EU:C:1963:1, para. 12.

limitation to the ability of the Union institutions in charge of conducting foreign relations: The ECJ opined that the EEA draft agreement, and specifically its dispute settlement mechanism was

> likely adversely to affect [...] the autonomy of the Community legal order, respect for which must be assured by the Court of Justice pursuant to Article 164 of the EEC Treaty.[22]

This, however, was not seen as a repudiation of international law: Treaty-based dispute settlement mechanisms are designed to ensure the effectiveness of international law and have been embraced, with the benefit of hindsight maybe even too much, by international lawyers and policy makers in the last 60 years. Thus, the Court recognised that the Union's

> competence in the field of international relations and its capacity to conclude international agreements necessarily entails the power to submit to the decisions of a court which is created or designated by such an agreement as regards the interpretation and application of its provisions.[23]

Thus, "an international agreement providing for [...] a system of courts is in principle compatible with" Union law.[24]

It will be recalled that the EEA agreement, not unlike some of the more recent association agreements, e.g. the EU—Ukraine DCFTA[25], was designed to expand the Single Market (Article 26 TFEU) to Non-member states, *in casu* the EFTA members. The Draft EEA Agreement set up an adjudicative body (the "EEA Court") with jurisdiction over all disputes arising out of the interpretation of the EEA agreement and involving non-EU-Member states. In light of the semi-identical body of law to be applied by the EEA Court, the ECJ had two major concerns: Firstly, it perceived the danger of being unduly influenced by "prior art" of the EEA court: As the EEA was supposed to be (and actually has

---

22   Opinion 1/91, *EEA I* EU:C:1991:490, para. 35; see H. G. Schermers, 'Opinion 1/91 of the Court of Justice, 14 December 1991; Opinion 1/92 of the Court of Justice, 10 April 1992', *Common Market Law Review* 29 (1992), p. 991.

23   Opinion 1/91, *EEA I*, para. 40.

24   Opinion 1/91, *EEA I*, para. 40 and para. 70.

25   Cf. G. Van der Loo, '*The EU-Ukraine association agreement and deep and comprehensive free trade area: a new legal instrument for EU integration without membership?*' (Brill, 2016), passim.

become) an extension of the EU Single Market,[26] the law of the EEA was (and is) to a large extent identical with EU Single Market law. The EEA agreement does not just internalize the wording of the Founding treaties: that would also be true for many of the first-generation FTAs concluded by the EEC with its EFTA-partners in 1972.[27] Rather, the explicitly stated goal is homogeneity with the Union legal order.[28] Of course, it is the very idea underlying the EEA to have the EFTA partners benefit from and apply the (primary and secondary) Single Market rules. The EEA Court's interpretation of norms which in essence constitute Union law (projected beyond the Union's territory) would have given it occasion to interpret and adjudicate on the basis of norms that represent the *inner sanctum* of Union law. Even if the primacy of the ECJ may have been established as a matter of principle,[29] this would have established an undue influence on the Court's freedom to develop independently its own reading of pertinent norms and decide pursuant to its own standards. The involvement of ECJ judges, intended as an institutional link to avoid such conflicts, was perceived as aggravating the indirect reduction of the ECJ's judicial independence: If the "wrong" approach was (even partly) attributable to some of their own, the subjective and systemic impediment to take a different position would be even greater.[30] In addition, the Court was not prepared to accept that

---

26   See the Conclusions of the 50th meeting of the EEA Council under: https://www.consil-ium.europa.eu/en/ press/press-releases/2018/11/20/conclusions-of-the-50th-meeting-of-the-eea-council/.

27   See, e.g., Agreement between the European Economic Community and the Portuguese Republic, OJ L 301, 31.12.1972, p. 165–356. Cf. Case 270/80, Polydor, ECR 1982, p. 329, ECLI:EU:C:1982:43, para. 14–15: The provisions of the Agreement on the Elimination of Restrictions on Trade between the Community and Portugal are expressed in terms which in several respects are similar to those of the EEC Treaty on the abolition of restrictions on intra-community trade [, ...] in particular the similarity between the terms of Articles 14 (2) and 23 of the Agreement on the one hand and those of Articles 30 and 36 of the EEC treaty on the other. However, such similarity of terms is not a sufficient reason for transposing to the provisions of the agreement the above-mentioned case-law, which determines in the context of the community the relationship between the protection of industrial and commercial property rights and the rules on the free movement of goods." This point is confirmed by Opinion 1/91, *EEA Agreement – I*, EU:C:1991:490, para. 14.

28   Cf. Art. 105 (1) EEA Agreement.

29   The mechanisms in place, even though ultimately deemed problematic by the ECJ, clearly reflected who was supposed to set the standards and who was to apply them. Protocol 34, to which Article 104(2) of the EEA agreement referred, established a specific preliminary procedure, under which the ECJ could, however, only express its views in a non-binding fashion; Opinion 1/91, *EEA Agreement – I*, EU:C:1991:490, para. 62 et seq.

30   Opinion 1/91, *EEA Agreement – I*, EU:C:1991:490, para. 35: "... the jurisdiction conferred on the EEA Court under Article 2(c), Article 96(1)(a) and Article 117(1) of the agreement is likely adversely to affect the allocation of responsibilities defined in the Treaties and,

its advisory opinions would have been just that: opinions, unlike the binding decisions pursuant to Article 267 or 218 (11) TFEU.[31]

As can be seen already from this briefest of overviews, the development of the concept of autonomy satisfied a real need: while it would have been difficult, if not impossible, to pinpoint what specific provision in the Founding Treaties would have been affected by the interference of the EEA and its institutional infrastructure, the Court recognised the systemic potential for destabilising *de facto* the *modus operandi* of the delicate EU institutional machinery; the latter has to integrate the Member states (in their capacity as EU actors *and* as friendly separate entities) and the institutions, most importantly the Commission, the legislative bodies and, of course, the ECJ itself. In the case at hand, this was in particular true due to the very close interworking between EEA and EU based on the legal semi-identity of the two agreements and their contracting parties, but also due to the mission of the EEA court: serving as an independent Court in charge of disputes arising out of the interpretation of a "mixed agreement" that was somewhat a mirror-image of the Treaty of Rome. The vulnerability of the EU system followed specifically from the other agreement's similarity. As a consequence, there was a genuine potential for a competitive relationship between the two courts, even though the status of the ECJ as ultimate interpreter of EU law had possibly not been put in question as a matter of law.

2.2   *The Implementation of Opinion 1/91's Concept of Autonomy in the EEA and the ECAA*

In response to the Court's decision, the EEA contracting parties separated the EEA pillar from the EU realm, replaced the EEA court by an EFTA court and eliminated the involvement of ECJ judges in the latter. Also, mechanisms were introduced that ensured that the ECJ had the last word in all questions of the externalised EU law that is the EEA law, if the matter deserved more than peripheral attention.[32] If the divergence of the two Courts' jurisprudence is not

---

hence, the autonomy of the Community legal order, respect for which must be assured by the Court of Justice pursuant to Article 164 of the EEC Treaty. This exclusive jurisdiction of the Court of Justice is confirmed by Article 219 of the EEC Treaty, under which Member States undertake not to submit a dispute concerning the interpretation or application of that treaty to any method of settlement other than those provided for in the Treaty. Article 87 of the ECSC Treaty embodies a provision to the same effect."

31   Ibid., para. 45, 61 et seq.

32   Approved by Opinion 1/92, *EEA Agreement – II*, EU:C:1992:189; cf. see B. Brandtner, 'The 'Drama 'of the EEA – Comments on Opinions 1/91 and 1/92', *European Journal of International Law* (1992), p. 300 – 328.

merely temporary or negligible, it may lead to the suspension of relevant treaty parts.[33] Interestingly, that institutional interface between the EEA and the EU legal order has so far not been used: the treaty speaks softly, but carries a big stick.[34]

The solution triggered by Opinion 1/91 and approved by Opinion 1/92[35] has allowed the EEA to become a success story.[36] It would seem that the key for this success was a small but indispensable element of trust by the Court: trust with regard to the EFTA Court's future commitment to follow the ECJ's jurisprudence, but also trust in the preparedness of the Commission to stand up for the Union legal order if necessary: While any direct threats to its position as the ultimate interpreter of Union law had been eliminated, the Court accepted *pro futuro* the possibility of temporary divergence. Granting the EFTA court enough space to develop its own profile, custom-tailored to the specific needs of the international treaty that it administers went hand-in-hand with weaving a safety-net ensuring homogeneity that consists of a substantive strand (addressed mainly at the EFTA Court) and a political strand, enabling the Commission to protect the ECJ's role at the apex of the Union legal order and thus its autonomy.

Pursuant to Article 6 EEA treaty the provisions of the EEA Agreement,

> in so far as they are identical in substance to corresponding rules of the [EU-Treaties] and to acts adopted in application of these [...] Treaties, shall, in their implementation and application, be interpreted in conformity with the relevant rulings of the Court of Justice of the European Communities given prior to the date of signature of this Agreement.

In the *Agreement on the establishment of a surveillance authority and a court of justice*[37], Article 3 (2) determines that

---

33   Cf. below and Art. 105 EEA Agreeement.
34   Cf. Theodore Roosevelt (1858–1919) to Henry L. Sprague, Albany, New York, January 26, 1900, Carbon copy letterbook, Manuscript Division, Gift of the heirs of Theodore Roosevelt, Jr., 1958–1965 (52A), to be consulted at https://web.archive.org/web/20160911173110/http://www.loc.gov/exhibits/treasures/images/at0052as.jpg.
35   Opinion 1/92, *EEA Agreement – II*, EU:C:1992:189.
36   See the Conclusions of the 50th meeting of the EEA Council under: https://www.consilium.europa.eu/en/ press/press-releases/2018/11/20/conclusions-of-the-50th-meeting-of-the-eea-council/.
37   OJ L 344, 31.1.1994, 3.

In the interpretation and application of the EEA Agreement and [the Agreement on the establishment of a surveillance authority and a court of justice] [...], the EFTA Surveillance Authority and the EFTA Court shall pay due account to the principles laid down by the relevant rulings by the Court of Justice of the European Communities given after the date of signature of the EEA Agreement and which concern the interpretation of that Agreement or of such rules of the Treaty establishing the European Economic Community [...] in so far as they are identical in substance to the provisions of the EEA Agreement [...].[38]

A chapter on *Homogeneity* defines the objective "to arrive at as uniform an interpretation as possible of the provisions of the Agreement and those provisions of Community legislation which are substantially reproduced in the Agreement".[39] The implementation of this goal depends in the first instance on the EFTA court's commitment to follow the ECJ's lead. However, this commitment is underwritten by the political strand of the 'safety net' mentioned *supra*: Article 105 (2) EEA Agreement tasks the EEA Joint Committee to "keep under constant review the development of the case law of the Court of Justice of the European Communities and the EFTA Court". If a difference in the case law of the two Courts is relevant enough to be brought before the Joint Committee, any contracting party – but for practical purposes the Commission as guardian of the Union interests in foreign relations – may propose that the Joint Committee requests a binding ECJ ruling on the interpretation of the relevant rules.[40] If this effort to allow an authoritative

---

38   Whereas no commensurate obligations of the ECJ exist to take the decisions of the EFTA Court into account, this has not kept it from citing EFTA Court decisions as persuasive; cf. V. Skouris, 'The ECJ and the EFTA Court under the EEA Agreement: A Paradigm for International Cooperation between Judicial Institutions', in C. Baudenbacher, P. Tresselt, T. Örlygsson (ed.), *The EFTA Court: Ten Years On,* (Hart, 2005), p. 123–129, at p. 127; A. Rosas, 'The European Court of Justice in Context: Forms and Patterns of Judicial Dialogue', *European Journal of Legal Studies* (2007), p. 1 -16, to be consulted at https://cadmus.eui.eu/bitstream/handle/1814/7706/EJLS_2007_1_2_7_ROS_EN.pdf?sequence=1&isAllowed=y.

39   Art. 105 (1) EEA Agreement.

40   Art. 105 (3) EEA agreement reads: "If the EEA Joint Committee within two months after a difference in the case law of the two Courts has been brought before it, has not succeeded to preserve the homogeneous interpretation of the Agreement, the procedures laid down in Article 111 may be applied." Art. 111 states in relevant parts: "If a dispute concerns the interpretation of provisions of this Agreement, which are identical in substance to corresponding rules of the [Founding treaties] and to acts adopted in application of these two Treaties and if the dispute has not been settled within three months after it has been brought before the EEA Joint Committee, the Contracting Parties to the dispute may agree to request the Court of Justice of the European Communities to give a ruling on the

resolution by the Court is blocked, the Commission may trigger commensurate rebalancing measures and the suspension of the pertinent parts of the agreement ensue.[41]

With its EEA Opinions, the Court has allowed the Union to achieve an unequivocal foreign relations success that is the small but economically and geopolitically important extension of the Union market to Western European market economies. The indispensable guarantee of the Court's position at the apex of the jurisdictional order was defended and enforced, without snuffing out an effective DSM that went on to establish an excellent reputation as "the little brother" of the ECJ.[42] Due to the modifications to EEA and the 'Agreement on the establishment of a surveillance authority and a court of justice'[43] the supremacy of the ECJ's jurisprudence is beyond doubt. In addition, without affecting the independence of the EFTA Court, mechanisms have been put in place that give teeth to the principled lead of the ECJ. The "judicial dialogue"[44] creates transparency and the building of mutual trust; the political mechanisms described above allow the Commission to enforce, if need be, the necessary homogeneity of the EEA with the Union legal order. The judicial dialogue has worked so well that the second element has not been used yet.

The short summary of the EEA's post-*EEA I* homogeneity provisions renders clear that the ECJ has the final say and is the fully autonomous arbiter of all

---

interpretation of the relevant rules. If the EEA Joint Committee in such a dispute has not reached an agreement on a solution within six months from the date on which this procedure was initiated or if, by then, the Contracting Parties to the dispute have not decided to ask for a ruling by the Court of Justice of the European Communities, a Contracting Party may, in order to remedy possible imbalances, - either take a safeguard measure in accordance with Article 112(2) and following the procedure of Article 113; - or apply Article 102 mutatis mutandis." Art. 102 reads in pertinent parts: "If, at the end of the time limit set out in paragraph 4, the EEA Joint Committee has not taken a decision on an amendment of an Annex to this Agreement, the affected part thereof, as determined in accordance with paragraph 2, *is regarded* as provisionally suspended, subject to a decision to the contrary by the EEA Joint Committee."

41   Art. 111, 102 EEA Agreement.

42   The former President of the EFTA Court, Carl Baudenbacher, has called his former Court the "little brother" of the ECJ and highlighted its influence on the jurisdiction of the ECJ (Der EFTA-Gerichtshof – der kleine Bruder des EuGH, 15. Oktober 2012, https://prisma-hsg.ch/articles/der-efta-gerichtshof-der-kleine-bruder-des-eugh/).

43   OJ L 344, 31.1.1994, 3.

44   Art. 106 EEA Agreement establishes a system of exchange of information concerning judgments by the EFTA Court, the ECJ and the Courts of last instance of the EFTA States "[i]n order to ensure as uniform an interpretation as possible of this Agreement [and] in full deference to the independence of courts".

disputes arising under EU law; because of the semi-identity of the EEA agreement with the TFEU's Single Market provisions this extends for all practical purposes to EEA law. This, however, is ensured in ways that leave room for an independent EEA court capable of administering justice within the realm of the EEA agreement. Despite the fact – absent in "normal" trade agreements – that the EEA agreement is identical in substance to corresponding rules in EU-Treaties, the EEA mechanism accepts the theoretical possibility of some "initial" divergence between the Court and its EFTA counterpart, given that mechanisms were put in place that credibly back up the role of the Court as ultimate interpreter of Union law.

Opinion 1/00 on the *European Common Aviation Area (ECAA)*,[45] the next case in the Court's autonomy jurisprudence, dealt with an agreement that was similar to the EEA in that it expanded the Union legal order to non-Member states. Opinion 1/00 confirmed the jurisprudence with regard to the requirements a DSM needs to meet in order to not infringe on the autonomy of the Union legal order.[46]

> Preservation of the autonomy of the Community legal order requires therefore, *first*, that the essential character of the powers of the Community and its institutions as conceived in the Treaty remain unaltered.
>
> *Second*, it requires that the procedures for ensuring uniform interpretation of the rules of the ECAA Agreement and for resolving disputes will not have the effect of binding the Community and its institutions, in the exercise of their internal powers, to a particular interpretation of the rules of Community law referred to in that agreement.[47]

In casu, the application of these principles posed few problems, because the effects on the Commission were marginal at best, and the Court was conferred with the competence to act as adjudicative body for all questions concerning the legality of decisions taken by Community institutions.[48] To the extent that

---

45   Opinion 1/00, E*uropean Common Aviation Area,* EU:C:2002:231.

46   Opinion 1/00, para. 3.: "3 The proposed agreement is inspired by aims similar to those of the EEA Agreement, two versions of which were the subject of Opinions 1/91 and 1/92, cited above. Although the proposed agreement, unlike the EEA Agreement, is limited to one sector, air transport, its aim, like that of the EEA Agreement, is to extend the acquis communautaire to new States, by implementing in a larger geographical area rules which are essentially those of Community law".

47   Opinion 1/00, para. 12–13, emphasis added, quoting Opinion 1/91, para. 61 to 65, and 1/92, para. 32 and 41.

48   Opinion 1/00, para. 20: "The Court has already recognised that an international agreement entered into by the Community with non-Member States may affect the powers of

the Joint Committee acted as adjudicator, the ECAA mandated that it had to be "in conformity with the case-law of the Court". The Court took in particular note of the fact that "the proposed agreement itself" mandated that "decisions of the Joint Committee taken in that context 'shall not affect the case law of the Court'."[49]

> Therefore, the mechanisms for ensuring uniform interpretation of the rules of the ECAA Agreement and for resolving disputes will not have the effect of binding the Community and its institutions, in the exercise of their internal powers, to a particular interpretation of the rules of Community law incorporated in the agreement.[50]

Like in *EEA I*, the concept of autonomy is used to preserve the integrity of the decision-making process, including the binding nature of all ECJ statements; only since Opinion 2/13 the concept internalises substantive standards.[51] In *ECAA*, the danger for the Union legal order followed from the friendly and consensual expansion of the crown jewel of the EU's legal regime, the Single Market, accompanied by efforts to involve their sovereign third-country-partners in ways that acknowledge their choice to abstain from EU-membership. Like in the EEA, potential effects on the EU's institutional autonomy were noted, but the containment measures considered sufficient.

---

the Community institutions, without, however, being regarded as incompatible with the Treaty [...]. Although the proposed CAA Agreement affects the powers of the Community institutions, it does not alter the essential character of those powers and, accordingly, does not undermine the autonomy of the Community legal order." See also Opinion 1/00, para. 24–26: " First, Article 17(3) of the proposed agreement makes the Court responsible for ruling on [a]ll questions concerning the legality of decisions taken by Community institutions under this Agreement. [...] Second, [...] in every case where the proposed agreement confers powers on the Court, the binding nature of the latter's decisions is safeguarded (see Opinion 1/91, paragraphs 59 to 65). In those circumstances, the provisions of the proposed ECAA Agreement do not alter the essential character of the powers of the Community and its institutions and thus to that extent do not adversely affect the autonomy of the Community legal order."

49   Opinion 1/00, para. 44.
50   Opinion 1/00, para. 45.
51   The argument can be made that already in Opinion 1/09, *European Patents Court*, para. 84–85 pertinent tendencies were developed: the ECJ argued that agreements that deprive individuals of access to judicial means of protecting rights violate the principle of autonomy; see also Opinion 2/13 *Accession to the ECHR*, para. 175–176.

3   The Development of the Autonomy Jurisprudence Post EEA *and* ECAA

Whereas the EEA and ECAA agreements had endangered the role of the Court and the autonomy of the Union legal order almost accidentally, as a consequence of the semi-identity of the original (EU) and the derivative (EEA and ECAA) regulations and the existence of an independent court, the following cases dealt with agreements that threatened rather direct interference into the Union legal order and endangered in particular the role of the Court itself. The aggressive edge the concept develops over time and with it the sometimes rather imperial language that seems to be commensurate with the existential threat these efforts constituted. The concept of "autonomy" turned into a tool of self-defence as it addressed treaty-based DSMs designed by the Commission and the Member states to allow regulatory and judicial parallelism, even sometimes competition, through parallel governance structures: the two-pronged test of autonomy requires not only to leave unaltered the "essential character of the powers of the Community and its institutions as conceived in the Treaty"[52] but also making sure that the DSM in question "will not have the effect of binding the Community and its institutions, in the exercise of their internal powers, to a particular interpretation of the rules of Community law".[53]

With regard to the *Mox* case,[54] it is noteworthy that the threat for the homogeneity of Union law and the autonomy of the EU legal order did not stem from the pertinent agreement as such which specifically provides for cases of potentially overlapping jurisdictions,[55] but rather from the disloyal behavior of Ireland.[56] Relying on its prior case law, the Court blocked the thinly veiled attempt to circumvent ECJ procedures by engaging the UK under the DSM of the United Nations Convention on the Law of the Sea (UNCLOS).[57]

---

52   Opinion 1/00, para. 12.

53   Opinion 1/00, para. 13.

54   Case C-459/03, *Commission of the European Communities v. Ireland (Mox)*, EU:C:2006:345.

55   Art. 282 UNCLOS reads: "If the States Parties which are parties to a dispute concerning the interpretation or application of this Convention have agreed, through a general, regional or bilateral agreement or otherwise, that such dispute shall, at the request of any party to the dispute, be submitted to a procedure that entails a binding decision, that procedure shall apply in lieu of the procedures provided for in this part, unless the parties to the dispute otherwise agree."

56   Case C-459/03, *Mox,* para. 168 et seq., 179 et seq.

57   Case C-459/03, *Mox,* para. 123: "[A]n international agreement cannot affect the allocation of responsibilities defined in the Treaties and, consequently, the autonomy of the Community legal system, compliance with which the Court ensures under Article 220 EC. That exclusive jurisdiction of the Court is confirmed by Article 292 EC, by which Member States undertake not to submit a dispute concerning the interpretation or application of

In contrast, Opinion 1/09 on the European Patents Court[58] dealt with a draft agreement between the EU-Members, the Union itself and third country parties of the European Patent Convention, which was supposed to establish a court with jurisdiction to hear actions related, *inter alia*, to EU patents. By establishing a European and Community Patents Court structured as a mirror image of the Court of Justice with a "court of first instance, comprising a central division and local and regional divisions, and a court of appeal",[59] the drafters endangered the role of the Court of Justice at two levels: Firstly, it would have been confronted with a European court that could have, mistakenly, been perceived as a co-equal EU High Court (albeit "only" in charge for certain IP disputes); in reality, a preliminary ruling procedure established (for those in the know) a clear hierarchy between the (junior) "other" court and the ECJ. Secondly, the replacement of national courts by the new specialised European patent courts, and the ensuing elimination of domestic courts as feeder courts for preliminary proceedings would have changed the judicial architecture of the EU.[60] Regardless whether the ECJ's tears shed for the Member states courts[61] were crocodile tears or not: the sectoral disappearance of national courts requesting reference decisions pursuant to Article 267 TFEU eliminates (for a small sector, admittedly), the ECJ as supreme authority for all things "European" for the EU courts of general jurisdiction that are the Member states courts since *Van Gend, Costa* and *Simmenthal*.[62]

In light of this challenge, the Court added the preservation of the usability of the preliminary reference procedure pursuant to Article 267 TFEU to the definition of "the essential character of the powers which the Treaties confer on the institutions of the European Union and on the Member States".[63]

---

the EC Treaty to any method of settlement other than those provided for therein (see, to that effect, Opinion 1/91 [1991] ECR I-6079, paragraph 35, and Opinion 1/00 [2002] ECR I-3493, paragraphs 11 and 12)."

58   Opinion 1/09, *European Patents Court*, EU:C:2011:123.

59   Opinion 1/09, *European Patents Court*, para. 8.

60   Opinion 1/09, para. 94–103.

61   Ibid., para. 80: "would deprive those courts of their task, as "ordinary" courts within the European Union legal order, to implement European Union law and, thereby, of the power provided for in Article 267 TFEU'; cf. the friendlier analysis by R. Baratta, 'National Courts as 'Guardians' and 'Ordinary Courts' of EU Law: Opinion 1/09 of the ECJ', *38 Legal Issues of Economic Integration* (2011), p. 297.

62   Cf. Case C-2/88 *Zwartfeld*, (1990) ECR I-3365 or Case T-51/89, *Tetrapak*, ECR II, p. 364: "... national Courts are acting as Community courts of general jurisdiction ..."; cf. J.Temple Lang, 'The duties of national courts under Community Constitutional Law', *22 European Law Review 3* (1997).

63   Opinion 1/09, para. 89; see also para 83 et seq.: "*83.* ...] Article 267 TFEU [...] is essential for the preservation of the Community character of the law established by the Treaties, aims

Logically, this argument is based on the following hypothesis: because every parallel system-of-governance structure (*in casu* the European Patent Court) will eliminate the usual avenues to access the ECJ – including, but not limited to Articles 258, 260 and 267 TFEU – and other tools developed to ensure the uniform application, such as the liability for domestic measures not compatible with EU law,[64] it violates the autonomy of the Union legal order. This hypothesis – the other treaty has a system of governance different from the EU and FEU Treaties, therefore it violates the autonomy of the legal order – is tenable only, if an argumentative stepping stone is impliedly added. That stepping stone is that the "other court" may compete with the ECJ (in the latter's realm) regarding the interpretation of EU law and thus endanger the homogeneity of Union law. On that basis, the Court determines all other agreements between Members within the field of gravity of the Founding Treaties are inherently accessory and must be structured in ways that do not affect the TEU- and TFEU-determined *modus operandi*.

> Consequently, the envisaged agreement, by conferring on an international court which is outside the institutional and judicial framework of the European Union an exclusive jurisdiction to hear a significant number of actions brought by individuals in the field of the Community patent and to interpret and apply European Union law in that field, [...] would alter the essential character of the powers which the Treaties confer on the institutions of the European Union and on the Member States and which are indispensable to the preservation of the very nature of European Union law.[65]

On the basis of this reading, the agreement in question would not have avoided the verdict of infringing the autonomy of the Union legal order, even if it had provided for a reference procedure similar to the one foreseen in Article 267 TFEU, thereby permitting a unitary interpretation of EU law: Still, that solution

---

to ensure that, in all circumstances, that law has the same effect in all Member States. [...] 84. The system set up by Article 267 TFEU therefore establishes between the Court of Justice and the national courts direct cooperation as part of which the latter are closely involved in the correct application and uniform interpretation of European Union law and also in the protection of individual rights conferred by that legal order. 85. It follows from all of the foregoing that the tasks attributed to the national courts and to the Court of Justice respectively are indispensable to the preservation of the very nature of the law established by the Treaties. [...]".

64   Opinion 1/09, para. 87, 88.
65   Opinion 1/09, para. 87, 89.

would have eliminated the domestic courts as street-level feeder courts pursuant to Article 267 TFEU.[66]

In a similar fashion, the draft Accession Agreement of the Union to the ECHR[67] would have endangered the Court's role as the Human Rights Court of the European Union.[68] Whereas the *Kadi* case[69] would today not need any invocation of a general principle such as "autonomy", as the Court now administers one of the most ambitious international human rights instruments,[70] accessing the ECHR would have endangered its supreme role as final arbiter of the totality of legal issues involving EU law, including primary law (such as the CFR) and, notably, secondary law.[71] Despite of the rather distant and limited possibility that the Strasbourg Court would be shaping the human rights regime in the Union[72], the ECJ found the accession agreement to violate the

---

66   H. Lenk, 'Prior Judicial Involvement in Investor-State Dispute Settlement: Lessons from the Court's Rhetoric in Opinion2/15', *Global Trade and Customs Journal 13* (2018), p. 19–26; A. Dimopoulos, 'The Validity and Applicability of International Investment Agreements Between EU Member States Under EU and International Law', *Common. Market. Law Review 48* (2011), p. 63, 91.

67   Opinion 2/13, *Accession of the European Union to the European Convention for the Protection of Human Rights and Fundamental Freedoms*, EU:C:2014:2454. From the literature see P. Eeckhout, Opinion 2/13 on EU Accession to the ECHR and Judicial Dialogue: Autonomy or Autarky?, *Fordham International Law Journal 38(4)* (2015), p. 955; T. Lock, Walking on a Tightrope: The Draft ECHR Accession Agreement and the Autonomy of the EU Legal Order, *Common Market Law Review* 48 (2011), p. 1025.

68   Whether this, in principle unacceptable consequence had been endorsed by the Founding Treaties through Art. 6 (2) TEU shall not be discussed here. See, *inter alia*, B. de Witte, 'A Selfish Court? The Court of Justice and the Design of International Dispute Settlement Beyond the European Union' in M. Cremona and A. Thies (ed.), *The European Court of Justice and External Relations Law: Constitutional Challenges* (Hart, 2014).

69   Joined Cases C-402/05P and C-415/05P, *Kadi and Al Barakaat v. Council*, EU: C:2008:461; cf. B. De Witte, The Relative Autonomy of the European Union's Fundamental Rights Regime, *Nordic Journal of International Law* (2019,) p. 65–85; T. Konstadinides, 'When in Europe: Customary international law and EU competence in the sphere of external action', German Law Journal 13 (2012), p. 1177–1201; G. de Búrca, The European Court of Justice and the International Legal Order After Kadi, *Harvard International Law Journal 51* (2010), p. 1–49; M. Scheinin, 'Is the ECJ Ruling in *Kadi* Incompatible with International Law?', *28 Yearbook of European Law* (2009), p. 637.

70   See the ambitious projection of Article 47 CFR on the rest of the world: Opinion 1/17, para. 189 et seq.

71   One of the central issues addressed by the ECJ was the lack of a mechanism, similar to Art. 267 TFEU, that would have obliged the ECtHR to refer questions related to secondary law to the ECJ; see Opinion 2/13, *Accession to the ECHR*, para. 245 and 247.

72   See the view of AG Kokott, Opinion 2/13, EU:C:2014:2475, para. 106 – 141; she came to the following conclusion in para. 142: "In summary, it must be stated that the draft agreement does not affect the powers of the Court of Justice of the EU in such a way as to be

autonomy of the Union legal order;[73] as a consequence, the Union's participation in the ECHR has been rendered impossible for decades to come, given
the need for approval by members such as Russia and Turkey. Again, the lack
of certainty to be the first call pursuant to Article 267 TFEU for Member states
courts played a major role. In addition, a new dimension was added by the
Court of Justice by expanding the scope of that concept. Whereas hitherto only
the procedural aspects of governance had been protected by that concept, the
Court adds, almost in passing, now the "constitutional founding principles" as
being an integral part of the "autonomy defence".

> As the Court of Justice has repeatedly held, the founding treaties of the
> EU, unlike ordinary international treaties, established a new legal order,
> possessing its own institutions, for the benefit of which the Member
> States thereof have limited their sovereign rights, in ever wider fields,
> and the subjects of which comprise not only those States but also their
> nationals.
>   The fact that the EU has a new kind of legal order, the nature of which
> is peculiar to the EU, its own constitutional framework and founding
> principles, a particularly sophisticated institutional structure and a full
> set of legal rules to ensure its operation, has consequences as regards the
> procedure for and conditions of accession to the ECHR.[74]

The inclusion of "constitutional founding principles" into the "autonomy defence" leads, in Opinion 1/17,[75] to an even more expansive notion of autonomy,
moving from a concept designed to protect *de iure* and *de facto* autonomous
decision-making to an all-encompassing basis for measuring, without specific
normative basis in the Founding Treaties, whether an international agreement
is compatible with EU law.

On the basis of Opinions 1/09 and 2/13 it was possible to predict that any
international agreement representing *some* form of regulatory competition
and establishing a DSM would be viewed as infringing the autonomy of the

---

incompatible with the first sentence of Article 2 of Protocol No 8, provided that the scope
of application of the prior involvement procedure is clarified as indicated in point 135".

73   Opinion 2/13, *Accession to the ECHR*, para. 200: "Having regard to the foregoing, it must
be held that the accession of the EU to the ECHR as envisaged by the draft agreement is
liable adversely to affect the specific characteristics of EU law and its autonomy."

74   Opinion 2/13, para. 157, 158, invoking *van Gend & Loos*, 26/62, EU:C:1963:1, p. 12, and *Costa*,
6/64, EU:C:1964:66, p. 593, and Opinion 1/09, EU:C:2011:123, para. 65.

75   Opinion 1/17, para. 150 et seq..

Union legal order by disrupting the EU and FEU-Treaty-mandated functioning of all institutions pursuant to Article 13 TEU, including the interaction between Member states and their creation. In particular, any interference with the role of the Court of Justice (and thus the uniform and consistent application of EU law), be it *directly*, by exposing the Court to judicial competition by an adjudicative body, or *indirectly*, by foreclosing Member states' courts from serving as entry-level feeder institutions for the ECJ, would lead to the regional treaty being found incompatible with the principle of autonomy.

It thus came as no surprise that *Achmea*[76] was decided as it was. There, the Court had to address the compatibility of pre-accession BITs between Slovakia and the Kingdom of the Netherlands, as the German Bundesgerichtshof had specifically asked whether "the Netherlands-Czechoslovakia BIT [had] the effect of undermining the allocation of powers fixed by the EU and FEU Treaties and, therefore, the autonomy of the EU legal system." Despite the explicit reference to the Court's "autonomy"-jurisprudence, AG Wathelet argued along the wording of the TFEU, and in particular the provisions of Articles 18, 267 and 344 TFEU. To him, the opportunity

> afforded by Article 8 of the BIT to Netherlands and Slovak investors to have recourse to international arbitration does not undermine either the allocation of powers fixed by the EU and FEU Treaties or the autonomy of the EU legal system, even if the Court should decide that the arbitral tribunals constituted in accordance with that article are not courts or tribunals of the Member States within the meaning of Article 267 TFEU.[77]

The Court rejected the AG's proposal to view Arbitral tribunals established pursuant to a BIT as standing in for domestic courts, and thus competent to request preliminary rulings, a novel proposal which attracted only limited support. More to the point for this paper, it stood by its reading of autonomy as preventing any interference into the organisational set-up of the Union: Allowing bilateral relationships *and* their respective DSMs into a Single Market that operates on the foundational premise that the pertinent constitutional and statutory rules have direct effect, are supreme (thus do not face regulatory competition as a matter of law) *and* are administered by the Union organs

---

76   Case C-284/16, *Slowakische Republik v. Achmea BV (Achmea)*, EU:C:2018:158.

77   Opinion of Advocate General Wathelet delivered on 19 September 2017, *Slowakische Republik v Achmea BV*, Case C-284/16, ECLI:EU:C:2017:699, para. 237.

pursuant to the treaties (for example pursuant to Articles 258, 260 or Article 267 TFEU) was seen as allowing to put an unacceptable crack into the Union legal order and its essential characteristics. It is noteworthy, that the principle of autonomy becomes more "meta" with every pertinent decision of the Court, distilling ever more specific provisions (such as Articles 26, 63, 267 and 344 TFEU) and case-law-based general principles and concepts of EU law (e.g., direct effect and supremacy). Thus, a *ménage à deux* between Member states dealing with issues falling within the scope of Single Market law will, for all practical purposes, not be reconcilable with the autonomy of the Union legal order.[78]

4   Opinion 1/17 and the Principle of Autonomy

Pursuant to the Belgian request, Opinion 1/17 had to find answers to the following question:

> Is Section F ('Resolution of investment dispute between investors and states') of Chapter Eight ('Investment') of the Comprehensive Economic and Trade Agreement between Canada, of the one part, and the European Union and its Member States, of the other part, signed in Brussels on 30 October 2016 (OJ 2017 L 11, p. 23; 'the CETA') compatible with the Treaties, including with fundamental rights?[79]

The Court concluded that it was; the structure of its analysis follows largely the structure of the Belgian brief, which addressed three categories of "doubts": Firstly, whether the envisaged ISDS mechanism was compatible with the "autonomy of the EU legal order";[80] secondly, whether CETA's ISDS mechanism was compatible with the principle of equal treatment and of effectiveness of EU law;[81] thirdly, whether CETA's ISDS mechanism sufficiently ensured the right of access to an independent tribunal pursuant to Article 47 CFR.[82] There is nothing useful to add to the previous chapter's summary of the decision.

---

78   On the implications of *Achmea* and *Opinion 1/17* on the intra- and extra-EU-BITs, see the contribution by G. Van der Loo in this volume.

79   Opinion 1/17, para. 1.

80   Opinion 1/17, para. 46–50.

81   Opinion 1/17, para. 51–55.

82   Opinion 1/17, para. 56–69.

4.1   An Addition to the Concept of Autonomy

The Court starts with the well-established recognition that the Union may conclude modern treaties that include a DSM. After restating its case-law on autonomy,[83] the Court turns to the issue at hand and extracts the following two requirements that the DSM of an agreement of the EU with a third country needs to meet in order to be compatible "with the autonomy of the EU legal order":[84] The agreement may not confer on its DSM

> any power to interpret or apply EU law other than the power to interpret and apply the provisions of that agreement having regard to the rules and principles of international law applicable between the Parties, and[85]

the examined agreement may not structure the powers of the DSM

> in such a way that, while not themselves engaging in the interpretation or application of rules of EU law other than those of that agreement, they may issue awards which have the effect of preventing the EU institutions from operating in accordance with the EU constitutional framework.[86]

Both points would seem fully in line with prior case-law: With regard to the first point, it is by now almost a matter of course, that it would be an infringement of EU autonomy, if the DSM was to "interpret or apply" EU law, save, of course, the agreement itself which becomes an integral part of the Union legal order. The Court then explains[87] why CETA, more specifically Section F of Chapter 8 restricts

> the power of interpretation and application [of the DSM in question] [...] to the provisions of the CETA and that such interpretation or application must be undertaken in accordance with the rules and principles of international law applicable between the Parties.

The second point picks up an issue well established since *EEA I*: a DSM may violate the principle of autonomy not just in the case of *de jure* interference; rather, there may be an unacceptable *de facto* impact that would restrict in

---

83   Opinion 1/17, para. 107–111.
84   Opinion 1/17, para. 119.
85   Opinion 1/17, para. 119.
86   Opinion 1/17, para. 119.
87   Opinion 1/17, para. 120 – 136.

an unacceptable manner the freedom of a Union institution to exercise its conferred competences. In *EEA I*, this impairment followed, *inter alia*, from the fact that the DSM in question had the task of interpreting a treaty that essentially restated EU law and was supposed to do so with the involvement of an ECJ judge. From this flowed, in the eyes of the Court, an undue *de facto* restriction of the Court's ability to pronounce itself freely when discharging its judicial functions. However, the concretisation of the "effects"-dimension adds a new attribute to the operational consequences of *this* "effects doctrine":

> If the Union were to enter into an international agreement capable of having the consequence that the Union – or a Member State in the course of implementing EU law – has to amend or withdraw legislation because of an assessment made by a tribunal standing outside the EU judicial system of the level of protection of a public interest established, in accordance with the EU constitutional framework, by the EU institutions, it would have to be concluded that such an agreement undermines the capacity of the Union to operate autonomously within its unique constitutional framework.
>
> It must be emphasized, in that regard, that EU legislation is adopted by the EU legislature following the democratic process defined in the EU and FEU Treaties, and that that legislation is deemed, by virtue of the principles of conferral of powers, subsidiarity and proportionality laid down in Article 5 TEU, to be both appropriate and necessary to achieve a legitimate objective of the Union. In accordance with Article 19 TEU, it is the task of the Courts of the European Union to ensure review of the compatibility of the level of protection of public interests established by such legislation with, inter alia, the EU and FEU Treaties, the Charter and the general principles of EU law.[88]

---

88   Opinion 1/17, para 150–151; see also para. 152: "With respect to the jurisdiction of the envisaged tribunals to declare infringements of the obligations contained in Section C of Chapter Eight of the CETA, Article 28.3.2 of that agreement states that the provisions of Section C cannot be interpreted in such a way as to prevent a Party from adopting and applying measures necessary to protect public security or public morals or to maintain public order or to protect human, animal or plant life or health, subject only to the requirement that such measures are not applied in a manner that would constitute a means of arbitrary or unjustifiable discrimination between the Parties where like conditions prevail, or a disguised restriction on trade between the Parties."

While the Court comes to the somewhat surprising conclusion that the CETA Tribunal did not have the requisite competence and capacity,[89] the quoted statement is nevertheless noteworthy. Taken at face value, it is a variation on the theme *The King can do no wrong*, the King, of course, being the EU legal order: because its system of governance is democratic and the judicial review by the ECJ ensures that any mistake would be corrected in due course, it would constitute *lèse-majesté*, if the adjudicate body established by the treaty found that measures by the contracting party EU are not in conformity with its obligations under CETA.

This would not only be the very negation of the endorsement for public international law that the EU and FEU Treaties give;[90] rather, such a statement would also be difficult to reconcile with the principled endorsement by the ECJ of the Union's capability to enter into treaty arrangements that include a robust DSM. Because the EU institutions typically and genuinely strive in good faith to comply with their international obligations to not violate international law (see, e.g., Articles 20 and 21 TEU), international wrongful acts of the type policed by the DSMs of CETA or other multilateral or bilateral trade agreements will be rare incidents, or so one would expect. But they will unavoidably happen, and the EU organs will then have to abide by the decision of the independent third-party arbiters that have found the EU to have been not complying with the EU's international obligations.

But maybe the quoted passage should not be taken at face value: it is positioned in the context of discussing whether the CETA investment tribunals *de facto* restrict the necessary autonomy of the Union, its Member states and their respective institutions; the preceding paragraph provides context:

> If the CETA Tribunal and Appellate Tribunal were to have jurisdiction to issue awards finding that the treatment of a Canadian investor is incompatible with the CETA because of the level of protection of a public interest established by the EU institutions, this could create a situation where, in order to avoid being *repeatedly* compelled by the CETA Tribunal to pay damages to the claimant investor, the achievement of that level of protection needs to be abandoned by the Union.[91]

---

89   Opinion 1/17, para 153; cf. E. Gaillard, 'Note sur Avis CJUE 1/17de la Cour de justice de l'Union européenne (CJUE) rendu le 30 avril 2019', *Journal du Droit International*, Juillet-Août-Septembre 2019, n°3/2019, p. 833–853, at p. 848 *et seq.*

90   Cf. Art. 3 TEU and 21 TFEU.

91   Opinion 1/17, para. 149, emphasis added.

Thus, the Court's subsequent discussion would refer to an exceptionally rare circumstance: While the CETA Investment court can award damages for EU measures, this entails, pursuant to EU law, no legal obligation to adapt its legal order: The violation of treaty obligations is, regrettably, always an option for Sovereigns. But the Court addresses whether the Union would *de facto* be forced to change its course as a consequence of multiple ("repeated") monetary awards; in contrast to a single award for damages, such a scenario might bend the will of the EU decision-makers, thus infringing the autonomy of the Union legal order. This specific circumstance – a "cluster" of awards reimbursing Canadian investors – would only be relevant as potentially infringing the autonomy of the Union legal order, if it concerned the "*level* of protection of a public interest established by the EU institutions".

As the Union has shown to be able to do "whatever it takes"[92] to pursue the policies it chooses, it may be far from certain that even *repeated* negative awards would exercise the kind of "Beugezwang" that would "compel" the EU into obedience for the purposes of Opinion 1/17; in this context it is noteworthy that pursuant to Article 8.81.3 CETA, the Joint Committee may adopt interpretations of the agreement that will be binding on the CETA Tribunal.[93] Hence the contracting parties can block any threat of being exposed to the consequences of a constant CETA tribunal jurisprudence deviating from the ECJ. The somewhat imperial statement that EU legislation is characterized by being brought forward through a

> democratic process defined in the EU and FEU Treaties, and that that legislation is deemed, by virtue of the principles of conferral of powers, subsidiarity and proportionality laid down in Article 5 TEU, to be both appropriate and necessary to achieve a legitimate objective of the Union[94]

would *a priori* be limited to a very small group of cases. According to the current President of the Court,[95] this latter view is the correct one. Being able

---

92   Speech by Mario Draghi, President of the European Central Bank at the Global Investment Conference in London, 26 July 2012, https://www.ecb.europa.eu/press/key/date/2012/ html/sp120726.en.html: "Within our mandate, the ECB is ready to do whatever it takes to preserve the euro. And believe me, it will be enough."

93   Cf. the discussion in Opinion 1/17, para. 232–244.

94   Opinion 1/17, para. 151.

95   K. Lenaerts, 'Modernising trade whilst safeguarding the EU constitutional framework: an insight into the balanced approach of Opinion 1/17', Speech – Belgian Ministry of Foreign Affairs – Seminar on Opinion 1/17, 6 September 2019. To be consulted at https://diplomatie.belgium.be/sites/default/files/downloads/   presentation_lenaerts_opinion_1_17.pdf.

to draw on privileged information, he has soothed concerns that Opinion 1/17 would, in the Court's reading, prevent the CETA tribunal from awarding damages for "discrimination or arbitrary treatment affecting a Canadian investor". That, we are told, is not so because a dispute-settlement mechanism such as that at issue is established by an agreement which, pursuant to Article 216(2) TFEU, is "binding upon the institutions of the Union". The implication would be that in such a case, even repeated and financially "compelling" awards would not fall into the prohibited zone pursuant to Opinion 1/17: "What the Court is protecting instead is the *essence of the democratic process* leading to the adoption of EU norms protecting public interests, a process which forms part of the EU constitutional framework." This almost poetic take-away would imply that the *quasi-ius cogens* status requested for EU law by the Court in paragraph 151 would be limited to the very specific case questioning the "level of protection of a public interest established by the EU institutions".[96] As already indicated, the Court describes *in casu* a victimless crime, as the Court opines (see infra 4.2) that the CETA tribunal does not have that competence.

4.2   *An Unexpected Appetite for Risk?*

This brings us to the Court's application of its principles to CETA: Again, the pertinent remarks can be short, as my co-editor *Van der Loo* has comprehensively presented and analysed the Court's application of its principles to the facts at hand.

The Court's considerate approach is evidenced by multiple examples: For example, the Court emphasises at the beginning of its analysis the respective autonomy of the three groups of adjudicators interpreting and applying the examined international agreement CETA: the EU courts (with the ECJ at their helm), Canadian Courts and the adjudicative bodies established by CETA, i.e. *in casu* the CETA Investment Tribunal. While this statement is self-evident from an international law perspective, it represents an unexpected courtesy to the CETA Tribunal:

> Accordingly, while those agreements are an integral part of EU law and may therefore be the subject of references for a preliminary ruling[97] they concern no less those non-Member States and may therefore also be interpreted by the courts and tribunals of those States. It is, moreover,

---

96   Opinion 1/17, para. 149.

97   Referring in the original to the "judgments of 30 April 1974, *Haegeman*, 181/73, EU:C:1974:41, paragraphs 5 and 6; of 25 February 2010, *Brita*, C-386/08, EU:C:2010:91, paragraph 39; and of 22 November 2017, *Aebtri*, C-224/16, EU:C:2017:880, paragraph 50".

precisely because of the reciprocal nature of international agreements
and the need to maintain the powers of the Union in international relations that it is open to the Union [...] to enter into an agreement that confers on an international court or tribunal the jurisdiction to interpret that
agreement without that court or tribunal being subject to the interpretations of that agreement given by the courts or tribunal of the Parties. [98]

This benevolent attitude is also manifest, when the Court swats away the argument that the two avenues for redress against BIT-incompatible measures by
EU companies owned by a Canadian investor – both the full protection of the
Union legal order for the EU operator and the ISDS protection for the investor – may be a problematic "double-dipping" in light of the principle of equal
treatment.[99]

Maybe the most obvious sign of the Court's CETA-friendly approach is the
unequivocal acceptance of the argument that the "the power of interpretation and application conferred on [the DSM] is confined to the provisions of
the CETA and that such interpretation or application must be undertaken in
accordance with the rules and principles of international law".[100] While this
follows directly from the wording of Article 8.31.1. CETA, it would seem more in
line with the Court's attitude evidenced in Opinions 1/09 and 2/13 to approach
that provision with a suspicious eye for what could go wrong, rather than to
rely fully on the *verbatim* reading of the pertinent CETA-provisions: Pursuant
to Article 8.31.2 CETA, the Tribunal may consider domestic law, including EU
law, "as a matter of fact" when it is called on to determine "consistency of a
measure with" CETA; in such circumstance, i.e. when applying EU law, "the
Tribunal shall follow the prevailing interpretation given" by the ECJ.[101]

The Court accepts that the mere consideration of EU law as a matter of fact,
combined with the proviso that the CETA tribunal would be "obliged to follow
the prevailing interpretation given to that domestic law"[102] would not permit a
scenario in which the CETA tribunal could unduly influence the Court, in contrast to pertinent threats spotted in previous decisions, including, for that matter, *EEA I*. This follows not the least, we are being told, from the CETA provision

---

98   Opinion 1/17, para. 117.
99   Opinion 1/17, para. 181.
100   Opinion 1/17, para. 122.
101   Opinion 1/17, para. 130.
102   Article 8.31.2 CETA reads: "any meaning given to domestic law by the Tribunal shall not be
      binding upon the courts or the authorities of that Party"; this half-sentence is specifically
      quoted by Opinion 1/17, para. 130.

stating that the domestic courts would not be "bound by the meaning given to" domestic law by the CETA Tribunal.[103]

In fairness, the Court's position that applying the law as a matter of fact is clearly discernible from interpreting and applying law as a matter of law is not limited to Opinion 1/17: for example, when it comes to the application of foreign law before Union courts, the Court similarly adheres to the "fiction"[104] that it is possible to cleanly separate the application as fact from the application of law; of course, a rich body of pertinent literature[105] and state practice[106] highlights the difficulty to do so.

This is not a purely theoretical or esthetical issue: the jurisprudence of the Court of Justice contains a significant number of surprising decisions concerning the compatibility of Member states' measures with EU law with

---

103   Opinion 1/17, para. 132.

104   C. Kuner, International agreements, data protection, and EU fundamental rights on the international stage: Opinion 1/15, EU-Canada PNR, *Common Market Law Review 55* (2018), p. 857–882, at 880.

105   K. Von Papp, Clash of Autonomous Legal Orders: Can EU Member State Courts Bridge the Jurisdictional Divide Between Investment Tribunals and the ECJ? A Plea for Direct Referral from Investment Tribunals to the ECJ, *Common Market Law Review 50* (2013), 1039–1082,p. 1039–1040; recently,S. Hindelang has regularly addressed this issue: S. Hindelang, Conceptualisation and Application of the Principle of Autonomy of EU Law – The CJEU's Judgment in Achmea Put in Perspective, *European Law Review 44* (2019), *p.* 383–400, where he highlights at p. 384 the "undetermined borderline between the expression "matter of fact" and the *de facto* interpretation of domestic law"; at p. 392 he states: "it might not make a difference that an investment tribunal does not apply EU law as law senso strictu but treats it merely as facts"; S.Hindelang, Repellent Forces: The CJEU and Investor-State Dispute Settlement, *Archiv des Völkerrechts 53* (2015), p. 68–88, at 76 and 79; see also C. Contartese and M. Andenas, EU Autonomy and Investor-State Dispute Settlement Under Inter Se Agreements Between EU Member States: Achmea, *Common Market Law Review 56* (2019), p. 157–192 at 186.

106   Pursuant to para. 137 of AG Bot's opinion, "it is indeed conceivable that [...] the Tribunal may be called upon to undertake *some* interpretation of EU law" (emphasis added). A comparative look at the WTO reveals that whereas the US characterisation of the Appellate Body as a "rogue actor" would seem less than convincing, the USTR can identify some difficulties by the Appellate Body to cleanly separate "application as fact" from interpretation as law: USTR Policy Agenda 2018 p. 27–28. (https://ustr.gov/sites/default/files/files/Press/Reports/2018/AR/2018%20Annual%20Report%20FINAL.PDF): "The United States has also noted with concern the Appellate Body's review of the meaning of Member's domestic law that is being challenged. In a WTO dispute, the key fact to be proven is what a Member's challenged measure does (or means), and the law to be interpreted and applied are the provisions of the WTO agreements. But the Appellate Body consistently asserts that it can review the meaning of a Member's domestic measure as a matter of law rather than acknowledging that it is a matter of fact and thus not a subject for Appellate Body review."

potential relevance for an investor.[107] Given the lack of a preliminary ruling procedure, it is possible that – on the base of existing, but not directly pertinent ECJ case-law – a CETA tribunal might determine the compatibility of a Member state's measure with a new Regulation or Directive in ways which differ from the Court's subsequent findings. Thus, there is the potential for divergence between the CETA Tribunal and the ECJ jurisprudence.[108] Or, *horribile dictu*, the CETA Tribunal advances a novel view, maybe seemingly questionable in the light of ECJ precedents, and the Court leans towards the same approach, creating unintentionally a perception that it follows rather than leads.

As the EU legislator will unavoidably produce completely new legislation answering to new or previously unaddressed topics or new problems arising out of "old" regulatory concerns – data, nanotechnology, public health, (internal and border) measures to foster CO_2-reduction[109] – a realistic possibility exists that a small number of *ad-hoc* divergences of jurisprudence may develop. However, CETA's (technical)[110] safety-net that "any meaning given to the domestic law by the Tribunal shall not be binding upon the courts or authorities of that Party" is only of limited value with regard to *de facto* reductions of the ECJ's autonomy. Of course, the very existence of this provision indicates that the legal advisors servicing the negotiations spotted this very issue and included redundancies that allowed the Court to approve CETA without modifying its jurisprudence. This, it will be recalled, is not only a different approach from the one taken in *EEA I*, but *very* different from what the Court of Justice was prepared to accept in Opinion 1/09, 2/13 or *Achmea*.

---

107   Recent pertinent examples would include the Judgments in Case C-592/14, *European Federation for Cosmetic Ingredients v Secretary of State for Business, Innovation and Skills and Attorney General*, EU:C:2016:703 and in Case C-528/16, *Confédération paysanne and Others v Premier ministre and Ministre de l'agriculture, de l'agroalimentaire et de la forêt*, EU:C:2018:583.

108   From the Board: 'The Paradox of Proliferation and Contestation of Economic Integration', *Legal Isues of European Integration* 46 (2019), p. 197–202 at 199, referring *inter alia* to a Twitter feed by *Simon Lester* adressing the statement in para. 156 of the Opinion that the "discretionary powers of the CETA Tribunal [...] do not extend to permitting them to call into question the level of protection of public interest determined by the Union following a democratic process": Lester wrote, it is reported, "We can all agree that this is incorrect, right?".

109   Cf. Z. Ahmad, WTO Law and Trade Policy Reform for Low-Carbon Technology Diffusion, PhD Thesis, University of Bern 2020.

110   In addition to the provision of Art. 8.31.3 CETA discussed below.

5   Conclusion: Never Get High on Your Own Supply

Why then this *ouverture d'esprit* of the Court, which is so obviously different from the attitude visible in *ECHR?* It would seem that at least two strands of possible explanations exist: The obvious first one has already been discussed *supra*: on the basis of the sketched case-law on autonomy, CETA can pass muster, provided it is read innocently – meaning *verbatim* – and not so much with a view to the potential divergences and possible difficulties. CETA and EU law are indeed not only separate as a matter of EU law and of public international law. They are also separate in the sense that CETA law is not substantially EU law. While some overlap between Single Market law and EU trade agreements will always exist (in the case at hand, e.g., an overlap between the provisions of Article 63 *et seq.* TFEU and the CETA investment chapter), this proximity is fundamentally different from an expansion of EU law as was the case in *EEA* and in *ECAA*. The contracting parties – not least due to the Wallonian prodding – went out of their way to underscore that EU law was only used as a matter of law and provided a safety-net by including the provision that, in any case, the Tribunal's interpretation would not be binding upon the Court.[111]

However, there is another strand of reasoning that the Court either does not openly address or rather touches upon outside of the context of autonomy: Article 8.31.3 CETA, pursuant to which the Joint Committee may react to a jurisprudence of the CETA tribunal that is not aligned with the political will of the contracting parties,[112] may have given the Court the confidence that – like in the context of the EEA – the Commission was prepared to play its part in preserving the autonomy of the legal order, if the CETA Tribunal would indeed act against CETA's brief to apply EU law as interpreted by the Court of Justice. Read in combination with the manifold provisions of the contracting parties in CETA and adjoined documents, amply cited in Opinion 1/17,[113] the Court seems

---

111   On this point, see the contribution by G. Van der Loo in this volume.

112   The provision reads: "Where serious concerns arise as regards matters of interpretation that may affect investment, the Committee on Services and Investment may [...] recommend to the CETA Joint Committee the adoption of interpretations of this Agreement. An interpretation adopted by the CETA Joint Committee shall be binding on the Tribunal established under this Section. The CETA Joint Committee may decide that an interpretation shall have binding effect from a specific date."

113   Opinion 1/17 para. 154, 155: "In the same way, [...] Article 8.9.1 of that agreement states explicitly that Parties have the right 'to regulate within their territories to achieve legitimate policy objectives, such as the protection of public health, safety, the environment or public morals, social or consumer protection or the promotion and protection of cultural diversity'. Further, Article 8.9.2 of that agreement provides that 'for greater certainty, the

to have felt confident that any deviation from its jurisprudence would make the Commission take up the case with its Canadian counterpart. In light of the political will to protect the political choices of both the European and the Canadian democratic processes, a CETA Tribunal "going rogue" would face the risk of a "nuclear option": getting reversed, if only *pro futuro*, by the contracting parties. Such a reaction by the political branches of government would pull the rug out from all previous efforts by the Tribunal and would inflict considerable damage to its credibility. Insofar, it is not unlike the possibilities open for the Commission in the EEA. There, the Commission can bring a partial and temporary end to the EEA, if the softer tools of persuasion do not work.[114] In the context of an advanced but nevertheless classic FTA with less probability of divergence, it seems that the CETA mechanism inspired enough trust in the Court that it was prepared to accept a residual risk of future divergence with the CETA's DSM jurisprudence.

It would seem that the most important reason for the Court's most 'pragmatic' application of the principle of 'autonomy of the Union legal order' is the absence of any realistic possibility of regulatory competition between CETA and EU law, and between the Court of Justice and the CETA DSM. As important as CETA is, and its DSM's jurisprudence will become, the two regimes are not positioned to be in a competitive relationship, even sectorally: insofar, the Court's remark that the three adjudicative bodies using and applying CETA were autonomous from each other, highlights the main difference from previous cases applying the principle of autonomy. Free trade agreements, even advanced ones such as CETA, are very different from agreements establishing potentially competing structures of European economic or human rights governance that have overlapping field of applications or expand the Union legal

---

mere fact that a Party regulates, including through a modification to its laws, in a manner which negatively affects an investment or interferes with an investor's expectations, including its expectations of profits, does not amount to a breach of an obligation under this Section'. Moreover, Point 1(d) and Point 2 of the Joint Interpretative Instrument provide that the CETA 'will ... not lower [the standards and regulations of each Party] related to food safety, product safety, consumer protection, health, environment or labour protection', that 'imported goods, service suppliers and investors must continue to respect domestic requirements, including rules and regulations', and that the CETA 'preserves the ability of the European Union and its Member States and Canada to adopt and apply their own laws and regulations that regulate economic activity in the public interest'." For an overview cf. Cf. C. Titi, 'Right to Regulate', in M. M. Mbengue, S. Schacherer (ed.) *Foreign Investment under the Comprehensive Economic and Trade Agreement* (CETA) (Springer, 2019), p. 159–183.

114   See *supra*, 2.2.

order to associated third countries, such as the EEA. The EU-Ukraine Agreement[115], the draft framework agreement between Switzerland and the EU[116], and possibly the future agreement between the EU and its former Member state UK are somewhat between these two endpoints of a continuum: Not coincidentally, the two former ones contain preliminary ruling procedures ensuring the autonomy of the Union legal order, by ensuring that Union law is authoritatively interpreted by the ECJ. One would hope that the Court spells out in more detail in future case-law how the principle of autonomy applies in a differentiated fashion to the different categories of treaties concluded by the Union. However, it is to be welcomed that the Court relies on the willingness of the Union's political branches to ensure that the homogeneity of the Union legal order will enforce *vis-à-vis* foreign partners.

While the business advice "to not get high on one's own supply" has its origins in an imaginary (and highly criminal) context,[117] it would seem to describe best practice in all sorts of contexts. Opinion 1/17 combines an ambitious and self-asserted further expansion of the concept of autonomy – the President of the Court views it as "a major contribution to [...] the EU's functional constitution, that is to say a Union founded on democracy, justice and rights",[118] no less – with a surefooted self-restraint with regard to the agreement at hand. While the former aspect will doubtlessly be used in future constellations in which the Court gains the impression that a genuine loss of autonomy looms for itself and the Union legal order, the self-restraint shown in Opinion 1/17

---

115   Association Agreement between the European Union and its Member States, of the one part, and Ukraine, of the other part, OJ L 161, 29.5.2014, p. 3–2137.

116   The text of the draft can be consulted at https://www.eda.admin.ch/dea/en/home/ verhandlungen-offene-themen/verhandlungen/institutionelles-abkommen.html.   Cf. Art. 4 and 10 of the draft agreement, in particular Art. 10 (3) ("3. Lorsque le différend soulève une question concernant l'interprétation ou l'application d'une disposition visée dans le deuxième paragraphe de l'article 4 du présent accord, et si son interprétation est pertinente pour régler le différend et nécessaire pour lui permettre de statuer, le tribunal arbitral saisit la Cour de justice de l'Union européenne. L'arrêt de la Cour de justice de l'Union européenne lie le tribunal arbitral") and the annexed Protocol 3 "sur le Tribunal Arbitral".

117   References to the motion picture *Scarface* and its lead villain *Tony Montana* to be consulted at Eugene Volokh, "Don't get high on your own supply, 'cause double jeopardy don't apply", Washington Post June 2, 2017, https://www.washingtonpost.com/news/volokh-conspiracy/wp/2017/06/02/tony-montana-montana-sup-ct-dont-get-high-on-your-own-supply-cause-double-jeopardy-dont-apply/.

118   K. Lenaerts, 'Modernising trade whilst safeguarding the EU constitutional framework: an insight into the balanced approach of Opinion 1/17', Speech – Belgian Ministry of Foreign Affairs – Seminar on Opinion 1/17, 6 September 2019. To consult at: https://diplomatie. belgium.be/sites/default/files/downloads/ presentation_lenaerts_opinion_1_17.pdf.

allows hope that the concept will not serve as a weapon of mass destruction, evaporating the linkage between the Union legal order and international law, and in particular the political branches' efforts to strengthen treaties concluded by the Union with effective and meaningful DSM s.

Rather it would seem that the ECJ is inclined to apply the principle of autonomy as "weaponised reasonableness", requiring on its basis full alignment with all standard tools of the Union legal order – and in particular all instruments required to protect the role of the Court – , if the agreement in question is characterised by a high degree of interconnectedness and interworking with the Union legal order. In contrast, agreements that facilitate cooperation and exchange at arm's length would benefit from a much more lenient approach. In this understanding, effective implementation of international law through the conclusion of treaties with effective DSM s and the protection of the Union and its legal order are not mutually exclusive concerns. In Opinion 1/17, the Court was prepared to take a leap of faith – because they both matter.

CHAPTER 6

Investment Screening – a New Era of European Protectionism?

Marc Bungenberg and Fabian Blandfort

1 Introduction

The admission of foreign investment is a basic sovereign right of States, as *inter alia* the United Nations General Assembly (UNGA) Resolutions on *Permanent Sovereignty over Natural Resources*[1] and on a *Charter of Economic Rights and Duties of States*[2] have reaffirmed. In the absence of an international commitment a State is under no obligation to liberalise the market access of foreign investments, to grant authorisations or admit a tender in a national procurement proceeding.[3] Since Bilateral Investment Treaties (BITs), especially those negotiated by the European Union (EU) Member States, traditionally do not contain provisions on the *pre-establishment phase*, but rather exclusively govern the *post-establishment phase*, the sovereign right of host States to regulate the market access of foreign investments in principle is not restricted through public international law.[4] Hence, the substantive standards of protection do only apply to State measures after the foreign investment has entered into the host State's market and has been established.[5] Thus, deriving from its sovereign

---

1   United Nations General Assembly Resolution 1803 (XVII), *Permanent Sovereignty over Natural Resources*, 14 December 1962.

2   United Nations General Assembly Resolution 3281 (XXIX), *Charter of Economic Rights and Duties of States*, 12 December 1974.

3   See M. Bungenberg, 'Evolution of Investment Law Protection as Part of a General System of National Resources Sovereignty (and Management)?', in M. Bungenberg, S. Hobe (eds.), *Permanent Sovereignty over Natural Resources* (Springer, 2015), p. 129; R. Dolzer, C. Schreuer, *Principles of International Investment Law*, 2nd edition (OPU, 2012), p. 88; A. Dimopoulos, *EU Foreign Investment Law* (OUP, 2011), p. 50. On the application of IIAs on public procurement proceedings, see M. Bungenberg, F. Blandfort, 'International Investment Law and Public Procurement – An Overview', in K. Gómez, A. Gourgourinis, C. Titi (eds.), *International Investment Law and Competition Law*, Springer, forthcoming.

4   On the different approaches in the transatlantic context see also R. Dolzer, C. Schreuer, (n. 3), p. 89; S. Schill, 'The Impact of International Investment Law on Public Contracts', *ACIL Research Paper* 2017-07, p. 16–17.

5   On the notion of investment as the decisive condition for an arbitral tribunal's jurisdiction and the application of the standards of protection alike, see i.a. J. Bischoff, R. Happ,

jurisdiction the host State can restrict the market access of foreign investments and regulate the criteria for admission.

Therefore, after the Second World War in particular newly-independent and developing States restricted their market access, opposing the interests of capital-exporting developed States.[6] However, in order to attract foreign investments, States have increasingly liberalised their market access provisions in the late 1980s, incentivising foreign investment inflows, leading not only to capital, but also to the transfer of technology and know-how.[7] In particular, developing countries rich in natural resources have traditionally had to rely on foreign capital and technology to foster their economy and therefore opened up their markets. But also the EU prohibits (nearly) all restrictions on the movement of capital not only between Member States but also between Member States and third countries, according to Article 63 TFEU.[8]

Although investment policies worldwide continue to promote inward investment flows and incentivise foreign investments in the form of direct investments and portfolio investments alike, the global foreign direct investment (FDI) flows fell by 13 per cent to US$ 1.3 trillion in 2018,[9] declining significantly compared to 2017 (US$ 1.5 trillion)[10] and 2016 (US$ 1.868 trillion).[11] The United Nations Conference on Trade and Development (UNCTAD) observes, *inter alia*, increasing concerns about the potential impact of foreign investments on national security, resulting particularly in amendments to national investment review mechanisms.[12] Besides such national legislation in EU Member States and third countries,[13] the Union itself enacted Regulation (EU) 2019/452 establishing a framework for the screening of foreign

---

'The Notion of Investment', in M. Bungenberg, J. Griebel, S. Hobe, A. Reinisch (eds.), *International Investment Law: A Handbook* (C.H. Beck, Hart, Nomos, 2015), p. 495–544; N. Rubins, 'The Notion of 'Investment' in International Investment Arbitration', in N. Horn (ed.), *Arbitrating Foreign Investment Disputes: Procedural and Substantive Legal Aspects* (Kluwer Law International, 2004), p. 283–324.

6   R. Dolzer, C. Schreuer (n. 3), p. 4.

7   K. Vandevelde, 'A Brief History of International Investment Agreements', *UC Davis Journal of International Law & Policy* 12 (2005), p. 178; R. Dolzer, C. Schreuer (n. 3), p. 87–88.

8   A. Dimopoulos (n. 3), p. 50 f.; J. Kotthaus, *Binnenmarktrecht und externe Kapitalverkehrsfreiheit*, (Nomos, 2012).

9   UNCTAD, World Investment Report 2019, Special Economic Zones, p. 2.

10   UNCTAD, World Investment Report 2019, Special Economic Zones, p. 3.

11   UNCTAD, World Investment Report 2018, Investment and New Industrial Policies, p. xi and 15.

12   UNCTAD, World Investment Report 2019, Special Economic Zones, p. 65–66.

13   See e.g. on the reform of the US Screening System CFIUS, Congressional Research Service, CFIUS Reform: Foreign Investment National Security Reviews, 2 May 2019.

direct investments into the Union on 19 March 2019.[14] The Regulation has officially entered into force on 10 April 2019 and is applicable since 11 October 2020, according to its Article 17. Moreover, the Commission has issued an in-depth analysis of foreign direct investment flows into the EU, concentrating on strategic sectors and assets.[15] The Regulation can be seen as a major measure of the autonomous Common Commercial Policy (CCP) in the investment sector after FDI-competences were transferred to the EU with the Lisbon Treaty in 2009.

This contribution aims to provide an overview of this new EU Regulation (2), assessing the economic and political background as well as the basic features of the screening framework with regard to the main objective of the Union measures. Furthermore, since the Member States screening mechanisms are decisive for the implementation of the Regulation, the existing national review procedures have to be taken into account as well, focussing illustratively on the German, Austrian and French systems (3). In an *excursus*, the investment screening mechanisms of the US and China are summarised (4).

2 The EU Regulation

2.1 *Economic and Political Background*

Reaching an FDI inflow of US$ 334 billion in 2017, the EU is a major destination for foreign direct investments, outpacing North America (US$ 300 billion) and following Asia (US$ 476 billion).[16] Indeed, with a stock of inward FDI of more than EUR 5.7 trillion at the end of 2015 and Union investors holding EUR 6.9 trillion in FDI in third countries, the EU was "the world's leading source and destination of foreign direct investment".[17] However, it was already suggested by the EU Commissioners *Tajani* and *Barnier* in 2011 to create a comprehensive

---

14   Regulation (EU) 2019/452 of the European Parliament and of the Council of 19 March 2019 establishing a framework for the screening of foreign direct investments into the Union (OJ 2019, L 79).

15   European Commission, Commission Staff Working Document on Foreign Direct Investment in the EU, Following up on the Commission Communication 'Welcoming Foreign Direct Investment while Protecting Essential Interests' of 13 September 2017, SWD(2019) 108 final, 13 March 2019.

16   UNCTAD, World Investment Report 2018, Investment and New Industrial Policies, p. 15.

17   European Commission, 'Welcoming Foreign Direct Investment while Protecting Essential Interests', COM(2017) 494 final, 13 September 2017, p. 3.

screening mechanism for FDI on the Union level, comparable to the Committee on Foreign Investment in the United States (CFIUS).[18]

The recently adopted EU Regulation providing for a framework for the screening of inward FDI was then proposed on 13 September 2017 by the European Commission President Jean-Claude Juncker, who emphasised in his State of the Union Address that "Europe must always defend its strategic interests".[19] The proposal was following-up on the "Reflection Paper on Harnessing Globalisation" of 10 May 2017, which had emphasised:

> Openness to foreign investment remains a key principle for the EU and a major source of growth. However, concerns have recently been voiced about foreign investors, notably state-owned enterprises, taking over European companies with key technologies for strategic reason. [...] These concerns need careful analysis and appropriate action.[20]

The Commission's proposal was further influenced by the initiative to implement a coherent framework for the market access of FDI that was launched by Germany, Italy and France in 2017.[21] The Member States criticised, *inter alia,* the acquisition of European companies "as part of other countries' strategic industrial policies".[22]

Hence, the Regulation has to be seen as a response to the increase of foreign investments in key European industries, including high-tech and advanced

---

18   European Commission, Cabinet Newsletter of Vice President of the European Commission Tajani, No. 33 of 11 February 2011, to consult at: http://ec.europa.eu/archives/commission_2010-2014/tajani/about/newsletter/files/2011-02/cabnews-33-20110211_en.pdf.

19   European Commission, Jean-Claude Juncker – State of the Union Address, 13 September 2017, to consult at: https://europa.eu/rapid/press-release_SPEECH-17-3165_en.htm.

20   European Commission, 'Reflection Paper on Harnessing Globalisation', COM (2017) 240, 10 May 2017, p. 15.

21   The first Member States' initiative 'Proposals for ensuring an improved level playing field in trade and investment' was published in February 2017, to consult at https://www.bmwi.de/Redaktion/DE/Downloads/E/eckpunktepapier-proposals-for-ensuring-an-improved-level-playing-field-in-trade-and-investment.pdf?__blob=publicationFile&v=4. The second initiative 'European investment policy: A common approach to investment control' followed on 28 July 2017, to consult at https://g8fip1kplyr33r3krz5b97d1-wpengine.netdna-ssl.com/wp-content/uploads/2017/08/170728_Investment-screening_non-paper.pdf. T. Schuelken, 'Der Schutz kritischer Infrastrukturen vor ausländischen Direktinvestitionen in der Europäischen Union. Zum Vorschlag der EU-Kommission für eine Verordnung zur Schaffung eines Rahmens für die Überprüfung ausländischer Direktinvestitionen – KOM (2017) 487 endg.', *EuR* 2018, p. 591.

22   *Ibid.,* p. 1.

manufacturing assets, thus in potentially sensitive sectors.[23] In recent years, the takeover of the German robotics maker *Kuka* by *Midea* in 2016,[24] the much debated stake of the *China General Nuclear Power Group* in *Hinkley Point C* in Somerset[25] or the interest of a Chinese investor in the German power network operator *50Hertz*[26] caused a stir among the public perception.[27] The "Chinese Dragon" seems to be the spectre within the rise of merger transactions in the European market from third countries,[28] although in reality Chinese FDI in Europe has declined in 2019.[29]

Albeit, the regularly implied imbalance concerning the flow of direct investments in- and outward the EU should not hide the fact that these investments are needed in the European Union industries as a "source of growth, jobs and

---

23   See T. Hanemann, M. Huotari, 'Record Flows and Growing Imbalances – Chinese Investment in Europe in 2016', *Merics Paper on China* No. 3 January 2017, p. 5 f. On the political background see also J.-C. Gottwald, J. Schild, D. Schmidt, 'Das Ende der Naivität gegenüber China? Die Reform des europäischen Investitionskontrollregimes', *Integration* 2019, p. 134 f.

24   Kuka, 'US Government Authorities grant clearances for take-over of KUKA by Midea', Press Release of 30 December 2016.

25   S. Thomas, 'China's nuclear export drive: Trojan Horse or Marshall Plan?', *Energy Policy* 101 (2017), p. 688.

26   C. Jungbluth, Kauft China systematisch Schlüsseltechnologien auf? Chinesische Firmenbeteiligungen in Deutschland im Kontext von "Made in China 2025", *GED Studie*, 2018, p. 8.

27   A. Zhang, 'Foreign Direct Investment from China: Sense and Sensibility', *Northwestern Journal of International Law & Business* 34 (2011), p. 434; T. Schuelken (n. 21), p. 578 f. On the energy sector, see B. Conrad, G. Kostka, 'Editorial: Chinese investments in Europe's energy sector: Risks and opportunities?', *Energy Policy* 101 (2017), p. 646–647. See also BDI Policy Paper China, 'Partner and Systemic Competitor – How Do We Deal with China's State-Controlled Economy?', January 2019; European Commission, 'EU-China – A strategic outlook', JOIN(2019) 5 final, 12 March 2019.

28   See M. Bungenberg, A. Hazarika, 'Chinese Foreign Investments in the European Union Energy Sector: The Regulation of Security Concerns', *Journal of World Investment and Trade* 20 (2019), p. 378; S. Hindelang, T. Hagemeyer, 'Enemy at the Gates? Die aktuellen Änderungen der Investitionsprüfvorschriften in der Außenwirtschaftsverordnung im Lichte des Unionsrechts', *EuZW* (2017), p. 882.

29   See EY, 'Chinesische Unternehmenskäufe und – beteiligungen in Europa: Eine Analyse von M&A-Deals 2006–2019', August 2019, to consult at https://www.ey.com/Publication/vwLUAssets/ey-chinesische-unternehmenskaeufe-und-beteiligungen-in-europa-august-2019/$file/ey-chinesische-unternehmenskaeufe-und-beteiligungen-in-europa-august-2019.pdf; Spiegel Online, Minus 84 Prozent: Chinas Investitionen in Europa brechen ein, to consult at https://www.spiegel.de/forum/wirtschaft/minus-84-prozent-chinas-investitionen-europa-brechen-ein-thread-940836-1.html .

innovation."[30] The numbers above, indeed, illustrate the significant importance of foreign capital for the Union industries. Besides, in the period of 2013 to 2016, more than 51% of all FDI towards EU Member States came from the United States of America and not the Eastern Hemisphere.[31]

The actual problem arises out of the influence of State-Owned Enterprises (SOEs),[32] whose proportion is particularly high in the case of China and Russia.[33] The Commission recognises a risk that (state-influenced) "foreign investors may seek to acquire control or influence in European undertakings whose activities have repercussions on critical technologies, infrastructure, inputs, or sensitive information."[34] Also in international investment law under investment agreements, SOEs are of increasing relevance. The main question to be answered in this regard will be whether these entities act as market driven players or as political instruments of their home States and thus need or need not protection under international investment agreements.[35]

Considering the importance of foreign capital, a balance between risks and benefits of FDI rather than a mere shielding of the Union's industries against foreign investors has been the key objective of the Union measure. Accordingly, the former EU's Trade Commissioner Cecilia Malmström specified that "[t]he aim of what we are proposing is to keep the EU open to foreign investment, with a non-discriminatory, transparent and predictable framework"[36], but at the same time to begin to provide the EU with at least some instruments to react to "foreign threats", if necessary.

However, the Regulation adopted on 19 March 2019 differs significantly from the original proposal of the EU Commission.[37] Whereas the Commission had proposed a cooperative framework implementing a screening procedure on

---

30   European Commission, 'State of the Union 2017 – Trade Package: European Commission proposes framework for screening of foreign direct investments', press release, 14 September 2017, IP/17/3183, p. 1.

31   E. Sunesen, M. Hansen, *Screening of FDI towards the EU*, Danish Business Authority, Copenhagen Economics January 2018, p. 18.

32   European Commission (n. 20).

33   E. Sunesen, M. Hansen (n. 31), p. 18.

34   European Commission, 'Welcoming Foreign Direct Investment while Protecting Essential Interests', COM(2017) 494 final, 13 September 2017, p. 5.

35   S. Konrad, 'Protection of Investments Owned by States', in M. Bungenberg, J. Griebel, S. Hobe, A. Reinisch (eds.), *International Investment Law: A Handbook*, (Hart, Nomos, 2015), p. 545 f.

36   European Commission (n. 32), p. 1.

37   European Commission, 'Proposal for a Regulation of the European Parliament and of the Council establishing a framework for screening of foreign direct investments into the European Union', COM(2017) 487 final, 13 September 2017.

the Union level in addition to the mechanisms of the competent national authorities, the adopted Regulation avoids the term of a "Commission Screening" and softens the regime in the light of mere administrative cooperation and coordination. Indeed, the Regulation contains various without-prejudice clauses, for example in Article 1(2) and (3), emphasising the cooperative nature of the framework and the ultimate responsibility of the Member States to take the final screening decision in recital 17, Article 6(9) second sentence and Article 8(2) in conjunction with Article 6(9), respectively. Considering the rather cautious approach of the Union, emphasising the sovereign rights of the Member States, the question of the division of competences in the field of FDI inflows has to be raised.

2.2   *The Union Competence for a Screening Framework*

The Lisbon Treaty implemented a broad Union competence for the Common Commercial Policy pursuant to Article 207(1) TFEU, governing, *inter alia,* foreign direct investments.[38] It is therefore unquestioned within academic literature that the competence for the CCP covers provisions on the market access of FDI,[39] whereas the regulation of portfolio investments was debated controversially.[40] The Court of Justice of the European Union (ECJ), however, ruled in the Opinion 2/15 (*Singapore FTA*) that the use, by the framers of the Treaties, of the words "foreign direct investment" in Article 207(1) TFEU is an unequivocal expression of their intention not to include other foreign investments than direct investments in the CCP.[41] Therefore, portfolio investments do not fall within the exclusive Union competence according to Article 3(1)(e) TFEU.[42]

---

38   M. Bungenberg, 'The Division of Competences Between the EU and Its Member States in the Area of Investment Politics', in M. Bungenberg, J. Griebel, S. Hindelang (eds.) *European Yearbook of International Economic Law Special Issue: International Investment Law and EU Law* (Springer 2011), p. 29; A. Dimopoulos (n. 3); A. Reinisch, 'The EU on the Investment Path – Quo Vadis Europe? The Future of EU BITs and other Investment Agreements', *Santa Clara Journal of International Law* 12 (2013), p. 115 with many further references.

39   See i.a. C. Herrmann, T. Müller-Ibold, 'Die Entwicklung des europäischen Außenwirtschaftsrechts', *EuZW* (2016), p. 646–647; M. Bungenberg, 'Going Global? The EU Common Commercial Policy After Lisbon', in C. Herrmann, J. Terhechte (eds.), *European Yearbook of International Economic Law* (Springer, 2010), p. 143.

40   M. Krajewski, 'External Trade Law and the Constitution Treaty: Towards a Federal and More Democratic Common Commercial Policy?', *Common Market Law Review* 42 (2005), p. 112; C. Herrmann, 'Die Zukunft der mitgliedstaatlichen Investitionspolitik nach dem Vertrag von Lissabon', *EuZW* 2010, p. 208–209.

41   ECJ, opinion 2/15, *Singapore*, ECLI:EU:C:2017:376, para. 83.

42   See also M. Bungenberg, in M. Pechstein, C. Nowak, U. Häde (eds.), Frankfurter Kommentar, Art. 207 AEUV, para. 23 et seq., before the Singapore Opinion was rendered.

In literature, it has been argued that due to a different definition of the term
FDI in Article 2 (1) of the Regulation on the one side and in paragraph 80 of the
Singapore Opinion[43] of the ECJ on the other side, the Union measure would
not fall under Article 207(1) TFEU.[44] However, it has to be considered that the
scope of application of the Regulation is explicitly limited to foreign direct investments[45] and according to the European Commission does not intend to
cover portfolio investments.[46] Furthermore, the provisions can be interpreted
compliant to primary Union law without changing the meaning of the regulation.[47] On the contrary, due to the explicit Union competence, the national
screening mechanisms most likely have not been in conformity with EU law
according to Article 2(1) TFEU, as long as there was no explicit permission
granted by the Union.[48] This finding has finally been altered by Article 3(1) of
the Regulation.[49] Hence, the Regulation falls under the exclusive Union competence for the CCP pursuant to Article 3(1)(e) and Article 207(1) TFEU.[50] However, the Union act does not prejudice "the right of Member States to derogate
from the free movement of capital as provided for in point (b) of Article 65(1)
TFEU".[51] Moreover, the "Regulation is without prejudice to each Member State
having sole responsibility for its national security, as provided for in Article

---

43   CJEU, opinion 2/15, *Singapore*, ECLI:EU:C:2017:376, para. 80.

44   J. Brauneck, 'Ausländische Direktinvestitionen nur mit Einverständnis der EU-
      Kommission?', *EuZW* 2018, p. 192.

45   See e.g. Art. 1(1) of the Regulation.

46   European Commission (n. 37), p. 12.

47   On an interpretation compliant to primary law, see e.g. ECJ, joint cases C-201/85 and
      C-202/85, *Klensch/Secrétaire d'État*, ECLI:EU:C:1986:439, para. 21; case C-314/89, *Rau/
      HZA Nürnberg-Fürth*, ECLI:EU:C:1991:143, para. 17; case C-98/91, *Herbrink/Minister
      van Landbouw*, ECLI:EU:C:1994:24, para. 9. See also C. Herrmann, *Rechtsgutachten zu
      europäischen Fragestellungen, die sich im Rahmen der Diskussion über einer Änderung der
      AWV ergeben haben ("Investment Screening") im Auftrag des BMWi* (Project I C 4 101/19),
      June 2019, p. 36–37.

48   See also C. Herrmann (n. 40), p. 209; V. Günther, 'Der Vorschlag der Europäischen
      Kommission für eine Verordnung zur Schaffung eines Rahmens für die Überprüfung
      ausländischer Direktinvestitionen in der Europäischen Union', in C. Tietje, G. Kraft,
      C. Kumpan (eds.), *Beiträge zum Transnationalen Wirtschaftsrecht*, Heft 157, 2018, p. 34.
      In contrast, S. Hindelang and T. Hagemeyer (n. 28) at p. 885 only assess the compatibil-
      ity of the German Screening mechanism with the fundamental freedoms. Differently,
      M. Clostermeyer, *Staatliche Übernahmeabwehr und die Kapitalverkehrsfreiheit zu
      Drittstaaten: Europarechtliche Beurteilung der §§ 7 Abs. 2 Nr. 6 AWG, 53 AWV*, (Nomos,
      2011), p. 116.

49   V. Günther (n. 48), p. 34.

50   See also Recital 5 of Regulation (EU) 2019/452.

51   Recital 4 of Regulation (EU) 2019/452.

4(2) TEU, and to the right of each Member State to protect its essential security interests in accordance with Article 346 TFEU".[52]

With regard to the Member States' rights pursuant to Article 65(1)(b) TFEU, the question occurs as to whether the Union would be prevented from regulating market access for FDI comprehensively at Union level. Within the literature it has been argued that the unambiguous wording of Articles 64 and 65 TFEU would mean that the right to regulate the movement of capital on grounds of public security falls in an exclusive competence of the Member States, as laid down in Article 65(1)(b) TFEU.[53] These provisions could lead to the conclusion that the CCP would be restricted to measures of liberalisation and therefore would not allow restrictions concerning the market access as a limitation of the free movement of capital. Hence, a regulation under Article 207(2) TFEU as secondary Union law would have to obey Article 65(1)(b) TFEU as primary Union law,[54] resulting in an invalidity of the Regulation if it would affect the Member States right to take measures on grounds of public security. However, the question whether Article 65(1) (b) TFEU has to lead to an invalidity of the proposed regulation is interrelated to the distinction of the scope of application of the exclusive Union competence according to Article 207(1) and (2) TFEU and of the Member States' competence under Article 65(1)(b) TFEU.

As stated above, the CCP post-Lisbon is undoubtedly covering direct investments, which, indeed, has to result in a precedency of Article 207(1) TFEU for those measures of the autonomous CPP regulating the market access of FDI from third countries.[55] It cannot be assumed that the drafters of the Treaties did intend to restrict the broadened competence for the CCP, which explicitly includes FDI, by the narrowly interpreted rights of the Member States according to Article 65(1)(b) TFEU,[56] which rather intends to enable the national

---

52   Article 1(2) of Regulation (EU) 2019/452.

53   J. Brauneck (n. 44), p. 195; S. Beuttenmüller, 'Das deutsche Außenwirtschaftsgesetz vor dem Hintergrund der neuen Unionskompetenz für ausländische Direktinvestitionen', *Ritsumeikan Law Review* 28 (2011), p. 286.

54   On the Union's obligation to obey the fundamental freedoms of the internal market see ECJ, case C-15/83, *Denkavit Nederland*, ECLI:EU:C:1984:183, para. 15; case C-51/91, *Meyhui*, ECLI:EU:C:1994:312, para. 11; case C-114/96, *Kieffer und Thill*, ECLI:EU:C:1997:316, para. 27; case C-284/95, *Safety Hi-Tech/S. u. T.*, ECLI:EU:C:1998:352, para. 63. See also H. Rosenfeldt, A. Würdemann, 'Schöpfer des Binnenmarktes im Käfig der Verträge – Die grundfreiheitliche Bindung des EU-Gesetzgebers', *EuR* (2016), p. 453.

55   See also C. Herrmann (n. 40), p. 209.

56   ECJ, Case C-463/00, *Commission/Spain*, ECLI:EU:C:2003:272, para. 34. See also case C-212/ 09, *Commission/Portugal*, ECLI:EU:C:2011:717, para. 83; case C-244/11, *Commission/Greece*, ECLI:EU:C:2012:694, para. 67. See also L. Gramlich, in M. Pechstein, C. Nowak, U. Häde (eds.), Frankfurter Kommentar, 2017, Art. 65 AEUV, para. 11; G. Ress, J. Ukrow in E. Grabitz,

authorities to restrict the movement of capital within the internal market. Thus, regarding the external dimension of regulating the access of FDI from third countries into the EU, Article 207(1) and (2) TFEU is indeed the more specific provision and confers a comprehensive competence upon the Union for measures concerning the market access of FDI.[57] Therefore, due to the broad Union competence, the national screening mechanisms most likely have not been in conformity with EU law until the Union in Article 3(1) of the Regulation empowered the Member State to adopt measures, pursuant to Article 2(1) TFEU.

The division of competences would therefore have allowed a comprehensive regulation at Union level, which, however, was not achieved,[58] as discussed in the following.

2.3 *The Key Characteristics of the Regulation*

The Regulation states in its first Article that it "establishes a framework for the screening by Member States of foreign direct investments into the Union on the grounds of security or public order and for a mechanism for cooperation between Member States, and between Member States and the Commission, with regard to foreign direct investments likely to affect security or public order", defining the relevant terms in its second Article. The need for such a legal framework is expressed, *inter alia*, in recital five of the regulation, which refers to the missing comprehensive framework at EU-level for the screening of FDI on the grounds of security or public order.

2.3.1 Cooperation Mechanisms

According to Article 3 of the Regulation, the "Member States may maintain, amend or adopt mechanisms to screen foreign direct investments in their

---

M. Hilf, M. Nettesheim (eds.), Das Recht der Europäischen Union, 2017, Art. 65 AEUV, para. 56; K.-P. Wojcik, in H. v. der Groeben, J. Schwarze, A. Hatje (eds.), Europäisches Unionsrecht, 2015, Art. 65 AEUV, para. 20.

57 See also S. Johannsen, 'Die Kompetenz der Europäischen Union für ausländische Direktinvestitionen nach dem Vertrag von Lissabon', in C. Tietje, G. Kraft, M. Lehmann (eds.), *Beiträge zum Transnationalen Wirtschaftsrecht*, Heft 90 (2009), p. 21; C. Herrmann (n. 47), p. 37. The broad competence of Article 207(1) TFEU is emphasised by S. Weiß, in E. Grabitz, M. Hilf, M. Nettesheim (eds.), Das Recht der Europäischen Union, 2017, Art. 207 AEUV, para. 40; M. Bungenberg, in M. Pechstein, C. Nowak, U. Häde (eds.), Frankfurter Kommentar, 2017, Art. 207 AEUV, para. 24; T. Cottier, L. Trinberg, in H. v. der Groeben, J. Schwarze, A. Hatje (eds.), Europäisches Unionsrecht, 2015, Art. 207, para. 60. See also Bungenberg (n. 39), p. 144.

58 T. Schuelken (n. 21), p. 592.

territory on the grounds of security or public order". Hence, the general responsibility for the screening of FDI lies with the Member States, who may decide whether to establish a respective administrative procedure or not. However, with regard to the abolition of an existing national screening mechanism the provision remains silent, although the wording "may maintain" implies the right to not maintain and, thus, to abolish it. Nevertheless, the principle of sincere cooperation pursuant to Article 4(3) TEU could, indeed, also argue for an obligation to maintain existing national mechanisms. Thus, a deliberate undermining or circumvention of the EU framework by abolishing an existing national screening mechanism could violate the Union treaties. Such an infringement would, however, certainly depend on the specific circumstances of the Member State's behaviour in question.

The functional administration of the screening framework through the Member States' authorities ensures the necessary flexibility of the different national mechanisms, enabling authorities to take into account the respective circumstances.[59] The implementation through the national authorities applies for the execution of the Commission's opinions issued under Article 6(3) and Article 8(1) alike. For both cooperation mechanisms Article 4 sets out a non-exhaustive list of factors that may be considered in the screening. Hence, the Member States and the Commission may consider, *inter alia*, the potential effects of the FDI on "critical infrastructure, whether physical or virtual, including energy, transport, water, health, communications, media, data processing or storage, aerospace, defence, electoral or financial infrastructure, and sensitive facilities, as well as land and real estate crucial for the use of such infrastructure", "critical technologies and dual use items" and "access to sensitive information, including personal data, or the ability to control such information". Furthermore, Article 4(2) states that the screening authorities may also take into account "whether the foreign investor is directly or indirectly controlled by the government, including state bodies or armed forces, of a third country, including through ownership structure or significant funding" (SOEs).

The various cooperation mechanisms are established by Articles 6 to 8 of the Regulation, which distinguishes between the cooperation mechanisms in relation to foreign direct investments undergoing screening in Article 6, the cooperation mechanism in relation to foreign direct investments not undergoing screening in Article 7 and the Commission's screening procedure in Article 8. However, the Regulation does not use the term of a "Commission

---

59   European Commission (n. 17), p. 9.

screening",[60] but rather only refers to the right to issue an opinion to the Member State, if the FDI is likely to affect projects or programmes of Union interest.

2.3.2   The Competences of the EU Commission

Since the main competence of the EU Commission conferred on it by the Regulation is the right to render an opinion to the Member State in which the investment is supposed to be established, the legal nature of the opinion is decisive for the functioning and efficiency of the regime. Article 6(3) allows the Commission to issue an opinion addressed to the Member State if it considers that an FDI is likely to affect security or public order in one or more Member States. If the Commission makes use of this provision, the respective Member State has to "take due consideration" of the opinion of the Commission pursuant to Article 6(9). Therefore, considering the unequivocal wording of the provision, the opinions are not legally binding in nature. Rather, the Member States have discretion to decide whether or not to follow the Commission's position.

Article 6(3) of the regulation applies if the Commission considers that an FDI might affect security of public order in one or more Member States, whereas the framework of Article 8(1) applies if there is a possible threat to the Union interests on ground of security or public order. In the latter case, the screening on the Union level applies. Article 8(2)(c) of the Regulation has to be considered as the main provision regarding the effective implementation of the screening framework. It states that the respective Member State "shall take utmost account of the Commission's opinion and provide an explanation to the Commission in case its opinion is not followed." However, according to the clear wording, the opinion is again not *legally* binding for the national authorities, but they have discretion as to whether they execute it unrevised or not.[61] Moreover, the Regulation does not include any provisions which regulate the legal consequences if the Member State responsible for the screening refuses to consider the concerns of other Member States or the Commission.[62]

---

60   Differently the title of Article 9 of the Proposal mentions "Framework for Commission Screening".

61   Critically also T. Schuelken (n. 22), p. 590. See also J.-C. Gottwald, J. Schild, D. Schmidt (n. 23), p. 146. Differently, J. Brauneck, (n. 44), p. 191 and 194.

62   N. Lavranos, *Some Critical Observations on the EU's Foreign Investment Screening Proposal*, Kluwer Arbitration Blog, 2 January 2018, p. 2, to consult at: http://arbitrationblog.kluwerarbitration.com/2018/01/02/critical-observations-eus-foreign-investment-screening-proposal/.

2.3.3   Access to Legal Remedies

The missing (legal) binding force of the opinion raises the question whether an investor affected by a negative opinion of the Commission has the option to litigate against the opinion of the Commission, besides the legal recourse before the EU Member State's courts. Article 3(5) of the Regulation states that "[f]oreign investors and the undertakings concerned shall have the possibility to seek recourse against screening decisions of the national authorities". If the national authority is implementing the opinion of the Commission due to its obligation to "take utmost account" of it without exercising its own discretion, the investor concerned could attempt to appeal against the Commission's opinion directly rather than to challenge the *implementing act* of the Member State. However, direct judicial redress against an act of the Commission before the CJEU would only be possible pursuant to Article 263(4) TFEU.[63] But since Article 263(1) TFEU provides that the act has to intend to "produce legal effects", recommendations and opinions don't fall within the scope of Article 263(4) TFEU as they have no binding legal force according to Article 288(5) TFEU. As stated above, the opinion under Article 8(2) of the Regulation is indeed not legally binding. Whether a different assessment might be justified in analogy to the jurisprudence of the ECJ regarding the "direct and individual concern" under Article 263(4) TFEU[64] has not yet been decided. Thus, on the basis of the current case-law, the foreign investor has to challenge the implementing act of the national authorities before the Member States' courts, even if these authorities did not exercise their discretion but rather executed the Commission's opinion unaudited. Within the national court proceeding, the investor's legal challenge can nevertheless end up before the CJEU in case the national judge would rely on a preliminary ruling according to Article 267 TFEU. Although the Recommendation is not *legally* binding, it, however, can have a *de facto* binding effect on the national authorities. Hence, if there is no direct legal remedy on the Union level against the Commission's opinion, it seems not far-fetched to consider a violation of the right to an effective legal remedy according to Article 47 of the Charter of Fundamental Rights of the European Union. Since an indirect legal recourse through the Member States' courts is highly time-intensive, the legal protection of foreign investors could effectively be undermined.

---

63   See i.a. M. Pechstein, N. Görlitz, in M. Pechstein, C. Nowak, U. Häde (eds.), Frankfurter Kommentar, 2017, Art. 267 AEUV, para. 1 f.

64   ECJ, case C-386/96 P, *Dreyfus*, ECLI:EU:C:1998:193, para. 44; case C-62/70, *Bock*, ECLI:EU:C: 1971:108, para. 6; case C-11/82, *Piraiki-Patraiki*, ECLI:EU:C:1985:18, para. 8.

2.3.4   Interim Conclusion: Possible Circumvention

For an effective implementation of the EU framework the national screening mechanisms are therefore decisive. This becomes even more manifest by taking account of the cooperative nature of the framework, providing for rather soft obligations and a mere harmonisation of factors relevant within the various screening proceedings. Furthermore, recital 17 emphasises:

> The final decision in relation to any foreign direct investment undergoing screening or any measure taken in relation to a foreign direct investment not undergoing screening remains the sole responsibility of the Member State where the foreign direct investment is planned or completed.

Moreover, the Regulation states in Article 3(6) that "Member States which have a screening mechanism in place shall maintain, amend or adopt measures necessary to identify and prevent circumvention of the screening mechanisms and screening decisions". Therefore, the Member States' screening mechanisms are crucial for achieving the objectives of the Regulation.

2.4   *Interaction with Other Union Instruments*

Foreign investment regularly takes the form of an acquisition of a domestic undertaking or the merger and acquisition of different foreign and domestic entities or the establishment of a joint venture in the host country.[65] Hence, FDI can constitute a concentration in the sense of the EU Merger Regulation (EC) 139/2004.[66] With regard to the interrelation of the two mechanisms, Recital 36 of the Investment Screening Regulation provides that:

> When a foreign direct investment constitutes a concentration falling within the scope of Council Regulation (EC) No 139/2004, the application of this Regulation should be without prejudice to the application of Article 21(4) of Regulation (EC) No 139/2004. This Regulation and Article 21(4) of Regulation (EC) No 139/2004 should be applied in a consistent manner. To the extent that the respective scope of application of those two regulations overlap, the grounds for screening set out in Article 1 of this Regulation and the notion of legitimate interests within the meaning of the third paragraph of Article 21(4) of Regulation (EC) No 139/2004

---

65   European Commission (n. 37), p. 5. On Merger Control and State Aid law see M. Bungenberg, A. Hazarika (n. 28), p. 393.

66   Council Regulation (EC) No 139/2004 of 20 January 2004 on the control of concentrations between undertakings (OJ 2004, L 24).

should be interpreted in a coherent manner, without prejudice to the assessment of the compatibility of the national measures aimed at protecting those interests with the general principles and other provisions of Union law.[67]

It is interesting to note that, in the context of the EU-China trade and investment relations, the Union recently published a joint communication, highlighting, *inter alia,* the necessary steps to establish a level-playing field in trade and investment activities.[68] One key aspect is to strengthen the Union's competitiveness, taking account of an increasingly global procurement market and current challenges of the merger control system.[69] Hence, according to the Union, "it is necessary to identify how the EU could appropriately deal with the distortive effects of foreign state ownership and state financing of foreign companies on the EU internal market".[70] Moreover, the Federation of German Industries (BDI) has published a policy paper on the challenges with regard to the Chinese state-controlled economy, emphasising the demands to amend EU competition and state aid rules, taking account of distortions caused by subsidised or state-owned Chinese enterprises taking over European companies.[71]

Finally, sector-specific review mechanisms in particular concerning security of energy supply are not altered by the Regulation.[72] Therefore, FDI, inter alia in energy supply facilities or network operators, can be scrutinised pursuant to the Gas Directive[73] or the Electricity Directive[74], additionally.

---

67 For a brief procedural comparison with EU competition law, see G. Pandey, D. Rovetta, A. Smiatacz, 'How Many Barriers Should a Steeple Chase Have? Will the EU's Proposed Regulation on Screening of Foreign Direct Investments Add yet More Delaying Barriers When Getting a Merger Deal through the Clearance Gate, and Other Considerations', *Global Trade and Customs Journal* 14 (2019), p. 62–63.

68 European Commission (n. 30).

69 *Ibid,* p. 7.

70 *Ibid,* p. 8 (highlights omitted).

71 BDI Policy Paper China, 'Partner and Systemic Competitor – How Do We Deal with China's State-Controlled Economy?', January 2019, p. 14.

72 On review mechanisms in the energy sector see M. Bungenberg, A. Hazarika (n. 28), p. 384. See also European Commission (n. 37), p. 5.

73 Directive (EC) 2009/73/EC of the European Parliament and of the Council of 13 July 2009 concerning common rules for the internal market in natural gas and repealing Directive 2003/55/EC (OJ 2009, L 211/94).

74 Directive (EC) 2009/72/EC of the European Parliament and of the Council of 13 July 2009 concerning common rules for the internal market in electricity and repealing Directive 2003/54/EC (OJ 2009, L 211/55).

3   EU Member States Screening Mechanisms

According to the EU Commission nearly half of EU Member States have established different forms of screening mechanisms already in place, including Germany, Austria, France, Italy, Spain and the United Kingdom,[75] thus most of the major economies in the EU. However, these existing national mechanisms differ with regard to their scope and procedure. Although most of them do apply to both intra-EU and extra-EU investments, they are partially limited to specific potentially sensitive sectors or establish certain thresholds as regards to the gained influence of the foreign investor in the Union undertaking or the like.[76] Furthermore, the Member States' mechanisms vary concerning the screening procedure, implementing either an ex-ante or ex-post control.[77] As mentioned above, provisions against a circumvention through investments in neighbour EU Member States not having an investment screening mechanisms are decisive for the effectiveness of the Union framework. In particular, northern European Countries such as Sweden, Finland and Denmark traditionally do not foresee broad review mechanisms of FDI.[78]

3.1   *Germany*

In Germany, foreign investments have traditionally been broadly scrutinised pursuant to the Foreign Trade and Payments Act (Außenwirtschaftsgesetz – AWG)[79] and the Foreign Trade and Payments Ordinance (Außenwirtschaftsverordnung – AWV).[80] According to Section 55 of the AWV the "Federal Ministry for Economic Affairs and Energy can investigate whether the acquisition of a domestic company by a non-EU resident or the direct or indirect acquisition within the meaning of Section 56 of a stake in a domestic company by a non-EU resident poses a threat to the public order or security of the Federal Republic of Germany." Sectors that particularly merit a screening procedure are, *inter alia*, critical infrastructure, telecommunications, computing services

---

75   European Commission (n. 17), p. 7. See also M. Swartling, *EU FDI Screening – Legal Consideration*, Report 2017, p. 3.

76   European Commission, *Ibid*, p. 7.

77   *Ibid.* See also M. Bungenberg, A. Hazarika (n. 28), p. 389 f.

78   Kommerskollegium, National Board of Trade Sweden, Department for WTO and Development Cooperation, Reg. no 2019/00331-1, p. 22.

79   An English version of the legislation is available at <http://www.gesetze-im-internet.de/englisch_awg/> accessed 14 January 2018 ['AWG'].

80   An English version of the legislation is available at <https://www.gesetze-im-internet.de/englisch_awv/englisch_awv.html>. On the German system see e.g. *Slobodenjuk*, BB 2019, p. 202; S. Hindelang, T. Hagemeyer (n 28), p. 882 f.

and the media industry. However, the screening mechanism is not limited to those sectors, as long as the non-EU foreign investors acquire a minimum of 25% voting rights of a national company, according to Section 56 subsection 1 no 2 of the AWV.[81] If the company is operating in a sensitive sector in the sense of Section 55 subsection 1 sentence 2, the screening is triggered by an acquisition of only 10% voting rights pursuant to Section 56 subsection 1 no 1. Amendments to the AWV in July 2017[82] and December 2018[83], therefore, provide greater powers to the government to scrutinise investments in critical areas and increase the review period from two to four months.[84] Moreover, the Ministry can scrutinise also "indirect" investments by foreign companies through the establishment of an EU company. Section 55 subsection 2 sentence 1 provides that "[a]cquisitions by EU residents shall also be subjected to an investigation pursuant to subsection 1 if there are indications that an abusive approach or a transaction circumventing the law has been undertaken". Anti-Circumvention provisions are, indeed, vital due to the missing obligation to adopt screening mechanisms according to Article 3(1) of the EU Regulation, as pointed out above. In a last amendment of July 2020 the revision of the Foreign Trade and Payments Act[85] foresees that screening will depend on whether an acquisition results in a "likely impairment" of public order or security. In addition to the effects of an acquisition in Germany, the screening will also focus more on effects on other EU Member States and on EU programmes and projects.

In practice, the German government has already intervened with regard to two major investments (i.e. a EUR 670 million bid for Chipmaker Aixtron SE,[86] and a EUR 400 million bid for lighting products maker Osram).[87] Also,

---

81   T. Jost, 'Sovereign Wealth Funds and the German Policy Reaction', in K. Sauvant, L. Sachs, W. Schmit Jongbloed (eds.), *Sovereign Investment – Concerns and Policy Reactions* (OUP, 2012), p. 458; M. Niestedt, D. Ziegenhahn, 'Germany', in O. Borgers (ed.), *Foreign Investment Review* 2014 (Getting the Deal Through, 2014), p. 36–37.

82   Neunte Verordnung zur Änderung der Außenwirtschaftsverordnung, 12 July 2017. Available at <http://dip21.bundestag.de/dip21/btd/18/134/1813417.pdf>.

83   Zwölfte Verordnung zur Änderung der Außenwirtschaftsverordnung (Twelfth Regulation Amending the Foreign Trade Regulation), BAnz AT 28.12.2018 V1.

84   §59 Abs. 1 AWV.

85   Erstes Gesetz zur Änderung des Außenwirtschaftsgesetzes und anderer Gesetze, 10.07.2020 - Bundesgesetzblatt Teil I 2020 Nr. 35 16.07.2020 S. 1637

86   J. Hemmings, A. Manzoor, 'Putting Security into Prime Minister May's New Industrial Strategy', *RUSI Newsbrief*, 37 (1) (2017), p. 1.

87   L. Hsu, 'The Role and Future of Sovereign Wealth Funds: A Trade and Investment Perspective', *Wake Forest Law Review* 52 (2017), p. 843. The deal for OSRAM was completed in March 2017.

the recent failure of the Chinese State Grid Corporation to acquire a stake in German Transmission Services Operator – '50Hertz' has been attributed to an intervention of the German government.[88] However, out of 1.313 completed procedures in 2018, the German *Bundeskartellamt* rendered not one negative decision with regard to merger control.[89] With regard to the investment screening according to section 55 of the AWV, the Federal Ministry for Economic Affairs and Energy (BMWi) in 2016 and 2017 has not rendered a negative decision pursuant to section 59 of the AWV due to security concerns.[90] However, several authorisations were granted subject to conditions or after the conclusion of a contract between the foreign investor and the BMWi.[91]

3.2   *Austria*

In Austria, Section 25a of the Foreign Trade Act (*Außenwirtschaftsgesetz 2011*)[92] provides for an *ex-ante* screening of FDI on grounds of public security and order. Thus, in potentially sensitive sectors such as, inter alia, defence, energy supply and telecommunication (Section 25a subsection 3 of the Act) the acquisition of more than 25 per cent of the voting rights of an Austrian company needs an authorisation pursuant to Section 25a subsection 2 and 4 of the Act if the investment is originating from a third country outside the EU, the European Economic Area or Switzerland.[93] However, also intra-EU investments are subject to scrutiny if there is a well-founded concern that the operation is intended to circumvent the authorisation requirement, according to Section 25a subsection 11 lit. 2 of the Act. As under German law, Austria therefore also has a special provision to prevent circumvention of the screening mechanism through an indirect investment in another EU Member State.

---

88   China's State Grid Unable to Buy Stake in 50Hertz, a German Electricity Network, *Chinascope* (2018) < http://chinascope.org/archives/14719>.

89   Das Bundeskartellamt, Jahresbericht 2018 (Annual Report), May 2019, p. 23.

90   Kleine Anfrage mehrerer Abgeordneter der Fraktion Bündnis 90/Die Grünen, 27 February 2018, p. 10 (Question No. 12).

91   Kleine Anfrage mehrerer Abgeordneter der Fraktion Bündnis 90/Die Grünen, 27 February 2018, p. 10 (Question No. 12).

92   Gesamte Rechtsvorschrift für Außenwirtschaftsgesetz 2011, consolidated version of 4 July 2019, available under https://www.ris.bka.gv.at/GeltendeFassung. wxe?Abfrage=Bundesnormen&Gesetzesnummer=20007221.

93   Section 25a subsection 2 lit. 3 of the Act.

3.3   *France*

France has also modified its legislation to screen foreign investments[94], presumably as a 'reaction' to General Electric's (GE) bid for Alstom in 2014.[95] The French Monetary and Financial Code (*Code monétaire et financier*) allows the review of FDI in certain sectors. The screening procedure differs between non-EU and EU investments and with regard to the sector of the acquired company as well as the degree of the gained control.[96]

In practice, the French Government recently acted to block the acquisition of French engineering company Alstom by General Electric, citing national security concerns.[97] The investment was completed after prolonged deliberations with the French government.[98] However, the scope of the national security defence remains vague. In accordance with the new regulations, which were introduced through Decree No. 2014–479 dated 14 May 2014, investments in sectors such as energy, transport, water, public health and telecommunications will now require prior authorisation from the French Minister of Economy, introducing an ex-ante screening.[99] Interestingly, unlike the German amendments, the French regulations also cover all investors from within the EU.[100] Therefore, circumvention through an acquisition of a company in EU Member States not having a national screening mechanism can be prevented under the French system, as well.

3.4   *Northern European Countries*

As stated above, northern European countries traditionally do not have a general screening for FDI. In Sweden a new Protective Security Act[101] entered into

---

94   J. Seaman, 'Chinese Investment in France: An Openly Cautious Welcome', in J. Seaman, M. Huotari, M. Otero-Iglesias (eds.) *Chinese Investment in Europe A Country-Level Approach*, (ifri, 2017), p. 60.

95   N. Petit, 'State Created Barriers to Exit: The Example of the Acquisition of Alstom by General Electric', *Competition Policy International* 11 (2015), p. 98.

96   See Mannheimer Swartling (n 75), p. 3.

97   N. Petit (n. 94), p. 100.

98   N. Petit (n. 94), p. 98.

99   Décret n° 2014–479 du 14 mai 2014 relatif aux investissements étrangers soumis à autorisation préalable.

100   The new regulations prescribe that prior authorisation has to be taken in the following three scenarios: a transaction where a non-EU investor acquires control or acquires all or part of a business or acquires 33,33% shareholding of a Company whose registered office is located in France; a transaction where an EU investor acquires control or acquires all or part of a business of a Company whose registered office is located in France; and a transaction where a French investor under foreign control acquires all or part of a business of a Company whose registered office is located in France.

101   Protective Security Act (1996:627) – *Säkerhetsskyddslagen*.

force on 1 April 2019, protecting sensitive information of security interest to Sweden.[102] However, the Act does not implement a review mechanism for FDI, since an acquisition potentially concerning sensitive information only has to be reported to the Swedish government and no approval is required.[103] Also, in Denmark there are solely rules governing the access to sensitive information, but no screening or review procedure regarding the market access of FDI.[104] In contrast, Finland does monitor acquisitions in certain sectors according to an Act on the Monitoring of Foreign Corporate Acquisitions of 2012.[105] Hence, foreign acquisitions in the defence and dual-use sectors require an approval by the State pursuant to Section 4 and Section 1 subsection 4 of the Act, whereas some acquisitions in other sectors have to be notified.[106] However, with regard to acquisitions outside of the defence sector, only investments not originating from the EU or the EFTA fall under the monitoring procedure, according to Section 1 Subsection 5 of the Act. Therefore, the Finish system does not prevent the potential circumvention of the EU Regulation through an investment in other EU Member States as long as the FDI does not affect the defence sector.

In general, the northern European countries do not review FDI with regard to security concerns on a broad basis, but rather only foresee sectoral-specific notification or (restrictively) approval requirements.[107]

4   Excursus: Investment Screening in the US and China

As mentioned above, increasing concerns with regard to FDI, in particular through state-owned entities or indirectly controlled undertakings, are not a European phenomenon, but lead to the adoption of review mechanisms or amendments worldwide.

4.1   *Investment Screening in the United States*
As for the United States, FDI traditionally has been scrutinised pursuant to the rules on the Committee on Foreign Investment in the United States (CFIUS).[108]

---

102   See Kommerskollegium (n. 78), p. 16.
103   Kommerskollegium (n. 78), p. 17.
104   Kommerskollegium (n. 78), p. 21.
105   Act *Lag om tillsyn över utlänningars företagsköp* 13 April 2012 (172/2012).
106   Kommerskollegium (n. 78), p. 7.
107   Kommerskollegium (n. 78), p. 22.
108   Regulations Pertaining to Mergers, Acquisitions, and Takeovers by Foreign Persons, Federal Register Vol. 73 No. 226 of 21 November 2008. On the CFIUS and its impact on mergers and acquisitions, see also J. Bellinger, N. Townsend, 'Inside 'the CFIUS': US

However, due to concerns over the risk caused by strategic FDI primarily by Chinese entities,[109] the CFIUS recently has been amended by the *Foreign Investment Risk Review Modernization Act (FIRRMA) of 2018*.[110] Although the main pillars of the CFIUS remain untouched,[111] FIRRMA increases the timeframes for investigations and broadens the scope of the review, *inter alia,* to any also non-controlling FDI in those US undertakings involved in critical technology or critical infrastructure.[112] Moreover, irrespective of the sector, foreign investments in which a foreign government has a substantial interest are subject to review under CFIUS.[113] In practice, also prior to the adoption of FIRRMA, the President has blocked six FDI transactions using CFIUS since its implementation in 1975, out of which five decisions were rendered since 2012, affecting four Chinese and one Singapore investor.[114] In general, CFIUS legally allows discrimination among foreign investors, although there are not specific provisions on certain countries of origin.[115] However, the political debate during the reform process was strongly influenced by a potential threat for national security through Chinese state-owned or state-controlled investors.[116] Thus, the parallels to the European debate are, indeed, obvious.

4.2   *The Chinese Foreign Investment Law*

Since its opening up and economic reform, China has grown up to a leading country of foreign investment import and export. Yet, up to the present, China has no specialized law on foreign investment screening. The major rules in this regard scatter in a number of national laws, regulations and rules, which were mostly adopted since the new millennium.[117]

National Security Review of Foreign Investments', *Global Trade and Customs Journal* 6 (2011), p. 1 f. Specifically with regard to Chinese investment, see P. Griffin, 'CFIUS in the Age of Chinese Investment', *Fordham Law Review* 85 (2017), p. 419 f.

109   Congressional Research Service, CFIUS Reform: Foreign Investment National Security Reviews, 2 May 2019, p. 1.

110   To consult at https://home.treasury.gov/sites/default/files/2018-08/The-Foreign-Investment-Risk-Review-Modernization-Act-of-2018-FIRRMA_o.pdf.

111   See on the criteria applicable e.g. S. Anwar, 'CFIUS, Chinese MNCs' Outward FDI, and Globalization of Business', *Journal of World Trade* 44 (2010), p. 434.

112   Congressional Research Service (n. 108), p. 1.

113   Congressional Research Service (n. 108), p. 1: Griffin (n 107), p. 1777–1778.

114   Congressional Research Service (n. 108), p. 1. For an overview on proceedings involving Chinese enterprises between 2002 and 2009 see S. Anwar (n. 108), p. 439–440.

115   Congressional Research Service (n. 108), p. 1.

116   P. Griffin (n. 107), p. 1787 and 1768 f.

117   This Section on the Chinese Foreign Investment law was written by Prof. Maniao CHI, Professor & Founding Director, Center of International Economic Law and Policy, University of International Business and Economics, Beijing, 100029, P.R.China.

China's investment screening has three major aspects: sectoral review, anti-monopoly review and national security review. Sectoral review is mainly based on the Catalogue of Industries for Guiding Foreign Investment ("Catalogue"),[118] jointly issued by the Ministry of Commerce (MOFCOM) and the National Development and Reform Commission (NDRC) of China. The Catalogue is updated every few years to keep pace with the need of China's industrial development. Before 2016, the Catalogue impliedly divided industries into four types, in which foreign investments are encouraged, restricted, prohibited or allowed. Yet, since 2016, China has adopted a new mode of foreign investment regulation based on "negative list", after a few years of experiment in some pilot free trade areas. Under the new regulation mode, if an industry is not listed on the negative list, it shall be allowed for foreign investment access.

National security review and anti-monopoly review of FDI are conducted concurrently by the same government body, as implied in the Anti-Monopoly Law of China and some ministerial rules and decrees.[119] At central level, a joint committee established by the Ministry of Commerce of China (MOFCOM) and the National Development and Reform Commission (NDRC) is responsible for the two reviews. While it is clear that anti-monopoly review aims at ascertaining whether and to what extent the access of an FDI will harm Chinese industry, the exact criteria for the review is not clarified sufficiently in these laws and rules. Similarly, national security review aims at assessing the potential impact of an FDI on China's national defense, national economic development, basic social order and research and development of key technologies. Due largely to the vagueness of the criteria and the non-transparent mode of review, the predictability of national security review is kept at a low level.

In March 2018, the Foreign Investment Law of China was adopted.[120] This law clearly requires national security review.[121] Hailed as a major legal development in China, this law provides no implementing rules of national security review. Unless the implementation rules of this law, which is likely to be issued

---

118   Available at http://www.fdi.gov.cn/1800000121_39_4851_0_7.html.
119   Article 31, Anti-Monopoly Law of China (Where a foreign investor merges and acquires a domestic enterprise or participate in concentration by other means, if state security is involved, besides the review on the concentration in accordance with this Law, the review on national security shall also be conducted in accordance with the relevant State provisions.), available at http://www.lawinfochina.com/display.aspx?lib=law&id=0&CGid=96789.
120   Available at http://en.pkulaw.cn/display.aspx?cgid=6a88714068b3724dbdfb&lib=law.
121   Article 35, Foreign Investment Regulation Law of China (The State establishes a system of security review for foreign investment to review the foreign investment that affects or may affect national security).

next year, incorporate concrete rules of national security review, the defects of national security review in China are unlikely to be cured.

5   Conclusion

The access of foreign investments into the internal market of the European Union is a highly sensitive and, thus, a politically-charged issue, as it is affecting the potential interference of foreign investors in those sectors which are crucial for the public security and public order, such as energy supply, military or high-tech industries. Therefore, a framework at the Union level, which enables a consistent and predictable screening of investments, which might compromise the above mentioned public interests, seems essential. The EU Regulation is addressing this issue by introducing an enabling framework which sets out basic requirements and installs cooperation mechanisms, especially the possibility for the Commission to render an opinion, if the Member States' public security and public order or the Union's interest might be affected.

However, regarding the effectiveness of the screening framework, doubts rise out of the missing binding legal force of the Commission's opinion.[122] Furthermore, there is no obligation to establish national screening mechanisms, which are indeed crucial for the efficiency of the Union framework. Therefore, the potential circumvention of the framework through strategic investments in those Member States not having a national screening mechanism is a valid risk. Although some Member States do foresee broad review procedures also scrutinising FDI from within the EU, such as France, others only provide for a screening if there is a well-founded concern that an FDI is supposed to circumvent the national review procedure, such as Germany and Austria. However, other Member States like, *inter alia*, Finland and Sweden do not have a broad screening mechanism, but only foresee sectoral-specific notification or approval requirements. In sum, future circumvention of the EU screening framework therefore cannot be excluded.

Since a broad competence for the CCP was conferred upon the Union through the Lisbon Treaty, a comprehensive investment screening mechanism on the Union level, indeed, would have been legally feasible, and remains open for further discussion in the future.

---

122   See also T. Schuelken (n. 22), p. 590. For a more optimistic view, see V. Günther (n. 48), p. 17 f.

PART 3

The Scope of the EU's Free Trade Agreements

∴

CHAPTER 7

Trade and Sustainable Development Post-Lisbon

Barbara Cooreman and Geert van Calster

1   Introduction

Trade and sustainable development have increasingly received attention, particularly following the debates on TTIP and CETA.[1] The core of the debate,
however, is not new. Free trade can have detrimental consequences for labour
and environmental conditions, often in developing countries. However, the
general assumption is that trade also plays a positive role, contributing to enhanced protection of the environment and of labour conditions. Trade, it is
argued, contributes positively to sustainable development by increasing real
income and standards of living, allowing countries to allocate more resources
to e.g. environmental protection. It is often heard that liberalisation can lead
to a "race to the bottom" as countries and companies are tempted to engage
in social and eco-dumping to become more attractive. Conversely, however,
the global value chains resulting from trade may also lead to higher standards
when powerful states promote a regulatory "race to the top".[2]

Arguably the best option to achieve global environmental and social progress is to adopt appropriate corrective policies. Trade is neither the only nor
the ideal tool to achieve environmental or social progress, but it can definitely
serve as a tool in a larger toolkit that includes binding international environmental agreements and labour laws. Powerful markets, and hence powerful
trading partners, such as the EU or the US have the capacity and arguably also
the responsibility to use that power to encourage positive change. Complying
with the rules of an attractive market is the price of trading with that market.[3]
Preferential access to such a market (positive approach) or restricted access
(negative approach) can have a strong, at times even coercive, effect on producers and exporters. It is worth noting in this context that higher sustainability

---

1   Sustainable development under EU trade law comprises three pillars: economic, environmental and social – the latter including both labour standards and respect for human rights.
2   D. Vogel, *Trading up: Consumer and environmental regulation in a global economy* (Harvard
University Press, 1997), 248 ff.
3   A. Bradford, 'The Brussels Effect', 107 *Northwestern University Law Review* 1 (2012); D. S. Grewal, *Network Power: The social dynamics of globalization* (Yale University Press, 2008).

standards do not only bring benefits to the local population in the developing country (such as better working conditions) or the global population (such as better environmental protection). They also create more of a level playing field with producers that already adhere to higher standards. Trade and Sustainable Development (TSD) standards viewed from this angle aim to abolish unfair or unethical competition from producers that employ for instance exploitative labour practices.

Since the Lisbon Treaty, the EU is formally committed to promoting environmental and social rights protection globally through Articles 3(5) and 21(2) TEU.[4] Furthermore, Article 11 TFEU prescribes an environmental integration requirement in other EU polices with a view to promoting sustainable development. While this requirement is important with regard to internal policy, it is also being applied externally, such as in trade agreements with third countries.[5] The EU has increasingly sought to assert itself as a prominent player in global environmental governance by gradually expanding its environmental policy from an internal policy to one with a marked external dimension. This is also an inevitable consequence of the aforementioned global value chains. If and when products and services exceed borders from the design to the final consumption stage, it is inevitable that their regulation implies external elements.

The increasingly elaborate and detailed TSD chapters in trade agreements are the flagship of the EU's commitments, as also emphasised in the 2015 "Trade for all" strategy.[6] However, it is not because current trade agreements are more

---

4   Article 3(5) TEU reads "In its relations with the wider world, the Union shall uphold and promote its values and interests and contribute to the protection of its citizens. It shall contribute to peace, security, *the sustainable development of the Earth*, solidarity and mutual respect among peoples, *free and fair trade*, eradication of poverty and the protection of human rights, in particular the rights of the child, as well as to the strict observance and the development of international law, including respect for the principles of the United Nations Charter" (emphasis added). Article 21(2) TEU reads "The Union shall define and pursue common policies and actions, and shall work for a high degree of cooperation in all fields of international relations, in order to: (d) foster the sustainable economic, social and environmental development of developing countries, with the primary aim of eradicating poverty; (f) help develop international measures to preserve and improve the quality of the environment and the sustainable management of global natural resources, in order to ensure sustainable development".

5   See for a study on this, G. Marin Duran, E. Morgera, *Environmental Integration in the EUs External Relations: Beyond Multilateral Dimensions* (Hart Publishing, 2012).

6   Stating that "the EU has been leading in integrating sustainable development objectives into trade policy and making trade an effective tool to promote sustainable development worldwide" (European Commission, 'Trade for all: Towards a more responsible trade and investment policy', 2015, p. 22).

explicit in their sustainable development objectives, that pre-Lisbon trade agreements or trade relations did not include those. Equally, neither does it automatically mean that recent actions have become more effective. TSD chapters have been subject to much criticism because of their perceived lack of effectiveness, both among EU institutional players and civil society.

The current chapter will take a closer look at the evolution of sustainable development provisions/chapters in the recent history of EU trade agreements, both going back to the roots as looking at recent developments. After giving a factual overview, the challenges of effective trade and sustainable development policy will be addressed. The chapter will conclude with an outlook and possible policy recommendations for the next decade of the Common Commercial Policy.

2   Sustainable Development Provisions in FTAS

2.1   *The Roots of Sustainable Development Provisions*
The linking of trade and sustainable development is not new. International core labour standards were for the first time explicitly linked to international trade in the Havana Declaration of 1948. The trade-environment relationship has been embedded in the GATT 1947, the predecessor to the current WTO agreements in the post-war global trading system. Article XX GATT 1947 included exceptions to the substantive GATT obligations, allowing Members to adopt measures "necessary to protect human, animal or plant life"[7] or "relating to the conservation of exhaustible natural resources".[8] Trade concerns also found their way into multilateral environmental agreements (MEAs) starting from the mid '70s, such as the 1975 CITES[9] (mandating a system of trade bans and restrictions on trade in endangered species), the 1987 Montreal Protocol[10] (trade restrictions for ozone-depleting substances) and the 1989 Basel Convention[11] (on hazardous wastes).[12]

---

7   Article XX (b) of GATT.
8   Article XX (g) of GATT.
9   Convention on International Trade in Endangered Species of Wild Fauna and Flora, 993 UNTS 243, 1973.
10   Montreal Protocol on Substances that Deplete the Ozone Layer, 1522 UNTS 3, 1987.
11   Basel Convention on the Control of Transboundary Movements of Hazardous Wastes and Their Disposal, 1673 UNTS 126; 28 ILM 657, 1989.
12   As different subsystems under international law, there is no hierarchy in norms between trade law and environmental law. Within the WTO dispute settlement, jurisdiction is limited to the WTO Agreements, but MEAs can serve as interpretative means to the

The beginning of the '90s was an important mark for the trade-environment debate. In 1992, the UN convened a landmark conference in Rio de Janeiro, the United Nations Conference on Environment and Development (UNCED, known as the '92 Rio Earth Summit), to set the tone and ambitions for global policy on development and environment. Leaders in Rio recognised the substantive links between international trade and environment by agreeing to strive for mutually supportive policies in favour of sustainable development.[13] It was acknowledged that international trade is a key component of sustainable development, through a more efficient allocation of scarce resources and easier access for countries to, for instance, environmental goods and technologies.[14] While Article XX GATT explicitly embedded an environmental element to trade policy, a similar social clause on human rights and labour rights was never introduced (apart from prison labour), despite regular calls for it and despite similar social clauses that can be found in regional, bilateral or unilateral initiatives such as the EU treaties, the EU Generalised System of Preferences, and EU trade agreements.

2.2   *Sustainable Development Conditionality in the E U GSP*

With regard to the EU's GSP, social and environmental clauses were added as a special incentive arrangement in 1998,[15] and further defined in the 2002–2004 GSP.[16] The aim of the clauses was to assist beneficiary countries in sustaining and improving their environmental and social standards, and to enable the EU to grant additional preferences to countries that respect minimum standards, such as the ILO labour conventions. In 2005, as a result of a dispute at the WTO brought by India concerning the EC's special arrangements to combat drug production and trafficking,[17] GSP+ arrangements for sustainable development

---

    Agreements (and in particular to Article XX GATT), as was held by the AB in *US-Gasoline*, referring to Article 3.2 DSU.

13 Rio Declaration on Environment and Development 1992, A/CONF.151/26 (Vol. I). See in particular principle 12 stating that "States should cooperate to promote a supportive and open international economic system that would lead to economic growth and sustainable development in all countries, to better address the problems of environmental degradation. Trade policy measures for environmental purposes should not constitute a means of arbitrary or unjustifiable discrimination or a disguised restriction on international trade. Unilateral actions to deal with environmental challenges outside the jurisdiction of the importing country should be avoided. Environmental measures addressing transboundary or global environmental problems should, as far as possible, be based on an international consensus".

14 WTO, *Harnessing Trade for Sustainable Development and a Green Economy* (2011), p. 1.

15 Council Regulation (EC) No 2820/98 of 21 December 1998.

16 Council Regulation (EC) No 2501/2001 of 10 December 2001.

17 Panel, *EC – Conditions for the Granting of Tariff Preferences to Developing Countries*, DS246.

and good governance were introduced, bringing under one heading the social and environmental clauses. In order to be eligible for GSP+, "vulnerable" countries must have ratified and implemented 16 UN/ILO core human and labour rights conventions, and at least 7 of 11 international conventions related to environmental and governance principles.[18] As of 2014, developing countries need to have ratified all 27 listed conventions to qualify for GSP+.[19] However, the 2005 GSP Regulation provided for a derogation in case of "specific constitutional constraints" where a "formal commitment to sign, ratify and implement any missing Convention" has been made. Only 14 developing countries applied for GSP+ treatment at the time, and currently there are 9 beneficiaries.[20] GSP+ status was lifted for Sri Lanka in 2010, but the country regained it in 2017.

In 2001, a third category of trade preferences for least-developed countries was introduced by the EU: the "Everything but Arms" status is being granted to countries when listed by the UN as LDC. While in principle unconditional, EBA preferences can be withdrawn in case of some exceptional circumstances, notably in case of serious and systematic violation of principles laid down in fundamental human rights and labour rights conventions.[21] This happened to Myanmar in 1997 (reinstated in 2013), and in October 2018 the European Commission announced it would start withdrawal procedures for Cambodia and again for Myanmar.[22] EBA status for Cambodia was withdrawn in August 2020, while formal procedures against Myanmar have yet to be started. The withdrawal procedure is a measure of last resort, when intensive dialogues fail to produce results.[23]

In 2017, the Commission evaluated the functioning and the impact of the revised GSP. Whereas positive economic impact could already be witnessed, as well as an overall positive impact on social development and human rights, the Interim Report indicates only a limited impact on sustainable development and environmental protection. The latter is difficult to determine due to a lack

---

18   Council Regulation (EC) No 980/2005 of 27 June 2005.

19   Regulation (EU) No 978/2012 of the European Parliament and the European Council of 25 October 2012.

20   In 2018, the GSP+ beneficiaries are Cape Verde, Armenia, Kyrgyzstan, Mongolia, Pakistan, Philippines, Sri Lanka, Bolivia and Paraguay. Sri Lanka re-entered GSP+ in May 2017, after having been removed in 2010. Classified for three consecutive years by the World Bank as an upper middle income country, Paraguay left GSP+ on 1 January 2019. Countries lose their GSP status when entering an FTA with the EU.

21   Regulation (EU) No 978/2012, Article 19.

22   Commission Implementing Decision of 11 February 2019, OJ [2019] C55/11 (Cambodia).

23   European Commission, 'Report on the Generalised Scheme of Preferences covering the period 2016–2017', COM (2018) 36 final, 16 January 2018.

of availability of environmental indicators and data over time. It is noted in the
EC report that the "GSP should be considered as a facilitator, because the nature and the extent of the positive impact is critically co-determined by the domestic priorities of the beneficiary countries as reflected in the human rights,
socio-economic and environmental policies adopted and implemented".[24]

2.3   *Sustainable Development Chapters in FTAs*

With regard to its bilateral free trade agreements, the EU has included social
clauses (human rights clauses) in all its agreements since 1995. All EU trade
agreements since EU-CARIFORUM in 2008 contain provisions on trade and
sustainable development, and the new generation of EU trade agreements,
launched by the "Global Europe" Strategy,[25] of which EU-Korea was the first
agreement in 2011, include a separate trade and sustainable development
chapter with more legal detail concerning elements such as civil society involvement. In contrast to the earlier agreements that only contained an agreement on trade, the new generation of agreements (since the EU-Korea FTA)
contain both a free trade agreement and a political framework agreement.
The framework agreements reiterate the political objectives of sustainable development for both parties.[26] Post-Lisbon, TSD chapters are pursued next to
the investment chapters, allowing the latter to be read in light of the former.[27]
Since trade and investment are split into separate agreements following the
ECJ's Opinion 2/15 in May 2017, the preamble to the investment agreements explicitly refer to the TSD provisions and commitments. In its Opinion 2/15, upon
questions put forward by the European Commission on competence and legal
basis, the ECJ found that the TSD provisions in the EU-Singapore agreement
formed an essential part of the agreement, did not require a separate legal basis and thus fell within the competence of the EU under the CCP.[28] TSD clauses

---

24   European Commission, 'Mid-Term Evaluation of the EU's Generalised Scheme of
      Preferences (GSP): Final Interim Report', 21 September 2017.
25   Communication from the European Commission COM(2006) 567, 'Global Europe
      competing in the world': https://eur-lex.europa.eu/legal-content/EN/TXT/HTML/
      ?uri=LEGISSUM:r11022&from=EN.
26   See e.g. Title V of the EU-Korea Framework Agreement.
27   See F. Hoffmeister, 'The Contribution of EU Trade Agreements to the Development of
      International Investment Law', in S. Hindelang, M. Krajewski (eds.), *Shifting Paradigms in
      International Investment Law* (OUP, 2016), p. 357–376.
28   For a discussion of competences for TSD chapters, see M. Cremona, 'Shaping EU Trade
      Policy post-Lisbon: Opinion 2/15 of 16 May 2017', *European Constitutional Law Review*
      14:1 (2018), p. 231–259; See also the contributions of M. Cremona and A. Rosas in this vol-
      ume on Opinion 2/15.

do preserve the right, however, of the parties to set their own standards in conformity with their international obligations and in accordance with their own internal legislative procedure.[29]

By including TSD provisions in FTAs, the EU seeks to "maximise the leverage of increased trade and investment on issues like decent work, environmental protection, or the fight against climate change in order to achieve effective and sustainable policy change".[30] Depending on the partner country, the objective of the TSD chapter may differ. With developed countries as trading partners that have similar levels of environmental protection and labour standards, the provisions serve to ensure that trade and investment liberalisation does not lead to a deterioration of environmental and labour conditions. In the case of developing countries the chapter may serve as an incentive to commit to and fully engage in the protection of environmental and labour standards.

TSD chapters have a common core, with possible additions that are specific to the partner country. In general, such a chapter contains provisions on core multilateral labour standards and ILO Conventions, common commitments to multilateral environmental conventions, climate change, and sustainable management of natural resources. The following example of the EU-Korea FTA may serve as an illustration:

> ... each Party shall seek to ensure that [...] laws and policies provide for and encourage high levels of environmental and labour protection, consistent with the internationally recognized standards or agreements referred to in Articles 13.4 and 13.5 [...].[31]
>
> The Parties [...] commit to respecting, promoting and realising, in their laws and practices, the principles concerning the fundamental rights, namely: (a) freedom of association and the effective recognition of the right to collective bargaining; (b) the elimination of all forms of forced or compulsory labour; (c) the effective abolition of child labour; and (d) the elimination of discrimination in respect of employment and occupation. The Parties reaffirm the commitment to effectively implementing the ILO Conventions that Korea and the Member States of the European Union have ratified respectively.[32]

---

29   ECJ, 'Free Trade Agreement with Singapore', Opinion 2/15 (2017), para. 165.
30   Non paper of the Commission services, 'Feedback and way forward on improving the implementation and enforcement of Trade and Sustainable Development chapters in EU Free Trade Agreements', 26 February 2018 (EC non-paper on trade and sustainable development), p. 1.
31   See Article 13.3 EU-Korea FTA.
32   See Article 13.4 EU-Korea FTA.

The chapter then proceeds with respect to multilateral environmental agreements as follows:

2. [...] The Parties reaffirm their commitments to the effective implementation in their laws and practices of the multilateral environmental agreements to which they are party.

3. The Parties reaffirm their commitment to reaching the ultimate objective of the United Nations Framework Convention on Climate Change and its Kyoto Protocol. They commit to cooperating on the development of the future international climate change framework in accordance with the Bali Action Plan.[33]

The EU-Korea FTA also states the parties' intention to facilitate and promote trade in environmental goods and services:

> The Parties shall strive to facilitate and promote trade and foreign direct investment in environmental goods and services, including environmental technologies, sustainable renewable energy, energy efficient products and services and eco-labelled goods, including through addressing related non-tariff barriers. The Parties shall strive to facilitate and promote trade in goods that contribute to sustainable development, including goods that are the subject of schemes such as fair and ethical trade and those involving corporate social responsibility and accountability.[34]

TSD chapters can include provisions on specific local challenges, such as for instance biodiversity loss caused by deforestation and intensification of agriculture. A typical example would be a provision on palm oil production in countries such as Malaysia or Indonesia. The EU-Singapore FTA has been branded as the EU's first "green" FTA, containing specific terms on the liberalisation of environmental services such as waste removal and rules on illegal fishing and logging.[35]

TSD chapters also contain provisions on upholding levels of domestic legislation and establish a monitoring mechanism, building on public scrutiny through involvement of civil society. While the objectives are set out, the parties to FTAs are free to regulate according to their own collective preferences. Harmonisation of social and environmental provisions with parties to trade agreements is not the aim, rather progressing through dialogue and

---

33   See Article 13.5 EU-Korea FTA.
34   See Article 13.6 EU-Korea FTA.
35   See Article 12.7, 12.8 EU-Singapore FTA. See also the draft Articles 15.7 and 15.8 in the EU-Vietnam FTA.

cooperation to make economic and trade-related endeavours sustainable in the long term:

> The Parties recognise that it is not their intention in this Chapter to harmonise the labour or environment standards of the Parties, but to strengthen their trade relations and cooperation in ways that promote sustainable development [...].[36]

TSD chapters are often associated with developing countries. However, as the above examples of Korea and Singapore have shown, these chapters are equally relevant to developed countries with regard to upholding high standards, both in the partner country and in the EU. The strong protests against the EU-US Transatlantic Trade and Investment Partnership (TTIP) and the "Wallonia-debacle" with the Canada-EU Comprehensive Economic and Trade Agreement (CETA) have shown growing concerns about the policy space for sustainability standards within the EU and the fear that such trade agreements may lead to lower standards. CETA contains three chapters (22–24) on trade-related sustainability provisions, including labour and environmental considerations. Chapter 22 of CETA concerns trade and sustainable development and serves as a framework chapter establishing institutional rules for the subsequent two chapters dealing with trade and labour (Chapter 23) and trade and environment (Chapter 24). The objective of the chapter is stated in Article 22.1, which stipulates:

> The Parties recognise that economic development, social development and environmental protection are interdependent and mutually reinforcing components of sustainable development, and reaffirm their commitment to promoting the development of international trade in such a way as to contribute to the objective of sustainable development, for the welfare of present and future generations.

The parties make the commitment "to review, monitor and assess the impact of the implementation of this Agreement on sustainable development" in their territories, and additionally they may carry out joint assessments (Article 22.3(3)). Furthermore, the agreement establishes the Committee on Trade and Sustainable Development (CTSD), an intergovernmental body made up of high level officials of the parties. The CTSD is to meet on an *ad hoc* basis and

---

36   See e.g. Article 13.1(3) EU-Korea FTA.

monitor the implementation of Chapters 22 to 24 and the review of the impact of the agreement on sustainable development (Article 22.4). Chapters 23 and 24 furthermore contain provisions on regulatory dialogue and on the parties' rights to regulate.[37]

The right to regulate includes the right of the parties to set their own priorities and modify and adapt their legislation. With regard to the potential lowering of standards, the right to regulate is limited in a twofold fashion: First, parties must not modify their laws in ways inconsistent with their international commitments including those of CETA. Second, CETA incorporates two articles (Article 23.4 for labour and Article 24.5 for environment) on 'Upholding levels of protection' that introduce an obligation

> not [to] waive or otherwise derogate from, or offer to waive or otherwise derogate from, its labour law and standards [environmental law], to encourage trade or the establishment, acquisition, expansion or retention of an investment in its territory.

In previous agreements, such as the EU-Cariforum EPA, the obligation to uphold the level of protection was put forward as a recommendation and not as an obligation.[38] The "level of protection" referred to in these titles are the levels as set by the respective parties to the agreement. In other words there is no ambition to agree to a common level.

3   Impact, Effective Implementation and Enforcement

Sustainability provisions do not have as their primary objective the liberalisation of trade, and do not follow the same logic as the pertinent core provisions. The provisions are not written in the same strict, detailed and binding manner as economic provisions, and monitoring their implementation and compliance is not as straight-forward and requires a different approach.[39] Also, one needs to be aware that trade policy is not and cannot be the best method to deal with labour market imperfections (such as child labour or discrimination of workers) or environmental distortions (such as polluting production or illegal logging) – the best method is to adopt appropriate corrective labour market

---

37   See Article 23.3 and 24.3 CETA.
38   See Article 193 EU-Cariforum EPA.
39   Kommerskollegium, 'Implementation and Enforcement of sustainable development provision in free trade agreements – options for improvement', 2016 (Kommerskollegium), p. 3.

or environmental policies.[40] However, trade policy can be a second-best where the first option is not available, in particular when higher standards are set than would otherwise be applicable. The bigger the market, the more powerful that standard-setting will be.[41] It has been suggested that the effects of sustainability provisions depend on a variety of factors, such as presence of strong domestic social partners, economic dependence of the trade partner on market access, and domestic technical capacity for the remediation of problems.[42] The EU undertakes Sustainability Impact Assessments (SIA) to assess the potential economic, social, human rights and environmental impact of ongoing trade negotiations, both in the EU and the partner countries.[43] They allow stakeholders to give input, and should help the negotiators to identify possible trade-offs and optimise the policy choices. The SIA is available to the public and includes policy recommendations, to which the European Commission answers in a position paper. The Commission also undertakes ex-post evaluations (implementation assessments), but they are more *ad hoc* and without a clear timeline. A systematic exercise would give great insights, also with a view to later agreements; beyond the impact assessment and the stakeholder views, little research has been undertaken into the actual negotiations of the sustainability provisions and the main challenges and hurdles during the negotiations of these chapters, which may in itself be telling.[44] Our assumption would be that due to the soft nature of the chapters combined with the *sine qua non* approach of the EU (the agreement needs to be taken – or not, as a whole), trading partners agree with the terms without extensive discussions.

The TSD provisions/chapters in EU trade agreements can be criticised for not going far enough, being too vague in their wording and too soft in the way violations are dealt with. As they strive for a balance between "imposing" norms on trade partners (often developing countries, such as the African, Caribbean and Pacific countries, as well as a number of Asian and Latin-American countries) and leaving sufficient policy space and ownership, they inevitably lead the EU to meet its partners "somewhere in the middle" (assuming that the

40   L. Cuyvers, 'The sustainable development clauses in recent free trade agreements of the EU: perspectives for ASEAN', *Journal of Contemporary European Studies* 22:4 (2014), p. 430.

41   A. Bradford, 'The Brussels Effect', 107 *Northwestern University Law Review* 1 (2012); D. S. Grewal, *Network Power: The social dynamics of globalization* (Yale University Press, 2008).

42   Kommerskollegium (n. 39), p. 15.

43   For the updated SIA methodology, see European Commission, 'Handbook for Trade Sustainability Impact Assessment', 2nd edition, 2016.

44   On labour rights provisions see J. Harrison et al., 'Governing Labour Standards through FTAs', *Journal of Common Market Studies* 57.2 (2018), p. 1–18.

EU starts from the higher ground – which may not be the case with some of its FTA partners). The TSD chapters do not contain specific requirements for modifications to domestic law as they leave discretion to governments as to how to implement the relevant standards and how to enforce them. The EU has traditionally based its enforcement system on a cooperative, managerial model, focusing on "managing" causes of non-compliance through positive means. The US for instance, applies a more sanctions-based model, in which cooperation is ensured through sanctions which create costs and remove benefits.[45] Interestingly the EU's cooperative approach has been suggested as a serious downside to TSDs, even though the sanctions based approach is not widely carried either.[46]

Trade sanctions can be justified when others are not "playing by the rules" of the international trading system, such as countervailing measures against foreign subsidies or to impose anti-dumping duties. It is attractive to suggest that this logic may be applied to social and environmental dumping, too. When countries gain their market advantage by not respecting labour or environmental standards, trading partners should not enable these practices. Nonetheless, there is little evidence that imposing sanctions will lead to a long-term strategy with permanent improvement.[47] Sanctions could trigger unwanted effects, especially in developing countries or least developed countries. A decrease of exports could lead to a reduction of investments and consequently jobs, hitting the very workers which are meant to be protected. Moreover, poverty reduction may (understandably) trump environmental or labour protection in terms of policy priorities in developing countries. Furthermore, the loss of market share of one country is likely to be filled by competitors from other countries which may not have similar, let alone higher sustainability standards.

There is not enough evidence to comment on the effectiveness of EU TSD chapters in comparison with U.S. and Canadian models which involve sanctions, and there are certainly pros and cons to every system.[48] However, following a public stakeholder consultation launched by the European Commission on the matter in 2017, it can be concluded that there is no consensus among European policy makers and stakeholders on the use of sanctions, while there

---

45   Kommerskollegium (n. 39), p. 5.
46   EC non-paper on trade and sustainable development (n. 30).
47   Kommerskollegium (n. 39).
48   Kommerskollegium (n. 39). For an interesting comparison between the EU and US approach, see J. L. Mortensen, 'Towards more effective sustainability provisions in future European trade agreements: can Europe learn from the US?', Discussion paper for the Danish Confederation of Trade Unions (2017).

is consensus on enhancing engagement and making more effective use of the toolbox already available under TSD chapters to increase effectiveness.[49] That toolbox contains structures to involve civil society organisations in the implementation of those commitments, as well as a dedicated dispute settlement mechanism through which the findings of independent arbitrators may highlight issues of compliance. Engagement and compliance can also be required before the actual conclusion of the agreement (pre-ratification conditionality): for instance in the case of the EU agreement with Peru and Colombia, the European Parliament in 2012 demanded the adoption by the Colombian governments of a Roadmap to protect trade unionists, human rights and environmental protection before giving its consent[50]; in 2016, the Parliament insisted on a human rights conditionality clause in CETA.[51]

3.1   *Monitoring and Civil Society Mechanisms*

Under EU FTAs, the implementation of commitments is ensured through the monitoring roles of the dedicated government bodies (TSD Committee, Trade Committee, Joint Committee) and the civil society structures (domestic advisory groups and civil society forums). The Committee is established to oversee the implementation of the chapter.[52] Within that committee, domestic advisory groups comprising of civil society organisations can be set up:

> Each Party shall convene new or consult existing domestic advisory group(s) on sustainable development with the task of advising on the implementation of this Chapter. Each Party shall decide on its domestic procedures for the establishment of its domestic advisory group(s) and appoint its (their) members. Such domestic advisory group(s) shall comprise independent representative organisations, ensuring a balanced representation of economic, social and environmental stakeholders, including among others employers' and workers' organizations, business groups, and environmental organizations. Each domestic advisory group may, on its own initiative, submit views or recommendations to its respective Party on the implementation of this Chapter.[53]

---

49   EC non-paper on trade and sustainable development (n. 30).
50   European Parliament Resolution of 13 June 2012 on the EU Trade Agreement with Colombia and Peru (2012/2628(RSP)).
51   CETA, Article 28(7).
52   Such committees have been set up in EU-Korea, Article 44; EU-Colombia/Peru (2014), EU-Central America (2014), as well as in the current draft FTAs.
53   Draft EU-Vietnam FTA, Article 15.4.

Civil society mechanisms are characterised by the participation of a group of domestic representatives of labour, environment and business constituencies in both trading partners (called the *Domestic Advisory Group* (DAG)); by a transnational forum where the members of the domestic groups meet; and by interaction between the civil society groups and government officials of both trading partners discuss the implementation of the TSD chapter. However, little is known about the functioning of these groups and they have been subject to criticism.[54] For instance, they are viewed as too improvised, lacking frequency and continuity.[55] The selection procedures are criticised for being not transparent, which may lead to representatives clearly not always being independent from the government.[56] Furthermore, it is often unclear whether and how governments follow up on the outcomes of these mechanisms, undermining their credibility and effectiveness.[57] Notwithstanding its flaws, in 2017 the Europe-Peru Platform (a network of 16 European NGOs created in 2005 to increase coordination of advocacy toward European institutions and the European public on the topic of human rights situation in Peru) as well as members of the EU DAG, filed a "complaint against the Peruvian Government for failing to fulfil its labour and environmental commitments under the Trade Agreement between Peru and the EU".[58] The European Commission has since been following up with the relevant authorities in Peru, as well as the ILO and civil society.[59]

Even if the mechanisms and the trade agreements as a whole may have obvious shortcomings, participation is an opportunity to highlight those

---

54   See among others J. Orbie, D. Martens, M. Oehri, L. Van den Putte, 'Promoting Sustainable Development of Legitimising Free Trade? Civil Society Mechanisms in EU Trade Agreements', *Third World Thematics: A TWQ Journal* 1:4 (2017) (Orbie et al.), p. 526–546.

55   J. Orbie, D. Martens, L. Van den Putte, *Civil Society meetings in European Union Trade Agreements: Features, Purposes and Evaluation* (CLEER papers, 2016/3); L. Van den Putte, J. Orbie, F. Bossuyt, D. Martens, F. de Ville, *What social face of the new EU Trade Agreements? Beyond the 'soft' approach* (ETUI Policy Brief, 13/2015).

56   Y. Altintzis, 'Civil society engagement and linkages in EU trade policy', in T. Takacs, A. Ott, A. Dimopoulos (eds.), *Linking Trade and non-commercial interests: The EU as a global role model?* (CLEER papers, 2013/4).

57   M. Muguzura, *Civil society and trade diplomacy in the 'Global Age': The European case: trade policy dialogue between civil society and the European Commission* (WWF European Policy Office, 2002).

58   'Complaint against the Peruvian Government for failing to fulfil its labour and environmental commitments under the Trade Agreement between Peru and the EU': http://ec.europa.eu/transparency/regexpert/index.cfm?do=groupDetail.groupMeetingDoc&docid=12295.

59   Commission Staff Working Document, 'Individual reports and info sheets on implementation of EU Free Trade Agreements', SWD (2018) 454 final, 31 October 2018, p. 49.

shortcomings and to try to make a change from within. Public protesting may be easier, but progress can only be made if all stakeholders engage to work together towards a better-functioning system – even if some civil society groups participate to oppose the very trade agreement.[60] Engaging private actors in the implementation of labour and environmental provisions may also be essential for compliance, in particular with regard to countries with limited engagement capacity.[61]

The European Commission has proposed to take further steps to support DAGs in the EU and in the partner countries: a project under the EU's Partnership Instrument has been launched to support trade unions and business in their roles. Also, an exchange of best practices between DAGs of different partner countries is set up in order to create rules and recommendations for establishment and functioning of DAGs and CSFs, and stimulate creation of guidelines for DAGs based on existing experience and practices in this context.[62] Furthermore, it is proposed to extend the scope of the civil society structure to cover the entire FTA instead of only the TSD chapter (DAGs are currently only allowed to discuss and advise on the implementation of the TSD chapters only). This legal limitation has constrained the ability of the groups to provide advice on the sustainability implications of other parts of agreements – e.g. technical barriers to trade, or sanitary and phytosanitary measures, etc.[63]

3.2   *Dispute Settlement Mechanisms*

Based on the example of the WTO dispute settlement system that has, despite the recent challenges and need for reform, mostly worked very well since its inception in 1995, the EU has included state-to-state dispute settlement mechanisms in its FTAs since 2000. Since 2009, the EU has also included investor-state dispute settlement mechanisms in trade and investment agreements. Disputes settlement mechanisms are set up to ensure that agreements are enforced and that disputes can be settled: it provides an effective means to establish whether a country has acted in conformity with its obligations and aims to avoid trade damaging unilateral action by having an independent body applying and interpreting the agreement. Where a party fails to comply with a commitment, the other party can resort to the dispute settlement mechanism,

---

60   Orbie et al. (n. 54), p. 535.

61   Kommerskollegium (n. 39), p. 26.

62   EC non-paper on trade and sustainable development (n. 30), p. 5.

63   EC non-paper on trade and sustainable development (n. 30), p. 6.

including recourse to the independent panel procedure leading to a public report with recommendations. Despite their potential, dispute settlement mechanisms in EU FTA s have not been triggered until very recently indeed.[64] Before these recent developments, the only known example of a "sustainability dispute" under a bilateral trade agreement was a dispute brought by US and Guatemalan labour unions on failure by Guatemala to implement labour rights provisions of the US-DR-CAFTA agreement.[65] The reason for the rare occurrence of relevant dispute settlement provisions being triggered, are most likely diverse. One reason is that in order to trigger dispute settlement, it must be demonstrated that the failure is due to a sustained or recurring course of action, and that the violation occurs in a manner affecting trade or investment between the parties.[66] Another reason could relate to the limited standing in the dispute settlement provisions: in addition to current state-to-state model, it is suggested to add a third-party-state dimension and a third party-third party component.[67]

Dispute settlement for TSD chapters differs from the general dispute settlement procedure established for the remainder of the FTA, which does provide an explicit role for civil society and international organisations. Under the TSD dispute settlement, civil society and international organisation can be involved at every stage. The outcome of the proceedings are a public report that can be monitored for implementation, but does not include sanctions. Rather, it focuses on mutually agreed solutions to problems. The European Commission has recently stepped up the monitoring and analysis of compliance with TSD commitments by a number of FTA partner countries: letters setting out compliance concerns and actions to be taken in the absence of which dispute settlement would need to be launched have been sent to a number of partner countries. Should the results of these actions not

---

64   EC non-paper on trade and sustainable development (n. 30), p. 7. For recent triggers see request for consultations under the EU-Korea FTA's sustainable development chapter: 17 December 2018. See 'EU steps up engagement with Republic of Korea over labour commitments under the trade agreement': http://trade.ec.europa.eu/doclib/press/index. cfm?id=1961. Labour rights are at the heart of the request. Subsequently see consultations with Ukraine over the country's ban on the export of unprocessed woods: http://trade. ec.europa.eu/doclib/press/index.cfm?id=1968.

65   Panel Report, *In the Matter of Guatemala – Issues Relating to the Obligations Under Article 16.2.1(a) of the* CAFTA-DR (adopted 14 June 2017), https://bit.ly/2tiQos4.

66   Kommerskollegium (n. 39), p. 14.

67   A. Marx, F. Ebert, N. Hachez, 'Dispute settlement for labour provisions in EU Free Trade Agreements: Rethinking current approaches', *Politics and Governance* 5:4 (2017), p. 49–59.

be satisfactory and compliance concerns persist, the Commission services take the view that dispute settlement proceedings should be launched "without hesitation".[68]

3.3   *Enhanced Engagement*

Another "soft" means of increasing the effectiveness and the impact of the trade preferences and relations, mostly applicable to GSP and EBA beneficiaries, is intensifying the dialogue through enhanced engagement. In the event of failure of the dialogue the EU may still withdraw the status and (part of) the preferential access. Dialogue rather than ready triggering of the dispute settlement provisions is the preferred option for the EU's approach towards FTA partner countries, too, as illustrated by its talks with South Korea on the ratification of outstanding ILO Conventions.

Examples of formalised enhanced engagement with EBA beneficiaries can be found in the Special Partnership for Democracy, Peace and Prosperity with Myanmar, a strategy laid down by the European Commission in May 2016,[69] or the 2013 Bangladesh Sustainability Compact for the clothing industry.[70] In the Myanmar Special Partnership, possible EU initiatives were proposed to improve democracy, the rule of law, the peace process, human rights, and sustainable development. The Bangladesh Sustainability Compact is a sectoral initiative, aimed at the promotion of labour rights and factory safety. In a coordinated effort by the EU, Bangladesh, the US, Canada and the ILO short and long-term commitments have been set. They bring together employers, trade unions and other key stakeholders to promote labour rights and factor safety. The Compact is underpinned by the possible action of withdrawing trade preferences should results not shows – a threat which was narrowly averted by the Bangladeshi government through sufficient progress made on its labour laws.

---

68   European Commission, 'Feedback and way forward on improving the implementation and enforcement of Trade and Sustainable Development chapters in EU Free Trade Agreements', non-paper of the Commission services, 26 February 2018, p. 8.

69   European Commission, 'Elements for an EU strategy vis-à-vis Myanmar and Burma: A Special Partnership for Democracy, Peace and Prosperity', (JOIN (2016) 24 final), 1 June 2016.

70   Joint Statement, 'Staying engaged: a Sustainability Compact for continuous improvements in labour rights and factory safety in the Ready-Made Garment and Knitwear Industry in Bangladesh', 8 July 2013 https://trade.ec.europa.eu/doclib/docs/2014/october/tradoc_152853.pdf.

4   Outlook

One can only truly measure performance and success when clear performance
indicators are set. What are the objectives, what are the aims to be achieved?
Without such objectives, one is left to judge based on differing expectations
and ideals. It is not difficult to criticise trade and sustainable development
chapters in FTAs if the expectation is that these will lead to a green and fair
planet for all. A TSD chapter in a trade agreement has its obvious limits. Firstly,
they exist within the context of a trade agreement, and any action must thus
somehow be related to that. Secondly, the levels of development between the
EU and its trading partners may differ considerably, which often has an impact on the institutional set-up, legal framework and rule of law of the trading
partner. The EU can assist developing countries because of the hard lessons
it learnt itself in the past and continues to learn. Thirdly, the EU cannot just
impose its (relatively recent) "superior" norms on trade partners: local circumstances, cultural differences and geographical aspects may require a different approach. Effective long-term policy depends on the engagement and
ownership of local partners. Fourthly, sanctions run the risk of being counterproductive, harming those who are in most need of help due to loss of jobs and
increased poverty. Any type of sanction needs to contain strong incentives and
cooperation mechanisms to have a positive effect. However, as noted above,
there is no consensus among EU stakeholders on the use of sanctions. The jury
is still out on what is empirically the most effective measure available pursuant
to the EU's recent FTAs.

    One could argue that TSD chapters are only included in free trade agree-
ments to mobilise sufficient public and political support for those trade agreements in times where globalisation and free trade are increasingly contested in
developed countries.[71] It could also be argued that (some) civil society support
in developed countries is related to the extent that they are exposed to unfair or unethical competition from producers that employ exploitative labour
practices. There may even be true believers in the idea of using trade policy
as a means to incentivise better global labour and environmental protection.
However, whatever the rationale, it is in everyone's best interest to ensure
that the TSD chapters are as impactful and effective as possible. Any criticism
should thus be framed constructively, and all stakeholders need to cooperate
to the extent possible to ensure the success. This requires efforts from different

---

71   J. Orbie et al. (n. 54), p. 530; K. Ulmer 'Trade embedded development models', *The
       International Journal of Comparative Labour Law and Industrial Relations* 31:3 (2015),
       p. 303–326.

stakeholders to engage partners in their "field of expertise": amongst industry, amongst social partners – especially if the institutional set-up in either country is not yet what it should be. As has been shown above, the larger the group that implements high TSD standards, the stronger those standards become, which may then have an impact on regional trade in other regions of the world and may eventually result in a general uptake of the higher standard. Trade can in that regard serve as leverage and a positive incentive for more ambitious norms.

The link between trade and sustainable development is not new as has been demonstrated in this chapter. However, the TSD provisions and chapters have become the subject of scrutiny and debate, which can only be seen as a positive development. The current challenge is to increase their effectiveness and maximise results, whether through dispute settlement or otherwise.

CHAPTER 8

Technical Barriers to Trade in the New Generation of EU Trade Agreements

Isabelle Van Damme

1 Introduction

The objective of this contribution is to map the evolution of the chapters on technical barriers to trade in goods and related obligations in other chapters in the European Union's trade agreements concluded since the establishment of the World Trade Organization (WTO) and thus the entry into force of the Agreement on Technical Barriers to Trade (TBT Agreement). Those developments relate to, in particular, the mutual recognition or equivalence of standards, the definition of relevant international standards and cooperation in the field of especially conformity assessment procedures. The overall objective of this chapter is to reach conclusions on the degree of regulatory cooperation and possible convergence achieved by those agreements. Those conclusions are based on, in particular, the EU-Canada Comprehensive Economic and Trade Agreement (CETA),[1] the EU-Singapore Free Trade Agreement (EU-Singapore FTA)[2] and the EU-Japan Economic Partnership Agreement (EU-Japan EPA)[3] but take into account also examples of recent association agreements, certain proposals for new agreements and standalone agreements regarding the mutual recognition of conformity assessment procedures and emerging initiatives for engagement on regulatory issues with certain third countries (such as the United States[4]).

European Union (EU) trade agreements set out obligations regarding technical barriers to trade in, in particular, separate chapters or protocols on

---

1   Comprehensive Economic and Trade Agreement (CETA) between Canada, of the one part, and the European Union and its Member States, of the other part (OJ 2017, L 11), p. 23.

2   EU – Singapore Free Trade Agreement: http://trade.ec.europa.eu/doclib/press/index.cfm?id=961.

3   EU – Japan Economic Partnership Agreement: http://trade.ec.europa.eu/doclib/press/index.cfm?id=1684.

4   See European Commission, DG Trade, 'Note for the Attention of the Trade Policy Committee', 3 October 2018, available at http://www.foeeurope.org/sites/default/files/eu-us_trade_deal/2018/181003_com_proposals_for_eu-us_regulatory_cooperation.pdf.

technical barriers to trade (laying down general and/or sector-specific obligations), horizontal chapters regarding regulatory cooperation, chapters relating to trade and sustainable development, trade and labour and/or trade and environmental cooperation[5] and chapters relating to non-tariff barriers and investment in renewable energy generation. As a result, assessing the regulation of technical barriers to trade in EU trade agreements requires taking into account all or various parts of those agreements.

That regulation (and possible convergence) of technical barriers to trade is based on different models. Those models include mutual recognition or equivalence of standards, the common development of standards, agreements on what international standards to use (direct and indirect harmonisation), forms of regulatory cooperation and a more detailed articulation of the rights and obligations found in the TBT Agreement. The European Union has summarised its approach to, for example, conformity assessment procedures in free trade agreements as follows:

> a joint commitment to choose the least-burdensome procedure on the basis of risk assessment and GRP (Good Regulatory Practices) principles to ensure fitness for purpose; the reference to existing multilateral schemes (e.g. ILAC, IAF) where positive assurance of conformity is required; sector-specific provisions such as use of UNECE-type approval certificates for motor vehicles or supplier's declaration of conformity (SDoC) for some sectors, e.g. electronics; and, where appropriate, integration of existing bilateral MRAs into FTAs.[6]

After explaining what technical barriers to trade are, this chapter describes types of mutual recognition of results of conformity assessment procedures. Next, the chapter examines more closely the obligations assumed under recent trade agreements with third States, relating to horizontal chapters on good regulatory practices and regulatory cooperation, generally applicable obligations regarding technical barriers to trade, sector-specific obligations and chapters on trade and sustainable development, trade and labour and trade and environment as well as renewable energy.

---

5   On this issue, see the contribution by B. Cooreman and G. van Calster in this volume.
6   WTO, Committee on Technical Barriers to Trade, 'Eighth Triennial Review of the Operation and Implementation of the Agreement on Technical Barriers to Trade under Article 15.4, G/TBT/41, 19 November 2018, para. 4.7.

2   The Definition of "Technical Barriers to Trade"

Technical barriers to trade are a form of non-tariff barriers to trade. They may
be applied at and/or behind the border. The TBT Agreement applies to three
types of measure, namely technical regulations, technical standards and conformity assessment procedures. A technical regulation means a

> [d]ocument which lays down product characteristics or their related pro-
> cesses and production methods, including the applicable administrative
> provisions, with which compliance is mandatory' and 'may also include
> or deal exclusively with terminology, symbols, packaging, marking or la-
> belling requirements as they apply to a product, process or production
> method.[7]

A technical standard is defined as a

> [d]ocument approved by a recognized body, that provides, for common
> and repeated use, rules, guidelines or characteristics for products or re-
> lated processes and production methods, with which compliance is not
> mandatory. It may also include or deal exclusively with terminology,
> symbols, packaging, marking or labelling requirements as they apply to a
> product, process or production method.[8]

A conformity assessment procedure is "[a]ny procedure used, directly or indirectly, to determine that relevant requirements in technical regulations or
standards are fulfilled".[9]

Certain EU trade agreements also include commitments regarding so-called
"market surveillance", which is a function distinct from conformity assessment
procedures, and refers broadly to "activities conducted and measures taken by
public authorities on the basis of procedures of a Party to enable that Party to
monitor or address compliance of products with the requirements set out in
its laws and regulations".[10]

Conformity assessment procedures, if mandatory, are often specific to
the sector at issue. The least intrusive process involves that a manufacturer

---

7   Agreement on Technical Barriers to Trade (TBT Agreement), Annex 1 TBT Agreement,
     para. 1.
8   Annex 1 TBT Agreement, para. 2 (n. 7).
9   Annex 1 TBT Agreement, para. 3 (n. 7).
10   See, for example, Art. 7.10.1 EU-Japan EPA (n. 3); Art. 11 CETA (n. 1); Art. 4.9 EU-Singapore
     FTA (n. 4).

prepares a declaration of conformity. In case of higher risks, third party conformity assessment will be required and no self-declaration of conformity will be accepted.

Technical standards, technical regulations and conformity assessment procedures may be issued at the state, federal, regional or international level. They may be developed by public or private bodies.

The TBT Agreement applies to the preparation, adoption and application of such measures. The scope of most TBT chapters in the European Union's trade (and association) agreements is similar.[11] Most agreements expressly refer to the definitions in Annex 1 to the TBT Agreement.[12]

Technical barriers to trade in essence result primarily from differences in the preparation, adoption and application of technical regulations, technical standards and conformity assessment procedures. Convergence of such measures, through direct or indirect harmonisation, is the main tool through which such barriers might be reduced. However, in so far as such convergence implies that different trading partners align their technical regulations, technical standards and conformity assessment procedures, the question arises of whether those measures are to be defined jointly and through common processes or whether, instead, one party is to design those measures and thus to set also the underlying objective and level of protection whereas the other party becomes a rule taker. Those questions typically relate to the respective sizes of the market of each party to the trade agreement and each party's interest in market access.

The types of obligation through which the TBT Agreement seeks to reduce technical barriers to trade include a wide non-discrimination obligation (comprising both most-favoured nation treatment and national treatment[13]), an obligation not to create unnecessary obstacles to trade, meaning that such measures should not be more trade restrictive than what is necessary to achieve legitimate objectives,[14] and different types of transparency and due process

---

11 See, for example, Art. 4.1.1 CETA (n. 1); Art. 53(1) Association Agreement between the European Union and its Member States, of the one part, and Ukraine, of the other part (OJ 2014, L 161) (EU-Ukraine Association Agreement); Art. 7.2.1 EU-Japan EPA (n. 3); Art. 4.2.1 EU-Singapore FTA (n. 2); Art. 44.1 Association Agreement between the European Union and the European Atomic Energy Community and their Member States, of the one part, and Georgia, of the other part (OJ 2014, L 261) (EU-Georgia Association Agreement).

12 See, for example, Art. 4.2.3 EU-Singapore FTA (n. 2). See also, Art. X.2 Chapter XX (Technical Barriers to Trade) of the European Union's proposal for the EU-New Zealand (http://trade.ec.europa.eu/doclib/docs/2018/july/tradoc_157208.pdf) and Australia FTA (http://trade.ec.europa.eu/doclib/docs/2018/july/tradoc_157195.pdf); Arts. 7.2.1 and 7.4 EU-Japan EPA (n. 3).

13 Art. 2.1 TBT Agreement (n. 7).

14 Art. 2.2 TBT Agreement (n. 7).

obligations. Similar obligations apply as regards, in particular, conformity assessment procedures.[15] A certain degree of deference is also given to technical regulations adopted in accordance with international standards. In that manner, indirect harmonisation is encouraged by WTO law, although the WTO itself is not a harmonising body.[16] Another means to promote harmonisation (indirectly) is the obligation of WTO Members to play a full part in the preparation of international standards by international standardising bodies.[17]

Those WTO obligations being the baseline, this chapter seeks to identify the contribution of recent EU trade agreements to the objective of reducing technical barriers to trade.

3   Models of Mutual Recognition of the Results of Conformity Assessment Procedures

Before looking in greater detail at the provisions on technical barriers to trade in selected EU trade agreements, this chapter discusses the European Union's policy of concluding mutual recognition agreements with certain third countries in order to facilitate market access by providing for the recognition of the results of conformity assessment procedures completed by relevant bodies of the exporting country.[18] Some of those agreements are in the process of being renegotiated or replaced by mutual recognition obligations in trade agreements.

Mutual recognition agreements apply specifically to conformity assessment procedures. Their objective is not necessarily to achieve regulatory convergence. Thus the assumption is that the agreement applies to the assessment of conformity with technical regulations that might be different. In that regard, the generally applicable obligation under the TBT Agreement is that, in principle,

> Members shall ensure, whenever possible, that results of conformity assessment procedures in other Members are accepted, even when those

---

15   Art. 5 TBT Agreement (n. 7).

16   Arts. 2.4, 2.5 TBT Agreement (n. 7). See also Art. 5.4 TBT Agreement (n. 7).

17   Art. 2.6 TBT Agreement (n. 7). See also Art. 5.5 TBT Agreement (n. 7).

18   For an overview, see European Commission, 'Trade Issues … Technical Barriers to Trade, Mutual Recognition Agreements and Agreements on Conformity Assessment and Acceptance of Industrial Products, Newsletter No 10, February 2018': http://trade.ec.europa.eu/doclib/docs/2018/february/tradoc_156599.pdf.

procedures differ from their own, provided they are satisfied that those procedures offer *an assurance of conformity with applicable technical regulations or standards equivalent to their own procedures.*[19]

Furthermore, Article 6.3 of the TBT Agreement encourages WTO Members to enter into negotiations for concluding mutual recognition agreements.

The European Union currently has Mutual Recognition Agreements (MRAs) with at least the following countries: the United States;[20] Canada;[21] Japan;[22] Switzerland;[23] Australia;[24] New Zealand;[25] and Israel.[26]

MRAs typically include sectoral annexes for products such as telecommunication equipment, electrical safety, medical devices or pharmaceuticals and with respect to which conformity assessment bodies of both parties to the MRA are recognised. Despite the entry into force of those MRAs, certain sectoral annexes are suspended, have been amended separately from the MRA or have been replaced by regulatory cooperation in the sector concerned.

With certain of those countries, the European Union has either concluded trade agreements (for example, Canada) or is in the process of negotiating such agreements (for example, New Zealand and Australia). As a result of

---

19   Art. 6.1 TBT Agreement (emphasis added) (n. 7).

20   Council Decision 1999/78/EC of 22 June 1998 on the conclusion of an Agreement on Mutual Recognition between the European Community and the United States of America (OJ 1999, L 31), p. 1, as amended by Council Decision 2002/803/EC of 8 October 2002 (OJ 2002, L 278), p. 22. The European Union and the United States are currently initiating negotiations on a more comprehensive agreement on the mutual recognition of conformity assessment procedures; see, for example, European Commission, 'Recommendation for a Council Decision authorising the opening of negotiations of an agreement with the United States of America on conformity assessment', COM (2019) 15 final, 18 January 2019.

21   CETA (n. 1), p. 23.

22   Council Decision 2001/747/EC of 27 September 2001 on the conclusion of an Agreement on Mutual Recognition between the European Community and Japan (OJ 2001, L 284), p. 1, as amended by Council Decision 2002/804/EC (OJ 2002, L 278), p. 23.

23   Council and Commission Decision 2002/309/EC of 4 April 2002 on the conclusion of an Agreement on Mutual Recognition between the European Community and Switzerland (OJ 2002, L 114), p. 1.

24   Council Decision 98/508/EC (OJ 1998, L 229), p. 1, as amended by Council Decision 2002/800/EC (OJ 2002, L 278), p. 19 and Council Decision 2012/837/EC (OJ 2012, L 359), p. 1.

25   Council Decision 98/509/EC (OJ 1998, L 299), p. 61, as amended by Council Decision 2002/801/EC (OJ 2002, L 278), p. 20 and Council Decision 2012/828/EU (OJ 2012, L 356), p. 1.

26   Agreement on mutual recognition of OECD principles of good laboratory practice (OJ 1999, L 263), p. 7; Protocol to the Euro-Mediterranean Agreement establishing an association between the European Communities and their Member States, of the one part, and the State of Israel, of the other part, on conformity assessment and acceptance of industrial products (OJ 2013, L 1), p. 1.

subsequent trade agreements between the relevant parties, MRAs might be replaced. This is the case, for example, regarding the Protocol on conformity assessment and the Protocol on the mutual recognition on the compliance and enforcement programme regarding good manufacturing practices for pharmaceutical practices for pharmaceutical products included in CETA which have replaced the MRA between the European Union and Canada.

An essential element underpinning most MRAs is the certification of conformity assessment bodies. This also means that if one party changes its legislation regarding the requirements that its conformity assessment bodies must satisfy, adjustments might need to be made in the certification of the other party's conformity assessment bodies.

There are three main models of mutual recognition under MRAs.

Under a traditional MRA, country A will agree to assess the conformity of products with the technical regulations of country B. Thus, by means of a single conformity assessment procedure, it is possible to obtain a determination that a product complies with the technical regulations of countries A (the home market) and B (the export market). By agreeing to such commitments, country A seeks to facilitate market access for its exports. Under that model, there is no alignment of technical regulations. Examples of this model are found in the MRAs with the United States, Australia and New Zealand.

Under enhanced MRAs with equivalence of rules, countries A and B apply equivalent but not identical technical regulations. Thus, a conformity assessment procedure for determining assessment of a product with the technical regulation of country A results also in a determination that the product satisfies the equivalent technical regulation of country B. That model is found in Article 1(2) of the MRA with Switzerland.

Another model is that of an enhanced MRA with common rules. Under that model, countries A and B apply the same technical regulations (set through common processes or, more commonly, by the European Union) and recognise each other's conformity assessment determinations. For example, under the EU-Georgia Association Agreement,[27] Georgia accepts to take

> [t]he measures necessary in order to gradually achieve approximation with the Union's technical regulations, standards, metrology, accreditation, conformity assessment, corresponding systems and market surveillance system, and undertakes to follow the principles and the practice

---

27   EU-Georgia Association Agreement (n. 11), p. 4.

laid down in the relevant Union acquis (indicative list in Annex III-B to this Agreement).[28]

Article 56.1 the EU-Ukraine Association Agreement contains a similar commitment.

MRAS are a useful tool to facilitate the recognition of the results of conformity assessment bodies of other WTO Members and therefore to facilitate trade (because fewer resources are required for testing, inspection and/or certification). Their use is nonetheless often predicated on a determination that the technical regulations of the parties to the agreement are, albeit not necessarily identical, equivalent. This means that MRAS often might be available only for certain (well-defined) categories of goods.

4   Horizontal Chapters on Good Regulatory Practices and Regulatory Cooperation

The European Union's new trade agreements typically include a horizontal chapter concerning good regulatory practices and/or regulatory cooperation that applies to the development, review and methodological aspects of regulatory measures (in the sense of measures of general applicability[29]) issued in respect of any matter covered by the free trade agreement or matters covered by certain WTO agreements and specific chapters of the free trade agreement (such as matters falling within the scope of the TBT Agreement, the SPS Agreement, the GATT 1994, the GATS, the additional obligations regarding TBT and SPS measures, cross-border trade in services, trade and sustainable development, trade and labour and trade and environment).[30] Those horizontal chapters on regulatory cooperation also seek to involve private parties that are stakeholders and interested parties in the parties' process of cooperation.[31]

One of the first of such chapters was included in the EU-Japan EPA. Chapter 18 of the EU-Japan EPA has been described as "one of the hardest and

---

28   Art. 47 EU-Georgia Association Agreement (n. 11).

29   See, for example, Art. 18.2(b) EU-Japan EPA (n. 3); Art. 4.4.2(a) EU-Singapore FTA (n. 2).

30   See, for example, Chapter 21 CETA (in particular Art. 21.1 CETA) (n. 1); Chapter 18 EU-Japan EPA (the latter chapter is not subject to the general dispute settlement chapter: Art. 18.19 EU-Japan EPA) (n. 3).

31   See, for example, Art. 21.8 CETA (n. 1); Art. 18.7 EU-Japan EPA (n. 3); Art. 4.4.2(d) EU-Singapore FTA (n. 2).

full-fledged FTAs in terms of regulatory coherence".[32] Although the obligations have a potentially wide scope, certain types of regulatory measure are treated separately. That is the case, for example, for animal welfare in the EU-Japan EPA.[33] That agreement also exempts regulatory cooperation on financial regulation from the scope of the horizontal chapter on regulatory cooperation and good regulatory practices.[34]

Those horizontal chapters seek to find a balance between the need for increased regulatory cooperation in, in essence, all fields of trade and the respect for each party's right to regulate and to define its own levels of protection regarding the achievement of legitimate policy objectives.[35] In CETA, this balance is expressly confirmed by both parties in the Joint Interpretative Instrument:

> CETA preserves the ability of the European Union and its Member States and Canada to adopt and apply their own laws and regulations that regulate economic activity in the public interest, to achieve legitimate public policy objectives such as the protection and promotion of public health, social services, public education, safety, the environment, public morals, social or consumer protection, privacy and data promotion and the promotion and protection of cultural diversity.[36]

Likewise, Article 18.1.2 of the EU-Japan EPA states that nothing in the chapter on good regulatory practices and regulatory cooperation "shall affect the right of a Party to define or regulate its own levels of protection in pursuit or furtherance of its public policy objectives in areas such as" those listed in that provision (covering, for example, public health; human, animal and plant life and health; occupational health and safety; labour conditions; the environment including climate change; consumers; social protection and social security; personal data and cybersecurity; cultural diversity; financial stability; and energy security).

Despite their right to define their own level of protection, the parties to CETA and other agreements nonetheless accept a common baseline. For example,

---

32   C.-F. Lin, H.-W. Liu, 'Regulatory rationalisation clauses in FTAs: a complete survey of the US, EU and China', *Melbourne Journal of International Law* 19(1) (2018), p. 172.

33   Art. 18.17 EU-Japan EPA (n. 3).

34   Art. 18.18 EU-Japan EPA (n. 3).

35   See, for example, Art. 18.1 EU-Japan EPA (n. 3).

36   See point 2 of the Joint Interpretative Instrument on the Comprehensive Economic and Trade Agreement (CETA) between Canada and the European Union and its Member States (OJ 2017, L 11).

CETA refers to the need to ensure "high levels of protection for human, animal and plant life or health, and the environment".[37] Similarly, the EU-Japan EPA states that "each Party shall strive to ensure that its laws, regulations and related policies provide high levels of environmental and labour protection and shall strive to continue to improve those laws and regulations and their underlying levels of protection"[38] precludes parties from "encourag[ing] trade or investment by relaxing or lowering the level of protection provided by their respective environmental or labour laws and regulations".[39] Furthermore, despite the recognition of each party's right to regulate, the chapters provide that "[r]egulatory measures shall not constitute a disguised barrier to trade".[40] For example, Article 16.2.3 of the EU-Japan EPA precludes the parties from using their environmental or labour laws and regulations in a manner which would constitute a means of arbitrary or unjustifiable discrimination against the other party or a disguised restriction on international trade.

The obligations under these horizontal chapters concern the regulatory practices of each individual party as well as the cooperation between both parties in this area. Most of the general obligations regarding good regulatory practices and regulatory cooperation relate to making the processes through which each party adopts regulatory measures more transparent, predictable and understandable.[41] For that purpose, for example, CETA envisages that a party may receive access to (certain) information from the other party's alert system regarding the product safety of consumer products. Whilst horizontal chapters also seek to have each party carry out impact assessments of major regulatory measures and retrospective evaluations of regulatory measures, those obligations are typically aspirational. For example, the EU-Japan EPA states that a regulatory authority of a party "shall endeavour to systematically carry out [...] an impact assessment"[42] and "shall maintain processes or mechanisms to promote periodic retrospective evaluation of regulatory measures in force".[43]

The objective of these horizontal chapters is not to harmonise. To that effect, most chapters state expressly that the obligations assumed under

---

37   Art. 21.2.1 CETA (n. 1).

38   Art. 16.2.1 EU-Japan EPA (n. 3).

39   Art. 16.2.2 EU-Japan EPA (n. 3).

40   See, for example, Art. 18.4 EU-Japan EPA (n. 3).

41   See, for example, sub-section 2 of section A of chapter 18 EU-Japan EPA (n. 3); chapter 21 CETA (n. 1).

42   Art. 18.8.1 EU-Japan EPA (n. 3).

43   Art. 18.9.1 EU-Japan EPA (n. 3).

the chapter are not to be construed as requiring the parties to achieve any particular regulatory outcome.[44] The parties nonetheless commit to consider typically two main types of cooperation in order to promote regulatory compatibility.[45] The first type involves the promotion of common principles, guidelines, codes of conduct, mutual recognition of equivalence and implementing tools to avoid unnecessary duplications of regulatory requirements. The second type involves bilateral cooperation and cooperation with third countries with a view to developing and promoting the adoption and implementation of international regulatory standards, guidelines or other approaches. Those types of obligation may not be enforced through the inter-state dispute settlement mechanism for which the agreement otherwise provides.[46]

Although the obligations in such horizontal chapters are typically defined in a detailed manner, they do not go beyond cooperation and the exchange of information. Even if these agreements thus offer a platform to facilitate regulatory cooperation, that cooperation remains voluntary.[47] Nor do they undermine the right of each party to adopt different measures or pursue different initiatives.[48] In other words, the right of each party to regulate and to set its values or priorities remains unaltered.

Finally, also outside the context of a comprehensive trade agreement, the European Union engages with certain third States on regulatory issues. One example is the new initiative between the European Union and the United States regarding regulatory issues and standards. That initiative is based on the following principles: (i) cooperation must be limited to areas in which regulators identify a common interest; (ii) full respect for domestic law and regulatory procedures and for the maintenance of levels of protection; (iii) regulatory cooperation must be on a voluntary basis and respect each party's regulatory autonomy; and (iv) application of the highest levels of transparency and accountability.[49] Against the background of those principles, the European Union and the United States have started negotiations on a horizontal

---

44   See, for example, Art. 18.5 EU-Japan EPA (n. 3).
45   See Art. 18.13 EU-Japan EPA (n. 3).
46   Art. 18.19 EU-Japan EPA (n. 3).
47   See, for example, point 3 of the Joint Interpretative Instrument to CETA (n. 36).
48   See, for example, Art. 21.5 CETA (n. 1); Art. 18.13 EU-Japan EPA (n. 3).
49   European Commission, DG Trade, 'Note for the Attention of the Trade Policy Committee', 3 October 2018 (n. 4); European Commission, Progress Report on the implementation of the EU-US Joint Statement of 25 July 2018 – Greater together: Slashing billions in industrial tariffs and boosting transatlantic trade, Chapter 1; USTR, United States – European Union Negotiations – Summary of Specific Negotiating Objectives (January 2019).

agreement that is envisaged to cover all industrial sectors in which third-party conformity assessment is required by either side. They are also discussing co-operation on standards and sectoral cooperation (in particular, in the sectors of pharmaceuticals, medical devices and cybersecurity).

5 Chapters on Technical Barriers to Trade: Generally Applicable Obligations Regarding Technical Barriers to Trade

5.1 *Introduction*

The European Union's trade agreements contain chapters, entitled "Technical Barriers to Trade", the objective of which is to facilitate trade by preventing, identifying and eliminating technical barriers to trade. In that manner, the European Union seeks to facilitate market access between trading partners. Those chapters follow a similar structure to that of the TBT Agreement by addressing separately technical regulations, technical standards and conformity assessment procedures.

The agreements typically confirm the application of (parts) of the TBT Agreement which is used, in essence, as a baseline for the additional obligations assumed under the agreement. Significantly, the agreements incorporate certain instruments adopted by the TBT Committee. Building on the horizontal chapters relating to cooperation, the TBT chapters contain more detailed obligations regarding cooperation and information sharing, including regarding the development of (international) standards. Despite the fact that no general harmonisation of standards is envisaged, they nonetheless seek to enhance the compatibility and convergence of technical regulations. In association agreements, a different model is used because, in certain areas, the third State accepts to conform to EU law.

TBT chapters also introduce mutual recognition and other forms of facilitating trade in order to reduce the costs involved in conformity assessment procedures. Apart from those generally applicable obligations, most agreements provide for closer approximation of technical barriers to trade and models of mutual recognition for specific categories of goods.

Finally, certain agreements contain a jurisdictional clause that is specific to the TBT chapter and provisions of the TBT Agreement which it incorporates. For example, Article 7.3.3 of the EU-Japan EPA provides that

> [w]here a dispute arises regarding a particular measure of a Party which the other Party alleges to be exclusively in breach of the provisions of the TBT Agreement [incorporated into the agreement], that other Party

shall, notwithstanding paragraph 1 of Article 21.27, select the dispute settlement mechanism under the WTO Agreement.

In other words, as a result of such a clause, dispute settlement under the EU-
Japan EPA will, in principle, be limited to the interpretation and application
of TBT obligations that are separate and additional to those assumed under
the TBT Agreement. This type of clause seeks to confirm the role of the WTO
dispute settlement system as the preferred forum for enforcing the core obligations governing technical barriers to trade and to avoid divergent interpretations of the same obligation under different agreements. At the same time,
although perhaps not envisaged by the parties to the agreement, arguably its
effectiveness depends on the existence of a fully functioning WTO dispute settlement system.

5.2   *Using the TBT Agreement as the Baseline*
The baseline for specific commitments in the chapters on "Technical Barriers
to Trade" are the obligations laid down in the TBT Agreement,[50] taking into
account also the reports of WTO panels and the Appellate Body regarding the
interpretation of that agreement and (certain) decisions and recommendations of WTO Members acting within the framework of the WTO Committee
on Technical Barriers to Trade.[51]

Most TBT chapters in essence start by incorporating the main obligations
of the TBT Agreement. Certain agreements incorporate specific provisions of
the TBT Agreement (in particular the obligations found in Articles 2 to 9 of
that agreement and Annexes 1 and 3),[52] whereas others incorporate the entirety of the TBT Agreement.[53] Another model is that of agreements that "affirm
their rights and obligations under the TBT Agreement" and then incorporate
specific provisions of the TBT Agreement into the free trade agreement.[54] By

---

50   See, for example, Art. 4.3 EU-Singapore FTA (n. 2); Art. 45 EU-Georgia Association
       Agreement (n. 11); Art. 54 EU-Ukraine Association Agreement (n. 11).

51   See, for example, WTO, Committee on Technical Barriers to Trade, 'Eighth Triennial
       Review of the Operation and Implementation of the Agreement on Technical Barriers to
       Trade under Art. 15.4', G/TBT/41, 19 November 2018 (n. 6).

52   See, for example, Art. 4.2.1 CETA (n. 1); Art. 7.3.2 EU-Japan EPA (n. 3).

53   See, for example, Art. 4.3 EU-Singapore FTA (n. 2); Art. 54 EU-Ukraine Association
       Agreement (n. 11). See also Art. X.3.1 Chapter XX (Technical Barriers to Trade) of the
       European Union's proposal for the EU-New Zealand and Australia FTA (n. 12); Art. 45 EU-
       Georgia Association Agreement (n. 11).

54   See Art. 7.3.1 and 7.3.2 EU-Japan EPA (incorporating Arts. 2 to 9 TBT Agreement and
       Annexes 1 and 3 TBT Agreement) (n. 3).

incorporating all of or parts of the TBT Agreement, those WTO obligations thus also become enforceable, in the relations between the parties to the trade agreement, though the WTO dispute settlement mechanism might, under certain agreements, remain the preferred forum.

Typically, the obligations regarding technical regulations, standards and conformity assessment procedures build on existing provisions of the TBT Agreement. Apart from addressing separately, similar to the TBT Agreement, technical regulations, standards and conformity assessment procedures, most chapters lay down additional and more detailed obligations regarding joint cooperation, transparency, market surveillance, marking and labelling and contact points.

Many agreements include, for example, a separate set of obligations regarding marking or labelling requirements.[55] Such measures fall within the scope of the definition of technical regulations within the meaning of paragraph 1 of Annex 1 to the TBT Agreement. Apart from confirming the application of Article 2.2 of the TBT Agreement, the agreements impose further restrictions on the use of marking and labelling requirements in the form of a technical regulation. Those requirements concern, for example, the conditions under which a party may require prior approval or certification of labels and markings as a precondition for the sale of the products on its markets, the need for requirements to be relevant for consumers or users, the conditions under which unique identification numbers by economic operators may be required, the conditions under which information in other languages and internationally accepted nomenclatures, pictograms, symbols and graphics may be used, and a commitment to accepting non-permanent or detachable labels.[56] To take the example of the marking and labelling obligations under the EU-Ukraine Association Agreement, each party to that agreement may continue to determine the form of a label or mark or to require that information on that label or mark is in a specific language. However, they may not require the approval, registration or certification of a label. A separate provision expresses a commitment to minimising marking or labelling requirements but provides for an exception in case such requirements are needed for adopting the EU acquis and for protecting health, safety, the environment or for other "reasonable public policy purposes".[57]

In accordance with Articles X.4.1 and X.4.2 of Chapter XX (Technical Barriers to Trade) of the European Union's proposal for the EU-New Zealand and

---

55   See, for example, Art. 4.10 EU-Singapore FTA (n. 2).

56   See, for example, Art. 4.10 EU-Singapore FTA (n. 2); Art. 7.11 EU-Japan EPA (n. 3).

57   See, for example, Art. 58 EU-Ukraine Association Agreement (n. 11).

Australia FTA, the parties to those agreements would be obliged to prepare a regulatory impact assessment of planned technical regulations and assess the availability of regulatory and non-regulatory alternatives to the proposed technical regulation taking into account the legitimate objectives pursued. This type of provision gives further effect to Article 2.2 of the TBT Agreement by imposing certain procedural steps in preparing a technical regulation. Likewise, that proposal envisages additional process-based obligations in case a party sets a technical regulation without using an international standard. Thus, in accordance with Article X.4.6 of Chapter xx of the European Union's proposal for the EU-New Zealand and Australia FTA, the parties would need, upon the request of another party, to

> identify any substantial deviation from the relevant international standard and explain the reasons why such standards have been judged inappropriate or ineffective for the aim pursued, and provide the scientific or technical evidence on which this assessment is based.

5.3   *Increased Cooperation and Transparency*

The remaining obligations set out in the TBT chapters in EU trade agreements focus on, in particular, increased cooperation between treaty partners, including through the development of good regulatory processes[58] and greater transparency.[59] The agreements also establish new fora for the parties to discuss draft or proposed technical regulations or conformity assessment procedures[60] and, in general, any matter arising under the chapter.[61] In order to facilitate the implementation of the chapters on technical barriers to trade, certain agreements provide for the operation of TBT chapter coordinators or committees, appointed by each party.[62]

---

58   See, for example, Arts. 4.3, 4.4 and 4.5 CETA (n. 1), Art. 7.12 EU-Japan EPA (n. 3); Art. 55 EU-Ukraine Association Agreement (n. 11).

59   See, for example, Art. 4.6 CETA (n. 1); Art. 7.9 EU-Japan EPA (n. 3); Art. X.7 Chapter xx (Technical Barriers to Trade) of the European Union's proposal for the EU-New Zealand and Australia FTA (n. 12); Art. 4.8 EU-Singapore FTA (n. 2); Art. 49 EU-Georgia Association Agreement (n. 11).

60   See, for example, Art. X.9 Chapter xx (Technical Barriers to Trade) of the European Union's proposal for the EU-New Zealand and Australia FTA (n. 12).

61   See, for example, Art. X.9 Chapter xx (Technical Barriers to Trade) of the European Union's proposal for the EU-New Zealand and Australia FTA (n. 12).

62   See, for example, Art. X.10 Chapter xx (Technical Barriers to Trade) of the European Union's proposal for the EU-New Zealand and Australia FTA (n. 12); Art. 7.13 EU-Japan EPA (n. 3); Art. 4.7.1 CETA (n. 1).

Cooperation can take different forms. The softest model is that included in, for example, the EU-Singapore FTA. That model aims to strengthen cooperation in the field of technical barriers to trade by establishing various processes through which parties to the agreement obtain a better mutual understanding of their measures and may facilitate market access.[63]

Another form of cooperation is the establishment of a process through which the parties undertake to cooperate in order to ensure that their technical regulations are compatible with one another.[64] Yet another means of cooperating is the possibility of one party requesting the other party to recognise that its technical regulation, which it considers to be equivalent to a technical regulation of that party, has a compatible or equivalent objective and product scope.[65] If the other party refuses recognition, it must, upon request, state reasons for its decision.[66]

5.4   *Cooperation and Information Sharing Regarding the Development of (International) Standards*

Subject to those agreements by which a third State joins the EU single market (such as the EEA Agreement), no free trade agreement to which the European Union is a party envisages, in a general manner, the harmonisation of standards. Typically the European Union and its trading partners affirm their commitment to comply with Article 4.1 of the TBT Agreement which provides that:[67]

> Members shall ensure that their central government standardizing bodies accept and comply with the Code of Good Practice for the Preparation, Adoption and Application of Standards in Annex 3 to this Agreement (referred to in this Agreement as the "Code of Good Practice"). They shall take such reasonable measures as may be available to them to ensure that local government and non-governmental standardizing bodies within their territories, as well as regional standardizing bodies of which they or one or more bodies within their territories are members, accept and comply with this Code of Good Practice. In addition, Members shall not take measures which have the effect of, directly or indirectly, requiring or encouraging such standardizing bodies to act in a manner inconsistent

---

63   Arts. 4.4, 4.8 and 4.8 EU-Singapore FTA (n. 2); Arts. 7.9, 7.10 and 7.12 EU-Japan EPA (n. 3).
64   See, for example, Art. 4.4.1 CETA (n. 1).
65   See, for example, Art. 4.4.2 CETA (n. 1); Art. 7.5.2 EU-Japan EPA (n. 3).
66   See, for example, Art. 4.4.2 CETA (n. 1); Art. 7.5.2 EU-Japan EPA (n. 3).
67   See, for example, Art. 4.5.1 EU-Singapore FTA (n. 2); Art. 7.7.1 EU-Japan EPA (n. 3).

with the Code of Good Practice. The obligations of Members with respect to compliance of standardizing bodies with the provisions of the Code of Good Practice shall apply irrespective of whether or not a standardizing body has accepted the Code of Good Practice.

Other generally applicable obligations relate to cooperation between the parties' respective standardising bodies in international standardisation activities[68] and the exchange of information regarding the use of standards in support of technical regulations, the parties' standardisation processes, the extent of the use of international or regional standards and cooperation agreements on standardisation implemented by the parties.[69]

5.5   *Enhancing the Compatibility and Convergence of Technical Regulations*

Many of the agreements provide for a deeper commitment, going beyond Articles 2.4 and 2.8 of the TBT Agreement, to achieve compatibility and convergence of technical regulations through the use of international standards and the need for justification of the decision to depart from those standards, guides or recommendations.[70] One of the means through which this is done is agreeing to commitments on good regulatory practice.[71]

Specifying relevant international standards can take the form of defining the criteria that such standards must satisfy or of listing the relevant standards by name (which is particularly the case for certain sectoral arrangements). Often the agreements will include an annex listing the specific organisations which, for the purposes of the agreement, may develop international standards that are, in accordance with the agreement, relevant international standards.[72] For example, Article 7.6 of the EU-Japan EPA identifies the relevant international standard-setting bodies for the purposes of Chapter Seven on technical barriers to trade and also Articles 2 and 5 of the TBT Agreement and Annex 3 to the TBT Agreement. Those bodies are the International Organisation for Standardisation (ISO), the International Electrotechnical Commission (IEC), the

---

68   See, for example, Art. 4.5.2 EU-Singapore FTA (n. 2); Art. 7.6.2 EU-Japan EPA (n. 3).
69   See, for example, Art. 4.5.3 EU-Singapore FTA (n. 2); Art. 7.7.4 EU-Japan EPA (n. 3); Art. X.4.4 Chapter XX (Technical Barriers to Trade) of the European Union's proposal for the EU-New Zealand and Australia FTA (n. 12).
70   See, for example, Art. 7.6.2 and 3 EU-Japan EPA (n. 3); Art. 4.6 EU-Singapore FTA (n. 2).
71   See, for example, Art. 4.6 EU-Singapore FTA (n. 2); Art. 18 EU-Japan EPA (n. 3).
72   See also, Art. X.4.4 Chapter XX (Technical Barriers to Trade) of the European Union's proposal for the EU-New Zealand and Australia FTA (n. 12).

International Telecommunication Union (ITU), the Codex Alimentarius Commission, the International Civil Aviation Organisation (ICAO), the World Forum for Harmonization of Vehicle Regulations (WP.29) within the framework of the United Nations Economic Commission for Europe (UNECE), the United Nations Sub-Committee of Experts on the Globally Harmonized System of Classification and Labelling of Chemicals (UNSCEGHS), and the International Council for Harmonisation of Technical Requirements for Pharmaceuticals for Human Use (ICH).

Furthermore, the development of those standards must be in accordance with the principles and procedures laid down in the Decision of the WTO Committee on Technical Barriers to Trade on Principles for the Development of International Standards, Guides and Recommendations with Relation to Articles 2 and 3 of the TBT Agreement and Annex 3 to the TBT Agreement (TBT Committee Decision).[73] That suggests that, in defining the baseline, it is in fact insufficient to consider only the terms of the TBT Agreement. Rather, it is necessary to take into account also the activity of the TBT Committee which, as the WTO case-law has shown, might be normatively relevant even if it is not binding.[74] That means that rules developed in the WTO having no binding force might become treaty law and thus binding as a result of their incorporation in trade agreements to which the European Union is a party. Most agreements also envisage that, in particular, the TBT chapter is to be reviewed in light of any developments in the WTO Committee on Technical Barriers to Trade.[75]

5.6 *Harmonisation*

Similar to the TBT Agreement, the European Union's trade agreements seek to achieve harmonisation through primarily indirect means. Typically, no common standards are set. Apart from recognising what are relevant international standard-setting bodies, the parties commit to being active in the standard-setting bodies and to use relevant international standards.[76] Thus, the agreements identify relevant international standard-setting bodies and the parties commit to using those standards as the basis for their own standards, technical

---

73 See, for example, Art. 7.6.1 EU-Japan EPA (n. 3). See also, for example, Art. X.4.4 Chapter XX (Technical Barriers to Trade) of the European Union's proposal for the EU-New Zealand and Australia FTA (n. 12).

74 D. McDaniels, A. C. Molina, E. Wijkström, 'How does the regular work of the WTO influence regional trade agreements?', *Staff Working Paper* ERSD-2018-06.

75 See, for example, Art. 7.13.2(c) EU-Japan EPA (n. 3); Art. 4.7(f) CETA (n. 1).

76 See, for example, Art. 7.6.2 EU-Japan EPA (n. 3); Art. 4.6(b) EU-Singapore FTA (n. 2); Art. X.4.3 Chapter XX (Technical Barriers to Trade) of the European Union's proposal for the EU-New Zealand and Australia FTA, Art. 4.6(b) EU-Singapore FTA (n. 12).

regulations and conformity assessment procedures.[77] Parties may depart from those international standards in case it can be shown, subject to certain conditions, that using the standards would be ineffective or inappropriate for the fulfilment of the legitimate objectives pursued.[78] These obligations confirm mostly the main principles of the TBT Agreement.

A different model appears in association agreements. In those types of agreement, there might be some tension between, on the one hand, commitments to incorporate the EU *acquis* and, on the other hand, the recognition of the trading partner's right to regulate. For example, in the EU-Ukraine Association Agreement, the parties recognise their right

> to establish and regulate their own levels of domestic environmental and labour protection and sustainable development policies and priorities, in line with relevant internationally recognised principles and agreements, and to adopt or modify their legislation accordingly

and they commit to "ensure that their legislation provides for high levels of environmental and labour protection and shall strive to continue to improve that legislation".[79] At the same time, Article 56.1 of the EU-Ukraine Association Agreement provides that:

> Ukraine shall take the necessary measures in order to gradually achieve conformity with EU technical regulations and EU standardisation, metrology, accreditation, conformity assessment procedures and the market surveillance system, and undertakes to follow the principles and practices laid down in relevant EU Decisions and Regulations.

To that effect, Ukraine is to, for example, "incorporate the relevant EU acquis into its legislation",[80] "progressively transpose the corpus of European

---

77   See, for example, Arts. 7.6.2 and 7.6.3 EU-Japan EPA (n. 3); Art. X.4.3 Chapter XX (Technical Barriers to Trade) of the European Union's proposal for the EU-New Zealand and Australia FTA; Art. 4.6(b) EU-Singapore FTA (n. 12).

78   See, for example, Art. 7.6.3 EU-Japan EPA (n. 3); Art. 4.6(b) EU-Singapore FTA (n. 2); Art. X.4.6 Chapter XX (Technical Barriers to Trade) of the European Union's proposal for the EU-New Zealand and Australia FTA (n. 12).

79   Art. 290.1 EU-Ukraine Association Agreement (n. 11); Art. 228.1 EU-Georgia Association Agreement (n. 11).

80   Art. 56.2(i) EU-Ukraine Association Agreement (n. 11); see also Art. 290.2 EU-Ukraine Association Agreement (n. 11); Art. 47.2(a) EU-Georgia Association Agreement (n. 11).

standards (EN) as national standards",[81] "withdraw conflicting national standards",[82] and

> ensure that its relevant national bodies participate fully in the Europe-an and international organisations for standardisation, legal and funda-mental metrology, and conformity assessment including accreditation in accordance with its area of activity and the membership status available to it.[83]

Furthermore, Annex III to the agreement contains a list of both framework and sectoral legislation, specifying for each type of legislation a deadline with-in which Ukraine is to align its legislation with the relevant EU *acquis*. Ukraine accepts also to "progressively transpose the corpus of European standards [...] as national standards, including the harmonised European standards". Fur-thermore, under that agreement, the parties commit

> to add an ACAA [the Agreement on Conformity Assessment and Accep-tance of Industrial Products] as a Protocol to this Agreement, covering one or more sectors listed in Annex III to this Agreement once they have agreed that the relevant Ukrainian sectoral and horizontal legislation, in-stitutions and standards have been fully aligned with those of the EU.[84]

As a result, upon Ukraine's alignment of its legislation in accordance with An-nex III, the parties may then agree to add a protocol to the association agree-ment. That ACAA, which would cover one or more sectors listed in Annex III (though the scope may, over time, be further widened[85]) is to "provide that trade between the parties in goods in covered sectors is to take place under the same conditions as those applying to trade in such goods between the Member States of the European Union".[86]

---

81   Art. 56.8 EU-Ukraine Association Agreement (n. 11); Art. 47.5(a) EU-Georgia Association Agreement (n. 11).
82   Art. 56.8 EU-Ukraine Association Agreement (n. 11); Art. 47.2(b) EU-Georgia Association Agreement (n. 11).
83   Art. 56.7 EU-Ukraine Association Agreement (n. 11); Art. 47.4 EU-Georgia Association Agreement (n. 11).
84   Art. 57.1 EU-Ukraine Association Agreement (n. 11); Art. 48 EU-Georgia Association Agreement (n. 11).
85   Art. 57.4 EU-Ukraine Association Agreement (n. 11).
86   Art. 57.2 EU-Ukraine Association Agreement (n. 11).

As a result, the EU-Ukraine Association Agreement offers an example of one of the most advanced models of cooperation in the area of technical barriers to trade, whereby one party becomes a "rule taker" and in essence accepts that relevant parts of EU law are "exported" to a wider geographical area, namely that covered by the trade agreement. As a result of transposing the EU *acquis* in this manner, the party that becomes the rule taker must also accept the jurisdiction of the Court of Justice of the European Union as regards the interpretation and application of those rules. This is not the case for other types of regulatory cooperation.

5.7   *Conformity Assessment Procedures: Testing and Certification*

Separate obligations apply with respect to the results of conformity assessment procedures. At a general level, TBT chapters frequently envisage the various mechanisms through which the acceptance of the results of conformity assessment procedures may be facilitated (in the same manner as stand-alone mutual recognition agreements, discussed previously).[87] Such mechanisms include reliance on a supplier's declaration of conformity, accreditation procedures in order to qualify as conformity assessment bodies, government designation of conformity assessment bodies, unilateral recognition of the results, voluntary arrangements between conformity assessment bodies and use of regional or international recognition agreements. The agreements then lay down how both parties may, through subsequent actions (such as the exchange of information), put in place these mechanisms.[88]

One illustration, in this regard, is CETA. In addition to generally applicable obligations regarding conformity assessment procedures, two protocols attached to CETA address mutual acceptance or recognition of the results of conformity assessment. One protocol (namely the Protocol on the mutual acceptance of the results of conformity assessment) applies to a list of different products for which a party recognises non-governmental bodies for the purposes of conformity assessment (such as electrical and electronic equipment, radio and telecommunications terminal equipment, toys, machinery). It envisages that the product scope may be widened. Subject to certain conditions, each party accepts to recognise (accredited) conformity assessment bodies of the other party on national treatment terms and to accept the results of the conformity assessment activities carried out by those bodies. The second

---

87   Art. 4.7.1 EU-Singapore FTA (n. 2); Art. 7.8.3 EU-Japan EPA (n. 3); Art. 3 CETA (n. 1); Art. X.6 Chapter XX (Technical Barriers to Trade) of the European Union's proposal for the EU-New Zealand and Australia FTA (n. 12).

88   Art. 4.7.2 EU-Singapore FTA (n. 2); Arts. 7.8.4 and 7.8.5 EU-Japan EPA. (n. 3).

protocol applies with respect to pharmaceutical products (that is, the Protocol on the mutual recognition of the compliance and enforcement programme regarding good manufacturing practices for pharmaceutical products). It lays down detailed obligations regarding the recognition of certificates attesting to the compliance of a manufacturing facility with Good Manufacturing Practices and the conditions under which batch certificates are to be accepted and on-site evaluations may be carried out.

6 Sector-Specific Obligations Regarding Technical Barriers to Trade

Sector-specific obligations appear in the form of annexes and protocols (of which some have already been discussed in this chapter). Although the generally applicable obligations are aimed mostly at confirming the WTO obligations in the TBT Agreement and enhancing regulatory cooperation, the sector-specific obligations are more ambitious.

What sectors are covered by such specific obligations depends on the agreement at issue. Relevant sectors often include motor vehicles and equipment and parts thereof, electronics and pharmaceutical products. The types of sector-specific obligation may relate to the definition of common standards or regulations or processes for mutual recognition of standards or regulations but also the results of conformity assessment procedures. A few illustrations of such annexes or protocols help to explain the scope of these commitments.

The first example is Annex 4-A to the EU-Singapore FTA concerning electronics. It applies to standards, technical regulations and conformity assessment procedures of either party related to the safety and electromagnetic compatibility of electrical and electronic equipment, electrical household appliances and consumer electronics.[89] The TBT Agreement does not define what international standards or international standard-setting bodies are relevant to particular sectors of goods. By contrast, Annex 4-A identifies the ISO, the IEC and the ITU as the relevant international standard-setting bodies.[90] By decision of the Committee on Trade in Goods, the parties may add other bodies to that list.[91] The parties commit to consulting within the framework of the relevant international standard-setting bodies with a view to establishing a common approach in that body.[92] They accept to use relevant international

---

89 Art. 1(2) of Annex 4-A EU-Singapore FTA (n. 2).
90 Art. 2(1) of Annex 4-A EU-Singapore FTA (n. 2).
91 Footnote 1 of Annex 4-A EU-Singapore FTA (n. 2).
92 Art. 2(4) of Annex 4-A EU-Singapore FTA (n. 2).

standards produced by those bodies. An exception applies in case the standards would be an ineffective or inappropriate means for fulfilling the legitimate objective pursued but the party deciding not to use the standard might need to justify that decision[93] and will need to review at regular intervals the technical regulations at issue.[94] The other two main sets of obligations relate to conformity assessment procedures and safeguards. There is a commitment to rely, in principle, on a supplier's declaration of conformity and/or post market surveillance mechanisms instead of using mandatory third party conformity assessment.[95] Mandatory third party testing or certification or administrative procedures for approving or reviewing test reports are still possible (under the conditions for imposing safeguard measures), in particular where compelling reasons related to the protection of human health or safety exist that justify the introduction of such requirements or procedures, supported by substantiated technical or scientific information.[96] Furthermore, a provision (entitled "Exceptions") concerns the specific commitments undertaken by Singapore to reduce substantially the list of products for which it requires a positive conformity assessment with its mandatory safety and/or EMC requirements in the form of third party certification.[97] Finally, the parties commit not to prevent or unduly delay the placing on their respective markets of a product on the ground that that product incorporates a new technology or a new feature which has not yet been regulated.[98]

The second example is Annex 4-A to CETA, entitled "Cooperation in the field of motor vehicle regulations". That annex is aimed at strengthening

> cooperation and communication [...] on motor vehicle safety and environmental performance research activities related to the development of new technical regulations or related standards, to promote the application and recognition of the Global Technical Regulations under the framework of the 1998 Global Agreement [the 1998 Global Agreement administered by the World Forum for the Harmonization of Vehicle Regulations of the United Nations Economic Commission for Europe] and possible future harmonisation.[99]

---

93   Art. 2(2) of Annex 4-A EU-Singapore FTA (n. 2).
94   Art. 2(3) of Annex 4-A EU-Singapore FTA (n. 2).
95   Art. 4 of Annex 4-A EU-Singapore FTA (n. 2).
96   Art. 5 of Annex 4-A EU-Singapore FTA (n. 2).
97   Art. 6 of Annex 4-A EU-Singapore FTA (n. 2).
98   Art. 3 of Annex 4-A EU-Singapore FTA (n. 2).
99   Art. 1.6 of Annex 4-A CETA (n. 1).

The object of that annex is, in essence, to further develop regulatory cooperation in the area of motor vehicle regulations. Article 5 of that Annex requires
each party to consider the technical regulations of the other party when it decides to develop a new or modify an existing technical regulation for motor
vehicles and their parts. Various types of information sharing obligations appear in this chapter. One of the more far-reaching obligations concerns Canada's obligation to inform the European Union before it amends or revises its
laws.[100] Article 6 of Annex 4-A to CETA also includes cooperation obligations
with reference to a possible future EU-US agreement. Should the European
Union and the United States conclude an agreement or arrangement on the
harmonisation of their respective technical regulations relating to motor vehicles, the European Union and Canada commit to cooperation "with a view
to determining whether they should conclude a similar agreement or arrangement". In addition, CETA contains a separate Protocol on the mutual recognition of the compliance and enforcement programme regarding good manufacturing practices for pharmaceutical products.[101]

The third example is Annex 2-C to the EU-Japan EPA on "Motor vehicles and
parts". In that annex, the parties agree, inter alia, to:

> recognise that the [World Forum for Harmonization of Vehicle Regula-
> tions, acting within the framework of the United Nations and the Eco-
> nomic Commission for Europe or "WP.29"] is the relevant international
> standardising body for the covered products, and that UN Regulations
> [meaning UN Regulations established in accordance with the Agree-
> ment concerning the Adoption of Harmonized Technical United Na-
> tions Regulations for Wheeled Vehicles, Equipment and Parts which can
> be Fitted and/or be Used on Wheeled Vehicles and the Conditions for
> Reciprocal Recognition of Approvals Granted on the Basis of these Unit-
> ed Nations Regulations] and GTRs [meaning a global technical regula-
> tion established and placed on the Global Registry in accordance with
> the 1998 Agreement] are relevant international standards for covered
> products.[102]

Both parties also commit to accept on their market, without requiring any further testing, documentation, certification or marking,

---

100   Art. 4.2 of Annex 4-A CETA (n. 1).
101   See, for example, Art. 4.5 CETA (n. 1).
102   Art. 4 of Annex 2-C EU-Japan EPA (n. 3).

products which are covered by a type approval certificate, under the 1958 Agreement, for the UN Regulations specified in Appendix 2-C-1 as compliant with its domestic technical regulations and conformity assessment procedures, in the area regulated by the relevant UN Regulation.[103]

Furthermore, the parties agree to cooperate closely in the establishment of new UN regulations.[104] In accordance with Article 12 to Annex 2-C, the parties are also to

refrain from introducing any new domestic technical regulations or conformity assessment procedures which have the effect of preventing or increasing the burden for the importation and the putting into service on their domestic market of products for which type approvals have been granted under UN Regulations applied by both Parties, for the areas covered by those UN Regulations unless such domestic technical regulations or conformity assessment procedures are explicitly provided for by those UN Regulations.

The parties commit not to prevent or unduly delay the placing on their respective markets of a product on the ground that the pertinent product incorporates a new technology or a new feature for which regulation does not yet exist.[105] A general exception clause offers a legal basis for a party to refuse placing the product on its market or to require the withdrawal of the product from the market if "there are urgent and compelling risks for human health, safety or the environment",[106] provided that "[s]uch a refusal or requirement shall not constitute a means of arbitrary or unjustifiable discrimination against the products of the other Party or a disguised restriction on trade". When that right is exercised, Article 15.2 requires notification of the other party as well as of the manufacturer or the importer; it must be "accompanied by an objective, reasoned and detailed explanation of the risks and the measures and any relevant scientific and technical evidence". Finally, Article 16 confirms each party's

right to adopt regulatory measures necessary for safety, environmental protection or public health and the prevention of deceptive practices, provided that such measures are based on substantiated scientific or

---

103   Art. 5.1 of Annex 2-C EU-Japan EPA (n. 3).
104   Art. 7 of Annex 2-C EU-Japan EPA (n. 3).
105   Art. 14 of Annex 2-C EU-Japan EPA (n. 3).
106   Art. 15 of Annex 2-C EU-Japan EPA (n. 3).

technical information and that the relevant cooperation provided for in this Annex has been undertaken in good faith.

A final example is chapter 2 of the EU-Japan EPA, addressing trade in goods, which contains specific obligations relating to wine products. It lays down a phased process according to which the European Union and Japan agree to authorise importation and sale of wine products for human consumption produced in accordance with specified product definitions and oenological practices authorised and restrictions applied in the respective countries.[107] For Japanese wine products, a certificate issued in conformity with Japanese laws and regulations, including a producer's self-certificate, is sufficient for access to the European market.[108] For European wine products, no certificate or equivalent documentation is required for market access in Japan.[109] There is also a catch – all provision according to which both parties must refrain from nullifying or impairing the market access benefits accruing to the other Party under Annex 2-C through other regulatory measures specific to the sector covered by the Annex.[110]

Apart from general means of enforcement through dispute settlement, certain agreements provide for types of sector-specific safeguard to be applied with respect to the failure to apply commitments relating to technical barriers to trade. One example is Article 18 of Annex 2-C (on motor vehicles and parts) of the EU-Japan EPA. That provision gives each party a right to apply a safeguard, during ten years following the entry into force of the agreement to:

> suspend equivalent concessions or other equivalent obligations in the event that the other Party:
>
> (a) does not apply or ceases applying a UN Regulation as specified in Appendix 2-C-1; or (b) introduces or amends any other regulatory measure that nullifies or impairs the benefits of the application of a UN Regulation as specified in Appendix 2-C-1.

---

107   Arts. 2.25 to 2.27 EU-Japan EPA (n. 3).

108   Art. 2.28(1) EU-Japan EPA (n. 3). The EU-Japan Working Group on Wine has already adopted further implementing action in respect of, in particular, Article 2.28: Decision No 1/2019 of the EU-Japan Group on Wine of 1 February 2019 on the forms to be used for certificated for the import of wine products originating in Japan into the European Union and the modalities concerning self-certification (2019/224), (OJ 2019 L 35, p. 36).

109   Art. 2.28(3) EU-Japan EPA (n. 3).

110   Art. 16 of Annex 2-C EU-Japan EPA (n. 3).

Those safeguards may remain in force "only until a decision is made in accordance with the accelerated dispute settlement procedure referred to in Article 19 of this Annex or a mutually acceptable solution is found".

For sector-specific obligations relating to regulatory convergence commitments, an accelerated dispute settlement procedure is sometimes included. That is the case for, again, Annex 2-C (on Motor vehicles and parts) to the EU-Japan EPA. The particularities of that procedure include the fast-tracking of disputes concerning the interpretation and application of the Annex: they are to be considered as matters of urgency and time lines for consultations, for the issuance of the interim report and the final report and for the reasonable period of time and for the implementation of countermeasures are shorter than normal.

These examples show that there is no single model for sector-specific obligations. Although it is common for the agreements to define for specific sectors the pertinent international standard-setting bodies that are relevant for the parties' development of technical regulations in accordance with international standards, other sector-specific obligations vary: they include diverse approaches such as rules exempting exporters from the need for conformity assessments; the (gradual) phasing out of mandatory conformity assessments by third parties in favour of self-certification (subject to possible safeguards); and, last but not least, multilateral recognition of results of conformity assessment procedures of the other party.

7   Chapters on Trade and Sustainable Development, Trade and Labour and Trade and Environment, Renewable Energy

The TBT chapters in the European Union's new trade agreements cannot be read in isolation of the chapters on trade and sustainable development, trade and labour and trade and environment or chapters relating to non-tariff barriers to trade and investment in renewable energy generation. To a large extent, obligations in those chapters seek to promote adherence to and the implementation of labour and environmental standards laid down in other international agreements or in so-called soft law instruments.[111] Some link those commitments with technical barriers to trade. For example, Article 24.8 of CETA expresses the parties' resolution "to make efforts to facilitate and

---

111   See, for example, Chapter 12 EU-Singapore FTA (n. 2); Chapters 22, 23, 24 CETA (n. 1); Chapter 16 EU-Japan EPA (n. 3); Chapter 13 EU-Ukraine Association Agreement (n. 11); Chapter 13 EU-Georgia Association Agreement (n. 11).

promote trade and investment in environmental goods and services, including through addressing the reduction of non-tariff barriers related to these goods and services".

Whilst in the context of the TBT Agreement, the relevance of such treaties and soft law instruments is to be considered on a case-by-case basis in WTO dispute settlement, their importance in the enforcement of obligations under the TBT chapters, including the provisions of the TBT Agreement that are incorporated therein, is generally recognised by the parties to the European Union's trade agreements. This may result in more progressive interpretations and applications of identical obligations under those trade agreements as compared to the available practice under the TBT Agreement.

Despite the common emphasis on each party's right to regulate, chapters on, for example, trade and environment may interfere with the exercise of that right. For example, Article 24.5.1 of CETA states that "[t]he Parties recognise that it is inappropriate to encourage trade or investment by weakening or reducing the levels of protection afforded in their environmental law".[112] A sharper contrast is found in Article 290 of the EU-Ukraine Association Agreement. It recognises each party's right to establish and regulate its own levels of domestic environmental and labour protection and sustainable development policies and priorities (para. 1), but adds that "Ukraine shall approximate its laws, regulations and administrative practice to the EU acquis" "[a]s a way to achieve the objectives referred to in this Article" (para. 2).

The EU-Singapore FTA and the EU-Vietnam Agreement contain a separate chapter on non-tariff barriers to trade and investment in renewable energy generation. The objectives of, for example, Chapter Seven of the EU-Singapore FTA are twofold: to establish cooperation between the two parties towards removing or reducing tariffs and non-tariff barriers and to foster regulatory convergence with or towards regional and international standards.[113] In particular, the parties to that agreement accept to use, in principle, international or regional standards with respect to products for the generation of energy from renewable and sustainable non-fossil sources and recognise that in particular ISO and IEC are relevant international standard-setting bodies.[114] They commit to specify, where appropriate, technical regulations based on product requirements in terms of performance, including environmental performance and not on design or descriptive characteristics.[115] For certain products, defined by

---

112   See also point 9.b of the Joint Interpretative Instrument to CETA (n. 36).
113   Art. 7.1 EU-Singapore FTA (n. 2).
114   Art. 7.5 EU-Singapore FTA (n. 2).
115   Art. 7.5 EU-Singapore FTA (n. 2).

reference to their Harmonized System (HS) numbers, the European Union accepts Singaporean suppliers' declaration of conformity under the same terms as from Union suppliers for the purpose of placing the products on the European market, and Singapore accepts EU conformity declarations or test reports.

8   Conclusion

There is no single model in the European Union's recent trade agreements for the regulation of technical barriers to trade. Agreements typically incorporate (large parts of) the TBT Agreement and possibly also certain decisions or other instruments adopted by the WTO TBT Committee. In that manner, such instruments thus become legally binding whereas they do not have such a status as a matter of WTO law.

Building on the obligations laid down in the TBT Agreement, those agreements seek to establish various forms of closer cooperation regarding the development and application of technical barriers to trade and to promote the compatibility and convergence of regulations based on international standards which are, for certain sectors, specifically defined. Taking into account that these agreements are typically not directly aimed at achieving harmonisation and therefore that each party maintains its right to regulate, facilitating (or omitting) conformity assessment (by promoting recognition of assessments) is a central theme of many of the TBT chapters in removing barriers to trade. The specific model used for achieving that objective will depend on the type of good though there are some attempts to develop a model that could be used for a wider group of goods.

Acknowledgement

The author is grateful for the helpful comments received from the participants of the workshop on the Law and Practice of the Common Commercial Policy: The First 10 Years after the Treaty of Lisbon, organised by the University of Berne (Institute for European and International Law (IEW) and World Trade Institute (WTI)), the Ghent European Law Institute, and CEPS (Brussels, 7–8 June 2018) and for the editorial assistance provided by Victoria Ciudin.

CHAPTER 9

Public Procurement in EU FTAS

Stephen Woolcock

1   The Wider Context

With multilateralism stalled during the 2000s most of the developments in trade and investment, and thus the extension of the rules-based trading system have taken place through the vehicle of preferential trade and investment agreements (PTAS). The debate on the pros and cons of preferential versus plurilateral or multilateral approaches is now giving way to a concern about the stability of the rules-based trading system *per se*.[1] One source of instability is whether there is support for an extension of the multilateral trading system beyond the existing WTO rules from China and other emerging markets. Another source of uncertainty is whether the apparent US shift towards a power-based approach to trade is a temporary phenomenon or something more structural. Finally, there is the general backlash against globalisation as a result of populist pressures.

In this environment it is in the interests of the EU to defend and ideally promote a stronger rules-based trading system. This is because the EU represents the most comprehensive application of a rules-based order. The EU has generally gone further in applying the norms and codes developed internationally, including in public procurement.[2] The EU has also gone further in the sense that EU rules are binding and subject to direct effect, thus introducing a form of "constitutionalisation" of international best practice in public procurement practice as expressed in OECD,[3]

---

1   A rules-based order means one that provides a framework of agreed rules that promotes predictability and stability in international trade and investment. This can be contrasted with a power-based order in which more powerful or larger economies shape the conditions of trade unilaterally (see J. Jackson, 1995).

2   For example, voluntary codes of conduct or conventions such as those developed in the OECD have been implemented in EU law. This is the case for public procurement, in which the rules developed in the OECD have been applied by the EU in binding legislation. It is also true in other areas such as the financial market regulations, or labour standards, where ILO conventions have formed the basis of relevant EU provisions.

3   See for example OECD Recommendation of the Council on Public Procurement (2015): http:// www.oecd.org/gov/public-procurement/recommendation/OECD-Recommendation-on-Public-Procurement.pdf.

© KONINKLIJKE BRILL NV, LEIDEN, 2021 | DOI:10.1163/9789004393417_011

WTO[4] or UNCITRAL[5] codes and instruments. Deeper integration in the EU has gone hand-in-hand with the adoption of a comprehensive, rules-based order at the EU level. The EU is therefore understandably interested in rolling out comprehensive rules internationally. The comprehensive nature of EU provisions on transparency in public contracts means it is generally easier for non-EU suppliers to be aware of EU calls for tender and how these will be awarded than it is for EU suppliers in many third countries. The nature of EU decision-making, based on a *de jure* qualified majority but *de facto* on consensus, also means that there is little prospect of the EU shifting to adopt a power-based trade policy, should this be the trend in trade policy in general and procurement markets in particular (F. Hoffmeister, 2016).[6]

The key question is therefore whether the EU can defend and ideally extend the rules-based order. In this context extending the scope of rules on procurement represents something of a litmus test for the ability of the EU and the international trading system as a whole to retain and build a rules-based order.

2   Why Include Public Procurement?

Public procurement represents an important share of GDP in most countries. Although data is generally patchy, public procurement at the central and sub-central government levels as well as procurement by state-owned/parastatal enterprises accounts for around 12% of GDP in developed economies.[7] It is probably the most important policy area, in terms of funding, in which governments retain discretionary powers. The EU supports the inclusion of public procurement in trade rules for a range of reasons, both normative and commercial.

---

4   See WTO Revised Government Procurement Agreement (2014 entry into force): https://www.wto.org/english/docs_e/legal_e/rev-gpr-94_01_e.htm.

5   UNCITRAL Model Law on Public Procurement (2014): https://www.uncitral.org/pdf/english/texts/procurem/ml-procurement-2011/2011-Model-Law-on-Public-Procurement-e.pdf.

6   This can also be illustrated by the case of public procurement. For some time there has been a debate on whether the EU should adopt an International Procurement Instrument (IPI) that would in effect enable the EU to threaten to close its market if it does not get "fair" access to other key markets, see Commission (2016). The European Council has called for the resumption of discussions on the IPI but to date, not been possible to reach an agreement on the adoption of such an instrument. Commission Guidance on the participation of third country (China is referred to several times) bidders and goods in the EU procurement market (C 2019) 5494 of July 2019 is based on existing legislation.

7   This is the OECD 34 average: http://www.oecd.org/gov/public-procurement/.

In normative terms, rules on procurement can help ensure value for money and counter corruption in the awarding of public contracts. The fact that discretionary power remains in the hands of government means that public contracts represent a major vehicle for and source of corruption, when there are inadequate forms of scrutiny and control. Corrupt practices can be found in countries at all levels of development, including within the EU, but the implications in terms of economic losses and the undermining of confidence and legitimacy of government is more pronounced in the less developed economies.[8] The adoption of rules on transparency and due process and objective criteria in the award of public contracts can therefore contribute to the better use of limited public funds and thus contributing to sustainable development.

In commercial terms, the fact that the EU regime for public procurement is more comprehensive than any other national or international agreements, means that the EU is more transparent and arguably more open than other markets.[9] In the EU, comprehensive rules cover all levels of procurement with transparency and national treatment obligations.[10] This contrasts with the absence of any binding obligations on the procurement in emerging economies that have not signed the WTO's Government Procurement Agreement (GPA) and often have extensive public and state-owned enterprise sectors. The state and state-owned enterprises in these countries can use discretion in the awarding of contracts to promote national champions and to keep out EU suppliers. In other words the EU is seeking a "level playing field" or reciprocity in public procurement that accounts for about 15% of world markets.

3   Why Preferential Trade Agreements?

One short answer to the question of why the EU seeks to include rules on public procurement in the PTAs it negotiates is that the multilateral and plurilateral

---

8   While figures are by definition difficult to obtain on the waste caused by corrupt practices, surveys show that bribes are more common in public contracts than any other field and as much as 20% of the value of public contracts could be lost due to corruption. See UN Office on Drugs and Crime: https://www.unodc.org/documents/corruption/Publications/2013/Guidebook_on_anti-corruption_in_public_procurement_and_the_management_of_public_finances.pdf.

9   There has been a debate on this topic in the context of the TTIP negotiations with the US and some literature that has sought to measure the relative degrees of openness of the EU market with others, see S. Woolcock and J. H. Grier, 2015.

10   See Annex 1 for a summary of the topics generally included in agreements on public procurement.

alternatives have failed or are too slow. Public procurement was explicitly excluded from the scope of the GATT in1947. In 1963, work began in the OECD on the topic. In line with the normal development of trade rules (at least until the 2000s), the code developed in the OECD was then carried over into GATT rules in the form of the 1979 Agreement on Government Procurement (GPA). The next major advance came in 1994 with the revised plurilateral GPA another 15 years on. The 1994 GPA was more extensive and included enforcement provisions in the shape of the bid challenge procedures. Bid challenge that enables companies to seek review of contract award decisions was first introduced in the Canada – US FTA in 1988. The advances in the 1990s also owed much to the comprehensive rules on procurement introduced by the EU as part of the Single European Market (SEM). The latest revision of the GPA rules was agreed in 2011 and that for commitments on coverage in 2014, so another 20 years later. And by 2014 the number of countries and types of public procurement covered is still far from complete.

International agreements on public procurement have two main elements: rules and coverage.[11] The rules (see Annex 1 for a listing of the details) emerged from the work in the OECD and have both shaped and been shaped by the EU, which has incorporated the OECD approach in binding EU legislation. The voluntary UNCITRAL model law on procurement that has been used by many developing countries is also based on the OECD approach. Donors, such as the World Bank, also require developing countries to follow very similar rules when the former fund public expenditure. It could therefore be argued that there is a *de facto* international norm or best practice in public procurement based on the OECD norm.

In terms of the coverage – of these rules – both in terms of the countries that sign up to them and which types of purchasing entity they agree to cover, there has been much less progress. Coverage has been negotiated within the GATT/WTO but has been signed only by OECD economies and a few others such as Hong Kong. Even some OECD economies such as New Zealand and Australia have only recently joined.

The EU preference was to include greater coverage of the rules on procurement in the WTO as reflected in the EU efforts to include procurement as one

---

11   A distinction has been made between transparency and liberalisation. This facilitated international agreement, it being thought easier to agree on transparency than specific commitments. In practice the distinction is a less clear. Most impediments to competition in public contracts take the form of *de facto* – rather than specific *de jure* (i.e. price margins favouring local suppliers) – preferences. This means that transparency can have the effect of enhancing competition.

of the so-called "Singapore issues" from the mid-1990s. In the subsequent debate in the WTO, developing countries opposed any "liberalisation" so the discussions were limited to transparency. In this the EU also sought to be comprehensive. EU experience internally had been that this was necessary in order for transparency to be effectively achieved.[12] The EU, supported by the USA, also argued that *all* procurement should be covered by transparency requirements, not just procurement covered by schedules, and that this should be subject to dispute settlement.[13] Developing country WTO members opposed detailed transparency rules, arguing that only "covered procurement" should be subject to transparency requirements, and opposed the use of dispute settlement. In the end, these countries accepted the normative case for transparency, but not the case for inclusion of rules in the WTO.[14]

The EU has also promoted plurilateral efforts. In the text of the 2011 revised GPA rules there were provisions on special and differential treatment (see Annex 1) that had been added in order to encourage developing country signatories, but with few concrete results thus far. In the negotiations on coverage, the EU and other signatories sought extensions on coverage and the inclusion of China in particular. China agreed to negotiate accession to the GPA when it joined the WTO. Increases in the value of procurement covered by the GPA of some $18 billion were agreed by 2014, but there remain gaps in coverage of existing signatories, such as at the sub-central government level. And in the end, China could not be persuaded to join.

Inevitably, negotiations on rules and coverage of public procurement have been multi-level in nature. As well as pressing the case at the multilateral and plurilateral levels, the EU has sought to include procurement in the PTAs it negotiates. This has been in part driven by competition, such as from the USA and other OECD countries that negotiate PTAs including procurement (S. Khorana and M. Garcia, 2016). But the US and others have domestic constraints on what they can offer, in particular offers on coverage of sub-federal level procurement. The EU policy on procurement in PTAs is therefore shaped

---

12   The EU sought to include for example, requirements to publish all laws and regulations, information on planned procurement, contact points, information on the type of contract award procedure followed for each call for tender, the contract award criteria, calls for tender as well as any *de jure* preferences or local content requirements (S. Arrowsmith, 1996).

13   This is in line with the UNCITRAL approach, which is intended to apply to all procurement. The difference between UNCITRAL and the efforts in the WTO or in PTAs is that the adoption of UNCITRAL rules is voluntary.

14   More recently there appears to be more interest from a number of non-OECD economies, which have become observers in the GPA with some considering a move to accession.

by the normative belief that comprehensive rules promote objective contract award criteria, and by the fact that the EU has gone further than others in implementing a rules-based regime for procurement.

4   How Successful?

The EU approach to negotiating procurement provisions in PTAs has varied according to the negotiating partner. Broadly speaking, it is possible to differentiate between PTA partners that are signatories to the GPA, in other words developed market economy countries; neighbouring states with deep and comprehensive trade agreements; middle or high income developing economies; smaller or less developed economies; and significant emerging market economies (see also S. Woolcock, 2017).

In terms of the first group of GPA signatories, the EU has succeeded in enhancing the coverage beyond that in the 2014 GPA schedules in some cases, most significantly in the case of the CETA with Canada. For the EU's neighbouring states, such as the Ukraine, the deep and comprehensive trade agreements envisage the progressive adoption of the EU regime for procurement. For the middle income developing economies, the EU has succeeded in getting some partners to sign up to GPA type rules on transparency and some commitments on coverage. Examples here are the Columbia/Peru and Central American PTAs. There has however, been less progress with the more significant emerging market economies. Negotiations with Mercosur have also now been completed and include extensive provisions on procurement.[15] Negotiations with India do not appear to be making much progress and, if agreed, are likely to cover only transparency. Finally, with regard to smaller or less developed economies, the EU has succeeded in concluding an agreement with CARICOM on transparency rules. Table 9.1 provides a summary overview of the provisions in existing PTAs completed by the EU.

4.1   *Agreements with GPA Signatories*
Of the agreements with GPA signatories, the procurement provisions in the CETA are the most significant in that they include for the first time comprehensive coverage of provincial and municipal purchasing as well as that of the Crown Companies, in other words the para-statal bodies or type III entities

---

15   See http://trade.ec.europa.eu/doclib/press/index.cfm?id=2048. However, there appear to be no details yet on the scope of coverage.

TABLE 9.1 Summary of procurement provisions in PTAs concluded by the EU

Preferential trade agreement	GPA signatory	Transparency provisions	Coverage	NT	No off-sets	Bid/challenge	Comment
CETA	yes	GPA rules	GPA plus type II and III	yes	yes	yes	Procurement key issue in CETA, precedent for other federal states
Japan	yes	GPA rules	GPA plus; Japan higher thresholds for type II and III works	yes	yes	yes	Special arrangements to facilitate transparency for EU bids in rail sector
Singapore	yes	GPA rules	GPA plus; e.g. Singapore adds utilities	yes	yes	yes	Adoption of up to date GPA rules
Korea	yes	GPA rules	GPA plus build transfer and operate contracts; Korea higher thresholds for type II and III works	yes	yes	yes	Minimal additions to GPA due to timing
Ukraine	no	Progressive approximation of EU rules	Nominally covers all procurement				Effectively means reform of existing Ukraine provisions in line with EU *acquis*

TABLE 9.1 Summary of procurement provisions in PTAs concluded by the EU (*cont.*)

Preferential trade agreement	GPA signatory	Transparency provisions	Coverage	NT	No off-sets	Bid/ challenge	Comment
Mexico revision of 2001 PTA not yet finalised	No, but signed GPA like NAFTA	GPA type but less comprehensive	Type I and some type III; type II under discussion; higher threshold for works	yes	Most likely	Most likely	Illustration of extended coverage in revised agreements
Columbia/ Peru/	no	Very similar to GPA rules (best endeavours on some aspects)	Coverage of Type I, II and III with GPA thresholds	yes	yes	yes	Fairly comprehensive with EU offering some asymmetric coverage benefiting Colombia and Peru
Central America	no	GPA type	Type I, II and III, higher thresholds for smaller countries	yes	yes	yes	Fairly comprehensive
Vietnam	no	Broadly in line with UNCITRAL	Type I with some type III; phased reduction of thresholds over 16 years	yes	yes	yes	Use of phased reduction of thresholds
Cariforum	no	Similar but less detailed than GPA	Type I	no	no	yes	Transparency only, commitments to be negotiated; EU offers asymmetric coverage

Euromed partners	no						Simple reference to the aim of mutual access to procurement markets; current EU proposed text for DCFTA draws on GPA
East African Community, EPA	no						Rendezvous clause to negotiate
Mercosur	no	Agreement on a text	In principle types I, II and III	yes	yes	yes	Text agreed but no details of coverage yet
India	no	Slow progress					Procurement a problem topic

SOURCE: TEXTS OF VARIOUS AGREEMENTS: HTTP://EC.EUROPA.EU/TRADE/POLICY/COUNTRIES-AND-REGIONS/; TYPE I = CENTRAL GOVERNMENT; TYPE II SUB-CENTRAL/PROVINCES AND STATES; TYPE III PARA-STATAL COMPANIES/UTILITIES. SEE ALSO S. WOOLCOCK, 2017

as they are known in WTO terminology. The EU made inclusion of sub-federal procurement a condition for CETA. It may also serve as a precedent for negotiations with similar federal states, such as Australia. But success including procurement will depend on how much the EU's trading partner needs a PTA with the EU. Canada had been keen to negotiate for some time because of its desire to diversify from its dependence on the USA.

The agreements with Korea, Singapore and Japan were GPA plus in a number of respects. The least ambitious being the EU – Korea PTA, as it was completed in 2010. But the EU – Korea agreement did add "build, transfer and operate" (BTO) contracts to the coverage. The FTA with Japan raised some challenging questions concerning coverage. Although the Japanese commitments under the GPA include prefectures (47 in all), there was limited coverage of the municipal level procurement. As noted in the table, Japan also has some higher thresholds for works (i.e. construction projects) at the sub-national level; also, the EU is also especially interested in effective access to the Japanese market, i.e. not just in what is listed in the schedules but what happens in practice. For example, while Japan conforms to the GPA rules it does not provide systematic English translations of information. Another controversial question was the technical specifications for contracts with *Japan Railways* (the so-called Operational Safety Clause), which can be – and was – seen by EU suppliers of rail equipment as a technical barrier to access in the rail sector.[16] *Japan Railways* were privatised and thus seen to be subject to normal market conditions and so removed from the list of public entities subject to the discipline of the GPA rules, whereas most EU rail operators remain in the public ownership or regulated sectors, which brings them under the EU regime for type III procurement.

The EU – Singapore FTA has added more coverage of utilities in Singapore, which has been reciprocated by the EU thus resulting in greater coverage. In terms of FTAs under negotiation, the EU is likely to seek better than GPA coverage from Australia and New Zealand.

4.2   High- and Middle-Income Developing Countries

With the high and middle income developing economies, such as Colombia, Peru and Central America, the EU has effectively extended the GPA type transparency provisions as well as receiving coverage commitments.[17] These are

---

16   As Annex 1 shows, technical specifications can be seen as one means of providing a *de facto* preference for local suppliers. This is especially the case when equipment is supplied to a network provider or when technological change takes place fairly slowly. In these cases purchasing entities can be "locked in" to a specific standard for some time, which is why there are rules requiring technical specifications to be performance based.

17   These countries have also negotiated FTAs with the US that include similar provisions.

comprehensive agreements, but coverage is determined by schedules and reciprocity, as usual. Thus, given the smaller scale of the markets, the EU coverage commitments have tended to be less than GPA coverage. But the EU has offered asymmetric (i.e. more) coverage. The agreement with Central American partners also includes a further element of differentiation in that the smaller, less developed Central American states have higher thresholds. Generally speaking, most high value procurement will be carried out by central government so the coverage of sub-central government is relatively less important for small states than is the case in large federal states. Smaller, developing economies also tend to be more open because they lack the supply capacity of bigger, more developed economies and so must inevitably import more goods and services.

The agreement with Vietnam illustrates how the EU has been able to include GPA type rules, coverage of central government and some coverage of the important state owned enterprise sector. The Vietnam agreement provides another form of differentiation in the form of a transitional arrangement in which Vietnam starts with high thresholds (which reduce coverage and compliance costs) and only moves to GPA type thresholds over an extended transition period (of 16 years).[18]

4.3   *Smaller and Less Developed Partners*
With regard to the EU PTAs with smaller or less developed economies, there is the example of the CARIFORUM Economic Partnership Agreement (EPA). This provides for rules similar to but less comprehensive than the GPA transparency. There is an open-ended rendezvous clause (Article 167(3)) on the negotiation of coverage commitments. In other words, commitments to national treatment will only be made when the Joint Council (of the EU and Cariforum) agrees on a schedule of purchasing entity coverage. The experience with regard to Cariforum provides an illustration of how procurement norms and practices are being defused as much by cognitive learning on the part of the developing parties as by more coercive commitments in PTAs. Most Cariforum states have – or are in the process of introducing – transparency provisions in national legislation.[19] These all follow the UNCITRAL/GPA type rules and – depending on the size and capacity of the states – the Cariforum countries are

---

18   See EU – Vietnam FTA Chapter 9, Annex 9-B, Section A: http://trade.ec.europa.eu/doclib/press/index.cfm?id=1437.

19   See the Caribbean Single Market Economy (CSME) Protocol on Procurement that is now open for signature by CARICOM states: https://cpressrelease.com/public-procurement-protocol-to-be-signed/.

making progress towards effective application of such international best practice. Cariforum also shows how the pace of reform depends on the capacity of the administrations and on cognitive learning or buy-in from leading decision makers. Many countries in the region rely on development support to implement procurement reform programmes. Cariforum is also an example of the use of PTA s by the EU to promote regional integration in the sense that there is explicit provision for a Caribbean preference in procurement.

For other ACP states, the EPA s include only a rendezvous clause to negotiate on the topic as a whole. This is the case for the EPA with the East African Union (within a period of five years). In the case of other EPA s, such as the EU – SADC, there is no timing given in the rendezvous clause. The EU – SADC EPA simply recognises the importance of transparency in public contracts. Here opposition from South Africa was important and was based on the view that procurement rules would limit the scope to use procurement in promoting industrial development and the Black Empowerment programme. Here then is a case for the EU making clear that procurement rules do not reduce the ability to pursue strategic procurement, provided this is done in a transparent manner and is based on objective criteria.

4.4   *The Emerging Markets*

Finally, when it comes to PTA s with significant emerging markets, the EU has made less progress. The resumed negotiations currently underway between the EU and MERCOSUR appear to have now been concluded and adopt the GPA type rules for transparency and contract award procedures. In general, the EU has made much less progress extending a rules-based system to the emerging markets, which because of the scale of their public procurement and the significant role played by state-owned enterprises, are likely to be important.

4.5   *The Challenges Establishing (and Defending) a Rules-based Order in Procurement*

This section discusses some of the challenges or difficulties in negotiation provisions on public procurement in trade agreements.

4.5.1   Resistance to Rule-making

The first major challenge is the general resistance to inclusion of public procurement in trade agreements that constitute any form of binding obligation or a restriction of discretionary powers for states and other entities. The award of public contracts can be used as a discretionary policy instrument to promote national champions, infant industries or development. The political economy argument is that countries cannot benefit from more competitive public procurement markets unless they have the supply capacity to do so. The conventional infant industry argument favouring local suppliers is also still widespread although the development case is less clear-cut. Given limited resources, developing country governments are least able to carry the economic costs of inefficient allocation of public funds. There is also the risk that discretion in contract award procedures will invite corruption and undermine governance. This has been all too often the case, with public contracts frequently cited as the vehicle for corruption. International competition in public contracts also tends to come via indirect imports, in other words, contracts are supplied by the local affiliate of a foreign company. The local affiliate will then contribute to the national economy and employment. Thus, greater transparency and predictability in the award of public contracts can provide an incentive for potential suppliers to invest in capacity and thus contribute to economic growth and employment in the host state.

An additional factor in any cost-benefit analysis of procurement rules is the cost of compliance. This is often used as an argument to oppose rules including those on transparency. Compliance costs can be mitigated by setting the threshold for coverage at a suitable level that captures the significant contracts but avoids complex rules for small scale purchasing (see Annex 1). But there is still resistance to rules, especially when these are complex or necessitate a change from established procedures. Such resistance also comes from parastatal or state-owned enterprises that operate in competitive markets, but which are still subject to potential government influence and should therefore be covered.

In addition to the economic utility function of competitive public procurement, there is also often a significant political utility function at work. In most democratic systems, votes are still sought through the timely granting of a contract for an infrastructure project that helps create or preserve local employment. There are few votes to be gained from using local or national tax revenue to pay for contracts awarded to non-local or foreign suppliers. These considerations are present in discussions on "buy national" policies in all countries, including in leading OECD economies. In developing economies, or in political systems in which there is less democratic accountability, high-level corruption in the form of applying political pressure to distort or short cut contract award procedures may be a significant means of retaining political patronage and thus power. Low-level corruption in terms of officials turning a blind eye to illegal practices or in their awarding of smaller contracts (which generally fall below the thresholds of all procurement rules) can be a means of augmenting the income of lowly paid administrators.

Finally, in terms of the sources of resistance there is the general backlash against globalisation. The introduction of more competition in public contracts represents the latest frontier in the fight against neo-liberal globalisation. Introducing greater transparency or competition in certain services sectors or the utilities therefore faces considerable opposition.

4.5.2 Shaping Normative Views

A second, and related, challenge in defending and extending a rules-based order in public procurement is the need to achieve a buy-in for such policies. Experience has shown that the adoption of new laws or agreements in procurement is not sufficient. Many countries have adopted reform legislation on procurement, but then failed to implement it. The case of procurement has also shown that finding a broad consensus on the rules and getting such a buy-in takes time. As noted above, the OECD started work on norms in the 1960s, but there is still only very partial support. The OECD has, as in other areas of trade and investment rule-making, played an important role and continues to do so by seeking to improve the provision of information and promoting improvements, such as in the integrity in procurement initiative. But the OECD is no longer seen by all key EU trading partners in the emerging markets as the legitimate source of rule-making.

The challenge for the EU is therefore how to make the normative case for a rules-based order in public procurement. In this effort, it is unlikely to get much coherent support from the United States. The US administration has had limited power to negotiate on procurement because most (about two thirds of) US public procurement is at the state or municipal level and the federal government has no competence to negotiate sub-federal commitments in international agreements. In the past, the executive branch has made efforts to get state governors to support more coverage, but some states have now legislated to prevent this. The Congress has also pushed for Buy America provisions, as in 2008. The current Trump administration is more likely to extend Buy America or Buy American provisions than push the states or municipalities to offer more coverage.

4.5.2.1 *Conflating Normative and Commercial Arguments*

There is a strong case to be made for more transparency and competition in public procurement markets. This should not run counter to development aims and the use of public contracts to promote other legitimate public policy objectives, such as in the form of green procurement policies. The aim of the rules-based system should be that contracts are awarded according to predetermined, objective criteria and that public funds are not diverted to serve short term political or corrupt interests.

In negotiating trade agreements on procurement however, this normative case for rules is conflated with commercial interests in gaining access to markets. One of the reasons developing countries opposed the inclusion of procurement in the WTO was that the debate on transparency was linked to the bargaining process of the WTO on liberalisation in general and liberalisation of procurement markets in particular. This is also a challenge for the EU in negotiating procurement provisions in PTAs. Asymmetry in market size has effects here that go beyond relative bargaining power. As noted above, smaller, less developed economies have less supply capacity and generally fill more public contracts through foreign suppliers. The EU, due to its size, has supply capacity to satisfy almost all demands so that a smaller share of public contracts are satisfied by foreign suppliers, especially if one takes the EU-market as a whole. The case for transparency and best practice in procurement is therefore often interpreted in developing countries as simply serving EU vested interests in access.

4.5.2.2   *A General Dilemma*

This brings us back to the general dilemma facing the EU in its PTA strategy. On the assumption that little progress can be expected at the multilateral or plurilateral levels for the foreseeable future, it is in the interests of the EU to actively negotiate and conclude PTAs particularly with systemically important emerging market partners. But promoting a rules based order through PTAs is less likely if these potential PTA partners resist a comprehensive agenda. The question is therefore whether the EU can find sufficient flexibility in its approach to enable progress in concluding PTAs, whilst still promoting comprehensive rules-based trade. Public procurement is something of a litmus test in this respect, because it is one of the most sensitive and difficult topics to negotiate. In other words, should the EU conclude PTAs without effective provisions on public procurement, if this is the only way to conclude the PTA? Alternatively what provisions can or should be included, and how should the EU go about trying to persuade its trading partners to include procurement?

If buy-in is important for success in this field, then the EU needs to concentrate on making the normative case for the use of "international" best practice in procurement policies. This suggests a focus on transparency rather than pushing for market access as such. But the experience with procurement and the 70 years taken to get to where we are today suggests that this will be a slow process. For smaller developing countries the EU can – and is – focusing on transparency. But when it comes to the major emerging markets there is a commercial interest in ensuring reciprocal access. It is this objective that has driven demands for an International Procurement Instrument, which would provide more of a threat to close the EU market to major trading partners that do not offer reciprocal access to their public procurement markets.[20] One of the difficulties with these proposals however, has been how to coordinate procurement decisions taken by entities in the Member States that award almost all contracts and the Commission that negotiates PTA s. After much debate the solution proposed is a "centralised procedure" in which the Commission investigates possible discrimination against EU suppliers in third country procurement markets. If this exists the Commission is to seek redress. If this does not resolve the problem, the Commission, after consulting the Member States, can impose a price preference for contracts over Euro 5 million with more than 50% non-EU content. In other words an EU bid would be given preference unless the price is higher than the level of the price preference. The stated aim has been to enhance the EU's negotiating leverage rather than a means of protecting specific markets in the EU (Hoffmeister, 2016).

5   Conclusions on the Way Forward

The establishment of a predictable framework for competition in public procurement represents a high watermark for a rules-based international trading system. The codes and norms developed over the past 60 years or so, after the explicit exclusion of public procurement from the GATT, have only been partially applied in international agreements. To date it is the EU that has taken these codes and implemented them most comprehensively in binding EU legal instruments. This is the main reason the EU seeks comprehensive rules in procurement. As in other areas of trade and investment policy, PTA s have become the default option for the EU in the pursuit of such comprehensive agreements. This follows the EU's efforts to promote multilateral agreement on the topic and the real but limited progress in the plurilateral GPA. In the PTA s, the EU has been able to extend the coverage of what might be seen as

---

20   See Commission Staff Working Document; Impact Assessment accompanying the proposal for a Regulation of the European Parliament and of the Council establishing rules on the access of third country goods and services to the European Union's internal market in public procurement and procedures supporting negotiations on access of European Union goods and services to the public procurement markets of third countries SWD(2012) 57 final.

"international best practice" in public procurement markets, as defined in the OECD, UNCITRAL and other codes and guidelines.

The way ahead in promoting more comprehensive rules in procurement, as in trade and investment in general, requires the EU to differentiate between negotiating partners. In some cases it may be possible to use PTAs as a coercive instrument. This would be the case for example, when a more developed economy, with the capacity to adopt agreed international rules and procedures, but which has held back from doing so for industrial policy or other reasons. In such a case, coercion would take the form of a strong linkage between the conclusion of a PTA and the inclusion of comprehensive rules on public procurement. This approach appears to have worked in the case of CETA because Canada was very interested in negotiating an agreement with the EU. The EU was therefore able to make the inclusion of procurement a condition.

It has to be recognized, however, that rules ensuring the objective allocation and award of public contracts, and thus scope for international competition, require a long term investment and commitment on the part of governments and purchasing entities (as well as suppliers). The adoption of procurement laws or even regulations implementing such laws is not enough. Buy-in is also needed by key political decision-makers, who may well be tempted by the shorter term political utility of rather less objective contract award criteria. In such cases, the EU will need to adopt a more modest and progressive policy – and one based more on persuasion than coercion: for example, by persuading third country governments and stakeholders that transparency in public procurement has clear benefits and helps counter corruption.

The EU does in effect pursue such a differentiated approach to the inclusion of procurement in PTAs as the discussion above shows. For developed economies the approach is based on reciprocal coverage. For less developed PTA partners the focus is more on transparency and less on extensive coverage. There remains, however, a danger of confusing more coercive reciprocity or market access objectives with the normative case that adopting objective rules will serve the long-term interests of all stakeholders.

The case against inclusion of rules on procurement in PTAs has been made that these simply serve the interests of the EU suppliers. The EU therefore needs to continue to pursue a differentiated approach to the inclusion of rules on public procurement in its PTAs, including the promotion of capacity building in the field as it has also done. Combining the task of "norm entrepreneur" and trade negotiator during the negotiation of a PTA is a very challenging task indeed. Making the case for objective rules in procurement will therefore probably be best done via various channels including more soft law approaches. To date, this has been the OECD and to a lesser degree UN agencies.

Annex 1. The Scope of Provisions on Public Procurement

Coverage

Rules in international agreements generally cover procurement of supplies (goods), works (construction) and services. Coverage is defined by several elements: 1) thresholds (monetary values at and above which the agreement applies to procurement), which are designed to ensure that the most valuable contracts are open to competition and avoid the significant compliance costs of imposing international disciplines on smaller contracts; 2) the entities covered, as specified in three categories (central government, sub-central governments and other entities, such as utilities and SOE s); 3) negative list of goods, which means that the procurement of all goods is covered except those explicitly excluded; coverage of defence goods is generally based on a positive list; 4) services, including construction services, with coverage based on a positive list (only listed services are covered) or negative list (all services are covered except those listed); and 5) exclusions.

National Treatment

A cornerstone of public procurement agreements is non-discrimination. Parties must provide national treatment for all covered procurement. This requires parties to treat the goods, services, and suppliers of other parties no less favourably than domestic goods, services and suppliers. They may not apply domestic preferences and other discriminatory purchasing provisions for procurement covered by an international agreement. National treatment obligations are the main means by which *de jure* preferences for specific categories of suppliers are tackled.

Transparency

Central to the aim of facilitating increased international competition, more efficient purchasing and reduced scope for corruption in public procurement is the provision of information. Transparency and procedural obligations are aimed at ensuring that procurement covered by an international agreement is conducted in a manner that is transparent, predictable, fair and non-discriminatory. This encompasses both information on the procurement system, as well as information on each stage of the specific procurement, including development of technical specifications, publication of notices of intended procurement and invitations to request participation in procurements, provision of tender documentation, tendering process, use of negotiations and contract awards. It also includes post-contract award transparency in which purchasing entities are obliged to explain contract award decisions and publish awards.

Contract Award Procedures

In order to ensure flexibility, procurement rules in international agreements tend to provide for open, selective and limited tendering. Open tendering allows all interested suppliers to participate and may be based on price or most advantageous tenders. Selective tendering is used when the procuring entity invites only suppliers that meet certain qualification requirements to submit tenders. It requires competition and transparent procedures for the selection of qualified suppliers. Limited tendering is when the procuring entity invites specific suppliers to submit tenders. Agreements include more or less detailed rules on how invitations for tender are issued, what information is provided, and what time limits are set for bidding and for awarding contracts. Short time limits may put foreign bidders at a disadvantage, while long time limits may be detrimental to the work of the procuring entity.

Technical Specifications

Through specifications a procuring entity can tailor the requirements for a procurement to match the capabilities of certain (local) suppliers. To avoid this outcome, rules encourage the use of international standards and performance standards over design (or prescriptive) standards. Where design standards are used, tenders of equivalent goods or services should be allowed.

Exemptions or Exclusions

Agreements generally provide for exclusions of procurement from national treatment obligations for reasons of human health, national security and law enforcement.

Enforcement and Compliance

Experience has shown that without effective compliance, rules on public procurement will have little effect. Given the thousands of contracts that are awarded every day, central compliance monitoring is impracticable. Rules therefore provide bidders who believe they have not been fairly treated with an opportunity to seek an independent review of a contract award decision. Penalties in the case of noncompliance may involve project cancellation, requirements to retender or financial penalties (limited to the costs of bids or exemplary damages). Rules requiring information on contracts awarded and reasons why bids failed can also facilitate compliance.

Annex 2. Detailed comparison of procurement provisions in selected EU PTAs with international best practice

	GPA partners	UNCRITRAL	EU - CARIFORUM 2007	EU - Colombia/Peru 2010
Coverage	Cat I Central govt. Supplies and works – ve List. Service + ve list Thresholds supplies and services 130k SDR, works 5m SDR Cat II sub national Govt 'voluntary' upon first sub-national level no local govt. Thresholds supplies and services 200k SDR and works 5m SDR Cat III Other entities e.g. Utilities thresholds; supplies and services 400k SDR and works 5m SDR	Intended to cover all procurement no provision for schedules purchasing entities can decide to restrict to domestic suppliers if size of contract is small	central government only for CARIFORUM, central, sub-central and public enterprise for the EU (but not key utilities) (Annex 6) goods, services and works covered thresholds; as per GPA 1994 for the EU and for CARIFORUM 150k for goods and services and 6..5 mill SDR for works	Central government; goods, works and services through + ve listing; [with 200k threshold] sub-central govern-ment as in GPA for thresholds [threshold slightly lower than GPA, $50k for goods and services, $6.5m for works, $250k and $8m respectively for public enterprises;] [private companies not covered even regulated utilities;]

National treatment commitments	national treatment and MFN for signatories	participation without regard to nationality, but procuring entity can exclude foreign suppliers if grounds given	Joint Committee *may* decide on entities and procurement to be covered (Art. 167 (3)) NT for EU suppliers established in region; encouragement for the provision of national treatment within CARIFORUM	national treatment and non-discrimination for covered entities; NT for established suppliers of EU; no offsets;
Trans-parency	information to be provided on national procurement laws and rules; contracts to be advertised to facilitate international competition;	information on laws and rules to be provided invitations to tender to be published detailed records of contract awards to be kept	provision of information sufficient to enable effective bids no requirement on statistics	laws to be published; best endeavours for planned procurement; best endeavours for central information on contracts; post award transparency; detailed information on tenders and decisions to facilitate private actions reviews; information on why bids were not successful

Annex 2. Detailed comparison of procurement provisions in selected EU PTAs with international best practice (*cont.*)

	GPA partners	UNCRITRAL	EU - CARIFORUM 2007	EU - Colombia/Peru 2010
Contract award procedures	option of open, restricted or single tendering;	open, restricted or single tendering is possible	open, restricted or limited tendering;	open, restricted and single tendering; detailed procedures vary slightly from GPA;
Contract award criteria	lowest price or most economically advantageous bid	price but also contribution development and balance of payments position can be mentioned	lowest price or most advantageous bid based on previously determined criteria	[lowest-priced or most advantageous bid based on previously determined criteria]
Technical specifications	use of international standards encouraged; performance standards preferred to design standards	encourages use of standardised products; design standards to be avoided	no mention	Performance standards rather than descriptive standards; [encourages use of International standards, but exceptions always possible]

Exceptions	national security public interest override (Art. XXIII)	security can decide not to award a contract scope for review by administrative or judicial body choice of remedies	security	security
Bid challenge	bid challenge introduced in GATT for the first time; independent review interim remedies, but no contract suspension national interest waiver on contract suspension		bid challenge (Art. 179) independent review with administrative or judicial body; effective, rapid interim measures procuring entities to retain records to facilitate reviews	bid challenge provisions; independent review body [rapid interim measures including suspension and termination of contract] [national interest waiver on contract suspension]

Annex 2. Detailed comparison of procurement provisions in selected EU PTAs with international best practice (*cont.*)

	GPA partners	UNCRITRAL	EU – CARIFORUM 2007	EU – Colombia/Peru 2010
Technical cooperation and special and differential treatment	dcs can negotiate exclusions from national treatment to support balance of payments problems; to support the establishment or development of domestic industries; or for regional preferential agree-ments (Art. V1-7) non-binding technical assistance including help for dc bidders (Art V 8-10) dcs may negotiate offsets (which are otherwise banned under Art. xv) such as local content at time of accession (Art. xvi)	non-binding so developing countries can select which provisions they wish to follow	exchange of experience; EU support for capacity building;	[non-binding provisions on technical cooperation];

The texts of the various agreements are available on the WTO, UNCITRAL, EU and US Government websites.

CHAPTER 10

Prudential Carve-outs for Financial Services in EU FTAS

Bregt Natens and Claus D. Zimmermann

1   Introduction

In essence, prudential carve-outs enable a state to take measures that would otherwise be inconsistent with that state's financial services commitments under international law. The inclusion of a prudential carve-out in a treaty thus grants crucial regulatory autonomy to the parties.[1] As a result, prudential carve-outs have been included in many agreements dealing with international trade in financial services. The main agreement that covers trade in financial services is the World Trade Organization's (WTO) General Agreement on Trade in Services (GATS).[2] WTO Members have long steered away from invoking the GATS prudential carve-out in a dispute in order to maintain maximum regulatory autonomy. In 2016, the first, and to date only, dispute in which a WTO panel interpreted the GATS prudential carve-out was concluded. This case is *Argentina – Financial Services*.[3] Aside from the GATS, more recently negotiated "deep" trade agreements also include prudential carve-outs, often modelled on the one in GATS. While the prudential carve-outs included in those agreements are characterised by certain similarities, their exact wording also exposes some distinct differences. Perhaps surprisingly, this is even the case for the various prudential carve-outs that apply to the European Union (EU).[4] At first sight, this raises concerns of compatibility and legal certainty: a measure for

---

1 We use the term "regulatory autonomy" to denote the extent to which a regulator is constrained by the legal requirements in a prudential carve-out in adopting a policy measure that complies with these requirements.

2 General Agreement on Trade in Services, Apr. 15, 1994, Marrakesh Agreement Establishing the World Trade Organization, Annex 1B, 1869 U.N.T.S. 183 (1994).

3 See Panel, *Argentina – Measures Relating to Trade in Goods and Services*, DS453, (Panel, *Argentina – Financial Services*) and AB, *Argentina – Measures Relating to Trade in Goods and Services*, DS453 (AB, *Argentina – Financial Services*).

4 Financial services are among the most important sectors in the EU's trade relations (see G. Kemekliene and A. Watt, 'GATS and the EU: impact on labour markets and regulatory capacity', *European Trade Union Institute Report* 116 (2010), p. 23).

which justification is sought under a prudential carve-out (referred to in this article as "the measure") could be compatible with one but not with another EU agreement. To assess whether the differences in wording between EU prudential carve-outs indeed have (a substantial) legal significance or are rather evidence of an emerging common law of prudential carve-outs, we proceed as follows. In section 2, we analyse the GATS prudential carve-out in light of the Appellate Body and Panel's findings in *Argentina – Financial Services*. In section 3, on the basis of the GATS analysis, we provide an interpretation of the prudential carve-outs included in five recent EU trade agreements:

(1)   The Free Trade Agreement between the European Union and the Republic of Singapore (EU-Singapore FTA).[5] Singapore is the most important EU trading partner in ASEAN and serves as a hub for business in the entire region as evidenced by the EUR 30 billion bilateral trade in services.[6]

(2)   The Free Trade Agreement between the European Union and the Republic of Korea (EU-Korea FTA).[7] The EU-Korea FTA was hailed as the first of a new generation of trade agreements.[8]

(3)   The Free Trade Agreement between the European Union and the Socialist Republic of Vietnam (EU-Vietnam FTA).[9] The EU is one of the largest foreign investors in Vietnam.

(4)   The Trade in Services Agreement (TiSA). Although negotiations for the plurilateral TiSA are on hold, the agreement is formally still under

---

5   The negotiations on the EU-Singapore FTA were concluded in 2014. Following an advisory opinion by the European Court of Justice (Opinion of the Court 2/15 of 16 May 2017, EU:C:2017:376), the agreement was split into two standalone agreements: an FTA and an Investment Protection Agreement. Both agreements were signed on 19 October 2018. The European Parliament consented to the agreements on 13 February 2019. The following step is for the agreements to be ratified. The present analysis is based on the draft authentic text of the EU-Singapore FTA published by the European Commission on 18 April 2018.

6   See European Commission, 'Countries and Regions – Singapore': http://ec.europa.eu/trade/policy/countries-and-regions/countries/singapore/.

7   The EU-Korea FTA was signed on 15 October 2009. Having been provisionally applied from 1 July 2011, it entered into force on 13 December 2015, after having been ratified by all signatories. See Free Trade Agreement between the European Union and its Member States, of the one part, and the Republic of Korea, of the other part (OJ 2011, L 127/6).

8   The European Commission's website still describes the EU-Korea FTA in this way. See European Commission, 'Countries and Regions – South Korea': http://ec.europa.eu/trade/policy/countries-and-regions/countries/south-korea/.

9   The negotiations on the EU-Vietnam FTA were concluded in 2015. The EU and Vietnam agreed on the final text in July 2018, and the agreement was signed on 30 June 2019. The EU-Vietnam FTA has not yet been ratified. The present analysis is based on the final consolidated text published by the European Commission on 24 September 2018.

negotiation. Several draft negotiating texts have been leaked.[10] As the parties to the negotiation cover around 70% of global trade in services, if concluded, TiSA could be expected to become the successor to the GATS.[11]

(5)   The EU-Canada Comprehensive Economic and Trade Agreement (CETA).[12] Trade in services between the EU and Canada amounts to as much as EUR 30 billion.[13]

2   The Prudential Carve-out in the GATS

Paragraph 2(a) of the GATS Annex on Financial Services provides that:

> Notwithstanding any other provisions of the Agreement, a Member shall not be prevented from taking measures for prudential reasons, including for the protection of investors, depositors, policy holders or persons to whom a fiduciary duty is owed by a financial service supplier, or to ensure the integrity and stability of the financial system. Where such measures do not conform with the provisions of the Agreement, they shall not be used as a means of avoiding the Member's commitments or obligations under the Agreement.

This provision applies to measures affecting trade in services in any of the four modes of supply. Its broad wording, including the lack of definition of "prudential reasons", allows for a sufficiently wide "escape route" for WTO Members, and promotes liberalisation commitments for financial services.[14] However,

---

10   The present analysis is based on the leaked drafts of the Core Text of 21 June 2016 and Annex on Financial Services of 27 June 2016.

11   Currently, the parties to the negotiations are Australia, Canada, Chile, Chinese Taipei, Colombia, Costa Rica, the EU, Hong Kong China, Iceland, Israel, Japan, Korea, Liechtenstein, Mauritius, Mexico, New Zealand, Norway, Pakistan, Panama, Peru, Switzerland, Turkey, and the United States. See European Commission, 'In Focus: The Trade in Services Agreement (TiSA)': http://ec.europa.eu/trade/policy/in-focus/tisa/.

12   CETA entered provisionally into force in 2017. See Comprehensive Economic and Trade Agreement (CETA) between Canada, of the one part, and the European Union and its Member States, of the other part (2017) (OJ L11/13). It will enter into force fully and definitively when all EU Member States' Parliaments have ratified it.

13   See European Commission, 'Countries and Regions – Canada': http://ec.europa.eu/trade/policy/countries-and-regions/countries/canada/.

14   B. de Meester explains this lack of definition by the need for a sufficiently wide "escape route" for WTO Members, allowing them to make liberalisation commitments for financial services (see B. de Meester, 'Testing European Prudential Conditions for Banking Mergers in the Light of Most Favoured Nation in the GATS', *Journal of International Economic*

the primacy of the prudential carve-out over all provisions and commitments is not automatic, and depends on a case-by-case analysis of the parameters of the measure at issue.[15]

Under paragraph 2(a) of the GATS Annex on Financial Services, the applicable legal standard requires (i) that the measure at issue has been taken for prudential reasons and (ii) that it does not amount to a means of avoiding commitments or obligations under the GATS.[16] The Panel report in *Argentina – Financial Services* was the first to shed light on the applicable legal standard under the prudential carve-out contained in paragraph 2(a) of the GATS Annex on Financial Services, a provision that had never before been invoked in a WTO dispute.

The Panel found that since paragraph 2(a) is an "exception", the burden of proof lies with the respondent Member to demonstrate that the relevant measures are covered by the provision.[17]

As regards the first condition, the Panel examined the concept of "prudential reasons". It found that the expression refers to those "causes" or "reasons" that motivate financial sector regulators to act to prevent a risk, injury or danger, which do not necessarily have to be imminent.[18] The Panel also found that a measure taken "for" prudential reasons denotes a rational relationship of cause and effect between the measure and the prudential reason, and would be determined from a case-by-case analysis of the design, structure, and architecture of the measure.[19] A central aspect of this rational relationship of cause and effect is the adequacy of the measure to achieve the prudential reason, i.e., if the measure contributes to achieving the desired effect.[20]

Law 11(3) (2008), p. 643). On the implications of the lack of definition, see also M. Yokoi-Arai, 'GATS Prudential Carve out in Financial Services and its Relation with Prudential Regulation', *International and Comparative Law Quarterly* 57(3) (2008), p. 639.

15   P. Delimatsis, 'Transparent Financial Innovation in a Post-Crisis Environment', *Journal of International Economic Law* 16(1) (2013), p. 44.

16   The combination of these two elements leads to an enquiry of "whether the measure in question is genuinely for prudential reasons or rather for protectionist reasons, i.e. to avoid commitments and obligations" (B. de Meester, 'The Global Financial Crisis and Government Support for Banks: What Role for the GATS?' *Journal of International Economic Law* 13(1) (2010), p. 61). For a detailed analysis of this provision, see C. M. Cantore, "Shelter from the Storm": Exploring the Scope of Application and Legal Function of the GATS Prudential Carve-Out', *Journal of World Trade* 48(6) (2014), p. 1224–1229.

17   Panel, *Argentina – Financial Services* (n. 3), para. 7.816.

18   Panel, *Argentina – Financial Services* (n. 3), para. 7.859–7.944.

19   Panel, *Argentina – Financial Services* (n. 3), para. 7.891.

20   Panel, *Argentina – Financial Services* (n. 3), para. 7.905.

In *Argentina – Financial Services*, the Panel accepted as "prudential" the reasons given by Argentina, i.e., the protection of the insured, the solvency of insurers and reinsurers, the avoidance of the possible systemic risk of the insolvency, failure of direct insurance companies, investor protection, the reduction of systemic risk, and the prevention of money laundering and terrorist financing offenses. However, the Panel then concluded that the measures did not have a rational relationship of cause and effect with the reasons that Argentina had identified. Therefore, the measures could not be justified under the prudential carve-out.[21]

As regards the second condition, it essentially serves to ensure that the prudential carve-out is not invoked to bypass the disciplines under the GATS.[22] In *Argentina – Financial Services* the panel exercised judicial economy and did not examine whether the measures at issue satisfied this second condition.[23] It remains to be seen if adjudicators will opt for an interpretation of this condition similar to the test under the chapeau of Article XX of the GATT 1994, or for a more holistic interpretation, similar to a necessity test.[24] The first option would result in stricter control. If the second condition is interpreted in line with the test under the chapeau of Article XX, adjudicators would have flexibility to mold the test in order to prevent what they perceive as "abuse" of the prudential carve-out.[25] In contrast, if the second condition is approached as a necessity test, a measure would meet the condition if it makes a material contribution to its objective and there is no less-trade restrictive, reasonably available alternative.[26]

3 A Comparative Analysis of the Selected Prudential Carve-outs

In this section, we conduct a comparative analysis of the prudential carve-outs in (i) the EU-Singapore FTA, (ii) the EU-Korea FTA, (iii) the EU-Vietnam FTA,

---

21   Panel, *Argentina – Financial Services* (n. 3), para. 7.919.

22   J. Trachtman considers that the terms used in paragraph 2(a) "seem to call for some intent to evade GATS obligations" (J. Trachtman, 'Trade in Financial Services under GATS, NAFTA and the EC: a Regulatory Jurisdiction Analysis', *Columbia Journal of Transnational Law* 34:37 (1995), p. 72).

23   Panel, *Argentina – Financial Services* (n. 3), para. 7.945.

24   See, for instance, AB, *Brazil – Measures Affecting Imports of Retreaded Tyres*, DS332, para. 182; AB, *China – Measures Affecting Trading Rights and Distribution Services for Certain Publications and Audiovisual Entertainment Products*, DS362, para. 242.

25   See AB, *United States – Standards for Reformulated and Conventional Gasoline*, DS2, p. 22.

26   See AB, *Dominican Republic – Measures Affecting the Importation and Internal Sale of Cigarettes*, DS302, para. 72.

(iv) TiSA, and (v) CETA. We start by analysing the scope of each prudential carve-out (3.1) and continue with respectively the first (3.2) and second (3.3) condition of the prudential carve-outs.

3.1   *The Same Modal Scope*

As noted, the GATS prudential carve-out applies to measures affecting trade in services in *any* of the four modes of supply. This is also the case for the TiSA prudential carve-out.[27] Similarly, the prudential carve-out in the EU-Singapore FTA and the EU-Korea FTA applies to "financial services liberalised pursuant to" the sections on trade in services in the FTAs' equivalent of the four modes of supply.[28]

Negotiators took a different approach with the same outcome in the EU-Vietnam FTA and CETA. This is the result of the absence of specific provisions addressing Mode 3. Mode 3 disciplines are folded in the more general investment chapter.[29] The prudential carve-out in the EU-Vietnam FTA is part of the chapter "Liberalization of Investment, Trade in Services and Electronic Commerce" and provides that "[n]othing in this agreement shall be construed to prevent a Party from adopting or maintaining measures for prudential reasons ..."[30]

The prudential carve-out in CETA is part of the standalone chapter "Financial Services", which applies to measures adopted or maintained by a party relating to (i) financial institutions of the other party or (ii) trade in financial services in CETA's equivalent to Modes 1, 2, and 3, but not explicitly to Mode 4. That said, the prudential carve-out provides that "[t]his *Agreement* does not prevent a Party from adopting or maintaining reasonable

---

27   Article X.1.1 of the Annex on Financial Services to TiSA.

28   Article 8.49 of the EU-Singapore FTA; Article 7.37 of the EU-Korea FTA.

29   GATS, TiSA, and the EU-Korea FTA do not contain specific investment provisions and only address investment indirectly (i.e., mostly through Mode 3). After the EU-Singapore trade agreement was divided into two parts, the Mode 3 provisions remain in the FTA, while investment provisions are subject to a separate Investment Protection Agreement. The EU-Vietnam FTA and CETA only contain investment chapters.

      See, on the overlap between trade in services and investment, F. Ortino and A. Sheppard, 'International Agreements Covering Foreign Investment in Services: Patterns and Linkages' in L. Bartels and F. Ortino (eds.), *Regional Trade Agreements and the WTO Legal System* (OUP, 2006), p. 201; B. De Meester and D. Coppens, 'Mode 3 of the GATS: A Model for Disciplining Measures Affecting Investment Flows?' in Z. Drabek and P. C. Mavroidis (eds.), *Regulation of Foreign Investment: Challenges to International Harmonization* (World Scientific, 2013), p. 100–110.

30   Article 8.42.1 of the EU-Vietnam FTA.

measures for prudential reasons", and may thus also cover CETA's equivalent to Mode 4.[31]

3.2 *A Similar Approach to the First Condition*

In each of the five selected prudential carve-outs, the first condition is structured in a very similar manner to that in the GATS.[32] Each prudential carve-out provides that a party is not prevented by the agreement to adopt or maintain measures for prudential reasons.

First, like in the GATS, the prudential carve-outs in CETA, TiSA, and the EU-Vietnam FTA provide that a party is "not prevented" by the agreement to adopt and maintain measures for prudential reasons.[33] A party "may" however

---

31   Article 13.16.1 of CETA (emphasis added).

32   Article 8.50.1 of the EU-Singapore FTA provides that: Nothing in this Agreement shall be construed to prevent a Party from adopting or maintaining reasonable measures for prudential reasons, such as: (a) the protection of investors, depositors, policy-holders or persons to whom a fiduciary duty is owed by a financial service supplier; (b) the maintenance of the safety, soundness, integrity or financial responsibility of financial service suppliers; or (c) ensuring the integrity and stability of the Party's financial system.

Article 7.38.1 of the EU-Korea FTA provides that: Each Party may adopt or maintain measures for prudential reasons, including: (a) the protection of investors, depositors, policy-holders or persons to whom a fiduciary duty is owed by a financial service supplier; and (b) ensuring the integrity and stability of the Party's financial system. It is understood that the term 'prudential reasons' may include the maintenance of the safety, soundness, integrity or financial responsibility of individual financial service suppliers.

Article 8.42.1 of the EU-Vietnam FTA provides that: Nothing in this agreement shall be construed to prevent a Party from adopting or maintaining measures for prudential reasons, such as: (a) the protection of investors, depositors, policy-holders or persons to whom a fiduciary duty is owed by a financial service supplier; or (b) ensuring the integrity and stability of a Party's financial system.

Article X.16.1 of the Annex on Financial Services to TiSA provides that: Notwithstanding any other provision of the Agreement, a Party shall not be prevented from adopting or maintaining measures for prudential reasons, including for: (a) the protection of investors, depositors, policy-holders or persons to whom a fiduciary duty is owed by a financial service supplier; or (b) to ensure the integrity and stability of a Party's financial system.

Article 13.6.1 of CETA provides that: This Agreement does not prevent a Party from adopting or maintaining reasonable measures for prudential reasons, including: (a) the protection of investors, depositors, policy-holders, or persons to whom a financial institution, cross-border financial service supplier, or financial service supplier owes a fiduciary duty; (b) the maintenance of the safety, soundness, integrity, or financial responsibility of a financial institution, cross-border financial service supplier, or financial service supplier; or (c) ensuring the integrity and stability of a Party's financial system.

33   While the prudential carve-out of the GATS refers only to "taking" measures for prudential reasons, all the other analysed provisions seem to cover both existing and new measures, by reference to "adopting and maintaining" such measures.

adopt and maintain such measures under the EU-Singapore FTA and the EU-Korea FTA. Although "not prevented" may seem like more forceful language than "may", there does not appear to be a legal difference between both formulations. Nonetheless, there is a contextual nuance between the prudential carve-out and the general exceptions clauses (modelled after Article XIV of the GATS) in the EU-Singapore FTA and the EU-Korea FTA.[34]

Second, all prudential carve-outs in the selected agreements must be taken "for prudential reasons". In that regard, as to the term "prudential reasons", the prudential carve-outs in the selected agreements contain a non-exhaustive list of prudential reasons (as in the GATS). All agreements contain the two prudential reasons listed in the GATS, i.e., (i) protecting investors, depositors, policy holders, or persons to whom a fiduciary duty is owed by a financial service supplier, and (ii) ensuring the integrity and stability of the financial system.[35]

CETA, the EU-Korea FTA, and the EU-Singapore FTA refer to an additional example of a prudential reason, i.e., maintaining the safety, soundness, integrity, or financial responsibility of an individual financial service supplier. As noted above,[36] the Panel in *Argentina – Financial Services* considered that "prudential reasons" refers to those "causes" or "reasons" that motivate financial sector regulators to act to prevent a risk, injury or danger, which does not have to be imminent.[37] This broad definition likely captures this additional example, and explicitly adding it merely provides some additional legal certainty. In CETA, the scope of this example is further expanded to cover financial institutions. It is not clear to what extent this prudential reason is not already covered by "ensuring the integrity and stability of the financial system". The issue is currently being discussed in the context of the negotiations of TiSA. A number of States have proposed a footnote clarifying that "it is understood that the term "prudential reasons" includes the maintenance of the safety, soundness, integrity, or financial responsibility of individual financial service suppliers as well as the safety and financial operational integrity of payment and clearing systems". There is still no agreement on this point, with some negotiators

---

34   The general exceptions provisions for trade in services provide that "nothing in [the relevant chapters] shall be construed to prevent the adoption or enforcement" of a measure that satisfies the conditions of an exception. See Article 8.62 of the EU-Singapore FTA and Article 7.50 of the EU-Korea FTA.

35   For an analysis of these examples of prudential reasons, see A. D. Mitchell, J. K. Hawkins and N. Mishra, (n. 35), p. 787.

36   See above, section 2.

37   Panel, *Argentina – Financial Services* (n. 3), para. 7.879. See also C. M. Cantore (n. 16), p. 1227–1228.

opposing the entire footnote, and others (including the EU) opposing the last mention of "safety and financial and operational integrity of payment and clearing systems". The term "for" should be interpreted in the same manner as in the GATS, because its literal wording and its context as well as object and purpose are essentially identical in all of the selected EU prudential carve-outs and in the GATS.[38]

This is not the case for the CETA prudential carve-out. CETA contains an Understanding on the Application of Article 13.16.1 and 13.21 (Understanding). The Understanding provides that the application of the prudential carve-out by parties and by CETA dispute settlement tribunals should be guided by *inter alia* five high-level principles. Three principles directly inform the interpretation of the first condition of the CETA prudential carve-out:

- *First*, a party may determine its own appropriate level of prudential regulation, which may be higher than that in common international prudential commitments.[39]
- *Second,* those applying these principles shall defer to the highest degree possible to (i) regulations and practices in the party's jurisdiction and (ii) financial regulatory authorities' decisions and factual determinations. The rationale behind this principle is the highly specialised nature of prudential regulation.[40]
- *Third,* the relevant considerations in assessing whether a measure meets the requirements of the CETA prudential carve-out include (i) the extent to which the measure is required by the urgency of the situation and (ii) the information available to the party at the time when it adopted the measure.[41]

The first of these principles confirms established WTO case law on the general exceptions provisions of the GATS and the GATT 1994.[42] The second seems to spell out a deferential approach already indirectly adopted by the panel in *Argentina – Financial Services*.[43] The third principle puts the accent on the

---

38   See above, section 2.

39   Para. (a) of the Understanding.

40   Para. (c) of the Understanding.

41   Para. (b) of the Understanding.

42   See e.g., on Article XIV of the GATS, Panel, *United States – Measures Affecting the Cross-Border Supply of Gambling and Betting Services*, DS285, (*US – Gambling*), para. 6.461, and, on Article XX of the GATT 1994, AB, *Korea – Measures Affecting Imports of Fresh, Chilled and Frozen Beef*, DS161 (*Korea – Various Measures on Beef*), para. 176; AB, *European Communities – Measures Affecting Asbestos and Products Containing Asbestos*, DS135 (*EC – Asbestos*), para. 168.

43   Panel, *Argentina – Financial Services* (n. 3), para. 7.910.

urgency of a situation, in a manner slightly different than the GATS, under which the focus is less on urgency, and more on the nature of the situation that threatens a particular prudential objective.[44] Despite this nuance, it appears that the principles spelled out in the Understanding would not result in an interpretation or an application of the prudential carve-out that materially differs from the one under the GATS.

The two other principles of the Understanding contain alternative legal standards for both the first *and* the second condition of the CETA prudential carve-out. We address these alternatives below because they do not match our 'first' and 'second' condition framework.[45]

Table 10.1 below sets out an overview of the contents of the first condition in the selected prudential carve-outs.

3.3   *Substantial Variation in the Second Condition*

Contrary to what is the case for the first condition, the second condition substantially varies between the five selected prudential carve-outs. We start by analysing the second condition in the EU-Singapore FTA, which leaves the least regulatory wiggle room to regulators, and end with the widest second condition, i.e., that in CETA.

3.3.1   The EU-Singapore FTA

The prudential carve-out in the EU-Singapore FTA provides that each party may adopt or maintain *reasonable* measures for prudential reasons.[46] The prudential carve-out in the EU-Singapore FTA also provides that measures taken for prudential reasons:

> [...] shall not be more burdensome than necessary to achieve their aim and shall not constitute a means of arbitrary or unjustifiable discrimination against financial service suppliers of the other Party in comparison to its own like financial service suppliers or a disguised restriction on trade in services.[47]

A measure can thus be justified under the second condition of the prudential carve-out in the EU-Singapore FTA only if it fulfils three cumulative conditions,

---

44   Panel, *Argentina – Financial Services* (n. 3), para. 7.890.

45   See below, sections 3.3.5.2 and 3.3.5.3.

46   Article 8.50.1 of the EU-Singapore FTA.

47   Article 8.50.2 of the EU-Singapore FTA.

TABLE 10.1   The first condition in the selected EU prudential carve-outs

	Not prevented from adopting or maintaining / may adopt or maintain for prudential reasons	Protecting investors, depositors, policy holders or fiduciary duty beneficiaries	Ensuring integrity and stability of financial system	Maintaining safety, soundness, integrity, or financial responsibility of financial institution	Maintaining safety, soundness, integrity, or financial responsibility of individual financial service supplier
GATS	Not prevented	x	x		
CETA	Not prevented	x	x	x	x
TiSA	Not prevented	x	x		
EU-Vietnam FTA	Not prevented	x	x		
EU-Korea FTA	May	x	x		x
EU-Singapore FTA	May	x	x		x

i.e., that it (a) is reasonable, (b) is not more burdensome than necessary to achieve its aim, *and* (c) does not constitute a means of arbitrary or unjustifiable discrimination or a disguised restriction on trade in services. Below, we analyse these elements, which recur in various combinations in the second conditions of other selected prudential carve-outs.

3.3.1.1 *"Reasonable"*

A measure must be reasonable to be justified under the prudential carve-out in the EU-Singapore FTA. The notion of "reasonable" does not have a distinct meaning in WTO law and has been interpreted in light of its ordinary meaning as something that is "not irrational, absurd or ridiculous" or "of such an amount, size, number, etc., as is judged to be appropriate or suitable to the circumstances or purpose".[48]

It thus seems that this element requires little more than a marginal assessment of whether the measure is appropriate or suitable to achieve the prudential reason for which it is taken. Given that this element appears together with the two elements discussed next, we do not consider that such a narrow interpretation is problematic.

3.3.1.2 *"Not More Burdensome than Necessary to Achieve Its Aim"*

A measure can be justified under the prudential carve-out in the EU-Singapore FTA only if it is not more burdensome than necessary to achieve its aim. The legal standard of this element is also embedded in Article VI:4–5 of the GATS and is similar to Article 2.2 of the *TBT Agreement*,[49] which requires that a measure is not more *trade restrictive* than necessary. The difference between "burdensome" and "trade restrictive" is not straightforward. It has been suggested that "burdensome", the ordinary meaning of which is "onerous, cumbersome, oppressive, troublesome, wearisome",[50] is wider than "trade restrictive".[51] In our view, it is safer to say that, while the terms will often overlap, they do not

---

48   Panel, *Mexico – Measures Affecting Telecommunications Services*, DS204, para. 7.182. See also Panel, *Thailand – Customs and Fiscal Measures on Cigarettes from the Philippines*, DS371, para. 7.919 and 7.969; Panel, *Dominican Republic – Measures Affecting the Importation and Internal Sale of Cigarettes*, DS302, para. 7.385; Panel, *United States – Certain Country of Origin Labelling (COOL) Requirements*, DS384, para. 7.850.

49   Technical Barriers to Trade, April 15, 1994, Marrakesh Agreement Establishing the World Trade Organization, Annex 1A, 1868 U.N.T.S. 120 (1994) (TBT Agreement).

50   This is the definition provided in the Oxford English Dictionary.

51   See J. Neumann and E. Türk, 'Necessity Revisited: Proportionality in World Trade Organization Law After Korea – Beef, EC – Asbestos and EC – Sardines', *Journal of World Trade* 37(1) (2003), p. 223; M. Krajewski, *National Regulation and Trade Liberalization in Services* (Kluwer, 2003), p. 142.

necessarily do so. On the one hand, whereas measures that are more burdensome than necessary will often restrict trade, there may be situations in which they do not restrict trade.[52] On the other hand, there may be measures that are more trade restrictive than necessary but not more burdensome than necessary.[53] In any event, this element requires that the measure must not be more burdensome than necessary to achieve its (prudential) aim. The Appellate Body stated that, to ascertain whether a measure is *more* trade restrictive *than necessary*, the measure should be compared with reasonably available alternative measures.[54] By analogy to established WTO case law, in the context of the prudential carve-out in the EU-Singapore FTA, this means that (i) the measure must make a contribution to achieve the invoked prudential reason and (ii) there is no less burdensome and reasonably available alternative measure that would reach the same level of attainment of the said prudential reason.[55]

The division of the burden of proof to establish that these requirements are met depends on the legal nature of the prudential carve-out. In our view, the prudential carve-out in the EU-Singapore FTA constitutes an exception, as is the case under the GATS.[56] Consequently, it seems that the burden of proof is on the respondent to establish that the measure makes a contribution to achieve its aim; the complainant has to identify a *prima facie* alternative measure, which the respondent will then attempt to refute.[57]

In conclusion, a measure can only meet this element of the prudential carve-out in the EU-Singapore FTA insofar as it satisfies the well-known WTO necessity test. Although this test imposes a high threshold, WTO case law does

---

52   Regulations may be more burdensome than necessary to attain an objective without deterring service suppliers from actually conforming to them, for example because the expected gains are sufficient.

53   Trade restrictive measures that are very clear (e.g., an outright prohibition) do not necessarily impose a burden on economic entities, for example because the entity does not enter the market and thus does not engage in a process that is burdensome.

54   See, with respect to Article 2.2 of the TBT Agreement, AB, *United States – Measures Concerning the Importation, Marketing and Sale of Tuna and Tuna Products*, DS381 (AB, *US – Tuna II (Mexico)*), para. 320 and footnote 645.

55   See, with respect to Article 2.2 of the TBT Agreement (n 49), AB, *US – Tuna II (Mexico)* (n. 54), para. 322. Contrary to what is the case under Article 2.2 of the TBT Agreement, here is no need to take into account the risks non-fulfilment of the objective would create because the text of the prudential carve-out in the EU-Singapore FTA does not require this.

56   Panel, *Argentina – Financial Services* (n. 3), para. 7.816.

57   See, by analogy in the context of trade in services, AB, *China – Measures Affecting Trading Rights and Distribution Services for Certain Publications and Audiovisual Entertainment Products*, DS363, para. 319 and 324.

provide several examples of measures that were considered to be necessary under an exception.[58]

3.3.1.3   The Chapeau

A measure can only be justified under the prudential carve-out in the EU-Singapore FTA if it does not constitute a means of arbitrary or unjustifiable discrimination or a disguised restriction on trade in services. This element strongly resembles the chapeau of the general exceptions in the GATS (and the GATT 1994), but differs in one important aspect: contrary to the general exceptions in the GATS, it is not limited to the manner in which the measure is *applied*.[59] That said, WTO case law does not clearly distinguish between *to apply* and *to be*.[60] The function of the chapeau is to balance the right of a WTO Member to invoke an exception and that Member's duty to respect its obligations – i.e., to prevent a WTO Member from abusing its rights.[61]

To fulfil this function, the legal standards of the chapeau are "necessarily broad in scope and reach" so that, "[w]hen applied in a particular case, the actual contours and contents of these standards will vary as the kind of measure under examination varies".[62] This is also clear from the chapeau case law: in a nutshell, panels and the Appellate Body have made use of the chapeau to strike down (elements of) protectionist or arbitrarily discriminatory measures that managed to pass the "necessity" hurdle. Because the chapeau violation may concern a specific element of the measure (e.g., a built-in exclusion), such violations can sometimes be remedied without fundamentally changing the measure at issue (e.g., removing the exclusion).

In conclusion, the combination of these three elements makes the second condition of the prudential carve-out in the EU-Singapore FTA more narrow compared to that in GATS. This is because the three cumulative conditions of the EU-Singapore FTA set a higher threshold. Under the GATS, a measure is considered to be "for" prudential reasons if there is a rational relationship

---

58   See e.g., AB, *European Communities – Measures Prohibiting the Importation and Marketing of Seal Products*, DS401 (AB, *EC – Seal Products*), para. 5.204–5.290.

59   AB, *United States – Standards for Reformulated and Conventional Gasoline US*, DS2 (AB, *US – Gasoline*), para. 22.

60   Aside from the actual practice of application, the "application" of a measure in the sense of the chapeau is also determined on the basis of the text, design, architecture, and revealing structure of a measure. See AB, *EC – Seal Products* (n. 58), para. 5.302.

61   AB, *United States – Import Prohibition of Certain Shrimp and Shrimp Products*, DS58 (AB, *US – Shrimp*), para. 156; AB Report, *United States – Measures Affecting the Cross-Border Supply of Gambling and Betting Services*, DS258 (AB, *US – Gambling*), para. 339.

62   AB, *US – Shrimp* (n. 61), para. 120.

of cause and effect between the measure and the prudential reason.[63] Under the EU-Singapore FTA this is not enough. First, the measure also must make a contribution to achieve the invoked prudential reason. Second, there must not be a less burdensome and reasonably available alternative measure that would reach the same level of attainment of the prudential reason. Third, it must not constitute a means of arbitrary or unjustifiable discrimination or a disguised restriction on trade in services. A measure that could be justified under the GATS, might thus not fall within the scope of the prudential carve-out of the EU-Singapore FTA.

3.3.2   The EU-Korea FTA

The prudential carve-out in the EU-Korea FTA provides that measures taken for prudential reasons:

> [...] shall not be more burdensome than necessary to achieve their aim, and where they do not conform to the other provisions of this Agreement, they shall not be used as a means of avoiding each Party's commitments or obligations under such provisions.[64]

In other words, under the prudential carve-out in the EU-Korea FTA, a measure can only be justified if it complies with two cumulative elements, i.e., (i) the second condition of the GATS prudential carve-out *and* (ii) the second element of the second condition of the prudential carve-out in the EU-Singapore FTA. The wording of these elements is identical and we see no relevant differences in the context, object, and purpose of these provisions. These elements should thus be interpreted in the same manner as in the GATS and the EU-Singapore FTA.[65]

Compared to the GATS prudential carve-out, the scope of the prudential carve-out in the EU-Korea FTA is narrower because of the additional requirement that the measures shall not be more burdensome than necessary. By analogy, the scope of the prudential carve-out in the EU-Korea FTA is wider than that in the EU-Singapore FTA because it does not require that what we have called the chapeau element is met (whearas the prudential carve-out in the EU-Singapore FTA does).[66]

---

63   Panel, *Argentina – Financial Services* (n. 3), para, 7.891.
64   Article 7.38.2 of the EU-Korea FTA.
65   See above, sections 2 and 3.3.1.2.
66   See above, section 3.3.1.3.

3.3.3   The EU-Vietnam FTA

The prudential carve-out in the EU-Vietnam FTA provides that measures taken for prudential reasons "shall not be more burdensome than necessary to achieve their aim".[67] The wording of this condition is identical to the second element of the second condition of the prudential carve-out in the EU-Singapore FTA. The context, object, and purpose of these provisions also seem similar. The second condition in the EU-Vietnam FTA should thus be interpreted as discussed above.[68] Because the prudential carve-out in the EU-Vietnam FTA does not contain the requirement that the measure shall not be used as a means to avoid the party's commitments, its scope is wider than that in the EU-Korea FTA.

3.3.4   TiSA

The TiSA prudential carve-out repeats the second condition of the prudential carve-out in GATS: where the measure does not conform with the provisions of TiSA, it shall not be used as a means of avoiding the party's commitments or obligations under TISA.[69] The context, object, and purpose of the TiSA prudential carve-out also seem akin to those in GATS. The second condition in the GATS and TiSA prudential carve-outs should thus be interpreted identically.[70] As explained above,[71] it is not yet clear whether the second condition in the GATS prudential carve-out would be interpreted as a chapeau-like test, or more like a necessity test.

If the second condition in the prudentical carve-out in TiSA is interpreted as a necessity test, its scope would be very similar to that in the EU-Vietnam FTA, which essentially requires that the measure be necessary.

If the second condition is interpreted as a chapeau-like test, the scope of the TiSA (and GATS) prudential carve-out would seem to be wider than that of the prudential carve-out in the EU-Vietnam FTA. This is because, as explained,[72] the necessity test sets a higher threshold than the chapeau. A measure may not be used as a means of avoiding commitments or obligations under the GATS or

---

67   Article 8.42.2 of the EU-Vietnam FTA.

68   See above, section 3.3.1.2. Our view that the prudential carve-out in the EU-Vietnam FTA is an exception is supported by the language of the prudential carve-out in the EU-Vietnam FTA, which provides that nothing in the FTA shall be construed to prevent the adoption of measures for prudential reasons. This language mirrors that of the general and security *exceptions* in Articles XIV and XIV*bis* of the GATS.

69   Article X.16.2 of the Annex on Financial Services to TiSA.

70   See above, section 2.

71   See above, section 2.

72   See above, section 2.

the TiSA, but it can still not be, as required under the necessity test, the least burdensome possible option. On the other hand, it is difficult to conceive how a measure that is not more burdensome than necessary to achieve its prudential objective could be used as a means of avoiding commitments under TiSA.

3.3.5   CETA

The CETA prudential carve-out *sensu stricto* (i.e., the first paragraph of Article 13.16 of CETA – further referred to as "the CETA prudential carve-out") provides that the agreement does not prevent a party from adopting or maintaining *reasonable* measures for prudential reasons.[73] The fourth and fifth high-level principles of the CETA Understanding provide *two alternatives* to the legal standard of the CETA prudential carve-out. Finally, the CETA prudential carve-out *sensu lato* (i.e., the entire Article 13.16 of CETA) provides a *third alternative* for non-discriminatory measures. The Understanding does not apply to the CETA prudential carve-out *sensu lato*.[74]

A measure can thus be justified under the CETA prudential carve-out if it fulfils any one of four sets of elements of the second condition, i.e., those of (a) the text of the prudential carve-out, (b) the fourth principle of the Understanding, (c) the fifth principle of the Understanding, or (d) the exception for non-discriminatory prohibitions.

3.3.5.1   *The Text of the Prudential Carve-out*

A measure taken for prudential reasons is justified under the CETA prudential carve-out if it is reasonable. This is also the first element of the second condition of the prudential carve-out in the EU-Singapore FTA.[75] Contrary to what is in the EU-Singapore FTA, the context of this element in CETA includes the five high-level principles of the Understanding that guide the application of the CETA prudential carve-out.[76]

As further detailed below,[77] two principles contain alternatives to the legal standard of the CETA prudential carve-out. The other three principles directly inform the interpretation of the second condition of the CETA prudential carve-out, i.e., whether a measure is reasonable.

---

73   Article 13.16.1 of CETA.
74   The Understanding only applies to Article 13.16.1 of CETA, i.e., not to the CETA prudential carve-out *sensu lato*.
75   See above, section 3.3.1.1.
76   See above, section 3.2.
77   See below, sections 3.3.5.2 and 3.3.5.3.

– *First*, a party may determine its own appropriate level of prudential regulation, which may be higher than that in common international prudential commitments.[78] This codifies established WTO case law on the general exceptions provisions of the GATS and the GATT 1994.[79]
– *Second*, those persons applying the high-level principles shall defer to the highest degree possible to (i) regulations and practices in the party's jurisdiction and (ii) financial regulatory authorities' decisions and factual determinations. The rationale behind this principle is the highly specialised nature of prudential regulation.[80]
– *Third*, the relevant considerations in assessing whether a measure meets the requirements of the CETA prudential carve-out include (i) the extent to which the measure is required by the urgency of the situation and (ii) the information available to the party at the time when it adopted the measure.[81]

These principles confirm our above analysis that the "reasonable" element requires little more than a marginal assessment of whether the measure is appropriate or suitable to achieve the prudential reason for which it is taken.[82]

3.3.5.2   *In Particular the Fourth Principle of the Understanding*

Alternatively, the fourth principle of the Understanding provides that a measure is deemed to be justified under the CETA prudential carve-out if it meets three cumulative elements, i.e., (i) has a prudential objective, (ii) is not so severe in light of its purpose that it is manifestly disproportionate to the attainment of its objective, *and* (iii) is not a disguised restriction on foreign investment or an arbitrary or unjustifiable discrimination between investors in like situations.[83]

First, a measure must have a prudential objective. The panel in *Argentina – Financial Services* considered that a measure taken "for" prudential reasons under the GATS must have a "prudential cause",[84] i.e. there needs to be a rational

---

78   Para. (a) of the Understanding.
79   See e.g., on Article XIV of the GATS, Panel, *US – Gambling* (n. 42), para. 6.461, and, on Article XX of the GATT 1994; AB, *Korea – Various Measures on Beef* (n. 42), para. 176; AB, *EC – Asbestos* (n. 42), para. 168.
80   Para. (c) of the Understanding.
81   Para. (b) of the Understanding.
82   See above, section 3.3.1.1. Whereas in the EU-Singapore FTA, the proposed scope of the element "reasonableness" is counterbalanced by the other elements in the prudential carve-out, the proposed scope of the element "reasonableness" in CETA arguably reflects negotiators' intention to create a wide prudential carve-out.
83   Para. (d) of the Understanding.
84   Panel, *Argentina – Financial Services* (n. 3), para. 7.888.

relationship of cause and effect between the measure and the prudential reason.[85] Although the word "objective" adds a subjective aspect to the analysis, we believe that a measure having a "prudential objective" is not materially different from a measure "taken for prudential reasons".

Second, a measure must not be so severe in light of its purpose that it is manifestly disproportionate to the attainment of its objective. The wording of this element is notable as the terms "severe" and "manifestly disproportionate" are not common in trade law provisions. That said, the wording leaves regulators substantial regulatory autonomy as only *manifestly* disproportionate measures will fail to satisfy this element.

Compared to the condition that a measure is taken 'for prudential reasons', the combined first and second element result in a slightly higher threshold under the CETA. A measure "taken for prudential reasons" under the GATS may still be manifestly disproportionate to the attainment of the prudential reason, and thus not be justified under the CETA.

Third, a measure must not be a disguised restriction on foreign investment or an arbitrary or unjustifiable discrimination between investors in like situations. This element is very similar to the third element of the second condition of the prudential carve-out in the EU-Singapore FTA,[86] but adds the words "between investors in like situations".

These words again remind of the chapeau of Article XIV of the GATS, which speaks of "between countries where like conditions prevail".[87] This element of the chapeau has been interpreted very broadly; we are not aware of a successful claim that the conditions between countries were unlike (and, consequently, that the chapeau did not apply). As the Appellate Body clarified in its first report, the chapeau should mean:

> [T]aken to mean that the standards it sets forth are applicable to *all of the situations* in which an allegation of a violation of a substantive obligation

---

85 The Panel also noted that "measures taken for prudential reasons" is a broader concept than "prudential measures" (Panel, *Argentina – Financial Services* (n. 3), para. 7.861), demonstrating deference towards the WTO Members' autonomy to determine what a prudential reason is. See A. D. Mitchell, J. K. Hawkins and N. Mishra (n. 35), p. 805.

86 See above, section 3.3.1.3.

87 This element of the chapeau of Article XIV of the GATS has been interpreted by analogy to the words "between countries where the same conditions prevail" in the chapeau of Article XX of the GATT 1994. See Panel, *US – Gambling* (n. 42), para. 6.577–6.578 where the Panel relies on GATT 1994 case law.

has been made and one of the exceptions contained in Article XX has in turn been claimed.[88]

On the one hand, it can be argued that the function of the words "like situations" in CETA serve a similar purpose to the language "between countries where like conditions prevail" in the chapeau of Article XIV of the GATS. In that event, it is unlikely that there are many situations where the third element does not need to be met because investors' situations are not like. On the other hand, it can also be argued that the "like situations" element needs to be interpreted more narrowly, for instance with reference to the likeness criterion for service suppliers in the GATS non-discrimination obligations. In that event, there would be more situations where investors' situations are not "like", and this third element thus does not apply. An investor's situation could, for instance, not be like another investor's situation where both investors are not in a competitive relationship with each other.[89]

In conclusion, the alternative set of conditions for a measure to be justified, as provided in the fourth principle of the Understanding, appears to be more cumbersome than the conditions of the prudential carve-out itself. Nevertheless, the fourth principle creates a safe harbour for measures that might not pass the "reasonableness" test, but would still not be manifestly disproportionate to the attainment of their objective, as long as they do not discriminate between investors in like situations.

3.3.5.3   *In Particular the Fifth Principle of the Understanding*
Further, the fifth principle of the Understanding provides that a measure is also deemed to be justified under the CETA prudential carve-out if it (i) is not applied in a manner that constitutes a disguised restriction on foreign investment or an arbitrary or unjustifiable discrimination between investors in like situations and (ii) fits in one of four categories, i.e., is:
- In line with international prudential commitments that are common to the parties;
- In pursuance of the resolution of a financial institution that is no longer viable or likely to be no longer viable;

---

88   AB, *US – Gasoline* (n. 59), para. 23–24 (emphasis added).
89   See AB, *Argentina – Financial Services* (n. 3), para. 6.25.

- In pursuance of the recovery of a financial institution or the management of a financial institution under stress; or
- In pursuance of the preservation or the restoration of financial stability in response to a system-wide financial crisis.[90]

First, the measure must satisfy a chapeau-type element. Whereas the chapeaus in the prudential carve-out in the EU-Singapore FTA and under the fourth principle of the Understanding apply to the measure *as such*, this element only concerns the *application* of the measure (as in Article XIV of the GATS). As noted, under the current case law, this distinction does not seem to make a big difference.[91]

Second, the measure must only fit in one of four of the listed categories. Insofar as it does, the measure must not fulfil any other requirement. In conclusion, in view of its chapeau-like requirement, this fifth principle of the Understanding does not appear to set a lower threshold. Nevertheless, it allows for clarity when a measure is taken in pursuance of certain financial policies dictated by international commitments or required as a response to a system-wide financial crisis.[92]

3.3.5.4   *The Exception for Non-discriminatory Prohibitions*

Finally, the CETA prudential carve-out *sensu lato* provides that, subject to the national treatment and most-favoured-nation treatment obligations in the agreement, a party may prohibit a particular financial service or activity (but not all services or a complete subsector) for prudential reasons.[93]

This alternative leaves the most leeway to regulators as it allows any measure taken for prudential reasons that constitutes a non-discriminatory prohibition. The limit of this alternative is that it cannot be used to justify a ban on a complete subsector of financial services.

3.3.6   Overview

Table 10.2 below provides an overview of the second condition for justification of a prudential measure under the prudential carve-out in the selected case studies. Table 10.2 is organised from the strictest (in the EU-Singapore FTA) to the widest prudential carve-out (in CETA).

---

90   Para. (e) of the Understanding.
91   See above, section 3.3.1.3.
92   For further analysis, see A. D. Mitchell, J. K. Hawkins and N. Mishra (n. 35), p. 811.
93   Article 13.16.3 of CETA.

TABLE 10.2 The "second condition" in the selected EU prudential carve-outs

	Reasonable measures	Not avoiding commitments	Not more burdensome than necessary	Chapeau
EU-Singapore	X		x	x
EU-Korea		x	x	
EU-Vietnam			x	
GATS		x		
TiSA		x		
CETA	x (guided by Understanding)			
	Prudential objective + not manifestly disproportionate			x
	Fits in one of four categories of measures			x
	Non-discriminatory prohibitions			

3.4 A Specific Prudential Exception for Authorisation and/or Registration

Although the GATS and TiSA do not have a similar exception, all the selected EU trade agreements contain prudential exceptions for authorisation and/or registration, which are part of the same provisions as the prudential carve-outs discussed above. For instance, CETA contains the following registration exception:

> Without prejudice to other means of prudential regulation of cross-border trade in financial services, a Party may require the registration of cross-border financial service suppliers of the other Party and of financial instruments.[94]

There are similar provisions in the EU-Korea FTA, the EU-Vietnam FTA, and the EU-Singapore FTA.[95]

---

94   Article 13.16.2 of CETA.

95   Article 7.38.4 of the EU-Korea FTA provides that: Without prejudice to other means of prudential regulation of cross-border trade in financial services, a Party may require the registration of cross-border financial service suppliers of the other Party and of financial instruments.

These exceptions apply to (i) authorisation and/or registration require-ments of (ii) financial services suppliers and/or instruments for the purpose of supplying (iii) cross-border trade in financial services.[96] Beyond that, the authorisation and registration exception in the EU-Singapore FTA re-quires that the authorisation or registration requirement does not violate the national treatment obligation.[97] In contrast, the exceptions in the oth-er agreements do not impose any other requirement to the authorisation or registration. Consequently, the exceptions in these agreements may be con-strued as blanket waivers for requiring the authorisation and/or registration of financial service suppliers and instruments that are supplied via Modes 1 and 2. In other words, discriminatory, discretionary or overly burdensome authorisation and/or registration requirements could be justified under this exception.

To balance this broad right to require authorisation and/or registration, it is defensible to require that the authorisation and/or registration requirement bears *some* link to a prudential reason.[98] It is correct that these exceptions do not contain the requirement that the authorisation and/or registration is "for prudential reasons". Nonetheless, because the exceptions are part of provi-sions entitled "Prudential Carve-out", the context of the exception dictates that such a link must exist. That said, such nexus between the measure and the pru-dential reason can be much weaker than that under the prudential carve-outs.

4   Conclusions

In sum, the six analysed prudential carve-outs display a set of similarities and differences.

Article 8.42.6 of the EU-Vietnam FTA provides that: Without prejudice to other means of prudential regulation of cross-border trade in financial services, a Party may require the registration or authorization of cross-border financial service suppliers of the other Party and of financial instruments.

Article 8.50.5 of the EU-Singapore FTA provides that: Subject to Article 8.6 (National Treatment) and without prejudice to other means of prudential regulation of cross-bor-der trade in financial services, a Party may require the registration or authorisation of cross-border financial service suppliers of the other Party and of financial instruments.

96   In the EU FTAs, the term cross-border trade covers GATS Modes 1 and 2. See Article 9.1 of CETA; Article 7.4.3 (a) of the EU-Korea FTA; Article 8.4 of the EU-Singapore FTA; Article 8.2.1.c of the EU-Vietnam FTA. It is not clear whether Pakistan and Hong Kong intend to cover both modes with their proposal in TiSA.

97   Article 8.50.5 of the EU-Singapore FTA.

98   There is no reason why the same argumentation would not apply to the EU-Singapore FTA.

First, most of them address in a similar way the requirement that the measure at issue has been taken for prudential reasons. Despite some differences in wording, most of these carve-outs have the same, broad, modal scope. They cover measures affecting trade in financial services in any of the four modes of supply. They use similar wording in allowing (or not preventing) parties to adopt and maintain measures for prudential reasons. They also usually contain a non-exhaustive list of prudential reasons, in particular (i) protecting investors, depositors, policyholders, or persons to whom a fiduciary duty is owed by a financial service supplier, and (ii) ensuring the integrity and stability of the financial system.

Second, differences in the wording of these prudential carve-outs can at least partly be explained by different negotiation dynamics, the different time at which the FTAs were negotiated and the length of the respective negotiations. An important aspect in the negotiation of the EU's FTAs is the involvement of different institutional actors, and the delicate relations between the EU institutions. These parameters are illustrative of the extent to which negotiations in different fora influence the text of each provision. For instance, the text of the prudential carve-out in the recent EU-Japan Economic Partnership Agreement (EU-Japan FTA) contains largely the same terms as the prudential carve-out in the GATS.[99] It remains to be seen what the prudential carve-out will look like in the new FTA between the EU and the Mercosur countries (Argentina, Brazil Paraguay and Uruguay), which took almost twenty years to conclude.[100] In our opinion, some of the differences in wording between the prudential carve-outs in the various agreements would ultimately not result in an interpretation or application of the prudential carve-out in one treaty that materially differs from the other treaties.

Third, in contrast, some other differences may result in a diverging interpretation and ultimately lead to situations where a measure would be justified under one treaty and not another. These differences concern a set of conditions required by FTAs on top of the requirements contained in the GATS, making

---

99   The EU-Japan FTA entered into force on 1 February 2019. Article 8.65 of the EU-Japan FTA
       provides, in relevant part, that:
       1.   Nothing in this Agreement shall prevent a Party from adopting or main-
            taining measures for prudential reasons, including for: (a) the protection of
            investors, depositors, policy-holders or persons to whom a fiduciary duty is
            owed by a financial service supplier; or (b) ensuring the integrity and stabili-
            ty of the Party's financial system.
       2.   Where such measures do not conform with this Agreement, they shall not be
            used as a means of avoiding the Party's obligations under this Agreement.
100   At the time of writing, the text of the prudential carve-out in the EU-Mercosur FTA was
       not yet available. The EU and Mercosur reached a political agreement on the FTA on
       28 June 2019.

recourse to the prudential carve-out more cumbersome. For instance, the EU-Singapore FTA and CETA require that the measure be reasonable. The FTAs between the EU and Singapore, Korea and Vietnam pose a further condition that measures not be more burdensome than necessary to achieve the prudential aim.[101] Finally, the EU-Singapore and EU-Korea FTAs require that the adopted measures must not constitute a means of arbitrary or unjustifiable discrimination or a disguised restriction on trade in services. In that respect, CETA provides by far the most sophisticated – and flexible – set of conditions, including for alternative scenarios where a measure is deemed to be justified under the prudential carve-out.

Thus, a measure that would be justified under the GATS might not fall within the scope of the prudential carve-out of some FTAs. Therefore, the additional requirements result in a further limitation of the regulatory autonomy of the parties to these FTAs.

The differences in the wording are not necessarily constitutive of fragmentation, as long as interpretation remains consistent. Nevertheless, the different requirements create incoherence. This is particularly cumbersome for the EU, which is party to each one of these agreements. It would be required to abide by the highest threshold with respect to each condition. At the same time, prudential measures taken by its trading partners would have to meet the requirements of the GATS (as a minimum), and further requirements (if any) provided in each of the analysed FTAs.

On a final note, while a certain set of conditions appears throughout different agreements, possibly as a sign of a common law of prudential carve-outs (*in statu nascendi*), there are still important inconsistencies in the combination of these conditions. These differences occasionally have substantial legal significance, to the extent that they limit the regulatory autonomy of the parties to the FTA.

Acknowledgement

The authors are grateful to our former colleagues Jung-ui Sul and Dr. Jenya Grigorova for providing helpful comments on earlier drafts and during discussions.

---

101   A similar necessity test is included in the Commission's proposals for negotiations with Mexico and Chile. The Commission's decision to include a necessity test in its proposals will be "decided on a case by case basis in future negotiations". See Commissioner for Trade, 'Cecilia Malström's letter to MEP Mosca' (25 June 2018): http://ec.europa.eu/carol/?fuseaction=download&documentId=090166e5bbb939d5&title=3447492-_CM%20Letter%20to%20MEP%20Mosca.pdf.

We also owe thanks to our colleague Dr. Asja Serdarevic for their valuable help in finalising this chapter. Any errors or omissions are our own. The final manuscript for this chapter was completed in June 2019. Subsequent developments could not be taken into account.

CHAPTER 11

The Evolution of the EU Digital Trade Policy

Pierre Sauvé and Marta Soprana

1 Introduction

Major technological advances over the past two decades have led to the development of new business models, an increase in the complexity of production systems and a sharp rise in the volume of cross-border transactions conducted over digital networks. Launched in 1998 with the putative aim of building consensus over the key parameters of global digital governance, the World Trade Organization's (WTO) Work Programme on Electronic Commerce has achieved little progress in the past two decades. Rather, preferential trade agreements (PTAs) have increasingly served as laboratories in which to experiment with and adopt elements of a nascent regulatory regime governing electronic transactions and digital trade.

This chapter chronicles the evolution of the European Union's (EU) approach to digital governance since the Treaty of Lisbon entered into force in 2009. It dissects this evolution by looking at a sample of twelve PTAs entered into or negotiated by the EU with a diversity of trading partners over the past decade. In doing so, the chapter assesses the influence the EU exerts on emerging multilateral trade disciplines governing electronic commerce and in setting global norms addressing the delicate balance between the freedom to transact online and the protection of digital users' personal data.

The chapter starts by reviewing the burgeoning body of literature on electronic commerce, with particular attention paid to what existing studies say about the nature and depth of electronic commerce-related provisions found in PTAs. It then proceeds to analyse a representative universe of PTAs negotiated by the EU over the past decade. In so doing, the chapter explores how the nature, scope and depth of e-commerce provisions have evolved over this short time span. The chapter further takes up the EU's approach to data protection in discussing whether and how the experience of the EU's General Data Protection Regulation (GDPR) can inform and potentially shape digital trade norms at the regional and multilateral levels. The chapter concludes with conjectures on the likely direction of the EU's digital trade policy agenda.

2 Literature Review

The policy research literature on the treatment of digital trade in the context of preferential trade agreements is of relatively recent vintage. While extensive attention has been dedicated to the political economy forces underpinning the sharp recent rise in PTAs and their growing influence in norm-setting, research devoted to analysing the digital trade-related provisions found in PTAs and the factors influencing their inclusion and substantive remit remains largely incipient. This can be explained in part by the fact that digital technology for commercial purposes is itself a relatively recent phenomenon dating back to the mid- to late 1990s, as can be seen by the scant (explicit) attention paid to electronic transactions in the relevant legal texts establishing the World Trade Organization in 1994. This can also be inferred from the fact that the first PTA featuring specific provisions on e-commerce – on paperless trading – was that entered into by New Zealand and Singapore in 2000.

Several studies devoted to e-commerce have allowed for a finer understanding of how to identify and classify provisions relating to digital trade based on their content and scope of application.[1] Other studies have focused on all disciplines and obligations that impact digital trade, beyond e-commerce.[2] In overall terms, disciplines deemed of direct relevance to digital trade include provisions on data and consumer protection; rules on paperless trade, electronic authentication and digital signatures; provisions governing cross-border data flows and measures relating to data localization; the (temporary) prohibition of custom duties levied on electronic transactions; provisions on regulatory cooperation; and definitions of e-commerce and digital products.

The studies cited above usefully track the evolving scope and depth of disciplines governing electronic commerce in PTAs. Monteiro and Teh, for instance, found that almost 30 per cent of all 275 PTAs notified to the WTO (by May 2017) featured e-commerce provisions.[3] They also found that the number

---

1   L. Herman, 'Multilateralising Regionalism: The Case of E-Commerce', OECD Trade Policy Papers, N. 99 (2010); R.H. Weber, 'The Expansion of E-Commerce in Asia-Pacific Trade Agreements', *The E15 Initiative*, (2015), to consult at: http://e15initiative.org/blogs/the-expansion-of-e-commerce-in-asia-pacific-trade-agreements/; J. A. Monteiro, R. Teh, 'Provisions on Electronic Commerce in Regional Trade Agreements', WTO Staff Working Paper, No. ERSD-2017-11 (2017).
2   J. P. Meltzer, 'A New Digital Trade Agenda', *E15 Initiative*, (2015), to consult at: http://e15initiative.org/publications/a-new-digital-trade-agenda/; N. Mishra, 'Data Localization Laws in a Digital World: Data Protection or Data Protectionism?', *The Public Sphere*, (2016); M. Wu, 'Digital Trade-related Provisions In Regional Trade Agreements Existing Models and Lessons for the Multilateral Trade System', *ICTSD Overview Paper*, (2017).
3   J. A. Monteiro, R. Teh (n. 1).

of PTAs incorporating disciplines on e-commerce had increased over time, a conclusion also reached by Hofmann, Osnago, and Ruta in 2017.[4] Moreover, the work of Monteiro and Teh shows that, for most countries, the PTAs signed between 2009 and 2016 typically feature a greater number of provisions on e-commerce compared to PTAs concluded before 2009. The above studies concur that the EU stands out among those WTO Members having made the greatest changes in their approach to e-commerce in PTAs over the years. Wu corroborates the above findings, noting that the scope of e-commerce provisions found in PTAs has progressively expanded to encompass an ever-broader range of issues.[5] He further finds that PTAs featuring an advanced economy trading partner, such as the United States (US) or the European Union, tend to address a broader and deeper range of digital trade issues than do PTAs conducted along South-South lines.

Much attention has also been devoted in the academic literature to uncovering the underlying political economy of PTAs and the forces influencing a country's recourse to bilateral or regional trade agreements to advance its digital trade policy agenda.[6] An important strand of the above literature has concerned itself with the study of the role that various economic and geopolitical factors play in shaping the content of specific disciplines found in PTAs. For instance, in assessing the provisions of the PTAs entered into by the EU and the US, Horn, Mavroidis and Sapir determined that the EU showed a tendency to use trade policy as a vehicle for "declaratory diplomacy", whereas the US tended to ensure that any so-called WTO+ provisions found in its PTAs serve the commercial interests of its leading exporting firms and are enforceable.[7] Wunsch-Vincent[8] and Ferracane and Lee-Makiyama,[9] whose work explored the conceptual framework underpinning the negotiation of digital trade disciplines, found that the EU, the US, and China relied on different negotiating

---

4   C. Hofmann, A. Osnago, M. Ruta, 'Horizontal Depth: A New Database on the Content of Preferential Trade Agreements, World Bank Policy Research Working Paper 7981, (2017); B. Hoekman, M. Kostecki, *The Political Economy of the World Trading System: the WTO and Beyond* (OUP, 2009); P. Van den Bossche, W. Zdouc, *The Law and Policy of the World Trade Organization* (CUP, 2013).

5   M. Wu (n. 2).

6   C. VanGrasstek, 'The Political Economy of Services in Regional Trade Agreements', *OECD Trade Policy Papers* N. 112, (2011); and B. Hoekman, M. Kostecki (n.4).

7   H. Horn, P. Mavroidis, A. Sapir, 'Beyond the WTO? An Anatomy of EU and US Preferential Trade Agreements', *Bruegel* Blueprint Series (7), (2009).

8   S. Wunsch-Vincent, *The WTO, the Internet and Digital Products: EC and US Perspectives*, (Hart Publishing, 2006).

9   M. Ferracane, H. Lee-Makiyama, 'China's Technology Protectionism and Its Non-Negotiable Rationales', *ECIPE Working Paper*, (2017).

parameters. Such differences have seen the EU carve-out cultural and au-
dio-visual services from its Common Commercial Policy whilst reconciling
the differing policy perspectives of DG Trade and DG Justice towards digital
governance. Meanwhile, the US has pursued a more activist free trade agenda in matters of digital content and cross-border data flows in its preferential
trade agreements, while China has adopted a more restrictive stance towards
information and communication technologies and, consequently, its negotiation of disciplines on digital trade, driven by non-trade considerations (e.g.
national security and public order concerns; and the operation of state-owned
enterprises).

Building on the above literature, the chapter moves on to examine the
evolving approach taken by the EU in regulating digital trade in the context
of the PTAs it has negotiated since the entry into force of the Treaty of Lisbon
in 2009.

3   Analysis of EU PTAS

The analysis that follows is rooted in a sample of thirteen PTAs linking the EU
to a diverse group of developed and developing country trading partners from
South America, Asia and the Commonwealth of Independent States (CIS) that
were either concluded or entered into force over the past decade. This sample
comprises two types of preferential trade agreements:
- PTAs that are part of a broader framework agreement, which encompass
  the *Deep and Comprehensive Free Trade Agreements* (*DCFTAs*) included in
  the Association Agreements (AAs) with the Eastern Partnership countries
  (i.e. the EU-Georgia AA (2014),[10] the EU-Moldova AA (2014)[11] and the EU-
  Ukraine AA (2014)[12]), and the EU-Serbia (2013)[13] *Stabilisation and Association Agreement* (SAA);

---

10   Association Agreement between the European Union and the European Atomic Energy
     Community and their Member States, of the one part, and Georgia, of the other part (OJ
     2014, L 261/4).
11   Association Agreement between the European Union and the European Atomic Energy
     Community and their Member States, of the one part, and the Republic of Moldova, of
     the other part (OJ 2014, L 260/4).
12   Association Agreement between the European Union and its Member States, of the one
     part, and Ukraine, of the other part (OJ 2014, L 161/3).
13   Stabilisation and Association Agreement between the European Communities and their
     Member States of the one part, and the Republic of Serbia, of the other part (OJ 2013,
     L 278).

- Stand-alone PTAs, which include the *Comprehensive Economic and Trade Agreement* (CETA) between the EU and Canada (2016)[14], *Economic Partnership Agreements* (EPAs) (i.e. the EU-CARIFORUM EPA (2008)[15], and the EU-Japan EPA (2017)[16]), and *Free Trade Agreements* (FTAs) (i.e. the EU-South Korea FTA (2010)[17], the EU-Colombia and Peru FTA (2012)[18], the EU-Singapore FTA (2018)[19], and the EU-Vietnam FTA (2019)[20]).

The chapter also draws attention to two additional PTA negotiations:

- between the EU and the United States (better known as the currently suspended Transatlantic Trade and Investment Partnership (TTIP), for which the EU produced a draft text of an e-commerce chapter in July 2015[21]; and
- between the EU and Mexico, with the draft text of the digital trade chapter made available in April 2018[22].

The analysis that follows adopts the methodological approach favoured by Wu and Monterio and Teh in identifying PTA provisions relating to digital trade.[23] While the analysis is primarily grounded in a study of provisions found in the PTA chapters specifically dedicated to e-commerce, analytical attention is also devoted to provisions that may impact e-commerce but are found in other PTA chapters.

In understanding the evolution of the EU's digital trade policy since the entry into force of the Treaty of Lisbon, this chapter focuses on three key dimensions of the e-commerce provisions under examination: (i) their type; (ii) their scope; and (iii) their depth.

---

14 Comprehensive Economic and Trade Agreement (CETA) between Canada, of the one part, and the European Union and its Member States, of the other part (OJ 2017, L 11/1).

15 Economic Partnership Agreement between the CARIFORUM States, of the one part, and the European Community and its Member States, of the other part (OJ 2008, L 289/I/3).

16 Agreement between the European Union and Japan for an Economic Partnership (OJ 2018, L 330).

17 Free trade Agreement between the European Union and its Member States, of the one part, and the Republic of Korea, of the other part (OJ 2011, L 127).

18 Trade Agreement between the European Union and its Member States, of the one part, and Colombia and Peru, of the other part (OJ 2012, L 354).

19 Free Trade Agreement between the European Union and the Republic of Singapore (OJ 2018, L 267/1).

20 Free Trade Agreement between the European Union and Vietnam (OJ 2019, L 177) (the conclusion of this agreement is pending).

21 European Commission, 'EU negotiating texts in TTIP (2016), to consult at: https://trade.ec.europa.eu/doclib/press/index.cfm?id=1230

22 European Commission, 'New EU-Mexico agreement: The Agreement in Principle and its texts' (2018), to consult at: https://trade.ec.europa.eu/doclib/press/index.cfm?id=1833.

23 M. Wu (n. 2); and J. A. Monteiro, R. Teh (n. 1).

3.1   *Dedicated E-commerce Provisions*

All EU PTA s examined in this chapter feature provisions relating to e-commerce under the trade in services chapter, with the exception of the SAA with Serbia, in which only a handful of provisions relating to electronic commerce can be found scattered across various parts of the Agreement.[24] A further exception can be found in the far more ambitious (and recent) CETA, which features an entire chapter specifically dedicated to e-commerce.

Important differences in the scope and depth of e-commerce-related provisions emerge over time. Before 2014, EU PTA s typically limited themselves to a few provisions explicitly prohibiting the application of customs duties to electronic transactions (i.e. giving permanency to the WTO moratorium that has been renewed every two years in the context of Ministerial meetings since 1998), alongside non-binding provisions calling on the Parties to promote e-commerce and cooperate on related regulatory issues (e.g. the EU-CARIFORUM EPA; the EU-South Korea FTA; and the EU-Ukraine DCFTA).[25] Starting in 2016, the EU has shown an interest in expanding the scope of its PTA provisions dealing with e-commerce-related issues by tackling a range of new issues. These include: cybersecurity, prior authorizations, the treatment of source code, as well as specific provisions relating to electronic authentication and electronic signatures; consumer protection; unsolicited commercial electronic messages (so-called spam) and the free flow of data (subject to justifiable exceptions). The EU-Japan EPA exemplifies this more comprehensive approach.[26]

Over time, changes are also noticeable in the EU's approach towards certain digital trade issues. For instance, all EU PTA s entered into force until 2015 feature an article describing the objectives and principles of the section on electronic commerce that mandated the Parties to refrain from levying customs duties on products delivered by electronic means insofar as they were considered as services transactions.[27] However, since 2016, the e-commerce sections or chapters of EU PTA s no longer define the nature of electronic transmissions, and address the issue of customs duties in a separate article rather than under

---

24   See for example Art. 81 on Protection of personal data under Title VII (Justice, Freedom and Security) and Art. 106 on Electronic Communications Networks and Services under Title VIII (Cooperation Policies).

25   See for example Art. 120 EU-CARIFORUM EPA; Art. 7.49 EU-South Korea FTA; Art. 140 EU-Ukraine DCFTA.

26   See for example Art. 8.73 on Source Code; Art. 8.79 on Unsolicited Commercial Electronic Messages; Art. 8.81 on Free Flow of Data.

27   See for example Art. 119 EU-CARIFORUM EPA; Art. 162 EU-Colombia and Peru FTA; Art. 139 EU-Ukraine AA.

objectives and principles, stating that the Parties shall not impose customs duties on electronic transmissions.[28]

The substantive remit of e-commerce provisions found in EU PTAs also varies across negotiating partners. For example, the EU-CARIFORUM EPA, the EU-Japan FTA and the EU-Serbia SAA do not contain articles specifically addressing the liability of intermediary service providers that are present in all the other PTAs in this chapter's sample.[29] The EU-Canada CETA, on the other hand, is the only agreement that clarifies that in the event of an inconsistency between its e-commerce chapter and another chapter of the agreement, the latter prevails to the extent of the inconsistency.[30]

It bears noting however that the wider scope of e-commerce provisions found in the most recent EU PTAs falls short of a number of disciplines found in the e-commerce chapter of the Comprehensive and Progressive Agreement for Trans-Pacific Partnership (CPTPP) whose precursor, the Trans-Pacific Partnership Agreement (TPP), was centrally shaped by the United States before its government opted to withdraw from it in early 2017. This broader scope relates to provisions such as those targeting the non-discriminatory treatment of digital products; the adoption of the UNCITRAL Model Law framework governing electronic transactions; Internet interconnection charge sharing; and the location of computing facilities (so-called localization requirements).[31]

3.2   *Recurring Provisions in E-commerce Sections*

Three provisions recur most frequently in the e-commerce sections of the PTAs entered into by the EU over the past decade. First, all PTAs include a provision stating the objective and principles of the section and calling on Parties to recognise that electronic commerce increases trade opportunities in many sectors and to cooperate in promoting the development of electronic commerce between them.[32] In the PTAs signed before 2015, such a provision also included a reference to the confidence of e-commerce users by ensuring that the development of electronic commerce was fully compatible with the highest international standards of data protection. It is notable that the Parties couched such an undertaking in legally binding and enforceable language (e.g.

---

28   See for example Art. 8.58 EU-Singapore FTA; and Article 8.72 EU-Japan FTA.
29   Provisions on the liability of intermediary service providers can be found either in the e-commerce section (e.g. CETA) or in the intellectual property section (e.g. EU-Vietnam, and EU-Singapore FTAs) of EU agreements.
30   Art. 16.7 CETA.
31   See for example Art. 14.4, Art. 14.5, Art. 14.12, and Art. 14.13 CPTPP.
32   See for example Art. 119 EU-CARIFORUM EPA, and Art. 8.50 EU-Vietnam FTA.

"must be fully compatible"; "shall be consistent with").[33] Though the above reference to data protection is no longer found in the EU's latest PTAs (with the exception of the EU-Singapore FTA), the EU-Japan EPA clarifies that the objective of the section on e-commerce is to contribute to creating an environment of trust and confidence in the use of electronic commerce.

The second most recurring provision found in EU PTAs concerns the prohibition of custom duties on electronic transmissions. All EU PTAs examined in this chapter enshrined this commitment in legally binding terms (e.g. "cannot be subject to"; "shall not impose").[34]

Provisions calling on the Parties to cooperate on regulatory issues relating to electronic commerce through regular dialogue and exchanges of information are also among the most frequently found in the PTAs signed by the EU during the last decade. The issues most frequently listed in the vast majority of EU PTAs include: (i) recognition of certificates of electronic signatures issued to the public and the facilitation of cross-border certification services; (ii) the liability of intermediary service providers with respect to the transmission or storage of information; (iii) the treatment of unsolicited electronic commercial communications; and (iv) the protection of consumers in the ambit of electronic commerce. Other issues that can be found in EU PTAs signed in the early 2010s called for regulatory cooperation relating to paperless trading and the protection of personal data.[35] Meanwhile, the EU-Japan EPA calls for the Parties to maintain a dialogue on regulatory matters relating to a range of newer issues, such as cybersecurity and electronic government.[36]

3.3   *Newest E-commerce Topics*

The most recent PTAs signed or negotiated by the EU address a range of new topics, with the EU-Japan EPA being at the forefront of such an expansion in scope. Among the newest issues taken up is the principle of "no prior authorization", according to which the supply of services should not be subject to prior authorisation requirements specifically and exclusively targeting services provided by electronic means, in order to avoid additional costs and negative effects on business decisions that would impact both domestic and cross-border

---

33   See for example Art. 162 EU-Colombia and Peru FTA.
34   See for example Art. 8.51 EU-Vietnam FTA; Art. 119 EU-CARIFORUM EPA; and Art. 127 EU-Georgia AA.
35   See for example Art. 7.49 EU-South Korea FTA and Art. 163 EU-Colombia and Peru FTA.
36   Art. 8.80 EU-Japan EPA.

electronic commerce.[37] This provision, which the EU has taken up in the context of the exploratory WTO discussions implementing the 11th Ministerial Conference (MC11) Joint Statement on e-commerce[38], is present in the EU-Japan EPA[39], in the draft chapter on digital trade of the EU-Mexico FTA, the draft chapter on trade in services of the EU-Mercosur FTA, as well as the EU's draft TTIP e-commerce chapter. In all four cases, however, these provisions do not entail binding obligations (i.e. "shall endeavour not to impose" and "may not be subject to").

The EU-Japan EPA is the only agreement in force that includes a provision specifically addressing issues relating to source code. While the Parties committed to refrain from enacting requirements for the transfer of, or access to, source code of software owned by a person of the other Party, the language adopted is once more of a non-binding nature (i.e. "may not") and several caveats apply.[40] In contrast, Article 14.7 of the CPTPP on source code contains strong binding obligations (i.e. "no Party shall require"), signalling a greater concern for the potential backdoors embedded in certain technology products that may threaten national security.[41]

Recent EU PTA s have also included a specific provision on the recognition of electronic contracts. This is exemplified by the agreement with Japan[42] and the chapter on digital trade of the revised EU-Mexico FTA. As clarified by the EU's submission of its PTA best practices during the exploratory work towards future WTO negotiations on electronic commerce launched at MC11 in Buenos Aires, such a provision signals the EU's interest in "ensuring that national legal systems allow contracts to be concluded by electronic means and that legal requirements for contractual processes neither create obstacles nor result in such contracts being deprived of legal effectiveness".[43]

---

37 WTO General Council, Joint statement on electronic commerce, Establishing an enabling environment for electronic commerce, Communication from the European Union, JOB/GC/188 of 16 May 2018.

38 Frustrated with the lack of progress under the 1998 Work Programme on E-commerce and convinced that electronic commerce deserves more focused attention in the WTO – considering the rising importance of global electronic commerce, the opportunities it creates for inclusive trade and development, and the technological advances made in the digital economy – 71 members, including the EU, issued a Joint Statement at the 11th Ministerial Conference stating that, as a group, they would "initiate exploratory work towards future WTO negotiations – with participation open to all members – on the trade-related aspects of e-commerce".

39 Art. 8.75 EU-Japan EPA.

40 Art. 8.73 EU-Japan EPA.

41 On this point, see M. Wu (n. 2).

42 Art. 8.76 EU-Japan EPA.

43 WTO General Council (n. 20).

Cybersecurity also ranks among the newer issues found in EU PTAs. Article 8.80 of the EU-Japan EPA explicitly singles out cybersecurity among the regulatory matters relating to electronic commerce that the Parties are called upon to cooperate. While a specific reference to cybersecurity only appears in one of the EU PTAs reviewed in this chapter, several agreements concluded by the EU over the past decade have acknowledged the need to improve the security of electronic transactions, promote electronic governance (e-government) and the protection of personal data.[44]

The EU-Japan EPA also contains a provision on the principle of technological neutrality in electronic commerce.[45] This signifies that any provision relating to trade in services should make no distinction between the different technological means through which services may be supplied.[46] Since no other EU PTA reviewed in this chapter features such a provision, which is found in many Japanese PTAs, one can safely deduce that this principle was agreed at the behest of Japan.

3.4   *Other Digital Trade-related Provisions*

In addition to the digital trade-related provisions specifically included in the e-commerce sections of EU PTAs, most preferential agreements signed by the EU also contain provisions addressing issues relating to electronic commerce that are treated in other parts of the agreements.

Most frequently, such provisions can be found under a different section within the PTA chapters dedicated to trade in services, investment and electronic commerce. Examples include PTA provisions prohibiting Parties from requiring the establishment of any form of commercial presence as a precondition for the supply of a service or the adoption of any measure restricting the cross-border provision of electronic communication services.[47] Further examples relate to provisions governing access to, and use of, the Internet, which can typically be found in PTA sections addressing electronic communication networks and services.[48] Similarly, several EU PTAs address issues relating to

---

44   See for example Art. 109 EU-Colombia and Peru FTA; Art. 325 EU-Georgia AA; and Art. 99 EU-Moldova AA.

45   Article 8.70 EU-Japan EPA.

46   J. A. Monteiro, R. Teh (n. 1).

47   See for example Art. 110 EU-Georgia AA; and Art. 237 EU-Moldova AA.

48   Art. 107 EU-Georgia AA; Art. 234 EU-Moldova AA; and Art. 118 EU-Ukraine AA. Measures that mandate data (or their copy) to be kept locally – i.e. data localization requirements – would not be allowed under these provisions.

data processing under the section on financial services rather than that on electronic commerce.[49]

Provisions relating to digital trade can also be found in separate PTA chapters. For example, in chapters addressing trade-related intellectual property rights, EU PTAs feature disciplines on Internet use for trademarks and geographical indications,[50] information on electronic rights management,[51] and the protection of data submitted to obtain a marketing authorisation for pharmaceutical or plant protection products.[52]

Interestingly, provisions addressing the centrally important – and politically sensitive – issue of personal data protection are typically scattered across various parts of the agreements. This recalls the strength of sentiments towards an issue EU Members consider as a fundamental right that forms a cornerstone of the Union's digital trade policy. While the EU-CARIFORUM EPA has a separate chapter entirely dedicated to this issue,[53] AAs concluded with the Eastern Partnership countries and the Western Balkan address matters relating to data protection through a single specific article under the Title on Freedom, Security and Justice that mandates the Parties to cooperate with a view to ensuring a high level of protection of personal data in accordance with EU, Council of Europe and international legal instruments and standards.[54] Meanwhile, other PTAs include a specific non-binding provision calling on the Parties to adopt or maintain measures for the protection of personal data in their e-commerce section.[55] Moreover, almost all EU PTAs examined in this chapter – irrespective of the EU trading partner – include a specific provision mandating the Parties to adopt appropriate safeguards to protect privacy and confidentiality with regard to the transfer of data and data processing for the supply of financial services.[56] Similarly, most PTAs in the sample under review include a reference to the protection of privacy and personal data as a legitimate policy

---

49   See for example Art. 7.43 EU-South Korea FTA; Art. 118 EU-Georgia AA; Art. 157 EU-Colombia and Peru FTA; Art. 8.54 EU-Singapore FTA.

50   Art. 144–145 EU-CARIFORUM EPA.

51   Art. 10.33 EU-South Korea FTA; Art. 161 EU-Georgia AA; Art. 288 EU-Moldova AA.

52   Art. 10.36–10.37 EU-South Korea FTA.

53   Art. 197–201 EU-CARIFORUM EPA.

54   The Title on Freedom, Security and Justice belongs to the 'political' part of the AAs, rather than to the DCFTA part of the agreement, which is usually identified by the Title on Trade and Trade-related Matters. Art. 81 EU-Serbia SAA; Art. 14 EU-Georgia AA; Art. 13 EU-Moldova AA; and Art. 15 EU-Ukraine AA.

55   Art. 164 EU-Colombia and Peru FTA; Article 16.4 CETA.

56   Art. 157 EU-Colombia and Peru FTA; Art. 245 EU-Moldova AA; Art. 8.54 EU-Singapore FTA; Art. 5–33 of the draft text the EU proposed for the TTIP negotiations.

objective covered by the general exception clause that is most frequently found in PTA chapters dealing with trade in services, establishment and electronic commerce.[57]

3.5   *Future Directions in EU PTAs*

EU PTAs have evolved markedly in scope and depth over the past decade. There are strong reasons to believe – and early signs suggesting – that such a trend is not about to abate. New PTAs negotiated and entered into by the EU will almost certainly further expand the scope and depth of provisions relating to electronic commerce and digital trade. A case in point is the recently revised EU-Mexico FTA, whose chapter on digital trade includes provisions on source code, online consumer protection, unsolicited commercial electronic messages, electronic contracts, the principle of prior authorization, and open internet access.[58] Other examples include PTAs under discussion with Australia and New Zealand, for which the EU negotiating mandate calls for the inclusion of disciplines covering digital trade and cross-border data flows, the improvement of conditions for international roaming, as well as provisions targeting unjustified or unduly burdensome data localization requirements.[59]

More significantly, future EU trade deals appear certain to include provisions specifically dedicated to ensuring the protection of personal data in the wake of the adoption of the EU General Data Protection Regulation (GDPR) regime. In February 2018, following a long and hard-fought debate between DG Justice and DG Trade that saw the former prevail, the European Commission developed a set of draft horizontal provisions for cross-border data flows (Article A) and for personal data protection (Article B) that the EU henceforth aims to include in any potential new PTA.[60] By incorporating such new language in all future trade agreements, which aims at ensuring that the fundamental right to privacy is not undermined by trade disciplines, the EU expects its trading partners to comply with Union-wide privacy rules, thus setting a potential international standard likely to shape policy debates at the global level. Already

---

57   See for example Art. 7.50 EU-South Korea FTA; Art. 167 EU-Colombia and Peru FTA; Art. 134 EU-Georgia AA; and Art. 141 of EU-Ukraine AA.
58   European Commission, (n. 20).
59   Council of the European Union, 'Negotiating directives for a Free Trade Agreement with New Zealand', 8 May 2018 (7661/18 Add 1, DCL 1); and Council of the European Union, 'Negotiating directives for a Free Trade Agreement with Australia', 8 May 2018 (7663/18 Add 1, DCL 1).
60   European Commission, DG Justice and Consumers, 'Horizontal provisions on cross-border data flows and personal data protection' (2018), to consult at: https://ec.europa.eu/newsroom/just/item-detail.cfm?item_id=627665.

the EU proposed to include these horizontal provisions in the PTA currently negotiated with Indonesia as well as in the context of the exploratory work on electronic commerce at the WTO.[61]

Although the obligation to protect personal data that arises from Article B.2 is non-binding, the draft proposal presented by the EU has met with some uneasiness, especially within the EU business community. For example, DIGITALEUROPE (2018) has voiced concerns over the perceived *de facto* nullification of the principle of unrestricted data flows arising from the right to protect personal data, as well as over the risks implicit in restricting the right to cross-border data flows through recourse to self-declaratory exceptions.[62]

4   The EU General Data Protection Regulation

What exactly is the GDPR and why has it come to play such a central role in the formulation of the EU's digital trade policy? Regulation 2016/679, which entered into force in May 2018, establishes a new EU data privacy regime that aims to protect and regulate the use of personal information by companies that have access to – and the means to transfer – the data of individuals in the EU.[63]

The GDPR, which supersedes the 1995 Data Protection Directive (95/46/EC)[64], seeks to harmonize data privacy laws across Europe, enhance the rights of EU citizens to manage their personal data, and reshape the way business

---

61   European Commission, 'The texts proposed by the EU for the trade deal with Indonesia', to consult at: https://trade.ec.europa.eu/doclib/press/index.cfm?id=1620; European Union, 'Joint Statement on Electronic Commerce, EU Proposal for WTO Disciplines and Commitments Relating to Electronic Commerce, Communication from the European Union', INF/ECOM/22 of 26 April 2019.

62   DIGITALEUROPE, 'Comments on European's Commission Draft Provisions for Cross-border Data Flows' (2018), to consult at: www.digitaleurope.org/Search-Results/categoryID/2.

63   The GPDR protects such data as basic identity information including personal names, addresses and ID numbers, web data such as location, IP addresses, cookie data and RFID tags, health and genetic data, biometric data, racial or ethnic data, political opinions, and sexual orientation (Regulation (EU) 2016/679 of the European Parliament and of the Council of 27 April 2016 on the protection of natural persons with regard to the processing of personal data and on the free movement of such data, and repealing Directive 95/46/EC (OJ 2016, L 119)).

64   Directive 95/46/EC of the European Parliament and of the Council of 24 October 1995 on the protection of individuals with regard to the processing of personal data and on the free movement of such data (OJ 1995, L 281).

entities across the Union operate in the digital domain through a comprehensive set of rules.[65]

This new EU Regulation covers – under Chapter III – the rights of "data subjects" (i.e. people residing in the territory of the EU), including the right to information, the right of access, the right to rectification (also known as the *right to be forgotten*), and the right to erasure of personal data. It also imposes numerous obligations on businesses dealing with the data of EU residents, including limitations on storage and process, the duty to report breaches and carry out risk assessments and the obligation to have a data protection officer (DPO) if processing large amounts of data.[66]

From a digital trade policy perspective, the adoption of the GDPR is significant for a number of reasons, not least of which because of its extraterritorial application to all companies doing business within the territory of the EU Single Market, regardless of where such companies are located. Indeed, Article 3 of the GDPR applies to the processing of personal data of data subjects who are in the EU by a EU-based controller or processor,[67] regardless of whether the processing takes places in the EU or not, as well as by a controller or processor not established in the EU, where the processing of activities relates to the supply of goods or services to such data subjects in the EU.[68]

Secondly, the GDPR imposes a common set of rules throughout the Union which, whilst benefiting domestic and foreign firms doing business in the EU through greater predictability, increased transparency, and reduced red tape, are nonetheless viewed as inflicting high implementation costs on business operators, especially micro-, small- and medium-sized firms (so-called MSMEs). Fears have been expressed of seeing firms pass on GDPR-related costs to consumers or of business losses and dampened digital competitiveness owing to decreased access to data.[69]

---

65   ICTSD, 'Europe's Data Privacy Rules Set New Global Approach to Consumer Rights', Bridges (2018), Vol. 22, N. 19.

66   K. Suominen, 'No Choice? GDPR's Impact on the U.S., UK and the EU', Centre for Strategic & International Studies, to consult at: www.csis.org/blogs/future-digital-trade-policy-and-role-us-and-uk/no-choice-gdprs-impact-us-uk-and-eu.

67   A controller is a natural or legal person, public authority, agency or other body that collects data and determines the purposes and means of the processing of personal data whereas a processor (e.g. cloud service provider) is a natural or legal person, public authority, agency or other body that processes data on behalf of the data controller (Art. 4 GDPR).

68   Art. 27(1) of the GDPR clarifies that when the controller is not established in the EU, it shall designate (in writing) a representative in the Union.

69   K. Suominen, (n. 20).

Thirdly, by imposing sanctions and penalties on firms found in breach of the GDPR, the new Regulation marks a striking departure from the 1995 Data Protection Directive. Article 83 of the GDPR establishes that infringements can lead to fines capped at 4 percent of a company's total worldwide annual turnover or € 20 million (whichever is greater). Financial penalties were absent from the enforcement mechanism of the 1995 Directive.

A further notable feature of the GDPR that is particularly relevant to how the EU is shaping its digital trade policy concerns the Regulation's approach to the transfer of data to third countries (Chapter 5). This issue was already addressed by the 1995 Directive but is expanded by the GDPR with the introduction of new tools for international transfers and the extension and simplification of cross-border data transfers. Article 45 GDPR establishes that a transfer of personal data to a country outside the EU may take place once the EU Commission determines that an adequate level of data protection is maintained abroad. The GDPR offers three different mechanisms to ensure that the personal data of EU residents is adequately protected when transferred abroad: (i) adequacy decisions[70], through which the European Commission establishes that the third country provides a level of protection of personal data comparable to that of the EU, either through domestic laws or international commitments (e.g. with Japan[71]); (ii) transfers subject to appropriate safeguards, which include binding corporate rules (BCRs), standard contractual clauses (SCCs), codes of conduct, and accredited certification mechanisms; and (iii) derogations for specific situations, which include consent by the data subject, transfers necessary for the performance of a contract between the data subject and the controller, and transfers necessary for the purposes of a legitimate interest pursued by the controller.

Chapter 5 of the GDPR governing the transfer of data to third countries is particularly relevant to the future of global digital trade because it leaves countries that want to access a market of over 500 million EU consumers with no alternative other than to update their domestic laws to comply with the new EU privacy regime or enter into specific arrangements like the EU-US Privacy

---

70   Art. 45(2) GDPR establishes that adequacy assessments shall take into account the existence of the rule of law; legislation including public security, national security and criminal law; whether there are effectively enforceable rights including administrative and judicial redress for data subjects; and, any international commitments entered into by the third country.

71   Commission Implementing Decision (EU) 2019/419 of 23 January 2019 pursuant to Regulation (EU) 2016/679 of the European Parliament and of the Council on the adequate protection of personal data by Japan under the Act on the Protection of Personal Information (OJ 2019, L 76).

Shield.[72] As of September 2019, the European Commission has rendered favorable adequacy decisions with regard to only 13 countries, including Japan, Israel and Switzerland, and the US remains the only economy with which the EU signed a sector-specific privacy arrangement that the European Commission deemed "adequate" under the GDPR framework, though this is no longer the case following the Schrems II ruling of the CJEU.[73]

5   EU Digital Trade Policy and the WTO

The former European Commissioner for Justice, Consumers and Gender Equality, Vera Jourova, left no doubts as to how the EU saw its role in the future of global digital governance when she opined that the EU – through the adequacy decisions of the GDPR – "aims to set the global standard for privacy".[74]

Is the former EU Commissioner overly optimistic or is the GDPR destined to become the *de facto* global norm governing the protection of personal data in the years to come? Though the EU's new privacy regime entered into force only recently, there is already some evidence to support the EU Commissioner's claim regarding the GDPR's global normative impact. For example, Colombia, South Korea and Bermuda are all currently revisiting domestic legislative instruments to mirror EU standards on privacy protection.[75] Similarly, the Chinese data protection regime, which comprises the 2017 Cybersecurity Law and a handful of accompanying measures and standards, draws to a large degree on the EU approach, as the Chinese authorities used the GDPR as the primary

---

72   The Privacy Shield is a new arrangement concluded between the EU and the US that applies only to specific sectors and was deemed adequate under Article 45.3 GDPR. It replaces the Safe Harbor Framework that, according to a 2015 ruling by the European Court of Justice, lacked appropriate redress mechanisms for EU citizens with respect to government access to their data. A. Mattoo, J. P. Meltzer, 'International Data Flows and Privacy: the Conflict and its Resolution', *World Bank Policy Research Working Paper* 8431 (2018).

73   *Data Protection Commissioner v. Schrems*, CJEU, C-311/18, 16 July 2020; and European Commission, Adequacy Decisions, to consult at: https://ec.europa.eu/info/law/law-topic/data-protection/international-dimension-data-protection/adequacy-decisions_en.

74   Politico, 'Europe's new data protection Politico rules export privacy standards worldwide' (2018), to consult at: www.politico.eu/article/europe-data-protection-privacy-standards-gdpr-general-protection-data-regulation/.

75   Ibid.

model in developing the Personal Information Security Specification – known as 'the Standard'.[76]

In determining whether the EU's quest to use its *first regulatory mover* advantage to set a global standard for data protection will materialize, one must acknowledge that the combination of the EU's sizeable internal market and its highly developed institutional (and hence enforcement) capacity afford it significant regulatory clout vis-à-vis third countries. Already, the EU's 1995 Data Protection Directive, which the GDPR builds on and today extends, served as an important reference framework for other countries as they developed their own privacy laws, with 39 countries outside the EU adopting data protection laws since 1995, 13 of which were closely aligned to the Directive while another 19 were broadly similar.[77]

An important additional contextual consideration shaping evolving attitudes on where the regulatory cursor should be placed at the interface of internet freedoms and data protection arises from growing public awareness – and concerns – over recent documented cases of widespread mishandling and abuse of personal data stemming from headline-grabbing data breaches. Recent scandals have led to stepped-up calls for stricter norms of digital governance, fueling support for more stringent privacy protection standards modeled on the EU's GDPR approach.

In its quest to set the global standard for privacy, the EU has recently tabled a proposal for multilateral disciplines on data protection and privacy in the context of the structured discussions that have proceeded among a group of like-minded WTO Members in the wake of the MC11 Joint Statement on e-commerce. The proposed provision mirrors the language of the GDPR-inspired draft horizontal provisions agreed to by DG Trade and DG Justice in February 2018.[78]

However, the ability of the GDPR to set a global privacy standard in the context of digital trade regulation may be open to debate given lingering uncertainty over its compatibility with Article XIV (General Exceptions) of the

---

76   The Personal Information Security Specification is a new national standard on personal information protection adopted by the Chinese government, laying out detailed new regulations for user consent, as well as how personal data is collected, stored, and shared. Of the six elements that make up China's new Cybersecurity Law, this standard belongs to the fourth, called "personal information and important data protection system" (S. Sacks, 'New China Data Privacy Standard Looks More Far-Reaching than GDPR', Centre for Strategic and International Studies (2018), to consult at: www.csis.org/analysis/new-china-data-privacy-standard-looks-more-far-reaching-gdpr.

77   A. Mattoo, J. P. Meltzer, (n. 20).

78   European Commission, (n. 20).

WTO's General Agreement on Trade in Services (GATS). While WTO Members generally exercise significant judicial restraint in challenging measures justified on general exception grounds, the argument has been made that the GDPR could be open to challenge by failing to pass the necessity test found in Article XIV by giving countries undue scope to decide what data protection measures provide "adequate safeguards", thus making any law justifiable as a privacy exception.[79]

6   Concluding Remarks

In a world where digital technologies are developing at breakneck speed and electronic commerce, including that transacted across online borders, has become an integral part of everyday life, the EU, by virtue of its size, income level and institutional sophistication, plays a crucial role in defining international regulation in an area that has long been characterized by "light touch" regulatory approaches and the absence of global governance norms.

This chapter has chronicled the evolution of the EU's treatment of e-commerce and digital trade in a representative sample of preferential trade agreements negotiated in the aftermath of the 2009 entry into force of the Lisbon Treaty.

The analysis on offer in this chapter reveals the incremental nature of EU rule-making, marked by the significant (and useful) doses of learning by doing and policy experimentation that PTAs make possible. The EU's e-commerce journey over the past decade reveals a rule-making landscape characterized by considerable diversity depending on the timing of agreements and the nature (and development level) of the Union's trading partners. Still, iterative advances made in PTAs have progressively shaped the emergence of an EU e-commerce model featuring a combination of binding and non-binding provisions in a policy domain that continues to elicit strong doses of regulatory precaution even on the part of technologically advanced countries.

The emergence of a EU digital trade model has paralleled major regulatory developments within the Single Digital Market. The source of long drawn-out debates and policy tensions between different components of the European Commission – DG Justice vs DG Trade – on how best to reconcile the needed freedom of cross-border data flows with legitimate calls to afford EU citizens

---

79   M. Burri, 'The Governance of Data and Data Flows in Trade Agreements: The Pitfalls of Legal Adaptation', *UC Davis Law Review*, Vol. 51 (2017), p. 65–133.

adequate levels of data protection appears largely settled. The adoption of the GDPR positions the EU as the global champion of data privacy. This raises important questions regarding the Union's ability to project its own internal norms externally. It is arguably too early to determine whether the GDPR will become the leading global norm on matters of data privacy, with pushback likely to emerge from large industry players, small scale digital operators and leading trading partners, particularly the United States. For now, the EU approach, in both its latest PTA s and multilaterally at the WTO, is to promote the emergence of vibrant digital ecosystems through the adoption of negotiated provisions focusing on key pillars of e-commerce facilitation while preserving needed Union-wide autonomy on the fundamental right to data protection.

PART 4

Trade Defence

∵

CHAPTER 12

The EU's Anti-Subsidy Practice during the Last Decade

Increasingly Aggressive Application

Edwin Vermulst and Juhi Dion Sud

1   Introduction

This contribution provides an overview of the anti-subsidy ("AS") law and practice of the European Union ("EU") over the last decade (2008–2018) as regards the determination of subsidisation. The injury, causation and Union interest determinations as well as procedural issues are not discussed as they have been touched upon in a previous article by the authors.[1] As the contribution was completed in 2018, subsequent developments are not discussed.[2]

The basic Anti-subsidy Regulation is Regulation (EU) 2016/1037 of the European Parliament and the Council of 8 June 2016[3] ("basic AS Regulation"), as amended in 2017 and 2018.[4] In addition to the basic AS Regulation, non-binding guidelines for the calculation of the subsidy amount in AS investigations

---

1   See E. Vermulst, J. Sud, 'Anti-Subsidy Law and Practice of the European Union', in H. C. H. Hofmann, C. Micheau (eds.), *State Aid Law of the European Union* (OUP, 2016), p. 508–563. Furthermore, injury, causation and Union interest determinations in AS cases are similar to those in anti-dumping cases, see for more detail in that regard, E. Vermulst, *EU Anti-dumping Law and Practice* (Sweet & Maxwell, 2010).

2   Notably the EU's countervailing foreign direct investment, as discussed in S. Evenett, E. Vermulst, J. Sud, The EU's New Move Against China: Countervailing Chinese Outward Foreign Direct Investment, 15:9 Global Trade and Customs Journal, 413-422 (2020).

3   For text, see OJ 2016, L176/55.

4   By Regulation (EU) 2017/2321 of the European Parliament and of the Council of 12 December 2017 amending Regulation (EU) 2016/1036 on protection against dumped imports from countries not members of the European Union and Regulation (EU) 2016/1037 on protection against subsidised imports from countries not members of the European Union OJ 2017, L338/1 and Regulation (EU) 2018/825 of the European Parliament and of the Council of 30 May 2018 amending Regulation (EU) 2016/1036 on protection against dumped imports from countries not members of the European Union and Regulation (EU) 2016/1037 on protection against subsidised imports from countries not members of the European Union OJ 2018, L143/1.

("Guidelines")[5] have existed since 1998. Although non-binding, the Guidelines have been referred to and applied in many AS cases, as will be demonstrated in Section 3.[6]

The present contribution is divided into three sections. Section 2 gives an insight into the use of the AS instrument by the EU since 2008. Section 3 represents the most extensive part of the article and discusses the EU's practice with respect to the key elements of a countervailable subsidy. Finally, Section 4 sets out the authors' conclusions.

2   Use of the Anti-subsidy Instrument from 2008–2018

2.1   *Overview*

Compared to the anti-dumping ("AD") instrument, the use by the EU of the basic AS Regulation has been relatively modest, although it has clearly increased over time. In addition, the EU has become increasingly aggressive in countervailing domestic subsidies, particularly in cases against China where export subsidies are rare.

In the 2008–2018 period, the EU initiated 35 AS cases.[7] Countervailing duties were imposed in 16 cases and in one case[8] undertakings were accepted; 17 cases were terminated without imposition of measures.

The products subject to AS investigations during the period considered include, *inter alia*, biodiesel, bioethanol, fasteners, solar panels and cells, different types of fish, bikes and e-bikes, bus and truck tyres, different types of steel, PET, PTA, and WWAN modems.

During the 2008–2018 period, China has been the most frequent target of the EU's AS investigations (12) and measures (8), followed by India (6).

2.2   *Developments and Trends*

An important change in the EU's AS practice occurred in 2010, when the EU launched the first AS case against a country considered to be a "non-market

---

5   Guidelines for the Calculation of the Amount of Subsidy in Countervailing Duty Investigations, OJ 1998, C394/6.

6   See, *e.g. HRF from China*, recital 212.

7   A single investigation initiated against several countries has been counted as several investigations. A list of all the AS cases initiated in the 2008–2018 period is provided in Annex 1. The detailed references to the publication in the Official Journal of the EU for all cases are also provided in Annex 1.

8   Solar cells and panels.

economy". Based on a complaint from the Confederation of European Fine Paper Industries, the EU launched an AS investigation against imports of *CFP from China*. This was followed by investigations against several other products from China such as *WWAN modems*, various *steel products, Bicycles, Solar panels and cells, Solar glass, Filament glass fibre products, Polyester staple fibres, E-bikes* and *Tyres*. In December 2013, the EU initiated the first AS case against Vietnam, which it also considers to be a "non-market economy".[9]

Another recent development in the EU's practice pertains to indirectly countervailing export taxes imposed by exporting country governments on raw materials. Following an unsuccessful attempt to address export taxes via the AD instrument in the context of *Biodiesel from Argentina and Indonesia*, the EU now addresses the effect of export taxes in AS cases.[10] In 2016, in the AS case concerning *Ductile cast iron tubes and pipes* ("DCIT") from India, the EU countervailed the Indian export tax on iron ore – which is the basic raw material to make DCIT – in an indirect manner by finding that through the export tax/restraints the Indian government induced and entrusted the iron ore producers to artificially lower the iron ore prices for the DCIT producers in India, resulting in iron ore being provided at less than adequate remuneration.[11] A similar approach was applied in the AS investigation concerning *Biodiesel from Argentina* with respect to the Argentine export tax on soybeans.[12]

In general, the EU's approach has been to pair AS investigations with AD investigations against the same product from the same country.

During the period 2008–2018, the EU applied the lesser duty rule in imposing AS measures which implies that the duty imposed is based on the lower of the subsidy or injury margins. Through the lesser duty rule, the EU avoided the problem of "double remedies"[13] when the same product originating in a non-market economy was subject to both AD and AS investigations and measures. This is due to the fact that the injury margin served as the cap for the total duty that can be imposed in the AD and AS cases. In other words, even though the EU imposed both an AD duty ("ADD") and a countervailing duty ("CVD") with

9   *Polyester staple fibres from inter alia Vietnam* (initiation). The case was terminated without the imposition of measures.

10   AB, *European Union — Anti-Dumping Measures on Biodiesel from Argentina*, DS473; Panel, *European Union — Anti-Dumping Measures on Biodiesel from Indonesia*, DS480.

11   *DCIT from India* (definitive), recitals 131–226.

12   *Biodiesel from Argentina*.

13   For further explanation of the term see, AB, *United States-Anti-Dumping and Countervailing Duties (China)*, DS379, para. 542–543. See also E. Vermulst, B. Gatta, 'Concurrent Trade Defence Investigations in the EU: The EU's New Anti-Subsidy Practice against China', *World Trade Review*, 11:3 (2012), p. 527–553.

the latter based on the subsidy margin – which was generally lower than the injury margin – and the former based on the difference between the injury and subsidy margins, the maximum duty that was imposed did not exceed the injury margin. Therefore, the AS case did not add anything further in terms of protection of the domestic industry because generally the ADD in cases against China was based on the injury margin as the dumping margin calculated on the basis of analogue country producers' data was almost always higher. However, it is politically more palatable in the EU to impose CVDs because they enjoy more Member States' support than ADD.

It is important to note that since the amendments to the EU's basic AD and AS Regulations ("TDI amendments") have entered into force,[14] the EU no longer applies the lesser duty rule in AS investigations.[15]

Additionally, over the years, in AS investigations, the EU has been countervailing subsidies that were not alleged in the complaints but "discovered" during the investigations. This approach has now been formalised and included in Article 10(7) of the basic AS Regulation.[16]

3   Key Elements of a Countervailable Subsidy

Article 3 of the basic AS Regulation sets out two key requirements for the determination of a subsidy, namely the existence of a financial contribution by a government or public body (or that there is some form of income or price

---

14 Regulation (EU) 2018/825 of the European Parliament and of the Council of 30 May 2018 amending Regulation (EU) 2016/1036 on protection against dumped imports from countries not members of the European Union and Regulation (EU) 2016/1037 on protection against subsidised imports from countries not members of the European Union OJ 2018, L143/1.

15 See the revised Article 15 of the Basic AS Regulation. After five years of negotiations, a political agreement on the substance of the changes to the basic AD and AS Regulations was reached between the Commission, the Council and the European Parliament. The International Trade Committee of the European Parliament endorsed this agreement on 23 January 2018, and it entered into force after the respective approval procedures within the European Parliament and the Council. For further details see European Commission's memo: 'Europe's trade defence instruments now stronger and more effective', 7. June 2018, available at: http://trade.ec.europa.eu/doclib/docs/2018/june/tradoc_156921.pdf.

16 Regulation (EU) 2017/2321 of the European Parliament and of the Council of 12 December 2017 amending Regulation (EU) 2016/1036 on protection against dumped imports from countries not members of the European Union and Regulation (EU) 2016/1037 on protection against subsidised imports from countries not members of the European Union OJ 2017, L338/1.

support) and a resulting benefit to the recipient. If these two broad conditions are fulfilled, a subsidy is deemed to exist. However, only those subsidies that are "specific" within the meaning of Article 4 of the basic AS Regulation are countervailable.

3.1   *Financial Contribution by a Government*
Article 3(1) of the basic AS Regulation elaborates the concept of a financial contribution made by a government or public body as well as a private body which has been entrusted or directed in this regard.

3.1.1   Government or Public Body
Article 2(b) of the basic AS Regulation defines a "government" as a "government or any public body within the territory of the country of origin or export". The basic AS Regulation does not contain a definition of "public body" nor criteria for the categorisation of an entity as a public body. The determination of a public body has been a cardinal issue in several EU AS cases and especially in those concerning China.

In all the AS cases completed against China thus far, the EU has determined, on the basis of *facts available*, that the Chinese policy and state-owned banks[17] are public bodies.[18] In the first AS case concerning China namely CFP, the EU considered policy and state-owned banks to be public bodies on the grounds that they are "[...] more than 50% state-owned and are thus controlled by the government", the banks effectively exercise government authority since there is state intervention in the manner in which commercial banks take decisions on loan interest rates, and various government documents, including the Commercial Banking Law, require banks to pursue government industrial policies.[19]

In subsequent AS cases targeting China, the EU has attempted to justify its findings more explicitly within the framework of the criteria set out by the Appellate Body in the WTO dispute *US-Anti-Dumping and Countervailing Duties (China)*.[20] In *Solar panels and cells from China* and *Solar glass from China*, for example, the EU's public body determination was premised on the finding that state-owned banks are controlled by the Chinese government and

---

17   In AS cases against China, state-owned commercial banks are referred to by the EU as including state-owned banks and banks where the state has a controlling interest in terms of shareholding, see *Solar glass from China* (definitive), recital 71.

18   A similar finding was reached by the EU as regards policy banks in *CFP from China* (definitive), recitals 58, 90.

19   *CFP from China* (definitive), recitals 74–90.

20   AB, *United States-Anti-Dumping and Countervailing Duties (China)*, DS379.

perform governmental functions. The EU held that: (i) the Chinese financial market is characterised by government intervention because most of the major banks are state-owned, these banks hold the highest market share and are "predominant players in the Chinese market"; (ii) the state-owned banks are controlled by means of ownership and administrative control over their behaviour; (iii) these banks are subject to legal rules, notably the Commercial Banking Law, which requires banks to carry out lending activities according to the "needs of the national economy", and other legal documents which require the banks to provide credit support to encouraged projects and give priority to the development of high and new technology industries. In *Hot-rolled flat products from China*, developing this approach further, the EU made separate analyses for the cooperating and non-cooperating banks that provided loans to the investigated exporters. With regard to each of the cooperating banks, the EU first assessed the "formal indicia of government control", and then relying on the macro level policies and documents, such as the five year and steel plans, held that the government of China has created a normative framework in order to exercise meaningful control over the functioning of those banks and confirmed this assessment on the basis of the specific loans given to the investigated Chinese exporters.[21]

Overall, on these bases, the EU has consistently held that "state-owned commercial and policy banks perform government functions on behalf of the (Chinese government), namely mandatory promotion of certain sectors of the economy in line with planning and policy documents".[22]

In *OCS from China*, the EU held that the state-owned enterprises ("SOEs") from which the exporting producers purchased hot- and cold-rolled steel were public bodies. This determination was based on the finding that SOEs perform governmental functions and are controlled by the government. As regards the former aspect, the EU relied on government policy documents concerning the sector to hold that "[...] concrete actions by the state-owned steel enterprises [are] orchestrated by the government".[23] It considered that the concerned SOEs performed governmental functions prescribed in the sectoral plans for the iron and steel industry, and that the implementation of the plans by the

21   *Hot-rolled flat products from China* (definitive), recitals 87–130.

22   See *e.g. Solar panels and cells from China* (definitive), recitals 158–168; *Solar glass from China* (definitive), recitals 71–87; *Hot-rolled flat products from China* (definitive), recitals 83–140. See also the EU's findings of public body regarding China Export and Credit Insurance Corporation, SINOSURE, in *Solar panels and cells from China* (definitive), recitals 225–235.

23   *OCS from China* (definitive), recital 57.

SOE s was tantamount to governmental practice. The EU furthermore held that the Chinese government "[...] is using the iron and steel (SOE s) as a prolonged arm of the state in order to achieve goals and targets set in the plans".[24] As regards government control, and again relying on facts available, including those provided by the complainant, the EU held that the government had ownership in many of the enterprises, that it controlled to a high degree the composition of the Boards of the various SOE s and these SOE s had to mandatorily follow government plans and policies.[25]

In AS cases against India, the EU has consistently held the Reserve Bank of India to be a public body mainly on account of 3 factors: (i) 100% government ownership; (ii) pursuance of government policy objectives such as the monetary policy; and (iii) the appointment of the bank's management by the Government of India.[26]

In PET from, inter alia, Iran, the EU held the Iran National Petrochemical Company to be a public body on the basis of its 100% government ownership,[27] the exercise of total control by the government, and because the company was responsible for the development and operation of Iran's petrochemical sector and for this reason had been entrusted to manage the Petrochemical Special Economic Zone.[28]

3.1.2 Forms of Financial Contribution

Financial contributions in various forms by a government have been treated as countervailable subsidies by the EU.

3.1.2.1 Direct and Indirect Transfer of Funds, Revenue foregone, Provision of Goods and Services

Article 3(1)(a)(i) of the basic AS Regulation refers to a financial contribution in the form of direct or potential direct transfer of funds and liabilities. Grants of various kinds have routinely been countervailed by the EU.[29] For instance, in Biodiesel from the USA, a Texan grant scheme by virtue of which a biodiesel producer that paid a fee of $0.032 per gallon of biodiesel produced in a registered

---

24   *Ibid.*, recitals 49–58.

25   *Ibid.*, recitals 59–71.

26   SSW *from India* (provisional), recital 98. See also the EU's finding of public body as regards the State Bank of Pakistan on similar grounds in PET *from inter alia Pakistan* (provisional), recital 128.

27   This company was a subsidiary of the National Iranian Oil Company which was fully owned by the Ministry of Petroleum.

28   PET *from inter alia Iran* (provisional), recital 52.

29   See *e.g. Hot-rolled flat products from China* (definitive), recitals 365–393.

plant was entitled to receive $0.20 for each gallon of biodiesel produced in each registered plant until the tenth anniversary of the start of production was countervailed.[30]

Loans by various Chinese state-owned banks as well as private banks located in China – pursuant to a finding of entrustment and direction – have been held in all the AS cases against China as providing a financial contribution.[31]

The basic AS Regulation outlines in Article 3(1)(a)(ii) certain examples of situations where government revenue, which is otherwise due, is foregone or not collected, including fiscal incentives such as tax credits as well as illegal duty drawback schemes.

In *Bioethanol from the USA*, the EU held a scheme by virtue of which blenders of bioethanol received a $0.45/gallon tax credit – for blending bioethanol with taxable fuels – which could be used to offset excise or income tax liability or received in cash, to provide a countervailable subsidy on the ground that there was a direct grant from or revenue foregone by the US government.[32] In *CFP from China* and *Solar glass from China*, the EU countervailed a subsidy scheme involving an exemption of dividend income for resident enterprises in China which are shareholders in other resident enterprises in China. The financial contribution was held to be in the form of revenue foregone.[33]

Article 3(1)(a)(iii) of the basic AS Regulation refers to financial contribution through government provision of goods and services other than general infrastructure. In all Chinese AS cases, the EU has systematically held the provision of land-use rights by the Chinese government to be at less than adequate remuneration ("LTAR").[34] In *OCS from China*, the EU additionally determined that the key raw materials, hot- and cold-rolled steel provided by SOEs – which were held to be public bodies – and private suppliers had been provided at LTAR.[35] In *Solar panels and cells from China*, the EU furthermore considered

---

30   *Biodiesel from the USA*, (provisional), recital 140. See also for instance, *Solar glass from China*, (definitive), recitals 122–136.

31   See *e.g. Hot-rolled flat products from China* (definitive), recitals 152–244.

32   *Bioethanol from the USA* (termination), recitals 67–69. See also in *Biodiesel from the USA* (provisional), tax reductions from the "Business and Occupation tax" imposed on manufacturing activities and tax exemption from property tax and leasehold excise tax provided to producers of biofuels.

33   *CFP from China* (definitive), recitals 125–136. See also *Solar glass from China* (definitive), recitals 153–159.

34   See *e.g. CFP from China* (definitive), recitals 248–263; *OCS from China* (definitive), recitals 107–126; *Solar panels and cells from China* (definitive), recitals 354–375; *Solar glass from China* (definitive), recitals 172–195; *Hot-rolled flat products from China* (definitive), recitals 281–311.

35   *OCS from China* (definitive), recitals 45–106.

the provision of credit lines by banks determined to be public bodies as provision of financial services at LTAR.[36] In *DCIT from India*, the Commission considered that iron ore had been provided at LTAR to producers of ductile cast iron tubes and pipes on account of the Indian government's export tax on this raw material.[37]

3.1.2.2   *Government Entrustment and Direction; Payments via a Funding Mechanism*

Article 3(1)(a)(iv) of the basic AS Regulation considers the financial contribution by a "government" requirement to be satisfied when a government "entrusts or directs a private body" to make one of the sorts of contributions enumerated in Article 3(1)(a)(i)-(iii) or makes payment to a funding mechanism.

In *SSW from India*, the EU held that the credits provided by commercial banks to the Indian exporters at preferential rates set by the RBI, were pursuant to government direction within the meaning of Article 3(1)(a)(iv) of the basic AS Regulation.[38]

In all Chinese cases investigated thus far, the EU has held that the *private* commercial banks – including branches of international banks – operating in China are entrusted or directed by the Government of China to provide preferential loans to encouraged industries on the ground that there is a Chinese government policy of providing preferential loans to the investigated industries and this extends to the private banks as well because the Commercial Banking Law – which equally applies to private banks – instructs banks to "[...] carry out their loan business upon the needs of the national economy and the social development and with the spirit of state industrial policies".[39] The EU also held that various policy documents mandate preferential lending to the investigated industries and tied this to a finding of distortion of the financial market.[40] The above reasoning and logic has also been extended by the EU to private finance companies.[41]

In *OCS from China*, the EU made a finding of entrustment and direction as regards state-owned and private enterprises supplying hot-and cold-rolled

---

36   *Solar panels and cells from China* (definitive), recital 213.
37   *DCIT from India* (definitive), section 3.2.4.
38   *SSW from India* (definitive), recital 39.
39   See *e.g., Solar glass from China* (definitive), recitals 89–94.
40   *OCS from China* (definitive), recitals 170–180; *Solar panels and cells from China* (definitive), recitals 169–184; *Solar glass from China* (definitive), recitals 89–93; *Hot-rolled flat products from China* (definitive), recitals 141–148.
41   *Hot-rolled flat products from China* (definitive), recital 132.

steel. It held that these enterprises act in accordance with government planning and policy documents and that the export restrictions on steel in the form
of a VAT system, depress prices and prevent these enterprises from acting independently. Moreover, according to the EU, due to the predominance of state-
owned suppliers, the private enterprises were forced to align their prices with
those of the SOE s.[42]

In the context of payments via a funding mechanism within the meaning of
Article 3(1)(a)(iv), in *Biodiesel from the USA* the EU found that the Government
of North Dakota made payments to a funding mechanism called the biodiesel partnership in assisting community expansion fund. The funds were used
to reduce the interest rate on loans made by lead local financial institutions
in conjunction with the North Dakota bank to a qualifying biodiesel production facility. The latter simply paid the reduced interest rate payment while the
difference between the normal and reduced interest rate was received by the
lending bank from the fund.[43]

3.2   *Specificity*

Article 4(1) of the basic AS Regulation provides that a subsidy can be countervailed only if it is specific. The various sub-paragraphs of Article 4 refer to the
different forms of specificity such as when a subsidy is limited to an enterprise,
industry or a group of enterprises or industries (sector specificity), is region-
ally specific, export contingent or dependent upon the use of domestic over
imported goods.

3.2.1   Sector Specificity

Article 4(2) of the basic AS Regulation establishes principles for determining
whether a subsidy is specific to an enterprise or industry or a group of enterprises or industries within the jurisdiction of the granting authority. Article
4(2)(a) provides that a subsidy is specific where the granting authority or
the legislation pursuant to which the granting authority operates expressly limits access to certain enterprises. This is commonly termed as *de jure*
specificity.

Article 4(2)(b) goes on to provide that specificity shall not exist if the granting authority or the legislation pursuant to which the granting authority operates, establishes objective criteria or conditions governing the eligibility for,
and the amount of, a subsidy and provided that the eligibility is automatic.

---

42   OCS *from China* (definitive), recitals 87–94.
43   *Biodiesel from the USA* (provisional), recitals 117–122.

Article 4(2)(c) further specifies that notwithstanding any appearance of non-specificity, if there are reasons to believe that the subsidy may in fact be specific, other factors may be considered including the use of a subsidy programme by a limited number of enterprises, predominant use by certain enterprises, the granting of disproportionately large amounts of subsidy to certain enterprises, and the manner in which discretion has been exercised by the granting authority in the decision to grant a subsidy. In other words, a subsidy may be *de facto* specific. The examples below illustrate that, in most cases, the EU has interpreted sectoral specificity in a rather broad manner, often by applying facts available.

In virtually all initial cases against Chinese products, the EU countervailed tax programmes among others concerning an exemption from income tax for 2 years and application of half the tax rate for the next 3 years ("two free, three half programme") provided to foreign invested enterprises. The EU considered this subsidy to be *de jure* specific as the legislation itself limited access to the programme to foreign invested enterprises.[44]

In *SSF from inter alia Malaysia*, a scheme called "pioneer status" was held to be a countervailable subsidy. Under this scheme, an investment tax allowance was given to all companies producing a promoted product listed in the Malaysian Promotion of Investments Act and categorised on the basis of certain criteria such as economic, national and strategic requirements of Malaysia, local content, and value added. The EU held that this scheme was specific because it was accessible only to enterprises producing the limited list of promoted products, and the criteria for the designation of a promoted product were vague and undefined with the Government having significant discretion to designate products as promoted. The EU furthermore considered that differential tax exemption rates for different products showed that certain enterprises were favoured over others.[45]

In *CFP from China*, the EU considered several subsidy schemes including preferential lending, provision of land-use rights and tax benefits to be specific on the basis that according to policy documents and the sectoral Papermaking Plan, the subsidies available to the paper making industry were not generally available and were targeted to the paper making industry which was

---

44   See *e.g. Solar panels and cells from China* (definitive) recital 295. See also *CFP from China* (definitive). As this programme was terminated and the period during which its benefits could be "grandfathered" has also expired, it is no longer countervailed. See *Hot-rolled flat products from China* (definitive), recitals 312–316.

45   *SSF from inter alia Malaysia* (provisional Malaysia, Philippines, no measures Thailand, Singapore), recitals 38–41.

an "encouraged" industry.[46] In subsequent cases against China, the EU again found specificity on the basis of the "encouraged" industries approach.[47] In *ocs from China*, the EU found specificity as regards the provision of hot- and cold-rolled steel at LTAR because these inputs were used only by a limited number of enterprises in China.[48] A similar approach was taken as regards iron ore in *DCIT from India*.[49]

3.2.2   Regional Specificity

Article 4(3) of the basic AS Regulation provides that a subsidy which is limited to certain enterprises located within a designated geographical region within the jurisdiction of the granting authority is specific. The setting or changing of generally applicable tax rates by all levels of the government entitled to do so is not deemed to be specific.

In *CFP from China*, grants available to companies in Shandong province and Suzhou industrial park were found to be limited to companies within these designated geographical areas.[50]

3.2.3   Export Contingent Subsidies

A subsidy which is contingent in fact or law upon export performance within the meaning of Article 4(4)(a) of the basic AS Regulation is deemed to be an export subsidy. The EU's practice regarding countervailing of export subsidy programmes has included illegitimate duty drawback schemes, import duty exemptions or reductions on imported capital goods for production of export-ed goods, and benefits available in export processing zones. Subsidies counter-vailed in cases concerning India are mostly export subsidies.

3.2.3.1   *Duty Drawback Schemes*

Under the basic AS Regulation, properly functioning duty drawback schemes are not subsidies.[51] Thus far, the EU has examined the duty drawback systems

---

46   *CFP from China* (definitive), recitals 92–93, 254–255.

47   See as regards preferential lending and land-use rights, *e.g.*, *Hot-rolled flat products from China* (definitive), recitals 149–151; 297–299.

48   *ocs from China* (definitive), recital 84. Compare *Hot-rolled flat products from China* (defin-itive), where the EU rejected allegations that Chinese hot-rolled flat products' producers benefitted from the provision of iron ore, coke, cooking oil and power at LTAR, recitals 267–280. In *Bicycles (electric)*, the EU considered that batteries and engines had been provided to e-bikes' producers at LTAR.

49   *DCIT from India* (definitive), recitals 272–275.

50   *CFP from China* (definitive), recitals, 193–202; 213–245.

51   Art. 3(1)(a)(ii) of the basic AS Regulation.

of several countries including India, Indonesia, Korea and Pakistan and has countervailed them in virtually all instances by finding that the duty drawback systems did not meet the requirements in Annex I (i), Annex II and Annex III of the basic AS Regulation.

In the Indian context, three key schemes have been countervailed, namely the Duty Entitlement Passbook Scheme ("DEPBS"), the Advanced Authorization Scheme ("AAS"), the Focus Market Scheme ("FMS") and the Focus Product Scheme ("FPS").

The DEPBS was considered countervailable *inter alia* because the exported products did not have to incorporate imported raw materials. While the programme was terminated in September 2011, it was then replaced by a similar scheme called the duty drawback scheme ("DDS") which functions in a somewhat similar manner as the former scheme and has been countervailed by the EU for the same reasons.[52]

The AAS basically permits the duty-free imports of inputs incorporated into the exported product. The main reason for not considering this scheme as a permissible duty drawback scheme is the absence of a verification mechanism by the Government of India regarding the actual use and amounts of the inputs used in the exported products.[53] Even where exporting producers were found to have maintained production and consumption registers, the EU found deficiencies in the system such as the absence of proper audits and intervention/control in case of excess remission.[54]

Exceptionally, in *PTY from, inter alia, India*, the EU did not countervail this scheme as the investigated companies were able to demonstrate that the quantities of imported materials, which were exempted from import duties, did not exceed the quantities incorporated in the exported goods.[55]

The FMS, pursuant to which exporters were provided duty credits for exports of all products to certain specified countries (which did not include the EU Member States), and FPS pursuant to which exporters were given duty credits equivalent to a certain percentage of the FOB export value for exports of specific products, have been considered impermissible duty drawback schemes

---

52   For further details on countervailing of DDS see *DCIT from India* (definitive), section 3.2.3. For similar reasons, the Pakistani Manufacturing Bond Scheme was considered an impermissible duty drawback scheme in *PET from inter alia Pakistan* (provisional), recitals 75–76; *PET from inter alia Pakistan* (definitive), recital 50.

53   See for instance, *SSW from India* (provisional), recitals 65–80; *PET film from India* (amendment definitive pursuant to partial interim review 2005), recital 58.

54   *SSF and parts thereof from India* (provisional), recital 48.

55   *PTY from inter alia India* (provisional India, no measures Indonesia), recital 66.

on similar grounds as the DEPBS.[56] These two schemes were terminated in 2015 and a new scheme called Merchandise Exports from India Scheme was instituted which is considered by the EU as a replacement of FPS and FMS.[57]

The EU generally countervailed the entire benefit from a duty drawback scheme, not merely the excess remission, if it found the scheme not to be a permissible duty drawback scheme. This approach was applied by the EU in *PET from Pakistan* with regard to the Pakistani manufacturing bond scheme ("MBS"). The EU considered MBS as an impermissible duty drawback system owing to the failures or malfunctions in the Government of Pakistan's system of verification and considered it an export contingent subsidy.[58] This approach was successfully challenged in the WTO by Pakistan.[59] Indications are that the EU has changed its approach since.

3.2.3.2   *Export Oriented Units ("EOUs")] and Special Economic Zones ("SEZs")*
In several Indian cases the EU has held that companies located in EOUs/SEZs which undertook export obligations could obtain various tax benefits.[60] Since these benefits were contingent, in law, upon export performance, they were held to be export subsidies. However not all the EOU/SEZ sub-schemes have been held to be countervailable. For instance, in *SSB from India*, the EU held that while the sales tax reimbursement for EOUs was countervailable, the excise duty exemption was not.[61]

In *SSF from, inter alia, Malaysia,* the EU investigated the import duty exemption on raw materials, machinery and equipment in so-called Free Zones and considered it to be countervailable. Specificity was found in the export contingency of the exemption as a company established in a Free Zone was obliged to export 80% of its production[62] and alternatively on the assessment that the

---

56   For FMS see *SSW from India* (provisional), recital 109, and for FPS see *DCIT from India* (definitive), recitals 85–86.

57   *DCIT from India* (definitive), recitals 87–89.

58   *PET from inter alia Pakistan* (definitive), recitals 43–53.

59   Panel, *European Union — Countervailing Measures on Certain Polyethylene Terephthalate from Pakistan*, DS 486, para. 7.37, 7.50–7.58, further confirmed by the Appellate Body in DS 486, para. 5.138–5.139.

60   These benefits included exemption from customs duties on purchases of capital goods, raw materials and consumables; exemption from excise duty on goods from indigenous sources; exemption from income tax normally due on profits from export sales; reimbursement of central sales tax paid on goods procured locally; and exemption from tax on profits from export.

61   *SSB from India* (provisional), recitals 72–74.

62   *SSF from, inter alia, Malaysia* (provisional Malaysia, Philippines, no measures Thailand and Singapore), recital 63.

subsidy is limited to companies located in certain areas. It was considered to be an impermissible duty drawback scheme because the Malaysian government could not prove that it applied a proper verification system.[63]

3.2.3.3   *Import Duty Exemption Capital Goods*
Duty-free/reduced duty imports of capital goods used for the production of exported products have consistently been considered countervailable subsidies. Thus, for example, the Indian scheme called the Export Promotion Capital Goods Scheme has been countervailed in all the AS cases against India where the scheme was used by the investigated exporters.[64]

3.2.3.4   *Export Credits and Export Credit Insurance*
The EU has countervailed export credits or other export-related financing in several cases.

An Indian subsidy scheme called the Export Credit Scheme involving the grant of credits to exporters was countervailed by the EU in a string of Indian cases. Under this scheme the RBI set the maximum ceiling interest rates applicable to export credits in Indian Rupees and foreign currencies. It was considered countervailable because the exporters got credits on preferential interest rates set by the RBI which reduced the interest costs of the exporters, and the subsidy was deemed to be specific for being export contingent.[65]

On similar grounds, the Pakistan Export Long-Term Fixed Rate Financing Scheme was countervailed in *PET from, inter alia, Pakistan*.[66]

In *Solar panels and cells from China*, the EU considered the short-term export credit insurance provided by the Chinese Export Credit and Insurance Corporation, SINOSURE, to be a countervailable subsidy as it was linked to the export sales of the exporting producers. The EU also considered – on the basis of facts available – that SINOSURE's premiums did not cover the long-term

---

63   *Ibid*, recital 65.

64   Compare also *PSF from, inter alia, Thailand*, (provisional Australia, Taiwan, termination Korea, Thailand), where a similar Thai scheme was considered countervailable. It is noted that a similar scheme, called "VAT and Tariff exemption on imported equipment", was investigated and considered countervailable in *CFP from China, Solar panels and cells from China* and subsequent Chinese cases. However, in those cases it was not considered an export subsidy because the receipt of the benefit was not linked to export performance or export commitments. See *e.g. CFP from China*, (definitive), recitals 137–147; *Solar panels and cells from China* (definitive), recitals 331–335.

65   See *e.g. ssw from India* (provisional), recital 98.

66   *PET from Iran, Pakistan and UAE* (provisional), recital 129.

operating costs of the programme within the meaning of item (j) of Annex I of the SCM Agreement.[67]

3.2.3.5   Tax Exemptions

In *SSF from, inter alia, Malaysia*, the EU countervailed the double deduction of business expenses for export promotion by exhibiting products in an international trade fair recognised by the Malaysian authorities[68] and for cargo insurance premium for exports.[69] In the same case, as regards sales tax exemption, the EU justified the export contingent nature of the scheme on the ground that the exemption was applicable only on machinery and raw materials used for the production of goods destined for export and the companies located in the Free Zone had to export 80% of their products.[70]

In *PET from, inter alia, Pakistan*, the EU countervailed a programme in which Pakistani export sales were taxed at a lower rate than domestic sales.[71]

3.2.4   Import Substitution Subsidies

According to Article 4(4)(b) of the basic AS Regulation, a subsidy which is contingent upon the use of domestic over imported goods is deemed to be specific. In *PET from, inter alia, Pakistan*, the EU investigated a scheme according to which a refund was provided to buyers of domestically produced PTA. It held that the scheme involved direct financing to the polyester industry and favoured the procurement of domestically produced PTA and was thus contingent upon the use of domestic over imported goods.[72]

3.3   *Benefit and Subsidy Margin Calculation*

According to Article 3(2) of the basic AS Regulation, a subsidy exists only if in addition to the financial contribution by a government or public body, a benefit is received by the recipient. While the term "benefit" is not defined in the basic AS Regulation (nor in the WTO ASCM), it is widely accepted that a government financial contribution confers a benefit if it makes the recipient "better

---

67   *Solar panels and cells from China* (definitive), recitals 236–246. See also *Solar panels and cells from China* (extension), recitals 276–304.
68   *SSF from, inter alia, Malaysia* (provisional Malaysia, Philippines, no measures Thailand, Singapore), recitals 18–25.
69   *Ibid.*, recitals 26–33.
70   *SSF from, inter alia, Malaysia* (provisional Malaysia, Philippines, no measures Thailand, Singapore), recitals 23, 31 and 50.
71   *PET from Iran, Pakistan and UAE* (provisional), recitals 111–113.
72   *PET from, inter alia, Pakistan* (provisional), recital 100.

off than it would otherwise have been, without that contribution",[73] and that the amount of the subsidy to be calculated is the difference between where the recipient is after the subsidy and where it would have been absent the subsidy. The implication of this is that a financial contribution must confer a *benefit to the recipient* (which is typically higher than the *cost to the government*).[74]

In *Biodiesel from the USA*, the EU countervailed certain federal and state excise and income tax credit schemes of which the most prominent was the biodiesel mixture credit. The EU found a benefit to the investigated producers, although the credits had been given to the blender who was not necessarily the producer. The EU held that in order to obtain the credits the blender had to obtain a biodiesel certificate from the producer mentioning the quantity of biodiesel and this was transferable and therefore conferred a right to a \$1/ gallon tax credit.[75]

It is important to note that Article 5 of the basic AS Regulation states that the amount of countervailable subsidies shall be calculated in terms of the benefit to the recipient found to exist during the investigation period ("IP") set in the investigation. Thus, the EU countervails all benefits received during the IP regardless of whether the subsidy scheme was terminated prior to or after the IP.[76] However, when investigated exporters could prove that the subsidy scheme was not continued in the same or a variant form, and there would be no continuing benefits, the EU has made exceptions.[77]

Article 6 of the basic AS Regulation provides the rules for the calculation of the benefit in case of government provision of equity, loans, loan guarantees, provision of goods or services or purchase of goods and for the calculation of benchmarks. Article 7 further states that the amount of the subsidy is to be established per unit of the subsidised product exported to the EU and permits certain types of deductions, such as the costs incurred to qualify or obtain the

---

73   See for example AB, *United States – Anti-Dumping and Countervailing Duties (China)*, DS379, para. 436, citing the Appellate Body in *Canada – Aircraft*, para. 157.

74   A noteworthy exception to this principle concerns certain forms of export credit financing referred to in paragraph 2 of item (k) of the *Illustrative List of Export Subsidies* of the EU's basic AS Regulation, providing for a situation in which a benefit to the recipient may not be considered countervailable if it does not also constitute a cost to the providing government.

75   *Biodiesel from the USA* (definitive), recitals 58–59.

76   *PET from, inter alia, Pakistan* (provisional), recital 124 as regards the Export Long-term Fixed Rate Financing.

77   Compare on the one hand *Solar panels and cells from China* (definitive), recitals 288–299, 338 and on the other hand *Solar glass from China* (definitive) recitals 141–142 and *Bioethanol from the USA* (termination) recitals 145–147.

subsidy and export taxes levied on the product. Additionally, it provides the methodology for the allocation of subsidy amounts. The Guidelines further elaborate the provisions in Articles 5–7 of the basic AS Regulation and also provide concrete examples.

3.3.1   Calculation of the Subsidy Amount in Practice

The calculation of the subsidy amount can be divided into methodical steps. The first step entails the assessment of the total benefit involving the determination of the benefit amount from the subsidy scheme based on the relevant parameters and benchmarks. This is adjusted on two counts:

- Deduction of expenses incurred to obtain the subsidy permitted by Article 7(1)(a) and (b) in terms of costs incurred to qualify for or obtain the subsidy and for export taxes, duties or other charges levied on the exports specifically intended to offset the subsidy.[78] However, the Guidelines qualify that "[n]o allowance can be made for any tax effects of subsidies or for any other economic or time value effect beyond that which is specified in this communication".[79]
- Interest adjustment involving the addition of the commercial interest rate to the basic benefit amount in order to "reflect the full amount of benefit". The interest adjustment is provided in the Guidelines.[80]

Once the benefit amount is calculated, the next step involves the allocation of the benefit to the IP. According to Article 7(3) of the basic AS Regulation, where a subsidy can be linked to the acquisition or future acquisition of fixed assets, the subsidy amount is to be calculated by allocating the subsidy over a period (useful life) which reflects the normal depreciation of such assets in the industry concerned. Article 7(4) further clarifies that "[w]here a subsidy cannot be linked to the acquisition of fixed assets, the amount of the benefit received during the investigation period shall in principle be attributed to this period [...] unless special circumstances arise justifying attribution over a different period".

---

78   See for instance *SSB from India* (provisional), recital 76.

79   Section G (2) of the Guidelines.

80   Section C of the Guidelines explains the need for such interest adjustment as follows: "Pursuant to the rule laid down in Article 5 of Regulation 2026/97, the calculation of the benefit shall reflect the amount of subsidy found to exist during the investigation period and not simply the face value of the amount at the time it is transferred to the recipient or foregone by the government. Thus the face value of the amount of the subsidy has to be transformed into the value prevailing during the investigation period through the application of the normal commercial interest rate".

These provisions imply that a recurring subsidy, such as an income tax exemption or illegal duty drawback received during the IP, will be allocated to the IP.[81] However, where a – typically non-recurring – subsidy received in the IP is linked to the acquisition of fixed assets such as a customs duty exemption on imports of capital equipment and machinery, the benefit is allocated over the useful life of the equipment/machinery.[82] In AS cases concerning China, the benefit from the provision of land-use rights at LTAR has been allocated over the normal lifetime of industrial land in China, *i.e.* 50 years.[83]

In the context of grants, the general practice of the EU has been to take the whole grant amount as the benefit and add the commercial interest rate.[84] In *SSF from, inter alia, Malaysia*, for example, the EU countervailed the sales tax exemptions granted to exporters on all imported machinery, equipment and raw materials used directly in the manufacturing of finished goods destined for export. The benefit amount was calculated as the difference between the 10% sales tax payable and the amount which was actually paid. The EU considered that as the benefit from sales tax exemptions was obtained regularly during the IP, it was equivalent to a series of grants made between the first and the last day of the IP. Accordingly, the EU held that in such a case, an average grant is deemed to be received at the mid-point of the IP and it added an interest rate "[...] on the whole amount of non-paid duties over a period of six months using the average commercial lending rate".[85]

The EU's benchmarking methodology for computing the benefit from loans at preferential rates has been straightforward when there were no allegations of a distorted domestic financial market.

However, the benchmark calculation for loans in AS cases concerning China is complicated as the Chinese financial market is considered to be distorted by government intervention and the benchmark calculation has consistently been based on facts available. The same applies with regard to the provision of land-use rights and inputs at LTAR.

---

81   *SSF from inter alia Malaysia* (provisional Malaysia, Philippines, no measures Thailand, Singapore), recital 68.

82   *SSF from, inter alia, Malaysia* (provisional Malaysia, Philippines, no measures Thailand, Singapore), recital 70; *Hot-rolled flat products from China* (definitive), recital 353.

83   *CFP from China* (definitive), recital 262. *Solar panels and cells from China* (definitive), recital 374.

84   See for instance *CFP from China* (definitive), recitals 182–192 concerning "special funds for encouraging foreign investment projects". See however the non-application of this approach in *Hot-rolled flat products from China* (definitive), recital 370.

85   *SSF from, inter alia, Malaysia*, (provisional Malaysia, Philippines, no measures Thailand, Singapore), recital 55.

326 VERMULSTVERMULST AND SUD

Thus, in the context of preferential lending assessed in AS cases against China, the EU has consistently determined that, due to the predominant role of the policy and state-owned banks in the domestic financial market and of the People's Bank of China in setting interest rates legally or informally, there is substantial government intervention in the financial market as a result of which there is no undistorted financial market in China. Additionally, it has held that the loans provided by private banks were pursuant to government entrustment and direction. Based on a sum of these two findings, the EU has constructed in each case, on the basis of facts available, a benchmark for the loans. The benchmark for RMB-denominated loans has been established by applying a mark-up[86] to the standard interest rate set by the People's Bank of China, in order to reflect the "normal market risk". The mark-up has varied in the different cases. For instance, in *Solar glass from China*, the mark-up was the absolute difference between "AAA" and "BB+" and "BB-" rated bonds.[87] As regards foreign currency loan benchmarks, in *CFP from China*, the EU used the USD LIBOR and EUR LIBOR rates for "BB" rated corporate bonds and added a mark-up for the duration.[88] A different benchmark was established in *Solar panels and cells from China*.[89] In *Hot-rolled flat products from China*, for RMB denominated loans, the EU used a mark-up based on the relative spread between the indexes of US A-rated to US BB-rated corporate bonds based on Bloomberg data for industrial segments.[90] Furthermore, loans granted to loss-making subsidiaries of two Chinese producers were treated as grants.[91] Additionally, "revolving loans" were treated as exceptionally high-risk loans and subject to very high benchmark rates.[92]

In the context of provision of inputs at LTAR, as regards land-use rights, in all cases against China, the EU has used an external benchmark, *i.e.* the land prices in Taiwan (adjusted in certain cases for inflation and GDP growth), on the grounds that there is no functioning land-use rights market in China.[93]

---

86 *CFP from China* (definitive), recitals 98–99; *OCS from China* (definitive), recitals 191–192; *Solar panels and cells from China* (definitive), recital 198; *Solar glass from China* (definitive), recitals 101–110; *Hot-rolled flat products from China* (definitive), recitals 152–242.

87 *Solar glass from China* (definitive), recitals 101–110.

88 *CFP from China* (definitive), recital 328.

89 Information known to the authors.

90 *Hot-rolled flat products from China (definitive)*, recital 169.

91 *Hot-rolled flat products from China (definitive)*, recitals 212, 235. A similar approach was taken in *Tyres (definitive)*.

92 *Hot-rolled flat products from China (definitive)*, recitals 171–172.

93 *CFP from China* (definitive), recital 260; *OCS from China* (definitive), recitals 107–118; *Solar panels and cells from China* (definitive), recitals 361–368; *Solar glass from China* (definitive), recitals 173–182; *Hot-rolled flat products from China (definitive)*, recitals 300–311.

Additionally, in *ocs from China*, for the benefit calculation for hot- and cold-rolled steel, the EU relied on its approach of "distorted market prices" for these inputs as a result of the predominance of SOEs and based the benchmark on the world market prices of these products derived from steel journals.[94] A similar approach was followed in *DCIT from India* as regards iron ore and the benchmark was based on the Australian FOB price of iron ore.[95]

In addition to the foregoing, in *Solar panels and cells from China*, the EU countervailed short-term export credit insurance provided by SINOSURE, which was held to be a public body. The benefit calculation was based on an external benchmark which was taken to be the premium rates applied by the US EXIM Bank.[96]

3.3.2   Subsidy Margin Calculation

For the calculation of the subsidy margin, the numerator is the benefit amount and the denominator the company's export turnover[97] or its entire turnover[98] depending upon whether the subsidy is export contingent or a domestic subsidy. Article 7(2) of the basic AS Regulation lays down the basic rule for the allocation of subsidies and provides that where a subsidy

> [...] is not granted by reference to the quantities manufactured, produced, exported or transported, the amount of countervailable subsidy shall be determined by allocating the value of the total subsidy, as appropriate, over the level of production, sales or exports of the products concerned during the investigation period for subsidisation.[99]

Furthermore, the Guidelines note that if the benefit of a subsidy is limited to a particular product, the subsidy should be allocated over the (export) turnover of that product. This also suggests that subsidies linked to non-investigated products should not be attributed to the product concerned. However, this logic has not been applied consistently.

---

94   *ocs from China* (definitive), recital 103.

95   *DCIT from India* (definitive), recitals 244–245.

96   *Solar panels and cells from China* (definitive), recitals 252–255.

97   See *e.g. ssb from India* (provisional), recitals 40 and 57 concerning the allocation of the benefit from the DEPBS and AAS.

98   See *e.g. Solar panels and cells from China* (definitive), recital 200 concerning the allocation of benefits from loans at preferential rates.

99   Section F (b) of the Guidelines elaborates the above provision.

In *ssw from India,* for example, the EU countervailed duty credits useable for the payment of customs duties, received by exporters upon exports of all products to certain countries other than the EU Member States pursuant to FMS. The EU justified its position on the grounds that the benefit from the scheme can be used for the product concerned because the duty credits are freely transferable and can be used for payment of customs duties on subsequent imports of any inputs or capital goods.[100] This approach amounts to the adoption of the *fungibility of money* concept.

3.3.3   Instances When Subsidies Were Not Countervailed

Routinely complainants allege a wide range of subsidies in a complaint to "cast the net wide" but very often it happens that some of the alleged subsidy schemes are not used by the investigated exporting producers.[101] Consequently, there is no legal basis for countervailing such subsidy schemes except if the cooperation of exporting producers is low and facts available are applied.[102]

Moreover, in certain cases, programmes alleged to be subsidies by the complainants were upon investigation by the EU found not to be granted directly or indirectly, for the manufacture, production, export or transport of the product concerned as required by Article 1(1) of the basic AS Regulation. For instance, in *Biodiesel from the USA*, the EU held that the tax exemption scheme of Illinois was not countervailable because the benefit was received by the consumers of biodiesel and biodiesel blends.[103]

In *ssf from, inter alia, Malaysia,* the industrial building allowance ranging from two to ten percent of the building expenditure was considered not to be a subsidy on account of the absence of a financial contribution. The EU held that it complied with the international accountancy standards on depreciation and it was a standard depreciation practice for production-oriented buildings used across the manufacturing and services sectors, thereby signifying the lack of specificity as well.[104]

---

100   *Stainless steel wires from India* (definitive), recital 42. See also *Broad spectrum antibiotics from India* (continuation pursuant to interim and expiry review 2003), recitals 78–85.

101   *ssf from, inter alia, Malaysia and Thailand* (provisional Malaysia, Philippines, no measures Thailand, Singapore), recitals 77, 81. See also assessment as regards the reinvestment allowance scheme in the same case at recital 76. Compare *Hot-rolled flat products from China,* (definitive), recitals 394–399.

102   See *ocs from China* (definitive).

103   *Biodiesel from the USA* (provisional), recital 97.

104   *ssf from, inter alia, Malaysia* (provisional Malaysia, Philippines, no measures Thailand, Singapore), recital 61. On the lack of specificity, see also *Hot-rolled flat products from China* (definitive), recitals 279–290 as regards the provision of power.

Exceptionally, when subsidy schemes were withdrawn during the course of the investigation by the exporting country government, the benefits from such schemes were not countervailed.[105]

In addition to the foregoing, when the subsidy obtained is insignificant or negligible, *i.e.* less than 0.1%,[106] the EU's practice has been to not countervail it.

4 Conclusions

After a hesitant start, since 1995 the EU has progressively – and increasingly aggressively – used the AS instrument to act against subsidisation by third country governments. This trend has accelerated in the last decade with the EU countervailing perceived Chinese subsidy schemes.

While initially focusing on relatively clear-cut export subsidies, over time the EU has more and more also countervailed domestic subsidy programmes. This is clearest in the AS cases initiated against China since 2010 where the vast majority of countervailed programmes have consisted of domestic subsidies. In this context, it is important to note that the findings of specificity reached by the EU in cases concerning China are largely based on the use of facts available, resulting from the imposition of very high burden of proof on the Chinese government that domestic subsidies in fact are not specific. This applies particularly to important elements of the Chinese economic system, such as land-use rights, loans by Chinese banks and purchases of inputs from SOEs. It seems a question of time before the EU's "broad brush" approach regarding specificity of Chinese subsidies is challenged in the WTO.[107]

Noteworthy from a systemic perspective is also the occasional (not consistent) adoption by the EU authorities of the "fungibility of money" concept.

From a policy perspective, one may wonder whether the increasingly aggressive approach by the EU is wise. As Lee Makiyama has noted,[108] those who

---

105   *PET from, inter alia, Pakistan* (definitive), recital 61. See also *Bioethanol from the USA* (termination); *PET from India* (2015 interim review), recital 106.

106   See for instance the North Dakota biodiesel production equipment tax credit and North Dakota biodiesel income tax credit. *Biodiesel from the USA* (provisional), recital 128. See also *SSB from India* (amendment definitive pursuant to partial interim review 2012), recital 17.

107   The same applies to treating loans as grants. The WTO compatibility of these and other aspects of EU TDI law and practice are discussed in more detail in Vermulst, Sud, Are the EU's Trade Defence Instruments WTO Compliant?, in *Global Politics and EU Trade Policy: Facing the Challenges* (eds. Weiss, Furculita 2020).

108   H. L. Makiyama, 'Chasing Paper Tigers: Need for caution and priorities in EU countervailing duties (CVDs)', *ECIPE Policy Brief* 1(2011), p. 7.

live in glass houses should not throw stones. Hopefully, therefore, the EU's aggressive AS practice will not come back to haunt EU producers/exporters in AS cases initiated by third countries. This appears to be a risk particularly in the agricultural sector.

Acknowledgement

The authors would like to thank Antoine Reco for his helpful comments and input.

Annex 1 EU Anti-subsidy cases from 2008 to 2018

Product	Country	Year	Parallel AD investigation or AD measures	Reason for termination of case without measures if applicable
Biodiesel[a]	USA	2008	Parallel AD investigation	-
Sodium metal[b]	USA	2008	Parallel AD investigation	Withdrawal of complaint
Stainless steel fasteners and parts thereof[c] ["SSF"]	India, Malaysia	2009	Parallel AD investigation	Withdrawal of complaint
Polyethylene terephthalate[d] ["PET"]	Iran, Pakistan, United Arab Emirates	2009	Parallel AD investigation	- (expired)
Purified terephthalic acid and its salts[e] ["PTA"]	Thailand	2009	Parallel AD investigation	*De minimis* subsidy margin
Stainless steel bars[f] ["SSB"]	India	2010	Parallel AD investigation	-
Coated fine paper[g] ["CFP"]	China	2010	Parallel AD investigation	-
Wireless wide area networking modems[h] ["WWAN modems"]	China	2010	Parallel AD and Safeguards investigations	Withdrawal of complaint
Polyethylene terephthalate[i] ["PET"]	Oman, Saudi Arabia	2011	Parallel AD investigation	Withdrawal of complaint
Stainless steel fasteners and parts thereof[j] ["SSF"]	India	2011	Parallel AD investigation	Absence of causal link as majority of the imports were found to be not subsidized
Bioethanol[k]	USA	2011	Parallel AD investigation	Subsidy scheme expired during the investigation

Annex 1 EU Anti-subsidy cases from 2008 to 2018 (*cont.*)

Product	Country	Year	Parallel AD investigation or AD measures	Reason for termination of case without measures if applicable
Organic coated steel products[l] ["ocs"]	China	2012	Parallel AD investigation	-
Bicycles[m]	China	2012	Previous AD measures	Withdrawal of complaint
Stainless steel wires[n] ["ssw"]	India	2012	Parallel AD investigation	-
Crystalline silicon photovoltaic modules and key components[o] ["Solar panels and cells"]	China	2012	Parallel AD investigation	-
Biodiesel[p]	Argentina and Indonesia	2012	Parallel AD investigation	Withdrawal of complaint
Solar glass[q]	China	2013	Parallel AD investigation	-
Filament glass fibre products[r]	China	2013	Previous AD measures	-
Polyester staple fibres[s] ["PSF"]	China, India and Vietnam	2013	AD measures against China existed until 10 June 2011	*De minimis* subsidy margin
Rainbow trout[t]	Turkey	2014	Terminated AD investigation	-
Stainless steel cold-rolled flat products[u] ["SSCR"]	China	2014	-	Withdrawal of complaint
European sea bass and gilthead sea bream[v]	Turkey	2015	-	Withdrawal of complaint

Annex 1 EU Anti-subsidy cases from 2008 to 2018 (*cont.*)

Product	Country	Year	Parallel AD investigation or AD measures	Reason for termination of case without measures if applicable
Tubes and pipes of ductile cast iron[w] ["DCIT"]	India	2015	Parallel AD investigation	-
Hot-rolled flat products of iron, non-alloy or other alloy steel[x] ["HRF"]	China	2016	Parallel AD investigation	-
Bicycles (electric)[y]	China	2017	Parallel AD investigation	-
Tyres for buses or lorries (new and retreaded)[z]	China	2017	Parallel AD investigation	-
Biodiesel[aa]	Argentina	2018		-
Biodiesel[bb]	Indonesia	2018		Pending

[a] OJ 2008, C147/10 (initiation); OJ 2009, L67/50 (provisional); OJ 2009, L179/1 (definitive); OJ 2010, L211/6 (initiation circumvention); OJ 2011, L122/1 (extension circumvention); OJ 2013, C124/10 (initiation partial interim review); OJ 2014, L115/14 (termination partial interim review); OJ 2014, C217/25 (initiation expiry review); OJ 2015, L239/99 (definitive expiry review); OJ 2015, C162/9 (initiation partial interim review); OJ 2016, L116/27 (definitive partial interim review).

[b] OJ 2008, C186/35 (initiation); OJ 2009, L149/74 (termination).

[c] OJ 2009, C190/32 (initiation); OJ 2010, L180/28 (termination).

[d] OJ 2009, C208/7 (initiation); OJ 2010, L134/25 (provisional); OJ 2010, L254/10 (definitive); OJ 2013, C138/32 (partial reopening); OJ 2013, L253/1 (amendment definitive pursuant to partial reopening 2013); OJ 2015, C319/6 (expiry).

[e] OJ 2009, C313/22 (initiation); OJ 2011, L15/17 (termination).

[f] OJ 2010, C87/17 (initiation); OJ 2010, L343/57 (provisional); OJ 2011, L108/3 (definitive); OJ 2012, C239/2 (initiation partial interim review); OJ 2013, L202/2 (amendment definitive pursuant to partial interim review 2012).

[g] OJ 2010, C99/30 (initiation); OJ 2011, L128/18 (definitive); OJ 2016, C172/19 (initiation expiry review); OJ 2017, 171/134 (definitive).

[h] OJ 2010, C249/7 (initiation); OJ 2010, L243/37 (registration); OJ 2011, L58/36 (termination).

[i] OJ 2011, C49/21 (initiation); OJ 2011, L330/43 (termination).

[j] OJ 2011, C142/36 (initiation); OJ 2012, L38/6 (provisional); OJ 2012, L134/31 (termination).

[k] OJ 2011, C345/13 (initiation); OJ 2012, L229/20 (registration); OJ 2012, L352/70 (termination).

[l] OJ 2012, C52/4 (initiation); OJ 2013, L73/16 (definitive); OJ 2018, C96/21 (initiation expiry review).

Annex 1 EU Anti-subsidy cases from 2008 to 2018 (*cont.*)

ᴹ OJ 2012, C122/9 (initiation); OJ 2013, L136/15 (termination).

ᴺ OJ 2012, C240/6 (initiation); OJ 2013, L126/19 (provisional); OJ 2013, L240/1 (definitive); OJ 2017, L214/1 (definitive).

ᴼ OJ 2012, C340/13 (initiation); OJ 2013, L61/2 (registration); OJ 2013, L209/26 (undertaking); OJ 2013, L325/66 (definitive); OJ 2013, L325/214 (undertaking definitive); OJ 2015, L132/53 (initiation circumvention); OJ 2016, L37/56 (definitive circumvention); OJ 2017, L289/1 (definitive circumvention); OJ 2015, C405/20 (initiation expiry review); OJ 2017, L56/1 (definitive expiry review).

ᴾ OJ 2012, C342/12 (initiation); OJ 2013, L102/13 (registration); OJ 2013, L315/67 (termination).

ᑫ OJ 2013, C122/24 (initiation); OJ 2014, L142/23 (definitive).

ᴿ OJ 2013, C362/66 (initiation); OJ 2014, L376/22 (definitive).

ˢ OJ 2013, C372/31 (initiation); OJ 2014, L360/65 (termination).

ᵀ OJ 2014, C44/9 (initiation); OJ 2014, L319/1 (provisional); OJ 2015, L56/12 (definitive); OJ 2017 C234/6 (initiation partial interim review).

ᵁ OJ 2014, C267/17 (initiation); OJ 2015, L196/4 (termination).

ⱽ OJ 2015, C266/4 (initiation); OJ 2016, L215/31 (termination).

ᵂ OJ 2015, C83/4 (initiation); OJ 2016, L73/1 (definitive); OJ 2016, L217/4 (definitive).

ˣ OJ 2016, C172/69 (initiation); OJ 2017, L147/17 (definitive).

ʸ OJ 2017, C440/22 (initiation); OJ 2019, L16/5 (definitive).

ᶻ OJ 2017, C346/9 (initiation); OJ 2018, L283/1 (definitive).

ᵃᵃ OJ 2018, C24/27 (initiation); OJ 2019, L40/1 (definitive).

ᵇᵇ OJ 2018, C439/16 (initiation).

CHAPTER 13

The Devil is in the Detail – a First Guide on the EU's New Trade Defence Rules

Frank Hoffmeister

1   Introduction

As of June 2018, the European Union's trade defence action operates under a new set of rules. On the one hand, some third-country exporters believe that the Union has created a "monster" which is very hard to tame. On the other hand, some Union industry representatives jubilee that the Union has become tougher vis-à-vis a growing trend of unfair practices world-wide. They hence view the new rules more like a "saviour" from the sin of others. A third point of view could be not to associate the EU's new TDI arsenal with either position. Looking through the neutral lawyer's lenses, one might rather ask how much the devil is in the detail of the new rules.

The purpose of this chapter[1] is two-fold. We will first trace back briefly the historical development to better understand the political context in which the legislation on the new methodology (Regulation (EU) 2017/2321[2]) and on the modernisation package (Regulation (EU) 2018/825[3]) came into being. Second, we will analyse the main features of the two texts, in order to review some legal questions arising from the new rules. A conclusion will contain a first assessment.

---

1   This chapter is a slightly enlarged version of an article that was published first in W. Weiß and C. Furculita (eds.), European Yearbook of International Economic Law, Special Issue: Global Politics and EU Policy – Facing the Challenges to a Multilateral Approach, Springer 2020, p. 211-230.

2   Regulation (EU) 2017/2321 of the European Parliament and of the Council of 12 December 2017 amending Regulation (EU) 2016/1036 on protection against dumped imports from countries not members of the European Union and Regulation (EU) 2016/1037 on protection against subsidised imports from countries not members of the European Union (OJ 2017, L 338/1).

3   Regulation (EU) 2018/825 of the European Parliament and of the Council of 30 May 2018 amending Regulation (EU) 2016/1036 on protection against dumped imports from countries not members of the European Union and Regulation (EU) 2016/1037 on protection against subsidised imports from countries not members of the European Union (OJ 2018, L 143/1).

2   Historical Development

Back in 2006, the British Trade Commissioner Mandelson started a public debate about TDI modernisation by launching a Green Paper.[4] However, his ideas
were perceived to be one-sided benefitting mainly exporters by shielding them
from EU action. Considerable opposition arose both in the European Parliament and the Council. Once the Commissioner realised that there was no sufficient support for the project, he abandoned it.[5]

In the second half of Commissioner de Gucht's mandate, the issue came
back on the table. In spring 2013, the Commission made a formal legislative
proposal, accompanied by four draft guidelines.[6] The Belgian Commissioner
took a conscious decision to include elements which would be of interest to
either side. Some pro-industry elements would strengthen the efficiency of the
instrument and the fight against retaliation, while some pro-importer elements
would increase the predictability of TDI action and optimise the review practice. Moreover, as a sort of house-keeping exercise certain modifications were
deemed necessary to take account of relevant WTO and ECJ jurisprudence.[7]

In the first reading of the European Parliament in 2014, the proposal received
some support; nevertheless, its balance was radically changed. Although the
Swedish *rapporteur* Fjellner was known to hold pro free-trade views, the majority of MEPs favoured an approach favouring the Union industry. The Parliament hence voted down the Commission ideas on pre-disclosure of provisional measures and the reimbursement of duties collected during an expiry
review which does not result in a renewal of measures.

In return, the Council was deeply split. While Member States agreed that the
proposal was much more balanced than Mandelson's Green Paper, they nevertheless saw no urgent need to tackle the issue. Moreover, De Gucht's proposal

---

4   European Commission, 'Europe's trade defence instruments in a changing global economy?',
    COM (2006)763 final, 6.December 2006.
5   For details on the green paper debate see F. Graafsma, J. Cornelis, 'The EC's Green Paper
    on Trade Defence Instruments: Guillotine on Anti-Dumping or Smokescreen for More Basic
    Predicaments?', *Global Trade and Customs Journal* 2 (2007), p.255–263.
6   European Commission, 'Proposal for a Regulation of the European Parliament and of the
    Council amending Council Regulation (EC) No 1225/2009 on protection against dumped im-
    ports from countries not members of the European Community and Council Regulation (EC)
    No 597/2009 on protection against subsidised imports from countries not members of the
    European Community', COM (2013) 192 final, 10 April 2013.
7   For details of the proposal see F. Hoffmeister, 'Modernising the EU's Trade Defence Instru-
    ments: Mission Impossible?', in C. Herrmann, B. Simma, R. Streinz, *Trade Policy between Law,
    Diplomacy and Scholarship – Liber amicorum in Memoriam Horst G. Krenzler* (Springer, 2015),
    p. 365–376.

to modify the lesser duty rule with regard to two scenarios – subsidy cases and structural distortions on raw materials – was considered as opening a Pandora's Box. A number of over ten traditionally liberal Member States feared that the proposal would turn into an inward-looking exercise where the traditional checks and balances of TDI in the EU would be tilted towards a protectionist approach. Accordingly, the Council did not give a mandate to any of its Presidencies during De Gucht's term. When he left office at the end of 2014, some even speculated that the proposal would be silently abandoned and buried in the graveyard of unpopular Commission initiatives.

A new wind blew, though, through the Council during the term of Trade Commissioner Malmström. The Swedish Commissioner first tackled the issue of calculating the normal value. After an internal impact assessment indicated that the Commission should respond to challenges emanating from certain WTO members, such as China, and the experience gained from case-law, she proposed in November 2016 to adapt the basic Regulation. In her view, the EU should operate on the basis of a non-discriminatory new methodology for calculating normal value in cases where significant distortions in an exporting WTO Member state existed. Council and Parliament (despite the quite different views in the political families[8]) agreed in record speed on the approach and the details,[9] and the new Regulation was enacted in December 2017.

With this new impetus, the Council also reconsidered its position on the modernisation proposal. In December 2016, the Slovak Presidency received a mandate to negotiate with the goal to emphasising more the importers' interests.[10] As it was very close to the Commission's original proposal for the remainder, earnest negotiations could take place with the Parliament in trilogues, and the institutions reached a final compromise a mere year later, on 5 December 2017. After formal voting in both the Parliament and the Council, the new Regulation came into force in June 2018.

When considering the outcome of the two processes together, one can conclude that the political context allowed for achieving a certain balance. While

---

8   For a description of the different views on TDI in the political families of the European Parliament see B. Petter, R. Quick, 'The Politics of TDI and the Different Views in EU Member States: Necessary Safety-Valve or Luxurious Rent-Seeking Device?', in M. Bungenberg et al. (eds.), *European Yearbook of International Economic Law* (Springer, 2018), p. 29–30.

9   For details of the legislative history see E. Vermulst, J. Sud, 'The New Rules Adopted by the European Union to Address "Significant Distortions" in the Anti-Dumping Context', in M. Bungenberg et al. (eds.), *European Yearbook of International Economic Law* (Springer, 2018), p. 66–69.

10   W. Müller, 'The EU's New Trade Defence Laws: A Two Steps Approach', in M. Bungenberg et al. (eds.), *European Yearbook of International Economic Law* (Springer, 2018), p. 47.

the new methodology and the reform of the lesser duty rule in the modernisation exercise can be seen as important tools to maintain an efficient anti-dumping system in the European Union in a time of increasing challenges, the Union still kept an eye on the interests of importers and maintained its basic approach to keep the instrument as a quasi-judicial and proportionate remedy against unfair practices. Let us now have a closer look at the technical details of the new rules.

3   The New Anti-dumping Methodology

3.1   *The Determination of Significant Distortions in the Exporting Country*

Since dumping occurs when the export price of the product concerned is lower than its normal value, the determination of the normal value is of crucial importance. According to Article VI (1) GATT and Article 2.1 of the Anti-Dumping Agreement (ADA), normal value is usually derived from the domestic price of the like product concerned in the ordinary course of trade in the exporting country. However, when there are no such sales or because of the particular market situation or the low volume of the sales in the domestic market of the exporting country, such sales do not permit a proper comparison, the normal value can be construed by using cost data in the country of origin or representative export prices to appropriate third countries (Article 2.2 ADA). The provision is, however, silent about the question what happens if also the costs in the country of origin are significantly distorted.

Against that background, Article 2 (6a) (a) of the EU's amended basic Antidumping Regulation (EU) 2016/1036 (basic AD Regulation) directs the Commission to make a determination whether or not it is appropriate to use domestic costs for constructing normal value. In doing so, the Commission shall look at six elements, listed in Article 2 (6a) (b) of the basic AD Regulation. The common characteristic of these elements is that they undermine the free-market principle. Costs and prices are not the result of offer and demand anymore, when they are influenced by heavy state intervention. Such intervention can exist when there is

- significant market-share of State-owned enterprises;
- State presence in (non-state owned) companies which allows that state to influence prices and costs;
- a State strategy or measure favouring domestic suppliers or otherwise influencing the free play of market forces;

- a lack of or the discriminatory application of insolvency, company or property law;
- distorted wage costs;
- access to financing by institutions which implement State objectives or do not act independently from the State.

As the wording "inter alia" shows, the list is non-exhaustive. Moreover, there is no need to show that all elements exist cumulatively. Rather, if it follows from one or several of the elements that there are significant distortions in the country of origin, the Commission shall make such a determination.

Evidently, such determinations will pose challenges to the investigators. How to collect relevant knowledge about the legal, institutional and macro-economic environment in the exporting country? How to make sure that broader observations on a country-wide level are also relevant for the product under investigation? In that respect, the new rules also offer some procedural novelties.

Under Article 2 (6a) (c), 1st sentence of the basic AD Regulation, the Commission shall produce, make public and regularly update a report, when it has well-founded indications of the possible existence of significant distortions in a certain country or sector. The first report was issued with respect to China as a staff working paper on the day the new methodology was adopted, on 20 December 2017.[11] Over 400 pages long, the report shows a considerable level of detail. Describing the general political system and the influence of the ruling party and State-owned enterprises in China's economy, it then sets out the financial, procurement and investment framework. Important factors of production, such as land, energy, capital, raw materials and labour are also analysed. The report concludes with three chapters on important sectors where trade defence measures have been taken in the past, namely steel, aluminium and ceramics. As mentioned by the Commission Director in charge of anti-dumping matters, Mr. Rubinacci, in a civil society dialogue of March 2018, the second report is likely to address Russia.[12] In drawing up such reports, the Commission may use its own expertise, but should also be receptive to international reports. Recital 4 of the amending Regulation (EU) 2017/2321 mentions in this context that "relevant standards, including core conventions of the International Labour Organisation (ILO) and relevant multilateral environmental conventions should be taken into account, where appropriate".

---

11   Commission Staff Working Document: http://trade.ec.europa.eu/doclib/docs/2017/december/tradoc_156474.pdf.
12   Civil Society Dialogue: http://trade.ec.europa.eu/doclib/docs/2018/march/tradoc_156630.pdf.

From an operational point of view, the report is the starting point for the application of the new methodology. It helps the applicant to produce *prima facie* evidence in the complaint.[13] Once the Commission decides to initiate a new investigation, it will put it on the open file of that case as well. As stated in Article 2 (6a) (c) 2nd sentence of the basic AD Regulation, interested parties then have the opportunity to rebut, supplement, comment or rely on the report and the evidence on which it is based. In practice, this means that the government of the exporting country may react to the report within 37 days after initiation of the case (country-wide defence). In addition, during the course of the investigation, the exporting producers or their associations may question whether the findings in the report are relevant for their sector. For example, they could contest a distorting effect of SOEs in their specific sector (sectoral defence). Finally, any individual exporting producer may challenge provisional or definitive findings of the Commission that its costs of production are influenced by significant distortions. A producer could, for example, challenge a finding that labour costs are significantly distorted in its business (product related defence).

The consequences of the different defences vary, however. A successful country-wide defence would close the avenue to the application of Article 2 (6a) of the basic AD Regulation altogether. In that case, the Commission would have to go back to the normal method of determining normal value under Article 2 (1) – (6) of the basic AD Regulation. A successful sectoral defence may have the same effect or the effect that the Commission may revisit for which factors of production it cannot replace the domestic cost with another benchmark. A product-related defence would usually not affect the application of Article 2 (6a) of the basic AD Regulation, but rather direct the Commission to make a precise determination which factors of production of the product concerned can be relied upon and which not. That is a question to which we now turn.

3.2 *The Appropriate Benchmarks for Replacing Distorted Cost Factors*
If the Commission has determined that significant distortions exist in the country of origin, it shall replace domestic prices and costs by other sources of data. Article 2 (6a) (a), 2nd paragraph of the basic AD Regulation, lists three non-exhaustive benchmarks: costs of production and sale in an appropriate

---

13   E. Vermulst, J. Sud, 'The New Rules Adopted by the European Union to Address "Significant Distortions" in the Anti-Dumping Context', in M. Bungenberg et al. (eds.), in M. Bungenberg et al. (eds.), *European Yearbook of International Economic Law* (Springer, 2018), p. 71.

representative country; undistorted international benchmarks, or undistorted domestic costs.

The list does not establish any strict hierarchy between these alternative benchmarks.[14] Recital 5 of the amending Regulation 2017/2321 contains a slight preference, though, when stating that costs should be established on:

> any reasonable basis, including information from other representative markets or from international prices or benchmarks. Domestic costs may also be used, but only to the extent that they are positively established not to be distorted, on the basis of accurate and appropriate evidence.

This preference has to do with the above-mentioned defences: only where an exporting producer can show with a sectoral or product specific defence that there are no significant distortions affecting certain cost factors of the product under consideration, and the Commission accepts this as accurate, the absence of significant distortions is "positively established". If such defence is neither made, nor successful, the Commission would resort to the other two benchmarks.

The first practice shows that among these two alternatives, the "corresponding costs from an appropriate representative country with a similar level of economic development" is the more promising. In China-related cases, countries with a similar level of economic development can be found in the World Bank list of middle income countries. The first candidates were Korea, Thailand, Brazil, Mexico or Turkey. If there are several countries available, a choice must be made. In that operation, several factors play a role: the relevant data must be "readily" available and preference should be given, where appropriate, to countries with an adequate level of social and environmental protection. Recital 6 of the amending Regulation 2017/2321 directs the Commission in this respect to analysing "whether those countries comply with core ILO and relevant environmental conventions". While the pertinent standards can be derived from the relevant list establishing additional incentives in the Generalized System of Preferences (GSP plus),[15] it is less obvious that a trade defence investigation can provide a detailed performance analysis of the actual performance record of several potential representative countries on labour and environmental matters. Hence, it is more crucial to establish which potential representative country offers the best available data for constructing normal

---

14   W. Müller (n. 9), p. 58.
15   See Annex VIII to Regulation (EU) 978/2012, OJ 2012, L 303/1.

value. The Commission hence produces a note to the file on the "factors of production", available data from representative third countries and shares this with the interested parties. After having considered the respective comments and additions, a qualitative comparison of the data sets derived from publicly available resources will then usually produce the "best" candidate, where the information is "most easily" available. Importantly, as these data are distilled from data bases and other publicly available sources, and not from specific sampled companies, the Commission services will not carry out verification visits at company premises anymore for the construction of normal value.

Finally, the Commission may also decide to resort to undistorted international prices, costs or benchmarks. This alternative may particularly come into play when international spot prices apply, as is the case for certain commodities. However, even in this alternative, finding the correct comparable like product to the raw material at issue, which is used in the production of the product concerned, may pose challenges.

3.3   *WTO Dimension*

As a full WTO member in its own right, the EU has taken on the obligation to ensure the conformity of its laws, regulations and administrative procedures with the provisions of the covered WTO Agreements (Article XVI:4 WTO Agreement). Among the pertinent provisions are Article VI GATT and the Anti-Dumping Agreement (ADA). In addition, specific rights may flow from obligations undertaken by other Members in their respective Accession protocols.[16] A good example is China's Accession Protocol of 2011 which contains additional obligations.[17]

In the WTO case DS516, the Chinese government attacked the EU's use of the non-market economy method under Article 2 (7) of the basic AD Regulation for cases launched after 15 December 2016. In Beijing's view, this method violates the EU's WTO commitments to apply the regular rules on establishing dumping under Article 2.2.1.1 of the ADA, as the 15-years transitional period under Section 15 of China's Accession Protocol[18] had expired by that date. In

---

16   M. Kennedy, 'The Integration of Accession Protocols in the WTO Agreement', *Journal of World Trade* 47 (2013), p. 45–75.

17   See M. Hahn, 'The Multilateral and EU Legal Framework on TDIs: An Introduction', in M. Bungenberg et al. (eds.), *European Yearbook of International Economic Law* (Springer, 2018), p. 6–10.

18   For discussion of the different interpretations of this provision see D. Fang, 'EU – Price Comparison Methodologies (DS516): Interpretation of Section 15 of China's Accession Protocol', in M. Bungenberg et al. (eds.), *European Yearbook of International Economic Law* (Springer, 2018), p. 107–124.

addition, the Chinese government sought to enlarge the scope of this case by portraying the new methodology as a continuation of the old analogue-country method in disguise. The EU is actively defending itself on the principle and the additional claims. As the panel decided on 17 June 2019 to suspend the case on China's request under Art. 12.12 of the DSU, it will not be discussed in detail here.[19] However, with regard to the procedural question of "continuity" one remark is merited, as there are a couple of important differences between the methodologies under Articles 2 (6a) and (7) of the basic AD Regulation. While the latter only applies to the countries specifically mentioned in the footnote thereto, the former is country-neutral. Moreover, in a non-market economy case under Article 2 (7) of the basic AD Regulation, the entire benchmark for construing normal value is taken from sampled companies in the analogue country, whereas the substitution of domestic costs in the new methodology is specific to those factors of production only which are tainted by significant distortions. Moreover, unlike in the former NME-cases under Article 2 (7) of the basic AD Regulation, data from high-income countries such as the US cannot be used under the new methodology in Article 2 (6a) of the basic AD Regulation with its focus on representative countries with a similar economic development as the source for benchmarks. Hence, it seems hardly convincing to argue that Article 2 (6a) of the amended basic AD Regulation essentially reproduces Article 2 (7) of the original basic AD Regulation.

4 The Main Features of TDI Modernisation

According to Recital 3 of the amending Regulation 2018/825, the basic AD Regulation should be updated "in order to improve transparency and predictability, to provide for effective measures to fight against retaliation by third countries, to improve effectiveness and enforcement, and to optimise review practice". In addition, it should also give room to codify certain standard practices. It is thus useful to present the main features of modernisation in line with the five main objectives, which had already been identified in the Commission proposal of April 2013.[20]

---

19   For a discussion of the WTO compatibility of the new methodology see C. Tietje, W. Sacher, 'The New Anti-Dumping Methodology of the European Union: A Breach of WTO Law?', in M. Bungenberg et al. (eds.), in M. Bungenberg et al. (eds.), *European Yearbook of International Economic Law* (Springer, 2018), p. 89–105; and E. Vermulst, J. Sud (n. 12), p. 78–85.

20   W. Müller (n. 9), p. 46. The Commission had also pursued a sixth objective, namely to facilitate the investigation. According to the Commission Communication of 2013, that

4.1   Improved Transparency and Predictability

The key instrument to improve transparency and predictability is the new system of advance disclosure for provisional measures under Article 19a (1) of the basic AD Regulation. While the Parliament argued for two weeks, the Council insisted on four weeks. In the end, a Salomon-like solution of three weeks was agreed. However, the Commission is empowered to modify this deadline in view of the experience gained in the first two years of application. As no major stock-piling problems were observed in this period, the Commission decided in mid-August 2020 that pre-disclosue of provisional measures will hitherto occur four weeks before publication.

The advance notification of provisional measures shall be given to all interested parties. However, it is not a disclosure inviting substantive comments. Rather, parties are given the opportunity to check the figures – and if there are obvious clerical errors, the Commission can still correct them in the regulation imposing provisional measures.

In the legislative process, advance notification was seen by representatives of the EU industry as a means for allowing importers to stockpile. They could be tempted to accelerate imports to escape the announced provisional duties. In order to mitigate this risk, the legislator introduced as a precautionary measure a system of compulsory registration. At the same time as advance information is forwarded, the Commission shall direct national customs authorities to register imports. If it is shown that in the four weeks preceding provisional duties the imports increased, that fact can be taken into account when determining the injury margin for definitive measures.

4.2   Fight against Retaliation by Third Countries

At the time when Commissioner De Gucht made his proposal, a high-profile TDI case was ongoing vis-à-vis China on telecommunication networks. The Commission had taken a decision of principle to investigate allegations of dumping and subsidy *ex officio*. One reason for this unusual step was the fear of the handful of telecommunication companies in Europe that their business in China would suffer if they lodged a formal complaint with the Commission on the matter. The *ex-officio* initiation of a case would not expose them and could thus tackle a perceived or real retaliation threat from the Chinese authorities. The second sentence of Recital 6 acknowledges the Commission approach in more general terms. According to the legislator, those threats indeed

---

would not require a legislative change. However, with the new SME provision in Article 5 (1a) of the basic AD Regulation, the co-legislator also integrated this idea into the new legislation.

constitute special circumstances within the meaning of Article 5 (6) of the basic AD Regulation.

However, at the next stage, i.e. during the investigation, the same issue could arise. A company which is seen as cooperating with the investigation could face negative consequences in its China business. Against that background, Recital 7 of Regulation 2018/825 makes the point that Union producers should provide the Commission with the necessary information. Under the new Article 6 (10) of the basic AD Regulation, Union producers are now "requested to cooperate" with the Commission. This expression falls short of a hard duty to cooperate, but it should nevertheless serve as a shield: since all EU companies are requested to cooperate, no one can be singled out for retaliatory action. On the other hand, the legislator did not follow the Commission's proposal to add specific enforcement powers. If any EU company chooses to withhold information from the Commission during an *ex-officio* investigation, it cannot be compelled to cooperate. The fight against retaliation was thus somewhat watered down by Council and Parliament.

4.3 *Improved Effectiveness and Enforcement*
4.3.1 Lesser Duty Rule
The corner-stone of the modernisation package are the provisions to improve effectiveness and enforcement. As explained in Recitals 8–10 and 21 of the amending Regulation 2018/825, there are two situations, where the Commission shall no longer impose the lesser duty, laid down in Article 9 (4) of the basic AD Regulation.

The first situation concerns systemic distortions on raw materials in the exporting country, such as in particular export taxes and dual pricing schemes. In such scenario, the Commission shall verify under Article 7 (2a) of the basic AD Regulation whether a distortion on raw materials forms part of the relevant OECD catalogue and accounts for at least 17 % of the cost of production of the product concerned. Two points merit particular attention here: Firstly, as long as a specific distortion is not listed in the relevant OECD catalogue, Article 7 (2a) of the basic AD Regulation does not come into play. This question can already be verified by the Commission's complaint office before a case is initiated. Secondly, the 17 % threshold is to be applied country-wide. In other words: the Commission shall determine whether the average of the sampled exporting producers use a raw material, of which the price is distorted and the proportion of the costs of production crosses the 17 % mark. If that is the case, the new Union interest test comes into play, and its result will be applicable for all exporting producers (sampled or not). Only where an exporting producer can clearly show that he does not benefit from the distortion on the raw material in place (e.g. because he uses another substitute material, of which the price is not distorted) he could then plead for being excluded from the application of Article 7 (2a) of the basic AD Regulation.

When conducting the test, the Commission shall make an assessment of the spare capacity in the exporting country, competition for raw materials and the effect on supply chains for Union companies. These issues are not completely new for the investigators. The question of spare capacity in the exporting country is regularly analysed in expiry review cases. In the tungsten carbide case, the Commission carried out an analysis of the competitive situation for this rare earth material.[21] In the hot-rolled flat steel case on imports from Brazil, Russia, Ukraine, Iran and Serbia the impact on downstream users was at the core of an extensive Union interest analysis.[22]

Importantly, these three competing interests must not be seen in isolation. Article 7 (2b), 3rd sentence of the basic AD Regulation expressly states that the Commission shall examine "all pertinent information". Moreover, unlike in Article 21 (1) of the basic AD Regulation, there is no particular emphasis to protect the interests of the Union industry. In other words: the Commission must positively establish that the reasons for imposing the higher duty prevail over the reasons for not doing so – a "positive" Union interest.[23] In this exercise, all EU producers (and not just the complainants) shall be heard (Recital 20 of amending Regulation 2018/825), and the Commission shall actively seek information also from other interested parties. In order to assess the "effect on supply chains", this includes also upstream and downstream users. Importantly, Article 7 (2b), 4th sentence of the basic AD Regulation contains a new procedural default rule. In the absence of cooperation (from interested parties in the EU arguing for the lower duty) the Commission may conclude that it is in the interest of the Union to apply the higher duty.

If the Commission does not have sufficient material to apply the higher duty, it will fall back on Article 7 (2) of the basic AD Regulation. This, in turn, brings back the "negative" Union test under Article 21 (2) of the basic AD Regulation, as confirmed in Recital 21 of the amending Regulation 2018/825.

The second situation is more straightforward: the Union considers the granting of countervailable subsidies by third countries as particularly distortive of trade. Hence, when determining the level of countervailing measures, it is no longer possible to apply the lesser duty rule. This is an important piece

---

21   Commission Implementing Regulation (EU) 2017/942, Recitals 213–220, OJ 2017, L 142/53.

22   Commission Implementing Regulation (EU) 2017/1795, Recitals 414–553 and 625–636, OJ 2017, L 258/24.

23   W. Müller (n. 9), p. 50.

in stepping up the EU's fight against subsidies worldwide. It will also make the recourse to the anti-subsidy instrument more interesting for the EU industry, as the countervailing duties will not be capped anymore by the injury margin.

4.3.2 Profit Target

Another important novelty is the new Article 7 (2c) of the basic AD Regulation on establishing the profit target. The profit target is a concept used to establish how much profit a company can be expected to make in the absence of injurious dumping under normal conditions of competition.[24] The higher the profit target is set, the higher the injury margin becomes and – if the measures are set at the level of injury and not at the level of dumping – the higher the duties will be set as well. Accordingly, the Union industry favoured a new mechanism, which would allow it to claim higher target profits than before. Article 7 (2c) of the basic AD Regulation reflects that wish in fairly broad terms. After modernisation, the Commission shall not only look at the profitability to be expected under normal conditions of competition, but also look at additional factors.[25] Among them is the profitability before the increase of imports from the country under investigation and the level of profitability needed to cover full costs and investments, research and development and innovation. The Commission has thus a new duty to look into historic profitability data and to make a prospective analysis what profitability is "needed" for a company to maintain a high-quality business. As Article 7 (2d) of the basic AD Regulation lays down, particular attention is to be given to future costs, which will result from the implementation of multilateral environmental agreements and core ILO conventions. While this sounds attractive as a concept, its implementation is fairly time-consuming. The Commission will have to make an assessment which costs are triggered by the need to comply with environmental or labour standards today. This will pose difficult questions to investigators, such as: "Was the modernisation of a furnace a normal measure to uphold efficiency, or was it made in order to comply with certain (stricter/increased) environmental standards flowing from the Paris agreement?" "Is the salary of a steel worker a couple of Euros higher than it would otherwise be, because the company is complying with ILO Conventions on working time and minimum holidays?" To make it even more complicated, the new Article 7 (2d) also mentions "future costs", which result from those international standards. Thus, the company must also demonstrate that a planned modernisation of a furnace or

---

24   Case T-210/95, *EFMA v. Council*, EU:T:1999:273, para. 60.
25   W. Müller (n. 9), p. 48.

a future increase of worker's salary was triggered by a need to comply with a stricter regulatory framework "resulting from" these international conventions. Clearly, this will entail a lot of work for both the EU industry and the Commission investigators.

Against that background, the last sentence of Article 7 (2c) of the basic AD Regulation is much more user-friendly. It simply states that the profit margin shall not be lower than 6 %. This figure serves as a floor and will rule out some lower figures from the past, in which sometimes profit margins of 3 % or 5 % were used.

4.3.3   Additional Reasons for Interim Reviews

Another difficult provision is the new Recital 12 of amending Regulation 2018/ 825. Under this provision, the Commission should initiate interim reviews, where appropriate, in cases where the Union industry faces increased costs resulting from higher social and environmental standards. Conversely, if the social and environmental costs in an exporting country are decreasing, because it withdraws from a multilateral environmental convention or from core ILO Conventions, this should also constitute a reason to initiate interim reviews. This Recital should inform Article 11 (2) of the basic AD Regulation, which requires that interim reviews are successful, when there is a lasting change of circumstances. Clearly, regulatory changes are difficult to grasp, as by very nature they can change again. In how far such increase or decrease of costs fulfils the legal requirements under Article 11 (2) of the basic AD Regulation remains to be seen.

4.3.4   Refined Test for Expiry Reviews

The new version of Article 11 (2) on expiry reviews complements the picture in this regard. After 5 years, when a measure is due to expire, the Union industry can ask for a sunset review. Its request must contain sufficient evidence that the expiry of the measure would likely result in a continuation or recurrence of dumping and injury. The new second subparagraph now specifies that such likelihood may be indicated by ... , "or by evidence of continued distortions on raw materials". While the wording "or" seems to indicate that distortions on raw materials could constitute a new self-standing ground for expiry reviews, it has to be read against the EU's WTO obligations. Under Article 11.3 of the ADA, a measure can only be prolonged if it is shown that the expiry of the duty would "likely lead to a continuation or recurrence of dumping and injury". A simple reference to continuing distortions on raw materials in the exporting countries alone is thus not sufficient. Accordingly, the new Article 11 (2) 2nd subparagraph of the basic AD Regulation should rather be interpreted in a WTO-compatible way – it directs the Commission to take into account the detrimental effects of continuing distortions on raw materials when assessing the likelihood of recurring dumping and injury.

4.3.5   Stricter Conditions for Accepting Undertakings

Finally, Recital 17 of amending Regulation 2018/825 and the new version of Article 8 of the basic AD Regulation on price undertakings impose stricter conditions for accepting undertakings. The Parliament introduced this topic into the debate with the objective of reducing the Commission's discretion in this field.

Undertakings are an alternative means to remedy the injury suffered by the EU industry. Rather than imposing duties on the imported products, the Commission accepts a price undertaking from the importers. For them, that may be a much better solution, as they do not have to pay duties, but rather can earn more by taking higher prices in the Union (at the risk of lowering their market shares, though). Before the modernisation package, the Commission was able to reject undertakings because they were either impracticable, could not be monitored or were contrary to the EU's general policy. Now, the new version of Article 8 (1) of the basic AD Regulation contains a test: the Commission must be satisfied that the price increases under an undertaking shall be less than the dumping margin, provided such increase would be adequate to remove the injury of the Union industry. This entails the calculation of a margin in line with the new provisions on the lesser duty rule under Articles 7 (2a), (2b), (2c) and (2d). Moreover, the legislator included a strict time-limit to introduce undertaking offers in Article 8 (2), 3rd subparagraph, countering the practice of some exporting producers to come up with such offers (and their updates) in the "last minute" before the adoption of definitive measures. Finally, Article 8 (3) makes it clear that policy grounds to reject an undertaking offer may again be linked to social and environmental standards. This could mean that undertakings by an exporter from a country with very low standards should generally not be accepted. If the exporting country is at the same time a developing country in WTO terms, this principle needs to be weighed with the opposing principle under Article 15 ADA. Under this general obligation, every WTO member, including the EU, must assess whether to resort to "constructive remedies", including undertakings, as an alternative to imposing measures on developing countries.

4.3.6   Trade Unions and SMEs

Responding to an old idea, Parliament also included special provisions on trade unions. Under the new version of Article 5 (1) of the basic AD Regulation, complaints can now also be brought by trade unions alone. In practice, that possibility seems to be rather remote. If a trade union wishes to bring a case to the Commission against the will of its own executive board, its ability to demonstrate *prima facie* evidence in a complaint (including on injury) is hampered, as the evidence on injury normally emanates from the Union industry.[26] Therefore, it is more likely that the second alternative in that provision will be used in practice, namely that a case is "supported by trade unions". This, in turn, does not change much the course of the investigation other than increasing the visibility of the concern of workers.

Moreover, a new Article 5 (1a) of the basic AD Regulation on SMEs is introduced with the idea of facilitating their access to trade defence instruments. The Commission shall operate a dedicated SME helpdesk, which is supposed to make it easier for these actors to take the necessary steps and avoid paying highly specialised lawyers. Moreover, some simplified questionnaires may be used. Probably the most important novelty lies, however, in another provision. Under Article 6 (9) 2nd sentence of the basic AD Regulation, "investigation periods shall, whenever possible, especially in the case of diverse and fragmented sectors largely composed of SMEs, coincide with the financial year". While this article is inspired by the wish to help SMEs, its formulation is of a general nature. Currently, the Commission determines the investigation period (IP) as close as possible to the recent past. This means that sometimes, it falls on the last quarter of one year, and three quarters of the next year. This is impracticable, as audited financial statements and other important documents usually cover the full financial year (and not quarters). Under the new Article 6 (9) of the basic AD Regulation, the Commission is now expected to make an effort to define the investigation periods more user-friendly. This could mean that, generally, IPs should only start on 1 January of a given year. If the case is lodged in the 2nd half of a year, that would then trigger an IP running from 1 July of that year. However, IPs involving quarters should be regularly avoided in the future, unless the Commission can justify the need for such an IP.

4.3.7   Shorter Deadline for Provisional Measures

Finally, the legislator has shortened the deadline for imposing provisional measures. Before modernisation, the Commission had nine months to prepare this step. Under the new Article 7 (1) of the basic AD Regulation, provisional duties shall be imposed no earlier than 60 days from initiation and "normally not later than seven months, but in any event not later than eight months, from the initiation of proceedings". This puts considerable pressure on investigators

---

26   W. Müller (n. 9), p. 52.

and interested parties to advance the case in a timely fashion. As a practical consequence, the time-span for choosing the appropriate sample of exporting producers and EU industry companies at the beginning of the case will have to be shortened considerably. Moreover, requests from interested parties to prolong deadlines for comments will most likely not succeed anymore. When combined with the new methodology, where a couple of crucial issues on the appropriate benchmarks have to be resolved before taking provisional measures, seven months appear to be very short. In those circumstances, it makes sense to make use of the eight-month fall-back provision.

4.4   *Optimising Review Practice*
While the many novelties mentioned in the previous paragraph may mostly be seen as Union industry friendly, other aspects of modernisation favour the importers. Under the previous regime, a Union industry could prolong the duration of a measure by simply lodging an expiry review request under Article 11 (2) of the basic AD Regulation. Once the Commission accepts the *prima facie* evidence, the measure would continue while the Commission verifies whether the likelihood of continuation or recurrence of dumping and injury can really be affirmed. On top of this, even if the Commission was to come to a negative result at the end of an expiry review examination, the importer would not benefit from this decision, as the duties paid during an unsuccessful expiry review would not be repaid.

When submitting his proposal in April 2013, Commissioner De Gucht argued that this system is unfair. In a system based on the rule of law, one party should not be able to make the adversary party pay on the basis of an unfounded request. Accordingly, Recital 11 of amending Regulation 2018/825 states that those duties paid should be reimbursed. Article 11 (5) 3rd subparagraph of the basic AD Regulation creates a new legal basis to that effect and clarifies that no interest is to be paid.

4.5   *Codifications Issues*
The modernisation package also addresses certain codification issues, as explained in Recitals 14–16 of amending Regulation 2018/825. The definition of the Union industry in Article 4 (1) of the basic AD Regulation is now done by reference to the initiation thresholds. If an exporter falls under the *de-minimis* threshold, the case against it should be terminated (Article 7 (3) of the basic AD Regulation). This follows the AB report in the "Beef and Rice" case.[27]

---

27   AB, *Mexico – Definitive Anti-Dumping Measures on Beef and Rice,* DS295.

Moreover, Recitals 18–19 of amending Regulation 2018/825 touch upon a thorny issue of the past in the anti-circumvention field. In such cases, the Commission may extend existing measures against one country (e.g. China) to exporting producers from another country (e.g. Malaysia) when there is suspicion that Chinese goods are transhipped through Malaysia and wrongly declared as being of Malaysian origin. However, such a country-wide extension may also affect bona fide producers of the product concerned in Malaysia, which are *not* involved in such practices. These bona-fide Malaysian producers may apply for an exemption to the Commission. Under the previous version of Article 13 (3) 3rd subparagraph of the basic AD Regulation, the Commission was obliged to refuse such exemption requests for the sole reason that a Malaysian company had a legal relationship with a company from China, even if it was not engaged in circumvention activities. As of 2010, the Commission had stopped applying this rule,[28] as punishing law-compliant Malaysian companies for their mere relationship with companies from a country under measures would have been disproportionate pursuant to EU law and possibly incompatible with the EU's obligations under the WTO Agreement. With the new version of Article 13 (3) 3rd paragraph of the basic AD Regulation, this anomaly is eliminated. Finally, Recital 20 makes clear that the Commission may sample companies from the entire Union industry and not only from the complainants.

4.6   *Institutional Issues*

The modernisation regulation takes a position on the somewhat protracted discussion on guidelines. As noted before, the Commission had also published a set of four draft guidelines next to the legislative proposal. They related to the choice of the analogue country in non-market economy cases; to injury calculations; to the duration of measures and to Union interest. They were supposed to lay down some administrative guidance as to how these concepts are to be applied by the Commission. However, the draft guidelines were not met with much sympathy. Some circles in the Parliament and the Council protested that they had not been consulted before; others took issue with the content. In particular, EU industry and some Southern and East European Member States thought that the Union interest guidelines and the guidelines on duration were too "liberal". In their view, the Commission would become too

---

28   Regulation No. 400/2000 of the Council – Steel ropes from China, extended to Korea), OJ 2010, L 117, Recital 80; Regulation No. 723/2011 of the Council – Fasteners from China, extended to Malaysia, OJ 2011, L 194, Recital 64.

importer-friendly by advocating a broad approach to the Union interest test[29] and legitimising the shortening of ordinary measures to less than five years more frequently. The other two guidelines proved less controversial, but were overcome by events: with the adoption of the new methodology and a complete set of rules on target profits in the legislation, there was no need to adopt separate guidelines on these topics anymore.

Accordingly, Commissioner Malmström silently dropped the guidelines from the modernisation exercise. However, in the legislation, an echo of the discussion can be found. Recital 13 of the amending Regulation 2018/825 recalls that the Commission can adopt interpretative notices providing general guidance which, however, are not legally binding and cannot modify mandatory rules of Union law. However, the following two sentences are less convincing. First, the law states that the Commission "cannot waive by [the adoption of the notices providing general guidance] the discretion it enjoys in the area of common commercial policy". However, it is precisely the purpose of such guidelines to explain how the Commission will generally interpret certain concepts on which it has discretion. Second, according to the last sentence of Recital 13, the Commission should carry out consultations with the other two institutions under Article 11 (3) TEU before adopting guidelines. The latter provision refers to a "hearing of the concerned". Clearly, interested parties in TDI cases are concerned by the adoption of guidelines, but does this rule of transparency expand to the other two institutions as well? In any case, Commissioner Malmström has unilaterally committed to consult the Parliament and the Council in such instances. Most likely, this will not facilitate the adoption of any guidelines under the new Article 11 (8) of the basic AD Regulation in the future, as the political directions in Council and in Parliament may differ quite substantially on critical issues.

Another inter-institutional issue is brought up in the new version of Article 23 of the basic AD Regulation. In the future, the Commission shall write one comprehensive annual report on its own TDI practice and on third country-measures (instead of two separate ones as in the past). A curiosity is the last sentence of Recital 23 of amending Regulation (EU) 2018/825. It expresses the wish that the Council may participate in the parliamentary discussion of this report.

Under Article 23a of the basic AD Regulation, the Commission received the power to enact two delegated acts: in summer 2020 it shall assess how the new

---

29   For details see B. Hartmann, Commentary on Article 21 of the Basic AD Regulation, in: H. G. Krenzler, C. Herrmann, *EU-Aussenwirtschafts- und Zollrecht*, Ergänzungslieferung 2019.

pre-notification system for provisional measures has fared in practice. If there will be no substantial problems of stockpiling, it shall prolong the period under Article 19a of the basic AD Regulation from three to four weeks; conversely, if experience shows that importers abuse their knowledge about impending duties by massive imports after notification, that period shall be reduced to two weeks. The second delegated act allows the Commission to update the OECD inventory of relevant distortions on raw materials, which are important for the assessment whether a lower duty can be applied or not under Article 7 (2a) of the basic AD Regulation. In addition, the Commission is also preparing a new implementing act foreseen under Article 14a of the basic AD Regulation, which would extend the territorial scope of the anti-dumping instrument to the continental shelf if certain products concerned (such as tubes and pipes) are used there in considerable quantities.[30]

5   Conclusion

The overhaul of the EU's trade defence instruments constitutes a remarkable political achievement. The institutions were able to enact a solid response to challenges stemming from a changing environment in world trade with the new methodology, and updated the rulebook on many salient issues. The key for success was that both EU industry and importers received due attention. With pre-notification before provisional measures a long-held wish of importers to render EU trade defence measures less disruptive for their business found its way into the rulebook. The reimbursement of duties paid during an unsuccessful expiry review also provides more procedural fairness. In return, EU industry will benefit from the new rules about the lesser duty rule and several other provisions, which direct the Commission to take account of distortions on raw materials in the exporting country. Moreover, the question of level playing fields in social and environmental matters pops up on several occasions with the likely result that more protection is given to the EU industry. While the political balance of the Commission proposal was thus more or less preserved, the new legal texts pose a fairly high number of technical challenges. Many of the novelties require from the investigators and interested parties additional time-consuming analysis, and all users will be required to adapt to the new realities. I am thus of the opinion that the new rules have neither created a "monster" nor a "saviour". But it has to be admitted after a first guide to the EU's new trade defence rules that the devil is indeed in the detail.

---

30   For details on this provision see W. Müller (n. 9), p. 52–53.

CHAPTER 14

The EU's Amended Basic Anti-dumping Regulation – a Practitioner's View

Philippe De Baere

1 Introduction

Following several years of intense debate, the EU finally adopted two legislative acts amending Regulation (EU) 2016/1036 on protection against dumped imports from countries not members of the European Union[1] (basic AD Regulation).

The first act, Regulation (EU) 2017/2321,[2] sets out new rules for establishing normal value in case of "significant distortions" in the market of the exporting country and was published in the Official Journal on 19 December 2017 (new methodology).

The second act, Regulation (EU) 2018/825 (modernisation package),[3] was published on 7 June 2018 and introduces, amongst other matters, new rules on the partial non-application of the lesser-duty rule (LDR), the relevance of social and environmental standards in anti-dumping investigations and the issue of "pre-disclosure".

While these two sets of amendments were agreed upon independently and result from different necessities and political motives, together they constitute a major overhaul of the EU's existing anti-dumping rules.

---

1 Regulation (EU) 2016/1036 of the European Parliament and of the Council on protection against dumped imports from countries not members of the European Union (OJ 2016, L 176/21).

2 Regulation (EU) 2017/2321 of the European Parliament and of the Council of 12 December 2017 amending Regulation (EU) 2016/1036 on protection against dumped imports from countries not members of the European Union and Regulation (EU) 2016/1037 on protection against subsidised imports from countries not members of the European Union (OJ 2017, L 338/1).

3 Regulation (EU) 2018/825 of the European Parliament and of the Council of 30 May 2018 amending Regulation (EU) 2016/1036 on protection against dumped imports from countries not members of the European Union and Regulation (EU) 2016/1037 on protection against subsidised imports from countries not members of the European Union (OJ 2018, L 143/1).

In a first part, this chapter will describe the changes made in order to introduce in the basic AD Regulation a new methodology for determining normal value in cases where significant distortions exist in the market of the exporting country and analyse the WTO compatibility of the amendments. In a second part, the main features of the modernisation package focusing on the conditions for the non-application of the LDR and the WTO-compatibility of these conditions will be discussed. The final part gives an overview of the concerns raised by other WTO members regarding the amended EU anti-dumping regulation and the possibility for them to initiate WTO dispute settlement proceedings.

2   The New Normal Value Methodology Introduced by Regulation (EU) 2017/2321

Through the addition of a new paragraph 6a to Article 2 of its basic AD Regulation, the EU introduced a new methodology for establishing the normal value in case of "significant distortions" in the market of the exporting country, which render the use of domestic prices and costs in that country inappropriate.[4]

Formally, the new EU methodology provides for a country-neutral approach, abolishing the current distinction between market and non-market economies. Instead, the new methodology now applies to all countries where "significant distortions" are deemed to exist.

In practice, however, China is the main target of the new legal regime. This follows from the *raison d'être* of the new methodology, which was implemented in order to bring the EU's basic AD Regulation in line with the changes resulting from China's WTO Accession Protocol and, more precisely, the expiry of the alternative methodologies contained in Section 15(a)(ii) of China's WTO Accession Protocol on 11 December 2016.[5] The new methodology was expressly designed to ensure that the EU industry continues to enjoy a level of protection

---

4   For a detailed description of the EU anti-dumping legislation and practice prior to the amendments, see Van Bael & Bellis, *EU Anti-Dumping and Other Trade Defence Instruments* (Wolters Kluwer, 2019).

5   For an overview of the discussion on the legal consequences of the effect of the expiry of Section 15(a)(ii) of China's WTO Accession Protocol, see C. Tietje and V. Sacher, 'The New Anti-Dumping Methodology of the European Union – A Breach of WTO Law?' *Essays on Transnational Economic Law*, 153 (2018): http://tietje.jura.uni-halle.de/sites/default/files/BeitraegeTWR/Heft%20153.pdf.

against imports from China that was equivalent to the high duties resulting from the former non-market economy methodology.[6]

2.1   *Significant Distortions*

The new regulation defines "significant distortions" as "distortions which occur when reported prices or costs, including the costs of raw materials and energy, are not the result of free market forces because they are affected by substantial government intervention". In assessing the existence of significant distortions, Article 2(6a)(b) of the new basic AD Regulation provides a non-exhaustive list of elements to take into account: (i) the market being served to a significant extent by enterprises which operate under the ownership, control or policy supervision or guidance of the authorities of the exporting country; (ii) state presence in firms allowing the state to interfere with respect to prices or costs; (iii) public policies or measures discriminating in favour of domestic suppliers or otherwise influencing free market forces; (iv) the lack, discriminatory application or inadequate enforcement of bankruptcy, corporate or property laws; (v) wage costs being distorted; and (vi) access to finance granted by institutions which implement public policy objectives or otherwise not acting independently of the state.

2.2   *Undistorted Prices and Benchmarks*

In a scenario where the Commission finds that it is not appropriate to use domestic prices and costs in the exporting country due to the existence of "significant distortions", the normal value will be "constructed exclusively on the basis of costs of production and sale reflecting undistorted prices or benchmarks".

In determining such "undistorted prices or benchmarks", the Commission may use: (i) corresponding costs of production and sales in an appropriate representative country with a similar level of economic development as the exporting country; (ii) if it considers it appropriate, undistorted international prices, costs, or benchmarks; or (iii) domestic costs, but only to the extent that they are positively established not to be distorted, on the basis of accurate and appropriate evidence.

---

6   Commission Staff Working Document, SWD(2016) 370 final, 'Impact Assessment – Possible change in the calculation methodology of dumping regarding the People's Republic of China (and other non-market economies)': http://trade.ec.europa.eu/doclib/docs/2016/november/tradoc_155080.pdf.

2.3   *International Social and Environmental Standards*

The reference to international social and environmental standards is one of the main innovations introduced by the new set of rules. However, the role of such standards in the determination of the normal value remains unclear.

While Recital (4) of Regulation (EU) 2017/2321 states that when assessing the existence of significant distortions, "relevant international standards, including core conventions of the International Labour Organisation (ILO)[7] and relevant multilateral environmental conventions, should be taken into account, where appropriate", Article 2(6a)(b) of the new basic Anti-Dumping Regulation does not explicitly include social and environmental standards in the list of elements to be taken into account when assessing whether significant distortions exist.

Therefore, it appears that the Commission is under no obligation to take into account the social and environmental standards in a certain country when deciding on the existence of significant distortions and, as a consequence, when deciding whether or not to disregard the domestic prices and costs in the exporting country.

Once the Commission has determined that significant distortions exist and decides to construct the normal value on the basis of undistorted prices or benchmarks, Article 2(6a)(a) of the new basic Anti-Dumping Regulation states that the Commission may base itself on "corresponding costs of production and sale in an appropriate representative country with a similar level of economic development as the exporting country, provided the relevant data are readily available". Article 2(6a)(a) goes on by stating that where there is more than one such country, "preference shall be given, where appropriate, to countries with an adequate level of social and environmental protection".

It follows that social and environmental standards may play a role in the Commission's choice of the third country to use for the constructed normal value, provided that several countries with a similar level of economic development as the exporting country exist. In such a scenario, EU investigators would be encouraged to choose a third country with higher social and environmental standards rather than other possible choices.[8] Inadequate social

---

7   As listed in Annex Ia of Reg. (EU) 2016/1036, as amended (n. 1).

8   In *Organic Coated Steel from China*, R683, Regulation imposing definitive anti-dumping measures, the Commission selected Mexico over Malaysia as representative third country on the basis of Mexico having ratified more core ILO conventions as well as all major environmental conventions, (OJ 2019, L 116/5).

and environmental standards cannot, however, *per se* constitute a significant distortion under Article 2(6a).[9]

In any event, these changes might not result in an outcome which differs substantially from the current regime in terms of the choice of an analogue country, as investigating authorities enjoy wide discretion in this regard.[10]

2.4 Burden of Proof

The new methodology predominantly places the burden of proof on the exporting producers, who must establish that their domestic prices and costs are undistorted before normal value can be established on that basis. Article 2(6a)(a) of the new basic AD Regulation indeed provides that the sources for constructing normal value which the Commission may use include domestic costs, "but only to the extent that they are positively established not to be distorted, on the basis of accurate and appropriate evidence".

In contrast, the complainants do not face a similar burden of proving the existence of significant distortions, and the European Commission has repeatedly stated that "the Commission will ensure that the Union industry incurs no additional burden when seeking protection under the anti-dumping instrument".[11] This is mainly achieved by the preparation by the Commission staff of the necessary evidence on which the complainants can rely in the form of country reports.

On the basis of Article 2(6a)(c) of the new basic AD Regulation, the Commission will provide assistance in determining the existence of "significant distortions" by publishing reports describing the market circumstances in a certain country or sector for which the Commission has well-founded indications of the possible existence of significant distortions.[12] The reports and the evidence on which they are based will be placed on the file of any

---

9 Committee on Anti-Dumping Practices / Committee on Subsidies and Countervailing Measures, 'Replies to the questions posed by Mexico regarding the notification of the European Union' (G/ADP/Q1/EU/10, 9 October 2018), p. 3.

10 See Panel, *EU – Footwear (China)*, DS405, para. 7.295. In this respect, practice reveals that the European Union has frequently used data from countries with higher levels of development and GDP per capita in normal value determinations concerning imports from so-called non-market economies.

11 Commission Declaration on Transition (OJ 2017, L 338/7).

12 According to the EU, the choice of country on which a report may be prepared is determined by its relative weight in terms of the EU's anti-dumping activity. Committee on Anti-Dumping Practices / Committee on Subsidies and Countervailing Measures, 'Replies to the questions posed by Mexico regarding the notification of the European Union' (G/ADP/Q1/EU/10, 9 October 2018), p. 3.

investigation relating to that country or sector. They take the form of European Commission staff working documents and are of a technical nature. The report does not have any separate and self-standing legal value, and no opportunity will be given to stakeholders to comment on the report during the drafting phase. Interested parties will only be able to provide comments or submit rebuttals in the context of individual anti-dumping proceedings.[13] Consistent with the new legislation's aim to provide for a substitute for the analogue country methodology that was previously applied for determining normal value in anti-dumping investigations against exports from China, the Commission has – for the time being – only published a report on the market circumstances in China.[14]

In practice, it appears that for the purpose of filing a complaint requesting the initiation of an anti-dumping proceeding on the basis of the new methodology, it is sufficient for the EU industry to simply refer to the report of the Commission.[15] The absence of a report does not, however, preclude a finding that significant distortions exist and the application of the new methodology by the Commission.[16]

2.5   *Grandfathering Provisions*

For interim reviews and new exporter reviews of existing anti-dumping measures, Articles 11(3) and 11(4) of the new basic AD Regulation provide that the new EU methodology "shall replace the original methodology used for the determination of the normal value only [from/after] the date on which the first expiry review of those measures, after [19/20] December 2017, is initiated".

---

13   Committee on Anti-Dumping Practices / Committee on Subsidies and Countervailing Measures, 'Replies to the questions posed by Mexico regarding the notification of the European Union', (G/ADP/Q1/EU/10, 9 October 2018), p. 2.

14   Commission Staff Working Document, SWD(2017) 483 final/2, 'Significant Distortions in the Economy of the People's Republic of China for the Purposes of Trade Defence Investigations': http://trade.ec.europa.eu/doclib/docs/2017/december/tradoc_156474.pdf. A second report addressing the market distortions in the Russian Federation is expected to be published in the course of 2019.

15   See for instance, *Bicycles,* R688, Notice of Initiation (OJ 2018, C 189); *Ironing Boards,* R693, Notice of Initiation, (OJ 2018, C 253/30); *Tungsten Electrodes,* R685, (OJ 2018, C 186/13); and *Malleable Pipe Fittings,* R692, (OJ 2018, C 162/11). In a number of other proceedings, the complainants additionally refer to sources of information other than the Commission report. This is for instance the case in *Ceramic Tableware and Kitchenware* (R687) (OJ 2018, C 167/6).

16   Committee on Anti-Dumping Practices / Committee on Subsidies and Countervailing Measures, 'Replies to the questions posed by the Kingdom of Saudi Arabia regarding the notification of the European Union' (G/ADP/Q1/EU/11, 9 October 2018), p. 6.

It follows that the new rules will not be applied for the calculation of normal value in the context of an interim review. The old methodology will continue to apply for existing measures until an expiry review is initiated, irrespective of any request for an interim review. The same applies to new exporter reviews. Moreover, pursuant to Article 11(6) second paragraph of the basic AD Regulation, any future expiry review can only result in the continuation or repeal of the existing measures. It is therefore to be expected that most expiry reviews will result in the continuation of measures determined on the basis of the old analogue country methodology.

Finally, the mere fact that the rules governing the determination of normal value have changed cannot be invoked by exporters or importers as constituting evidence of changed circumstances sufficient to justify the initiation of an interim review.[17] They will additionally need to demonstrate that the application of the new methodology results in a lower dumping margin and that the reduction is of a lasting nature.

2.6 Consistency of the New Methodology with WTO Rules

The avowed purpose of the introduction of the new methodology for the determination of normal value was to bring the basic AD Regulation in compliance with the EU's WTO obligations following the expiry of certain provisions of Section 15 of China's WTO Accession Protocol. As acknowledged by then Trade Commissioner Karel de Gucht during the 2014 Workshop on the Modernisation of the EU's Trade Defence Instruments organised by the European Parliament, reform was necessary since "in 2016 China will receive market economy status".[18] As a result, the EU would no longer be able to apply to China the special "analogue country" methodology whereby the domestic costs and prices of the Chinese exporters were replaced by the costs and prices of producers in a so-called analogue market economy country. In order to maintain an equivalent level of protection as the one offered to EU producers under the analogue country methodology, the Commission was forced to develop a methodology which was *prima facie* horizontally applicable to all WTO members, would still make it possible to reject the Chinese domestic costs and prices, grandfather the existing high duties applicable to Chinese exports and would not increase the burden of proof for the EU complainants. As explained above, all of these

---

17   Rec. (9) of Reg. (EU) 2017/2321 (n. 2).
18   E. Vermulst and O. Prost, 'Workshop – Modernisation of the EU's trade defence instruments (TDI)' (Directorate-General for External Policies of the Union, April 2014), p. 13: www.europarl.europa.eu/RegData/etudes/workshop/join/2014/433842/EXPO-INTA_AT(2014)433842_EN.pdf.

objectives were achieved. The WTO compatibility of the rules that were necessary to achieve these objectives is, however, highly questionable.

2.6.1   Rejecting Domestic Prices as a Basis for Normal Value Due to the
          Existence of Significant Distortions

Article 2.1 of the WTO Anti-Dumping Agreement (ADA) requires that the normal value used for determining whether dumping exists should be based on the comparable price, in the ordinary course of trade, for the like product when destined for consumption in the exporting country. It is only where there are no domestic sales in the ordinary course of trade or when such sales do not permit a proper comparison because of their low volume or the existence of a particular market situation that the investigating authority may ignore them and rely on an alternative method for the determination of normal value, namely export sales to a third country or constructed normal value.[19] Thus, before an investigating authority may resort to the use of a constructed normal value, it must first determine that domestic prices cannot be relied on because of the existence of one of the circumstances set out in Article 2.2 of the ADA.[20]

New Article 2(6a) of the basic AD Regulation authorises the Commission, where appropriate, not to use domestic prices in the exporting country due to the existence in that country of significant distortions within the meaning of Article 2(6a)(b) and to use a constructed normal value instead. Such a determination will be inconsistent with the Union's obligations under Article 2.1 and 2.2 of the ADA unless the Union demonstrates that the existence of significant distortions result in the domestic sales not being in the ordinary course of trade or in the existence of a particular market situation.

2.6.2   Replacing Distorted Costs by Undistorted Costs

Where it is decided, that it is appropriate to reject domestic prices because of the existence of significant distortions, the Commission will construct normal value. In doing so, the Commission will need to replace the distorted cost factors by undistorted costs. According to Recital (5) of Regulation (EU) 2017/2321,

> where there are direct or indirect significant distortions in the exporting country with the consequence that costs reflected in the records of the party concerned are artificially low, such costs may be adjusted or

---

19   Art. 2.2 of the ADA.
20   AB, *EC – Tube or Pipe Fittings*, DS219, para. 94.

established on any reasonable basis, including information from other representative markets or from international prices or benchmarks.

This possibility of rejecting the actual costs of the exporting producer and replacing or adjusting them on the basis of international prices or benchmarks seems contrary to established WTO case law. According to the WTO Panel in *EU – Biodiesel*,

> the object of the comparison is to establish whether the records reasonably reflect the costs actually incurred, and not whether they reasonably reflect some hypothetical costs that might have been incurred under a different set of conditions or circumstances and which the investigating authority considers more 'reasonable' than the costs actually incurred.[21]

Likewise, the fact that the cost adjustment will be based on information from other representative markets or from international prices or benchmarks is difficult to reconcile with the EU's WTO obligations as interpreted by the Appellate Body in *EU – Biodiesel*:

> Thus, whatever the information that it uses, an investigating authority has to ensure that such information is used to arrive at the 'cost of production in the country of origin'. Compliance with this obligation may require the investigating authority to adapt the information that it collects. It is in this sense that we understand the Panel to have stated that Article 2.2 of the Anti-Dumping Agreement and Article VI:1(b)(ii) of the GATT 1994 'require that the costs of production established by the authority reflect conditions prevailing in the country of origin'.[22]

Under the new EU rules, the objective of using information from other representative markets or from international prices or benchmarks is manifestly not to arrive at a cost reflecting the conditions prevailing in the country of origin. The opposite is true. The Commission's aim is precisely to construct a cost which is not the cost in the country of origin, as further evidenced by the requirement to give preference to cost information from countries with an adequate level of social and environmental protection.

---

21   Panel, *EU – Biodiesel (Argentina)*, DS473, para. 7.242.

22   AB, *EU – Biodiesel (Argentina)*, DS473, para. 6.73; see also Panel, *Biodiesel (Argentina)*, DS473, (n. 21), para. 7.258.

2.6.3   Grandfathering Existing Measures

The new rules contain a specific transitional rule for existing measures and for measures adopted following an investigation initiated before the entry into force of the new rules on 20 December 2017. Under this rule, the original methodology will continue to apply until the initiation of the first expiry review following the transition to the new methodology. In practice, this means that for the determination of normal value in interim and newcomer reviews of existing measures imposed on China, the former analogue country methodology will continue to be used. Also, it is expressly stated that the

> transition from a normal value calculated pursuant to Article 2(7) to a normal value calculated in accordance with the methodology set out in Regulation (EU) 2016/1036 as amended by this Regulation would not in itself constitute sufficient evidence within the meaning of Article 11(3) of Regulation (EU) 2016/1036.[23]

Thus, exporters will be unable to invoke the change in the normal value methodology to request an interim review.

In practice, this means that the new methodology will only have a practical impact on existing measures during the first interim review following the expiry review. Article 11(6), second paragraph of Regulation (EU) 2016/1036 does not foresee the amendment of the measures as a result of an expiry review. They can either be repealed or maintained at the existing level and in the same form. Since expiry reviews usually take one year and an interim review itself takes at least another year to be concluded, the life span of the measures based on the analogue country methodology may well be extended with a further two or three years beyond the normal date of expiry of the measures.

For instance, the anti-dumping investigation against imports of electric bicycles from China was initiated on 20 October 2017[24] and definitive measures were imposed on 18 January 2019.[25] The first expiry review will take place five years later and will take one year. Pursuant to Article 11(2) of the basic AD Regulation, existing measures remain in force during an expiry review investigation. Thus, the measures based on the old methodology will remain in force at least until January 2025. If the expiry review concludes that there is a likelihood of a renewal of dumping and injury on the basis of the new methodology, the

---

23   Rec. (9) of Reg. (EU) 2017/2321 (n. 2); Art. 11(3) and (4) of Reg. (EU) 2016/1036 (n. 1), as amended.

24   *Bicycles*, Notice of Initiation (n. 15).

25   *Bicycles*, AD653, Regulation imposing definitive measures (OJ 2019, L 16/108).

measures based on the old methodology will be extended for a further five years. This will even be so where the dumping margin calculated on the basis of the new methodology during the expiry review would have shown a significantly lower dumping margin. In such a case, the exporters may request an interim review. If the request is granted, the interim review investigation will take another year. In other words, under the scenario foreseen in the new regulation, the new methodology will only have an effect on the antidumping measures applicable to imports of electric bicycles as of January 2026 at the earliest.

Considering that the provisions in China's Accession Protocol authorising the use of the analogue country methodology expired on 11 December 2016, the continued application of measures based on this methodology seems difficult to reconcile with the EU's WTO obligations. China has brought WTO dispute settlement proceedings against the EU claiming the as such incompatibility of the basic AD Regulation with the ADA and GATT 1994.[26] If the WTO dispute settlement proceedings in DS516 were to conclude that the analogue country methodology following the expiry of the relevant provisions in China's WTO Accession Protocol is illegal, the continued levying of duties calculated on the basis of the old methodology will by itself constitute a violation of the EU's WTO obligations and will fall under the obligation of the EU to put itself in compliance with the findings and recommendations of the Dispute Settlement Body in DS516. On 14 June 2019, however, China asked the panel to suspend its work and, hence, the issuing of its decision. By a communication of 17 June 2019, the panel accepted this request. As the work of the panel remained suspended for more than 12 months, the authority for the establishment of the panel has now lapsed.[27]

The special transitional rules in Regulation (EU) 2017/2321 also violate Articles 11.1 and 11.2 of the ADA. Under Article 11.1, anti-dumping duties may only remain in force as long as and to the extent necessary to counteract dumping which is causing injury. Article 11.2 requires that the "authorities shall review the need for the continued imposition of the duty, where warranted, on their own initiative [...]". By making it impossible for exporters to request an interim review invoking a reduction of their dumping margin as a result of the new methodology until after the initiation of the first expiry review, the EU manifestly violates both provisions. Indeed, on the basis of these provisions, the EU

---

26   *European Union – Measures Related to Price Comparison Methodologies,* DS516, Request for the establishment of a panel by China, Panel composed on 10 July 2017.

27   *European Union – Measures Related to Price Comparison Methodologies,* DS516, communication from the panel of 17 June 2019.

should have initiated *ex officio* reviews of any measures imposed on the basis of the old methodology which remain in force after 20 December 2017. As held by the Appellate Body,

> [w]here the conditions in Article 11.2 have been met, the plain words of the provision make it clear that the agency has no discretion to refuse to complete a review, including consideration of whether the duty should be terminated in the light of the results of the review.[28]

2.6.4 Burden of Proof

One of the main concerns of the EU producers was that following the entry into force of the new methodology the presumption would disappear that Chinese exporters operated on the basis of non-market economy principles and that, consequently, the burden of proving the existence of distortions would shift to the complainants. The new rules contain several provisions aimed at maintaining the *status quo ante* in this respect. The Commission even found it necessary to publish together with Regulation 2017/2321 a Declaration on Transition confirming that

> the purpose of the new methodology is to maintain the continued protection of the Union industry against unfair trade practices, in particular those arising from significant market distortions. In that respect, the Commission will ensure that the Union industry incurs no additional burden when seeking protection under the anti-dumping instrument, in particular in the context of potential expiry reviews requests lodged after the entry into force of the new methodology.[29]

As already mentioned above, this objective was achieved by mandating the Commission to prepare country reports setting out the significant distortions identified in the market of the country concerned.[30] Consonant with the objective of maintaining high duties on imports from China, the first and currently only country report covers distortions in the Chinese market and was made available the day the new rules entered into force.

These publicly available reports will be included in any investigation file relating to that country. Interested parties will be given an opportunity "to rebut, supplement, comment or rely on the report and the evidence on which

---

28   AB, *Mexico – Anti-Dumping Measures on Rice,* DS295, para. 314.

29   Commission Declaration on Transition (n. 11).

30   Art. 2(6a)(c) of Reg. (EU) 2016/1036, as amended (n. 1).

it is based".[31] Complainants will be able to rely on the country reports when filing requests for expiry reviews.[32] In the eight investigations initiated against imports from China since the entry into force of the new methodology, the complainants systematically substantiated the allegations of significant distortions, on the Commission Staff Working Document dated 20 December 2017 'Report on Significant Distortions in the Economy of the PRC for the purposes of the trade defence investigations.'[33]

In contrast, pursuant to Article 2(6a)(a), domestic costs in China may be used "only to the extent that they are positively established not to be distorted, on the basis of accurate and appropriate evidence [...]. Moreover, any evidence regarding the existence of significant distortions may only be taken into account if it can be verified in a timely manner within the investigation".[34]

The net outcome of these provisions is that where a country report exists, the burden of proof shifts to the exporters. It is highly questionable whether such a shift is consistent with the EU's WTO obligations. Article VI:1(b)(ii) of the GATT 1994 and Article 2.2 of the ADA require that the cost of production must be the cost of production in the country of origin. Likewise, Article 2.2.1.1 of the ADA states that "costs shall normally be calculated on the basis of records kept by the exporter or producer under investigation". The ADA therefore contains a clear preference for the use of domestic costs on the basis the exporter's own cost accounts.

In a similar situation where the EU automatically presumed that Chinese exporters formed a single entity with the State, the Appellate Body ruled that:

> placing the burden on NME exporters to rebut a presumption that they are related to the State and to demonstrate that they are entitled to individual treatment runs counter to Article 6.10, which "as a rule" requires that individual dumping margins be determined for each known exporter or producer, and is inconsistent with Article 9.2 that requires that individual duties be specified by supplier. Even accepting in principle that there may be circumstances where exporters and producers from NMEs may be considered as a single entity for purposes of Articles 6.10 and 9.2, such singularity cannot be presumed; it has to be determined by the investigating authorities on the basis of facts and evidence submitted or gathered in the investigation.[35]

---

31   Ibidem.
32   Art. 11(9), second paragraph of Reg. (EU) 2016/1036 (n. 1) as amended.
33   See e.g. *Bicycles,* Notice of Initiation (n. 15); see footnote 16 above for further examples.
34   Art. 2(6a)(e) of Reg. (EU) 2016/1036 (n. 1) as amended.
35   AB, *EC – Fasteners (China),* DS397, para. 364.

The EU approach, whereby the existence of a country report suffices to create a general presumption of the existence of distortions in a specific country and sector and then to leave it to each individual exporter to rebut this presumption as far as that specific exporter is concerned, seems equally WTO inconsistent. The burden of proving conclusively that the costs of each individual producer are significantly distorted must rest with the investigating authorities.

2.7   De Facto Discriminatory Treatment of China

Although the new rules were intended to replace the special regime applicable to a number of non-market economy countries and, in particular, China by non-discriminatory rules equally applicable to all WTO members, the close link with the expiry of parts of Section 15 of China's Accession Protocol as demonstrated by the many official statements made during the legislative process leading up to the adoption of the new methodology leaves little doubt about the aim of the EU, namely to maintain the same level of protection against imports from China as was available under the analogue country methodology. The manner in which the new methodology is being applied confirms the fact it is targeted at China. A Commission services' report on the existence of significant distortions in the Chinese market was released immediately after the new rules entered into force. Since then, no other country report has been released. Out of 14 investigations covering 11 exporting countries that were initiated under the new rules, the new methodology has only been invoked against imports from China. This is even so in investigations where the complainants raise the existence of significant raw material distortions justifying the non-application of the LDR in the market of the exporting country. Finally, the grandfathering clause results in the extension of duties that were based on the analogue country methodology which was predominantly used in investigations against China. Such *de facto* discriminatory treatment of Chinese imports appears in violation of Article 9(2) of the ADA requiring that duties are imposed and collected on a non-discriminatory basis.

2.8   Conclusion

While formally abolishing, for the determination of normal value, the distinction between market and non-market economies, the new EU anti-dumping methodology is designed to target China and other countries which the EU previously qualified as non-market economies. Despite the EU's efforts, the relabelling of "non-market economy" countries as "distorted economies" is unlikely to avoid new legal challenges in the WTO or other fora.

It is doubtful that the application of the new rules will be consistent with, amongst other provisions, Articles 2.1, 2.2 and 2.2.1.1 of the WTO ADA and

Article VI:1 of the GATT 1994 to the extent that they lead the Commission to reject the domestic prices and to determine constructed normal value for exporting producers on the basis of data other than their domestic costs. Problems also emerge with regard to a possible violation of Article 11.2 of the WTO ADA, since the new rules deny exporters the possibility of requesting an interim or new exporter review on the basis of the changed circumstances resulting from the entry into force of the new EU methodology. Moreover, where an interim or new exporter review is initiated, the old analogue country methodology will continue to apply and the EU will continue to collect anti-dumping duties determined on the basis of this illegal methodology, thereby violating Article 1 of the ADA. Furthermore, the *de facto* discriminatory treatment of China under the new rules runs counter to the non-discrimination obligation in Article 9.2 of ADA.

Finally, the newly introduced concepts of "significant distortions" and "undistorted prices and benchmarks", the role of international social and environmental standards in the calculation of the normal value and the burden of proof under the new rules remain unclear. The fact that only one country report has been published to date raises questions regarding the "uniform, impartial and reasonable administration" of the new rules. A challenge under Article X.3(a) can therefore not be excluded.

It is therefore highly unlikely that the new rules could survive WTO dispute settlement proceedings, either on an "as such" or "as applied" basis. At the most, it will offer the European Commission an excuse to continue applying a refurbished non-market economy methodology against Chinese exports for several years longer than was permitted on the basis of China's WTO Accession Protocol.

3   Modernisation of the EU's Anti-dumping Legislation

Following the Commission's 2013 proposal on the modernisation of the EU's trade defence instruments, and subsequent struggles amongst the EU Member States to arrive at a joint position, the Commission, the Council and the European Parliament only managed to reach a political agreement on the modernisation of the EU's anti-dumping rules on 5 December 2017. The regulation was finally published on 7 June 2018.[36]

---

36   See n. 3.

The most important amendments relate to non-application of the LDR and the determination of the target price when calculating the injury margin, the relevance of social and environmental standards in anti-dumping investigations, the issue of "pre-disclosure" and the possibility to impose duties on goods destined for a Member State's continental shelf or exclusive economic zone. In addition, the new rules on the modernisation of the EU's trade defence instruments purport to shorten the time before duties can be imposed, enhance the transparency of the system and facilitate the participation of smaller companies by providing them with assistance from a specific help desk. Finally, a number of changes were made to reflect the case law of the European Court of Justice and the recommendations of the WTO Dispute Settlement Body.

3.1   *Partial Non-application of the Lesser-duty Rule*

The LDR found in Articles 7(2) and 9(4) of the basic AD Regulation mandates the Commission to impose an anti-dumping duty which does not exceed the lower of the injury or dumping margin. This gives rise to situations where the dumping margin found may significantly exceed the anti-dumping duty actually imposed. Such lower duty will be justified if the Commission considers that such lower duty is sufficient to eliminate the injury margin which it has determined in the course of the investigation, generally by comparing the import price of the dumped goods with a profitable price, which may be a constructed target price, of the EU producers.

Anti-dumping duties are neither remedial of past injury nor punitive in nature. The rationale for imposing further measures will therefore normally disappear once the price of the imports is increased as a result of the imposition of the anti-dumping duty to a level sufficient to remove any further injury to the EU producers. From an economic viewpoint, the imposition of a lower duty also makes sense since it avoids undue harm to consumers and downstream users and acts as a brake on excessive price increases by EU producers once the market is shielded by prohibitively high import barriers.

Application of the LDR is not mandatory under the WTO ADA. Article 9.1 of the ADA describes the application of the LDR as merely "desirable". For this reason the LDR is frequently described as a WTO+ obligation.

Not surprisingly, the LDR has been a target of the EU industry lobbies for many years and the most recent amendment must therefore be seen as a partial step towards the complete elimination of the LDR. The new rules now foresee that the LDR may not apply in case of significant distortions on raw material (including energy) in the exporting country under investigation.

In addition, a number of rules have been adopted to increase the target price which needs to be used for the calculation of the injury margin.

3.1.1   Non-Application of the LDR in Case of a Significant Distortion on
            Raw Materials

Further to new Article 7(2b) and 9(4) of the EU basic Anti-Dumping Regulation, the LDR will no longer apply in determining the level of provisional and
definitive anti-dumping duties where the Commission, on the basis of all the
information submitted, can clearly conclude that a significant distortion on
raw materials (including energy) exists and that it is in the Union's interest not
to apply the LDR. The text does not clarify whether this determination will be
made for each exporting producer individually or for the exporting country as
a whole. In the only case until now, one determination on the Union interest
not to apply the LDR was made for the country as a whole.[37]

Article 7(2a) defines the types of raw material distortions which are covered
by the new rule by reference to the OECD "Inventory on export restrictions on
industrial raw materials". The restrictions listed mostly consist of export duties
or quota as well as dual pricing systems which have as a common feature that
they reduce the cost of raw material for the downstream users in the exporting country. In order to qualify as a distortion, the cost of the distorted raw
material (including energy) must account for not less than 17 % of the cost of
production of the exported product under investigation. This percentage will
be calculated on the basis of the undistorted price of the raw material as established in representative international markets. In addition, the Commission
must conclude that it is manifestly in the Union's interest not to apply the LDR.

It is unclear to what extent a finding of the existence of a significant distortion under Article 7(2a) will necessarily lead to a similar finding under Article
2(6a)(a) and trigger the rejection of the domestic prices and costs of the exporter. In the only case brought until now in which the complainants invoke
the existence of a significant distortion within the meaning of Article 7(2a), no
allegation was made that domestic prices and costs may not be used for the
determination of normal value due to the existence of said distortion.[38]

3.1.2   Target Price

The injury margin is normally calculated by comparing the price of the imported product with a profitable target price of the Union industry. In cases where
the LDR still applies, the new rules will result in higher target prices being set.

---

37   *Urea and Ammonium Nitrate*, AD649 Commission Implementing Regulation (EU) 2019/
      576 of 10 April 2019 imposing a provisional anti-dumping duty on imports of mixtures of
      urea and ammonium nitrate originating in Russia, Trinidad and Tobago and the United
      States of America, para. 205 to 237 (OJ 2019, L 100/7).
38   *Urea and Ammonium Nitrate*, AD649 Notice of Initiation (OJ 2018, C 284/9).

Higher target prices will result in higher injury margins and, unless the dumping margin is lower, higher anti-dumping duties. This objective is achieved by, first, imposing a minimum profit margin of six percent which needs to be added to the full production cost of the EU producers and second, by including already as a current cost of production future costs which result from multilateral environmental agreements, and protocols thereunder, to which the Union is a party, or from International Labour Organisation (ILO) Conventions listed in Annex Ia to the EU basic Anti-Dumping Regulation.

3.2 *Social and Environmental Standards*

Social and environmental standards will not only be taken into account when determining the target price used for the calculation of the injury margin in anti-dumping investigations but also in the context of interim reviews and in deciding whether or not to accept undertaking offers. According to Recital (12), the

> Commission should initiate interim reviews, where appropriate, in cases where the Union industry faces increased costs resulting from higher social and environmental standards. Furthermore, the Commission should also initiate interim reviews in cases of changed circumstances in exporting countries relating to social and environmental standards.

The content of this recital is, however, not transposed into the new provisions. At the most, Article 8(3) now expressly states that undertakings offered by exporters may be refused for reasons comprising "the principles and obligations set out in multilateral environmental agreements and protocols thereunder, to which the Union is a party, and of ILO Conventions listed in Annex Ia".

3.3 *Four-Week Notice Period*

Article 19a introduces a "pre-disclosure" prior to the entry into force of provisional duties. Interested parties will have three working days to comment on the accuracy of the Commission's calculations once they receive the disclosure. This notice period effectively puts in place an early warning mechanism and ensures that interested parties are informed of anti-dumping duties before their imposition. This should allow importers to anticipate the duty liability on future imports. For the same reason, notice will also be given in case the Commission does not intend to impose provisional duties.

The length of the notice period was the subject of intense discussion. Eventually, the European Parliament accepted a three-week notice period afforded to interested parties for impending measures, two weeks longer than what had been initially proposed. In exchange, the rules require the national customs authorities to register imports "whenever possible", allowing duties to be collected retroactively in certain circumstances such as stockpiling. Under the current rules, such registration is optional.

The three-week notice period was reviewed after two years by the Commission. As the review did not confirm that the three-week notice period led to significant stockpiling, the notice period has now been extended to four weeks.[39]

3.4 Application of Duties to the Continental Shelf and Exclusive Economic Zone

Pursuant to new Article 14a of the EU basic Anti-Dumping Regulation, antidumping measures may now also be imposed on any dumped product brought in significant quantities to an artificial island, a fixed or floating installation or any other structure in the continental shelf or the exclusive economic zone of a Member State, where this would cause injury to the Union industry. The Commission recently adopted an implementing act laying down the modalities governing the imposition and collection of such duties (the so-called "Customs Tool").[40] Duties will only be imposed on goods intended for the continental shelf or exclusive economic zone where the regulation imposing the provisional or definitive anti-dumping duties expressly refers to such imposition.

3.5 WTO Consistency of the New Rules

The main concern relates to the discriminatory application of the LDR to exports from countries applying policy measures, such as dual pricing or export duties, aimed at restricting the export of their raw materials. Although identified as distortions, most of the measures thus labelled are WTO consistent and legitimate industrial policy instruments.

More importantly, the selective use of the LDR may run counter to the nondiscrimination obligation of Article 9.2 of the ADA:

---

39   Commission Delegated Regulation (EU) 2020/1173 of 4 June 2020 amending Regulation (EU) 2016/1036 on protection against dumped imports from countries not members of the European Union and Regulation (EU) 2016/1037 on protection against subsidised imports from countries not members of the European Union as regards the duration of the period of pre-disclosure (OJ 2020, L 259/1).

40   Commission Implementing Regulation (EU) 2019/1131 of 2 July 2019 establishing a customs tool in order to implement Article 14a of Regulation (EU) 2016/1036 of the European Parliament and of the Council and Article 24a of Regulation (EU) 2016/1037 of the European Parliament and of the Council (OJ 2019, L 179/12).

> When an anti-dumping duty is imposed in respect of any product, such anti-dumping duty shall be collected in the appropriate amounts in each case, on a non-discriminatory basis on imports of such product from all sources found to be dumped and causing injury.

Previous WTO case law has clarified that the obligation in Article 9.2 does not only apply to the collection of anti-dumping duties but also to their determination and imposition. Therefore, the determination of different duty levels for exporters from the same exporting country could be contrary to Article 9.2. Prohibited discrimination will, however, only arise where the criteria used to distinguish between otherwise similarly situated exporters result in the imposition or collection of duties in amounts which are "inappropriate". The question is therefore whether or not the imposition of a higher anti-dumping duty on otherwise similarly situated exporters depending on whether or not they benefit from distortions on raw materials will result in the collection of the duty "in the appropriate amounts".

The panel in *EC – Salmon (Norway)* defined the term "appropriate amount" as the amount which is "proper" or "fitting" in the context of an anti-dumping investigation. The criteria used to differentiate between suppliers must have a connection with the objective of an anti-dumping investigation, namely to offset injurious dumping. Different duties which reflect different dumping or injury margins clearly meet this objective. It is, however, likely that the use of raw material distortions as a criterion would fail this test. Indeed, lower raw material costs will result in lower export prices and will therefore necessarily lead to a higher injury margin. This means that the price effect of raw material distortions will already be captured by the injury margin and the non-application of the LDR can therefore not be justified by the need to offset any additional injurious effect of such distortions.

Although in a different context, the Appellate Body has held in *EC – Tariff Preferences*[41] that the mere fact that different treatment is based on objective criteria which relate to a legitimate objective is not sufficient to conclude that the difference in treatment is non-discriminatory. It was additionally required that the differences respond positively to the aims pursued by the GSP programme concerned, namely the varying development, financial and trade needs of developing countries. It is precisely this link between the ADA and the EU's aim of addressing policies limiting the export of raw materials which appears to be missing.

---

41   AB, *EC – Tariff Preferences*, DS246, para. 162.

4 Possibility of a WTO Challenge of the New Rules

Several WTO Members have raised questions concerning the new methodology introduced by Regulation (EU) 2017/2321 in the Committee on Anti-Dumping Practices. During the regular meeting held on 27 April 2017,[42] Russia, Bahrain, Pakistan, China, Kazakhstan and Indonesia expressed their concerns regarding the proposed amendments to the EU basic AD Regulation. During the regular meeting held on 25 October 2017,[43] Russia reiterated its concerns and was joined by Kazakhstan, Egypt, Saudi Arabia, Bahrain, Kuwait, Oman and Qatar. China and Colombia also voiced their concerns about the WTO consistency of the proposed amendments. Mexico, Saudi Arabia, Russia, Kazakhstan and the United States subsequently submitted written questions to the EU to which the EU responded orally during the regular meeting held on 25 April 2018[44] and subsequently in writing.[45] During this last meeting, Argentina also stated its view that the new rules were WTO-incompatible citing *EU – Biodiesel (Argentina)*.

The concerns expressed focus mainly on the legality of replacing the actual costs of producers in the exporting country with allegedly "undistorted" out-of-country costs in the light of the Appellate Body report in *EU – Biodiesel (Argentina)*, the role played by social and environmental criteria in the assessment of whether costs or prices were distorted, how the "significance" of distortions would be assessed and the risk that the use of country reports prepared by the Commission would infringe procedural fairness. Certain Members also

---

42 Committee on Anti-Dumping Practices, Minutes of the regular meeting held on 27 April 2017, G/ADP/M/52: https://docs.wto.org/dol2fe/Pages/FE_Search/DDFDocuments/237961/q/G/ADP/M52.pdf.

43 Committee on Anti-Dumping Practices, Minutes of the regular meeting held on 25 October 2017 G/ADP/M/53: https://docs.wto.org/dol2fe/Pages/FE_Search/DDFDocuments/241760/q/G/ADP/M53.pdf.

44 Committee on Anti-Dumping Practices, Minutes of the regular meeting held on 25 April 2018, G/ADP/M/54: https://docs.wto.org/dol2fe/Pages/FE_Search/DDFDocuments/247297/q/G/ADP/M54.pdf.

45 Committee on Anti-Dumping Practices / Committee on Subsidies and Countervailing Measures, 'Replies to the questions posed by Mexico regarding the notification of the European Union' (G/ADP/Q1/EU/10, 9 October 2018); 'Replies to the questions posed by Saudi Arabia regarding the notification of the European Union' (G/ADP/Q1/EU/11, 9 October 2018); 'Replies to the questions posed by the Russian Federation regarding the notification of the European Union' (G/ADP/Q1/EU/12, 9 October 2018); 'Replies to the questions posed by Kazakhstan regarding the notification of the European Union (G/ADP/Q1/EU/13, 22 October 2018); 'Replies to the questions posed by the United States regarding the notification of the European Union' (G/ADP/Q1/EU/14, 30 October 2018).

pointed out that distortions as a result of government policy should be addressed through the anti-subsidy instrument and that, if justified, countervailing duties can be imposed.

The EU provided a number of clarifications in relation to the role of social and environmental protection in assessing market distortions, the case-by-case nature of the determination whether distortions are significant, the non-exhaustive nature of both the list of sources in Article 6(2a)(a) and the list of distortive elements in 6(2a)(b). The EU repeatedly stated that it is confident that there is no conflict between the EU's new dumping calculation rules and the Covered Agreements.[46] At the same time, the EU refused to enter into a legal discussion on this issue arguing that the Committee on Anti-Dumping Practices was not the forum to have a sophisticated legal debate.[47]

The EU will not be able to avoid such debate in case a WTO Member initiates dispute settlement proceedings challenging the WTO compatibility of the new rules. China already unsuccessfully tried to do so by including the two legislative proposals that lead to the amendment of the basic AD Regulation within the scope of the dispute regarding the legality of the EU's analogue country methodology after the expiry of the relevant provisions in China's Protocol of Accession.[48]

A WTO challenge can take the form of a direct challenge of the new rules as being "as such" incompatible with the EU's WTO obligations. In such a case, the

---

46   See for instance, Committee on Anti-Dumping Practices / Committee on Subsidies and Countervailing Measures 'Replies to the questions posed by Kazakhstan regarding the notification of the European Union' (G/ADP/Q1/EU/13, 22 October 2018), p. 3.

47   Committee on Anti-Dumping Practices, Minutes of the regular meeting held on 25 April 2018, (n. 43), p. 4.

48   *European Union – Measures Related to Price Comparison Methodologies* (n. 26) Request for Consultations, Footnote 2: 'At present, China is aware of two legislative processes implicating potential changes to relevant provisions of the basic Regulation: (i) the legislative process initiated by the European Commission's Proposal for a Regulation of the European Parliament and of the Council amending Regulation (EU) 2016/1036 on protection against dumped imports from countries not members of the European Union and Regulation (EU) 2016/1037 on protection against subsidised imports from countries not members of the European Union, dated 9 November 2016 (COM(2016) 721 final); and, (ii) the legislative process initiated by the European Commission's Proposal for a Regulation of the European Parliament and of the Council amending Council Regulation (EC) No 1225/2009 on protection against dumped imports from countries not members of the European Community and Council Regulation (EC) No 597/2009 on protection against subsidised imports from countries not members of the European Community (COM(2013) 192 final). This request includes any changes made to the basic Regulation pursuant to the legislative processes initiated by these proposals.'

complainant will need to demonstrate that under certain circumstances the challenged measures necessarily lead to a WTO incompatible outcome. An "as such" challenge will therefore require that where such circumstances arise, the WTO Member concerned does no longer have the discretion to act in a manner that is consistent with its WTO obligations.

The above analysis of the new rules shows that it will be difficult to bring an "as such" challenge of the new normal value methodology. The use of the wording "[i]n case it is determined, [...] that it is not appropriate to use domestic prices and costs in the exporting country due to the existence in that country of significant distortions" in Article 2(6a)(a) suggests that the European Commission has the discretion not to use the new methodology even where significant distortions exist. Likewise, the fact that the non-application of the LDR is made subject to a public interest test and therefore is non-automatic is an obstacle to a finding that an "as such" violation exists.

Likewise, the grandfathering provisions in the amended basic AD Regulation do not preclude "as such" the initiation of an interim review or newcomer review. They do mandate the use of the old analogue country methodology in interim and newcomer reviews but the fact that the old methodology continues to apply is presented as a specific application of the rule in Article 11(9) of the basic AD Regulation.[49]

The situation would be different if the ongoing dispute brought by China against the former analogue country methodology were to end with a finding that such methodology is not WTO compatible. Such outcome, which is now unlikely in view of the suspension of the panel proceedings, would mean that the grandfathering provisions mandating the continued use of this WTO-incompatible methodology in reviews would themselves become "as such" in violation of the EU's WTO obligations.

In contrast, the fact that a reduction of the dumping margin on the basis of the new methodology may not be considered as a change in circumstances justifying the initiation of an interim review arguably constitutes an "as such" violation of Article 11.2 of the ADA.[50]

China could also try to bring an "as such" challenge in relation to the *de facto* allocation of the burden of proof to the exporting producers and the *de facto*

---

49   Art. 11(9) of the basic Anti-Dumping Regulation states that "[i]n all review or refund investigations carried out pursuant to this Article, the Commission shall, provided that circumstances have not changed, apply the same methodology as in the investigation which led to the duty".

50   See above, section 2.8.

discriminatory treatment of China resulting from the new rules as evidenced by the legislative process leading up to their adoption, the fact that only China is covered by a country report and the consistent application of the new methodology to China alone. Bringing an "as such" claim against rules which are *de facto* WTO inconsistent is however seldom successful.[51]

Faced with the difficulties in bringing an "as such" challenge, WTO Members will most likely prefer to wait until the rules, as applied, lead to a WTO inconsistent outcome. This could be the imposition of anti-dumping measures as a result of a dumping margin established on the basis of the new methodology or the continuation of existing measures following an expiry review applying the new methodology.

Likewise, the non-application of the LDR to some countries only on the basis of export restrictions on raw materials or dual pricing systems can only be challenged where such non-application results in the imposition of anti-dumping duties in a discriminatory manner.

5   Conclusion

Several aspects of the EU's new anti-dumping legislation are unlikely to survive a WTO challenge. This is most notably so for the new methodology for determining normal value whereby local prices and costs may be rejected and replaced with so-called "undistorted" costs from outside the country of origin of the exports.

The EU has however taken great care in drafting the new rules in such a way that, on their face, they apply equally to all WTO Members and leave discretion to the Commission services whether or not to apply WTO inconsistent methodologies in a given case. As discussed above, the circumstances surrounding their adoption and the Commission's subsequent practice make it clear that, *de facto*, the new methodology is targeted at China and will be automatically applied in investigations concerning imports from China.

The net result is that other WTO members will need to wait until definitive measures are adopted on the basis of the new methodology before they will be able to bring dispute settlement proceedings. In view of the current stalemate at the WTO's Appellate Body, this may well mean that the EU will manage to extend the application of its analogue country methodology, albeit dressed up

---

51   See, for example, how similar claims failed in Panel, *Russia – Tariff Treatment,* DS485, and Panel, *Russia – Railway Equipment,* DS499.

differently, for at least six to seven years after what should have been its normal expiry date.

Acknowledgement

This chapter was written with the help of Sidonie Descheemaeker and Victor Crochet.

PART 5

The Nexus between the CCP and Other EU External Policies

∵

CHAPTER 15

Tightening the EU's Trade-Development Nexus

A Strategic Turn in Search for Enhanced Effectiveness

Sieglinde Gstöhl

1 Introduction: the Trade-Development Nexus from an EU Perspective

The European Union (EU) and its Member States are important trading partners and donors for many developing countries. This chapter explores the intersection between the common commercial policy and the European development policy, arguably the most developed nexus of the EU's external policies. Through the concept of policy coherence for development, introduced by the Maastricht Treaty and reinforced by the Lisbon Treaty (Article 208 TFEU), the EU seeks to take account of development objectives in all of its policies that are likely to affect developing countries. It aims at minimising contradictions and building synergies between different EU policies to benefit developing countries and increase the effectiveness of development cooperation. Young and Peterson identify three key dimensions of the trade-development nexus: (1) trade *as* development policy; (2) development considerations *in* trade policy more broadly; and (3) the development effects of *internal* EU policies.[1] The focus of this chapter is on the first two aspects, that is, the potential trade-offs and synergies between the external policies of trade and development.

The rationale underlying the EU's current approach to the linkage of trade and development can be summarised as follows: first, preferential market access for developing countries is expected to generate export-led growth and thus promote economic development. Second, increased competition through reciprocal trade liberalisation is believed to increase efficiency and thus stimulate development. Third, aid for trade and other financial or technical assistance as well as the promotion of domestic reforms (e.g. to strengthen the rule of law and good governance) are meant to build up countries' capacity for trade. Fourth, political conditionality in favour of democratic reforms and

---

1 A. R. Young, J. Peterson, ' "We Care about You, but ...": The Politics of EU Trade Policy and Development', *Cambridge Review of International Affairs* 26(3) (2013), p. 499.

human rights (such as 'essential elements' clauses) as well as sustainable development chapters in free trade agreements (FTAS), which involve stakeholders and civil society in the monitoring process, and increasingly also aspects of gender equality, are deemed to render development policy more effective and help sustain development. Fifth, regional integration among neighbouring developing countries should be promoted to create larger markets which contribute to attracting foreign direct investment (FDI) and locking in the reforms conducive to development. Finally, one might add geopolitical reasons for the nexus given Europe's colonial history and the growing differentiation of developing countries from least developed countries (LDCs) to emerging economies.

In the words of the European Commission, trade is a necessary, but not sufficient condition for development: "Trade can foster growth and poverty reduction, depending on the structure of the economy, appropriate sequencing of trade liberalisation measures and complementary policies."[2] This thinking is in line with the Sustainable Development Goals (SDGs) of the United Nations (UN). According to the Agenda 2030, "[i]nternational trade is an engine for inclusive economic growth and poverty reduction, and contributes to the promotion of sustainable development".[3] Already in 2001 the European Council had adopted an EU Strategy for Sustainable Development in order "to meet the needs of the present generation without compromising those of future generations" by "dealing with economic, social and environmental policies in a mutually reinforcing way" both internally and externally.[4]

This chapter asks how and why the connection between the EU's common commercial policy and its development policy has changed over the past decade. It argues that the trade-development nexus has become more intertwined and more strategic. The EU draws on its economic power for leverage in the pursuit of trade liberalisation with developing countries beyond trade in goods, based on increased reciprocity and offensive interests as well as a more assertive promotion of own, respectively Western values. Two emblematic cases illustrate the tightening of the trade-development nexus: the EU's longstanding relations with the group of African, Caribbean and Pacific (ACP)

---

2 European Commission, 'Trade, Growth and Development: Tailoring Trade and Investment Policy for those Countries most in Need', COM (2012) 22, 27 January 2012, p. 5.

3 UN General Assembly, 'Transforming our World: The 2030 Agenda for Sustainable Development', Resolution adopted by the General Assembly on 25 September 2015, A/RES/70/1, 21 October 2015, para. 68.

4 European Council, 'Presidency Conclusions – Göteborg, 15 and 16 June 2001', SN 200/1/01 REV 1, para. 19.

countries and with the beneficiaries of its Generalised System of Preferences (GSP). Both cases underwent radical changes in terms of form, contents and partners, and are arguably the most important EU trade *as* development and development considerations *in* trade policies. The GSP reform also affected the negotiation of Economic Partnership Agreements (EPAs) with the ACP countries.

The reasons for the tightening of the trade-development nexus are both internal and external and generally linked to the EU's search for enhanced effectiveness, understood as goal attainment: on the one hand, the reforms of the Lisbon Treaty recalibrated the goals and the competences in the field of EU external action for the sake of stronger coherence, while on the other hand the global power shift in favour of emerging economies and the policies of the World Trade Organisation (WTO) and the United Nations have also shaped the nexus.

The following section addresses this broader context relevant for the trade-development nexus before the subsequent sections analyse the two case studies. The conclusions provide a short summary and discuss some implications.

2   New Goals, Actors and Instruments in the Post-Lisbon Era

In the post-Cold War era the ideas of market economy, trade liberalisation and democracy seemed to celebrate a worldwide triumph. At the beginning of the new millennium, the big states with large populations and often rapid economic growth – such as Brazil, Russia, India, and especially China (BRIC) – appeared to be rising as first collective rival to the global economic dominance of the West. Yet, neither the expectation that the BRIC countries would act as a new bloc, nor that the emerging powers would behave as co-opted responsible stakeholders of the international liberal order has been fulfilled. The BRICs' levels of trade protection are still much higher, and they have continued to pursue *dirigiste* models of development and often with authoritarian, illiberal political systems.[5]

With the inception of the WTO in 1995, its dispute settlement system was strengthened, membership grew and the coalition patterns changed. The stagnation of the Doha Round negotiations, the new assertiveness of the emerging economies, and the 'competitive liberalisation', in which the United States and

5   M. D. Stephen 'Rising Powers, Global Capitalism and Liberal Global Governance: A Historical Materialist Account of the BRICs Challenge', *European Journal of International Relations* 20(4) (2014), p. 912–938.

others engaged, contributed to the proliferation of bilateral trade agreements. The EU has since 2006 refocused its FTA policy on growth and jobs, reinforced by an economic crisis and reconfiguring global supply chains.[6] The new strategy led to negotiations with bigger and more strategic partners – such as South Korea, the US, Canada or Japan.

The Lisbon Treaty placed both the common commercial policy and the development policy under the TFEU's external action chapter. The overall goals of Article 21 TEU apply to these policies, although the Treaty made the eradication of poverty the primary objective of development cooperation. The EU is to help all countries to integrate in the world economy and to foster sustainable development (see also Article 11 TFEU and Article 3(5) TEU). Whereas all trade policy became an exclusive competence of the Union,[7] development policy has remained a shared parallel competence, requiring close coordination, coherence and complementarity between the action of the EU and that of its Member States. The Lisbon Treaty also strengthened the value-based agenda by bestowing the European Parliament – often an advocate for the promotion of values such as human rights, democracy and sustainable development – with new powers in the conclusion of trade agreements and in the implementation of the common commercial policy.[8] Both the Council and the Parliament have to ratify trade agreements, co-decide on the Commission's proposals for regulations (e.g. the GSP regulation) under the ordinary legislative procedure, and co-monitor the implementation by the Commission.

The Commission's 2015 "Trade for All" strategy intends to use trade and investment to support inclusive growth in developing countries by providing an open market for their exports, by enabling them to integrate into and move up regional and global value chains, by taking into account policy coherence for development, and by promoting respect for human rights and high labour and environmental standards.[9] Moreover, bilateral "FTAs must provide reciprocal and effective opening, based on a high level of ambition".[10] In its Global Strategy adopted one year later, the EU explicitly confirms its intention to use trade

---

6   European Commission, 'Global Europe: Competing in the World: A Contribution to the EU's Growth and Jobs Strategy', COM (2006) 567, 4 October 2006.

7   On the scope of the EU's exclusive competences in the area of trade, see the contributions by Allan Rosas and Marise Cremona in this volume.

8   On the role of the Parliament and the Council in the CCP, see, respectively, the chapters by Andrej Auersperger Matić and Bart Driessen in this volume.

9   European Commission, 'Trade for All: Towards a More Responsible Trade and Investment Policy', COM (2015) 497, 14 October 2015, p. 16–20.

10   *Ibid*, p. 22.

agreements to "underpin sustainable development, human rights protection and rules-based governance".[11] According to the Strategy's "principled pragmatism", the EU should act in accordance with universal and own values, but in doing so follow a pragmatic approach that also takes into account its interests. Finally, the European Consensus on Development Policy revised in 2017 endorses the SDGs and "a rights-based approach to development cooperation" with greater coherence and inclusiveness.[12]

On the institutional level, the European External Action Service (EEAS) began to participate in the preparation and programming of certain financial instruments together with the Commission's Directorate-General (DG) International Cooperation and Development. The EEAS provides in particular strategic political guidance. Moreover, the EU Delegations, which are part of the EEAS, play a role in the formulation and implementation of development assistance.

As a result of these changes in the post-Lisbon era, one might expect more policy coherence and effectiveness of the trade-development nexus. The two case studies that follow address this question by focusing on the changing form, contents and partners before briefly reflecting on the impact.

3 EU-ACP Relations: 'Privilege Erosion' and the Strategic Turn

The trade and aid relationship between the European Union and the ACP countries underwent considerable changes over time:[13] from the association of dependent territories (1958–1963) to the Yaoundé Conventions I and II (1964–1974) in the wake of decolonisation, the Lomé Conventions I-III (1975–1990) with the newly established ACP group and the current Cotonou Agreement (2000–2020). Reflecting the prevailing discourse on development strategies at the time, the EU's approach shifted from reciprocal trade relations under Yaoundé, to non-reciprocal trade under Lomé in 1975, and back to

---

11 European External Action Service, 'Shared Vision, Common Action: A Stronger Europe – A Global Strategy for the European Union's Foreign and Security Policy', June 2016, p. 26–27.

12 Joint Statement by the Council and the Representatives of the Governments of the Member States Meeting within the Council, the European Parliament and the Commission: 'The New European Consensus on Development: Our World, Our Dignity, Our Future', 8 June 2017.

13 S. Gstöhl, D. De Bièvre, *The Trade Policy of the European Union* (Palgrave Macmillan, 2018), p. 139–175.

reciprocity in 2008 with the comprehensive EPA s negotiated under the Cotonou Agreement.

In 1990 the Lomé IV Convention had introduced a human rights clause as a 'fundamental part' of cooperation. This did not allow for the suspension of the agreement in case of serious violations under the 1969 Vienna Convention on the Law of Treaties. The 1995 revision turned the human rights clause into an 'essential element' of the agreement, making suspension legally possible. The Cotonou Agreement of 2000 added a political dialogue that clarified the procedure to follow for the suspension and resumption of relations. The suspension clause was extended to include good governance, but as a mere 'fundamental' and not an 'essential' element of the agreement – except for serious cases of corruption. In the 2005 revision of the Cotonou Agreement, cooperation on the non-proliferation of weapons of mass destruction was added as an 'essential element', and the parties were encouraged to join the International Criminal Court.

EU development policy has since the Rome Treaty been characterised by a controversy between the regionalists (mainly composed of France, Belgium and the Southern Member States) and the globalists in the North. Whereas the regionalists emphasised the historical links with their former colonies, the globalists stressed poverty eradication worldwide. The regionalists dominated the debate and the European Commission services for a long time, but the influence of the globalists was growing with the EU's changing membership.[14] In the context of the Lisbon Treaty and the debate on the EU's post-2020 relations with the ACP countries, a further shift towards globalism has occurred. There is no special division in the EEAS or in the Commission anymore dedicated to the ACP countries, as the pre-Lisbon DG Development was, and any Treaty reference to the ACP was dropped. Nevertheless, the ACP countries still benefit from a close institutional association with the EU and the exclusive, intergovernmental European Development Fund (EDF).[15] By comparison, the Asian and Latin American countries have not been subject to a single, overarching EU approach, nor profited from special trade privileges or funds. Their trade relations with the EU have mainly been governed by the GSP and since the 2000s increasingly by FTA s.

---

14   M. Carbone 'Mission Impossible: The European Union and Policy Coherence for Development', *Journal of European Integration* 30(3) (2008), p. 31–37.

15   This could, however, change with the new Multiannual Financial Framework 2021–2027 in light of the expiry of the Cotonou Agreement in 2020 (and Brexit), which might finally lead to a 'budgetisation' of the EDF.

3.1   *Changing Form, Contents and Partners*

Under the Lomé Conventions the ACP countries enjoyed almost full, non-reciprocal duty-free access for all their exports. Only their products directly competing with products under the Common Agricultural Policy were restricted, but these still enjoyed more favourable treatment than under most-favoured nation (MFN) terms. For a long time, no objections were raised in the General Agreement on Trade and Tariffs (GATT) against the EU's discrimination between ACP and non-ACP developing countries. The EU only asked for and obtained a waiver in 1994, in the course of the protracted banana disputes and just before the WTO was established and the veto in the dispute settlement system was abolished.[16] EU-ACP relations under Lomé were increasingly considered a disappointment since years of privileged trade and aid relations had still left many ACP states economically marginalised, impoverished and uncompetitive – especially compared to Asia and Latin America.[17]

The Cotonou Agreement introduced the new principles of differentiation and regionalisation. With the expiry of the WTO waiver at the end of 2007, the Agreement's trade chapter was to be replaced by several EPA s with regional groupings of ACP countries, whereby the latter were free to choose which group to join. Due to multiple, partly overlapping organisations in Africa, this choice was not always obvious. The EPA s aimed at a phased establishment of WTO-compatible free trade areas based on asymmetrical reciprocity, in compliance with the requirement of Art. XXIV GATT to cover "substantially all trade". In addition, regional integration among the ACP countries was expected to boost local trade and attract investment. The EPA negotiations started in 2002, right after the EU launched the *Everything but Arms* (EBA) initiative at the beginning of the Doha Round in 2001. The EBA initiative opened the European market for the first time equally for all LDC s and all agricultural products. Yet, it undermined the EU's bargaining leverage in the EPA negotiations as most LDC s are Sub-Saharan members of the ACP group. In addition, several reforms of the Common Agricultural Policy have in fact over the past three decades removed many, though not all, trade-distorting features.

The ACP countries negotiated with DG Trade instead of DG Development, which was interpreted as a shift from the promotion of social development to the

---

16   This was not a complete waiver as challenges to the quota-based Banana Protocol were still allowed (on this issue, see E. Guth 'The End of the Bananas Saga', *Journal of World Trade* 46(1) (2012), p. 1–32).

17   European Commission, 'Green Paper on Relations between the European Union and the ACP Countries on the Eve of the 21st Century: Challenges and Options for a New Partnership', COM (1996) 570, 20 November 1996.

promotion of deep free trade.[18] The negotiations mobilised non-governmental organisations (NGOs) and civil society and led to growing criticism of the Commission. Many African countries and some EU Member States feared that the long-term sustainable development of ACP countries and their regional integration processes would be undermined. Under pressure for demonstrating a more development-friendly approach and of meeting the deadline set by the WTO waiver, the Commission in 2007 offered 100 per cent tariff- and quota-free market access as well as more aid.[19] A full and comprehensive EPA covers not only trade in goods, as the Lomé and Cotonou Agreement did, but also trade in services and a host of provisions in other trade-related areas such as investment, competition policy, government procurement, intellectual property rights and labour and environmental standards.[20] After the collapse of the WTO Ministerial Conference in Cancún in 2003, the three most controversial 'Singapore issues' (competition policy, public procurement and investment) were dropped from the Doha agenda. Hence, the proposed scope of the EPAs was broader than required by WTO rules, and "the Commission could no longer hide behind the pretext of WTO compatibility".[21]

On the eve of the expiry of the WTO waiver, the European Commission decided to permit individual countries and regions to initial 'goods only' interim EPAs with a view to the completion of full region-wide EPAs at a later date. Interim EPAs therefore contain *rendez-vous* clauses which foresee further talks. As a bridging solution, a Market Access Regulation was adopted to provide temporary duty-free market access as of 2008 for those ACP countries that had at least initialled an interim agreement. This led to the conclusion of some EPA negotiations, but thereafter the negotiations slowed considerably. In response, the EU attempted to regain some of the leverage by letting the Market Access Regulation expire in 2014 (a deadline which was later extended to 2016). Nevertheless, among the seven regional groups, only Cariforum has so far concluded a full regional EPA. Some members of the Southern African Development Community (SADC), the Economic Community of West African States (ECOWAS), the East African Community and the other groups

---

18   O. Elgström, M. F. Larsén 'Free to Trade? Commission Autonomy in Economic Partnership Agreement Negotiations', *Journal of European Public Policy* 17(2) (2010), p. 214.

19   *Ibid,* 215.

20   In addition to the reciprocity of trade and the legal certainty of an agreement, this is an important difference compared to the unilateral EBA initiative which is restricted to non-reciprocal trade in goods (and with less beneficial rules of origin).

21   T. Heron 'Trading in Development: Norms and Institutions in the Making/Unmaking of European Union-African, Caribbean and Pacific Trade and Development Cooperation' *Contemporary Politics* 20(1) (2014), p. 20.

have concluded regional or bilateral interim EPAs restricted to trade in goods. Table 15.1 summarises the trade status of the 77 ACP countries that have participated in the EPA negotiations.[22]

Overall, the form of EU-ACP relations changed from a 'one-size-fits all' approach to differentiation; the contents shifted towards more comprehensive and reciprocal trade; and the partners were subject to a regionalisation. Nevertheless, Poletti and Sicurelli consider the EPAs the most development-friendly FTAs concluded by the EU in the 2000s because of the asymmetrical market liberalisation, long transition periods, flexible rules of origin, protection for infant industries and high standards for sustainable development.[23] They explain this in particular with the mobilisation of NGOs and the lack of offensive European interests given the low levels of EU-ACP trade, the weak integration of ACP countries in the global value chains and the absence of relevant 'domino effects' from other FTAs.

3.2 Impact: from a Group-to-Group Approach to a Patchwork

The biggest impact of the EPAs was, first of all, a 'patchwork effect' on the regions although most ACP countries now benefit either from the EBA initiative or have concluded, or are still in the process of concluding, an EPA. However, many EPAs still need to be signed, ratified or implemented, and the interim EPAs are supposed to be further developed into full regional agreements.

Second, the EPA negotiations have been highly controversial with regard to their expected economic impact. The main criticism concerns the protection of nascent agro-processing and manufacturing sectors in developing countries in light of cheaper, potentially even subsidised, imports from Europe, which could act as a barrier to diversification and value addition, keeping African countries dependent on exporting raw materials.[24] This concern was reinforced by the prospect of significant tariff revenue losses – to be (partially) compensated by more EU aid for trade –, by the reduced policy space for governments, and by the fact that the EPA regions in most cases do not correspond to the regional integration schemes on the ground, leading to trade diversion and the disruption of existing or planned regional customs unions.[25] Moreover,

---

22   The ACP country Cuba is not a signatory of the Cotonou Agreement, and South Sudan is not yet a member of the ACP group.

23   A. Poletti, D. Sicurelli, *The Political Economy of Normative Trade Power Europe* (Palgrave Macmillan, 2018), p. 91.

24   M. Langan, *Neo-Colonialism and the Poverty of 'Development' in Africa* (Palgrave Macmillan, 2018), p. 120.

25   European Parliament, *African, Caribbean and Pacific (ACP) Countries' Position on the Economic Partnership Agreements (EPAs)* (Study PE 433.843, April 2014).

TABLE 15.1   ACP countries' current trade relations with the EU (July 2019)[a]

EPA group	Number of countries	Members and their EU trade status
Caribbean (CARIFORUM without Cuba)	15	full regional EPA (provisionally applied), *except* for Haiti (EBA, yet EPA signed)
Central Africa	8	regional EPA (provisionally applied) for Cameroon only; EBA for the others, *except* for Congo-Brazzaville (GSP) and Gabon (MFN)
East African Community (without South Sudan)	5	regional EPA (Kenya ratified, Rwanda signed, signatures pending for the others, which are covered by EBA)
Eastern and Southern Africa (without Somalia)	11	EPA (provisionally applied) for Comoros, Madagascar, Mauritius, Seychelles and Zimbabwe; EBA for the others
Pacific (Pacific Islands Forum without New Zealand & Australia)	15	regional EPA for Papua New Guinea (in force) as well as Fiji and Samoa (provisionally applied); Solomon Islands and Tonga are joining; EBA or GSP for the others (*except* for the Marshall Islands which have no preferential status)
SADC EPA (partial SADC)	7	regional EPA (provisionally applied) for Botswana, Eswatini, Lesotho, Namibia, South Africa (which form the South African Customs Union) and Mozambique, *except* for Angola (EBA)
West Africa (ECOWAS & Mauritania)	16	EPA provisionally applied for Ivory Coast and Ghana; regional EPA signed by all, incl. Cabo Verde (GSP+) and Mauritania (EBA), *except* for Nigeria (GSP)

[a] . Based on European Commission, 'Economic Partnerships', http://ec.europa.eu/trade/policy/ countries-and-regions/development/economic-partnerships (accessed July 2019). See below for further explanations on GSP, GSP+ and EBA.

the Commission's political pressure through setting deadlines and threatening default options (such as the GSP or MFN) was condemned.

Third, the trade preferences for the ACP group have very much been 'stream-lined' with the EU's FTAs with other countries, a move that was further rein-forced by the GSP reform (see below). As a result, the ACP countries have been facing a 'privilege erosion' over the past ten years. Furthermore, the EU and the ACP countries are since September 2018 renegotiating their partnership for the time after 2020, when the Cotonou Agreement will expire. The Euro-pean Commission proposed an umbrella agreement defining common prin-ciples and priorities and three distinct regional partnerships with Africa, the Caribbean and the Pacific.[26] As the African Union is working on an African continental FTA, Commission President Juncker envisioned for the long run a continent-to-continent free trade area.[27] At the same time, however, the rel-evance of the EU as a trade and development partner has been challenged by the rise of the BRIC countries, which for some ACP countries represent an alternative source of (unconditional) aid and trade as well as potential allies in international fora.[28]

Fourth, a growing literature has been addressing the (lack of) effectiveness of the EU's conditionality policy, which in practice has been mainly focused on the ACP countries. The only action under a human rights clause in any of the EU's trade agreements was in the context of the Lomé/Cotonou Agreements. Moreover, the EU's measures have been limited to delays in and suspension of financial cooperation with the ACP countries concerned. No sanctions in terms of disrupting trade with a contracting party have been implemented. A study confirms that the EU most often responds to violations of political rights (in particular *coups* and flawed elections) and that enforcement is a more power-ful catalyst for change in highly aid-dependent states.[29]

The ACP countries played a pioneer role not only with regard to human rights conditionality but the EU-CARIFORUM EPA included a novel chapter on environmental and social aspects. The parties' commitments to core labour

---

26 Council of the EU, 'Negotiating directives for a Partnership Agreement between the European Union and its Member States of the one part, and with countries of the African, Caribbean and Pacific Group of States of the other part', 8094/18 ADD1, 21 June 2018.

27 Jean-Claude Juncker 'State of the Union 2018', 12 September 2018, 8, https://ec.europa.eu/commission/sites/beta-political/files/soteu2018-speech_en_0.pdf (accessed July 2019).

28 M. Lipton 'Are the BRICS Reformers, Revolutionaries, or Counter-revolutionaries?' *South African Journal of International Affairs* 24(1) (2017), p. 41–59.

29 D. Donno, M. Neureiter 'Can Human Rights Conditionality Reduce Repression? Examining the European Union's Economic Agreements', *The Review of International Organizations* 13(3) (2018), p. 335–357.

standards and environmental protection are monitored by mechanisms including civil society, and the CARIFORUM EPA is to date the only agreement where the dispute settlement mechanism is applicable to the sustainable development provisions (yet without the possibility of suspending trade concessions or financial cooperation in case of violations).[30] Hence, paradoxically, the human rights clause is enforceable but has no specific monitoring bodies, while the sustainable development provisions come with monitoring procedures and civil society involvement but lack enforceability and have to rely on 'naming and shaming'. Effectiveness has arguably remained mixed: whereas Bastiaens and Postnikov see environmental reforms in developing countries spurred by the policy dialogue established by EU FTAs, Harrison *et al.* argue that the new trade and sustainable development chapters have so far delivered little improvements in labour standards.[31] The Commission has been reviewing the functioning of these chapters in practice and proposed an action plan to improve their implementation.[32]

In sum, the EU's goal of full and comprehensive EPAs has – so far – only been met in the Caribbean region. The ACP countries' alternatives to an EPA were either the GSP or the less attractive MFN treatment as WTO member (or in exceptional cases even no preferences at all). The expiry of the Market Access Regulation strategically coincided with the GSP reform, thus increasing the pressure on those ACP countries that would in 2014 fall out of the new GSP.

4   The 2012 Reform of the GSP: Preference Erosion and the Strategic Turn

The GSP goes back to a recommendation of the second United Nations Conference on Trade and Development in 1968, calling on the industrialised countries

---

30   L. Bartels, 'Human Rights and Sustainable Development Obligations in EU Free Trade Agreements', in J. Wouters *et al.* (eds.), *Global Governance through Trade: EU Policies and Approaches* (Edward Elgar, 2015), p. 73–91.

31   I. Bastiaens, E. Postnikov, 'Greening up: The Effects of Environmental Standards in EU and US Trade Agreements', *Environmental Politics* 26(5) (2017), p. 847–869; J. Harrison *et al.* 'Governing Labour Standards through Free Trade Agreements: Limits of the European Union's Trade and Sustainable Development Chapters', *Journal of Common Market Studies* 57(2) (2019), p. 260–277.

32   See European Commission, 'Feedback and way forward on improving the implementation and enforcement of Trade and Sustainable Development chapters in EU Free Trade Agreements', non-paper, 26 February 2018, https://trade.ec.europa.eu/doclib/html/156618.htm (accessed July 2019).

to grant non-reciprocal trade preferences to all developing countries. It was expected that such preferences would increase their export earnings and promote their industrialisation. The European Community was among the first actors to create a GSP in 1971 which has since undergone many reforms.[33] The UN only provides a definition of least developed countries. According to the principle of self-election, countries can designate themselves as developing countries in the WTO and they are thus potential GSP beneficiaries. However, the developed countries had reserved the right to exclude countries from their tariff concessions and to use graduation mechanisms that phase-out non-reciprocal preferential market access for beneficiaries (or for product sectors from specific countries) which had made progress. The GSP also allows for EU safeguard measures.

The EU's GSP is since 2006 composed of three schemes: first, the general or standard arrangement grants duty-free access for non-sensitive products and tariff reductions for sensitive products (mainly agriculture and textiles); second, the "special incentive arrangement for sustainable development and good governance" (GSP+) provides duty-free access to all the products covered by the standard GSP without distinction in terms of their sensitivity;[34] and third, the EBA offers duty-free and quota-free access to all products (except arms) from LDCs. Whereas eligible countries benefit automatically from the standard GSP and EBA, those wishing to be granted the extended preferences of GSP+ have to apply and qualify as 'vulnerable' economies (with poorly diversified exports and very low benefits under the standard GSP).

4.1 *Changing Form, Contents and Partners*

The entry into force of the Lisbon Treaty in late 2009 accelerated the negotiation of a new GSP system before its ten-year cycle 2006–15 was over. The revised GSP regulation of 2012 came into force in 2014, starting another ten-year cycle.[35] For the first time, the European Parliament had participated in the drafting of the regulation in the framework of the ordinary legislative procedure.

---

33   S. Gstöhl, 'No Strings Attached? The EU's Emergency Trade Preferences for Pakistan', in
      I. Govaere, S. Poli (eds.), *EU Management of Global Emergencies: Legal Framework for
      Combating Threats and Crises* (Brill, 2014), p. 52–62.

34   The GSP(+) covers around two thirds of all EU tariff lines.

35   Regulation (EU) No 978/2012 of the European Parliament and of the Council of 25 October
      2012 *applying a scheme of generalised tariff preferences and repealing Council Regulation
      (EC) No 732/2008* (OJ 2012, L 303/1).

The EU's foremost objective of the GSP reform was to focus on the countries 'most in need' in view of the increasing erosion of preferences. Moreover, the new regulation aimed at strengthening the support for sustainable development and good governance as well as the consistency with the EU's overall trade objectives. The main changes thus concerned the coverage of countries, the criteria for graduation and vulnerability, and political conditionality. The product coverage was only marginally altered.

Countries which the World Bank classifies as either high-income or – new – upper-middle income countries are no longer eligible, and beneficiaries covered by other trade arrangements were also removed. This halved the number of beneficiaries from 177 developing or transition countries and territories to around 90 in 2014. By July 2019, only 15 countries were in the standard GSP, 8 in the GSP+ and 48 in the EBA (see Table 15.2). Among the beneficiaries excluded from the GSP as a result of the reform were the 33 overseas countries and territories, the high-income countries (such as Saudi Arabia and the United Arab Emirates), the upper-middle income countries (e.g. Argentina, Brazil, Malaysia, Russia, and China) and the increasing number of countries that have concluded FTAs with the EU (e.g. Mexico, Morocco, Tunisia, or the ACP countries with EPAs).

The management of the GSP's new focus on fewer, poorer and less diversified countries has been facilitated by the Lisbon Treaty. The European Commission can directly amend the list of eligible countries via delegated acts or implementing acts. This makes also the withdrawal or reinstatement of preferences easier and quicker.

While the GSP still offers unilateral market access , the EU regained some bargaining power vis-à-vis the non-LDCs with which it was negotiating or intended to negotiate FTAs (such as the EPAs). Siles-Brügge thus argues that the GSP reform was part of a broader "reciprocity agenda" with which the EU aimed in particular at recapturing leverage with emerging economies such as the members of the Association of Southeast Asian Nations.[36]

By contrast, for the GSP+ the entry criteria were lowered, the graduation mechanism was abolished and the promotion of values strengthened. GSP beneficiaries are expected to abide by a number of core conventions of the UN and the International Labour Organisation (ILO). In case of serious and systematic violations, the trade preferences can temporarily be withdrawn by

---

36   G. Siles-Brügge 'EU Trade and Development Policy beyond the ACP: Subordinating Developmental to Commercial Imperatives in the Reform of GSP', *Contemporary Politics* 20(1) (2014), p. 49–62.

TABLE 15.2 Beneficiaries of the EU's GSP (July 2019)[a]

Scheme	Number of countries	Beneficiaries
Standard GSP	15 (of which 9 ACP)	Congo-Brazzaville, Cook Islands, Federate States of Micronesia, India, Indonesia, Kenya, Nauru, Niue, Nigeria, Samoa, Syria, Tajikistan, Tonga, Uzbekistan, Vietnam
GSP+	8 (of which 1 ACP)	Armenia, Bolivia, Cabo Verde, Kyrgyzstan, Mongolia, Pakistan, Philippines, Sri Lanka
EBA	48 (of which 39 ACP)	Afghanistan, Angola, Bangladesh, Benin, Bhutan, Burkina Faso, Burundi, Cambodia, Central African Republic, Chad, Comoros, DRC Congo, Djibouti, Equatorial Guinea, Eritrea, Ethiopia, Gambia, Guinea, Guinea-Bissau, Haiti, Kiribati, Lao PRD, Lesotho, Liberia, Madagascar, Malawi, Mali, Mauritania, Mozambique, Myanmar, Nepal, Niger, Rwanda, Sao Tome & Principe, Senegal, Sierra Leone, Solomon Islands, Somalia, South Sudan, Sudan, Tanzania, Timor-Leste, Togo, Tuvalu, Uganda, Vanuatu, Yemen, Zambia

[a] Based on European Commission, 'Generalised Scheme of Preferences (GSP)', http://ec.europa. eu/trade/policy/countries-and-regions/development/generalised-scheme-of-preferences (accessed July 2019). Note that transition periods apply to move from one trade regime to another. Equatorial Guinea, for instance, is no longer classified as an LDC and will be removed from the EBA at the end of 2020.

the Commission. In addition to the 15 international conventions relevant for all three GSP schemes, the GSP+ covers 12 additional international conventions, including multilateral environmental agreements as well as anti-drug trafficking and anti-corruption conventions. In order to further strengthen conditionality in the GSP+, the burden of proof for compliance was put on the beneficiary and no longer on the EU side, and the monitoring of effective implementation of the ratified conventions was enhanced. The European Commission has also provided several grants to the ILO and other partners for projects in GSP beneficiary countries to help them meet their commitments.

Overall, the GSP still takes the form of a regulation but the European Parliament acquired a new role in the shaping of this regulation and the Commission in its implementation. The biggest change in contents occurred in the GSP+ which removed graduation and increased conditionality. The number of partners in the standard GSP was radically downsized by focusing on those countries most in need. Only the EBA remained the same.

4.2 Impact: from a Generalised to a Select System of Preferences

First of all, the GSP reform has pushed many developing countries to negotiate FTAs with the EU. For upper middle-income ACP countries not signing up to their region's EPA would have meant a return to MFN status. This is what Gabon opted for, whereas Botswana and Namibia finally signed the SADC EPA. There are currently six trade regimes for developing countries, namely FTAs, the standard GSP, the GSP+, the EBA, MFN treatment, or no preferential status at all (outside the WTO).

Second, since the reform, India and Vietnam are the largest GSP beneficiaries, Bangladesh the dominant beneficiary under the EBA and Pakistan under the GSP+.[37] The EU has in June 2019 signed bilateral trade and investment protection agreements with Vietnam, while the FTA negotiations with India have de facto faced a standstill since 2013. The mid-term evaluation of the new GSP found some positive economic effects for the two more advanced schemes: the shares of EU imports under the GSP+ and the EBA have grown since 2014, the beneficiaries in these arrangements have significantly increased their utilisation rates and many of them strengthened their export diversification as well.[38] Yet, textiles and clothing are still the main category of EU imports under the GSP. More trade did not necessarily go hand-in-hand with improvements in labour and human rights, and the environmental impact has also been very mixed.

Third, despite its new focus on the poorer and more vulnerable countries, the GSP is still suffering from preference erosion given the further increasing number of FTAs that the EU is concluding. Young and Peterson thus argue that in a paradoxical way, the EU has placed greater emphasis on trade as a tool for development, while the general neoliberal thrust of its trade policy at the same time eroded the value of preferential market access.[39] A major challenge remains the under-utilisation of preferences due to the need to comply with EU product standards and rules of origin.

---

37   European Commission 'Report on the Generalised Scheme of Preferences Covering the Period 2016–2017', COM (2018) 36, 19 January 2018.
38   European Commission Mid-Term Evaluation of the EU's Generalised Scheme of Preferences (GSP): Final Report, prepared by DEVELOPMENT Solutions, July 2018, p. 7–11.
39   A. R. Young, J. Peterson (n. 1).

Fourth, the goal of the GSP+ to attract more countries has not been reached as currently only 8 countries benefit from this scheme. In 2013 the Commission had listed 35 countries as eligible to apply for GSP+, among them nine ACP countries.[40] However, only Cabo Verde applied when it had to leave the EBA scheme, and it also signed the West African EPA. The Republic of Congo (Brazzaville), Nigeria and six Pacific islands chose not to apply, which left them in the GSP (from which the Marshall Islands, as upper-middle income country, were excluded in 2017). Among the 26 eligible non-ACP candidates, as of July 2019, only seven have joined GSP+, while three have remained in the GSP. 10 countries have so far concluded trade agreements with the EU, whereas two have MFN and four no preferential status.

Fifth, the effectiveness of political conditionality has also been questioned due to the EU's rather inconsistent application of sanctions. The EU has withdrawn the trade preferences only in very few cases (and considered but not implemented it for some other beneficiaries): for serious violations of labour rights in Myanmar (1997–2013) and Belarus (2007–14, as the country was in 2014 anyway removed by the GSP reform) and under the GSP+ for human rights abuses in Sri Lanka (2010–17, yet the country remained in the standard GSP). In addition, the Commission has in February 2019 initiated a temporary withdrawal procedure for Cambodia (with a final decision to be taken within one year), and it has stepped up its engagement with Bangladesh and Myanmar in light of their poor human rights records.

In sum, the impact of the GSP reform has been considerable in terms of reducing the number of beneficiaries and rather varied with regard to its effectiveness.

5   Conclusion: the EU's Continuing Quest for Trade-Development Coherence

This chapter explored how and why the nexus between the EU's common commercial policy and its development policy has changed in the Lisbon Treaty era. It argued that the nexus has become tighter: the EU's trade policy towards developing countries has become more strategic, pursuing reciprocal trade liberalisation going beyond trade in goods, with a more geopolitically

---

40   European Commission 'Information Notice for Countries which May Request to be Granted the Special Incentive Arrangement for Sustainable Development and Good Governance under Regulation (EU) No 978/2012 of 31 October 2012', 2013.

motivated choice of trade partners and a more pronounced value orientation. The achievement of the goals, or the effectiveness of this nexus management, has overall been positive yet limited. Trade preferences, and for the ACP countries also other privileges, have over time eroded as the EU sought to improve its leverage. Siles-Brügge argues that "the GSP reform appears to be driven by commercial interests to which developmental considerations have been subordinated", thus blurring the differences between *developmental* trade policy-making (e.g. ACP countries) and *commercial* trade policy-making (e.g. emerging economies).[41] The GSP reform "is thus a stark reminder of the problems associated with the entwinement of commercial and developmental trade policy already brought to the fore by the previous controversy surrounding the EPA negotiations".[42]

Among the external factors behind the EU's changing approach to the trade-development nexus are in particular the global power shifts, but also the sluggishness of the Doha Round negotiations, the expiry of the WTO waiver and the adoption of the SDG s. In the past few years, EU trade policy has increasingly come to reflect the insight that "the notion of 'developing countries' as a group is losing relevance".[43] With the EPA s the 'one-size-fits-all' arrangement for the big and heterogeneous ACP group has been abandoned, and the non-LDC s have been facing more ambitious demands from the EU. Differentiation also took place in the reform of the EU's Generalised System of Preferences.

These changes have led to more reciprocity in the EU's trade relations with different groups of developing countries. The degree of reciprocity and the comprehensiveness of FTA s thereby tends to vary with the level of economic development. Moreover, the GSP is no longer the safe fallback position for all self-declared developing countries which are not willing to sign an FTA with the EU. The LDC s can rely on the EBA as long as the UN classifies them as such, and other developing countries may benefit from the GSP(+) as long as they fulfil all the criteria set by the EU. Table 15.3 summarises the findings.

Despite many changes, trade policy tends to be mainly driven by commercial interests, while development policy primarily aims to eradicate poverty. This has led some scholars to argue that EU trade policy falls short of being an effective and coherent tool of foreign policy whose multiple policy

---

41   G. Siles-Brügge (n. 36), p. 50.
42   *Ibid*, p. 59.
43   European Commission, 'Trade, Growth and Development: Tailoring Trade and Investment Policy for those Countries most in Need', COM (2012) 22, 27 January 2012, p. 2.

TABLE 15.3   Summary of changes in the EU's trade-development nexus management

Case criteria	EU-ACP relations	GSP reform
Form	shift from 'one-size-fits-all' to several EPA s (and in future three regional partnerships)	new powers for European Parliament and Commission in shaping resp. implementing GSP regulation
Contents	shift from non-reciprocal trade in goods to reciprocal and comprehensive trade	exclude competitive GSP beneficiaries, facilitate GSP+ entry, no change in EBA
Partners	EPA s with regional groups	fewer beneficiaries with focus on those 'most in need'
Impact	'privilege erosion', patchwork of trade relations, limited effectiveness	shift from generalised to rather select system to counter preference erosion, push to conclude FTA s, limited effectiveness

subsystems come with different constellations of societal and policy-makers' preferences and institutions.[44] The quest for horizontal coherence regarding the trade-development nexus remains a challenge; institutional coherence is still confronted with problems of compartmentalisation; and for non-exclusive competences like development policy vertical coherence between the EU and the Member States adds an additional layer to the nexus.

Acknowledgement

The author would like to thank the participants of the conference "Law and Practice of the Common Commercial Policy: The First 10 Years after the Treaty of Lisbon" (CEPS, Brussels, 7–8 June 2018) for their valuable feedback.

44   A. R. Young, J. Peterson (n. 1).

CHAPTER 16

The Nexus between the CCP and the CFSP

Tamara Perišin and Sam Koplewicz

1   Introduction

In the light of the first ten years of the entry into force of the Treaty of Lisbon, this chapter aims to examine the relationship between two dimensions of the European Union's (EU) external relations – the economic dimension as expressed through the Common Commercial Policy (CCP), and the security one embodying the Common Foreign and Security Policy (CFSP), as well as some other measures taken by the EU or its Member States.

One of the main aims of the Treaty of Lisbon in respect of external relations was to make EU action more coherent (consistent)[1] and effective.[2] However, even after the Treaty of Lisbon, EU external relations remain divided into a number of categories, each involving different decision-makers (i.e. EU institutions and Member States) and different processes, including different voting rules. Roughly speaking, in the CCP, the EU might seem more united because this falls within its exclusive competences,[3] with a significant role attributed to all its institutions, including the Council, the Commission, the Parliament and the Court. The Council votes in principle with a qualified majority, so a single Member State cannot easily disrupt Union action. In the CFSP, the European Council and the Council have a leading role while the voting rule is in principle unanimity so the interests of a single Member State affect what the Union as a whole can achieve. In addition, the Court's review is limited.[4] It is for these

---

1   On the difference between coherence and consistency in this context, see C. Hillion, 'Tous pour un, un pour tous!' Coherence in the External Relations of the European Union', in M. Cremona (ed.), *Developments in EU External Relations Law* (OUP, 2008), p. 12 -29.

2   See Communication from the Commission to the European Council of June 2006: Europe in the World – Some Practical Proposals for Greater Coherence, Effectiveness and Visibility, COM (2006) 278 final, 8 June 2016. See also on this M. Cremona, 'Coherence through Law: What Difference Will the Treaty of Lisbon Make?' *Hamburg Review of Social Sciences* 3(1) (2008), p. 13–17.

3   Art. 3 TFEU.

4   On the scope of judicial review over the CFSP, see C. Hillion, R. Wessel, 'The Good the Bad and the Ugly': Three Levels of Judicial Control over the CFSP', in S. Blockmans, P. Koutrakos (eds.), *Research Handbook on EU Common Foreign and Security Policy*; (Edward Elgar Publishing, 2018), p. 91–98.

reasons that EU policies and rules are often just a snapshot of the current balance of power and interests, and not necessarily part of one consistent external policy. This becomes problematic in situations where it would be good for the EU to act in a consistent and united way in the external sphere. For example, when the former EU Trade Commissioner, Cecilia Malmström, reacted to the US imposition of tariffs on EU goods, she stated: "When they say American first, we say Europe united".[5] However, the set-up of the EU's external policies that resembles a patchwork of many different competences and legal bases in reality makes "united" action quite difficult.

This chapter first examines three sets of issues bordering between the CCP and CFSP (2): trade in dual-use items (2.1), arms trade (2.2), and restrictive measures (2.3). This is followed by a case study on the EU's relations with Iran (3), focusing on the developments that happened in 2018 related to the Joint Comprehensive Plan of Action. Finally, some concluding remarks are formulated (4).

2 EU Rules in Sectors on the Borderline between Trade and Security

Before going into the specific regimes dealing with dual use items, arms trade and restrictive measures, two issues are especially worth highlighting. The first issue is consistency. Article 21(3) TEU in its second subparagraph provides that:

> [t]he Union shall ensure consistency between the different areas of its external action and between these and its other policies. The Council and the Commission, assisted by the High Representative of the Union for Foreign Affairs and Security Policy shall ensure that consistency and shall cooperate to that effect.

However, achieving consistency between the EU's trade agenda and its foreign and security policy is challenging.[6] Due to variance in EU foreign policy agendas and economic realities of the Member States, the EU may advocate for an

---

5 Speech of Commissioner Malmström available at https://twitter.com/nbcnews/status/1002605269141086210?lang=en on 10 Dec 2018.! (Brussels, 1 June, 2018).
6 On the balance between the CCP objectives and the general objectives of Art. 21 TEU, see C. Kaddous, 'The Transformation of the EU's Common Commercial Policy', in P. Eeckhout, M. Lopez-Escudero (eds.), *The European Union's External Action in Times of Crisis* (Hart Publishing, 2016), p. 440–444.

arms embargo on a third country while several of its Member States continue to provide significant amount of arms to that state.

The second issue relates to the legal limits between the CFSP and other EU competences. Article 40 TEU (ex Article 47 TEU) provides for a *non-affect clause* under which the implementation of the CFSP must not affect the procedures and powers of EU institutions exercising other Union competences (listed in Articles 3 to 6 TFEU), and *vice versa*. This clause prevents the Council, i.e. the Member States acting unanimously, from using a CFSP legal basis to circumvent the competences that EU institutions have under the TFEU (and *vice versa*). It is also worth recalling that the Member States are also limited in pursuing their security policies individually if the matter lies in the field of the CCP. This was made clear in the *Centro-Com* case concerning sanctions on Serbia and Montenegro where the Court found that the UK was limited in adopting an additional security measure which went beyond Community law in the field.[7]

2.1   *EU Rules on Dual-use Items*

Dual use items are goods, software and technology that "can be used for both civil and military purposes".[8] It is nowadays considered that trade in dual use items falls under the CCP as will be seen below.

Historically, however, trade in dual use items has been seen as a matter that also partly falls within the CFSP. Thus, trade in such items was regulated by two measures – one adopted on the basis of the CCP, i.e. Regulation 3381/94,[9] and another one adopted within the CFSP, i.e. Council Decision 94/942/CFSP.[10] The regime changed in response to the Court's case law on dual use goods where the main issue was the balance between, on the one hand, the free movement of goods and trade, and security, on the other hand. For example,

---

7   Case C-124/95, *The Queen, ex parte Centro-Com Srl v HM Treasury and Bank of England*, EU:C:1997:8.

8   Article 2(1) Council Regulation (EC) No 428/2009 of 5 May 2009 setting up a Community regime for the control of exports, transfer, brokering and transit of dual-use items (OJ 2009, L 134/1).

9   Council Regulation (EC) No 3381/94 of 19 December 1994 setting up a Community regime for the control of exports of dual-use goods (OJ 1994, L 367/1) (no longer in force).

10   Council Decision 94/942/CFSP of 19 December 1994 on the joint action adopted by the Council on the basis of Article J.3 of the Treaty on European Union concerning the control of exports of dual-use goods (OJ 1994, L 367/8). See on this point P. Koutrakos, 'Security and Defence Policy within the Context of EU External Relations: Issues of Coherence, Consistency and Effectiveness', in M. Trybus, N. White (eds.), *European Security Law* (OUP, 2007), p. 256.

in the *Richardt* case, Luxembourg required a special licence for certain goods that were transiting through its territory from France to the Soviet Union and which could have been used for strategic purposes.[11] The goods were accompanied by relevant documents issued by the French authorities, and the issue was whether Luxembourg's requirement of an additional licence was compatible with Regulation 222/77 on Community transit.[12] The case is relevant because the Court held that this Regulation applied not only to ordinary goods, but also to goods of a strategic nature such as those that were at issue in the case.[13] However, the Court also found that it was possible for a Member State to invoke justifications for restrictions to the free movement of goods listed in what is now Article 36 TFEU (then Article 36 EEC Treaty).[14] As the public security exception under Article 36 EEC applied equally to internal and external security,[15] it was possible for Luxembourg to justify the special authorisation and licence procedure applied to the strategic goods. The proportionality analysis was left to the national court.[16] The two following cases, *Werner*[17] and *Leifer*,[18] decided on the same day, did not concern transit licences as did *Richardt*, but export licences that Germany imposed on the export of dual use goods. In the proceedings before the national court, the parties argued that this was contrary to the principle of free exportation embodied in the Export Regulation.[19] The main issue was whether a Member State can impose restrictions on the export of such goods to third countries or whether it is precluded from doing so because the CCP falls under the exclusive competences of the European Community (now Union). The Court was asked to clarify "whether the common commercial policy solely concerns measures which pursue commercial objectives, or whether it also covers commercial measures having foreign policy and security objectives".[20] It was held that the CCP must be interpreted broadly and that its uniform application mandates that Member States cannot be free to decide whether a matter is covered by the CCP or not on the basis of their own

---

11   Case C-367/89, *Richardt*, EU:C:1991:376.
12   Council Regulation (EEC) No 222/77 of 13 December 1976 on Community transit (OJ 1977, L 38/1).
13   *Richardt* (n. 11) para. 8, 11.
14   *Ibid.*, para. 19–23.
15   *Ibid.*, para. 22.
16   *Ibid.*, para. 25.
17   Case C-70/94, *Werner*, EU:C:1995:328.
18   Case C-83/94, *Leifer*, EU:C:1995:329.
19   Regulation (EEC) No 2603/69 of the Council of 20 December 1969 establishing common rules for exports (OJ 1969, L 324/25), no longer in force.
20   *Werner* (n. 17), para. 10.

foreign policy and security policies.[21] This did not mean that Germany was prevented from imposing export restrictions, but merely that such restrictions could only be adopted if they were in accordance with Community legislation in the field. The relevant legislation, Article 11 of the Export Regulation, provided for exceptions, i.e. Member States were allowed to adopt export restrictions on grounds of public security. Thus, the Court left it to the national court to decide whether the facts of the case came under this exception.[22] It did point out "that the exportation of goods capable of being used for military purposes to a country at war with another country may affect [...] public security".[23]

Due to this case law on dual use goods, Community secondary law in the field changed. It had become possible to regulate dual use goods solely on the basis of the CCP. In 2000, a new Regulation 1334/2000[24] was thus adopted on the basis of the CCP, and later so was Regulation 428/2009 which is currently in force.

For the purposes of this chapter, it is relevant to note that the Dual-Use Items Regulation puts in place common export control rules, and a common EU list of dual-use items. However, Member States are still permitted to adopt their own export rules on the grounds of security or human rights considerations. This can lead to a situation where States have different export regimes for certain dual use items, especially in the case of quickly developing technologies (e.g. cyber-surveillance) where codification at the EU level is too slow. For example, it has been reported that out of "[m]ore than 300 export licenses for surveillance technology [that] were granted in the EU between 2014 and 2016, 30% were for goods destined for countries the watchdog organization Freedom House has deemed 'not free' ".[25] This is an example of a situation where the practical life of the CCP in the context of commerce in dual use items is inconsistent with the EU's foreign or security objectives.

2.2   EU Rules on Arms Trade

The Treaties have a special provision concerning arms trade, Article 346 TFEU (ex Article 296 TEC), according to which a Member State is not prevented by the Treaties from taking measures which "it considers necessary for the

---

21   *Ibid.,* para. 8–11.

22   *Ibid.,* para. 28.

23   *Ibid.*

24   Council Regulation (EC) No 1334/2000 of 22 June 2000 setting up a Community regime for the control of exports of dual-use items and technology (OJ 2000, L 159/1).

25   M. Goslinga, D. Tokmetzis, 'The Surveillance Industry Still Sells to Repressive Regimes. Here's What Europe Can Do about It', *de Correspondent,* 23 February 2017.

protection of the essential interests of its security which are connected with the production of or trade in arms, munitions and war material" as long as those "measures [do] not adversely affect the conditions of competition in the internal market regarding products which are not intended for specifically military purposes".[26] And the Council acting unanimously and on the proposal of the Commission can update the list of products to which this applies.[27] Due to this special provision, arms trade has for a long time been seen as related solely to the CFSP, and not to the CCP.[28]

However, since the negotiation of the Arms Trade Treaty (ATT), it has also been recognised that arms trade is linked to the CCP and to the internal market. The ATT has been adopted as a UN Resolution[29] and then opened for signature to states, so the parties are EU Member States (and not the EU). However, since some of the aspects of the ATT fall within EU exclusive competence (Article 3(2) TFEU), Member States needed the Council's permission to conclude this agreement, and the Council gives this permission on the basis of the Commission's proposal. The fact that the ATT covers parts of the EU's exclusive competence in the CCP is explicitly mentioned in the Explanatory Memorandum accompanying the Council Decision authorising Member States to sign, in the interests of the Union, the ATT.[30] This means that the link between commerce and security is now also recognised in respect of arms trade.

Currently, a major issue regarding arms trade in which one can see the interplay between the interest of trade and security is the sales of weapons to countries allegedly endangering international security. For example, several EU Member States are continuing to export arms to Saudi Arabia despite reports suggesting that those weapons are being used in the conflict in Yemen where there have been grave violations of human rights, civilian victims, outbreaks of cholera, etc. The UK seems to be the largest exporter of arms to Saudi Arabia,[31]

---

26   Art. 346 TFEU (ex Art. 296(1)b TEC).

27   Art. 346 TFEU (ex Art. 296(2) TEC).

28   See on this point, e.g., Q. Michel, 'Arms Trade Exception to the EU Common Commercial Policy: A Soft Law Exception to a Hard Law Principle' (available at: http://www.esu.ulg. ac.be/file/20140209183637_Exception-to-the-EU-Common-Commercial-Policy-rev.pdf.

29   United Nations Resolution 67/234 adopted by the General Assembly on 2 April 2013, The Arms Trade Treaty, A/RES/67/234 B, 18 February 2019.

30   European Commission, 'Proposal for a Council Decision authorising Member States to ratify, in the interests of the European Union, the Arms Trade Treaty', COM (2013) 482 final, 6 June 2013. This proposal led to the adoption of Council Decision 2013/269/CFSP of 27 May 2013 authorising Member States to sign, in the interests of the European Union, the Arms Trade Treaty (OJ 2013, L 155/9).

31   E. Beswick, 'Which EU Countries Sell Arms to Saudi Arabia?', Euronews, 30 November 2018.

but some other Member States are also exporters (e.g. France, Germany, Italy, Croatia,[32] Greece[33]).

The European Parliament has recently urged for an EU-wide arms embargo in respect of Saudi Arabia.[34] The Parliament's Resolution "[c]alls on the Council to reach a common position in order to impose an Union-wide arms embargo on Saudi Arabia and to respect Common Position 2008/944/CFSP; calls for an embargo on the export of surveillance systems and other dual-use items that may be used in Saudi Arabia for the purposes of repression".[35] Thus, while trade can be a way of fostering security (since economic cooperation brings stability, mutual dependence, and the raising of the average standard of living), one can again observe how particular commercial interests can go against international security. It can also be seen that the EU may be unable to achieve consistency in its external policies.

2.3   EU Rules on Restrictive Measures

Restrictive measures are a type of sanctions that the Union can adopt against a third country or against natural or legal persons.[36] They can involve "interruption or reduction, in part or completely, of economic and financial relations",[37] so they are connected both to commerce and to foreign and security policy. The Treaties contain special legal bases for their adoption.

Typically, restrictive measures are adopted through two steps.[38] The first step is the adoption of a CFSP decision which presupposes the unanimity of Member States.[39] In the second step, provided for by Article 215 TFEU, the

---

32   *Ibid.*

33   'Athens Would Abide by EU Sanctions on Saudi Arabia, Spokesman Says', *Ekathimerini*, 29 November 2018.

34   See European Parliament resolution of 25 October 2018 on the killing of journalist Jamal Khashoggi in the Saudi consulate in Istanbul (2018/2885(RSP)). See also European Parliament, 'MEPs condemn attacks on civilians, including children, in Yemen', Press Release, 4 October 2018.

35   European Parliament, (n. 34), at 14.

36   For a detailed analysis of restrictive measures after the Treaty of Lisbon see e.g. C. Eckes, 'EU Restrictive Measures against Natural and Legal Persons: From Counterterrorist to Third Country Sanctions', *CMLRev* 51(3) (2014), p. 869–905.

37   Art. 215(1) TFEU.

38   On the relationship between the two-step procedure provided for in Art. 215 TFEU and the fact that Art. 21(2) TEU lists economic, security, environmental, humanitarian and other aims of EU external actions, see E. Cannizzaro, 'The EU Antiterrorist Sanctions', in P. Eeckhout, M. Lopez-Escudero (eds.), *The European Union's External Action in Times of Crises* (Hart, 2016), p.531–537.

39   Art. 31 TEU.

Council can adopt "necessary measures" against a third country (Article 215(1) TFEU) or against natural or legal persons (Article 215(2) TFEU). Here the Council acts on the basis of a qualified majority, and on the joint proposal of the Commission and the High Representative, and it must inform the European Parliament about the taken measures.

The Treaty of Lisbon also introduced a special legal basis, Article 75 TFEU, for the adoption of counter-terrorist financial sanctions. Measures founded on this legal basis are adopted through the ordinary legislative procedure, involving co-decision making of the Council and the Parliament (and not merely informing the Parliament as under Article 215 TFEU). In *Parliament v. Council*, the Parliament challenged the Regulation on restrictive measures directed against persons and entities associated with Usama bin Laden, the Al-Qaeda network and the Taliban, considering, inter alia, that the measure was wrongly based on Article 215 TFEU and that Article 75 TFEU should have been used instead.[40] The Court rejected this argument and upheld a broader interpretation of Article 215 under which this provision can be used in the fight against terrorism, even for the freezing of assets. The fact that the Parliament has different powers under two legal bases is only relevant in cases where both legal bases are used, so then the procedure giving more power to the Parliament ought to be used.[41] In contrast, the Court found that in this situation the framers of the Treaty deliberately opted for the lesser involvement of Parliament.[42]

It is especially worth noting that restrictive measures are the only substantive part of the CFSP over which the Court has been explicitly granted jurisdiction (alongside the general clause that it observes the application of Article 40 TEU).[43] The Court's jurisdiction is limited to the review of legality of Council decisions providing for restrictive measures against natural or legal persons.[44] Before the Treaty of Lisbon, restrictive measures against individuals could only be based on Article 308 TEC (which was the broadest competence allowing for measures to be taken in the absence of a specific legal basis, although subject to certain conditions).[45] When the Treaty of Lisbon introduced the special provision allowing for restrictive measures against individuals (Article 215(2) TFEU), it also introduced a special provision allowing these persons to challenge such measures (Article 275(2) TFEU), subject to the general rules on the

---

40   Case C-130/10, *Parliament v. Council,* EU:C:2012:472.

41   Case C-300/89, *Commission v. Council (Titanium Dioxide)*, EU:C:1991:244.

42   *Parliament v. Council* (n. 41), para. 82.

43   Art. 275 TFEU.

44   Art. 275(2) TFEU.

45   Art. 308 TEC (ex Art. 235 TEC pre-Treaty of Amsterdam).

standing of individuals.[46] At first instance, these cases are handled by the General Court, with the possibility of an appeal to the Court of Justice. The Court is also able to award material and immaterial damages to persons whose rights have been breached in the process of adopting restrictive measures (under the general conditions for Union liability for damages, as, for example, in *Safa Nicu Sepahan*).[47] Furthermore, in *Rosneft*, the Court found that it had jurisdiction to review legality of restrictive measures not only in direct actions, but also in the preliminary reference procedure[48] (according to the *Foto-Frost* doctrine[49]). In *Rosneft*, the Court found that it can review both a regulation adopted on the basis of Article 215 TFEU as well as the Council's CFSP decision.

This broadens the scrutiny of the Court over CFSP measures in a way which contributes to the coherence of EU action. This is particularly so because in practice adopting, maintaining, and modifying restrictive measures are also connected with other EU policies, even a commercial one (as, for example, in the cases of sanctions against Côte d'Ivoire[50] or Russia[51]). A case study on Iran will show that the EU can have an economic and security interest in keeping some, while lifting other, restrictive measures against the same third country.

3   Case Study: EU Relations with Iran

This brief case study intends to show how complex the EU's external relations are. In the fabric of external relations, economic and security threads are thickly interwoven, and the relations with one third country are dependent on the relations with another. Thus, analysing any situation is not only an analysis of

---

46   See e.g. Case T-715/14, *Rosneft*, EU:T:2018:544.

47   *Safa Nicu Sepahan* was the first case on restrictive measures where the General Court awarded damages (Case T-384/11, *Safa Nicu Sepahan* v. *Council*,EU:T:2014:986), but this was not upheld by the Court on appeal (Case C-45/15 P, *Safa Nicu Sepahan* v. *Council*, EU:C:2017:402).

48   Case C-72/15, *Rosneft*, EU:C:2017:236.

49   Case C-314/85, *Foto-Frost*, EU:C:1987:452.

50   See e.g. F. Hoffmeister's example of EU sanctions against Côte d'Ivoire, in F. Hoffmeister, 'The European Union's Common Commercial Policy a Year after Lisbon – Sea Change or Business as Usual?' in P. Koutrakos, *The European Union's External Relations a Year after Lisbon, CLEER Working Papers* 2011/3, p. 89.

51   See e.g. in F. Hoffmeister, 'Of Presidents, High Representatives and European Commissioners: The External Representation of the European Union Seven Years after Lisbon Making Transnational Markets: The Institutional Politics behind the TTIP", *Europe and the World* 1(1) (2017,), pp. 1–46, p. 23–32.

the interaction between economic aims and security aims, or CCP and CFSP, but there is also a much broader plethora of issues.[52]

The EU's relations with Iran mainly concerned the so-called Iran deal. This is the Joint Comprehensive Plan of Action (JCPOA), adopted in July 2015.[53] Under this deal, the EU lifted all nuclear-related economic and financial sanctions on Iran, starting from 16 January 2016. The political deal was reached between, on the one hand, the Islamic Republic of Iran, and, on the other hand, the group called "E3/EU+3", composed of three EU Member States – Germany, France and the United Kingdom, and three third countries – the United States of America, Russia and China.[54] The JCPOA states that the E3/EU+3 states were "with" the EU High Representative for Foreign and Security Policy.[55] Here we see the complex nature of Member States acting both on their own accord and simultaneously in coordination with a separate entity of which they are a part. The UN Security Council endorsed the JCPOA through a Resolution on 20 July 2015.[56] On 31 July, the Council adopted a Decision and a Regulation de facto turning the JCPOA into EU law, i.e. lifting some of the earlier restrictions.[57]

The EU's relations with Iran became more complex in May 2018 when the United States pulled out of the Iran deal claiming that the deal was not working, i.e. that Iran was violating it. By contrast, the official position has been that the deal has to be maintained for both security and economic reasons. However, for Iran, the deal became significantly less attractive once the US was no longer committed to it as it lost the economic benefits of US partnership and became subject to US sanctions. The EU thus had to find ways of compensating Iran for the economic loss that it sustained due to US withdrawal from the deal.

At the same time, the Union has continuously kept and wants to maintain a number of other "proliferation-related sanctions and restrictions".[58]

---

52 For more examples on the interaction between the CCP and other EU external policies, see F. Hoffmeister, (n. 51).

53 Joint Comprehensive Plan of Action, Vienna, 14 July 2015. On the JCPOA negotiating history and the EU's representation, see F. Hoffmeister (n. 51), p. 18–23.

54 See JCPOA (n. 53), p. 2.

55 Ibid.

56 Resolution 2231 (2015), Adopted by the Security Council at its 7488th meeting, on 20 July 2015.

57 Council Decision (CFSP) 2015/1336 of 31 July 2015 amending Decision 2010/413/CFSP concerning restrictive measures against Iran (OJ 2015, L 206/66); Council Regulation (EU) 2015/1327 of 31 July 2015 amending Regulation (EU) No 267/2012 concerning restrictive measures against Iran (OJ 2015, L 206/18).

58 Citations taken from the official EU website https://eeas.europa.eu/delegations/iran/44232/cooperation-between-eu-and-iran_en, last consulted at 18 February 2019.

The EU thus offered Iran several types of measures that were jointly proposed by the Commission president and the High Representative, and "[f]ollowing the unanimous backing of EU Heads of State or Government at the leaders' informal meeting in Sofia".[59]

One of these EU measure aimed at tackling the negative effects of the US withdrawal from the JCPOA by allowing the European Investment Bank (EIB) to finance activities in Iran. This also borders between economic interests and security, but the legal basis for the relevant measures[60] is Article 209 TFEU (development cooperation) and Article 212 TFEU (economic, financial and technical cooperation with third countries), thus avoiding a CCP or CFSP legal basis. On the basis of secondary law, the EU grants the European Investment Bank a budgetary guarantee for financing operations carried out outside the Union

---

59   European Commission, 'European Commission Acts to Protect the Interests of EU Companies Investing in Iran as Part of the EU's Continued Commitment to the Joint Comprehensive Plan of Action', Press Release, 18 May 2018. Legally, the most interesting one is the EU Blocking Regulation that has been amended so that it would also cover US sanctions on Iran. This measure was originally adopted in 1996 to tackle the negative effects of US sanctions on Cuba, Libya and Iran. It was adopted on three legal bases: the CCP (ex Article 113 TEC), restrictions on the movement of capital to third countries (ex Article 73c TEC), and the flexibility clause (ex Article 235 TEC). The Regulation "provides protection against and counteracts the effects of the extra-territorial application of the laws specified in the Annex [...] where such application affects the interests of [European Union] persons [...] engaging in international trade and/or the movement of capital and related commercial activities between the Community and third countries". In principle, it forbids EU persons from complying with US extraterritorial sanctions (except exceptionally when authorised under special procedures to comply fully or partially to the extent that non-compliance would seriously damage their interests or those of the EU). EU persons must notify the Commission of any effects on their economic and/or financial interests caused by a measure blocked in the Annex. The Regulation also nullifies the effect in the EU of any foreign court judgments based on them as these cannot be enforced in the EU. Further, it contains a "clawback" measure allowing persons to recover damages arising from such sanctions from the person causing them. Finally, it requires each Member State to determine effective, proportional and dissuasive sanctions for breaches of the Blocking Regulation. The new Blocking Regulation entered into force on 7 August 2018, when US sanctions started taking effect. It is accompanied by an Implementing Regulation and a Guidance Note.

60   Decision No 466/2014/EU of the European Parliament and of the Council of 16 April 2014 granting an EU guarantee to the European Investment Bank against losses under financing operations supporting investment projects outside the Union (OJ 2014, L 135/1); Decision (EU) 2018/412 of the European Parliament and of the Council of 14 March 2018 amending Decision No 466/2014/EU granting an EU guarantee to the European Investment Bank against losses under financing operations supporting investment projects outside the Union (OJ 2018, L 76/30).

in eligible countries.[61] In order for a country to become an "eligible country", the Council and the Parliament need to add a country to the list of "potentially eligible regions and countries", and this was done in respect of Iran in March 2018.[62] Then the Commission is authorised to amend the list of "eligible countries" in a way that it can move a third country from the list of "potentially eligible" to the list of "eligible" countries.[63] The Commission does this in the form of a delegated act.[64] The Commission adopted the Delegated Decision adding Iran to the list of eligible countries in May 2018.[65]

In addition, the EU has undertaken many other measures seeking to support Iran, including strengthening "the ongoing sectoral cooperation with, and assistance to, Iran, including in the energy sector and with regard to small and medium-sized companies",[66] and "encouraging Member States to explore the possibility of one-off bank transfers to the Central Bank of Iran".[67] Furthermore, some EU Member States are also finding ways to boost trade with Iran and circumvent US sanctions. For example, recently France, Germany and the UK have set up INSTEX (Instrument for Supporting Trade Exchanges) with the support from the EU.[68] The idea is that there would be no financial transfers between the EU and Iran.[69] Instead of an EU exporter receiving money from an Iranian purchaser and an EU importer paying money to the Iranian exporter, there would be exchanges only within the EU and within Iran.[70] The exchange would take place within the EU between the banks of an EU importer and exporter, and similarly within Iran between the Iranian importer and exporter.[71]

All these measures highlight the interplay between the CCP and security issues. If the EU sees a security threat, it will adopt restrictive measures – and in

---

61   Ibid.
62   Annex II of Decision 2018/412 (n. 71).
63   Art. 4 Decision No 466/2014/EU (n. 71).
64   *Ibid.*
65   Commission Delegated Decision (EU) 2018/1102 of 6 June 2018 amending Annex III to Decision No 466/2014/EU of the European Parliament and of the Council granting an EU guarantee to the European Investment Bank against losses under financing operations supporting investment projects outside the Union, as regards Iran (OJ 2018, L 199/11).
66   European Commission, 'European Commission Acts to Protect the Interests of EU Companies Investing in Iran as Part of the EU's Continued Commitment to the Joint Comprehensive Plan of Action', Press Release, 18 May 2018.
67   *Ibid.*
68   Statement by High Representative/Vice-President Federica Mogherini on the creation of INSTEX, Instrument for Supporting Trade Exchanges, Brussels, 31 January 2019.
69   Euractiv, 'Le troc UE-Iran en place pour contrer les sanctions américaines', 1 February 2019.
70   *Ibid.*
71   *Ibid.*

fact it still has a number of these in force for Iran. If its own NATO ally, the US, sees a security threat in keeping the Iran deal, while the EU assesses that the security interest is to keep the Iran deal in place, it will then adopt measures which are partly based on the CCP to nullify the effects of US sanctions.

4   Conclusion

The chapter has illustrated that the EU's competences and decision-making procedures for the CCP and the CFSP are still significantly different, jeopardising the coherence in the Union's external action.

We can see that the EU's external action greatly depends on the balance of power between the Union and its Member States and interinstitutional developments. The Court, the Commission and Parliament seek to play a greater role in all security issues that also touch upon trade. The Court has interpreted the balance between the internal market and the CCP on the one hand and the CFSP on the other hand in a way that an increasing number of situations have been covered by the former category.[72] It has also interpreted its own jurisdiction so as to cover the review of legality of CFSP decisions on restrictive measures in preliminary reference procedures.[73] The Commission has been keen for arms trade to stop being seen as exclusively a part of the CFSP. As a consequence, the Council has recognised that the Arms Trade Treaty is linked to the CCP and that it also has implications for the Internal Market.[74] The Parliament has been attempting to exert pressure on the High Representative to propose an arms embargo on Saudi Arabia.

Furthermore, EU action depends on the balance of power between different types of Member States. For example, the balance of power between the *centre v. the periphery* or perhaps between *big v. small* states can be seen from the fact that the Iran deal was negotiated by only three Member States, namely Germany, France and the UK, supported by the High Representative. After the deal was struck, and endorsed through the US Resolution, the Council unanimously adopted the CFSP decision; and then withdrew restrictive measures in a Regulation based on Article 215. The relevance of the balance of power between arms-producing countries and others can be seen from the fact that due to the UK's significant export of arms to Saudi Arabia it is likely that it would block any proposal for an arms embargo.

---

72   E.g. *Richardt* (n. 11), *Werner* (n. 17).

73   *Rosneft* (n. 48).

74   See the Explanatory Memorandum in the Proposal for a Council Decision (n. 30).

Consequently, in cases where external relations are most complex, such as the relations with Iran, EU action depends on a large amount of political will at so many different levels that fast and consistent action is difficult. So, Iran is in many ways the EU's partner in which it wants to invest. But at the same time the EU keeps in place its own restrictive measures against Iran. Achieving consistency in these actions is very difficult, and in areas where unanimity is the voting rule, any Member State can prevent consistent Union action.

CHAPTER 17

The Nexus between the Common Commercial Policy and Human Rights

Implications of the Lisbon Treaty

Peter Van Elsuwege

1 Introduction

The use of trade instruments for the promotion of non-trade objectives, including respect for human rights, pre-dates the entry into force of the Lisbon Treaty.[1] Typical examples concern the inclusion of so-called "essential element clauses" in bilateral trade agreements,[2] the application of human rights conditionality within the context of the EU's system of generalised preferences for developing countries (GSP+)[3] and the establishment of human rights dialogues as part of the broader framework of bilateral relations with third countries.[4] Whereas the EU's common commercial policy (CCP) has thus never been *apolitical*, the Lisbon Treaty strengthened the link between trade and human rights in several aspects.

First, the nexus between CCP and human rights is now firmly anchored in the EU's primary law. Of particular significance is the provision in Article 207 TFEU that "[t]he common commercial policy shall be conducted in the context of the principles and objectives of the Union's external action". The latter, enshrined in Articles 3 (5) and 21 TEU, explicitly refer to respect for and

---

1 It is noteworthy that the early case law of the ECJ already confirmed that non-economic objectives could fall within the scope of the CCP. See e.g. Opinion 1/78 *Natural Rubber*, EU:C:1979:224; Case C-45/86, *Tariff Preferences*, EU:C:1987:163, para. 19–20; Case C-70/94, *Werner*, EU:C:1995:328, para. 10; Case C-124/95, *Centro Com*, EU:C:1997:8.

2 Communication from the Commission on the inclusion of respect for democratic principles and human rights in agreements between the Community and third countries, COM (95) 216 final, 23 May 1995.

3 S. Velluti, 'Human Rights Conditionality in the EU GSP Scheme: A Focus on Those in Need or a Need to Refocus?', in N. Ferreira and D. Kostakopoulou (eds.), *The Human Face of the European Union. Are EU Law and Policy Humane Enough?* (CUP, 2016), p. 342–366. The EU's GSP scheme is discussed in the chapter by Sieglinde Gstöhl in this volume.

4 Guidelines on human rights dialogues with third countries: https://eeas.europa.eu/headquarters/headquarters-homepage_en/6987/EU%20Human%20rights%20guidelines.

© KONINKLIJKE BRILL NV, LEIDEN, 2021 | DOI:10.1163/9789004393417_019

promotion of human rights. Even though the precise meaning of the partly overlapping provisions may be subject to discussion, it is obvious that the integration of human rights in EU external trade relations is a constitutional obligation and not a mere policy choice.

Second, the Lisbon Treaty shifted the institutional balance in the CCP. In particular, the European Parliament acquired the power to give or withhold consent to trade agreements (Article 218 (6) (a) TFEU) whereas it only used to be consulted on trade deals in the past. Moreover, the Parliament is to be kept informed about the progress of trade negotiations (Article 207 (3) TFEU) and acts as a co-legislator with the Council under the ordinary legislative procedure for the adoption of measures defining the framework for implementing the CCP.[5] On several occasions, the European Parliament underlined its ambition to safeguard the strong connection between trade and human rights in the conduct of its activities.[6]

Third, the integration of the EU Charter of Fundamental Rights in EU primary law strengthened the EU's commitment to the protection of human rights. In this respect, it is noteworthy that the term "fundamental rights" is used within the specific context of the EU legal order whereas the term "human rights" derives from international law. However, there is a significant overlap in terms of substance as can be derived from a comparison between the content of the Charter and the core UN conventions on human rights.[7] Moreover, as can be derived from Article 6 TEU, the protection of fundamental rights in the EU legal order consists of different, partly overlapping, layers including the Charter of Fundamental Rights, the European Convention for the Protection of Human Rights and Fundamental Freedoms and the constitutional traditions common to the Member States.

The aim of the contribution is to analyse the impact of the identified normative changes for the law and practice of the CCP in the post-Lisbon era. After an analysis of the evolution of the general policy framework, in particular as far as the introduction of human rights impact assessments is concerned, the

---

5   On the role of the European Parliament in the CCP, see the chapter by Bart Driessen in this volume.

6   See e.g. A7-0312/2010, Report on Human rights and social and environmental standards in international trade agreements. On the role of the European Parliament and its influence on the EU's trade agenda, see also: F. Hoffmeister, 'The European Union as an International Trade Negotiator', in J. Koops and G. Macaj (eds.), *The European Union as a Diplomatic Actor* (Palgrave Macmillan, 2015), p. 144–146.

7   On this terminological distinction, see: European Commission, 'Guidelines on the analysis of human rights impacts in impact assessments for trade-related policy initiatives': http://trade.ec.europa.eu/doclib/docs/2015/july/tradoc_153591.pdf, p. 3.

relevant case law of the Court of Justice will be scrutinised. Particular attention will be devoted to the discussion surrounding the extraterritorial application of the Charter of Fundamental Rights and the legal obligations of the EU institutions in the framework of trade agreements with third countries. Finally, the challenges surrounding the effective enforcement of human rights clauses and social norms in EU Free Trade Agreements will be tackled.

Accordingly, it will be argued that the innovations of the Lisbon Treaty significantly affected the CCP in the sense that human rights considerations have become an integral part of the EU's trade policy. This is reflected both at the procedural level, with the practice of human rights impact assessments as a clear example; at the judicial level, with the Charter of Fundamental Rights as a key point of reference for assessing the legality of the EU's external action; and at the practical level, with the introduction of new initiatives and mechanisms aiming at the promotion of respect for human rights in the framework of the CCP.

2   Policy Impact of the Lisbon Treaty: the Practice of Human Rights Impact Assessments

The constitutionalisation of the trade-human rights nexus significantly affected the EU's policy documents related to the implementation of the CCP. In 2010, the European Commission Communication *Trade, Growth and World Affairs* already emphasised the ambition to use trade policy as an instrument in order "to encourage our partners to promote the respect of human rights, labour standards, the environment and good governance".[8] The subsequent Joint Communication of the European Commission and the EU High Representative for Foreign Affairs and Security Policy, entitled *Human Rights and democracy at the heart of EU external action – towards a more effective approach*, confirmed the "mainstreaming" of human rights and democratisation as a horizontal objective permeating all the EU's actions. This implies, amongst others, that "[t]he human rights situation in the partner country should be considered when the EU decides whether or not to launch or conclude FTA negotiations".[9] The 2012 EU Strategic Framework and Action Plan on Human Rights and Democracy provided the first attempt to operationalise the EU's commitment under Article 3 (5) TEU.[10]

---

8   COM (2010) 612, p. 15.
9   COM (2011) 886, p. 12.
10   Council of the EU, Doc. 11855/12.

The envisaged measures *inter alia* concerned the development of a methodology "to aid consideration of the human rights situation in a third country in connection with the launch or conclusion of free trade and/or investment agreements", the reinforcement of human rights dialogues with FTA partners, the inclusion of human rights considerations in the unfolding EU investment policy and a revision of the CFSP Common Position on arms export and the Regulation on trade in goods which can be used for capital punishment or torture. Subsequent policy documents reiterated and reinforced the values dimension of the EU's trade policy. For instance, the 2015 *Trade for all* strategy explicitly defined the promotion of sustainable development, human rights and good governance as a key pillar of the CCP.[11]

Whereas the Lisbon Treaty thus provided new impetus to the policy framework of the trade-human rights nexus, the implementation of this ambitious framework faced significant legal and political challenges. A good illustration concerns the discussion surrounding the failure of the European Commission to conduct a specific human rights impact assessment (HRIA) in anticipation of the conclusion of a Free Trade Agreement (FTA) with Vietnam. In the Commission's view, a separate HRIA concerning the FTA with Vietnam was unnecessary taking into account that the negotiations with Vietnam were taking place under the legal framework established for the ASEAN free trade negotiations. The latter had started before the entry into force of the Lisbon Treaty. It further argued that a standalone HRIA would be against the established integrated approach, implying that economic, social, environmental and – as of 2011 – human rights impacts are considered side by side. Moreover, the Commission pointed at the existence of other human rights instruments such as human rights clauses in the Partnership and Cooperation Agreement (PCA) with Vietnam, the enhanced human rights dialogue as well as public statements and foreign policy *démarches*.[12] These arguments could not convince the European ombudsman, who concluded that the Commission's refusal to carry out a HRIA constituted an example of maladministration. While acknowledging that "there appears to be no express and specific legally binding requirement to carry out a human rights impact assessment concerning the relevant free trade agreement", she took the view that such an obligation

---

11   European Commission, 'Trade for all. Towards a more responsible trade and investment policy', October 2015: http://trade.ec.europa.eu/doclib/docs/2015/october/tradoc_153846.pdf.

12   European Ombudsman, Decision in case 1409/2014/MHZ on the European Commission's failure to carry out a prior human rights impact assessment of the EU-Vietnam free trade agreement: https://www.ombudsman.europa.eu/en/decision/en/64308, para. 5.

can be derived from the spirit of Article 21 (1) TEU and Article 21 (2) (b) TEU in conjunction with Article 207 TFEU.[13]

The Ombudsman closed her inquiry with a critical remark concerning the Commission's approach without drawing any further conclusions, particularly because the analysis of human rights impacts in impact assessments for trade-related policy initiatives has now become a standard practice. In response to the 2012 Strategic Framework on Human Rights and Democracy (cf. *supra*), DG Trade has developed a set of relevant guidelines for this purpose. Moreover, the Commission's Better Regulation package also includes a specific tool regarding fundamental rights and human rights.[14] In this context, the impact of proposed trade-related policy initiatives is assessed against the normative framework of the EU Charter of Fundamental Rights and a number of international sources. Significantly, the Commission guidelines entail a broad definition of the scope and depth of the analysis, including "the potential impact of the proposed initiative on human rights in both the EU and the partner county/ ies" with respect to "civil, political, economic, social, cultural and core labour rights".[15] Moreover, in the case of negotiations of major trade and investment agreements, Sustainability Impact Assessments (SIAS) are undertaken in parallel with the negotiations and allow the Commission to conduct an extended analysis of the potential human rights impacts. This involves an extensive consultation of stakeholders, including those in the partner country/ies.[16]

Whereas this practice reveals the increased attention to the trade-human rights nexus in the post-Lisbon era, several questions remain concerning the precise implications of the HRIAS for the conduct of the CCP. For instance, the ombudsman firmly stated that "when negative impacts are identified, either the negotiated provisions need to be modified or mitigating measures have to be decided upon before the agreement is entered into".[17] The Commission, on the other hand, does not envisage such far-reaching implications. It rather sees the HRIAS as a tool to inform policy-makers about the potential impacts of the different options under consideration:

> An impact assessment should verify the existence of a problem, identify its underlying causes, assesses whether EU action is needed, and analyse

---

13   *Ibid*, para. 11.
14   See TOOL #28: https://ec.europa.eu/info/better-regulation-toolbox_en.
15   Guidelines on the analysis of human rights impacts in impact assessments for trade-related policy initiatives (n. 7), p. 5.
16   *Ibid*, p. 6.
17   European Ombudsman (n. 12), para. 25.

the advantages and disadvantages of available solutions. *It is not intended to pass a judgment on the actual human rights situation in a country nor to decide whether a country is eligible for a trade agreement.*[18]

In other words, whereas the duty to conduct HRIAS in relation to trade-related policy initiatives may be regarded as a procedural obligation stemming from the combined reading of Article 207 TFEU and Articles 3 (5) TEU and 21 TEU, the substantive obligations are less evident. In particular, the question remains to what extent human rights considerations can be balanced with other interests. May certain negative impacts on human rights be compensated by gains in other areas, for instance the creation of job opportunities thanks to economic growth, or the introduction of cleaner technologies in a country allowing for progress in relation to sustainable development?[19] Arguably, the principle that the EU institutions enjoy a wide margin of discretion in areas which involve political, economic and social choices and in which it is called upon to undertake complex assessments is relevant in this respect.[20] This margin of discretion also applies in the field of external economic relations.[21] It follows that judicial review is limited to the question whether the competent EU institutions made "manifest errors of assessment".[22] As argued by the General Court in the *Frente Polisario* case, this implies that the assessment is to be based on a careful and impartial analysis of all relevant facts of an individual case, with facts supporting the conclusion reached.[23]

3 The Trade-human Rights Nexus before the Court of Justice and the External Dimension of the EU Charter of Fundamental Rights

The EU's duty to take into account fundamental rights when it acts in the area of its external policies, including the CCP, is confirmed in the case law

---

18 Guidelines on the analysis of human rights impacts in impact assessments for trade-related policy initiatives (n. 7), p. 2.

19 O. De Schutter, 'The implementation of the Charter of Fundamental Rights in the EU institutional framework', Study for the AFCO Committee, 2016, p. 60.

20 See e.g. Case C-72/15, *Rosneft*, para. 146; Case C-348/12 P, *Council v Manufacturing Support & Procurement Kala Naft*, EU:C:2013:776, para. 120.

21 See e.g. Case T-572/93, *Odigitria* v *Council and Commission*, EU:T:1995:131, para. 38; Case T-512/12, *Frente Polisario v. Council*, EU:T:2015:953, para. 164.

22 Case T-512/12, *Frente Polisario v. Council*, EU:T:2015:953, para. 224.

23 *Ibid*, para. 225.

of the EU Court of Justice (ECJ). In the *Air Transport Association of America* (*ATAA*) case, the Court derived from Article 3 (5) TEU an obligation for the EU "to observe international law in its entirety, including customary international law".[24] Whereas the precise scope of international customary law in relation to human rights is subject to discussion, the Universal Declaration of Human Rights (UDHR) and the core human rights conventions used for the GSP+ system constitute an important source of reference.[25] Of course, as also observed by the Court in ATAA, "since a principle of customary international law does not have the same precision as a provision of an international agreement, judicial review must necessarily be limited to the question whether, in adopting the act in question, the institutions of the European Union made manifest errors of assessment concerning the conditions for applying those principles".[26]

Hence, apart from the EU's obligations with respect to the observance of (customary) international law, the EU Charter of Fundamental Rights (CFR) constitutes a crucial source of reference. As observed in the Commission's guidelines on human rights impact assessments, respect for the CFR is "a binding legal requirement in relation to both internal and external policies".[27] In other words, the CFR has certain extraterritorial implications in the sense that it applies in relation to all EU activities irrespective of whether they take place within or outside its territorial boundaries. In this respect, it has been argued that the CFR differs from other human rights treaties, most notably the European Convention on the Protection of Human Rights and Fundamental Freedoms (ECHR), which usually contain a specific clause delimiting their application to acts with the State Parties' jurisdiction.[28] Article 51 (1) of the Charter defines its field of application in relation to its addressees, i.e. the institutions, bodies, offices and agencies of the Union and the Member States when they are implementing Union law, and in connection to the powers of the EU as conferred on it in the Treaties. It does not entail any reference to the territorial scope of application, implying that the obligations of the Charter apply whenever the EU acts. Hence, as observed by Moreno-Lax and Costello, "The key question is not whether the Charter applies territorially or extraterritorially,

---

24   Case C-366/10, *ATAA*, EU:C:2011:864, para. 101.

25   V. Kube, 'The European Union's External Human Rights Commitment: What is the Legal Value of Article 21 TEU?', *EUI Department of Law Research* Paper, No. 2016/10, p. 20.

26   Case C-366/10, *ATAA*, EU:C:2011:864, para. 110.

27   Guidelines on the analysis of human rights impacts in impact assessments for trade-related policy initiatives (n. 7), p. 5.

28   See Art. 1 ECHR.

but whether a particular situation falls to be governed by EU law or not".[29] Or, to use the metaphor of Koen Lenaerts and Gutierrez-Fons, "the Charter is the 'shadow' of EU law. Just as an object defines the contours of its shadow, the scope of EU law determines that of the Charter".[30]

The view that the Charter applies in relation to the EU's external policies seems supported by the case law of the ECJ. In *Mugraby*, a Lebanese applicant claimed that the Council and the Commission failed to suspend economic aid programmes under the human rights clause in the EU-Lebanon Association Agreement. Whereas the action failed, essentially in light of the institutions' broad margin of discretion in the management of the EU's external relations, it is noteworthy that neither the General Court nor the Court of Justice questioned the extraterritorial application of the EU Charter of Fundamental Rights.[31] A more explicit reference to the role of the Charter in relation to the EU's external trade relations occurred in the *Frente Polisario* case. In this case, the *Frente Polisario* sought the annulment of the EU Council decision approving the agreement concerning the progressive liberalisation of trade in agricultural and fisheries products.[32] In support of its action, the applicant set out not less than eleven pleas which all directly or indirectly touched upon the EU's commitments to respect the right to self-determination of the people of the Western Sahara and the rights which derive from it.

After recalling the settled case law concerning the EU institutions' wide discretion in the field of external economic relations, the General Court pointed at the EU's human rights obligations. Even though it found that there is "no absolute prohibition on concluding an agreement which may be applicable on disputed territory, the fact remains that the protection of fundamental rights of the population of such a territory is of particular importance and is, therefore, a question that the Council must examine before the approval of such an agreement".[33] In particular, the Council is bound "to examine, carefully and impartially, all the relevant facts in order to ensure that the production of goods for export is not conducted to the detriment of the population of the territory

---

29   V. Moreno-Lax and C. Costello, 'The Extraterritorial Application of the EU Charter of Fundamental Rights: From Territoriality to Facticity: the Effectiveness Model', in S. Peers et. al. (eds.), *Commentary on the EU Charter of Fundamental Rights* (Hart, 2014), p. 1682.

30   K. Lenaerts and J.A. Gutierrez-Fons, 'The place of the Charter in the EU Constitutional Edifice', in S. Peers et. al. (eds.), *Commentary on the EU Charter of Fundamental Rights* (Hart, 2014), p. 1568.

31   L. Bartels, 'The EU's Human Rights Obligations in Relation to Policies with Extraterritorial Effect', *European Journal of International Law* (2014) 25 (4), p. 1076 and Kube (n. 25), p. 25.

32   Case T-512/12, *Front Polisario v. Council*, EU:T:2015:953.

33   *Ibid*, para. 227.

concerned, or entails infringements of fundamental rights".[34] Significantly, the Court referred to a wide range of Charter rights thus confirming the latter's extraterritorial application. Whereas it agreed with the Council that the EU cannot be held responsible for actions committed by Morocco, this does not erase the EU from its obligation to prevent that it indirectly encourages a third country's human rights violations or profits from them by allowing the export to its Member States of products which have been produced or obtained in conditions which do not respect the fundamental rights of the population of the territory from which they originate.[35] For this purpose, the Council should have examined that there was no risk and could not simply conclude that it was for the Kingdom of Morocco to ensure that the rights of the Sahrawi population are guaranteed.[36] In other words, the General Court views the existence of a human rights impact assessment prior to the adoption of the Council decision as a crucial procedural requirement.

In his opinion in the appeal procedure, Advocate General Wathelet agreed with the requirement of a human rights impact assessment but explicitly dismissed the General Court's reliance on the provisions of the Charter of Fundamental Rights. In his view, Article 51 of the Charter does not allow for an extraterritorial effect, unless an activity is "governed by EU law and carried out under the effective control of the EU and/or its Member States outside their territory".[37] This "effective control" doctrine is inspired by the case law of the European Court of Human Rights but, as argued before, such parallelism is not very convincing taking into account that the Charter does not include a provision comparable to Article 1 ECHR. Hence, the Advocate General's view that the scope of the human rights impact assessment should be confined to checking compliance with *jus cogens* and *erga omnes* norms as derived from the EU's obligations under international law seems to deny the role of the Charter of Fundamental Rights in the EU legal order.[38]

In its appeal judgment, the Court of Justice did not explicitly engage in the discussion regarding the extraterritorial application of the Charter. In contrast to the General Court, it concluded that the Association Agreement and

---

34   *Ibid*, para. 228.

35   *Ibid*, para. 231.

36   *Ibid*, para. 241.

37   Opinion of Advocate General Wathelet in Case C-104/16 P, *Council v. Front Polisario*, EU:C:2016:677, para. 270.

38   For a similar view, see: V. Kube, 'The Polisario Case: Do Fundamental Rights matter for EU trade policies?', https://www.ejiltalk.org/the-polisario-case-do-eu-fundamental-rights-matter-for-eu-trade-polices/.

the ensuing agreement on the liberalisation of trade in agricultural products did not apply to the Western Sahara, implying that the Polisario Front had no standing to seek the annulment of the decision at issue.[39] Significantly, the Court of Justice based its reasoning on the principle of self-determination, which it defined as "a legally enforceable right *erga omnes* and one of the essential principles of international law".[40] Proceeding from the application of the principle of the relative effect of treaties of Article 34 of the VCLT, the people of the Western Sahara are defined as a "third party" implying that their consent is needed for the application of the agreement.[41] Without entering into the background and the practical implications of this reasoning,[42] it is sufficient to observe that "the ECJ left the door open for a fundamental rights assessment".[43] In any event, the *Frente Polisario* case revealed the significance of fundamental rights considerations in relation to the CCP.

Finally, it is noteworthy that in *Opinion 1/17*, both the Council and several Member States contested the applicability of the EU law principle of equal treatment (Articles 20 and 21 of the Charter) and the right of access to an independent tribunal (Article 47 of the Charter) in relation to the Comprehensive Economic and Trade Agreement with Canada (CETA).[44] The Court of Justice used this opportunity to stress, once again, that "international agreements entered into by the Union must be entirely compatible with the Treaties and with the constitutional principles stemming therefrom".[45] Taking into account that the Charter of Fundamental Rights has the same legal value as the treaties, as expressed in Article 6 (1) TEU, it logically follows that the EU's trade agreements must be fully compatible with the Charter. Of course, certain Charter provisions have a limited personal scope of application. This is, for instance, the case with Article 21 (2) of the Charter, which explicitly provides that the prohibition of discrimination on grounds of nationality shall be prohibited "within the scope of application of the Treaties". As can be derived from the Explanations relating to the Charter, this corresponds to the first paragraph of Article 18 TFEU and is, therefore, limited to situations involving EU Member State nationals. As a result, Article 21 (2) of the Charter is of no relevance in

---

39   Opinion of AG Wathelet in Case C-104/16 *Council v. Front Polisario*, EU:C:2016:677, para. 49.

40   Case C-104/16 P *Council v. Front Polisario*, EU:C:2016:973, para. 88.

41   *Ibid*, para. 106.

42   See: G. Van der Loo, 'The Dilemma of the EU's Future Trade Relations with Western Sahara: Caught Between Strategic Interests and International Law?', CEPS Commentary, 20 April 2018.

43   V. Kube (n. 38).

44   Opinion 1/17 (*CETA*), EU:C:2019:341, para. 81 and 87.

45   *Ibid*, para. 165.

relation to the question of potential discrimination between nationals of the Member States and those of third countries.

Significantly, the non-application of Article 21 (2) CFR does not affect the applicability of other provisions of the Charter which do not have a similar limitation and are, therefore, applicable to all situations governed by EU law, including those falling within the scope of international agreements entered into by the EU.[46] This is, for instance, the case with Article 20 of the Charter, which provides that "everyone is equal before the law". This implies that the Court may be called to examine whether an agreement which leads to a difference in treatment within the Union between third country nationals and Member State nationals is contrary to Article 20 CFR.[47]

Fundamental rights concerns may not only relate to the material provisions of international agreements, but may also arise in relation to the established procedures for dispute settlement. For instance, in *Opinion 1/17*, Belgium raised a question concerning the compatibility of the Investor-State Dispute Settlement (ISDS) mechanism under the CETA with Canada with the fundamental right of access to an independent tribunal, as enshrined in Article 47 CFR. The Belgian government expressed its concern about the difficulties for small and medium-sized enterprises to obtain access to the CETA Tribunal given the high cost of such a dispute settlement procedure. In addition, uncertainties about the remuneration, appointment procedures, conditions for removal and the applicable rules of ethics for the Members of the CETA Tribunal and Appellate Tribunal all required an interpretation in light of Article 47 CFR. In this respect, the Court quickly rejected the argument put forward by the Council and the Member States that the Charter is inapplicable in relation to the envisaged ISDS mechanism. Whereas it is uncontested that the Charter is not binding for a non-Member State, in this case Canada, the Charter is binding for the Union. As a result, the Union cannot enter into an agreement that establishes judicial bodies that can issue binding awards and deal with disputes brought by EU litigants if the safeguards foreseen in the Charter are not guaranteed.[48]

As a result, the Court assessed the compatibility of the CETA ISDS mechanism with the requirements of accessibility and independence as derived from Article 47 CFR. As far as the requirement of accessibility is concerned, the Court found that the financial cost could deter natural persons or small-sized

---

46   *Ibid,* para. 171.
47   *Ibid,* para. 172–175.
48   *Ibid,* para. 192.

enterprises from initiating proceedings before the CETA Tribunal and that the CETA did not contain legally binding commitments to address this problem.[49] The agreement only provides that the CETA Joint Committee "may" take decisions and "consider" additional rules to reduce the financial burden for natural persons or small-sized enterprises. However, the Court pointed at the crucial role of Statement No 36, which implies a commitment of the Commission and the Council to tackle the financial accessibility of the CETA Tribunal even if the CETA Joint Committee would not be able to adopt the necessary additional decisions.[50] Without elaborating upon the legal nature of this statement, which was adopted on the occasion of the adoption by the Council of the decision authorising the signature of CETA,[51] the Court simply concluded that this commitment "is sufficient justification, in the context of the present Opinion proceedings, for the conclusion that the CETA, as an 'agreement envisaged', within the meaning of Article 218(11) TFEU, is compatible with the requirement that those tribunals should be accessible".[52]

Whereas it may well be argued that the Statement does not involve any hard legal guarantee but only a political commitment on behalf of the EU institutions, the Court defended its approach by pointing at the close connection between the financial accessibility of the CETA dispute settlement mechanism and the conclusion of the CETA.[53] In particular, the Member States can consider the progress regarding the review of the dispute settlement mechanism as part of their national ratification process. Taking into account that the Council only adopts the decision concluding the agreement after the ratification by all Member States, there is thus a strict political control on the implementation of the commitments laid down in Statement No 36. This line of reasoning allowed the Court to confirm the compatibility of the envisaged agreement with Article 47 Charter. Of course, in principle, there is still a possibility of *ex post* judicial review under the form of an action for annulment against the Council decision concluding the agreement, should there be any issues regarding the accessibility to the CETA Tribunal after the entry into force of the agreement. Taking into account the absence of explicit legal guarantees in the agreement and the essentially political control mechanism

---

49   *Ibid*, para. 211–216.

50   *Ibid*, para. 217–218.

51   See: Council of the EU, Statements and Declarations entered into on the occasion of the adoption by the Council of the decision authorising the signature of CETA, doc. 13463/1/ 16, 27 October 2016.

52   Opinion 1/17 (*CETA*), EU:C:2019:341, para. 219.

53   *Ibid*, para. 221.

on the implementation of the commitment to reduce the financial burden of accessibility for natural persons and small-sized enterprises, such an option cannot be totally excluded when the envisaged initiatives of the CETA Joint Committee or the Commission and the Council would not lead to any concrete results.

Finally, as far as the condition of independence of the CETA Tribunals is concerned, the Court applied its two-prong approach as defined in relation to the EU's domestic legal order.[54] This involves an external dimension, which implies that a judicial body is to function autonomously without being subject to any external interventions or pressure, and an internal dimension, implying the maintenance of an equal distance from the parties to the proceedings and the absence of any personal interest of the judges in the outcome of the proceedings.[55] With respect to the external dimension, the Court recalled that the CETA Joint Committee, which plays a key role in the appointment, removal and remuneration of members of the CETA Tribunals, cannot affect the handling of disputes under the ISDS mechanism. Moreover, the EU's consent to any decision of the CETA Joint Committee has to comply with EU primary law, including the right of an effective remedy enshrined in Art. 47 CFR.[56] As far as the internal dimension is concerned, the Court concludes that the CETA provisions about the composition of the Tribunal as well as the references to the International Bar Association (IBA) Guidelines on Conflicts of Interest in International Arbitration are sufficient to satisfy the requirement of independence.[57]

4   The Practice of Human Rights Clauses and Social Norms in EU Free Trade Agreements and the Challenge of Enforcement

Apart from the evolving practice of human rights impact assessments and the external implications of the Charter of Fundamental Rights, which may be directly attributed to the new legal and political framework of the Lisbon Treaty, the trade-human rights nexus is also visible through the inclusion of human rights clauses and social norms in EU Free Trade Agreements. Whereas this

---

54   See e.g. Judgment of 25 July 2018, *Minister for Justice and Equality*, C-216/18 PPU, EU:C:2018:586.

55   Opinion 1/17 (*CETA*), EU:C:2019:341, para. 202–203.

56   *Ibid*, para. 237.

57   *Ibid*, para. 238–244.

practice pre-dates the entry into force of the Lisbon Treaty,[58] some significant developments can nevertheless be observed.

First, in light of the Treaty objectives defined in Articles 3 (5) and 21 TEU, the inclusion of human rights clauses and social norms in FTAS is no longer a matter of foreign policy choice.[59] Rather, it is the expression of a constitutional obligation to ensure that the EU's external action respects the "principles of democracy, the rule of law, the universality and indivisibility of human rights and fundamental freedoms, respect for human dignity, the principles of equality and solidarity and [...] the principles of the United Nations Charter and international law".[60]

Second, in line with the well-established pre-Lisbon practice, international agreements concluded on behalf of the Union generally include an "essential element" clause in combination with a "non-execution" (suspension) clause as an expression of the parties' commitment to respect core common values. The drafting of the respective clauses gradually developed over time and typically includes references to democratic principles, human rights and fundamental freedoms and the rule of law.[61] Whereas the EU only uses this form of human rights conditionality in very exceptional circumstances (such as a *coup d'état*), it is noteworthy that the post-Lisbon practice increasingly uses the essential element clause as a normative framework for a positive and institutionalised dialogue on political reform in a partner country which underpins all instruments – including trade instruments – deployed by the EU.[62]

Third, the EU's post-Lisbon trade agreements all include a chapter on Trade and Sustainable Development (TSD) with references to labour and environmental standards that are based on multilateral instruments such as Conventions of the International Labour Organisation (ILO) and the United Nations Convention on Climate Change. Whereas such references were already

---

58   On the pre-Lisbon practice, see e.g. E. Fierro, *The EU's Human Rights Approach to Human Rights Conditionality in Practice* (Martinus Nijhoff, 2013) and L. Bartels, *Human Rights Conditionality in the EU's International Agreements* (OUP, 2015).

59   L. Bartels, 'Human Rights and Sustainable Development Obligations in EU Free Trade Agreements', *Legal Issues of Economic Integration* 40 (4) (2013), p. 311.

60   Art. 21 (1) TEU.

61   N. Hachez, 'Essential Element Clauses in EU Trade Agreements Making Trade Work in a Way That Helps Human Rights?', Leuven Centre for Global Governance Studies, Working Paper No. 158, April 2015.

62   N. Ghazaryan, 'A New Generation of Human Rights Clauses? The Case of Association Agreements in the Eastern Neighbourhood', *European Law Review* (2015), p. 391–410.

included in pre-Lisbon trade agreements, the new generation of trade agreements are more explicit in their sustainable development objectives.[63] Moreover, as observed in *Opinion 2/15*, TSD chapters now fall within the scope of the EU's exclusive competence in relation to the CCP.[64] In other words, making the liberalisation of trade relations with a third country subject to the condition of the parties' compliance with international obligations concerning social protection of workers and environmental protection is a logical consequence of the post-Lisbon orientation of the CCP.

Significantly, there is a certain overlap between the social norms included in the TSD chapter and the protection of human rights in the sense that core labour standards as defined within the framework of the ILO are also human rights which the parties are deemed to respect under the human rights clause.[65] In this respect, it is noteworthy that the EU-Korea FTA, which has been used as a template for other FTAs, identifies four "fundamental rights" which the parties promise to respect: freedom of association and the effective recognition of the right to collective bargaining; the elimination of all forms of forced or compulsory labour; the effective abolition of child labour and the elimination of discrimination in respect of employment and occupation. Moreover, they commit themselves "to make continued and sustained efforts" towards ratifying the fundamental ILO Conventions.[66]

A recurring criticism concerns the weak enforcement mechanisms in relation to human rights clauses and social norms in EU free trade agreements[67].[68] The monitoring of implementation of the relevant commitments is essentially based on dialogue and cooperation without a possibility to use the normal dispute settlement procedures. The TSD chapters generally provide for the establishment of a specialised Committee with senior officials from the respective parties, accompanied by a civil society mechanism that may take the form of a Domestic Advisory Group. Disputes are to be resolved within a system of consultations with a possible referral to a Panel of Experts. This panel has the power to draw up a report and to make non-binding recommendations for the

---

63   On the nexus between trade and sustainable development, see also the chapter by Sieglinde Gstöhl in this volume.
64   Opinion 2/15 (*Singapore FTA*), EU:C:2017:376, para. 141–167.
65   L. Bartels (n. 58), p. 312.
66   Art. 13.4 (3) of the EU-Korea FTA (OJ 2011, L 127/62).
67   On this issue, see also the chapter by G. Van Calster and B. Cooreman in this volume.
68   C. Gammage, 'A Critique of the Extraterritorial Obligations of the EU in Relation to Human Rights Clauses and Social Norms in EU Free Trade Agreements', *Europe in the World: A Law Review* (2018) 2, p. 1.

solution of the matter. It has been argued that this soft approach is one of the main weaknesses of the EU's trade-human rights nexus.[69] Without a more robust and formal dispute settlement mechanism, the effectiveness of including human rights clauses and social norms in EU free trade agreements remains questionable.

A look at the available *ex post* impact assessments seems to confirm the rather weak enforcement of human and labour rights.[70] The report on the EU-Mexico FTA found that "the commitments to human rights in the agreement still lack effective mechanisms through which human rights could be better monitored or defended".[71] The evaluation report of the implementation of the EU-Korea FTA bluntly concluded that "the EU-Korea FTA is assessed to have not changed the status quo of human and labour rights in Korea as they were when the FTA came into effect, in the sense that little change (positive or negative) over the 2011 situation and/or longer term trends can be observed".[72] However, it would be too easy to reduce the soft approach to an exercise of mere window dressing without any concrete implications. A good example is the EU's initiative to request, for the very first time, formal consultations with the Republic of Korea in relation to the country's non-compliance with international labour standards as defined in the TSD chapter of the EU-Korea FTA.[73] This initiative, which was launched in December 2018, reveals a more assertive approach on behalf of the EU and a clear willingness to use the available mechanisms under free trade agreements in order to ensure compliance with standards that go beyond the traditional scope of international trade relations.[74] Significantly, this approach seemed to produce some effect in the

---

69   *Ibid.*

70   The ex-post evaluations are available at the website of the European Commission, DG Trade: http://ec.europa.eu/trade/policy/policy-making/analysis/policy-evaluation/ex-post-evaluations/.

71   Ex-post Evaluation of the Implementation of the EU-Mexico Free Trade Agreement, February 2017: http://trade.ec.europa.eu/doclib/html/156011.htm, p. 161.

72   Evaluation of the Implementation of the Free Trade Agreement between the EU and its Member States and the Republic of Korea, May 2018, p. 244 available at: http://trade.ec.europa.eu/doclib/html/157716.htm.

73   Request for consultations by the European Union: http://trade.ec.europa.eu/doclib/docs/2018/december/tradoc_157586.pdf.

74   In this respect, it is noteworthy that adopting a more assertive approach towards the enforcement of commitments made under the TSD chapters was one of the recommendations included in a non-paper of the Commission services in February 2018, entitled 'Feedback and way forward on improving the implementation and enforcement of Trade and Sustainable Development chapters in EU Free Trade Agreements'.

sense that the Korean government announced the objective to ratify three key
ILO Conventions by the end of 2019.[75]

5   Conclusions

The constitutionalisation of the trade-human rights nexus with the Treaty of
Lisbon influences the law and practice of the CCP in several aspects. Most notably, it resulted in the adoption of new policy frameworks and strategies ensuring the mainstreaming of human rights considerations in all EU external
policies, including the CCP. Of particular significance is the inclusion of human rights impact assessments for trade-related policy initiatives. As observed
by Advocate General Wathelet in the *Frente Polisario* case, "the Council and
the Commission have set the bar very high for themselves".[76] The discussion
surrounding the absence of a prior impact assessment for the conclusion of
the FTA with Vietnam and the critical remarks of the European ombudsman
in this respect, as well as the *Frente Polisario* case, reveal the political and legal
significance of human rights impact assessments in relation to the conclusion
of international trade agreements.

Whereas there is a general consensus that the EU must take into account
fundamental rights in its external action, the precise implementation and op-
erationalisation of these duties remains subject to discussion.[77] The increased
attention to human rights as a "founding value" (Article 2 and 3 (5) TEU), "guiding principle" (Article 21 (1) TEU) and "objective" (Article 21 (2) (b) TEU) implies at least a duty to put human rights on the agenda of trade negotiations.
Arguably, it involves certain procedural obligations such as conducting human
rights impact assessments prior to concluding trade agreements, ensuring that
adequate monitoring mechanisms are in place and establishing accountability
mechanisms.[78] The effectiveness of EU human rights conditionality in external trade instruments is yet another discussion which largely depends upon
a variety of factors such as the integration of trade instruments in a broader

---

75   Kim Hyun-Bin, 'Gov't aims to ratify 3 key ILO Conventions within this year', *Korean Times*,
        13 June 2019: http://www.koreatimes.co.kr/www/nation/2019/06/371_270584.html.
76   Opinion of Advocate General Wathelet in Case C-104/16 P, *Council v. Front Polisario*,
        EU:C:2016:677, para. 263.
77   O. De Schutter (n. 19).
78   V. Kube (n. 25), p. 28.

human rights agenda, the position of third countries and the interests of the various actors and institutions.[79]

---

79   See e.g. L. McKenzie and K. L Meissner, 'Human Rights Conditionality in European Union Trade Negotiations: The Case of the EU Singapore FTA', *Journal of Common Market Studies* (2017), p. 832–849; S. Velluti, 'The Promotion and Integration of Human Rights in EU External Trade Relations', *Utrecht Journal of International and European Law* (2016), p. 41–68.

CHAPTER 18

The European Union and the Multilateral Trade Regime

Reciprocal Influences

Pieter Jan Kuijper and Geraldo Vidigal

1 Introduction

The European Union (EU) and the World Trade Organization (WTO) are often described as "rules-based" organisations. In both organisations, the adjudicators established to oversee implementation of the core treaties – the WTO Appellate Body and the Court of Justice of the European Union (ECJ) – have played a significant role in establishing the principle that commonly agreed rules and principles constitute an integral legal framework rather than a mere juxtaposition of bilateral relations between parties.[1] From the viewpoint of the EU's institutions, the EU's Membership in the WTO means that, while they remain chiefly submitted to the political and legal imperatives of the European Union, they must also take into account external constraints established by the WTO Agreements.

The internal imperatives of the European Union, governed by the rules and procedures of its founding treaties and subject to adjudication by the ECJ, include the unification of the internal market and the defence at its external borders.[2] By directing the economic policies of EU Members States and controlling access to the world's largest market, EU regulations and practices inevitably affect economic agents in third countries. Given the extent of its legal and economic influence, it is not far-fetched to describe the EU as a regulatory superpower.[3]

Externally, the EU is constrained by its engagements towards its economic partners. While "regional" trade agreements (RTAs) are acquiring growing

---

1 See e.g. AB, *EC – Large Civil Aircraft*, DS316, para. 845; AB, *Peru – Agricultural Products*, DS457, para. 5.106; Case 6/64 *Flaminio Costa v E.N.E.L.*, [1964] ECR 585, 593.

2 See Treaty on the European Union, preamble, Recitals 8–9, 11.

3 D. W. Drezner, *All Politics is Global: Explaining International Regulatory Regimes* (Princeton University Press 2007); A Bradford, 'The Brussels Effect', *Northwestern University Law Review* 107 (2012), p. 1.

importance, adjudication of trade disputes has taken place overwhelmingly at the WTO.[4] The WTO Dispute Settlement Understanding provides WTO Members with the ability to seek authoritative rulings from panels and the Appellate Body on the WTO-consistency of other Members' measures, and then employ political pressure and trade retaliation to induce compliance with these rulings.

This chapter examines the reactions by the EU's different organs to adverse decisions adopted at the WTO level. It begins by describing the rejection by the Court of Justice of direct effect of WTO law and panel and Appellate Body reports on EU law. It then examines different types of responses by the EU to WTO rulings that required it to change its policies. We divide responses into three types. First are the cases in which, in response to adverse rulings, the EU established an internal mechanism to ensure not only case-specific compliance but also the dynamic adaptation of its policies to decisions made at the WTO level. Second are two cases in which the EU has complied with decisions of panels and the Appellate Body, significantly changing its own policies to adapt to the WTO's rulings. Third are two cases in which the EU has responded to rulings by the WTO with attempts to change the global regulatory regime. While in one high-profile case (hormone-treated beef), this involved contradicting the findings of WTO adjudicators, in another case (agricultural subsidies) the EU's compliance with adverse rulings led it to mobilise other countries to concur in accepting its own way of complying with global agreements.

2 WTO Law and the EU Legal Order

2.1 *WTO Law and the EU Legal Order*
It is briefly recalled here that the ECJ has rejected the direct effect of GATT provisions almost from the start of the EEC common commercial policy (CCP) in 1970, even when it recognised the succession of the EEC in the rights and obligations of the Member States that were Contracting Parties to the GATT.[5] There is little doubt that a certain fear of contamination must have played a role in this judgment, so close was the resemblance between key provisions of

---

4 See G. Vidigal, 'Why Is There So Little Litigation under Free Trade Agreements? Retaliation and Adjudication in International Dispute Settlement', JIEL 20 (2017), p. 927 (noting that RTA adjudication occurs essentially only where RTAs give individuals and private entities standing before the adjudicator).

5 Case 21–24/72, *International Fruit,* EU:C:1972:115, para. 20–27.

both treaties.[6] The ECJ's view on this matter did not change when the GATT was succeeded by the WTO, of which the EC was one of the founding Members. Direct effect of WTO provisions, which would set aside EU secondary law, remained beyond the pale for the Court.[7] A clearer interpretation of the relevant provisions of the different WTO Agreements could not change this rejection of direct effect.[8] On the other hand, the ECJ maintained its traditionally monist position where it concerned the relation between international law and Union law also in respect of the WTO Agreements. This implied that the Court was willing to interpret and apply Union law so that it would be in conformity with the WTO Agreements.[9] Such interpretation can be quite stringent in some cases and come close to direct effect in practice.[10] In itself this approach followed by the ECJ is in line with Article XVI:4 of the WTO Agreement, which reads: "Each Member shall ensure the conformity of its laws, regulations and administrative procedures with its obligations as provided in the annexed Agreements". This provision leaves room both for monist and dualist Members of the WTO to fulfill their WTO obligations, each in their own way.[11]

On the other hand, the ECJ has been extremely reluctant to be seen to have taken into account, in its interpretation of WTO rules, the interpretations of WTO law by panel and Appellate Body reports. This has been most evident in the attitude of the ECJ to the report of the Appellate Body (AB) in *EC – Bed Linen*, which condemned the so-called *zeroing* practice of the Commission for calculating the dumping margin for imports of bed linen from India into the EU.[12] In the end, the ECJ followed the example of the AB without ever referring

---

6   See Art. XI:1 GATT and Art. 30 EEC; Art. XX GATT and Art. 36 EEC; Art. III:2 GATT and
       Art. 91 EEC; Art. XXI GATT and Art. 223 EEC etc. The "eternal" provisional application of
       the GATT may also have played a role.

7   Case C-149/96, *Portugal v Council,* EU:C:1999:574, para. 36–48.

8   Case C-377/02, *Léon Van Parijs v BIRB,* EU:C:2005:121, in particular para. 42–48 and
       para. 50–54.

9   Case C-53/96, *Hermès v FHH,* EU:C:292, para. 39–44; Joined Cases C-390 and 392/98, *Dior
       et al.,* EC:C:2000:688, no direct effect of the TRIPs Agreement, but harmonious interpretation acceptable.

10   Case C-89/99, *Schieving-Nystad v Robert Groeneveld,* EU:C:2001:438, in which the Court
       gives an extensive interpretation of Art. 50(6) of TRIPs, with instructions to the Dutch
       tribunal that asked the questions on how to implement this interpretation.

11   It is interesting to note, however, that the practice of the WTO Secretariat has always been
       that strongly monist Members could not rely on their monism to argue that they did
       not need to write, for instance, their own anti-dumping legislation, since the WTO Anti-
       Dumping Agreement was detailed enough to be applied directly by their courts. Personal
       knowledge of the authors.

12   AB, *EC –Anti-Dumping Duties on Imports of Cotton-type Bed-Linen from India,* DS141.

in any way to the AB's report adopted by the DSB condemning this practice.[13] In this respect, there has been lately a considerable divergence in judicial style, if perhaps not substance, between the Court of Justice and the General Court, with the latter having developed familiarity with the WTO case law in the field of anti-dumping (AD) and countervailing duties (CVD) and not shying away from referring to this case law in support of its own positions.[14]

The ECJ's view that WTO law requires political implementation may have contributed to the EU's developing legislative tools that are supposed to work seamlessly with the WTO legal instruments. Some of these instruments allow EU executive organs to access the WTO dispute settlement system or directly exercise certain rights that the EU may have under the WTO rules, including as a consequence of an adopted Panel or Appellate Body report. However, international influence also played a role in the creation of these instruments.

Thus the so-called *Trade Barriers Regulation*, which was part of the Uruguay Round implementation package, was supposed to be the European response to Section 301 of the US Trade Act 1974. It created a procedure by which representatives of economic sectors or individual companies could launch a complaint to the Commission so that it would investigate allegedly unfair or illegal trade legislation of a third State.[15] Normally these complaints were related to trade legislation or practices that were allegedly contrary to WTO provisions. Originally this instrument attracted a fairly steady stream of complaints, but, after some ten years of its existence, this slowed to a trickle and now seems to have petered out altogether.[16] Of late, most complaints from economic sectors or individual enterprises are channeled to the Commission informally, either through the authorities of a Member State or directly.[17]

---

13   Case C-351/04, *Ikea Wholesale v Commissioners of Customs and Excise*, EU:C:2007:547, para. 50–57.

14   See in respect of the WTO Appellate Body on Bed-Linen from India, the Judgment of the General Court in Case T-274/02, *Ritek et al. v Council*, EU:C:2006:332, where at para. 97 ff. the Court refers extensively to the *Bed-Linen* report of the AB in order to argue that it differs fundamentally from the Ritek case. Another example of the General Court referring to WTO cases is Case T-67/14, *Viraj Profiles Ltd. v Council and Commission*, EU:2017:481, para. 98–99.

15   Council Reg. 3286/94 laying down Community procedures in the field of the common commercial policy in order to ensure the exercise of the Community's rights under international trade rules, in particular those established under the auspices of the World Trade Organization (OJ 1994, L 349/71–78).

16   For a brief perusal of the complaints brought under the Trade Barriers Regulation, see P. J. Kuijper et al. (eds.), *The Law of EU External Relations, Cases, Materials and Commentary on the EU as an International Legal Actor, 2nd ed.* (OUP, 2015), p. 442–443.

17   This is based on personal knowledge of one of the authors and is linked to the felt need of enterprises not to make themselves known to the country complained of for fear of

Whereas the Trade Barriers Regulation is about authorising the Commission to manage a procedure that may lead to the EU starting a WTO dispute settlement case, the 2014 Enforcement Instrument[18] authorises the Commission to implement the suspension of concessions and other obligations pursuant to a decision to this effect by the WTO DSB, after a third State has failed to carry out a report of a panel or of the Appellate Body favourable to the EU.[19] A similar authorisation enables the Commission to take so-called rebalancing measures in case it is not compensated by a third State that has taken safeguard measures (Article 8 of the Safeguards Agreement) or modified concessions under Article XXVIII of GATT.[20] In short, this instrument is about the Commission enforcing the EU's rights. It is interesting to note that the first major use of the Enforcement Instrument has been the taking of "rebalancing" measures against the US in response to the latter's tariff increases on steel and aluminum, allegedly taken for national security reasons.[21] Two successive Commission Implementing Regulations based on the Enforcement Instrument implicitly characterised these US measures as safeguard measures for which the US had not offered the required compensation.[22]

Much earlier, it had been found necessary that the Commission should be put in the position to implement Panel and Appellate Body reports requiring changes or amendments to EU Acts, notably in the field of anti-dumping and countervailing duties. After the EU lost the important *EC – Bed Linen* case,[23] it became obvious that the Union should be capable of implementing adverse panel and Appellate Body reports at relatively short notice in order to be able

being targeted by its authorities. In this regard, see the comments made in Panel Report, *Argentina – Import Measures*, DS438, DS444, DS445, para. 1.27–1.30 and 6.45 (noting companies' concerns about being identified as being at the origin of the dispute).

18   Regulation No. 654/2014 concerning the exercise of the Union's rights for the application and enforcement of international trade rules (OJ 2014, L 189/50–58).

19   Art. 3(a) of Reg. 654/2014.

20   Art. 3(c) and (d) of Reg. 654/2014.

21   Taken on the basis of Section 232 of the Trade Expansion Act 1962. The EU has attacked these measures in the WTO: DS/548. This case has been joined to a number of other such cases brought by other WTO Members and is presently before the panel, which has let it be known that its final report can only be expected by the autumn of 2020, see doc. WT/DS548/16.

22   Commission Implementing Regulation (EU) 2018/724 on certain commercial policy measures concerning certain products originating in the United States of America (OJ 2018 L 122/14) and Commission Implementing Regulation (EU) 2018/886, with the same title (OJ 2018 L 158/5). The US, after consultations, has initiated a dispute settlement procedure against the EU, DS559. The panel was composed on 28 January 2019 and the panel has stated that its final report can only be expected by the second half of 2020.

23   See n. 12.

to respect the time limits of Articles 21 and 22 DSU. Soon thereafter, in 2001, the Council adopted a Regulation that authorised the Commission to take "appropriate measures" to implement reports of the WTO, which was codified in a new Regulation in 2015 (the so-called "implementing regulation").[24] "Appropriate measures" may include measures which go beyond mere repeal or amendment of the condemned EU act or practice and seek more broadly to ensure the conformity of the EU legislation or practice in the field of anti-dumping and anti-subsidy to WTO rules.[25]

In respect of the actual application of the "implementing regulation" the following can be said, based on a terminological search in the EUR-Lex data base. Since 2001, there have been broadly six instances of the initiation of procedures for review or amendment of specific anti-dumping measures based principally on the "implementing regulation" as such.[26] And there have also been six instances of the "implementing regulation" being an accessory basis for an interim or expiry review of anti-dumping measures or of a renewed complaint of European producers of such measures that had been the subject of Panel or Appellate Body reports.

It is not always easy to be sure of the result of the initiation of these procedures under the "implementing regulation" as a principal or accessory basis, since some of the procedures initiated under this regulation as principal basis in the end were superseded and/or formally adopted as the result of an interim review of the anti-dumping duties concerned.[27] This meant that the delegation to the Commission laid down in the "implementing regulation" was no longer applicable, as the final anti-dumping measures after an interim review had to be imposed by the Council, which could decide not to follow the Commission. In theory this should have changed after 1 December 2009, when the new implementing powers of the Lisbon Treaty should have found application in anti-dumping, which made the decision-making procedures under the "implementing regulation" and under the Basic Anti-Dumping Regulation follow the general procedure for the exercise

---

24   Regulation (EU) 2015/476 (Parliament and Council) on the measures that the Union may take following a report adopted by the WTO Dispute Settlement Body concerning Anti-Dumping and Anti-Subsidy matters (OJ 2015 L 83/6–10).

25   See Art. 1(b) of Reg. 2015/476.

26   These were published as Notices in the OJ C series under the heading "Procedures relating to the implementation of the Common Commercial Policy".

27   See, for example, European Commission, *Notice regarding the termination of the process concerning implementation of the Panel report adopted by the WTO Dispute Settlement Body concerning the anti-dumping measure applicable on imports of farmed salmon originating in Norway* (2008/C 298/04), (OJ 2008, C 298/7–8).

of implementing powers by the Commission, pursuant to Article 291 TFEU.[28] In reality the Basic Anti-Dumping Regulation was only adapted to the general rules on implementing powers of the Lisbon Treaty in the framework of a broader reform of the Basic Anti-Dumping Regulation adopted by the Council and the Parliament in mid-2016.[29] This now makes implementation of panel and Appellate Body reports in the field of anti-dumping much easier across the board.

Shortly before the adaptation of the Basic Anti-Dumping Regulation to the general scheme of implementing powers, an *ad hoc* modification of certain provisions on non-market economy countries of this regulation was adopted by the Council and the Parliament in order to adapt EU anti-dumping law[30] to the Appellate Body report in *China – Fasteners*.[31]

In a similar vein as the "implementing regulation" in the field of anti-dumping and anti-subsidy procedures, the present general regulation on the common organisation of the different agricultural markets contains a number of different provisions authorising the Commission, following the general procedures for delegated powers and for implementing powers, to adapt import duties and tariff quotas on agricultural products to the Union's international obligations, including any obligations under the WTO.[32] This considerably simplifies EU implementation to changes in WTO rules and to panel and Appellate Body reports. In Section 4.2 below we will return to a specific regulation which played an important role in the solution of the problems confronted by the Union after the DSB report in *EC – Sugar*.[33]

---

28   Regulation (EU) 182/2011, laying down the rules and general principles concerning mechanisms for control by Member States of the Commission's exercise of implementing powers (OJ 2011, L 55/13).

29   Reg. (EU) 2016/1036 on protection against dumped imports from countries not members of the European Union (OJ 2016, L 176/21–54), Art. 14–15. On this issue, see the contributions of F. Hoffmeister and P. De Baere in this volume.

30   Reg. (EU) 765/2012 amending Council Regulation No. 1225/2009 on the protection against dumped imports from countries not members of the European Community (OJ 2012, L 237/1), Rec. 1 and Art. 1.

31   AB, *EU – Anti-dumping duties on certain iron and steel fasteners from China*, DS397.

32   Reg. (EU) 1308/2013 establishing a common organisation of the markets in agricultural products, in particular Rec. 146, Art. 180 ff. on import duties and Art. 184 ff. on tariff quotas.

33   Art. 44(b) of Council Regulation No. 318/2006 on the common organisation of the markets in the sugar sector (OJ 2006, L 58/1). This provision authorised the Commission, together with the management committee for the sugar sector, "to ensure compliance ... with [the EU's] international obligations" with regard to so-called C sugar, which had been found contrary to WTO rules by the panel and the Appellate Body in DS265 and DS266, *EC – Export Subsidies on Sugar*.

2.2   EU Law before Panels and the Appellate Body

On the side of the WTO, the panels and the Appellate Body, when they have to pronounce on the conformity of EU law with the WTO Agreements, have taken the position that they should treat EU law as "fact", in other words to treat it as any international court would treat national law.[34] That means that a panel or the AB should treat the question of what a certain national legal provision means on the basis of the arguments of the claimant and the defendant Member relating to their legality under WTO law. The view of the national law that a panel or the AB forms on this basis is said to be a factual assessment, while presumably the question of its conformity with the WTO agreements is a legal judgment. This argument was encountered by the EC early on in the existence of the WTO in the *EC – Bananas* dispute.[35] The EC argued to no avail that only itself (in particular the Court of Justice) could give an authoritative interpretation of the Lomé Convention and its successors, as it was an agreement concluded by the Community. In reality there is always an aspect of interpretative skill involved in construing a provision of national law even if it is formally a question of fact. Qualifying it nevertheless as a factual judgment serves the formal purpose of clarifying that what the WTO DS organs say about provisions of Union law has no legal value inside the EU legal system, but only within the "WTO sphere" with a view to judging whether such EU legislation is in conformity with WTO law. It is important to note that the ECJ itself has applied similar reasoning in the *Kadi I* case to explain to the UN side that its views about the EU implementation of Security Council sanctions in the EU had no legal value in UN law.[36]

On the "legislative side" of the WTO, recommendations and decisions of WTO Committees in the field of AD and CVD and of the SPS and TBT Committees have a legal status that is not always clear from the text of the WTO Agreements. Although the Appellate Body has sought to endow such instruments with a legal status on the basis of their text and multilateral character,[37] the lack of clear legal rules in the WTO Agreement on the matter renders panels wary of making any clear finding on the matter.[38] From earlier research, it

---

34   On national law as fact before international courts, see *Oppenheim's International Law, 9th edition* by Jennings and Watts, p. 83 and S. Bhuiyan, *National Law in WTO Law*, Cambridge 2007, p. 41–42.

35   AB, *EC – Bananas III*, DS27, para. 167 ff.

36   Case C-402/05 P, *Yassin Abdul Kadi & Al-Barakaat v Council and Commission*, EU:C:2008:461, para. 290 ff.

37   G. Vidigal, 'From Bilateral to Multilateral Law-making: Legislation, Practice, Evolution and the Future of Inter Se Agreements in the WTO, *EJIL* 24 (2013) 1027, p. 1033–1035.

38   See, e.g., Panel, *US – Poultry (China)*, DS392, para. 7.131–7.139 (on the *Decision* on the Implementation of *Article 4* of the SPS Agreement); Panel Report, *Australia – Plain*

would seem that the Commission's services have been following such texts as a matter of administrative practice, in particular in AD and CVD cases.[39] The EU has never adapted its regulatory texts to such WTO instruments.

3   Achieving Compliance

3.1   *EC – Bananas*

EC – Bananas was one of the longest-lasting disputes in the WTO history, having involved five complainants, including two that went all the way to requesting trade retaliations (the US and Ecuador). The period 1996–1999 saw the dispute go through all the regular steps of WTO litigation: original reports of the panel and Appellate Body, arbitration of a reasonable period of time for compliance, compliance reports by the panel and Appellate Body and arbitration of an amount of retaliation, which the US started applying in 2001.[40] This first stage of the dispute was followed in 2001 by a mutually agreed solution, within which the EU committed to replace its complex regime for bananas with a tariff-only regime by the end of 2006,[41] and a waiver granted for the EU to amend its banana regime, subject to an *ad hoc* arbitration procedure.[42] In 2005, proposals made by the EU for new tariffs and quotas were twice submitted to an *arbitrator*, who found that they did not eliminate the WTO-inconsistency.[43] New EU regulations were subsequently adopted, in 2005 and 2007, and condemned by a new compliance panel and by the Appellate Body in 2008.[44] New agreements were reached in 2009, followed by

---

Packaging, DS435, DS441, DS458, DS467, para. 7.2588 (on the Doha Declaration on TRIPS and Public Health).

39   P.J. Kuijper & F. Hoffmeister, 'WTO Influence on EU Law: Too Close for Comfort?', in Wessel and Blockmans (eds.), *Between Autonomy and Dependence, The EU Legal Order under the Influence of International Organisations* (Springer – Asser, 2013), 131–158, p. 142–143.

40   A fairly comprehensive report can be found here: https://www.wto.org/english/tratop_e/dispu_e/cases_e/ds27_e.htm.

41   *EC – Bananas*, Notification of a Mutually Agreed Solution, 2 July 2001 (WT/DS27/58), p. 2, 5.

42   Ministerial Conference, Decision of 14 November 2001 (WT/MIN(01)/15).

43   Award of the Arbitrator, *The EC–ACP Partnership Agreement*, 1 August 2005 (WT/L/616); Award of the Arbitrator, *The EC–ACP Partnership Agreement*, 27 October 2005 (WT/L/625).

44   AB, *EC – Bananas III*, adopted 11 December 2008 (WT/DS27/AB/RW2/ECU, WT/DS27/AB/RW/USA), para. 16.

the "Geneva Agreement on Trade in Bananas" in 2010[45] and, finally, a definitive mutually agreed solution in 2012.[46]

Despite the protracted negotiations and various adjudication stages, the outcome of *EC – Bananas* conformed fully with WTO orthodoxy: the mutually agreed solution involved the EU, after a number of agreed intermediate steps, replacing its complex mechanism which the Appellate Body found to be discriminatory with a tariff-only barrier.

At the same time, this dispute, which lasted for almost 17 years, was no doubt *the* case that fed the ECJ's conviction that negotiations and attempts at appropriate implementation could and would continue in certain cases even after all the steps of the WTO dispute settlement system had been gone through, even twice, with two *ad hoc* arbitrations in the middle. This justified the ECJ's concern about the negative effects on the EU separation of powers of granting direct effect even to the most straightforward provisions of the GATT. Granting such direct effect would effectively put the Court in the position of the negotiator of the mutually agreed solution, the Commission, and/or of the Council, as the authority which needed to approve such a solution or otherwise adapt the EU legislation on bananas.[47] It should be noted that the EU and world market for bananas changed considerably over the course of the dispute. Hence, the interests of both the EU and the different groups of banana-producing countries had shifted. Moreover, the EU and the ACP countries also needed time in order to perform a complete overhaul of the Association between them (and not just of the system of buying guaranteed quantities of bananas) and its conversion from a system of unilateral trade liberalisation in favour of the ACP countries to mutual liberalisation between the EU and the ACP countries.[48] In the light of the foregoing, it is not exaggerated to say that the bananas case has had an enormous influence on the EU's development and trade policy, in particular in its relations with Africa and the Caribbean.[49]

---

45   Geneva Agreement on Trade in Bananas (OJ 2010, L 141/3).

46   Notification of a Mutually Agreed Solution, *EC – Bananas III*, 12 November 2012 (WT/DS27/98).

47   Case C-377/02, *Léon Van Parijs v BIRB* (n. 8).

48   This was mainly done by concluding a large number of regional trade and cooperation agreements between the EU and regional groups of countries parties to the Cotonou Agreement, see for instance the first of these agreements, between the EU and Caricom (OJ 2008, L 289/I/3).

49   See Francis A.S.T. Matambalya & Susanna Wolf, 'The Cotonou Agreement and the Challenges of Making the New EU-ACP Trade Regime WTO Compatible', *Journal of World Trade* 35(1), 123–144 (2001).

3.2   *EC – Biotech*

In *EC – Biotech*[50] in which the EU's procedure for authorising the cultivation and marketing of genetically modified organisms (GMOs) was challenged by the US, Canada and Argentina, the outcome was difficult for the Union. The dispute challenged the decision-making rules of the EU in two ways. First, the question arose to what extent it was acceptable, in a centralised procedure for the admission of certain agricultural products and for the cultivation of such products, to give a certain leeway to the Member States to take their own decisions based on their specific circumstances (so-called safeguards) and what such specific circumstances could be restricted to. Secondly, the condemnation of the Members States' safeguards also immediately affected the new EU Regulation concerning the Member States' mechanisms for control of the Commission's exercise of its newly acquired implementing powers under the Treaty of Lisbon (under Article 292 TFEU).

The complainants (US, Canada and Argentina) had framed their attack on the EU regulation of GMO products so as to avoid a frontal attack on the approval of GMO products as such. Instead, they attacked the EU *method for approval* as being insufficiently based on science and leaving room for prevarication. The result was that the EU was condemned for having operated a *de facto* moratorium on approval of GMO products; having caused undue delays in 23 cases of approval of specific products; and, in 6 cases, for Member States' implementation of national safeguards without an appropriate risk assessment. The WTO Dispute Settlement Body duly adopted the relevant conclusions and recommendations in late 2006. The US then sought authorisation from the WTO Dispute Settlement Body to suspend concessions and other obligations, after the reasonable period of time for implementation by the EU had run out after an agreed prolongation. Since the EU objected to the level of retaliation requested by the US, the dispute was submitted to an arbitrator pursuant to Article 22(6) of the DSU. In February 2008, the US and the EU agreed to suspend the arbitration subject to a promise that the EU would apply its implementation mechanism for admission of GMO products on its market in an effective manner.[51] This agreement with the US was not in the form of a Mutually Agreed Solution (which the EU later adopted with regard to Canada and Argentina).[52] It was an informal arrangement, so-called "Agreed Procedures", which did not terminate

---

50   DS291, DS292 and DS293.

51   Art. 22.6 Arbitration, *EC – Biotech, Communication from the Arbitrator*, 19 February 2008 (WT/DS291/42).

52   See WTO Doc. WT/DS292/40 (EU-Canada) and WT/DS293/41 (EU-Argentina).

the dispute.[53] Hence, the US retains to this day the right to re-activate the arbitration on the level of the suspension of concessions and other obligations and the EU remains subject to the obligation to report on the implementation of the AB report to the DSU.[54]

In spite of the differences in form, the substance of the two mutually agreed solutions and the understanding with the US was broadly the same. The EU promised to make its procedures "really work" and to apply them in conformity with the relevant WTO agreements, notably the Sanitary and Phytosanitary (SPS) Agreement. A dialogue was to be instituted between the EU and the three complaining WTO Members on these matters. This dialogue on the functioning of the EU's approval procedures was to be held twice a year between the relevant government/Commission departments on a number of themes mentioned in the understanding.[55]

In order to make the approval procedure for GMO cultivation and GMO food and feed speedier and (thus) more compatible with WTO requirements, the Commission had to confront two problems. First, the frequency with which Member States applied so-called safeguards, which seemed to be incompatible with the Commission's science-based approach in its proposals for approvals.[56] Second, the unwillingness of Member State representatives to take any position at all during the implementation procedure with regard to individual approvals of GMO products (e.g. to be used for cultivation or as a part of another food or feed product), too often made any position of the implementing committee impossible, leaving the Commission to bear the burden of a positive or negative decision.[57]

The first problem was solved by organising the Member States' power to take national or even regional measures in respect of cultivation of GMOs and the marketing of GMO food and feed, only after these products have been

---

53 See WTO Doc. WT/DS291/38, Understanding between the EC and the US regarding procedures under Art. 21 and 22 of the DSU.

54 See WTO Doc. WT/DS291/137/ Add. 128 'Status Report of the European Union' (7 December 2018). The re-activation of the arbitration occurs in the event that the DSB finds that measures taken in compliance with the panel report by the EU are non-existent or inconsistent with a covered agreement (para. 6 of the Agreed Procedures mentioned in n. 53).

55 See the documents mentioned in n. 52.

56 Normally the Commission's proposals are based on a risk assessment of EFSA, the European Food Safety Authority.

57 See Communication from the Commission to the European Parliament, the Council, the Economic and Social Committee and the Committee of the Regions, *Reviewing the decision-making process on genetically modified organisms (GMOs)*, COM(2015) 176 final, para. 2.2.

authorised at the level of the Union. Thus, such national measures cannot affect the procedural and substantive conditions of the EU authorisations of GMOs and GMO food and feed. Moreover, the Member States can only base their national measures on elements other than those that are taken into account at the Union level, and the Union authorisation will in principle remain valid for the Union as a whole.[58]

In order to deal with the second problem, the Commission felt constrained to propose a modification of the standard decision making procedure that had been adopted after the entry into force of the Lisbon Treaty and laid down in the new Regulation on the exercise of the Commission's implementing powers.[59] The Commission's proposal aimed to reduce the risk that there would be no opinion of the implementing committee because of abstentions by the Member State representatives on the Committee. Hence, the Commission wanted to ensure that the Member States that are absent or do not vote are not counted in the calculation of the qualified majority and that a simple majority of the Member States constitutes a quorum. Moreover, the procedure in the appeal committee should be strengthened, the votes of the Member States should be made public and a referral to the Council should be made possible.[60] It can be argued that this proposal was actually an abdication by the Commission of its normal task in such situations and may not even lead to an improvement in the EU's implementation record. The case is unique insofar as it has led the European Commission to propose modification of important generally applicable decision-making procedures in the EU, inspired by considerations principally related to one kind of implementing decisions, namely those relating to GMOs.

Everything considered, it is reasonable to conclude that the EU in part has adapted, and is still adapting, its authorisation procedures in a way that guarantees that decisions concerning GMOs at the Union level are taken on the basis of a conformity assessment that will be based on science, while not affecting the Member States' right to exercise their residual competence to ban

---

58   See Art. 1(2) of Directive 2015/412 amending Directive 2001/18/EC as regards the possibility for the Member States to restrict or prohibit the cultivation of genetically modified organisms (GMOs) in their territory (OJ 2015, L 68/1) and Art. 1 of the Commission Proposal amending Reg. 1829/2003 as regards the possibility for the Member States to restrict or prohibit the cultivation of genetically modified food and feed in their territory, COM/2015/177 final (not yet enacted). See also Miranda Geelhoed, 'Divided in Diversity: Reforming The EU's GMO Regime', *Cambridge Yearbook of European Legal Studies*, 18, 20–44 (2016).

59   Reg. 182/2011 laying down the rules and general principles concerning mechanisms for control by the Member States of the Commission's exercise of implementing powers.

60   See COM(2017)85, p. 7–9. This proposal has not yet been adopted.

GMOs for reasons other than those addressed in the EU measure. The Member States may thus be constrained to face up to any complaint from WTO Members about such decisions concerning GMOs without being able to rely on any support from EU institutions, most notably the unrivalled WTO litigation experience of the Commission.

3.3 EC – Seals

The EC – Seals disputes[61] only came about because the EU authorities, principally the Commission, took a flight forward, when Belgium and the Netherlands decided to introduce a ban on seal products from Canada and Norway on their own. In the end, an EU-wide ban on the marketing of seal products and products made from seals was instituted.[62] In invoking the public morals exception of the GATT (Art. XX(a) GATT), the EU argued that the methods used for killing seals ran contrary to the concerns of EU citizens with animal welfare, which made the ban necessary to protect public morals.[63] The WTO panel and the Appellate Body upheld that view.[64] However, the EU's exception allowed the sale of products derived from seal hunted by Inuit communities, permitting cruel hunting, without clear criteria, and more easily accessible to Greenlandic Inuit communities than to Canadian ones. These elements of the seal regime were found to be discriminatory treatment that could not be justified by the "the objective of addressing EU public moral concerns regarding seal welfare".[65]

In order to address these shortcomings, the EU enacted in 2015 a new Regulation and a new Implementing Regulation. Regulation 2015/1850 required hunting conducted by Inuit communities to be conducted "in a manner which has due regard to animal welfare, taking into consideration the way of life of the community and the subsistence purpose of the hunt".[66] Implementing

---

61 DS400 and DS401.

62 Commission Regulation (EU) No. 737/2010 of 10 August 2010 laying down detailed rules for the implementation of Regulation (EC) No. 1007/2009 of the European Parliament and of the Council on trade in seal products (OJ 2010, L 216), p. 1–10. For a complete overview of the EU Seals saga, including the development of the internal legislation and the ECJ case law, see Julinda Beqiraj, 'The Delicate Equilibrium of EU Trade Measures: The Seals Case', *German Law Journal* 14 (1) 2013, 279–319.

63 AB, *EC – Seal Products*, DS401, para. 5.153–5.160. For a critical evaluation of the AB report, see Petros C. Mavroidis, 'Sealed with a Doubt. EU, Seals, and the WTO', *European Journal of Risk Regulation,* 3/2015, 388–395.

64 *Ibid*, para. 5.200.

65 *Ibid*, para. 5.338.

66 Regulation (EU) 2015/1775 of the European Parliament and of the Council of 6 October 2015 amending Regulation (EC) No 1007/2009 on trade in seal products and repealing Commission Regulation (EU) No 737/2010, OJ L 262, 1–6, Art. 3(1)(c).

Regulation 2015/1850 established clear criteria for the EU recognition of independent bodies able to certify compliance by Inuit communities with the hunting requirements set out in the regulation.[67]

The EU declared before the DSB that, with these regulations, it had achieved compliance with the recommendations and rulings in the *EC – Seals* Reports.[68] This declaration was met with a mixed reaction. Canada, which had signed a Joint Statement with the EU on access to the EU market for Inuit products, and had had a Canadian Inuit entity added to the EU's list of recognised bodies for the purposes of Inuit hunting, was pleased with the EU's path towards compliance.[69] On the other hand, Norway stated that the new EU regime had not had "any effect regarding seal products exported from Norway".[70] Despite this declaration, Norway did not request a compliance panel, suggesting that it accepted that the EU's measures, despite restricting rather than facilitating trade, addressed the problematic discrimination found by the Appellate Body in the original regulation.[71]

3.4   *Conclusion*

The *EC – Bananas*, *EC – Biotech* and *EC – Seals* disputes involved complex regulatory measures adopted by the EU. In all three cases, the EU implemented the DSB recommendations and rulings in the end. In the latter two cases, it also maintained certain essential features of its legislation, which were also considered of exemplary value for subsequent cases in which domestic regulation, adopted for non-economic reasons, affected international trade.

4   Influencing the Global Regime – Enforcing Rules, Developing Rules, and Breaking Rules

This section analyses cases in which the EU went beyond compliance, and employed its legal and political machinery, as well as its economic weight, to shape the global regulatory legal order. In the three cases examined, this

---

67   Commission Implementing Regulation (EU) 2015/1850 of 13 October 2015 laying down detailed rules for the implementation of Reg.(EC) No 1007/2009 [...] on trade in seal products, OJ L 271, 1–11.

68   Minutes of DSB Meeting of 28 October 2015 (WT/DSB/M/369), para. 1.45.

69   *Ibid*, para. 1.46.

70   *Ibid*, para. 1.47.

71   See E. Lygate, 'Is It Rational and Consistent? The WTO's Surprising Role in Shaping Domestic Public Policy' *JIEL* 20 (2017), p. 561–582.

attempt to influence the regime took different forms. In the case of zeroing, the EU sought to "level the playing field" by enforcing the interpretation adopted by the Appellate Body against the other Member using it (the US). In the case of agricultural subsidies, the EU *de facto* shifted sides in agricultural subsidies negotiations after having adapted its policies to the WTO rulings. Finally, in the case of the ban on hormone-treated beef, the EU's technical institutions failed to convince the EU political bodies to comply with the reports of the DSB that found the ban to be "not based on science". Unable to comply with the ruling, the EU first sought to change its legal position before the WTO. When this was ineffective, the EU opted for negotiation with the various claimants arrangements whereby they accepted the EU's ban in exchange for compensation.

4.1   *The Rule Enforcer: Zeroing*

This Section examines the case of the EU's reaction to the AB's ruling in *EC – Bed Linen*, brought by India and the first case in which the AB decided that the application of so-called *zeroing* methodology for calculating of AD duties was contrary to Article 2.4 and 2.4.2 of the WTO Anti-Dumping Agreement (ADA). *Zeroing* is the technique whereby the so-called positive dumping margins resulting from transactions in which the export price (price at which the good is exported) is *above* normal value (the price in the country of exportation) are set at *zero* (absence of dumping), while the transactions in which the export price is *below* normal value (presence of dumping) are averaged in order to yield the so-called overall dumping margin, which defines the maximum level for anti-dumping duties. Calculated in this way, dumping margins will be higher than when transactions with a positive dumping margin (above zero) had been included in the averaging (instead of being set at zero) and hence the dumping duties imposed will be higher than when the overall average dumping margin had been calculated by also taking into account positive dumping margins. Pursuant to the Appellate Body's reading of the ADA, this approach is incompatible with Article 9.3 ADA. Briefly summarised, the AB considered that this methodology prevented a "fair comparison" between normal value and export price that has pride of place in Article 2.4 ADA. Moreover, Article 2.4.2 ADA sets out the method for calculating the anti-dumping margins based on "a comparison between a weighted average normal value with a weighted average of prices of *all comparable* export transactions" and referred back explicitly to Article 2.4's "fair comparison". Thus, the Appellate Body supported the panel's conclusion that zeroing was contrary to Article 9.3 ADA.[72]

---

72   AB, *EC – Bed Linen*, DS141, para. 54–60.

One remarkable aspect of the aftermath of this case was that the EU adapted fairly quickly to the results of the case and enacted the "implementing regulation" as a consequence (see sec. 2.1 above). The US, the other major user of the zeroing technique, however, tried to escape in all possible ways from the consequences of this decision of the AB for its own anti-dumping practices and was supported in that approach by quite a few panel reports, which did not follow the AB's report in *EC – Bed Linen*.[73]

As a reaction to that, the EU began following a determined litigation policy in order to ensure that the US would also be fully subject to the AB's interpretation of the ADA Thus the EU and the US would be competing on a level playing field with regard to the WTO's anti-dumping rules. Initially, the EU intervened systematically in cases brought by other WTO Members against the US's *zeroing* practices. This intervention policy culminated in the EU's intervention in *US – Stainless Steel (Mexico)*, in which the EU strongly supported Mexico, arguing for the unlawfulness of *zeroing*, and encouraged the AB to make it unambiguous that panels are not only expected, but also obliged, to follow AB findings.[74] In response, the Appellate Body ventured to decide the question of the unlawfulness of the *zeroing* technique definitively[75] and also elegantly slammed the resistance of panels that refused to follow its earlier decisions on *zeroing* by intimating that such decisions in future might be deemed to be contrary to the duty of a panel to make "an objective assessment of the matter before it", as set out in Article 11 DSU.[76]

Subsequently, the EU directly attacked the US practices with respect to *zeroing* in *US – Continued Zeroing*.[77] This case concerned a large number of anti-dumping cases involving EU companies, in particular periodic and sunset reviews in which the US continued to apply zeroing because it was built into the computer programs that the US authorities used for the calculation of dumping margins in such reviews. This occurred despite "zeroing" having

---

73   See Panel Report, *US – Zeroing* (EC), DS294, paras. 7.220–7.221; Panel Report, *US – Zeroing* (*Japan*), DS322, para. 7.99 and footnote 733; Panel Report, *US – Stainless Steel (Mexico)*, DS344, paras. 7.106. For a comment on these cases: Thomas J. Prusa & Edwin Vermulst, 'A One-Two Punch on Zeroing, US-Zeroing (EC) and US-Zeroing (Japan)', *World Trade Review*, (2009) 8:1, 187–241 and Bernard Hoekman & Jasper Wauters, 'US Compliance with WTO Rulings on Zeroing in Anti-Dumping', *World Trade Review*, (2011) 10:1, 5–43, on the DSU 21.5 Implementation Reports.

74   AB, *US – Stainless Steel (Mexico)*, DS344, para. 149.

75   *Ibid*, para. 133-134,139 and 143.

76   *Ibid*, para. 162.

77   DS 350, See Thomas J. Prusa & Edwin Vermulst, 'Continued Existence and Application of Zeroing Methodology: The End of Zeroing?' *World Trade Review*, (2011) 10:1, 45–61.

already been found unlawful in the original imposition of the anti-dumping duties in these cases. The vexed question of zeroing was once again fully litigated, including the interpretation of the special standard of review for anti-dumping cases in Article 17.6(ii) ADA, with the Appellate Body reiterating its earlier interpretations on both issues.[78]

This case is an example for the the EU having brought its measures in conformity with WTO law in an important trade defence policy case, as required by the DSU, even though its anti-dumping authorities had been of the same opinion as their US counterparts, namely that applying zeroing was an appropriate methodology to calculate dumping margins. Once the EU had adapted to the Appellate Body's view, it played the role of a "private Attorney-General" in respect of the US, trying to ensure a level playing field for itself and all other WTO Members that had adapted their legal frameworks to implement the Appellate Body's rejection of "zeroing".

4.2 The Rule Developer: Agricultural Subsidies

Agricultural subsidies are historically a difficult area in trade negotiations, and one in which the European Union and its Member States traditionally appeared as the ones resisting disciplines. Under the GATT, Australia challenged French subsidies to wheat exports in 1958.[79] In the late 1970s and early 1980s, Australia and Brazil unsuccessfully sought agreement from the then European Economic Community on new disciplines on sugar subsidies.[80]

In the WTO, the big breakthrough on agricultural subsidies came in 2002. On a single day, Brazil requested consultations on agricultural subsidies granted by the United States (*US – Cotton*) and by the European Union (*EC – Sugar*). Australia, and later Thailand, joined the *EC – Sugar* dispute as complainants. In both disputes, the complainants achieved resounding victories. In *US – Cotton*,

---

78 AB, *US – Continued Zeroing*, DS350, para. 264–303. An anonymous concurring opinion was added to this part of the report in which the Appellate Body Member recalled that the matter had been litigated in great detail and from many different angles over the years and that every time the AB had considered numerous arguments, always ending with the same conclusion. The author pointed out that this was fully in conformity with the task of the AB, to cut difficult Gordian knots. It was now time to accept what it had decided. The US has not been willing to do this, and the AB's reports on zeroing and its interpretation of the special standard of review have still played an important role in its finally successful manoeuvers to render non-operational the AB, crippling the WTO dispute settlement system with it.

79 GATT, *French Assistance to Exports of Wheat and Wheat Flour*, Report by the Panel for Conciliation, 20 November 1958 (L/924).

80 GATT, Minutes of Meeting held in the Centre William Rappard on 31 March 1982, 7 May 1982 (C/M/156).

the Appellate Body concluded that the Agreement on Agriculture (AoA) did not create a comprehensive carve-out from the Subsidies Agreement with respect to agricultural products, but only exempted Members from the general disciplines on subsidies to the extent that the general rules were being specifically substituted by the *lex specialis* of the AoA.[81] In *EC – Sugar*, the Appellate Body found that guaranteed prices for sugar sold in the EU domestic market in fact provided price support for all sugar production. Coupled with a legislation that required non-subsidised sugar to be exported, this support was found to constitute a "payment on the export financed by virtue of governmental action" above the levels permitted by the EU schedule.[82]

The EU's response to the condemnation was to adopt, a few months before the expiry of the reasonable period of time for compliance, a framework for a comprehensive reform of the sugar sector.[83] Besides removing the requirement that non-subsidised sugar be exported, the 2006 EU regulation allowed dynamic compliance with "the Community's international obligations". Although the complainants were not satisfied that the regulation produced the required compliance, the EU's efforts were sufficient to prevent them from requesting either a compliance panel or authorisation for retaliation.[84]

Over the next decade, the EU reformed its common agricultural policy substantially. This process significantly decreased the weight of the CAP on the EU budget and was driven in large measure by internal pressures resulting from budgetary constraints and the recognition that it would be financially impossible to continue with the old ways of agricultural subsidies when several agricultural states were about to join the EU as new EU Members.[85] The WTO rulings and the prospect of a Doha Round agreement, whereby the EU would have had to reduce subsidies significantly, allowed reformers to reduce the level of trade-distorting subsidies, while being able to "blame it on Geneva".[86] In

---

81   AB, *US – Upland Cotton*, DS267, para. 532.

82   AB, *EC – Sugar*, DS265, para. 164, 278.

83   Council Regulation (EC) No 318/2006 of 20 February 2006 on the common organisation of the markets in the sugar sector.

84   *EC – Sugar*, Understanding between Brazil and the European Communities, 9 June 2006 (WT/DS266/36); Understanding between Australia and the European Communities, 9 June 2006 (WT/DS265/36); Understanding between Thailand and the European Communities, 9 June 2006 (WT/DS283/17).

85   See Johan F.M. Swinnen ed., *The Perfect Storm. The Political Economy of the Fischler Reforms of the Common Agricultural Policy,* Center of European Policy Studies, Brussels 2008.

86   J.C. Bureau, 'Does the WTO discipline really constrain the design of CAP payments?', CAPReform.eu, available at http://capreform.eu/does-the-wto-discipline-really-constrain-the-design-of-cap-payments/.

late 2017, the EU ended its system of quotas for domestic sugar production. Together with the opening of the EU's sugar market through special arrangements for least developed countries and Economic Partnership Agreements with developing countries, this development was the final step in the EU's transition towards "market orientation" in the Common Agricultural Policy.[87]

The shift in the EU's situation was such that, on the issue of agricultural subsidies, it effectively went from being a defendant to being one of the lead proponents of reforms. In 2015, it submitted, together with Brazil and other agricultural exporters, a proposal to restrict agricultural subsidies.[88] This proposal eventually developed into a decision issued by the 2015 Ministerial Conference in Nairobi. This Ministerial Decision required developed countries to eliminate immediately their "remaining scheduled export subsidy entitlements", including with respect to cotton, providing developing countries with a three-year period to do the same.[89] The decision also limited the granting of export credit, export credit guarantees and insurance programmes for export of agricultural products.[90] In implementation of this decision, the EU proposed a revised schedule in October 2017, eliminating its entitlements to agricultural export subsidies.[91] The EU was only the second Member, after Australia, to amend its schedules for this purpose.

The EU's newfound activism against agricultural subsidies did not end there. In the run-up to the 2017 Ministerial Conference in Buenos Aires, Brazil and the EU again submitted a joint proposal, supported by agricultural exporters, to curb "trade distorting domestic support".[92] Although no decision was reached on the matter, this confirmed that the EU – once a large provider of trade-distorting agricultural subsidies – now consistently co-authors proposals to restrict such subsidies, joined by developing, agricultural-exporting countries. The EU therefore not only abided by the WTO ruling requiring it to

---

87   European Commission, 'EU sugar quota system comes to an end', Press release, 29 September 2017 (quoting Phil Hogan, Commissioner for Agriculture and Rural Development).

88   WTO Committee on Agriculture, *Proposal on Export Competition from Brazil, European Union, Argentina, New Zealand, Paraguay, Peru, Uruguay and the Republic of Moldova*, 16 November 2015 (JOB/AG/48/Corr.1).

89   WTO, *Ministerial Decision of 19 December 2015* (WT/MIN(15)/45 – WT/L/980), para. 6, 7, 12 (with respect to cotton, developing countries had only one year to comply).

90   *Ibid*, para. 13.

91   Committee on Market Access, *Rectification and modification of schedules – Schedule CLXXV – European Union*, 17 October 2017 (G/MA/TAR/RS/506).

92   WTO Committee on Agriculture, *Proposal on Domestic Support, Public Stockholding for Food Security Purposes and Cotton from Brazil, European Union, Colombia, Peru and Uruguay*, 17 July 2017 (JOB/AG/99).

modify its agricultural support policies but also actively engaged in seeking a trade-facilitating modification of the multilateral regime governing the matter.

4.3   *The Rule-breaker: Hormone-treated Beef*

The dispute regarding the European Union's ban on hormone-treated beef, started in 1996, was one of longest-lasting ones in the WTO's history.[93] In 1998, the Appellate Body found in *EC – Hormones* that the EU had not produced a risk assessment to support its ban.[94] The EU failed to modify its measures within a reasonable period of time, leading the Dispute Settlement Body to authorise trade retaliation by Canada and the United States.[95]

The EU subsequently sought compliance by funding scientific work to justify the ban. This research was considered insufficient by the complainants, which refused to cease retaliation. In response, the EU initiated the *Canada/ US – Continued Suspension* dispute, arguing that its implementation measures had rendered the retaliation WTO-incompatible; it requested an end to those measures.[96]

In its 2003 report, the Appellate Body concluded that the mere taking of implementation measures did not preclude continued retaliation against a party found in breach. Instead, "substantive compliance" with the report was required.[97] In order to show substantive compliance, the EU would have to demonstrate either that its new reports had been produced with "the necessary scientific and methodological rigour to be considered reputable science"[98] or that they constituted "evidence from a qualified and respected source" putting into question "the relationship between the pre-existing body of scientific evidence and the conclusions regarding the risks".[99] Although the Appellate Body reversed the panel's finding that the EU's measures were not scientifically grounded, the Appellate Body set up more than a procedural requirement for the hormone ban to be lawful: the EU's risk assessment would have to be sufficiently rigorous and either demonstrate the existence of a health risk from hormone-treated beef or cast doubt on the pre-existing body of scientific evidence.

---

93   For a full and informative overview of the whole dispute up to and including 2016, when the US briefly revived the dispute, see Renée Johnson, *The US-EU Hormones Dispute*, Congressional Research Service, 7 January 2017, 35 pp.

94   AB, *EC – Hormones*, DS26, para. 208.

95   Arbitral Award (Article 22.6), *EC – Hormones*.

96   AB, *Canada/US – Continued Suspension*, DS321, para. 211.

97   *Ibid*, para. 321.

98   *Ibid*, para. 591.

99   *Ibid*, para. 703.

The EU did not seek a new adjudication on the basis of the research it had produced. Instead, it negotiated agreements with the complainants whereby, in exchange for tolerating non-compliance, Canada and the US were granted quotas for exporting "high-quality beef" (i.e. non-hormone-treated beef) to the European Union. In 2009, the US was granted an import quota of 20,000 metric tons of high-quality beef (increased to 45.000 in 2012).[100] In 2011, Canada was granted a quota of 1,500 metric tons,[101] replaced in 2017 with a mutually agreed solution that merely noted that the parties' "enhanced cooperation and deeper understanding" under the Comprehensive Economic and Trade Agreement (CETA) had resulted in a solution to the dispute.[102] Quotas for "high-quality beef" are available to other large beef exporters, including Argentina, Australia, Brazil, New Zealand and Uruguay.

In the case of hormone-treated beef, therefore, rather than complying with the WTO ruling, the EU has sought to change the international regulatory framework by entering into bilateral agreements with the complainants, and presumably by offering a degree of compensation to non-complaining WTO Members. Thus, the EU chose a course of action that is an anathema internally: allowing Member States to continue with treaty violations, while paying for their (ongoing) sins.

5   Conclusion

The WTO provides a forum where EU policies are regularly challenged by other Members, subjected to scrutiny by non-EU adjudicators,[103] and enforced through retaliatory measures under strict WTO surveillance.[104] This has compelled the various EU organs to make decisions on how to manage the interrelationship between the EU legal order and WTO rules. This included, on the one hand, the ECJ's rejection of direct effect of WTO rules within the EU legal order and its minimising of the authority of reports of panels and the Appellate Body. This rejection foreshadowed the separation of the EU's "new legal

---

100   *EC – Hormones*, Joint Communication from the European Communities and the United States, 17 April 2014 (WT/DS26/29).

101   *EC – Hormones*, Joint Communication from the European Union and Canada, 22 March 2011 (WT/DS48/26).

102   *EC – Hormones*, Notification of a Mutually Agreed Solution, 3 October 2017 (WT/DS48/27, G/L/91/).

103   This situation differs from the adjudication by the ECJ itself under Association Agreements. See e.g. C-65/16, *Istanbul Lojistik*, 19 October 2017, EU:C:2017:770.

104   Art. 22(3)-(8) Dispute Settlement Understanding (DSU).

order" from general international law, later expressed in the legal notion of "autonomy of the EU legal order", as advanced, among others, in the *Kadi* cases[105] on the implementation of so-called smart sanctions of the UN Security Council and in *Opinion 2/13* on the accession of the EU to the European Convention on Human Rights.[106] It also imposed on the EU's political organs the task of determining how and at what pace to comply with WTO rulings, managing the interaction between the EU legal order and the rules governing the EU's relations with its main trade partners.

Overall, the EU's political organs have sought to implement faithfully the rulings and recommendations adopted by the DSB. This has proven possible in cases, such as that of bananas and zeroing, in which WTO-inconsistent policies were based essentially on economic interests. In some cases, such as those of zeroing and agricultural subsidies, the EU has gone on to promote the Appellate Body's view, aiming to "level the playing field" so that the WTO-inconsistent benefits it had denied to its own economic agents would become unavailable also to their foreign competitors.

Changing policies based on politically sensitive "non-trade values", on the other hand, has proven much more difficult. In the case of Inuit indigenous communities, the EU was able to implement the Appellate Body's rulings while maintaining the bulk of its measure in place, and even furthering its objective, by further restricting the possibilities for cruel hunting, as well as by opening its market to Canadian Inuit products.[107] In the cases of rulings condemning its restrictions on GMOs and hormone-treated beef, however, the EU political organs were unable either to provide evidence that these products pose actual health risks or to override deeply held public suspicion that they do. In these cases, the EU has had to compromise, either by offering implementation measures that did not fully address the complainants' concerns (in *EC – Biotech*) or by agreeing with complainants to provide compensation through imports of other products ("high-quality beef") in *EC – Hormones*.

Overall, the means that the political organs have used to remedy adverse WTO reports have confirmed the ECJ's view that WTO rulings may not

---

105   Joined Cases C–402/05 P and C–415/05, P. *Kadi and Al Barakaat International Foundation v. Council and Commission* [2008] ECR I–6351; Joined Cases C-584/10 P, C-593/10 P and C-595/10 P, *European Commission and Others v Yassin Abdullah Kadi*, EU:C:2013:518.

106   *Opinion 2/13 ECHR Accession*, EU:C:2014:2454. The recent *Opinion 1/17*, EU:C:2019: 341 clarifies that binding international dispute settlement procedures are not at odds with the autonomy of the EU legal order, when they are inter-State mechanisms involving the EU and third States as parties, such as the WTO dispute settlement procedure.

107   Emily Lydgate, 'Is it Rational and Consistent? The WTO'S Surprising Role in Shaping Domestic Public Policy' 20 *Journal of International Economic Law* (2017) 561.

constitute the end of disputes, but merely a starting point for negotiations; this is contrasted with the role of ECJ decisions that have a significantly higher implementation rate. In these negotiations, the EU has generally aimed to address inconsistencies found by the panel and Appellate Body without harming the competitive conditions of its economic agents and without giving up its policies to protect non-trade values, irrespective of whether these values can be "objectively" (read: scientifically) justified.

Conflict therefore is more likely to occur in the latter cases: those in which the political opinions of EU citizens materialise in policies that run counter to WTO requirements of objectivity and non-discrimination. In these cases, the EU's political and economic weight may allow it to choose between addressing the issues internally, at the risk of lowering the EU's popularity with its citizens, or seeking to re-shape the global legal environment to level the playing field and project its preferences into the broader international legal order.

PART 6

The Institutional and Procedural Dimension of the CCP

∵

CHAPTER 19

The Legitimacy of 'EU-Only' Preferential Trade Agreements

David Kleimann

1 Introduction

This chapter examines three dimensions of legitimacy of the negotiation, signature, and conclusion of broader EU external economic treaties – i.e. preferential trade agreements (PTAs) – since the entry into force of the Lisbon Treaty in 2009 in comparison to pre-Lisbon law and practice. These three dimensions are the *de jure* legitimacy, output legitimacy, and input legitimacy of EU PTA governance. The focal point of this enquiry is whether the Lisbon Treaty reform of EU Common Commercial Policy (CCP) has resulted in the achievement of the reform objectives set out by the 2001 Laeken Council[1], notably the European Council's pledge to enhance the legitimacy of EU governance through "more democracy, transparency, and efficiency".[2] For the purposes of this chapter, the term governance is employed as a synonym for the process of negotiating, signing, and concluding EU PTAs.

Any assessment of the Lisbon reform of the CCP that is mindful of the Laeken objective of enhanced legitimacy can arguably not be limited to the positive analysis of black letter law but should account for the constitutional reality and practice that followed formal reform. Most importantly, in order to discern potential effects on political representation, transparency and efficiency of the decision-making process any such an assessment needs to

---

1 European Council, *Presidency Conclusions, European Council Meeting in Laeken*, 14–15 December 2001.

2 Already in 2011, Markus Krajewski noted that "the results of the EU reform process reached by the Lisbon Treaty, must be primarily assessed according to whether they have contributed towards an improvement in the transparency, efficiency and democratic legitimation of the Union. These aims which were set down by the European Council in the Laeken Declaration are the "raison être" of the Lisbon Treaty." M. Krajewski, 'New Functions and New Powers for the European Parliament: Assessing the Changes of the Common Commercial Policy from the Perspective of Democratic Legitimacy', in C. Herrmann, M. Bungenberg (eds.) *Common Commercial Policy after Lisbon* (Springer, 2013), p. 67–68.

examine whether primary law reform restructures the market for access to public decision-making.

Constitutional reform may reallocate institutional access points for political participation of stakeholders. If so, constitutional reform *a priori* alters the relative cost of political participation for a given set of diffuse or special interests that act upon the political institutions mandated with CCP governance. Formally institutionalized incentives guide interest group activity towards legitimate channels of influence. The variable efficiency of private interest organization[3] as well the structural characteristics of public decision-making bodies[4] – i.e. of the mandated political institutions – determine the quality of interest aggregation and the effectiveness of interest groups to skew the substance of policy in their favour.[5] Constitutional reform and practice by the mandated political institutions thereby determine the likelihood for diffuse (majoritarian) interest biases in decision-making or the success of attempts to capture the public policy agenda on behalf of special (minoritarian) interests.[6] Alternative institutional choices and the design of the institutional architecture implicate choices over process transparency, representation of stakeholders, policy objectives, and the likelihood of their accomplishment.[7]

This chapter argues that the Lisbon reform of CCP governance has triggered a process of institutional change that may now – 10 years after the entry into force of the reform – generate what Joseph Weiler calls a new "legal-political equilibrium".[8] At the time of writing, it is now evident that the new post-Lisbon legal-political equilibrium of CCP political transactions in the area of broader external economic treaty-making has fundamentally shifted to a *modus operandi* that arguably minimises transaction costs of CCP governance; alters the

---

3   M. Olson, *The Logic of Collective Action – Public Goods and the Theory of Groups* (Harvard University Press, 1965).

4   E. L. Rubin, 'The New Legal Process, the Synthesis of Discourse, and the Microanalysis of Institutions', 109 (6) *Harvard Law Review* (1996) p. 1428.

5   As Hauser notes: "Indeed, the very structure of a political institution influences the nature of interest representation." H. Hauser, 'European Union Lobbying Post-Lisbon: An Economic Analysis', 29 *Berkeley Journal of International Law* 680 (2011), p. 694.

6   N. K. Komesar, *Imperfect Alternatives – Choosing Institutions in Law, Economics, and Public Policy*, (University of Chicago Press, 1984), p. 81. Similarly, Olson discusses "latent" and "dormant" low-stake majorities that can be activated – say through high-profile misinformation campaigns - by high-stake special interest groups - to the disadvantage of the former and the advantage of the latter. M. Olson, (n. 3).

7   M. Olson (n. 3); N.K. Komesar (n. 6), p. 54; G. Stigler, 'The Theory of Economic Regulation', *Bell Journal of Economics and Management Science* 2(1) (1971), p. 3–21.

8   J. H.H. Weiler, 'The Transformation of Europe', *The Yale Law Journal* 100(8), Symposium: International Law (1991), p. 2429.

institutionalized sources of democratic legitimacy; and enhances democratic representation at the same time. It is the change of constitutional practice from a mixed to a non-mixed (*EU-only*) mode of signing and concluding broader EU external economic agreements, which creates this new balance. It is argued here that the achievement of the three Laeken objectives, which underpin the Lisbon reform, is further approximated in this new legal-political equilibrium.

As noted above, legitimation of post-Lisbon CCP governance can be conceptualized along the lines of three different dimensions of legitimacy, notably *de jure* legitimacy, output legitimacy, and input legitimacy. The formal reform of vertical (substantive) and horizontal (procedural) competences as a result of the Lisbon Treaty of 2009 and the legal clarity advanced through ECJ adjudication fall into the realm of the first – *de jure* – dimension to this end.[9] Beyond formal reform and legal certainty of policy-making, it is the powerful demand for the successful implementation of the EU's PTA agenda as well as enhanced democratic representation and transparency at the EU level through the empowerment of the European Parliament, which have enabled and incentivized the *transformation* of EU PTA governance to a new equilibrium.

The chapter is structured as follows. Section 2 examines the conditions for *de jure* legitimation of EU-only PTA governance and gives an overview of the formal reform and litigation of EU exclusive competence for Common Commercial Policy. Turning to output legitimacy, Section 3 contextualizes the debate over institutional effectiveness and efficiency of EU external treaty governance by reference to George Tsebelis "veto-player" analysis and provides evidence for adverse effects of comparatively high numbers of veto points on both quality and quantity of EU PTA output. Section 4 complements the forgoing analysis by presenting the latest evidence of changing EU institutional practice, notably the split of EU PTAs along the lines of EU exclusive and shared external competences and the shift to an EU-only mode of EU PTA governance. Section 5 discusses the input legitimation of EU-only external economic treaty governance and, to that end, examines the scope of changes in democratic representation and transparency of EU decision-making as afforded through the empowerment of the European Parliament and the subordination of national political institutions to the EU level. Section 6 concludes the chapter.

---

9 Most importantly: Case C-414/11, *Daiichi Sankyo* Co. Ltd and Sanofi-Aventis Deutschland GmbH v DEMO Anonimos Viomikhaniki kai Emporiki Etairia Farmakon, EU:C:2013:520; Case C-137/12, Commission v. Council (*Conditional Access Convention*), EU:C:2013:675; Opinion 2/15, The FTA with Singapore, ECLI:EU:C:2017:376; *Opinion 3/15, The Marrakesh Treaty* EU:C:2017:114.

2   De Jure Legitimation of EU External Economic Treaty-making

De jure legitimacy of external economic treaty-making denotes the scope of lawful treaty-making governance by the political institutions and actors mandated by EU primary law. The compliance of respective institutions and actors with the EU primary law provisions and relevant jurisprudence shall be – for the purposes of this chapter – characterized as *de jure* legitimate.

To begin with, the choice of the *de jure* legitimate external treaty-making procedure (EU-only *or* mixed) is a function of the delineation and scope of external treaty-making competences in EU primary law and the content of the respective treaty. The significance of the question over the existence and nature of EU external competence, in other words, derives from its link to the procedural modalities of treaty-making in the EU: if the content of a treaty falls within the scope of EU exclusive competence entirely, the conclusion of the treaty by the EU alone is a legal requirement (*mandatory EU-only agreement*). In contrast, where a treaty includes (just) a single provision that falls within the scope of exclusive competences of the Member States, the EU *must* conclude the treaty jointly with the Member States in their own right (*mandatory mixed agreement*). If, however, parts of the treaty fall under EU exclusive competence, whereas other parts of the treaty fall under competences shared with the Member States, it is left to the political discretion of the EU institutions to involve the Member States as parties in their own right or conclude the treaty alone (*facultative mixity*).[10] In other words, Member States in the Council may insist on their participation in their own right through mixed treaty-making.[11]

---

10   On this issue, see also the contributions by A. Rosas and M. Cremona in this volume.

11   In his submission in the Opinion 3/15 proceedings, Advocate General Wahl recalled that "the choice between a mixed agreement or an EU-only agreement, when the subject matter of the agreement falls within an area of shared competence (or of parallel competence), is generally a matter for the discretion of the EU legislature. That decision, as it is predominantly political in nature, may be subject to only limited judicial review." (Opinion 3/15: Opinion of the Advocate General Wahl, para. 119–120) Such discretion, however, is subject to procedural rules laid down in Article 218 TFEU: The Commission may propose the signing and conclusion of an external agreement as 'EU-only'. Member States represented in the Council can then decide to authorize the signature and conclude the treaty as an EU-only agreement by qualified majority voting (QMV) if TFEU-based unanimity requirements do not apply. Alternatively, the Council may adopt a unanimous decision to amend the Commission proposal for an EU-only agreement and mandate the independent ratification by each and every Member State - in addition to the Council decision on treaty signature and conclusion (Article 293(1) TFEU). The Court's wording in Opinion 2/15 (para. 244 and 292) cast doubts over the prevalence of the theory of facultative mixity. See, for instance: L. Ankersmit, *Opinion 2/15 and the Future of Mixity and ISDS*, European Law Blog (2017). The Court, however, reaffirmed the political discretion

Importantly, the Lisbon Treaty reform of EU primary law broadened the scope of EU exclusive competence for Common Commercial Policy and hence altered the conditions for the *de jure* legitimation of EU-only external economic treaty-making. The ECJ, moreover, clarified the precise delineation of EU external competence with regard to the EU's new generation of PTAs in Opinion 2/15.[12] Given the significance of the Lisbon reform of exclusive EU economic treaty-making competence and the Court's precise delineation of that very competence in Opinion 2/15, both issues are briefly discussed below.

2.1   *Exclusive Competence for Common Commercial Policy after Lisbon*

Under the Treaty of Rome of 1957, initially, the CCP only extended to basic border measures for trade in goods.[13] Consecutive reforms of the primary law provisions through the treaties of Amsterdam[14], Nice[15], and Lisbon[16] have widened the scope of the CCP to cover a broader realm of policy areas and instruments that affect external trade in goods and services as well as foreign direct investment at the border and beyond.

The latest EU primary law reform – the Lisbon Treaty of 2009 – considerably consolidated and simplified the provisions of the CCP. Most notably, the reform treaty added "services", "commercial aspects of intellectual property" and "foreign direct investment" to the text of the first paragraph of former Article 133 EC Treaty, now Article 207 (1) TFEU. Article 207 (1) TFEU reads as follows:

---

of the Council to adopt facultative 'EU-only' / 'mixed' agreements in C-600–14, *Germany v. Council* (ECLI:EU:C:2017:935), para. 68.

12   On Opinion 2/15, see also the contributions by M. Cremona and A. Rosas in this volume.

13   The original version of Article 113(1) of the 1957 Treaty Establishing the European Community reads: "The common commercial policy shall be based on uniform principles, particularly in regard to changes in tariff rates, the conclusion of tariff and trade agreements, the achievement of uniformity in measures of liberalisation, export policy and measures to protect trade such as those to be taken in the event of dumping or subsidies."

14   For a contextualization of Amsterdam Treaty amendments in ECJ jurisprudence and treaty negotiation see M. Cremona, *EC External Commercial Policy after Amsterdam: Authority and Interpretation within Interconnected Legal Orders,* in Weiler, JHHW (ed.): *The EU, the WTO, and the NAFTA: Towards a Common Law of International Trade?* (Oxford University Press, 2001), p. 5–34.

15   For a comprehensive discussion of the Nice treaty amendments, see C. Herrmann, 'Common Commercial Policy after Nice: Sisyphus would have done a Better Job', *Common Market Law Review* 39 (2002), p. 7–29.

16   M. Krajewski, 'The Reform of the Common Commercial Policy', in A. Biondi, P. Eeckhout, and S. Ripley (eds.) *EU Law after Lisbon* (Cambridge University Press, 2012).

> The common commercial policy shall be based on uniform principles, particularly with regard to *changes in tariff rates*, the conclusion of tariff and trade agreements *relating to trade in goods* and *services*, and the *commercial aspects of intellectual property, foreign direct investment*, the achievement of uniformity in measures of liberalisation, export policy and measures to protect trade such as those to be taken in the event of *dumping or subsidies*. The common commercial policy shall be conducted *in the context of the principles and objectives of the Union's external action*.[17]

The arguably most significant expansion of EU exclusive competence occurred in the area of foreign direct investment (FDI). The addition of FDI in Article 207(1) TFEU, however, raised a number of legal questions with regard to the scope of Union competence in this policy area as well as over the future substance of EU foreign direct investment policy.[18] Immediate challenges associated with the transfer of competence were, however, resolved through the adoption of a regulation establishing a transitional arrangement for bilateral investment agreements (BIT).[19] Yet, the exact scope of the Union's new exclusive external competence for FDI was only clarified by Opinion 2/15 in May 2017, as discussed further below.

The Commission had negotiated services and trade-related intellectual property rights (IPRS) – i.e. the two other areas that are now part of the scope of EU exclusive competence – since the coming into force of the 1997 Treaty of Amsterdam on the basis of Article 133(5) EC Treaty. The clarification and consolidation of EU exclusive competence in these areas, by means of their inclusion in the first paragraph of Article 207 TFEU nevertheless have important ramifications for Member States' involvement in the decision-making procedure. First, Member States' governments can no longer invoke the right to unanimous decision-making in the Council on the basis of their coverage in

---

17   Emphasis added.
18   On this issue, see the contribution by C. Brown in this volume.
19   Regulation (EU) 1219/2012 of the European Parliament and of the Council of 12 December 2012 establishing transitional arrangements for bilateral investment agreements between Member States and third countries (OJ 2012, L 351/40). In order to guarantee legal certain, the regulation grandfathers existing Member State BITs by authorising Member States to leave national agreements in force, while obliging Member States to bring these treaties into conformity with the regulation where necessary. The regulation also authorises Member States, subject to Commission approval, to negotiate individual BITs and envisages the formulation of a comprehensive EU investment policy at a later stage.
        M. Cremona (n. 14), p. 6.

legislation or external agreements. Secondly, the signature and conclusion of agreements covering only services- and trade-related IPR s and other EU exclusive competences requires the 'EU-only' *modus operandi*, which subordinates Member States' political institutions to the EU level of governance. Member States, in their own right, are then precluded from participation other than through their representation in the Council.

Article 207(4)(3) TFEU retains exceptions that apply to certain services sectors, which are regarded as politically sensitive, i.e. cultural and audiovisual services as well as social, health and education services. Compared to Article 133 EC Treaty, however, Article 207(4) TFEU has removed such services from the field of shared competences and added them to the scope EU exclusive competence under Article 207 TFEU. Article 207(5) TFEU, however, provides for the last bastion of services sectors that fall in the scope of shared external EU competence. The field of transport services remains subject to shared EU competence in accordance with Article 4(g) TFEU if Union competence is not otherwise rendered exclusive by implication via Article 3(2) TFEU.

Article 207 TFEU, in sum, is the latest result of 60 years of formal institutional change in Common Commercial Policy. As predicted by the Court in Opinion 1/78[20] and retrospectively observed by Richard Baldwin[21], the changing nature and increasing complexity of international trade and investment patterns in the past decades has generated a demand for a constitutional framework that adapted the powers of the Community (and Union) institutions to engage in the regulation of its external economic environment. The profit and welfare

---

20   In Opinion 1/78, the Court opted for a markedly dynamic interpretation of the scope of the CCP. More than two decades after the entry into force of the Treaty of Rome, the Court held that "it would no longer be possible to carry on any worthwhile common commercial policy if the Community were not in a position to avail itself also of more elaborate means devised with a view to furthering the development of international trade. It is therefore not possible to lay down, for Article 113 of the EEC Treaty, an interpretation the effect of which would be to restrict the common commercial policy to the use of instruments intended to have an effect only on the traditional aspects of external trade to the exclusion of more highly developed mechanisms such as appear in the agreement envisaged. A 'commercial policy' understood in that sense would be destined to become nugatory in the course of time." Opinion 1/78, *International Agreement on Natural Rubber*, ECLI:EU:C:1979:224, para. 44

21   In 2011, Baldwin noted that "[in the 20th century], trade mostly meant selling goods made in a factory in one nation to a customer in another. Simple trade needed simple rules. [...] Today's trade is radically more complex. The ICT revolution fostered an internationalization of supply chains, and this in turn created the 'trade-investment-services nexus' at the heart of so much of today's international commerce." R. Baldwin, '21st Century Regionalism: Filling the gap between 21st century trade and 20th century trade rules', World Trade Organization (2011), p. 3.

enhancing potential of commercial opportunities inherent to international trade, as well as the evolving complementary international legal institutions that have facilitated and regulated international commercial transactions catalysed the demand for reform of primary legal provisions governing the CCP.

The otherwise rare exclusive nature of EU competence for the CCP as well as the vagueness of its provisions with respect to its material scope and purpose(s), has, however, provided strong incentives for political and judicial conflict over the operation of the CCP.[22] It is in this context that the interplay between policy demand generated by international economic and legal institutions, the inter-institutional political process at Community and Union level, primary law reform, and ECJ litigation has created a dynamic of constructive tension. It is this interplay that has catalysed as well as constrained incremental progress towards an expansion of the scope within which EU unity in external commercial policy remains an *a priori* possibility. It is this interplay, moreover, that has set incentives for the EU's political institutions to seek greater legal clarity over the precise delineation of exclusive competence for external economic treaty-making through litigation – as, most recently, done in Opinion 2/15.

2.2   *Opinion 2/15: Litigating EU Exclusive Competence for External Economic Governance*

Whether the content of the new generation of broader external economic agreements matches or exceeds the scope of the CCP and implied EU exclusive competence for treaty-making is the very question that stood at the centre of the Opinion 2/15 proceedings. It was of particular concern here whether the Union's exclusive treaty-making competences extend to the entirety of the EU-Singapore FTA (EUSFTA), which makes for a blueprint for the latest generation of EU trade and investment agreements. In its questions submitted to the Court, the European Commission asked:

> Does the Union have the requisite competence to sign and conclude alone the Free Trade Agreement with Singapore? More specifically: Which provisions of the agreement fall within the Union's exclusive competence? Which provisions of the agreement fall within the Union's shared competence? and Is there any provision of the agreement that falls within the exclusive competence of the Member States?[23]

---

22   M. Cremona (n. 14), p. 6.

23   Request for an opinion submitted by the European Commission pursuant to Article 218(11) TFEU (Opinion 2/15) (2015/C 363/22), 3 November 2015.

In her submission to the Court in the Opinion 2/15 proceedings, Advocate General Sharpston argued that several parts and components of the EUSFTA fall under EU shared competence – including certain transport services[24], portfolio investment[25], labour rights and environmental protection obligations[26] – whereas the termination of Member States' BITs, in her view, fall within the scope of exclusive competence of the Member States.[27]

The Court's opinion, however, markedly differed from the legal view of the AG and broadly confirmed the tectonic shifts of competence that the Lisbon Treaty brought about in the area of Common Commercial Policy and EU external economic governance – with one notable exception.[28] At the most general level, the Court held that EUSFTA components governing trade in goods, services, commercial aspects of intellectual property, government procurement, competition policy, FDI admission and protection, transport services, e-commerce, and sustainable development provisions related to trade fall under EU exclusive external competence, whereas portfolio investment and the contentious investor-to-state dispute settlement (ISDS) mechanism are subject to shared external competence.[29] It follows that the Union can conclude treaties, which include wide-ranging substantive areas covered by exclusive external competence without the participation of the Member States in their own right – with the exception of portfolio investment and ISDS.

Compared to the legal view of the AG, the Court advanced a wider application of the "immediate and direct effects on trade" criterion, which it had developed in its earlier jurisprudence in an effort to add precision to the exact material scope of Common Commercial Policy.[30] By the same token, the Court's reasoning embeds the CCP into the context of EU external action

---

24   Opinion of Advocate General Sharpston delivered on 21 December 2016, Opinion 2/15, The FTA with Singapore: para. 268.

25   *Ibid*, para. 370.

26   *Ibid*, para. 502.

27   The AG opined that "the European Union has no competence to agree to Article 9.10(1) of the EUSFTA", which provides that existing EU Member States' bilateral investment treaties with Singapore "cease to have effect and shall be replaced and superseded" by the EUSFTA (Opinion of AG Sharpston, Opinion 2/15, para. 396).

28   For a first analysis of Opinion 2/15 see: Kleimann, David and Gesa Kübek, 'The Singapore Opinion or the End of Mixity as we know it', *Verfassungsblog* (23 May 2017).

29   By inference, in conclusion, Opinion 2/15, para. 305.

30   "[A] European Union act falls within the common commercial policy if it relates specifically to international trade in that it is essentially intended to promote, facilitate or govern trade and has direct and immediate effects on trade." Case C-414/11 (*Daiichi Sankyo v DEMO*), para. 51; C-411/06 (*Commission vs Parliament and Council*), para. 71; C-347/03 (*Regione autonoma Friuli-Venezia Giulia and ERSA*), para. 75.

objectives and thus gives full effect to the Lisbon reform of Article 207(1) TFEU in this regard.[31] The combination of these two contingencies led the Court to the rather historical conclusion that the EUSFTA provisions on labor rights and environmental protection fall within the scope of EU exclusive competence attributed to the CCP.[32]

The Court, moreover, cast a wider web for *incidental* treaty content than the AG. Incidental treaty components or provisions, according to the Court's jurisprudence, are subordinated to the agreement's predominant purpose (i.e. commerce within the meaning of the CCP Article 207 TFEU) if they are "extremely limited in scope" and thus do not have the potential to affect the allocation of competences.[33] In application of a more generous understanding of what is "extremely limited in scope", the Court dismissed the AG's findings that "moral rights"[34] and "inland waterway transport"[35] could make for autonomous EUSFTA components. The Court hence did not require reference to legal bases for which the Union shares competence with the member states.[36] The Court, compared to the AG, also advanced a more permissive interpretation of implied exclusive powers with respect to its ERTA case law[37], which resulted in a broader shelter for EUSFTA transport services commitments.[38]

In agreement with AG Sharpston's finding on portfolio investment, the Court's ruling dismissed the arguments of the Commission in favor of implied ERTA exclusivity on the basis of a primary law provision, notably Article 63(1) TFEU. In doing so, the Court set an important boundary for the ERTA doctrine: triggering Article 3(2)(3) TFEU requires the existence of internal EU legislation. Primary law provisions cannot be altered or affected by external EU agreements.[39] Yet, the Court found that the EU and the Member States share the power to conclude non-direct investment agreements on the basis of Article 216 (1) TFEU.[40]

---

31 The (added) final sentence of Art. 207(1) TFEU reads: "The common commercial policy shall be conducted in the context of the principles and objectives of the Union's external action."

32 Opinion 2/15: para. 147 and 157.

33 For instance, Case C-377/12 (*Commission vs. Council*), para 34.

34 Opinion of AG Sharpston, Opinion 2/15, para. 456.

35 *Ibid*, para. 244–246.

36 Opinion 2/15, para. 129; 216–217.

37 C-22/70 (*Commission vs Council*), para. 17.

38 Opinion 2/15, para. 192.

39 *Ibid*, para. 235.

40 *Ibid*, para. 239.

In a finding that has markedly changed the direction of the Union's policy in pursuit of external investment protection, the Court ruled that the EUSFTA's ISDS mechanism falls within the scope of a competence shared between the EU and the Member States and thus objected to AG Sharpston's reasoning. The AG had considered that the investor-state dispute settlement mechanism is accessory to the substantive investment protection obligations of the EUSFTA. According to the Court, however, a regime that removes disputes from the jurisdiction of domestic courts may not be regarded as ancillary (or: accessory) to such substantive obligations. Consequently, it "cannot be established without the Member States' consent".[41] It remains a mystery, however, why the Court did not endeavor to ground this finding on an appropriate – or any – legal basis. As it stands, it remains entirely unclear which TFEU provision the Court deems to confer a shared competence for the establishment of an ISDS regime.

In sum, the Court provided a much awaited clarification of the delineation of EU exclusive competence for the negotiation, signing, and conclusion of both narrow and broader external economic treaties. As a result, it shall be noted that the entire content of the EUSFTA – with the exception of ISDS and portfolio investment – falls within the scope of exclusive external competence and, if limited to that scope, allows for EU-only signature and conclusion.

Having examined the scope for the *de jure* legitimacy of EU-only external economic treaty-making with respect to the realm of vertical competence, I now turn to a discussion of output legitimation of such treaty-making practice.

3   Output Legitimation of EU-only External Economic Treaty-making

Drawing from Fritz Scharpf's famous conceptual distinction between input and output legitimacy of public decision-making, the legitimacy of political decision-making increases if it is effective in increasing the welfare for the people governed by the respective policy.[42] One condition for such output legitimation of policy is, to be sure, the capacity of a given institutional framework to produce policy outcomes at all. A second factor is its capacity to minimize rent-seeking opportunities for special interest advocacy, which, if successful, reduces economic welfare. The degree of output legitimacy, third, is also contingent on the efficiency of decision-making as societal welfare benefits

---

41   *Ibid*, para. 292.
42   F. Scharpf, '*Governing in Europe: Effective and Democratic* (Oxford University Press, 1999).

that would stem from a new policy are reduced commensurate to delays in policy implementation. Overall, the analytical benchmark for economic integration policies is whether an institutional framework is effective in delivering outcomes that maximize economic welfare, notwithstanding equality of distribution.[43]

Demonstrating the significance of institutional choice for international economic integration, various scholars have applied George Tsebelis' veto player model to compare the effectiveness of entire institutional architectures across countries.[44] This effort resulted in a comparative assessment of the performance of national institutional frameworks governing external economic integration with respect to the likelihood for deeper external economic integration,[45] the likelihood of a state to sign preferential trade agreements (PTA),[46] and the likelihood to reduce tariff and non-tariff barriers.[47] The findings consistently demonstrate that domestic demand for enhanced economic integration is significantly less successful in shaping policy outcomes commensurate to the increasing number of veto-players involved in the decision-making process. A series of empirical tests based on an analysis of PTA membership from 1950 to 1999 demonstrate that an increase in the number of domestic veto players can cut the probability of forming a PTA by as much as 50 per cent.[48]

Following the logic of these results, the allocation of a veto right to the European Parliament in respect of CCP agreements with third countries through the 2009 Lisbon Treaty reform would thus be expected to decrease the relative institutional effectiveness of the Commission and the Council in the CCP treaty-making process. However, the extension of qualified majority voting (QMV) in the Council to external services trade, intellectual property rights, and foreign direct investment following the Lisbon reform of 2009 would *a priori* result in increasing institutional effectiveness of the Commission and

---

43   With regard to external economic integration, unequal internal distributional effects of economic welfare gains derived therefrom frequently require domestic social policies that generate benefits for the society as a whole.

44   G. Tsebelis, 'Decision Making in Political Systems: Veto Players in Presidentialism, Parliamentarism, Multicameralism and Multipartyism', *British Journal of Political Science* 25(3) (1995), p. 289–325.

45   E. Mansfield, H. V. Milner, and J. C. Pevehouse, 'Democracy, Veto Players and the Depth of Regional Integration', *The World Economy* 31(1) (2008), p. 67–96.

46   E. Mansfield, V. Milner, and J. C. Pevehouse, 'Vetoing Co-operation: The Impact of Veto Players on Preferential Trading Agreements', *British Journal of Political Science* 37 (2007), p. 403–432.

47   R. O'Reilly, 'Veto Points, Veto Players, and International Trade Policy', *Comparative Political Studies* 38(6) (2005), p. 652–675.

48   E. Mansfield, V. Milner, and J. C. Pevehouse (n. 46), p. 432.

the EP vis-à-vis the Council, and increasing effectiveness of the institutional framework overall.

The benefits of QMV Council decisions on signature and conclusion, however, only extend insofar as external economic treaties are limited to substance covered by EU exclusive external competence. In practice, broader EU external economic agreements – i.e. EU PTAS – always included provisions falling under shared or Member States' exclusive competence until very recently, which allowed Member States to insist on their participation in their own right and to opt for the mixed modus of treaty-making. The veto-rights held by 27 Member State governments and their national (and even regional) parliaments in the *modus operandi* applicable to the signing and conclusion of mixed external economic agreements dramatically decrease the effectiveness and efficiency of the overall institutional architecture in the process of CCP governance if compared to a scenario of *EU-only (non-mixed)* signature and conclusion of said agreements. At the same time, they increase the likelihood of successful capture of veto-points by efficiently organized special interest advocacy, which has the potential to decrease the efficiency of the policy at stake.

It is a well-documented fact that the European and international political economy continues to aggregate a powerful demand for the success of the EU's trade and investment policy agenda,[49] the substance of which is reflected in the 2006 Global Europe strategy[50] and its more recent updates of 2010[51] and 2015.[52] Highly effective special interest advocacy has, on the other hand, demonstrated its capacity to capture veto-points in the mixed mode of external economic governance and to increase political transaction costs associated with the signing and conclusion of EU external economic agreements to nearly prohibitive levels. A requirement for unanimity in the Council as well

---

49   Dür presents empirical evidence on the coincidence between societal demands and the EU's position in trade negotiations, which is explained through "first rate access to decision-makers on trade policy issues" (A. Dür, 'Bringing Economic Interests Back into the Study of EU Trade Policy-Making', *The British Journal of Politics & International Relations* 10(1) (2008), p. 27–45). Moreover, Dür et al. show that both business and citizen groups enjoy considerable influence in EU legislative politics (A. Dür, et al. 'Interest Group Success in the European Union: When (and Why) Does Business Lose?' *Comparative Political Studies* 48(8) (2013), p. 951–983.).

50   European Commission: *Global Europe, Competing in the World – A Contribution to the EU's Growth and Jobs* Strategy, COM(2006) 567 final, 4 October 2006.

51   European Commission: *Trade, Growth, and World Affairs – Trade Policy as a Key Component of the EU 2020 Strategy* COM(2010) 612 final, Brussels, 9 November 2010.

52   European Commission: *Trade for All – Toward a more responsible trade and investment policy,* COM (2015) 497 final, 14 November 2015.

as Member State ratification of EU external agreements hence pose a credible threat to the success of the Union's external economic agenda, despite broad general Member State support.

Two examples of post-Lisbon practice serve as an illustration of the consequences of unanimous voting requirements in the mixed mode of signing and concluding EU PTAs. The episodes referred to describe the dynamics inherent to the procedure of authorising the signature of two of the most advanced and economically most significant trade and investment agreements negotiated in the post-Lisbon era.

The signature of the EU – Korea FTA in September 2010, first, was jeopardized by the Italian government, which threatened to veto the Council decision to authorize the signing of the agreement if the agreement's provisional application was not postponed for another year. The Italian government's position at the time was heavily guided by Italy's troubled small-car maker Fiat, which sought protection from Korean car exports to Europe. As the signing of the treaty by the President of the Council had been planned to take place on October 5, 2010, at the ASEAN summit in Brussels – the Commission and the Council Presidency found themselves under strong time pressure to forge a compromise. Eventually, the provisional application of the EU-Korea FTA was delayed by six months and commenced on July 1, 2011 as a result of the Italian intervention.[53]

Similar to the Italian opposition to the EU-Korea FTA, the veto threat of the regional Belgian government of Wallonia in the more recent episode over the signing of the EU-Canada Comprehensive Economic Trade and Trade Agreement (CETA) in October 2016 further increased awareness of the negative repercussions of mixed agreement governance. The episode raised serious concerns over the prospects of the overall post-Lisbon PTA agenda, the credibility of EU negotiators vis-à-vis foreign governments, and highlighted issues of democratic representation in context of the unanimity requirement where a regional constituency of 3.5 million EU citizens could block a policy supported by the governments of all other Member States.[54]

As argued elsewhere in greater detail, the scenario of Member State parliamentary rejection of a mixed agreement – such as CETA – continues to confront the Union's political institutions with significant legal and political

---

53   D. Kleimann, 'Taking Stock: EU Common Commercial Policy in the Lisbon Era', *Aussenwirtschaft* 66(2) (2011), p. 243–44.

54   D. Kleimann, G. Kübek, 'The Signing, Provisional Application, and Conclusion of Trade and Investment Agreements in the EU - The Case of CETA and Opinion 2/15', *Legal issues of Economic Integration* 45 (2018), p. 13–45.

challenges. At the same time, it has sharply increased incentives towards the adoption of a new EU-only design of EU external economic agreements.[55]

The two examples underscore the significance of institutional choice and institutional change in EU external economic governance for the pursuit of legitimate public goods, which affect the development path of the European political, social, and economic community in the decades to come.

It is arguable, therefore, that the most recent Council practice, which acquiesces to Commission proposals for *EU-only* negotiation, signature, and conclusion of broader external economic agreements further approximates the achievement of *enhanced legitimacy* in terms of *output* through more effective and efficient governance and more efficient policies.

4   The New EU Economic Treaty Architecture

By providing legal certainty over the treaty-making competences of the Union under the post-Lisbon primary legal framework, the conclusions of the Court in Opinion 2/15 authoritatively delineated the *de jure* legitimacy of EU external action in the area of trade and investment. Seen in context of past political and judicial battles over external competence and post-Lisbon episodes of *vetocracy*, the Court's decision set the stage for a seminal shift in the practice of multilevel governance of EU external economic treaty-making.[56]

For the former EU Commissioner for External Trade Cecilia Malmström "it's not about winning or losing in Court. It's about clarification. What is mixed? What is not mixed? And then we can design our trade agreements accordingly."[57] Malmström, in other words, saw an opportunity in the Court's delineation of exclusive external economic competence – an opportunity to depart from the practice of mixed signing and conclusion of EU trade and investment agreements.

To reiterate: EU-only – or non-mixed – negotiation, signature, and conclusion of PTAs significantly expedites the entry into force of respective agreements; renders provisional application obsolete; further elevates the role of the European Parliament vis-à-vis national parliaments; limits Member State participation to qualified majority voting in the Council; significantly reduces the number of veto-players involved in CCP governance; hence significantly

---

55   *Ibid,* p. 22–24; G. Van der Loo and R. Wessel, 'The non-ratification of mixed agreements: Legal consequences and solution's, *Common Market Law Review* (2017), p. 735–770.

56   D. Kleimann and G. Kübek (n. 54).

57   Brussels Close to Trade Deal with Japan, *Financial Times,* 4 December 2016.

limits the access points for special interest advocacy; and reduces prospects of non-ratification of EU external agreements that only cover EU exclusive competences.

In September 2017, to that very end, the European Commission proposed directives for FTA negotiations with New Zealand and Australia that are limited to substance covered by EU exclusive competence.[58] The negotiation directives were adopted by the Council shortly after.[59] If negotiated as such by the Commission, the agreements will require EU-only signature and conclusion.

By the same token, the Commission proposed to split – for the purposes of treaty signature and conclusion – already negotiated agreements with Singapore and Vietnam into components covered by EU exclusive and shared competence respectively in order to secure an expedited entry-into-force of treaty parts other than portfolio investment and investment protection and enforcement disciplines.[60] The Japan-EU Economic Partnership Agreement (JEEPA), moreover, does not cover policy areas subject to shared or exclusive Member State competences and thus required EU-only signature and conclusion in any case. As the first EU-only PTA in the history of the European Union, the JEEPA entered into force in on 1 February 2019 – only seven months after its signature by the parties and two months after the European Parliament had given its consent.[61]

Forshadowing this seminal shift in EU treaty-making practice, the Council, in its conclusions of 22 May 2018, took note of the fact that "the Commission intends to recommend draft negotiating directives for FTA s covering exclusive EU competence on the one hand and separate mixed investment agreements on the other, with a view to strengthening the EU's position as a negotiating

---

58   European Commission, 'Recommendation for a Council Decision authorising the opening of negotiations for a Free Trade Agreement with New Zealand', COM(2017) 469 final. European Commission, Recommendation for a Council Decision authorising the opening of negotiations for a Free Trade Agreement with Australia, COM(2017) 472 final.

59   Council of the European Union, 'Negotiating directives for a Free Trade Agreement with New Zealand', Brussels, 8 May 2018. Council of the European Union, 'Negotiating directives for a Free Trade Agreement with Australia', 8 May 2018.

60   Council Decision (EU) 2018/1599 of 15 October 2018 on the signing of the Free Trade Agreement between the European Union and Singapore (OJ 2018, L 267). Council Decision (EU) 2018/1676 of 15 October 2018 on the signing of the Investment Protection Agreement between the European Union and Singapore (OJ 2018, L 279). Council Decision (EU) 2019/1121 of 25 June 2019 on the signing, on behalf of the European Union, of the Free Trade Agreement between the European Union and the Socialist Republic of Viet Nam (OJ 2019, L 177).

61   Council Decision (EU) 2018/0091 of 12 December 2018 on the conclusion of the Agreement between the European Union and Japan for an Economic Partnership (OJ 2018, L 330).

partner."[62] Taking pains to emphasise "that it is for the Council to decide, on a case-by-case basis, on the splitting of trade agreements" the Council reluctantly agreed to the new approach proposed by the Commission in the aftermath of Opinion 2/15 and the *CETA drama*. At the same time, the Council determined that, "*depending on their content*, association agreements should be mixed. The ones that are currently being negotiated, such as with Mexico, Mercosur and Chile, will remain mixed agreements".[63]

The Council conclusions also mirror ubiquituos (input) legitimacy concerns. The Council notes that "for FTAs falling entirely within the EU's competence, which are approved at EU level and do not require ratification by Member States, the roles of the Council and the European Parliament ensure legitimacy and inclusiveness of the adoption process."[64] At the same time, the conclusions emphasize that "Member States should [...] continue to involve their parliaments and interested stakeholders appropriately, in line with their respective national procedures. More generally, the Council reiterates the importance it attaches to addressing citizens' concerns and expectations and recognizes the need to keep citizens continuously informed of the progress and contents of trade agreements under negotiation, thereby strengthening the legitimacy and inclusiveness of EU trade policy."[65]

5   Input Legitimation of EU-only Preferential Trade Agreements

The likely most contentious of all legitimacy debates surrounding the exercise of EU treaty-making competences concerns input legitimation, i.e. the responsiveness to citizens' concerns as a result of the political participation by the people governed.[66] While a measurement of *responsiveness* is elusive

---

62   Council of the European Union, 'Council Conclusions on the negotiation and conclusion of EU trade agreements', 22 May 2018, para 3.

63   *Ibid,* emphasis added. It should be noted at this point that Association Agreements are subject to a Council unanimity requirement codified in Article 218(8) TFEU in any case. Notwithstanding this unanimity requirement, association agreements are by no means mandatory mixed agreements. For instance, the Council had signed and concluded two facultative EU-only association agreements, notably with Kosovo and Cyprus. The signing and conclusion of association agreements as mixed agreements is, in other words, subject to *facultative mixity*, as they currently cover treaty content falling into the realm of both EU exclusive and shared competence.

64   *Ibid,* para. 7.

65   *Ibid,* para. 8.

66   F. Scharpf (n. 42).

in context of the limited scope of this chapter, the following considerations may help to evaluate the degree to which EU-only economic treaty governance increases or decreases input legitimation. The crucial question in regard of the shift from mixed to EU-only PTA governance is whether the given alteration of institutionalized sources of democratic legitimation can enhance democratic representation at the same time.

For starters, it is worth recalling that prior to the entry into force of the Lisbon Treaty in 2009, the European Parliament had little or no role in external economic governance. In many respects, the Council's Article 133 Committee (now: Trade Policy Committee) epitomized the *black box* character of the pre-Lisbon era trade policy governance process, which was characterized by a lack of parliamentary control, accountability, and transparency. The pre-Lisbon institutional framework left the exercise of EU exclusive external competence for Common Commercial Policy "largely in the purview of the generally free-trade oriented career officials in the Commission, with only attenuated connections to voters, constituencies or political concerns, and the economic affairs ministries of Member States through their collective participation in the Council."[67]

While the *technocratic* European Commission traditionally found itself wary of the politicisation of EU trade policy through the involvement European Parliament, it nevertheless advocated – under the leadership of former EU External Trade Commissioner Pascal Lamy – for the empowerment of the European Parliament in CCP matters via primary law reform as early as 2004.[68] Indeed, it was the Commissioner who suggested that "legitimacy is absolutely crucial to a successful EU trade policy. For example, it is scarcely credible that in 2004, nearly fifty years after the Treaty of Rome, that the European Parliament still has no formal involvement in EU trade policy."[69]

The empowerment of the European Parliament is thus among the most significant CCP reform that the Lisbon Treaty has brought about precisely because it put an end to the blatant lack of democratic (or input) legitimation of external economic governance.[70] First, Parliament gained decision-making powers in two main areas, notably co-decision powers applying to CCP

---

67   J. Hillman, D. Kleimann, 'Trading Places: The New Dynamics of EU Trade Policy under the Treaty of Lisbon, GMF Economic Policy Paper', German Marshall Fund, October 2010.

68   G. Rosen, 'A match made in heaven? Explaining Patterns of cooperation between the Commission and the European Parliament', *Journal of European Integration* 38(4) (2016), p. 409–424.

69   P. Lamy, 'Trade Policy in the Prodi Commission – an Assessment', speech, 19 November 2004.

70   On this issue, see also the contribution by A. Matic in this volume.

domestic framework legislation. Secondly, it received the right to consent to or reject trade and investment agreements following the authorization of their signature and before conclusion by the Council. Article 218(6) TFEU *per se* requires EU parliamentary consent to all external agreements "to which either the ordinary legislative procedure, or the special legislative procedure applies". This, in line with Article 207 (2) TFEU, applies to all CCP agreements.

Moreover, the Lisbon Treaty amendments equipped the European Parliament with formal rights that practically enable the Parliament to control the negotiation process and to condition the conclusion of EU trade and investment agreement on its consent. Most importantly, the TFEU provisions confer significant information rights onto the Parliament. Article 207(3) TFEU requires that the Commission "shall report regularly to special [Council TPC] committee and the European Parliament on the progress of negotiations". Moreover, Article 218(10) TFEU provides that "the European Parliament shall be immediately and fully informed at all stages of the procedure" applying to the negotiation and conclusion of agreements with third states and international organizations as laid down in Article 218 TFEU.[71]

Nevertheless, the TFEU falls short of granting Parliament a formal role in the decision on the mandate or in setting out objectives of trade negotiations more generally, nor does it provide for parliamentary participation in negotiations. The Commission, through proposal by virtue of Article 218(3) TFEU, and the Council, by adopting decisions on negotiation directives by virtue of Article 218(2) TFEU, formally retain this prerogative. The European Parliament's right to be informed, furthermore, – even if fully, immediately, and at all stages – does not match the Council Trade Policy Committee's prerogative "to assist the Commission in" the task of negotiating trade agreements in consultation with the Commission, which is codified in Article 207(3) TFEU. Finally, Parliament has no formal role in the signature and provisional application of external economic agreements. Article 218(5) TFEU, in this respect, mandates that "[t]he Council, on a proposal by the negotiator, shall adopt a decision authorising the signing of the agreement and, if necessary, its provisional application before entry into force." The Council, in other words, does retain the exclusive formal right to direct the Commission's conduct of negotiations, additional to the Council's exclusive role in amending and adopting proposed negotiation

---

71   The European Commission and the European Parliament have detailed the substance of the Parliament's information rights under Article 207 and 218 TFEU in the Framework Agreement on relations between the European Parliament and the European Commission (OJ 2010, L 304/74).

directives as well as proposed decisions on the authorization of the signature and provisional application of external economic agreements.

In practice, however, the European Parliament has compensated for the lack of its formal role in decision-making on the adoption of negotiation directives, on provisional application of treaties, and its passive formal role during negotiations. Parliament has done so by leveraging existing procedural rights and setting out its substantive and procedural demands through its various channels of communication. Parliament, assisted by its specialized Committee for International Trade (INTA), has various means to voice political preferences and set out preconditions for assenting to CCP agreements early on during negotiations. These include the use of non-binding parliamentary resolutions, hearings, opinions, exchanges with Commission officials in the course of regular Commission reports to the INTA committee on progress in negotiations, as well as written questions to the Commission.

The Parliament has, in fact, on many occasions, called "on the Commission [...] to take due account of Parliament's preconditions for giving its consent to the conclusion of trade agreements."[72] European Parliament resolutions on negotiations of PTAs with the United States[73] and Japan[74] have set significant precedents in this regard.

Against this background, parliamentary information rights vis-à-vis the Commission have an important political value: constitutionally guaranteed full and immediate information on the procedure applying to the proposal and adoption of decisions on negotiation directives and the adoption of

---

72   European Parliament, 'Resolution of 18 May 2010 on the EU Policy Coherence for Development and the "Official Development Assistance plus" concept' (2009/2218(INI)). In the same vein, in its Resolution of 7 May 2009 on the Parliament's new role and responsibilities in implementing the Treaty of Lisbon (2008/2063(INI)) Parliament "[w]elcomes the fact that Parliament's consent will be required for a wide range of international agreements signed by the Union; underlines its intention to request the Council, where appropriate, not to open negotiations on international agreements until Parliament has stated its position, and to allow Parliament, on the basis of a report from the committee responsible, to adopt at any stage in the negotiations recommendations which are to be taken into account before the conclusion of negotiations".

73   European Parliament resolution of 23 May 2013 on EU trade and investment negotiations with the United States of America (2013/2558(RSP); European Parliament resolution of 8 July 2015 containing the European Parliament's recommendations to the European Commission on the negotiations for the Transatlantic Trade and Investment Partnership (TTIP) (2014/2228(INI).

74   European Parliament resolution of 13 June 2012 on EU trade negotiations with Japan (B7-0297/2012). European Parliament resolution of 25 October 2012 on EU trade negotiations with Japan (2012/2711(RSP)).

agreements, as well as regular Commission reports on progress in negotiations enable Parliament to leverage its consent rights in order to influence the content of negotiation directives, the direction of bilateral and multilateral trade negotiations, and hence the substance of the final agreements.

Furthermore, Parliament shares a bicameral function in the process of adopting legislation necessary for the implementation of CCP agreements. Parliamentary powers to block the framework legislation necessary to implement provisions of a trade agreement adds additional procedural leverage for it to demand involvement in the political deliberation process that applies to the scope, objectives, and directions of the negotiation of external economic agreements.

In light of these multiple levers – through the Parliament's formal role in adopting implementing legislation and its right to veto the conclusion of CCP agreements, substantive and even procedural demands from the Parliament can hardly be ignored when the Commission and the Council determine negotiating objectives and EU positions in negotiations with third countries.

Another tangible outcome of the empowerment of the Parliament is enhanced transparency and public deliberation of EU external economic governance. The European Parliament has effectuated this change not only by creating a public platform for deliberation but has also – albeit indirectly – forced the Commission to seek legitimacy of its policy proposals through an enhanced practice of public consultations, exponentially increasing efforts to explain complex policy instruments to a broader public, and a dramatic increase of public access to trade negotiation documents. In this way, the emergence of the European Parliament has – overall – directly and indirectly resulted in enhanced transparency of CCP governance through the political institutions of the EU.

As an illustration, in the period of December 2009 until November 2013, the Directorate General for External Trade of the European Commission provided 155 informal technical briefings to members and staff of the INTA committee and European Parliament political groups on a diversity of CCP dossiers and presented over 50 times in INTA Committee sessions and monitoring group meetings.[75] Moreover, in response to the Parliament's ubiquitous calls for negotiation transparency, the European Commission's *Trade for All* communication of 2015 enhanced the previously highly restricted access to negotiation documents to unknown levels.[76]

---

75   Internal documentation obtained from DG TRADE – to be disclosed upon request.
76   European Commission, 'Trade for All – Toward a more responsible trade and investment policy' (2015). In the communication, the Commission notes that: "[t]ransparency should apply at all stages of the negotiating cycle from the setting of objectives to the

It is, in sum, difficult to argue with the general assessment that the Lisbon Treaty reform has institutionalized and vastly increased input legitimation of the exercise of EU exclusive competences for external trade and investment. The question remains, however, whether the most recent design of EU PTAs has factually diminished democratic representation by reducing their scope to content falling within the realm of exclusive external EU competence. The resulting subordination of Member State political institutions to decision-making by EU institutions could lead to the impression that EU-only PTAs suffer from a net loss of input legitimation.

A look back at scholars' expectations for post-Lisbon external economic governance facilitates an evaluation of the effect of the shift from mixed to non-mixed PTA negotiation, signature, and conclusion as regards the issue of input legitimation. In 2011, Krajewski anticipated that the "broadening of the scope of the common commercial policy by the Lisbon Treaty will lead to a disempowerment of the national parliaments." He further notes that the "loss of competencies in the Member States leads to a removal of the active participation of the parliaments of the member states. This loss is not just of a formal nature, but instead leads in practice to lesser parliamentary control over multilateral commercial agreements."[77]

Woolcock, on the other hand, observed that "in practice few Member State parliaments have exercised effective scrutiny of EU trade policy" prior to the entry-into-force of the Lisbon Treaty.[78] Adding to the lack of political participation prior to 2009, Krajewski considered that "the rejection of an international treaty can practically be ruled out" because, in parliamentary systems of government, the ruling government is frequently backed by voting majorities in parliament.[79] By distinction, the functioning of the European Parliament as a check and balance to the Council and the Commission, rather than approval of government in a parliamentary democracy, rendered the Parliament more autonomous from the decision-making of the executive

---

negotiations themselves and during the post-negotiation phase. On top of existing measures, the Commission will: at launch, invite the Council to disclose all FTA negotiating directives immediately after their adoption; during negotiations, extend TTIP practices of publishing EU texts online for all trade and investment negotiations and make it clear to all new partners that negotiations will have to follow a transparent approach; and after finalising negotiations, publish the text of the agreement immediately, as it stands, without waiting for the legal revision to be completed."

77   Krajewski (n. 2), p. 81–82.
78   S. Woolcock, 'The potential impact of the Lisbon Treaty on European Union External Trade Policy', SIEPS European Policy Analysis 8 (2008), p. 5.
79   Krajewski (n. 2), p. 69.

branch and more comparable to the US Congress than EU Member State parliaments.[80]

In contrast to some of these early expectations, Member State parliaments have since then markedly enhanced scrutiny of CCP negotiation dossiers commensurate to the perceived political value of respective negotiations and agreements as well as intensifying public concern. Jancic, for instance, observes that "[t]he developments in EU trade policy have provoked a remarkable reaction in national parliaments. [...] Specifically, TTIP negotiations have been discussed by no fewer than 32 parliamentary chambers" most of which engaged in substantive scrutiny.[81]

Moreover, as noted further above, it is only in the post-Lisbon era that Member States' *vetocracy* in the mixed mode of treaty-making[82] has become a credible threat to the Union's trade and investment policy agenda. This fact serves, by itself, as another indicator for enhanced political participation of Member State legislatures compared to the pre-Lisbon era. Political participation of the European legislatures has in fact dramatically increased at both the EU and Member State level.

But does the limitation of the political influence of individual Member State parliaments to the voting behaviour of *their* government in the Council diminish input legitimation of PTAs as compared to the mixed mode of PTA ratification? An affirmative answer to this question necessarily accepts the notion that, in extremis, democratic representation through the European Parliament and the legislatures of 26 Member States only provides sufficient input legitimation to EU external economic treaty-making if, and only if, the legislature of the 27th Member State – potentially representing a constituency as small as the population of Malta – concurs with the vote of parliamentary chambers representing 450 million EU citizens. This notion, however, seems to contradict ideas of both proportionate democratic representation in decision-making as well as output legitimation of the given institutional framework. The shift to a qualified majority voting in the Council – which requires at least four Member States that represent at least 35 percent of the EU population in order to block a Council decision – and the elevation of an increasingly effective and veto-armed European Parliament in the EU-only modus of treaty governance, appear to mend issues of both output and input legitimation discussed here.

---

80   *Ibid.*

81   D. Jancic, 'TTIP and legislative-executive relations in EU trade policy', *West European Politics* 40(1) (2017), p. 209.

82   F. Mayer, 'European Vetocracy? How to overcome the CETA problem?' *Verfassungsblog* (24 October 2016).

6   Conclusions

The Council's acquiescence to the Commission proposal for a new economic treaty architecture for Preferential Trade Agreements with third countries has fundamentally changed the *modus operandi* for Member State political participation in multilevel external economic governance of the European Union. *EU-only* external economic governance further channels the aggregation of policy demand and political transactions towards the EU triangular institutional framework epitomized by the Commission, the (qualified majority-voting) Council, and the European Parliament. It strips national political institutions of their veto-rights and yet incentivizes national legislatures to employ the rights of participation guaranteed under national constitutions to influence the voting behaviour of their respective governments in the Council throughout – and not only at the very end – of the negotiation process. The seminal shift from a mixed to EU-only mode of EU PTA governance further elevates the responsibilities of the European Parliament – in comparison to its previous marginalization in a multi-dozen veto-player setting – and allows for it to effectively fulfil its treaty-prescribed role as a check-and-balance of the Commission and the Council.

This chapter has advanced a comparative analysis of *de jure*, output, and input legitimacy of PTA governance in the mixed versus EU-only mode of economic treaty-making. Against the backdrop of the Laeken Council legitimacy benchmarks, this analysis has demonstrated that the *best-imperfect institutional alternative* to mixed EU external economic governance stems from the EU-only mode of negotiating, signing, and concluding of preferential trade agreements, which fully employs the available EU constitutional space for more representative, transparent, and efficient public decision-making.

The Council's preference for mixed signature and ratification of Association Agreements with Mercosur, Chile and Mexico retains a last bastion of Member State participation – in their own right – in EU PTA governance. By inference, the Council seems to prefer that the Laeken legitimacy standard does not apply these external action instruments. This circumstance, however, appears to be both politically arbitrary and anachronistic. The Council has, in the past, used its discretion for facultative mixity to allow for the EU-only signature and conclusion of Association Agreements with Cyprus and Kosovo. While it is *de jure* legitimate to do so, it does – in the Lisbon era – enhance output and input legitimacy at the same time. The Association Agreement treaty instrument as means to forge stronger political and economic ties with third countries, however, may soon be outdated: the more recent EU treaty design has seen a split of traditional Association Agreement content into political partnership agreements, on the one hand, and deep and comprehensive trade agreements, on the other. Adding a third separate – investment protection – agreement to this formula may thus make for the future approach to the design of broader EU external action instruments in line with the spirit of the Laeken Council declaration of 2001.

Acknowledgement

The preparation of this chapter was funded by the Horizon 2020 project RE-SPECT ('Realising Europe's soft power in external cooperation and trade') under grant agreement No. 770680. The grant is implemented by an EUI-led research consortium coordinated by Professor Bernard Hoekman (http://re-spect.eui.eu/).

CHAPTER 20

EU Trade Policy after Opinion 2/15

Internal and External Threats to Broad and Comprehensive Free Trade Agreements

Reinhard Quick and Attila Gerhäuser

1 Introduction

In 1995, the WTO started to work on the basis that it would engage its members to further trade liberalisation and rule-making either as a permanent negotiating forum or within multilateral rounds of trade negotiations. After the abysmal performance of the Doha Development Agenda (DDA), the EU moved its emphasis from multilateral to bilateral trade liberalisation. Under the leadership of Commissioners Mandelson, de Gucht and Malmström, the European Commission presented proposals on how the EU should engage bilaterally.[1] It proposed a new generation of free trade agreements (FTAs) encompassing traditional market access subjects, services, government procurement and intellectual property as well as regulatory cooperation, sustainable development and investment. At the beginning, the EU sought FTAs with emerging trading partners in Asia and Latin America (South Korea, India, Singapore, Vietnam and Mercosur), later traditional trading partners were added (Canada, USA, Japan, Australia and New Zealand). These developments reached their peak with the negotiations of TTIP, the Transatlantic Trade and Investment Partnership. Whilst TTIP was put on ice in early 2017, the EU has successfully concluded FTAs with Korea, Singapore, Vietnam, Canada, Japan and Mercosur. The Lisbon Treaty extended the Union's common commercial policy competence by adding trade in services, the commercial aspects of intellectual property rights

---

1 European Commission, 'Global Europe: Competing in the World. A Contribution to the EU's Growth and Jobs Strategy', COM (2006) 567 final, 4 October 2006; European Commission, 'Trade, Growth and World Affairs. Trade Policy as a core component of the EU's 2020 strategy', COM (2010) 612 final, 9 November 2010; European Commission, 'Trade for All. Towards a More Responsible Trade and Investment Policy', COM (2015) 0497 final, 14 October 2015; European Commission, 'A Balanced and Progressive Trade Policy to Harness Globalisation', COM (2017) 492 final, 13 September 2017.

and foreign direct investment[2] to the Union's existing trade competences. Moreover, trade policy was embedded into the European Union's overall objectives for external actions.[3] Following these changes, one would have expected a smooth working process between Member States and the Commission concerning trade agreements; yet competence issues remained high on the political agenda. The Member States wanted to retain some power regarding FTAS, probably also as a reaction to the public's critical perceptions and discussions of CETA and TTIP. They did not agree with the position of the Commission, i.e. that these agreements were "EU-only" agreements requiring only an EU signature and ratification.[4] To obtain clarity, the Commission in 2014 asked the Court of Justice of the European Union (ECJ) for an Opinion on the competence to sign and ratify the trade agreement which it had negotiated with Singapore.[5] In June 2016, President Juncker tried to sell CETA as an "EU-only" agreement, yet had to backtrack after a storm of protest from Member States.[6] CETA was declared "mixed", requiring not only the EU's signature and ratification but also those of the 28 Member States.[7]

The ECJ rendered its Opinion on 16 May 2017.[8] It held that the EU-Singapore FTA (EUSFTA) "cannot, in its current form, be concluded by the EU alone".[9] It considered that the provisions on non-direct foreign investment (portfolio investments) and on the dispute settlement regime between investors and the Member States (ISDS) fell into the category of "shared competences" between the European Union and the Member States. With respect to all other

---

2   The transfer of competence for foreign direct investment from the Member States to the EU represented a long and arduous process which already started in 1972. Some Member States, like Germany, the United Kingdom and France had voiced serious criticism to this transfer in the context of the Convention for a constitutional treaty in 2003/2004 but then they no longer raised objections in the context of the Lisbon Treaty.

3   See generally M. Cremona, 'A Quiet Revolution: The Common Commercial Policy Six Years After the Treaty of Lisbon', *Swedish Institute for European Policy Studies* (2017:2), p. 32.

4   See M. Greive, A. Tauber, '"Schnurzegal" – Juncker erzürnt deutsche Politiker': https://www.welt.de/wirtschaft/article156690315/Schnurzegal-Juncker-erzuernt-deutsche-Politiker.html.

5   European Commission, 'Singapore: The Commission to Request a Court of Justice Opinion on the trade deal', Press Release IP/14/1235, 30 October 2014.

6   P.J. Kuijper, 'Post-CETA: How we got there and how to go on': https://acelg.blogactiv.eu/2016/10/28/post-ceta-how-we-got-there-and-how-to-go-on-by-pieter-jan-kuijper; Kuijper points out that the Commission made this proposal to avoid a unanimous decision of the Council overturning the Commission's position.

7   European Commission, 'European Commission proposes signature and conclusion of EU-Canada trade deal', Press Release IP/16/2371, 5 July 2016.

8   Case A-2/15, *Opinion of the Court*, EU:C:2017:376.

9   ECJ, 'The free trade agreement with Singapore cannot, in its current form, be concluded by the EU alone', Press Release No/52/17, 16 May 2017.

substantive issues of the agreement the CJEU held that the European Union had exclusive competence.

Opinion 2/15 triggered a debate on how the European Union should, in the future, ratify broad and comprehensive free trade agreements. Following the ECJ's Opinion, the Commission, in April 2018, split the original EUSFTA into two agreements and proposed the "EU-Singapore Free Trade Agreement" as an "EU-only" agreement[10] and the "EU-Singapore Investment Protection Agreement" as a "mixed" agreement[11]. The Council accepted to proceed in this way for the Singapore agreements,[12] yet it also made clear that it will "decide whether to open negotiations on this basis"[13] and therefore confirmed its decision-making power on this issue.

In the following, we will analyse the impact of Opinion 2/15 on the CETA ratification process.[14] Will CETA be ratified by the Member States notwithstanding the outspoken opposition of some of them or will the Commission eventually also have to split CETA into two agreements? Thereafter, we will consider the EU's trade relation with the U.S. and China, and discuss the challenges for EU trade policy posed by these "heavy-weight" trading partners.

2   CETA Ratification: Rough Ride on a Rollercoaster or Plan B?

2.1   *Will CETA Be Ratified?*
Originally, the European Commission considered that "CETA has identical objectives and essentially the same contents as the Free Trade Agreement with

---

10   European Commission, 'Proposal for a Council Decision on the signing, on behalf of the European Union, of a Free Trade Agreement between the European Union and the Republic of Singapore', COM (2018) 197 final, 18 April 2018; European Commission, 'Proposal for a Council Decision on the conclusion of a Free Trade Agreement between the European Union and the Republic of Singapore', COM (2018) 196 final, 18 April 2018.

11   European Commission, 'Key elements of the EU-Singapore trade and investment agreements', MEMO 18/3327, 18 April 2018.

12   In October 2018, the Council adopted the decision to sign the two agreements. See Council of the EU, 'EU-Singapore: Council adopts decisions to sign trade and investment agreements', Press Release 563/18, 15 October 2018.

13   Council of the EU, 'Draft Council conclusions on the negotiations and conclusions of EU trade agreements', 8622/18, 8 May 2018. Adopted by the Foreign Affairs Council on 22 May 2018.

14   For an earlier version of this analysis cf. R. Quick and A. Gerhäuser, 'The Ratification of CETA and other trade policy challenges after Opinion 2/15', *Zeitschrift für Europarechtliche Studien* (ZEuS) 22 (2019), p. 505-528.

Singapore (EUSFTA); therefore, the Union's competence is the same in both cases"[15] and had the intention to propose CETA as an "EU-only" agreement. However, in reaction to Member States' protests it presented CETA as a mixed agreement in July 2016.[16] With the benefit of hindsight, one can say that it acted correctly; in fact, Opinion 2/15 confirms that some provisions of CETA fall into the category of "shared" competence. Notwithstanding the "satisfaction" given to the Member States, the signature of CETA[17] was preceded by some tumultuous events: most notably the rebellion of Wallonia[18] but also considerable opposition against CETA and TTIP in many Member States, particularly in Germany,[19] France,[20] Austria[21] and Belgium.[22] The NGO movement against TTIP[23]

---

15   European Commission, 'Proposal for a Council Decision on the conclusion of the Comprehensive Economic and Trade Agreement between Canada, of the one part, and the European Union and its Member States, of the other part', COM (2016) 443 final, 5 July 2016, p. 4.

16   Ibid.; European Commission, 'Proposal for a Council Decision on the signing on behalf of the European Union of the Comprehensive Economic and Trade Agreement between Canada of the one part, and the European Union and its Member States, of the other part', COM (2016) 444 final, 5 July 2016.

17   Council Decision 2017/37/EU of 28 October 2016 on the signing on behalf of the European Union of the Comprehensive Economic and Trade Agreement (CETA) between Canada, of the one part, and the European Union and its Member States, of the other part (OJ 2017, L 11/1).

18   G. Van der Loo, J. Pelkmans, *Does Wallonia's veto of CETA spell the beginning of the end of EU trade policy?* (CEPS Commentary, 2016).

19   In Germany, the opponents of CETA launched a constitutional challenge to CETA. The Bundesverfassungsgericht rejected the applications for a preliminary injunction on 13 October 2016, yet the case is still pending regarding the constitutional challenge. See C. Tietje, K. Nowrot, 'CETA an der Leine des Bundesverfassungsgerichts: zum schmalen Grad zwischen Ultra-vires-Kontrolle und Ultra-vires-Handeln', *EuR* 52 1 (2017), p. 137–154.

20   M. Orosz et al., '"Inside CETA", episode 6: is CETA unstoppable?': http://www.lemonde.fr/les-decodeurs/article/2016/11/14/inside-ceta-episode-6-is-ceta-unstoppable_5030670_4355770.html#7QM2GMMFwUAoe2sA.99.

21   S. Nasralla, G. Baczynska, 'Austria says it will start 'conflict' in EU about Canada trade deal': https://www.reuters.com/article/us-europe-trade-canada-austria/austria-says-will-start-conflict-in-eu-about-canada-trade-deal-idUSKCN1173Q4.

22   A. Crespy, 'CETA, Wallonia and sovereignty in Europe': https://www.euractiv.com/section/trade-society/opinion/ceta-wallonia-and-sovereignty-in-europe/.

23   One of the main arguments of NGOs against TTIP was the lack of transparency of the negotiations and the supposedly unwillingness of then Trade Commissioner Karel De Gucht while in fact the attempt of De Gucht to push for the declassification of the TTIP negotiations directives failed because of the resistance of Member States in the Council. See F. Hoffmeister, 'Of transferred competence, Institutional Balance and Judicial Autonomy – Constitutional Developments in Lisbon' in J. Czuczai, F. Naert (eds.), *The EU as a Global Actor – Bridging Legal Theory and Practice* (Brill Nijhoff, 2017), p. 323.

and CETA was no longer the isolated campaign of a few but had evolved into a mass mobilisation of "Joe Public". Some Member States' governments and deputies of national Parliaments and of the European Parliament joined in the criticism of both agreements. The Council's decision on signing CETA became possible only after the adoption by Canada, the EU and the Member States of a Joint Interpretative Instrument[24] and 38 statements or declarations[25] added to the decision.[26] The Joint Interpretative Instrument was considered necessary to overcome the opposition to CETA and to ease the tensions. The Instrument interprets in a legally binding way specific CETA concepts such as the much-disputed Investment Court System (ICS) or the right to impose regulation to achieve legitimate public policy objectives in the areas of public health, social services, education or environment as well as the concept that CETA will not lower food safety-, consumer protection-, health-, environment- and labour protection-standards.[27] Upon proposal of the Commission,[28] the Council also opened the way for the provisional application of CETA.[29] In February 2017, the European Parliament gave its consent to CETA[30] and after the Canadian ratification, parts of the agreement have been provisionally applied.[31] According to

---

24   Council of the EU, 'Joint Interpretative Instrument on the Comprehensive Economic and Trade Agreement (CETA) between Canada and the European Union and its Member States', 13541/16, 27 October 2016.

25   Council of the EU, 'Comprehensive Economic and Trade Agreement (CETA) between Canada, of the one part, and the European Union and its Member States of the other part – Statements to the Council Minutes', 13463/16, 19 October 2016 (Statements to the Council Minutes).

26   See G. Van der Loo, *CETA's signature: 38 statements, a joint interpretative instrument and an uncertain future* (CEPS Commentary, 2016).

27   Ibid., p. 2.

28   European Commission, 'Proposal for a Council Decision on the provisional application of the Comprehensive Economic and Trade Agreement between Canada of the one part, and the European Union and its Member States, of the other part', COM (2016) 470 final, 5 July 2016.

29   Council Decision 2017/38/EU of 28 October 2016 on the provisional application of the Comprehensive Economic and Trade Agreement (CETA) between Canada, of the one part, and the European Union and its Member States, of the other part (OJ 2017, L 11/1080).

30   European Parliament, 'MEPs back EU-Canada Trade agreement': http://www.europarl.europa.eu/news/en/press-room/20170209IPR61728/ceta-meps-back-eu-canada-trade-agreement.

31   Official Journal of the EU, 'Notice concerning the provisional application of the Comprehensive Economic and Trade Agreement (CETA) between Canada, of the one part, and the European Union and its Member States, of the other part', (OJ 2017, L 238/9).

the Council, "only matters within the scope of EU competence will be subject to provisional application".[32]

Three years after the heated CETA debates, the situation in Europe has changed. Of course, CETA will only come into force after all the national ratifications have been deposited (Article 30 CETA), and this will take time, as the example of the FTA with South Korea shows.[33] At the time of writing, 13 out of 28 Member States have ratified CETA;[34] more importantly, Brexit, the U.S. trade policy under President Trump, government changes in some of the Member States or regions, and the ECJ's reasoning in Opinion 1/17[35] allow a more positive outlook for a CETA ratification by the Member States notwithstanding the continuing NGO opposition.[36] Germany,[37] Austria[38] and France[39]

---

32 See Statement 15 of the above-mentioned 38 statements and declarations, note 24 above. With reference to past practice Kleimann and Kübeck argue that provisional application of other agreements do not necessarily concern only those provisions which fell under 'EU-only' competence; see D. Kleimann, G. Kübeck, 'The Signing, Provisional Application, and Conclusion of Trade and Investment Agreements in the EU – The Case of CETA and Opinion 2/15' (EUI Working Papers RSCAS, 2016/58), p. 17.

33 After the provisional application in July 2011, it took the Member States until October 2015 to fully ratify the Agreement with South Korea. See Council of the EU, 'EU-South Korea free trade agreement concluded', Press Release 691/15, 15 December 2015.

34 Council of the EU, Comprehensive Economic and Trade Agreement (CETA) between Canada, of the one part, and the European Union and its Member States, of the other part, Ratification Details, https://www.consilium.europa.eu/en/documents-publications/treaties-agreements/agreement/?id=2016017.

35 On 7 September 2017 Belgium requested under Article 218(11) TFEU the opinion of the Court of Justice concerning the compatibility of the CETA mechanism for the settlement of investment disputes with EU primary law. On 30 April 2019 the ECJ released its opinion in which it considered the respective mechanism in CETA to be compatible with EU law; see Opinion 1/17, EU:C:2019:341.

36 T. Bode, 'Trade by the People, for the People': https://www.politico.eu/article/opinion-trade-by-the-people-for-the-people/.

37 CDU/CSU, SPD, 'Ein neuer Aufbruch für Europa, Eine neue Dynamik für Deutschland, Ein neuer Zusammenhalt für unser Land. Koalitionsvertrag zwischen CDU, CSU und SPD, 19. Legislaturperiode', p. 65–6: https://www.cdu.de/koalitionsvertrag-2018.

38 NV, FPÖ, 'Zusammen. Für Unser Österreich, Regierungsprogramm 2017–2022', p. 141: https://www.wienerzeitung.at/_em_daten/_wzo/2017/12/16/171216_1614_regierungsprogramm.pdf; Austria has ratified CETA. The Austrian President gave up its opposition to CETA after the publication of Opinion 1/17, https://www.derstandard.at/story/2000102350295/handelsabkommen-ceta-muss-noch-einige-huerden-nehmen.

39 J.-B. Vey, B. Love, 'French parliament to ratify trade deal CETA in 2018: minister': https://www.reuters.com/article/us-canada-eu-trade-france/french-parliament-to-ratify-ceta-trade-deal-in-2018-minister-idUSKBN1CU1KB?il=0. On 23 July 2019 the French National Assembly ratified CETA, the French Senate is expected to ratify the agreement by the end of 2019, https://www.cbc.ca/news/politics/france-canada-ceta-trade-deal-1.5221766.

have declared that they will ratify CETA. Nevertheless, the case of CETA shows that the process of ratification of mixed agreements remains unpredictable. It cannot be said whether all EU Member States will eventually ratify CETA or whether one will reject it for specific reasons[40] and will, therefore, hold the EU and its trading partner hostage, just as the region of Wallonia did in 2016. Potential haphazardness is the political and legal consequence of "mixity".

Obliviously, mixed agreements do have their *raison d'être* in that Member States as parties to the agreement fulfill a role which the EU cannot (exclusive competence = "obligatory mixity") or should not fulfill (shared competence = "facultative mixity"). The distinction between "obligatory" and "facultative" mixity[41] is important for the ratification of the agreement. In the former case, a national ratification is "obligatory", whilst in the latter, the Council has political discretion to decide whether ratification by the EU is enough or whether a national ratification process is also necessary.[42] Given the ECJ's reference to "shared competences" in Opinion 2/15, a discussion has emerged on whether the ECJ implicitly ruled that national ratification is always required.[43] In our view and along the lines of AG Sharpston's reasoning,[44] as the ECJ's opinion does not relate to the Council's discretionary powers, the Council can

---

40   In an interview with La Stampa the Italian Agriculture Minister, Gian Marco Centinaio stated on 14 June 2018 that Italy would not ratify CETA given the lack of intellectual property protection for Italian agricultural goods. See M. Tropeano, 'Non ratificheremo il trattato Ceta. Altri ci seguiranno': http://www.lastampa.it/2018/06/14/italia/non-ratificheremo-il-trattato-ceta-altri-ci-seguiranno-vHOuiRxI91ipDozYJfGoNM/pagina.html.

41   A. Rosas, 'The European Union and Mixed Agreements' in A. Dashwood, C. Hillion (eds.), *The General Law of E.C. External Relations* (Sweet & Maxwell, 2000), p. 206.

42   As far as ratification is concerned, AG Sharpston clearly distinguishes between "shared" and "EU-exclusive"-competences: "In the former case, the Member States together (acting in their capacity as members of the Council) have the power to agree that the European Union shall act *or* to insist that they will continue to exercise individual external competence. In the latter case, they have no such choice, because exclusive external competence already belongs to the European Union." See Advocate General Sharpston, *Opinion procedure 2/15*, EU:C:2016:992, para. 72, 75; Kleimann and Kübek cite the Stabilization and Association Agreement with Kosovo as an example of the Council's discretion in favour of EU-ratification only. See D. Kleimann, G. Kübek 'The Singapore Opinion or the End of Mixity as We Know It' (2017): https://verfassungsblog.de/the-singapore-opinion-or-the-end-of-mixity-as-we-know-it/.

43   M. Bungenberg, 'Die Gemeinsame Handelspolitik, parlamentarische Beteiligung und das Singapur Gutachten des EuGH' in S. Kadelbach (ed.), *Die Welt und Wir: Die Außenbeziehungen der Europäischen Union* (Nomos, 2017), p. 146. See also D. Kleimann, G. Kübeck 2017 (n. 41), p. 3–4.

44   Sharpston (n. 41); See also Case C-600/14, *Germany v. Council of the European Union*, EU:C:2017:935, para. 67 et seq.

still decide that in cases of "shared competences" an "EU-only" ratification would be sufficient.

Before Opinion 2/15, there was a strong rationale that new FTAs fell into the category of "obligatory" mixed agreements. Opinion 2/15 has changed this rationale: in fact, the ECJ found that none of the provisions of EUSFTA was covered by exclusive Member States' competence. It therefore departed from the position held by AG Sharpston[45] and even more so from some legal opinions written in the context of CETA.[46] Given the political sensitivity of FTAs, the Commission's initiative to split the original EUSFTA into two agreements reflects political reality: with two agreements the Commission "throws-off the shackles of mixity"[47] for the part of the agreement for which the EU has exclusive competence and accepts Member States' ratification for the other agreement thus avoiding a complicated political discussion in Council on a discretionary "EU-only" ratification. In our view, the Commission's initiative constitutes an opportunity to strengthen the credibility and effectiveness of a common EU trade policy. It is a clear sign that the democratic control of new "trade agreements" lies first and foremost with the European Parliament. The role of national Parliaments is not diminished, though, rather it is redefined alongside their competences. For "EU-only" agreements, their role consists in controlling the position of their national government before, during and at the end of the negotiations, as highlighted by the *Trading Together Declaration*.[48]

Recent developments confirm this tendency: The Japan-EU Free Trade Agreement (JEFTA), negotiated without chapters on investment protection

---

45 AG Sharpston considered that the EUSFTA's provisions on the termination of Member States' bilateral investment treaties to fall under the Member States' exclusive competence. See CJEU, 'Advocate General Sharpston considers that the Singapore Free Trade Agreement can only be concluded by the European Union and the Member States acting jointly', Press Release 147/16, 21 December 2016.

46 F. C. Mayer, 'Rechtliche Aspekte des Freihandelsabkommens EU – Kanada (CETA)': https://www.bundestag.de/blob/348398/f864dce4b150e7f9af971286222c0c53/franz-c--mayer--uni-bielefeld-data.pdf; W. Weiss, 'Verfassungsprobleme des Abschlusses und der vorläufigen Anwendung des CETA Freihandelsabkommens mit Kanada': https://www.bundestag.de/blob/438052/9f45bd9ca1de30f51726df5d391b8702/stgn_weiss-data.pdf.

47 G. Van der Loo, *The Court's Opinion on the ET-Singapore FTA: Throwing off the shackles of mixity?* (CEPS Policy Insights, 2017).

48 'Trading Together Declaration': https://www.trading-together-declaration.org/. The Declaration signed by more than 60 academics from 15 countries distinguishes, inter alia, between "EU-only" and "mixed" agreements and elaborates on the role of national Parliaments in case of "EU-only" agreements. The Declaration is a reply to the "Namur Declaration" launched by the former Walloon Prime Minister Paul Magnette: https://www.sant.ox.ac.uk/sites/default/files/related-documents/en-declaration-de-namur.pdf

and dispute resolution, has consequently been proposed in May 2018 as an "EU-only" agreement.[49] Also in the case of Vietnam the Commission split the agreement into two. The Council approved on 25 June 2019 the EU-Vietnam trade and investment agreements:[50] The Free Trade Agreement is proposed as "EU-only" while the Investment Protection Agreement is proposed as "mixed"[51]. However as mentioned above, the Council[52] stresses its competence on how to classify trade and investment agreements. Hence the (future) association agreements with Mexico,[53] Mercosur[54] and Chile[55] will most probably be considered "mixed".

For the time being, the solution found for the Singapore and Vietnam Agreements is not feasible for CETA. The CETA national ratification processes have started and the European institutions will have to await their outcome. The Council has indicated, though, that CETA will only fail if the ratification fails *permanently* and *definitively, and* if the Member State in question formally notifies that it is unable to ratify the agreement.[56] The definition of what exactly "permanently and definitively" means will depend on the political situation in the country concerned and leaves the respective Member State with a certain degree of flexibility. Would a negative vote by a national or regional Parliament on CETA be immediately considered as "permanent or definitive" or would the Member State wait with the formal notification of that decision while trying to rescue the situation? In statement 37 of the above-mentioned statements and declarations,[57] the Kingdom of Belgium states that it has little flexibility in such a situation. Nevertheless, even this declaration reaffirms the notion of a "permanent and definitive decision not to ratify CETA" and allows for a notification period of one year during which a compromise could nevertheless be sought even after a negative vote of a regional Parliament. Another interesting example in this context is the negative Dutch referendum on the EU-Ukraine

---

49   In contrast to CETA, in the case of JEFTA the German government supported the European Commission in its decision to propose the agreement as EU-only. See http://dipbt.bundestag.de/dip21/btd/19/046/1904666.pdf.

50   European Commission, 'EU set to sign trade and investment agreements with Vietnam on Sunday': http://trade.ec.europa.eu/doclib/press/index.cfm?id=2036.

51   See 'EU-Vietnam Trade and Investment Agreements': http://trade.ec.europa.eu/doclib/press/index.cfm?id=1437.

52   Council Conclusions (n. 13).

53   https://ec.europa.eu/trade/policy/in-focus/eu-mexico-trade-agreement/.

54   http://trade.ec.europa.eu/doclib/press/index.cfm?id=2039.

55   https://trade.ec.europa.eu/doclib/press/index.cfm?id=1755&title=EU-and-Chile-to-start-negotiations-for-a-modernised-Association-Agreement.

56   Statements to the Council Minutes (n. 24).

57   Statements to the Council Minutes (n. 24), statement 37.

Association Agreement.[58] It is true that the referendum was not binding; on the other hand, it could not be ignored by the Dutch government either. The way out of this impasse was found in an explanatory declaration adopted by the EU summit in December 2016.[59] The declaration helped the Dutch government to argue that the criticism had been considered and therefore opened the way for the ratification of the agreement by both chambers of Parliament.[60] The national decision, i.e. the referendum, did not qualify as a permanent and definitive rejection of the agreement. Taking the various declarations and today's political mood into account and applying it to the CETA ratification process, we conclude that a full CETA ratification seems more possible today than it was at the time the decision on CETA was taken notwithstanding the recent opposition by the Italian government.[61]

2.2   Plan B: an EU-only Agreement?

If one Member State were unable to ratify CETA and notified the Council of its permanent and definitive decision, CETA would not enter into force lacking ratification by all parties (Article 30.7.2 CETA).[62] CETA, as such, would then be buried, yet not the idea of a comprehensive trade agreement with Canada. In Opinion 2/15 the ECJ confirmed the European Union's exclusive competence for almost all aspects of the new generation of free trade agreements. One can therefore reasonably assume that the Commission would work on a "Singapore-type" solution in such a situation, i.e. a proposal for a

---

58   See G. Van der Loo, *The Dutch Referendum on the EU-Ukraine Association Agreement, Legal options for navigating a tricky and awkward situation* (CEPS Commentary, 2016).

59   European Council meeting (15 December 2016) – Conclusions (34/16), para. 22–25.

60   The second chamber adopted the legislation on 23 February 2017. See M. Back, 'Kamer stemit in met alsnog ratificeren Oekraineverdrag': https://www.nrc.nl/nieuws/2017/02/23/kamer-stemt-na-10-maanden-debat-in-met-oekraineverdrag-a1547441. The first chamber adopted it on 30 May 2017. See NOS, 'Discussie Oekraine-verdrag nu definitief beslecht': https://nos.nl/artikel/2175769-discussie-oekraine-verdrag-nu-definitief-beslecht-eerste-kamer-stemt-voor.html.

61   M. Tropeano (n. 39).

62   This provision puts an end to the discussion on whether in case of a negative vote of a single Member State the agreement's EU-only provisions could nevertheless continue to be applied. Hoffmeister argues that the subsequent refusal of a Member State to ratify could then be linked to only the national provisions previously identified with the consequence that in such a situation the EU's provisional application for the remaining part of the treaty falling under EU competence remains unaffected. See F. Hoffmeister, in O. Dörr, K. Schmalenbach (eds.), *Vienna Convention on the Law of Treaties – A Commentary* (Springer, 2018), Art. 17 para. 12, p. 240.

"Comprehensive EU-Canada Trade Agreement" covering all those provisions of CETA for which the EU has exclusive competence.

The definitive and permanent decision by a Member State not to ratify CETA raises numerous issues. The first issue relates to the national rejection of CETA. Such a decision could, in principle, only be based on grounds for which the Member State has an "exclusive" or a "shared" competence. One of the problems with mixed agreements is the lack of demarcation between EU and national competences. Both sides seem to consider that they are one hundred percent competent for the full agreement. Neither side has an interest in spelling out which provision of the agreement falls under "exclusive EU", "shared" or eventually "exclusive Member States" competence. The Union's non-willingness to be more specific could be justified by the dynamic character of its competences in the area of external relations since, arguably, every time the Council adopts an internal regulation it broadens the Union's competence in relation to that specific issue.[63] It would therefore be counterproductive to specify the exact European competences in such an agreement. On the other hand, by proposing provisional application, the Commission specifies, to a certain extent, the areas of EU-competence.[64]

The practice of national Parliaments not to specify the areas of their national competences is more difficult to justify.[65] National Parliaments pretend to have the right to accept or reject the agreement as such.[66] This pretentiousness

---

63   G. Van der Loo, R. Wessel, 'The Non-Ratification of Mixed Agreements: Legal Consequences and Solutions', *Common market law review* 54(3) (2017), p. 753.

64   The Commission's proposal can only be seen as an indication since it is the Council's prerogative to decide on provisional application. G. Van der Loo and R. Wessel (n. 62) p. 755 point out that for political reasons parts of the agreement which fall under exclusive EU competence might not be applied provisionally. Critically also D. Kleimann, G. Kübeck (n. 31), p. 17.

65   See P.-J. Kuijper (n. 6), p. 3. Quite typically, the German ratification of the EU FTA with South Korea does not refer to those areas of the FTA for which Germany is competent. The 'Gesetz zum Freihandelsabkommen vom 6. Oktober 2010 zwischen der Europäischen Union und ihren Mitgliedstaaten einerseits und der Republik Korea andererseits vom 5. Dezember 2012' states in one paragraph that the Bundestag with the consent of the Bundesrat accepts the FTA. BGBL 2012, Teil II Nr. 39 vom 12. Dezember 2012, p. 1482 et seq.

66   This position is re-enforced by the so-called Pastis-theory introduced by AG Kokott in her Opinion in case C-13/07 where she stated: "Individual aspects of an agreement for which the Community has no competence internally 'infect' the agreement as a whole and make it dependent on the common accord of the Member States. The picture created by the Commission itself in another context is also absolutely true in relation to Article 133(6) EC. Just as a little drop of pastis can turn a glass of water milky, individual provisions, however secondary, in an international agreement based on the first subparagraph of Art. 133(5) EC can make it necessary to conclude a shared agreement". See

raises numerous constitutional issues.[67] A national Parliament could not vote against a provision of an FTA for which the EU has exclusive competence without violating both national constitutional law and European law.[68] The recent criticism by Italy on CETA's insufficient protection of Italian Geographical Indications is a case in point.[69] The EU alone is competent on IP issues in CETA; nevertheless, Italy pretends to have the right not to ratify CETA based on a perceived lack of IP protection.[70] Although it is convenient for national Parliaments not to clarify the demarcation of competences, we suggest that the national ratification act limits itself to areas of specific national competence.[71] Such an exercise would "improve transparency and legal certainty in Member States' domestic ratification procedures"[72] and it would help European citizens to better understand the allocation of competences between the EU and the Member States with the useful political consequence that citizens would be better empowered to allocate democratic responsibility in their votes for national Parliaments and for the European Parliament.

Secondly, there is the question of the necessity of a new negotiating mandate. Normally, the Council would have to agree to a negotiating mandate

---

Case C-13/07, *Commission v Council*, Opinion of Advocate General Kokott, EU:C:2009:190, para. 121.

67   C. Tietje, 'Ganz, aber doch nur teilweise – die Beteiligung des Deutschen Bundestages an gemischten völkerrechtlichen Abkommen': https://verfassungsblog.de/ganz-aber-doch-nur-teilweise-die-beteiligung-des-deutschen-bundestages-an-gemischten-voelkerrechtlichen-abkommen-der-eu/.

68   At the end of her Opinion AG Sharpston says: „The Court has held that, when an agreement requiring the participation of both the European Union and its constituent Member States is negotiated and concluded, both the European Union and the Member States must act *within the framework of the competences which they have while respecting the competences of any other contracting party* [see Case C-28/12, *Commission v Council*, EU:C:2015:282, para. 47]. It is true that, in principle, each party (including the Member States) must – as matters stand – choose between either consenting to or rejecting the entire agreement. However, that choice must be made in accordance with the Treaty rules on the allocation of competences. Were a Member State to refuse to conclude an international agreement for reasons relating to aspects of that agreement for which the European Union enjoys exclusive external competence that Member State would be acting in breach of those Treaty rules. See Sharpston (n. 41), para. 568.

69   M. Tropeano (n. 39).

70   In the meantime, the Italian Agricultural Minister corrected his earlier statement by saying that "nobody is in a hurry to bring CETA to the chamber". See F. Guarascio, P. Blenkinsop, 'Italy in no rush to reject EU-Canada trade deal: farm minister': https://www.reuters.com/article/us-eu-canada-italy/italy-in-no-rush-to-reject-eu-canada-trade-deal-farm-minister-idUSKBN1K61IT.

71   P.-J. Kuijper (n. 6) p. 4.

72   G. Van der Loo, R. Wessel (n. 62) p. 757.

for a Comprehensive EU-Canada Trade Agreement (Article 218 TFEU). Yet, it could be argued that such a mandate already exists, i.e. the original CETA mandates.[73] If we take the case of the EU-Japan agreement,[74] we note that the mandate was broader than the proposal made by the Commission. It could then be argued that also in the case of a Comprehensive EU-Canada Trade Agreement a new mandate is not necessary. However, the Japan case is different from the situation discussed here as plan B. The original CETA mandates have been adopted for an agreement which can no longer be concluded. It would therefore seem necessary for the Council to agree on a new negotiating mandate for the "Comprehensive EU-Canada Trade Agreement". Of course, the contents of the mandate could be quite similar to that of the original CETA mandate of 2011 (which did not contain any reference to "investment").[75]

Thirdly, Canada would have to accept a "Comprehensive EU-Canada Trade Agreement". Whether or not the two sides are able to conclude such an agreement rapidly depends on their political will and on the concessions made in respect of CETA. The concessions made by Canada and the EU on the investment part of CETA might in fact create some difficulties in the negotiations.

The fourth issue relates to how the provisional application of CETA would end after the non-ratification of the agreement by one Member State. The impossibility to conclude the agreement would also require the termination of the provisional application. Statement to the Council Minutes No. 20[76] confirms this view by reiterating that in this case "provisional application must be and will be terminated". It adds that "the necessary steps will be taken in accordance with EU procedures". The statements made by Germany, Poland, Belgium and Austria indicate[77] that these countries believe that they can

---

73   Council of the EU, 'Recommendation from the Commission to the Council on the modification of the negotiating directives for an Economic Integration Agreement with Canada in order to authorise the Commission to negotiate, on behalf of the Union, on investment', 12838/11; Council of the EU, 'Recommendation from the Commission to the Council in order to authorize the Commission to open negotiations for an Economic Integration Agreement with Canada', 9036/09 (both documents declassified 15 December 2015).

74   Council of the EU, 'Directive for the negotiation of a free trade agreement with Japan' (2012) 15864/12 (declassified 14 September 2017).

75   With respect to the recent EU-U.S. preliminary discussions on EU-U.S. negotiations, it could be argued that the Commission can rely on the existing TTIP mandate and does not need to restart the process of a Council agreement on a negotiating directive. This case is comparable to the EU-Japan situation where the Council adopted a broad mandate, the Commission however proposed a trade agreement only.

76   Statements to the Council Minutes (n. 24), statement 20.

77   Statements to the Council Minutes (n. 24), statements 21, 22, 37.

unilaterally terminate the provisional application of CETA and have triggered a debate[78] on how the provisional application of CETA should be ended in case of non-ratification. Since the Member States of the European Union are parties to CETA they can, in principle, terminate provisional application.[79] Yet at the European Union level the decision to adopt provisional application must be taken by the Council (Article 218 (5) TFEU) and consequently also the decision to revoke provisional application. The Council's above-mentioned Declaration that the necessary steps will be taken in accordance with EU procedures seems to confirm this view. If a Member State were to terminate provisional application unilaterally, this could have profound consequences for the functioning of the EU's internal market. Would the Member State impose tariffs on Canadian products imported from other EU-Member States? Not awaiting the Council decision to terminate provisional application, the Member State would probably violate the duty of sincere cooperation contained in Article 4 (3) TEU. Such violation could however also be assumed for other Member States if they prevented a decision in Council not to terminate provisional application. One could imagine for example that those Member States which had ratified CETA would not be inclined to adopt such a decision given the benefit they receive from provisional application.

Lastly, the Council would have to sign and conclude the "Comprehensive EU-Canada Trade Agreement" and the European Parliament would have to give its consent. Since both institutions have already ratified CETA it would be politically difficult for them to reject a "pure" trade agreement.

3   EU Trade Policy Vis-à-Vis the United States and China

The European Union, the United States and China are heavyweights in international trade. In 2017, the U.S. and China were the most important extra EU trading partners,[80] with the U.S. being the EU's most important export

---

78   See G. Van der Loo, R. Wessel (n. 62), p. 759 et seq.

79   Art. 30.7 (3) (c) CETA. Kuijper supports this view citing Art. 25 (2) Vienna Convention on the Law of Treaties. See P.-J. Kuijper, 'Of 'Mixity' and 'Double Hatting: EU External Relations Law Explained: Inaugural Lecture Delivered on the Appointment to the Chair of the Law of International (Economic) Organizations at the Faculty of Law at the University of Amsterdam on Friday 23 May 2008', p. 12.

80   European Commission, 'International trade in goods in 2017 – A third of EU trade is with the United States and China – At Member State level, trade within the EU largely prevails': http://europa.eu/rapid/press-release_STAT-18-2584_en.htm.

destination and China being the EU's major importing country.[81] Both countries pose challenges to the EU's trade strategy since they are not candidates for a new generation FTA.

3.1 The United States – Managed Trade Instead of Further Trade Liberalisation

"The international regulation of international trade has its genesis in the belief of national leaders that some international mechanism is essential to prevent the pursuit of self-interested national regulation of international trade in a manner that harms other nations and in a manner that, when combined with retaliatory actions, results in a sharp and chaotic restriction in the overall level of international trade."[82]

During the economic crisis of the 1920s, many countries adopted protectionist policies in the form of high tariffs and quantitative restrictions. The U.S. Smoot Hawley Tariff Act of 1930 and other protectionist measures taken in response to the crisis brought international trade virtually to a halt.[83] Recognising the serious impact of these policies on the economy, the U.S. then became an ardent supporter of global trade liberalisation. The U.S. pushed for and achieved trade liberalisation in eight GATT rounds and in the WTO but also bilaterally.[84] In the aftermath of the economic crisis of 2008, protectionist measures are again on the rise.

Donald Trump's "America First"-policy reflects the much feared "self-interested national regulations" and "retaliatory actions". The President considers the trade deals concluded by previous administrations as disadvantageous, "unfair" and responsible for the U.S. trade deficits and for job losses in the manufacturing industries.[85] He is critical towards the

---

81   For details see: http://ec.europa.eu/trade/policy/countries-and-regions/countries/united-states/ and http://ec.europa.eu/trade/policy/countries-and-regions/countries/china/.

82   J. H. Jackson, *World Trade and the Law of GATT* (Bobbs-Merrill, 1969), p. 9.

83   R. Senti, *GATT – Allgemeines Zoll- und Handelsabkommen* (Schulthess, 1986), p. 4.

84   P. Mavroidis, 'Guest Post: From Roosevelt to Reagan to Trump: the Decay of U.S. Internationalism': http://worldtradelaw.typepad.com/ielpblog/2018/09/guest-post-from-roosevelt-to-reagan-to-trump-the-decay-of-us-internationalism.html.

85   See generally Chapter I of the President's 2018 Trade Policy Agenda in: Office of the U.S. Trade Representative, '2018 Trade Policy Agenda and 2017 Trade Annual Report': https://ustr.gov/about-us/policy-offices/press-office/reports-and-publications/2018/2018-trade-policy-agenda-and-2017.

WTO[86] and its dispute settlement system.[87] The U.S. has withdrawn from the negotiations of the Transpacific Partnership Agreement, has re-negotiated the NAFTA and KORUS agreements and has put the TTIP negotiations on hold. Its trade policy strategy has become clear: the U.S. threatens trading partners with retaliatory actions (e.g. car tariffs[88], tax on French wine and spirits[89]), imposes new tariffs against them[90] and then engages in power-oriented bilateral negotiations to re-establish a favourable balance of concessions. These actions have brought the world to the brink of a trade war[91] since many U.S. trading partners (e.g. Canada, China, and the EU) have reacted with countermeasures while at the same time initiating WTO dispute settlement cases against the U.S. So far, the U.S. power politics have paid off in case of KORUS, albeit with a WTO-questionable outcome[92] and in the case of Canada and Mexico with a renewed "NAFTA" agreement, called USMCA which contains some trade liberalisation (e.g. US exports of dairy to Canada), but, overall, is more an agreement on industrial than trade policy, as demonstrated by the agreed minimum wages for Mexican autoworkers and the higher than the original NAFTA local content requirements in order to benefit from zero tariffs under the new rules of origin.

---

86   "Single worst trade deal ever", see J. Micklethwait et al., 'Trump threathens to pull U.S. out of WTO if it doesn't 'Shape up'": https://www.bloomberg.com/news/articles/2018-08-30/trump-says-he-will-pull-u-s-out-of-wto-if-they-don-t-shape-up.

87   Office of the U.S. Trade Representative (n. 84) p. 22.

88   U.S. Department of Commerce, 'U.S. Department of Commerce initiates section 232 investigation into auto imports': https://www.commerce.gov/news/press-releases/2018/05/us-department-commerce-initiates-section-232-investigation-auto-imports (U.S. Department of Commerce).

89   D. Shepardson, S. White, 'Trump says US could tax French wine in retaliation for digital tax',: https://www.reuters.com/article/us-usa-trade-france/trump-says-us-could-tax-french-wine-in-retaliation-for-digital-tax-idUSKCN1UL291.

90   Tariffs against China under Section 301 of the Trade Act of 1974. See Office of the U.S. Trade Representative, 'USTR Finalizes Second Tranche of Tariffs on Chinese Products in Response to China's Unfair Trade Practices': https://ustr.gov/about-us/policy-offices/press-office/press-releases/2018/august/ustr-finalizes-second-tranche. Tariffs on steel and aluminium imports under Section 232 of the 1962 Trade Expansion Act. See White House, 'President Trump Approves Section 232 Tariff modifications': https://www.whitehouse.gov/briefings-statements/president-trump-approves-section-232-tariff-modifications/.

91   P. Krugman, 'Thinking about a Trade War (Very Wonkish)': https://www.nytimes.com/2018/06/17/opinion/thinking-about-a-trade-war-very-wonkish.html.

92   It seems that South Korea has accepted, WTO illegal, voluntary export restraints on steel. See S. Lester, 'Will anyone file a WTO Complaint against the KORUS steel quotas?': http://worldtradelaw.typepad.com/ielpblog/2018/03/will-anyone-file-a-wto-complaint-against-the-korus-steel-quotas.html.

USMCA does not abolish the U.S. tariffs on steel and aluminium against Canada and Mexico and seems to accept voluntary export restraints in case the U.S. adopts punitive tariffs on cars.[93]

The European Union has reacted to the U.S. tariffs on steel and aluminium[94] by initiating a WTO dispute settlement proceeding[95] challenging the national security justification of the measures and by imposing "rebalancing" tariffs on certain U.S. products.[96] The EU/U.S. conflict came to a heat when the U.S., in May 2018, announced a Section 232 investigation on cars,[97] but was partially settled at a meeting between President Trump and President Juncker on 25 July 2018.[98] The agreed joint agenda contains the following main actions:

- Work towards zero tariffs, zero non-tariff barriers and zero subsidies tariffs on *non-auto* industrial goods (emphasis added). Both sides intend to increase trade in services, chemicals, pharmaceuticals, medical products and soybeans.

---

93   The text of USMCA can be found at https://ustr.gov/trade-agreements/free-trade-agreements/united-states-mexico-canada-agreement/agreement-between. See also M. Lanz, 'Trump will den Handel verwalten, nicht fördern': https://www.nzz.ch/wirtschaft/trump-will-den-handel-verwalten-nicht-foerdern-ld.1424807; A. Behsudi et al., 'Trump gets trade win with new NAFTA deal': https://www.politico.eu/article/us-reaches-nafta-deal-with-canada-providing-trump-crucial-trade-win-mexico-lighthizer/?utm_source=POLITICO.EU&utm_campaign=48df04fca7-EMAIL_CAMPAIGN_2018_10_01_04_25&utm_medium=email&utm_term=0_10959edeb5-48df04fca7-190009785.

94   European Commission, 'European Commission responds to the US restrictions on steel and aluminium affecting EU': http://trade.ec.europa.eu/doclib/press/index.cfm?id=1805.

95   WTO, Request for consultations by the European Union, *United States – Certain Measures on Steel and Aluminium Products: Request for Consultation by the European Union*, DS548, 1 June 2018.

96   European Commission, 'EU adopts rebalancing measures in reaction to US steel and aluminium tariffs', Press Release IP/18/4220, 20 June 2018. See also WTO, *Immediate Notification under Article 12.5 of the Agreement on Safeguards to the Council for Trade in Goods of proposed suspension of concessions and other obligations referred to in para. 2 of Article 8 of the Agreement on Safeguards*, G/L/1237, 18 May 2018. Whilst the EU 'rebalancing' tariffs are politically appealing, they raise some very interesting WTO legal issues which cannot be dealt with in this paper. See for further details C. Tietje, V. Sacher, *Stahl und Whiskey – Transatlantischer Handelskrieg als Bedrohung der Welthandelsordnung* (PPTEL, 2018:48), p. 6; N. Jung, A. Hazarika, *Trade Wars are Easy to Win? – National Security and Safeguards as the new weapon* (ZEuS, 2018:1), p. 1 et seq.; S. Lester, 'Litigating GATT Article XXI: the U.S. View of the Scope of Exception': http://worldtradelaw.typepad.com/ielp-blog/2018/03/litigating-gatt-article-xxi-the-us-view-of-the-scope-of-the-exception.html.

97   U.S. Department of Commerce (n. 87).

98   European Commission, 'Joint EU-U.S. Statement following President Juncker's visit to the White House', STATEMENT/18/4687, 25 July 2018.

- Strategic cooperation on energy with the EU intending to import more liquefied natural gas from the U.S.
- Dialogue on standards to ease trade, reduce bureaucratic obstacles and slash costs.
- Promotion of WTO reform to address unfair trading practices, theft of intellectual property, forced technology transfer, industrial subsidies and distortions created by state owned enterprises and overcapacity.

The U.S. and the EU are not negotiating yet, they rather explore the scope of the agreement to be negotiated.[99] The joint agenda though puts the EU into a difficult position conceptually. After the disastrous failure of TTIP, both sides can no longer negotiate a far-reaching and comprehensive FTA. However, it seems questionable whether a "more limited trade agreement"[100] with the U.S. is compatible with the EU's strategy for a trade policy to "harness" globalisation. The EU asks its trading partners to sign the new generation of comprehensive FTAS which require a substantial amount of trade and non-trade concessions. The non-trade concessions, but also other subjects such as government procurement, are absent in the discussions with the U.S. and hence put the EU into a credibility crisis. Moreover, the EU is bound by the rules-based international trading system and cannot take decisions which would jeopardise this allegiance. A zero-tariff agreement on non-auto industrial goods poses the immediate question on whether it would satisfy the requirements of GATT Article XXIV according to which an FTA should liberalise "substantially all trade".[101] The EU therefore rightly suggested to the U.S. to have all tariffs on industrial goods including car tariffs eliminated.[102] Zero tariffs for other industrial or agricultural products might help to increase trade, provided that the tariffs are not already at zero (as is the case for pharmaceuticals); yet as the

---

99   In the first year both partners made rather little progress and result have been achieved in only a limited number of areas such as on Conformity assessment or sectoral cooperation. See European Commission, Progress Report on the Implementation of the EU-U.S. Joint Statement of 25 July 2018': http://trade.ec.europa.eu/doclib/docs/2019/july/tradoc_158272.pdf.

100   Statement of Commissioner Malmström before the INTA Committee of the European Parliament on 30 August 2018. See H. von der Burchard, 'EU says it is willing to scrap car tariffs in US trade deal': https://www.politico.eu/article/eu-says-it-is-willing-to-scrap-car-tariffs-in-us-trade-deal/?utm_source=POLITICO.EU&utm_campaign=69ffb830e9

101   While there is a lot of discretion for WTO members and not much case law on GATT Article XXIV, any weak EU-U.S. agreement could nevertheless be open to a WTO attack. On GATT Article XXIV, see generally P. Mavroidis, *The General Agreement on Tariffs and Trade* (OUP, 2005), p. 225 et seq.

102   H. von der Burchard (n. 99).

TTIP discussions have shown, the far bigger trade obstacles lie in the domestic regulatory issues, hence the call for regulatory cooperation.[103] A dialogue on "standards" could be the right approach, yet again as the TTIP negotiations have illustrated, a meaningful regulatory cooperation is quite burdensome if the level of protection in the specifically regulated areas differs as much as it does between the EU and the U.S.: REACH, GMOs or "glyphosate" are telling examples. Since neither side will lower or increase its protective standard, regulatory cooperation can only result in technical improvements (e.g. testing requirements and criteria) not questioning the respective standard. The intention to strive for zero non-tariff barriers and zero subsidies is laudable in view of the many past EU/U.S. WTO dispute settlement cases (e.g. Airbus, GMOs, Chlorinated Chicken and Hormone-treated beef), but the solutions to be included in a "more limited trade agreement" require quite some imagination and might eventually be rejected.[104]

More importantly, if the U.S. continues to oppose the appointment of new members of the WTO Appellate Body, the WTO will be unable to perform its "judicial" function. The EU cannot allow that the international trading community returns to the "dark ages of the GATT 1947" when, at least in critical cases, GATT panel recommendations could be blocked by the loosing contracting party. WTO-reform is on the joint agenda, but unfortunately the reform of the dispute settlement system is not mentioned specifically. It will be difficult for the EU to promote WTO reforms if the U.S. continues to sabotage the WTO dispute settlement system. The international trading system is not sacrosanct, it allows for adjustments, adaptations and re-balancing through negotiations and legal proceedings, it is however adamant against power-based protectionism as the late John H. Jackson reminds us so forcefully.

The EU's answer to the joint agenda can therefore not lie in damage limitation to avoid a trade war, rather the EU must insist on WTO-reform and stand up for a rules-based international trading system. In parallel, the EU must pursue its FTA strategy by implementing the agreements with Canada, Japan, Mexico, Singapore, Vietnam, and by concluding agreements with Mercosur, Chile, Australia, New Zealand and other ASEAN countries.

---

103   European Commission, 'Transatlantic Trade and Investment Partnership – The Regulatory Part': http://trade.ec.europa.eu/doclib/press/index.cfm?id=1230#regulatory-cooperation

104   Note that the French President stated on 25 September 2018 that France would no longer accept "commercial agreements" with countries that do not respect the Paris Climate Agreement. See United Nations, 'General Debate France': https://news.un.org/en/story/2018/09/1020642. If the Council confirmed this view, a more limited EU-U.S. trade agreement would no longer be possible.

3.2   China – Not So Liberal after All?

The development of the Chinese chemical industry may be taken as an example to explain the rise of China to the manufacturing powerhouse of the world. At the time of China's accession to the WTO in 2001, the U.S. was the largest chemical producing nation followed by Japan and Germany. Recent developments have drastically changed this situation. In 2016, the Chinese chemical industry closed in on EUR 1.7 trillion annual turnover and today it is even larger than the EU and the U.S. chemical industry combined. The U.S. takes second place, followed by Japan and Germany. Between 2011 and 2016 the production average annual growth rate increased by 10.5 per cent. China not only produces commodity chemicals, but is also increasing its market share in fine and specialty chemicals as well as in pharmaceuticals. China's chemical industry currently shows the highest growth potential at international level.[105] These figures might help to understand why the mood in Europe towards China has changed considerably since its accession to the WTO. Originally, China was considered a partner with significant economic opportunities;[106] today, China is seen more as a threat than an opportunity. The EU is afraid of Chinese overcapacities, in particular in the steel sector, of cheap imports of industrial goods, of its appetite for taking over of European technology companies, of its "one-belt, one-road"- and "China Manufacturing 2025"- Initiatives, of the continuing discrimination of foreign investors in China, of forced technology transfer, of insufficient intellectual property protection and of its subsidised state-owned enterprises with which the European industries seem unable to compete. The EU's new strategy towards China is one of assertiveness and defence insisting on "reciprocity, a level playing field and fair competition across all areas of cooperation".[107]

China is not a candidate country for a new generation free trade agreement, but already in 2013, the EU and China started negotiations on a bilateral

---

105   Verband der Chemischen Industrie e.V., 'Länderbericht China. Daten und Fakten zur Chemieindustrie': https://www.vci.de/ergaenzende-downloads/laenderbericht-china-chemie-kurz-2.pdf; Verband der Chemischen Industrie e.V. and Prognos AG, 'The German Chemical Industry 2030. VCI-Prognos study – Update 2015/2016': https://www.vci.de/services/publikationen/broschueren-faltblaetter/vci-prognos-studie-die-deutsche-chemische-industrie-2030-update-2015-2016.jsp.

106   "The EU's fundamental approach to China must remain one of engagement and partnership". See European Commission, 'EU – China, Closer Partners, Growing Responsibilities', COM (2006) 631 final, 24 October 2006, p. 1.

107   European Commission, 'Joint Communication to the European Parliament and the Council. Elements for a new EU Strategy on China', JOIN (2016) 30 final, 22 June 2016, p. 2.

investment agreement. These negotiations are difficult to conclude since the agreement would provide for the governance structure of future bilateral economic relations and, even without a tariff component, would have to address many controversial issues, such as freedom of investment, reciprocity, and eventually subsidies (those to state-owned enterprises, in particular) and intellectual property protection.

The EU's actions and reactions to Chinese trade and investment issues further complicate the negotiations and demonstrate the new European assertiveness:

Firstly, the EU has not given China Market Economy Status (MES) in anti-dumping cases, but has tightened its anti-dumping Regulation instead:[108] the amended Regulation applies a new method of assessing market distortions in third countries when calculating anti-dumping duties; it allows the EU to continue its current practice not to use Chinese domestic prices in anti-dumping investigations with the consequence of high anti-dumping duties.[109] China considers that it is entitled to MES-treatment because of Article 15 of its WTO Accession Protocol and has initiated a WTO dispute settlement case against the EU.[110]

Secondly, the Regulation for a framework on investment screening.[111] The regulation is the result of intensive political discussions at national[112] and

---

108   Regulation (EU) 2017/2321 of the European Parliament and of the Council of 12 December 2017 amending Regulation (EU) 2016/1036 on protection against dumped imports from countries not members of the European Union and Regulation (EU) 2016/1037 on protection against subsidised imports from countries not members of the European Union (OJ 2017, L 338), Art. 11(4).

109   For an analysis of the EU anti-dumping activities against China, see B. Petter, R. Quick, 'The Politics of TDI and the Different Views in EU Member States – Necessary Safety-Valves or Luxurious Rent-Seeking Device?', in M. Bungenberg, M. Hahn, C. Herrmann, T. Müller-Ibold, *European Yearbook of International Economic Law* (Springer, 2018).

110   WTO, Request for consultations by China, *European Union – Measures Related to Price Comparison Methodologies*, DS516, 15 December 2016. See C. Tietje, V. Sacher, 'The New Anti-Dumping Methodology of the European Union – A Breach of WTO Law?', *Essays on Transnational Economic Law* (2018:153). Upon the request of China and after evaluationg the comments of the European Union, the panel decided on 14 June 2019 to suspend the proceeding. See: https://www.wto.org/english/tratop_e/dispu_e/cases_e/ds516_e.htm.

111   European Commission, 'Proposal for a Regulation of the European Parliament and of the Council establishing a framework for screening of foreign direct investments into the European Union', COM (2017) 487 final, 13 September 2017. The Regulation entered into force on 10 April 2019. See http://europa.eu/rapid/press-release_IP-19-2088_en.htm.

112   B. Zypries, M. Sapin, C. Calenda, 'Letter of the Economics Ministers of Germany, France and Italy to Commissioner Malmström': https://www.bmwi.de/Redaktion/DE/Downloads/S-T/schreiben-de-fr-it-an-malmstroem.pdf?__blob=publicationFile&v=5.

European level[113] on how to curtail the Chinese appetite to acquire European technology companies (e.g. KUKA, OSRAM and Aixtron). It does not provide for a European investment screening mechanism but leaves the final decision to the Member States who have such legislation in place (14 Member States in total); it introduces a cooperation mechanism for other Member States and the Commission to comment on the domestic proceedings. When deciding on the investment, the Member State should take the Commission's recommendations and other Member States' comments into account.[114] Member States not having an investment screening are not required to introduce one. It remains to be seen how actual cases will be dealt with under the new investment screening framework, its content does however reflect the new European strategy: The EU flexes its muscles and insists on reciprocal treatment in China notwithstanding some industry criticism.[115] The EU signals frustration with the lack of domestic reform in China despite the many announcements by the Chinese leadership to adopt such reforms. The European Chamber of Commerce in China criticises this difference between claim and reality complaining that regulatory obstacles are on the rise instead of being abolished. It openly supports the Commission's call for reciprocity in bilateral trade and investment relations and publishes case studies where China continues to restrict foreign investment together with a long list of Chinese discriminatory treatments against European companies.[116]

Thirdly, the EU has launched a WTO case against China's unfair technology transfers[117] and cooperates closely with Japan and the U.S. "to find effective

---

113   European Parliament, 'Debate on Foreign Investments in Strategic Sectors': http://www.europarl.europa.eu/sides/getDoc.do?pubRef=-//EP//TEXT+CRE+20170614+ITEM-018+DOC+XML+V0//EN&language=EN. On this issue see the contribution by M. Bungenberg in this volume.

114   For an analysis of the proposal, see V. Günther, 'Der Vorschlag der Europäischen Union für eine Verordnung zur Schaffung eines Rahmens zur Überprüfung ausländischer Direktinvestitionen in der Europäischen Union', *Essays on Transnational Economic Law* (2018:157).

115   Bundesverband der Deutschen Industrie e.V., 'China – Partner und systemischer Wettbewerber': https://bdi.eu/media/publikationen/?publicationtype=Positionen#/publikation/news/china-partner-und-systemischer-wettbewerber/ and 'Investment Screening in Germany and Europe': https://english.bdi.eu/article/news/investment-screening-in-germany-and-europe/.

116   European Union Chamber of Commerce in China, 'European Business in China – Position Paper 2018/2019': http://www.europeanchamber.com.cn/en/publications-position-paper.

117   WTO, Request for consultations by the European Union, *China – Certain Measures on the Transfer of Technology*, DS549, 6 June 2018. See also European Commission, 'EU launches WTO case against China's unfair technology transfers', Press Release IP/18/4027, 1 June 2018.

means to address trade-distorting policies of third countries".[118] Their statement on industrial subsidies, technology transfer policies, and practices and
market-oriented conditions targets China and shows dissatisfaction with
China's unwillingness to address these points in WTO negotiations. Japan,
the U.S. and the EU consider that the WTO Agreement on Subsidies needs re-
negotiation since it is ill-equipped to control subsidies given to state-owned
enterprises.[119]

In his key-note speech on economic globalisation, further trade liberalisation and multilateral approaches at the World Economic Forum in January
2017, Chinese President Xi Jinping[120] left no doubt that the world's second
largest economy would take over America's traditional role as the champion
of free trade and open markets which have become vacant since the election
of President Trump. China's quest for a bigger role at the global level was announced long before the present trade conflict with the U.S. started. In theory,
for the EU, China could be a natural ally to oppose U.S. isolationist policies and
to defend the rules-based international trading system. In practice, however, it
is unlikely that the EU and China can overcome their considerable differences
on the issues mentioned above. On Chinese trade and investment issues, the
EU rather seeks alliance with the U.S. and Japan. Therefore, it is doubtful that
the current U.S. – China "trade war" could serve as a catalyst to enhance closer
EU-China trade relations.

4   Conclusions

After Opinion 2/15, the future for EU trade agreements looks bright. The Commission can pursue its trade strategy, negotiate broad and comprehensive EU
trade agreements with partner countries and have them ratified at EU level
only. This clear allocation of competence allows the EU to remain a reliable
trading partner and strengthens the credibility and effectiveness of the common commercial policy. The practice of provisional application of some aspects of mixed agreements becomes superfluous as well as the decision which

---

118   European Commission, 'Joint Statement on Trilateral Meeting of the Trade Ministers of
        the United States, Japan and the European Union': http://trade.ec.europa.eu/doclib/docs/
        2018/may/tradoc_156906.pdf.
119   Critical H. Gao, 'What is "Socialist Market Economy"?': http://worldtradelaw.typepad.
        com/ielpblog/2018/07/index.html.
120   X. Jinping, 'Jointly Shoulder Responsibilities of Our Times, Promote Global Growth': http://
        www.china.org.cn/node_7247529/content_40569136.htm accessed 6 September 2018.

parts to apply provisionally. In fact, it is the whole agreement which enters into force. Criticism of and opposition to these agreements will continue to exist, yet only the EU itself will be able to block them and not a single Member State. The role of national Parliaments is limited to controlling the actions of the national governments in Council. National law makers can no longer pretend to have a competence which they themselves or their predecessors have transferred to the European level. European citizens can allocate democratic responsibility both at national and European level holding the European Parliament and the national governments accountable through their votes in national and European elections.

On the other hand, Opinion 2/15 has rendered the future of European BITs considerably difficult notwithstanding the recent legal clarifications contained in Opinion 1/17. As mixed agreements, these BITs will be ratified both at European and national level with all the uncertainty that this process entails. According to Opinion 2/15, some investment issues fall under "shared competences". This means that the Council could opt in favour of EU ratification only, although this is unlikely given the heated debate on investor-state dispute settlement even after Opinion 1/17. Nevertheless, more boldness on the Council's side when interpreting its discretionary powers in cases of mixed agreements would be in the interest of a stronger and more capable common commercial policy. We recommend that in such cases the Council always opts for EU-only. The practice of national Parliaments to adopt or reject these agreements as such, without indicating which part of the agreement falls under their competence, is regrettable but will not change. Apparently, national Parliaments consider that admitting to their constituencies that they no longer are competent on specific European trade policy issues is equal to a defeat.

In 2016, at the height of the heated and emotional debate on TTIP and CETA, the fate of CETA seemed doomed; today, mainly due to Brexit and to President Trump's aggressive trade policy, EU-internal opposition to trade agreements is fading. Compared to TTIP and CETA, the EU-Japan Trade Agreement JEFTA, hardly gave rise to public debate, let alone to huge demonstrations. These developments allow for a rather positive outlook on the CETA national ratification processes. Moreover, the Commission can demonstrate with data on EU-Canada trade[121] that many European companies have benefitted from

---

121   European Commission, 'CETA in your town (statistical data)': http://ec.europa.eu/trade/
       policy/in-focus/ceta/ceta-in-your-town/; European Commission, 'One year on EU-
       Canada trade agreement delivers promising results': http://trade.ec.europa.eu/doclib/
       press/index.cfm?id=1907.

improved market access since the provisional application of CETA.[122] National ratification of mixed agreements, however, remains unpredictable, as the remarks by the Italian Minister show. In case of a permanent and definitive rejection of CETA by a Member State, its provisional application would end, and the Commission would have to try again and propose an EU-only "Comprehensive EU-Canada Trade Agreement".

External challenges to EU trade policy coming from China and the U.S. are manifold. Both countries' trade and investment policies mean that the U.S. is no longer a candidate for a new generation FTA, and China has never been one.[123]

The EU's original intention for future transatlantic relations was a strong, modern and comprehensive FTA, called TTIP. TTIP was supposed to further liberalise transatlantic trade and to be a role-model for new trading rules bilaterally and multilaterally.[124] However, in 2016, TTIP came under considerable attack in Europe so that it was doubtful whether the EU would be able to deliver, and then, in 2017, it was put on ice by the U.S. President. In fact, the new U.S. trade policy consists of tariff increases, FTA re-negotiations and shutting down the WTO Appellate Body. Can the EU agree with the U.S. on a "TTIP-light" or will it have to insist on a broader outcome, thereby risking failure? Can the EU risk failure at all and face punitive tariffs which the WTO will not rule upon because of the U.S. sabotage of the Appellate Body? So far, the EU has avoided an outright trade war with the U.S. and discussions take place to avoid further escalation. The EU countermeasures as a reaction to the U.S. steel and aluminium tariffs can be seen as a targeted response to increase pressure of Congress on the White House to change course. In case of further U.S. protectionist measures, the EU will react, but at the same time should intensify its dialogue with Congress on trade policy in general but especially on WTO reform. It is of

---

122 The intensified EU-Canada cooperation on trade has also potential to stabilise the WTO Appellate Body. As a result of the EU-Canada Summit on 17–18 July 2019 both partners have agreed on an interim appeal arbitration arrangement to remedy the blockage of the Appelate Body by the US which may result in the unability of the Appellate Body to hear new appeals by 10 December 2019. See: http://trade.ec.europa.eu/doclib/press/index.cfm?id=2053&title=Joint-Statement-by-the-European-Union-and-Canada-on-an-Interim-Appeal-Arbitration-Arrangement.

123 China believes that it could become a candidate country for a new generation FTA with the EU, but only after a successful conclusion of the EU – China BIT. See The People's Republic of China-Information Office of the State Council, 'The Facts and China's Position on China – US Trade Friction', p. 70: http://english.gov.cn/archive/white_paper/2018/09/26/content_281476319220196.htm.

124 European Commission, 'What is TTIP about?': http://ec.europa.eu/trade/policy/in-focus/ttip/about-ttip/.

paramount importance for the EU to have a functioning WTO dispute settlement system in order to counter U.S. protectionist measures.

As for China, since entering the WTO in 2001, the country has shown an unprecedented development and has become the world's second largest economy. The list of EU-China contentious trade issues reflects the divergences on China's state capitalism and its quest to become a world leader in new technologies. This political reality will make it difficult for the EU to conclude the investment negotiations with China. Yet without such an agreement it will not be easy to find common ground at multilateral level on the indispensable WTO reform to redress the balance between market economy approaches and state capitalism. A first step has already been made by the Commission which, upon request of the European Council,[125] has prepared a concept paper on "WTO reform"[126] to be discussed within the EU and with other WTO members. The proposals are structured under the three headings rulemaking, regular work and transparency, and dispute settlement. They address the U.S. criticism on dispute settlement and the specific lacunae of WTO rules concerning China's economic structure. In sum, we believe that the concept paper should serve as a starting point for WTO negotiations. The EU has a particular interest to convince both the U.S. and China to join these reform efforts since the alternative will be an outright trade war.

125   European Council, 'Conclusions', Press Release 421/18, 29 June 2018, para. 16.
126   European Commission, 'WTO reform (Concept Paper)': http://trade.ec.europa.eu/doclib/
       docs/2018/september/tradoc_157331.pdf.

CHAPTER 21

The Integration of EU Trade Defence in the Horizontal Comitology Regime

Jacques Bourgeois and Merijn Chamon

1   Introduction

The integration of the Common Commercial Policy (CCP) in the horizontal comitology framework was not explicitly foreseen by the Lisbon Treaty itself but resulted indirectly from the Treaty's subjection of both the CCP and the comitology regime to the Community Method.[1] While the principal decision to integrate the CCP in comitology may therefore have been pre-ordained, it was far from accomplished with the entry into force of the Lisbon Treaty itself. From a political perspective a first issue was whether Member States could be convinced of letting go of the Council's primordial role in implementing the CCP in favour of the Commission and once this decision taken, whether the reconfigured institutional balance would have any impact on the actual decisions taken. In addition, the integration posed a number of challenges from a policy perspective and this both for the CCP and comitology: would the EU's autonomous trade policy retain its effectivity under the general comitology rules? Would the comitology regime be able to integrate the peculiarities of the CCP without losing its horizontal character? Finally, a question was whether the integration in the horizontal framework would in any way affect private parties impacted by CCP measures.

To keep a sufficient focus in our chapter we will concentrate on the adoption of anti-dumping measures. The chapter will then look into the reform brought by the Lisbon Treaty to both the CCP and comitology (2); the new framework for adopting CCP measures (3) and the practice under the new framework (4).

---

1   Arguing that the Lisbon Treaty introduced the Community Method to the CCP and comitology respectively, see Y. Devuyst, 'European Union trade policy after the Lisbon Treaty: the Community method at work', in N. Witzleb, A. Martinez Arranz, P. Winand (eds.), *The European Union and Global Engagement: Institutions, Policies and Challenges* (Edward Elgar, 2015), p. 138–158; M. Chamon, 'Institutional balance and Community method in the implementation of EU legislation following the Lisbon Treaty', *Common Market Law Review* 53 (2016), p. 1507.

EU TRADE DEFENCE AND COMITOLOGY

Before concluding our chapter we will wrap up the findings in an assessment of the law and practice in trade defence in light of the Lisbon Treaty.

2   The Lisbon Treaty's Reform of Comitology and the CCP

The comitology system is one of the unique features of EU decision-making and has been around since the 1960s. Originally developed without a clear legal basis in the Treaties, it was anchored in primary law by the Single European Act (then Article 145 EEC) and subsequently rationalised by horizontal (i.e. across the board) framework instruments: the first and second comitology decisions (1987 and 1999) and the Comitology Regulation (2011) currently in force. In essence, comitology implies that the EU Commission is granted the power to implement EU law but in doing so it is assisted (or controlled) by committees composed of national experts with a possibility (until 2011) that a committee refers a file to the Council, thereby divesting the Commission of its executive power.

2.1   *Comitology under the Treaty of Lisbon*
On paper, the Treaty of Lisbon fundamentally reformed the comitology system by drawing a distinction between two types of non-legislative rule-making: sometimes the Commission may be empowered to amend or supplement formal legislation while on other occasions its power is limited to implementing legislative acts (either through general or individual measures). Under the pre-Lisbon framework (Article 202 TEC and the second comitology decision) no distinction was made between these two normative activities and both were governed by comitology. Post-Lisbon however, the Commission amends or supplements legislation through delegated acts (Article 290 TFEU)[2] and implements EU law through implementing acts (Article 291 TFEU).[3] Under

---

2   Relying on an example outside the area of the CCP: legislative Regulation 2015/2283 prescribes that "novel foods" require an authorisation before they may be placed on the EU market. Art. 3(2) of the Regulation ensures that the notion of "novel food" is sufficiently broadly defined to also cover possible "engineered nanomaterials". To ensure that the notion of "engineered nanomaterial" in the Regulation remains up to date in light of "technical and scientific progress or to definitions agreed at international level", the legislator has also delegated a power to the Commission to amend the legislative regulation through delegated acts.
3   To illustrate the function of the implementing act, in the legislative Regulation 2015/2283 (n. 2), the Commission has been conferred the power to grant the EU authorisations for novel foods through implementing acts: allowing the different Member States to authorise (or not) novel foods would result in a disparate patchwork of (non-)authorisations even if every

Article 290 TFEU the Commission is controlled by the legislature (given that it exceptionally exercises a legislative function) while under Article 291 TFEU it is controlled (or assisted) by the Member States (given that under the EU's *Vollzugsföderalismus* EU law is normally implemented by the Member States). Under the Lisbon Treaty, the comitology system thus only applies to implementation in the strict sense (Article 291 TFEU).

While most commentators were positive about the Treaty reform of comitology, much evidently depended on the actual application of the new system. Given the constraints of space, this issue will not be explored further here.[4] Suffice to note that much of the Lisbon Treaty's reform has been undone, *inter alia* because the Court of Justice of the European Union (ECJ) confirmed that the EU legislature has significant discretion in choosing between Articles 290 and 291 TFEU when contemplating granting powers to the Commission.[5] Evidently this discretion undermines the categorical distinction introduced by the Treaty. This is all the more striking as the delegation of powers to the Commission is subjected to significant restrictions by Article 290 TFEU, while the conferring of implementing powers to the Commission contemplated in Article 291 TFEU is not subjected to similar restrictions.[6]

The pre-Lisbon comitology procedures (as laid down in the second comitology decision) were further rationalised by the 2011 Comitology Regulation. Post-Lisbon only two procedures remain: the advisory procedure pursuant to which a committee, by simple majority, delivers a non-binding opinion on the Commission's draft implementing act and the examination procedure pursuant to which a committee adopts an opinion by qualified majority voting (QMV). Under the examination procedure, a positive opinion requires the Commission to adopt its draft while a negative opinion bars the Commission from doing so and requires it to rework its draft or submit it to the Appeal

---

Member State acts based on a single set of EU criteria. To ensure uniformity in the internal market for foodstuffs, the Commission adopts one authorisation for the entire EU.

4   For a discussion, see *inter alia* M. Chamon (n. 1), p. 1501–1544; C. Tovo, 'Delegation of Legislative Powers in the EU: How EU Institutions Have Eluded the Lisbon Reform', *European Law Review* 42 (2017), p. 677 – 705; A. Buchet, 'La réforme des pouvoirs conférés à la Commission européenne, entre métamorphose et réminiscence', *Cahiers de droit européen* 54 (2018), p. 205-250.

5   See Case C-427/12, *Commission v. Parliament and Council*, EU:C:2014:170; Case C-88/14, *Commission v. Parliament and Council*, EU:C:2015:499. But see Case C-65/13, *Parliament v. Council*, EU:C:2014:2289, para. 45-56.

6   Some authors have argued that the conditions under Art. 290 TFEU should apply *mutatis mutandis* to conferrals under Art. 291 TFEU, while others have noted that the restrictions on the Commission under Art. 291 TFEU are implicit in the notion of implementation itself. On this debate, see M. Chamon (n. 1), p. 1528 at footnote 135.

Committee. In case the committee fails to deliver an opinion, the Commission may adopt its draft, unless the exceptions of Article 5(4) of the Comitology Regulation apply. One of these exceptions is that the Commission may not adopt the draft if a simple majority of the committee's members opposes this.[7]

2.2 Comitology and the CCP

While the Commission in pre-Lisbon times also had to cooperate with committees of national experts and the Council when adopting or proposing e.g. anti-dumping measures, these procedures were not formally governed by the horizontal comitology framework.[8] While the incorporation of the CCP in the comitology system may have been inspired by the Lisbon Treaty itself, it was far from a done deal when the Treaty entered into force. The new wording of Article 207(2) TFEU only foresees the adoption of "measures *defining the framework* for implementing the CCP", while Article 133(2) TEC and even Article III-317(2) of the draft Constitution provided for "measures implementing the CCP". As a result, the Council cannot anymore adopt implementing measures based directly on Article 207 TFEU,[9] such measures now require a framework instrument (e.g. the basic Anti-Dumping or the basic Anti-Subsidy Regulation) as a legal basis. However, it was not a given that such "typical" implementing measures would also be adopted under the "default" comitology system. Indeed, the Commission's proposal to this end initially led to a stalling of the negotiations on the new Comitology Regulation in the Council.[10] In its

---

7   As Blumann notes this effectively resurrects the contre-filet variant of the old regulatory procedure. See C. Blumann, 'Un nouveau départ pour la Comitologie. Le règlement n° 182/2011 du 16 février 2011', *Cahiers de droit européen* 47 (2011), p. 44.

8   See Recital 12 to the second Comitology decision of the Council 1999/468 (OJ 1999, L 184/23).

9   R. Streinz, C. Ohler, C. Herrmann, *Der Vertrag von Lissabon zur Reform der EU* (Beck, 2010), p. 152. Gosalbo Bono on the other hand found it was "*not clear what the terms 'framework for implementation' mean*." See R. Gosalbo Bono, 'The organization of the external relations of the European Union in the Treaty of Lisbon', in P. Koutrakos (ed.), *The European Union's External Relations a Year after Lisbon* (CLEER Working Paper 2011), p. 18.

10 See F. Hoffmeister, 'Of Transferred Competence, Institutional Balance and Judicial Autonomy – Constitutional Developments in EU Trade Policy Seven Years after Lisbon', in J. Czuczai, F. Naert (eds.), *The EU as a Global Actor – Bridging Legal Theory and Practice* (Brill/Nijhoff, 2017), p. 318. House of Commons European Scrutiny Committee, *Nineteenth Report of Session 2010–11*; p. 23. During the trilogues on the new Comitology RegulationComitology Regulation, the Belgian Presidency even proposed the following recital: "This Regulation does not apply to the specific procedures that were not subject to the Council Decision 1999/468/EC, in particular those created for the implementation of the common commercial policy and it does not prejudge the possibility to lay down specific procedures under article 291 TFEU." See proposed Recital 14a in the four column table NEGO_CT(2010)0051(REV-11-10-2010).

original proposal, the Commission had foreseen a straightforward integration of CCP measures in the horizontal comitology regime, but the final regulation effectively lays down a separate regime for CCP measures.[11] Still, the importance of the decision-making in the CCP being brought under the horizontal comitology framework remains significant and the European Parliament being a co-legislator proved to be crucial in securing this rationalisation.

As a consequence, today there are no implementing measures in the CCP anymore that are adopted by the Council. The only exception seems to be the adoption of retaliation measures for which Article 14(2) of Regulation 2015/1843 provides that these should be based directly on Article 207 TFEU.[12] This carve-out provision in secondary legislation seems itself problematic (i.e. impermissible or at the least an anomaly) in light of the fact that Article 207 TFEU refers to measures constituting the *framework* for implementing the CCP (see above) which hence would rule out the use of Article 207 TFEU as the direct legal basis for implementing measures.

3   The New Framework for CCP Measures

Following the principal decision to extend the scope of the Comitology Regulation (see above), the institutions still needed to amend the existing basic instruments in the CCP to the new Comitology Regulation. To this end the Commission proposed the Omnibus I package[13] to alter the references to *ad hoc* procedures in existing Basic instruments to the procedures laid down in the Comitology Regulation and the Omnibus II package[14] to change references to *ad hoc* procedures into references to delegated acts. Just like for the adoption of the Comitology Regulation, the Lisbon Treaty had also elevated the status of the European Parliament to that of a co-legislator for the adoption of the Basic acts under Article 207(2) TFEU. On these files, however, the Parliament was much less actively engaged. In this regard, the Parliament was mainly concerned with securing the use of delegated acts under Article 290 TFEU to grant GSP and GSP+ status to third countries.

The applicable GSP regulation at the entry into force of the Lisbon Treaty was valid until the end of 2011. Since the Commission could only propose

---

11   B. Daiber, 'EU-Durchführungsrechtsetzung nach Inkrafttreten der neuen Komitologie-Verordnung', *Europarecht* 47 (2012), p. 248–251.

12   See Regulation (EU) 2015/1843 (OJ 2015, L 272/1).

13   See COM (2011) 82 final.

14   See COM (2011) 349 final.

an amendment to "Lisbonise" the regulation following the adoption of the Comitology Regulation, it initially proposed a simple extension, by two years, of the GSP regulation.[15] The Parliamentary rapporteur recognised the need for an extension, in light of legal certainty, but nonetheless clearly voiced a certain dissatisfaction that the Commission's proposal "although published long after the entry into force of the Lisbon Treaty, did not take into account the [...] decision making procedures required by the Treaty, which enhanced powers of the European Parliament."[16] The Commission's limited proposal to amend the GSP Regulation in the Omnibus II package was then superseded by the Commission's proposal for a new GSP Regulation,[17] which was adopted in 2012.[18] The annexes listing the beneficiary countries can now only be amended through delegated acts, giving the European Parliament a formal veto right. So far however, in none of the 20 cases where the Commission has submitted a draft delegated act amending the basic GSP Regulation, has the European Parliament used this power. Furthermore, it only once used its power to extend the examination period from two to four months.

3.1 Pre-comitology Procedures under the Basic Anti-Dumping Regulation

To keep a sufficient focus, our chapter will predominantly look at the basic Anti-Dumping Regulation the amendment of which was foreseen in the Omnibus I package.[19] Under the pre-Lisbon regulation, the Commission could initiate proceedings following a complaint by the EU industry or a Member State. No later than 9 months following the initiation of the proceedings, the Commission could impose provisional duties unless the Council disagreed by QMV.[20] To impose definitive duties, the Commission needed to consult the Advisory Committee (composed of national experts) and make a proposal to the Council. Unless the Council rejected the proposal by

---

15   See COM (2010) 142 final.
16   See Report of Helmut Scholz on behalf of the Committee on International Trade, 7 March 2011, A7-0051/2011.
17   See COM (2011) 241 final.
18   See Regulation 978/2012, OJ 2012, L 303/1.
19   Ultimately however the regulation was amended by Regulation 37/2014, OJ 2014, L 18/1 (Omnibus II) rather than Omnibus I (Regulation 38/2014). The reason for this was practical rather than political since a parallel amendment of the Anti-Dumping Regulation had been required in light of WTO developments which slowed down the decision-making on this file.
20   See Art. 7(6) of the original Regulation 1225/2009.

simple majority, the proposal would be deemed adopted.[21] In what follows we will highlight some of the key elements of the new regime, juxtaposing the Commission's original proposal with the final Regulation as adopted by Parliament and Council.

3.2   The Commission's Proposal and the Updated Basic Anti-Dumping Regulation

In light of the new comitology regulation, the Commission proposed to do away with the Advisory Committee. The legislature agreed to this but each time also imposed an 'information+' requirement on the Commission to keep the Member States informed. The Commission also proposed to provide a possibility to extend the time limits to conclude investigations, impose provisional duties and conclude reinvestigations. The Commission surmised that these extensions would prove necessary since under the new comitology regime an extra procedural step (requiring extra time) could be triggered if a file would have to go to the Appeal Committee. The EU would thus run the risk of exceeding the time limits for terminating proceedings provided by the WTO Anti-Dumping Agreement (ADA). However, the Member States in Council rejected these elements of the proposal. Where the Commission had proposed the examination procedure to decide on provisional measures, the final regulation prescribes the lighter advisory procedure. The Commission and legislature agreed on adopting the decisions previously in the hands of the Council (i.a. imposition of definitive duties) pursuant to the comitology examination procedure. As regards the review of anti-dumping measures, the Commission had proposed to allow it to review anti-dumping measures out of its own accord but the legislature determined that the initiation of a review should be subject to the advisory comitology procedure, while the repeal, maintenance or amendment of the measures was to be subject to the examination comitology procedure. As to the suspension of measures, the Commission had proposed to decide itself on possible suspensions and subject the extension of suspensions to the examination procedure, but the legislature prescribed the advisory procedure for both the initial suspension and its extension. This conforms to the general principle that changes to the legal situation of third parties are to be effectuated pursuant to a formal comitology procedure. While an *ad hoc* procedure combined with an information+ requirement would be practically identical to the advisory comitology procedure, the latter is still required to decide on a suspension given that it evidently affects the legal position of third parties. Finally, whereas the Commission proposed a QMV threshold to end a

---

21   See Art. 9(4) of the original Regulation 1225/2009.

written comitology procedure, the legislature generally lowered the threshold to do so.[22]

Original commission proposal	Legislature's most significant changes
– Delete references to advisory committee – Extend time limits – Examination procedure for provisional measures – Commission may suspend measures itself – Extension of suspension subject to examination procedure – End written procedure by QMV – Review decisions by Commission	– Delete but add information+ requirement – Keep old time limits – Advisory procedure for provisional measures – Suspension of measures subject to advisory procedure – Extension of suspension subject to advisory procedure – Lower threshold to end written procedure – Reviews by Commission but initiation subject to advisory procedure and repeal, maintenance or amendment subject to examination procedure

The crux of the revision of the basic Anti-Dumping Regulation then lies in the formal excision of the Council from the decision-making process. Provisional measures are decided upon by the Commission under the advisory procedure, with no possible QMV veto for the Council. This means that Member States "only" require a simple majority to voice disagreement but that any such non-binding opinion also does not affect the provisional measures adopted. Definitive duties are decided upon by the Commission under the examination procedure where a simple majority of Member States can force a referral to the Appeal Committee. However, the Appeal Committee (composed of the permanent representatives or even the national ministers themselves) can only block the adoption of definitive anti-dumping or countervailing measures by QMV. If

---

22   To be precise, the legislature prescribed QMV to terminate written procedures on definitive measures or expiry review procedures, simple majority in other cases if drafts have been discussed and ¼ of the members if drafts have not been discussed.

a QMV cannot be mustered in the Appeal Committee the Commission is free to adopt its drafts (and in case there is a positive opinion it evidently has to adopt the draft).[23] In the well-known general terms of EU integration, the reform thus resulted in a shift towards the ideal type of the Community Method and away from intergovernmentalism in the adoption of trade defence measures.

The significance of this change may be illustrated by the so called footwear saga. In the pre-comitology but post-Lisbon period, the ECJ, on appeal, had annulled a Council Regulation imposing definitive anti-dumping duties on Chinese and Vietnamese footwear. Following these judgments in the *Brosmann*[24] and in *Zheijiang*[25] cases, the Commission resumed the anti-dumping proceeding, this time pursuant to the new (2009) anti-dumping regulation, at the point at which the illegality, vitiating the Council's original regulation, had occurred and proposed to the Council to re-impose a definitive anti-dumping duty. However, the Council considered that the re-imposition of anti-dumping duties would put the legitimate expectations of importers into question, since duties would be re-imposed retroactively, and rejected the Commission's proposal.[26] The Council could do so by simple majority. In the subsequent *Clark* and *Puma* cases,[27] the question of the validity of the same Council regulation was raised in a preliminary ruling procedure, given that the ECJ in *Brosmann* and *Zheijiang* had only annulled the regulation in so far as it related to the plaintiffs in those cases. The ECJ now declared the regulation to be invalid. Again the Commission resumed the anti-dumping proceeding at the point at which the illegality had occurred. However, by then the new comitology procedure applied and the Commission itself re-imposed the definitive anti-dumping duties.[28] For affected parties, this raised the question whether the Commission could indeed pursue the procedure according to the new Anti-Dumping Regulation or whether the proceedings needed to be pursued under the original Anti-Dumping Regulation (384/96). Another question is

---

23   This is different for definitive multilateral safeguard measures which may only be adopted by the Commission if the Appeal Committee adopts a positive opinion. See Art. 6(4) of the Comitology RegulationComitology Regulation.

24   Case C-249/10 P, *Brossman Footwear et. al. v. Council*, EU:C:2012:53.

25   Case C-247/10 P, *Zhejiang Aokang Shoes v. Council*, EU:C:2012:710.

26   Council Implementing Decision 2014/149, OJ 2014 L 82/27.

27   Joined Cases C-659/13 & C-34/14, *Clark*, EU:C:2016:74.

28   Commission Implementing Regulation 2016/1395, OJ 2016, L 225/52; Commission Implementing Regulation 2016/1647, OJ 2016, L 245/16. While the Commission's draft implementing regulation re-imposing duties for Vietnamese companies received a positive opinion from the Trade Defence Instruments (TDI) Committee, the draft regulation re-imposing duties for Chinese companies did not.

whether the Commission was not time-barred from pursuing proceedings and/or whether such duties could be imposed retro-actively. As will be noted below, the ECJ, in *Deichmann*,[29] addressed these issues in a manner that does not bode too well for parties affected by anti-dumping duties.

4 The Institutional Practice under the New Framework

As the discussion above shows, the integration of the CCP in the horizontal comitology framework was accompanied by a great deal of uncertainty: the Commission had difficulties in judging how the new procedures would affect its capacity to conduct its investigations within the prescribed time limits while the Member States had "psychological" difficulties in accepting their reduced role. Once the new system was in place, the question thus became how the adoption of trade defence measures would work in practice and whether the reform would result in a different institutional practice.

One of the first decisions of the Trade Defence Instruments (TDI) Committee[30] to take was the adoption of its own Rules of Procedure in light of the standard Rules of Procedure for comitology committees drawn up by the European Commission.[31] The differences between both are few and far between: substantially,[32] the rules of procedures of the TDI Committee are generally stricter on the confidentiality of the committee's proceedings. This translates in explicit provisions on the obligation, in certain cases, for representatives of acceding countries to withdraw from meetings and stricter rules on the correspondence between the chair and the members of the committee through secure electronic means.

The rules of procedure of the "horizontal" Appeal Committee also reflect the special place of the CCP in comitology by prescribing specific rules for the convening of meetings in cases of draft definitive anti-dumping or countervailing measures. In essence, these stress the need to have ongoing consultations

---

29   Case C-256/16, *Deichmann*, EU:C:2018:187.

30   This is the comitology committee for measures adopted under the following basic Regulations: Anti-Dumping Regulation (2016/1036); injurious pricing of vessels Regulation (2016/1035); EU measures following a report adopted by the WTO DSB concerning anti-dumping and anti-subsidy matters Regulation (2015/476); Safeguard combined effect Regulation (2015/477) and the Anti-Subsidy Regulation (2016/1037).

31   See OJ 2011, C 206/11.

32   An interesting purely procedural difference is that the minutes of the TDI Committee have to be circulated *normally* within one month following the meeting, rather than within one month following the meeting.

between the Commission and the Member States before the Appeal Committee meets and they lay down stricter time limits to refer a case to the Appeal Committee and to convene the committee.[33]

4.1   The Position of Private Parties in Comitology Procedures

In light of our topic and since the general procedural rights of private parties in anti-dumping procedures have been documented elsewhere,[34] we will focus on the specific question of how the position of private parties in anti-dumping procedures has been affected by the integration of the CCP in the horizontal comitology framework.

Because the Commission is now the sole authority to impose anti-dumping duties, the right to be heard, enshrined in Article 41(2) of the Charter, is arguably strengthened. After all, under the old regime, interested parties were only heard by the Commission, not by the final authority competent to impose definitive duties,[35] even if *de facto* the Commission was the only institution with a full understanding of the facts of the case.[36]

In the *Deichmann* case (cf. supra), the Court was confronted with some further questions on the effects of its findings in the *Clark* and *Puma* case. First was the question whether the Commission, rather than the Council, was competent to adopt definitive anti-dumping duties in a procedure that had originally been initiated pursuant to the old procedural framework. On this, Article 23 of Regulation 1225/2009 provided that the repeal of the old Regulation (384/96) did "not prejudice the validity of proceedings initiated thereunder."[37] The ECJ construed this simply as confirming the continued validity of the procedures initiated pursuant to the old regulation even after the latter's formal repeal. Applying the maxim *tempus regit actum*, the ECJ held that the new Regulation (1225/2009) had to apply to the proceeding initiated under the old

---

33   See Art. 2 of the Rules of Procedure for the Appeal Committee, OJ 2011 C 183/13.

34   Specifically on judicial review, see E. Vermulst, D. Rovetta, 'Judicial Review of Anti-dumping Determinations in the EU', *Global Trade and Customs Journal* 7 (2012), p. 240–247; I. Van Bael, J.-F. Bellis, *EU anti-dumping and other trade defence instruments* (Kluwer, 2011), p. 597–627. On the rights of interested parties, see Van Bael and Bellis, *EU anti-dumping and other trade defence instruments* (Kluwer, 2011), p. 496–510.

35   Criticising that state of affairs, see H. Hofmann, 'Private Interest Representation in Trade Policy Instruments – A Different View', *Legal Issues of Economic Integration* 31 (2004), p.131.

36   Y. Melin, 'Users in EU Trade Defence Investigations: How to Better Take their Interests into Account, and the New Role of Member States as User Champions after Comitology', *Global Trade and Customs Journal* 11 (2016), p. 100.

37   As the ECJ noted in *Deichmann* (n. 29), the German language version was markedly different as it provided that Regulation 384/96 was "*weiterhin auf Verfahren anwendbar, die während ihrer Geltungsdauer eingeleitet wurden.*"

Regulation since the Regulation imposing the anti-dumping duties in question had been adopted after 11 January 2010,[38] the date on which Regulation 1225/2009 had entered into force.[39]

A second issue in *Deichmann* revolved around the question whether the Commission is empowered by Article 14(1) of Regulation 1225/2009 (now 2016/1036) to instruct national authorities to withhold requests for reimbursement of duties, pending the re-imposition by the Commission of such duties. On this, the ECJ noted that it is clear from the wording of Article 14(1) that the EU legislature "did not intend to set out an exhaustive list of criteria relating to the collection of anti-dumping duties that may be set by the Commission."[40] Although the ECJ did not put it in this way, its finding implies that it agrees with the EU legislature in that the criteria for collection of duties are non-essential elements which the EU legislature does not need to define itself in light of Article ;290 TFEU. The ECJ furthermore held that the Commission's instructions did not conflict with Article ;236 of the customs code, which provides for the reimbursement of duties not legally owed, in light of the specific type of illegalities found in the *Clark* and *Puma* cases.[41]

---

38   However, when two Chinese interested parties invoked the expiry of paragraph 15(a)(ii) of the Protocol on the Accession of China to the WTO to challenge the Commission applying the non-market methodology to determine dumping from China in 2018, the Commission argued that the procedure was governed by the basic regulation as it stood at the time of the initiation of the investigation (which still allowed applying the non-market methodology) rather than the version applicable at the time of the adoption of the provisional anti-dumping duties. See para. 88 of Commission Regulation 2018/683, OJ 2018, L 116/8.

39   And since Regulation 1225/2009 had been amended in 2014 in order to allow the Commission to impose definitive duties, the contested regulation in casu had correctly reserved this power to the Commission. See *Deichmann* (n. 29), para. 45–55.

40   Ibid., para. 58.

41   The ECJ in *Deichmann* also further confirmed that the Commission could resume proceedings and re-impose duties at a point in time after the expiration of the period for which the original duties had been imposed. This notwithstanding the principle of non-retroactivity, on which the Council had relied to reject the Commission's first proposal following *Brosmann*, and the time-bar imposed by the customs code which requires the authorities to communicate any debts to the debtor within a period of three years. While these issues fall outside the scope of this contribution, it merits pointing out that private parties thus face an uphill struggle when contesting anti-dumping duties before the Court. Unless the *entire* procedure has been vitiated by irregularities the Court seems to accept that the Commission retroactively repairs irregularities, even if they have been deemed sufficiently serious to warrant annulment, and that it re-imposes duties. A successful legal challenge may therefore not produce any tangible benefits for litigants. See also Vermulst and Rovetta (n. 34), p. 244.

That the integration of the EU's unilateral trade policy in the horizontal comitology regime is not just of interest to the EU institutions and the Member States is further aptly illustrated by the recent *Tilly Sabco* case.[42] Although this case related to an export subsidy case under the Common Agricultural Policy (and not the CCP), it is of significant relevance for our present study precisely because of the General Court's clarifications on the position of private parties in comitology related matters now also apply to the EU's unilateral trade measures such as anti-dumping measures.

In casu, the Commission had reduced certain export subsidies for poultry meat to zero. The Commission had done so after sending a document on the EU market situation in poultry meat to the relevant comitology committee two days before the meeting. Only during the meeting itself did the Commission present its draft measure. Tilly Sabco, which exports poultry meat, argued that this violated Article 3(3) of the horizontal Comitology Regulation. This since the regulation provides (i) that, differently from the pre-Lisbon comitology decisions, meetings will be convened, except in duly justified cases, not less than 14 days after the submission of both the draft agenda and draft implementing acts and (ii) that the committee's chair will set the time limit for the committee to adopt its opinion in accordance with the urgency of the matter. On both time limits, Article 3(3) provides that they "shall be proportionate and shall afford committee members early and effective opportunities to examine the draft implementing act and express their views."

Before the General Court, Tilly Sabco argued that the committee members had not been given such an effective opportunity.[43] The General Court ruled, in our view correctly, that the Comitology Regulation in principle exceptionally allows draft implementing acts to be communicated during the committee's meeting itself.[44] As to whether the relevant conditions therefor were met *in casu*, the GC noted that the Commission had circulated a document on the market's situation two days before the meeting and that the draft agenda (circulated two weeks before the meeting) made clear that a draft act would be tabled.[45] According to the GC this allowed the Member States to hold the necessary consultations, even if the actual amount of the export subsidy (i.e. € 0/kg) was only communicated during the meeting itself.[46] Crucially, the GC accepted the Commission's argument that it only communicated the draft measure

42   Case T-397/13, *Tilly Sabco v Commission*, EU:T:2016:8.
43   Ibid., para. 70.
44   Ibid., para. 91.
45   Ibid., para. 93–95.
46   Ibid., para. 95–98.

during the meeting itself to counter the risk of leaks[47] and even though the actual urgency seems a factual issue,[48] the GC found that it could only verify whether the Commission had made a manifest error in qualifying the need to take a decision as urgent.[49] The GC further held that a private party, like Tilly Sabco, cannot invoke the committee's internal rules of procedure.[50] For the sake of completeness, the GC added that even if the Commission had violated Article 3(3) of the regulation, the proper respect of this provision would not have resulted in a different decision and would therefore not have amounted to a violation of an *essential* procedural requirement (thus warranting the annulment of the contested act).[51]

On appeal, the ECJ ruled that the Commission could not invoke a well-established practice in comitology decision-making, since the (new) Comitology Regulation, in contrast to the earlier comitology decisions, explicitly provided that the draft agenda and implementing acts had to be circulated, normally, 14 days in advance.[52] It further held that the Commission could not rely on a *general* risk of leaks to disregard that 14 days' time limit and submit the draft during the meeting itself.[53] The Court explicitly noted that it need not consider whether a violation of Article 3(3) of the Comitology Regulation could be invoked by a private party,[54] since it is competent to review violations of essential procedural requirements of its own motion. While this is true, it should be remarked that the Court did not indicate whether respect for Article 3(3) of the regulation is a matter of public interest, which also *requires* the Court to raise the issue of its own motion.

The *Tilly-Sabco* case illustrates how the procedural rules in comitology procedures, which henceforth also apply in the CCP, have been fine-tuned by the Comitology Regulation and how the Court is also willing to uphold them. At the same time, the Court has evaded the question whether and to which

---

47 Ibid., para. 115–116.
48 Earlier the Court had ruled "that whether a case is of extreme urgency is for the chairman of the particular management committee to decide. In view of the nature of the assessment which normally has to be made within a very short period the court can revoke a decision adopted by the chairman only in cases of obvious error or misuse of powers." See Case 278/84, *Germany v. Commission*, EU:C:1987:2, para. 13.
49 *Tilly-Sabco v. Commission* (n. 42), para. 114.
50 Ibid., para. 124. Tilly Sabco had done so because the rules of procedure prescribed a time limit of five days before the meeting to communicate draft measures, unless there is a risk of important perturbations in the relevant market.
51 Ibid., para. 125–128.
52 Case C-183/16 P, *Tilly-Sabco v. Commission*, EU:C:2017:704, para. 98.
53 Ibid., para. 108.
54 The Commission had explicitly argued against this, see ibid., para. 116.

extent private parties may invoke procedural irregularities in comitology proceedings. According to established case law, internal rules of proceedings only amount to essential procedural requirements if they are intended to guarantee legal certainty.[55] Although Article 3(3) of the Comitology Regulation is a proper legislative provision, AG Wahl still argued that "the comitology rules do not usually confer rights on private individuals [...], the time limits set in Article 3(3) of that regulation are too imprecise to confer an actionable right on private individuals."[56] With this issue held in abeyance, perhaps until another private party invokes the provisions of the Comitology Regulation, enforcing full compliance with the Comitology Regulation would seem to depend on the Court raising this procedural compliance of its own motion, without it being clear whether the Court is also required to do so.

4.2   Anti-dumping Cases

The data in the table below are compiled from the Commission's annual reports on the functioning of the comitology committees, the publication of which is a requirement under the horizontal Comitology Regulation, and relate to the functioning of the TDI Committee generally (i.e. the data are not just related to the anti-dumping basic regulation). Since the Omnibus II package was only adopted by the legislature in 2014 (cf. supra) no data are available prior to 2014. The first impression from the actual functioning of the TDI granted by these data is already revealing:

The TDI relies much more on the written procedure compared to the general population of comitology committees: for every physical meeting there are 1.57 written procedures, whereas this ratio is 1.37 for comitology committees in general.[57] Most strikingly, no referrals to the Appeal Committee were made in the first three years of the TDI's functioning when only in one case the TDI delivered a negative opinion. This case concerned the 2015 provisional anti-dumping duties on imports of certain grain-oriented flat-rolled products of silicon-electrical steel.[58] The lack of procedures going to the Appeal Committee results from the divisions among Member States. Thus, a first group of

---

55   K. Lenaerts, I. Maselis, K. Gutman, *EU Procedural Law* (OUP, 2014), p. 378.

56   Opinion of AG Wahl in *Tilly-Sabco v. Commission* (n. 52), para. 58.

57   These figures relate to the years 2014–2018 and were calculated based on the Commission's annual comitology reports.

58   Since this concerned provisional measures, this was a negative opinion in an advisory procedure. See the TDI Committee's vote of 27 May in dossier CMTD(2015)0585. For the provisional anti-dumping duties, see Commission Implementing Regulation 2015/763, OJ 2015, L 120/10.

TABLE 21.1 Functioning of the TDI committee

	Meetings	Written procedures	+ opinions	- opinions	no opinions	referral to AC	+ AC opinion	- AC opinion	no AC opinion	Acts adopted
2014	9	10	25	0	10	0	0	0	0	30
2015	12	19	44	1	4	0	0	0	0	52
2016	9	29	51	0	11	0	0	0	0	61
2017	13	15	41	1	7	2	0	0	2	58
2018	13	15	37	0	10	0	0	0	0	44

(protectionist) Member States agrees to any proposal put forward by the Commission, whereas a second group (free traders) principally rejects any measures. A third group will typically vote against measures if the third country involved has significant (political or economic) leverage over them. Finally, the fourth group will vote for or against measures depending on the actual merits of the case.

As one practitioner put it, "the Commission is therefore in the driving seat" when it comes to the imposition of duties. The only exception is when trade matters turn into politics. The three referrals to the Appeal Committee, two of which were bundled in one case (Chinese solar panels) in the year 2017 are an illustration of this. The anti-dumping measures on Chinese solar panels date back to 2013 and when the Commission simultaneously undertook an expiry and interim review, the duties proved too controversial for a majority of Member States. While the TDI did not muster a QMV against, it did refer the file, by simple majority, to the Appeal Committee (where no QMV could be found either).[59]

In the case of anti-dumping duties on imports of hot-rolled flat products of iron, non-alloy or other alloy steel, the decision-making became politicised after the relevant Union industry voiced its discontent with the Commission's proposal to impose capped *ad valorem* duties rather than fixed duties per ton. By reversing this following the referral to the Appeal Committee, the Commission prevented a qualified majority vote in the Appeal Committee from blocking the measure. In absence of an opinion of the Appeal Committee, the Commission was able to adopt the definitive anti-dumping duties.[60]

In terms of the interaction of the Commission and the Member States in the procedure of imposing anti-dumping duties it would thus seem that in its draft measures for definitive duties the Commission responds strategically to the message which the Member States have sent it when the provisional duties were adopted by the Commission.[61] Subsequently, the Commission will only adjust the measures it is proposing when there is a referral in the Appeal Committee to ensure that no QMV in the latter may be assembled against its measure.

---

59   See Commission Implementing Regulation 2017/367, OJ 2017, L 56/131.

60   See Recitals 628 & 671 of Commission Implementing Regulation 2017/1795, OJ 2017, L 258/24.

61   See also Y. Melin (n. 36), p. 101.

5   Reassessing the Law and Practice in Light of the Lisbon Treaty

Under the basic Anti-Dumping Regulation, duties are to be imposed when there is (i) dumping which (ii) causes injury and if (iii) the Union interest calls for intervention. While the first two requirements are still quantifiable (suggesting a measure of objectivity), the requirement that the EU interest necessitates intervention is rather malleable. In practice, the assessment of the Union (formerly: Community) interest was made in the TDI itself but today the assessment is effectively made by the Commission which has resulted in an erosion of Member States' powers over the question whether or not to impose duties. In legal terms the fact that the Commission has such great leverage in the interpretation of what constitutes the "Union interest" raises a question of constitutional nature. If this power of the Commission is conceived as allowing the Commission to de facto *supplement* the basic Regulation on one of its essential elements, current practice would be in breach of Article 290 TFEU which requires the EU legislature to define the essential elements of legislation itself. In contrast, if one applies constitutional avoidance, one would argue that the Commission is not really exercising a normative power but that instead it is merely *applying* a vague legislative norm.

Following the integration of the trade defence instruments in the horizontal comitology regime, Melin suggested that the new appeal procedure could give extra opportunities to the Member States to influence definitive anti-dumping duties and that (since the Council does not impose these duties anymore) they could be more inclined to challenge them before the ECJ (or at least intervene in support of private parties challenging the duties).[62] While the latter prediction has not materialised yet, there is limited evidence of the former. The appeal procedure indeed allows a further exchange of views or even negotiation, but getting to the appeal stage has proven to be exceptionally difficult.

All in all, evidence suggests that the EU's Trade Defence Policy has "survived" its incorporation in the horizontal comitology regime and has retained its effectiveness. The possible effects of the Commission's 2017 proposal to alter the Comitology Regulation are unclear in this regard.[63] In order to remedy the paralysis of comitology decision-making in controversial cases such as the authorisation of active substances in pesticides and GMO s, the Commission is proposing an across the board amendment of the examination procedure. The proposed amendments could therefore also have unintended consequences

---

62   Y. Melin (n. 36), p. 101.
63   See COM (2017) 85 final.

in other areas (such as trade defence) where the examination procedure has worked well. The soundness of the Commission's proposal has been questioned elsewhere,[64] but since the proposal has apparently fallen flat with the two co-legislators, it will not be further discussed here.

6   Conclusion

One of the major changes of the Lisbon Treaty to the CCP was that it subjected the latter to the ordinary legislative procedure. The further subjugation of the implementation of the CCP to the default comitology regime was a logical corollary to this, although far from a given. The role of the European Parliament, being a co-legislator for both CCP legislation and for the Comitology Regulation, proved to be instrumental in this regard.

While initially there were fears that the integration of the CCP in the horizontal comitology framework would negatively affect the effectiveness of both regimes, the integration was successful. Apart from some transitional issues, the EU's Trade Defence Policy is being implemented smoothly. Looking back with the benefit of hindsight, broadening the scope of the comitology regime to the EU's unilateral trade measures was the culmination point of an already ongoing evolution which has seen a progressive shift of power from the Member States in the committee to the Commission, in line with the Community Method.

---

64   M. Chamon, 'The Proposed Amendment of the Comitology Regulation – A Constitutional Perspective', *VerfBlog*, 19 February 2017.

CHAPTER 22

The Role of the Member States in the CCP

Sophie Gappa and Martin Lutz

1 Introduction

What role do the Member States play in the common commercial policy (CCP)? At first sight, the brief answer might be "none at all": according to the Lisbon Treaty (Article 207 TFEU) the key players *within* the CCP are the European Commission, the Council and the European Parliament.[1] The Member States as such only have a role of their own to play in specific areas, e.g. in comitology.[2] To the extent that the landmark opinion of the European Court of Justice on the EU's free trade agreement with Singapore (Opinion 2/15[3]) on the division of competences between the EU and the Member States in the field of commercial and investment policy recognises the existence of "shared competence" between the EU and the Member States, such shared competence exists *outside* the CCP. But does this mean that the Member States are truly irrelevant players in the CCP? This would be an oversimplification and thus wrong. The Member States are the "Masters of the Treaties", and form the membership of the Council, which remains a preeminent actor in the context of the CCP; in particular, it takes decisions on the commencement of free trade negotiations and on the signing and conclusion of pertinent agreements. Member States' participation provides "national" democratic legitimacy to decisions taken at European level which is of utmost importance in political terms. Nevertheless, there is no denying that Opinion 2/15 fundamentally changed the way the Member States understand their role in trade policy. An important

---

1   For example, Art. 207(2) TFEU states that "The European Parliament and the Council, acting by means of regulations in accordance with the ordinary legislative procedure, shall adopt the measures defining the framework for implementing the common commercial policy," whereas the Commission in particular conducts the negotiations with one or more third countries or international organisations to conclude agreements "in consultation with a special committee appointed by the Council to assist the Commission in this task and within the framework of such directives as the Council may issue to it" (Art. 207(3) sentence 2, 3 TFEU) and reports regularly to the European Parliament (Art. 207(3) sentence 2, 3 TFEU). In contrast, the Member States as such are not explicitly mentioned.
2   See the chapter by J. Bourgeois and M. Chamon in this volume.
3   Opinion 2/15, Singapore FTA, EU:C: 2017:376.

© KONINKLIJKE BRILL NV, LEIDEN, 2021 | DOI:10.1163/9789004393417_024

consequence of this could be seen in the conclusions on the negotiation and conclusion of EU trade agreements,[4] adopted unanimously by the Council of Trade Ministers at its meeting on 22 May 2018.

This article provides an overview of the core messages to be found in these conclusions (2.). A central aspect of the conclusions is the importance of keeping the stakeholders in the Member States, and particularly the parliaments, duly informed. We therefore explain the mechanisms to inform parliaments, taking Germany as an example (3.). At the same time, the Member States can only furnish their own stakeholders with information to the extent that they themselves are provided with that information. The article therefore also discusses current developments in transparency in the CCP (4.). Finally, we take a brief look at the comitology procedure in the CCP, where the Member States also have their own institutional part to play (5.).

2   The Council's Conclusions on the Negotiation and Conclusion of EU Trade Agreements

In the proceedings leading to Opinion 2/15, the European Court of Justice (ECJ) had to clarify whether the Union was competent to sign and conclude the envisaged free trade agreement with Singapore on its own, or whether the Member States were also contracting parties in their own right and therefore needed to ratify the agreement in line with their constitutional requirements. Specifically, then, the question was whether the agreement was "EU-only" or "mixed". The ECJ did find that the free trade agreement with Singapore (as it was structured at the time of the Opinion), could only be concluded by the EU and the Member States jointly, since the agreement also covered areas for which the Member States are competent. However, the ECJ also made it clear that the shared competence only extends to very specific sections of the agreement, such as portfolio investments and investor-state dispute settlement, whilst other important provisions of the agreement, e.g. on sustainable development or transport, fall within the exclusive competence of the EU.[5] This clarified important legal questions relating to the competence to conclude free trade agreements.

---

4   Council of the European Union, Draft conclusions on the negotiation and conclusion of EU trade agreements, 8622/18, 8 May 2018.

5   The Opinion is considered in greater detail in other contributions to this collection; see, in particular, the contributions by M. Cremona; A. Rosas; R. Quick and A. Gerhäuser.

At the same time, however, this raised the question of the future design of free trade agreements. The Council's conclusions on the negotiation and conclusion of EU trade agreements answer key questions raised by Opinion 2/15;[6] they were adopted approximately one year after the publication of the Opinion, after the European Commission had already drawn its own conclusions from the Opinion. The main conclusion drawn by the European Commission was that in the future, separate negotiating guidelines should be presented for trade agreements which fall within the exclusive competence of the EU and (partially) separate guidelines for specific, "mixed" agreements ("separation solution"). With this in mind, in its 2017 trade package, the Commission presented guidelines for the negotiation of trade agreements with Australia and New Zealand which only covered areas of exclusive EU competence.[7] In the related Communication "A Balanced and Progressive Trade Policy to Harness Globalisation", the Commission set out its motives:

> "To maximise the potential benefits of our trade policy, the EU must be a credible negotiating partner: our institutional decision-making must be clear, predictable and fit for purpose. This means ensuring that our institutional set-up allows us to ratify and implement our negotiated agreements in an accountable, legitimate and effective manner. The Opinion of the Court of Justice of the European Union on the EU-Singapore Free Trade Agreement provides welcome clarity on the division of competences in trade and investment agreements between the EU and its Member States.[8]"

2.1 Evaluation of Opinion 2/15 and the "Separation Solution"

When drawing up its conclusions, the Council was therefore able to take note not only of the relevant Opinion 2/15 (para. 2), but also of the conclusions presented by the European Commission regarding the separation of trade and investment agreements (para. 3 sentence 1). However, at the same time, the Council reserved the right, when issuing mandates, to decide on a case-by-case

---

6 Conclusions 8622/18 (n. 4).

7 Annex to the Recommendation for a Council Decision authorising the opening of negotiations for a Free Trade Agreement with Australia COM(2017) 472 final, Annex 1 and, Annex to the Recommendation for a Council Decision authorising the opening of negotiations for a Free Trade Agreement with New Zealand COM(2017) 469 final, Annex 1, 13 September 2017.

8 Communication from the Commission to the European Parliament, the Council, the European Economic and Social Committee and the Committee of the Regions, A Balanced and Progressive Trade Policy to Harness Globalisation, COM(2017) 492 final, 13 September 2017, p. 6.

basis whether it accepts such a separation solution or not (para. 3 sentence 2, but see below regarding para. 4). Equally, the Council stressed its right to decide on a retrospective separation of agreements with trade and investment sections which had already been fully negotiated before the Opinion. This has now taken place with respect to the agreements with Japan, Singapore and Vietnam (cf. also para. 6 in this regard). The comments on association agreements are also of importance: due to their general policy provisions, these tend to be categorised as mixed agreements. The Council did not state that association agreements will always have to be mixed agreements; rather, this will always depend on the specific text of the agreement (para. 3 sentence 4). However, the Council expressed a clear expectation that the association agreements currently being negotiated (or modernised) with Mexico, MERCOSUR and Chile will remain mixed agreements (para. 3 sentence 5).

2.2   *Relationship between Trade and Investment Provisions*

Further to this, the comments on the relationship between trade and investment rules are of considerable importance. Here, the conclusions take a multi-stage approach: the first step is to ascertain whether investment protection rules are actually needed with regard to a specific negotiating partner (para. 4 sentence 2). Once that question is answered in the affirmative, the second step is to examine whether such rules should be negotiated in parallel or together. The Council's conclusions suggest that the investment provisions should generally be negotiated in parallel to the trade rules (para. 4 sentence 3).

These statements are remarkable in several ways. Firstly, they show that the Council has arrived at a view that rejects a schematic negotiation of investment protection agreements with every negotiating partner – a view that was previously held by a group within the Council. Instead, a case-by-case consideration of the need for investment protection rules is preferred: it may be the case that investment protection can be dispensed with countries where the rule of law is strong. These statements in the Council's conclusions thus represent a departure of the European Commission's previous policy, which following the Lisbon Treaty had indeed urged a schematic negotiation of investment protection rules (e.g. with Canada or the United States). This discussion does, however, arise in the case of the free trade negotiations with Australia and New Zealand: so far, these do not include any negotiations on investment protection, not even separately from the negotiations on trade. However, the conclusions do state that this should not set a precedent (cf. para. 5). Beyond that, the reference to pursuing as standard procedure parallel negotiations of trade and investment agreements also implies a general acceptance of the separation solution pursued by the European Commission – a statement which the Council preferred not to make so clearly at the beginning (para. 3) of its conclusions.

2.3 Informing the Council and the Member States – Legitimacy of EU-only Agreements

The Council's conclusions underline how important it is that the European Commission provides the Council with comprehensive information about all phases of free trade negotiations (para. 7 sentence 1). Indeed, the Council needs to receive comprehensive information if it is to take informed decisions about the signing and conclusion of agreements – especially given that national parliaments and stakeholders are to be involved (para. 7 sentence 2, see below). Furthermore, it is also the duty of the European Commission, as laid down in Article 207(3) sentence 3 TFEU, to "report regularly to the special committee [i.e. the Trade Policy Committee] ... on the progress of negotiations".

Further to this, the conclusions stress the legitimacy and inclusiveness of EU-only agreements even if these are now to be approved not by the national parliaments, but solely by the European institutions, Council and European Parliament (para. 7 sentence 3). If an agreement does not legally require the approval of the Member States, there can be no objections in legal terms to sole approval by the EU institutions, i.e. the Council and the European Parliament. However, a distinction must be made between political legitimacy and legal requirements. In this context, the Council's emphasis on the principle of political consensus on trade policy decisions is an important response, "in order to ensure that all Member States' interests and concerns are adequately respected in trade agreements" (para. 9). This does not undermine the principle of the qualified majority in trade policy (Article 218(8) TFEU), but does underline the political goal of attaining the greatest possible consensus amongst the Member States.

2.4 Participation of Parliaments and Stakeholders

Building on this, the Council again highlights the importance of appropriate information for the Member States' parliaments and other stakeholders irrespective of the part they play in ratification – in line with the respective national procedures (para. 8 sentence 1 and 2). The emphasis on keeping citizens well informed about the progress and substance of free trade negotiations is also important (para. 8 sentence 3). Finally, the Council welcomes the steps taken by the European Commission and the Member States to improve transparency and calls on them to strengthen these measures (para. 8 sentence 4). In this context, the Council also recalls its decisions on the publication of negotiating directives for free trade agreements, e.g. recently on the free trade agreement with Japan (para. 8 sentence 5).

3   Participation of the National Parliaments: the German Example

3.1   *Basic Principles*
The Council's conclusions rightly flag up the importance of an intensive involvement of stakeholders in the Member States, and particularly the national parliaments. This section therefore provides a brief overview of the involvement of the parliaments, taking as an example that Member State with which the authors are most familiar: Germany. This does not imply that other Member States do not have similar or possibly even better consultation mechanisms[9] – merely that others are better placed to describe and analyse them.

The involvement of the national parliaments has particular relevance for Germany: the Bundesverfassungsgericht, which is the guardian of compliance with the Basic Law (Grundgesetz), Germany's constitution, emphasises the importance of the Member States as source of democratic legitimacy for EU policies. For example, in its judgment on the Lisbon Treaty, the Federal Constitutional Court found that, even in the European Union, which is conceived as an association of nations, the citizens *of the Member States* remain "subjects of democratic legitimation".[10] Therefore in principle the legitimation of the Member States imparted by the national parliaments and government suffices and is necessary to ensure the EU's democratic legitimacy. Against this background, the Federal Constitutional Court has held that Germany's Federal Government has a "special responsibility [...] to comply internally with the requirements under Article 23(1) of the Basic Law (responsibility for [European] integration)".[11] This results in the Federal Government's constitutional

---

9   Cf. in this regard S. Martini, 'Parlamentsbeteiligung im EU-Rechtsvergleich', in A. von Arnauld and U. Hufeld (eds.), *Systematischer Kommentar zu den Lissabon-Begleitgesetzen*, 2nd ed., Nomos 2018, p. 173.

10   Federal Constitutional Court, Judgment of the Second Senate of 30 June 2009 - 2 BvE 2/08 (Lisbon Decision), para. 229: "(...) [T]he Federal Republic of Germany takes part in the development of a European Union designed as an association of sovereign states (Staatenverbund) to which sovereign powers are transferred. The concept of Verbund covers a close long-term association of states which remain sovereign, a treaty-based association which exercises public authority, but whose fundamental order is subject to the decision-making power of the Member States and in which the peoples, i.e. the citizens, of the Member States, remain the subjects of democratic legitimation".

11   Ibid., para. 236.

obligation to inform the Bundestag and the Bundesrat (the representation of Germany's *Länder*) about the CCP.[12] In other words: the Federal Constitutional Court is of the view that an intensive involvement of national parliaments is a constituent element of ensuring adequate legitimacy for European action.

This is also true of the implementation of free trade agreements, as was stated by the Federal Constitutional Court in the expedited procedure initiated to stop the German representative in the Council of the European Union to give the go-ahead for the signing, conclusion and provisional application of CETA (Comprehensive Economic Trade Agreement between the EU and Canada). Here, however, it must be borne in mind that CETA is a "mixed agreement" which affects competences both of the EU and of the Member States. In its decision, the Federal Constitutional Court also considered the role of the Joint Committee pursuant to Article 26.1 CETA, which, as is customary in EU trade accords, is responsible for all questions relating to trade and investment activities between the contracting parties and the implementation and application (cf. Article 26.1(3) CETA). In the view of the Federal Constitutional Court, decisions by committees which affect the competences of the Member States[13] or the responsibility for European integration require German approval in order to avoid a violation of the Bundestag's legislative rights and its responsibility for European integration.[14] In order to take account of the concerns of the Federal Constitutional Court in this regard, the Council and the Member States jointly declared that the standpoint to be taken in the CETA Joint Committee on a decision by this committee which falls under the competence of the Member States should be adopted by common accord.[15] In another expedited procedure, the Federal Constitutional Court regarded this as being sufficient for the time being.[16]

The obligation under constitutional law to involve the Bundestag and the Bundesrat is directly derived from Article 23 Basic Law in order to permit scrutiny of compliance with the European integration programme by the European

---

12   Ibid., para. 375.

13   In its judgment, the Federal Constitutional Court assumes that there is a different division of competences than that set out later by the ECJ in its Opinion. This is – inter alia – the background of a recent constitutional complaint against the Free Trade Agreement of the EU with Singapore (2BvR 882/19).

14   Federal Constitutional Court, Judgement of the Second Senate of 13 October 2016 - 2BvR 1368/16, para. 65.

15   Statement 19: Statement from the Council and the Member States regarding decisions of the CETA Joint Committee (OJ 2017, L 11, 15).

16   Federal Constitutional Court, Judgement of the Second Senate of 7 December 2016 – 2 BvR 1444/16, para. 30.

Union and controls by the Federal Government.[17] Building on this legal basis, a network of laws which defines the relationship between executive and legislature on European affairs exists. These laws include the Integration Responsibility Act, the Act on Cooperation between the Federal Government and the German Bundestag on European Union Affairs, and the Act on Cooperation between the Federation and the *Länder* in the European Union.

3.2   *Information Requirements under the Act on Cooperation between the Federal Government and the German Bundestag on European Union Affairs*

This section outlines the main provisions in the Act on Cooperation between the Federal Government and the German Federal Parliament (Bundestag) on European Union Affairs (Gesetz über die Zusammenarbeit von Bundesregierung und Deutschem Bundestag in Angelegenheiten der Europäischen Union, EUZBBG)) governing the interaction of the Federal Government and the Bundestag, since these are of particular importance for the practical work of government.

The basic structure of the Act is explained in Section 1 subsection 1 EUZBBG, which states that the Bundestag plays a part in the decision-making of the Federal Republic in European Union affairs and has the right to make comments. The Federal Government must inform it comprehensively and as early as possible.

The ongoing and comprehensive providing of information to the Bundestag by the executive is clearly the main focus of the EUZBBG. This is particularly true with regard to the field of the CCP. Section 5 subsection 1 number 6 EUZBBG refers to "matters relating to discussion, initiatives, negotiating mandates and negotiating directives for the European Commission in the context of the common commercial Policy and the world trade rounds". All documents received in this context must be forwarded by the Federal Government to the Bundestag without delay (Section 4 subsection 1 number 1 EUZBBG). A similar obligation exists with regard to reports by Germany's Permanent EU-Representation and by the Federal Government on corresponding discussions at ministerial level, at the level of the Committee of Permanent Representatives or at council working party level (Section 4 subsection 1 number 2 EUZBBG). Hence, all documents sent to the Member States in connection with the discussions of the Trade Policy Committee must be forwarded to the Bundestag without delay. The same applies to reports of meetings of the Trade Policy Committee, and

---

17   Lisbon Decision (n. 10), para. 376.

for reports of meetings of the Committee of Permanent Representatives or of the trade ministers, even if they meet in an informal context.

The obligations on the part of the Federal Government to inform the Bundestag do not end here. For example, in addition to the above, specific projects (e.g. a project for a negotiating mandate to commence free trade negotiations with a third country) must be explained in a brief report (Section 6 subsection 2 EUZBBG). If a legislative instrument is involved (e.g. a Council decision on the signing of a free trade agreement by the EU), the Federal Government needs to provide the Bundestag with a "comprehensive evaluation" (Section 6 subsection 3 EUZBBG). These mechanisms also apply to any Council decisions pursuant to Article 218(9) TFEU – i.e. when it comes to stipulating the EU's standpoint in intergovernmental bodies.

The information obligations relating to meetings of the Council and other institutions are also important. Insofar, the Federal Government must report both before and after the session; pursuant to Section 4 subsection 4 EUZBBG, this obligation also extends to informal Council meetings (e.g. Informal Trade Ministers' Council meetings).

In addition to this, a German tradition has emerged to release "half-year reports", informing the Bundestag about current developments in the CCP during the respective (alternating) Council Presidency. It would seem appropriate to categorise this form of information provision as part of the general obligation to provide comprehensive information pursuant to Section 3 subsection 1 EUZBBG.

Ultimately, the goal of these comprehensive information obligations is to enable the Bundestag to form opinions on European projects. The EUZBBG actually envisages the Committee on European Union Affairs as the central place for discussing such matters (Section 2 EUZBBG). In fact, however, trade policy issues are primarily discussed in the expert committee (Committee on Economic Affairs and Energy) and, in some cases, subsequently in plenary session.

The Bundestag can intervene in trade policy with its own comments (Article 23(3) Basic Law). The Federal Government must "base its position" in discussions on such comments (Section 8 subsection 2 EUZBBG). In principle, it is required to lodge a parliamentary reservation, if it proves impossible to have key aspects of the comments accepted. As elsewhere, however, the Federal Government has a final decision-making power as the executive due to important foreign and integration policy reasons (for details cf. Section 8 subsection 4 EUZBBG).

Thus, German law obliges the Federal Government to provide the Bundestag with comprehensive information about EU trade policy projects. This gives the Bundestag the possibility to gain an overview of ongoing developments in the CCP and to influence these developments.[18] Increasingly, the Bundestag is making use of these possibilities: for example, it provided its own comments in relation to the signing of the free trade agreement with Canada (CETA) and discussed motions by the parliamentary opposition in relation to the signing of the free trade agreements with Japan and Singapore.

4 Transparency of Free Trade Negotiations: the Member States' Perspective

4.1 Efforts by the European Commission

Not least against the background of the critical public debate on CETA and the free trade agreement with the U.S. (Transatlantic Trade and Investment Partnership Agreement – TTIP), the European Commission has substantially increased its efforts to create greater transparency. In its communication entitled "Trade for all", it emphasised the importance of close cooperation with Member States, the European Parliament and civil society.[19] With a view to fostering a facts-based debate, one key step was the publication of studies on the likely impact and effects of free trade agreements ("impact and *ex post* assessments"). Also, the Commission invited the Council to publish all negotiating guidelines for free trade talks as soon as they were adopted.[20] In his State of the Union Address of 13 September 2017, then European Commission President Juncker again flagged the significance of a transparent trade policy ("Gone are the days of no transparency"[21]) and announced another "quantum leap" in the European Commission's transparency policy: the publication of proposals for negotiating guidelines ("mandates") by the European Commission. The proposed mandates for the negotiations with Australia and New Zealand, and regarding the multilateral court for investment disputes were indeed published on the day they were adopted.[22] Also, mention should be made of the EU's

---

18 Critics, however, describe this system as "based rather on documenting than on mandating"; cf. S. Martini, (n. 9), p. 194.

19 Communication from the Commission to the European Parliament, the Council, the European Economic and Social Committee and the Committee of the Regions: Trade for All – Towards a more responsible trade and investment policy, COM(2015) 497 final, 14 November 2015, p. 12.

20 Ibid., p. 13.

21 State of the Union Address 2017 of 13 September 2017: http://europa.eu/rapid/press-release_SPEECH-17-3165_en.htm.

22 COM(2017) 472 final, Annex 1; COM(2017) 469 final, Annex 1; COM(2017) 493 final, Annex 1, Annex to the Recommendation for a Council Decision authorising the opening of

proposals for legal texts in free trade agreements to be published on the website of the Directorate General for Trade as part of the European Commission's "transparency campaign". Furthermore, reports on completed rounds of negotiations with third countries are now regularly published online. The same appears for the text of an agreement as soon as a "political agreement" has been reached.[23] Another remarkable effort relating to CETA is the publication of the agendas and reports of the working groups and committees based on this agreement. On top of this, as part of the 2017 trade package, the Commission announced the formation of a Group of Experts on EU Trade Agreements, consisting of various representatives of non-governmental organisations such as trade unions, employers' organisations, industry associations and consumer organisations.[24] The Group of Experts was quickly rendered operational[25] and had already met nine times by September 2019.[26]

4.2   Evaluation from the Perspective of the Member States

From the Member States' perspective, the Commission's efforts to create greater transparency around free trade agreements are very welcome as a matter of principle, as they allow interested stakeholders, and citizens in particular, access to information about the goals, progress and outcomes of free trade negotiations. The involvement of civil society groups is an important supplement to the constitutionally mandated democratic legitimation. Pertinent efforts by the Commission to improve transparency may also put an end to accusations of "secret talks" and may help to address the growing scepticism of civil society about globalisation as such, but also about specific trade agreements. As such, they complement the various efforts of the Member States to ensure transparency to the public and the national parliaments by providing pertinent information.

Nevertheless, from the perspective of the Member States, some problems exist. One example is the publication of *proposals* for negotiating guidelines by

---

negotiations for a Convention establishing a multilateral court for the settlement of investment disputes.

23   An overview of these transparency measures can be found in the factsheet of the European Commission: http://trade.ec.europa.eu/doclib/docs/2017/september/tradoc_156041.pdf.

24   COM(2017) 492 final, 13 September, p. 7.

25   Commission Decision of 13 September 2017 setting up the Group of Experts on EU Trade Agreements, C(2017) 6113 final.

26   For further information on the Group of Experts on EU Trade Agreements (E03556) see:https://ec.europa.eu/transparency/regexpert/index.cfm?do=groupDetail.groupDetail&groupID=3556&Lang=DE.

the European Commission pursuant to Article 218(4) TFEU. In the guidelines, the Council defines the goals – based on proposals from the Commission – for the EU's chief negotiator, i.e. the European Commission. The Council decides on the publication of the finalised guidelines on a case-by-case basis.[27] This means that the Council controls whether and when the document is published. Its decision will have to consider that the publication reveals the goals not only to civil society, but also to the third country with which the negotiations are to take place. Publication of the "red lines" at the outset of the negotiations can, as the ECJ has recognised, impact negatively on the EU's negotiating position with the third country and thus harm the public interest.[28]

However, beyond such tactical considerations, publication of proposals for negotiating guidelines by the Commission also has an institutional effect: the finalised negotiating guidelines largely – apart from a few individual points – coincide with the Commission's original proposal. As soon as the proposed guidelines are published, the bulk of the EU's negotiating strategy with a third country enters the public domain, and the decision by the Council on whether to subsequently publish the finalised mandate is little more than a formality. It remains to be seen what effects this policy will have on the depth and the level of detail of future negotiating guidelines, and thus on the stipulation by the Council of the objectives to be pursued in the negotiations.

The online publication of reports about rounds of negotiations with third countries is another aspect. These published reports are identical to those received by the Council and the Member States on the rounds of negotiations. One consequence of the European Commission's new approach is that the published reports differ from the previous reports, which only went to the Member States, in terms of depth and the level of detail. It is fair to say that it would be very difficult politically for the European Commission to produce two reports, one for the public and one for the Council/the Member States. In practice, detailed debriefings about negotiating rounds shift to "technical meetings of experts", albeit often without any supplementary written documents.[29] These are useful and welcome, but take place outside the Trade Policy Committee, which is the central consultation body (Article 218(4) TFEU). Here, the outstanding role played by the Council in the CCP (Art. 218 TFEU) should be taken into consideration and strengthened.

---

27   Conclusions 8622/18 (n. 4), para. 8, sentence 6.
28   Case T-301/10, *In 't Veld v. Commission*, EU:T:2013:135, para. 124 f.
29   In Germany, these documents would need to be transmitted to the Bundestag, see Section 3.2. above.

5   Comments on Comitology in the CCP

Implementing acts of the European Commission are of considerable practical significance in the field of trade policy. This is particularly true of unilateral measures by the EU, e.g. the application of trade defence instruments. The further extension of the implementing powers of the European Commission in the field of the CCP resulting from Regulation (EU) No 654/2014 is of great political and practical significance. This Regulation gives the European Commission the power to suspend trade concessions and other obligations following corresponding authorisation from the Dispute Settlement Body of the WTO or from a bilateral tribunal. Pursuant to Article 3 of Regulation No 654/2014, the same mechanism applies with regard to the imposition of rebalancing measures as a consequence of multilateral or bilateral safeguard measures or the unilateral modification of tariff concessions pursuant to Article XXVIII GATT.

The Member States are involved in the adoption of implementing acts via the comitology procedure. The main legal basis for this is Regulation (EU) No 182/2011[30], which was enacted on the basis of Article 291(3) TFEU. In the case of implementing acts, the Member States' interest to be involved follows from the fact that the transfer of implementing powers to the European Commission constitutes a derogation from the fundamental principle that the Member States are responsible for implementing legal acts of the EU (cf. Article 291(1) TFEU).[31] This distinguishes the delegation of executive powers pursuant to Article 291 TFEU from the delegation of legislative powers pursuant to Article 290 TFEU – in the latter case, the Council and the European Parliament must play a part.

In this chapter, we shall limit ourselves to comment on a few of the special comitology rules in the CCP. However, these rules underscore the importance that the EU legislature attaches to comprehensive participation of the Member States in implementing acts in the CCP: for example, Article 2(2) (b) (iv) of the Comitology Regulation states that the examination procedure applies to implementing acts in the field of the CCP. In the examination procedure itself, the basic rule in the field of the CCP is that the European Commission adopts the implementing act if the committee approves by qualified majority (Article 5(2) Comitology Regulation) or does not issue an opinion – e.g. because there is no qualified majority for or against the implementing act (Article 5(4),

---

30   Hereinafter: "Comitology Regulation".
31   H. Hetmeier, *Art. 291 (Durchführungsmaßnahmen nach innerstaatlichem Recht)* in C. O. Lenz and K.-D. Borchardt (eds.), *EU-Verträge Kommentar nach dem Vertrag von Lissabon*, 5th edition, Bundesanzeiger Köln 2010, para. 2.

para. 1 Comitology Regulation). Only if a qualified majority in the Committee votes against the implementing act, the European Commission is unable to adopt the implementing act; in that case, it needs to call on the appeal committee if it wants to stick with its proposal (cf. Article 5(3) Comitology Regulation).

Since there is rarely a qualified majority opposed to the draft of an implementing act, the case where the committee has "no opinion" is especially important. In this regard, the Comitology Regulation contains important exceptions for the field of the CCP, e.g. when definitive multilateral safeguard measures (Article 5(4) para. 2(a) Comitology Regulation) or the adoption of definitive anti-dumping or countervailing measures (Article 5(5) Comitology Regulation) are involved. A corresponding exception applies pursuant to Article 8(2) Regulation (EU) No 654/2014: In these cases the lack of an opinion from the committee does not authorise the European Commission to adopt an implementing act: rather, the European Commission must either present an amended proposal or launch the appeal procedure (cf. Article 5(4) subpara. 3 Comitology Regulation). However, the European Commission's position is likely to prevail at the latest in the appeal procedure: in almost all cases, the European Commission can adopt the implementing act unless a qualified majority of the committee rejects it.[32]

Thus, while Member States still have an important role to play in the field of comitology, the Commission has been put in a particularly strong position, which has been further strengthened by the extension of the implementing powers by Regulation (EU) No 654/2014. A major argument in favour of empowering the Commission in the described fashion was the wish to ensure that the EU would be able to react more swiftly than would be possible within the timeframe of the ordinary legislative procedure.[33] This follows from the Lisbon Treaty's introduction of the co-decision procedure in the field of the

---

32 Cf. Art. 6(3) and (4) Comitology Regulation.

33 Cf. also Recital 2, sentence 3 of Regulation (EU) No 654/2014 of the European Parliament and of the Council of 15 May 2014 concerning the exercise of the Union's rights for the application and enforcement of international trade rules and amending Council Regulation (EC) No 3286/94 laying down Community procedures in the field of the common commercial policy in order to ensure the exercise of the Community's rights under international trade rules, in particular those established under the auspices of the World Trade Organization (OJ 2014 L 189/50): "The Union should be in a position to react swiftly and in a flexible manner in the context of the procedures and deadlines set out by the international trade agreements which it has concluded. There is therefore a need for rules defining the framework for exercising the Union's rights in certain specific situations". Meanwhile the European Commission has submitted a proposal to further extend the scope of this Regulation, in particular against the background of the current crisis of the WTO Appellate Body (COM (2019) 623 final).

CCP (Article 207(2) TFEU). The extension of the implementing powers has rendered this time-consuming and complex procedure superfluous when it comes to the adoption of any countervailing commercial policy measures. In essence, what began as an exercise in "parliamentarisation" of legislative acts in the field of trade policy has led to the strengthening of the EU executive.

On the other hand, the Regulation has already proven its great practical relevance. It was deployed for the first time when rebalancing measures which were imposed in response to the additional U.S. tariffs on steel and aluminium products.[34] The European Union thus gave a clear demonstration of its capacity to take rapid and decisive action where necessary.

6 Final Comments

Europe's CCP is characterised by a continuing need to balance efficiency with democratic legitimation, not least by and in the Member States. There are few areas in which a common EU policy makes as much sense as in the field of trade policy: the existence of the single market means that the Union needs to speak with one voice in relations with the rest of the world. In this sense, Opinion 2/15 has further strengthened the CCP. In the process, the institutional strength of the European Commission in the field of the CCP has become impressive: even if EU law determines the Council, the European Parliament and the European Commission as equal partners in the CCP, the European Commission, as the Union's chief negotiator, enjoys a pre-eminent position, even in comparison with other areas of exclusive EU competence.[35] In terms of substance, the commitment shown by the European Commission to the CCP in the current difficult trade policy environment merits unqualified praise. Nevertheless, the political debate about trade policy issues continues to run primarily along nation state lines, as exemplified by the sometimes heated debate about the then envisaged free trade agreement with the United States (TTIP). Insofar, the discussion in Germany was very different from that in fellow Member

---

34   Commission Implementing Regulation (EU) 2018/724 on certain commercial policy measures concerning certain products originating in the United States of America (OJ 2018 L 122/14).

35   One example is the exclusive competence for competition law (Art. 3(1)(b) TFEU), which does not cover supervision of competition, thus permitting the continued existence of national competition authorities. Cf. E. Lenski, *Art. 3 (Ausschließliche Zuständigkeit der Union)* in C. O. Lenz and K.-D. Borchardt (eds.), *EU-Verträge Kommentar nach dem Vertrag von Lissabon*, 5th edition, Bundesanzeiger Köln 2010, para. 10.

States such as Sweden or Poland. Despite certain similarities in the debate in certain parts of Europe, specific features of the various political cultures in the Member States created several distinct national discourses rather than a pan-European discussion theme.[36] Regardless of whether one regrets or praises this phenomenon: This conflict between a concentration of trade policy power in Brussels and a trade policy debate which is largely driven by the Member States does seem to be a reality, which creates certain risks for the public acceptance of Europe's CCP. It is therefore important to maintain and strengthen the involvement of the Member States in the CCP. The natural "forum" for the Member States in the field of the CCP is the Council, with its Trade Policy Committee as its working body. The Council's conclusions on the negotiation and conclusion of free trade agreements demonstrate assertiveness and the political will to embrace its institutional role. For this, it needs comprehensive and timely information from the European Commission; the conclusions rightly highlight this aspect. Therefore, the central role of the Trade Policy Committee as a forum for work and debate should be strengthened. But beyond this, there is a range of ways to further improve the involvement of the Member States in the CCP within the parameters of current primary law. For example, many Member States are willing to make use of their contacts with third countries to support the European Commission's efforts to modernise the World Trade Organization (WTO).

Other models are also feasible, from a strengthening of the role of the respective Council Presidency as an observer in trade talks between the European Commission and third countries, to an even greater degree of staff exchange between the Member States and the Directorate General for Trade, at all levels. Here, it is worthwhile reflecting on innovative approaches to cooperation rather than referring back to traditional institutional models. Ensuring the appropriate involvement of the Member States in the CCP remains as relevant as ever. It requires continuing reflection and debate.

---

36   This phenomenon sometimes even impacts the discussions in the European Parliament. One example was the announcement of the rejection of the Singapore free trade agreement by the *German* S&D MEP s, see: https://www.bernd-lange.de/content/522515.php.

CHAPTER 23

The Council, the Common Commercial Policy and the Institutional Balance

Recent Developments

Bart Driessen

1   Introduction

This Chapter focuses on the Council, the Common Commercial Policy (CCP) and the institutional balance in the area of the CCP.

Article 16(1) TEU defines the Council's general institutional role as "jointly with the European Parliament, exercis[ing] legislative and budgetary functions". Moreover, the Council carries out "policy-making and coordinating functions as laid down in the Treaties". As far as the CCP is concerned, then, the Council's role is that of co-legislator and of policy-maker. The Court of Justice has stressed that the Council possesses "discretion which it enjoys in an economic matter of such complexity" in implementing the CCP.[1]

A large component of the Council's institutional role – and a matter of great importance to the CCP – is its role in the negotiation and implementation of trade agreements. Apart from Article 207 TFEU, the procedure for this is spelled out in Article 218 TFEU. In the succinct summary by the Court's Grand Chamber, this latter provision

> [w]ith a view to establishing a balance between [the] institutions, [...] provides, in particular, that agreements between the European Union and one or more third States are to be negotiated by the Commission, in compliance with the negotiating directives drawn up by the Council, and then concluded by the Council, either after obtaining the consent of the European Parliament or after consulting it. The power to conclude such agreements is, however, conferred on the Council subject to the powers vested in the Commission in this field.[2]

---

1   Case 174/84, *Bulk Oil (Zug)*, EU:C:1986:60, para. 36.
2   Case C-425/13, *Commission v. Council (Gas emissions)*, EU:C:2015:483, para. 62 confirming Case C-327/91, *France v. Commission*, EU:C:1994:305, para. 28.

The TFEU, then, provides for a very substantial institutional role for the Council in both policy-making and the adoption of legal elements of the CCP.

Since the entry into force of the Lisbon Treaty, numerous aspects of the Council's handling of the CCP have changed. Some of these changes result from the Treaty of Lisbon; others were the effect of case law or pressures from other institutions. A part of these changes are specific to the CCP whilst others affect the Council's external policies altogether. A number of changes are procedural while others are substantive. Importantly, some of these changes affect the institutional balance.

In the coming pages I will endeavour to discuss the most important changes in the Council's CCP practice that in the last ten years have affected the institutional balance. Before doing so, it is to the latter notion that we must first briefly turn.

2 The Institutional Balance in EU Law

The concept of institutional balance has a long pedigree in EU law. As long ago as 1959 the Court of Justice spoke in *Fonderies de Pont-à-Mousson v. High Authority*[3] of "the separation between the powers vested in the High Authority alone and those vested jointly in the High Authority and the Council". The use of the words "separation of powers" is deceptive: what are separated are neither functions nor institutions, but the powers "vested" in them. That verb suggests that "powers" should be read as *competencies* so that, effectively, the Court spoke of the separation of competencies of the different institutions.

From the mid-1970s the Court filled the contours of its institutional balance doctrine with more colour. In *Rey Soda* it gave, as a reason for a strict interpretation of a Treaty provision on agriculture, the "preservation of the balance between the powers of the Council and the Commission".[4] Note that it referred not to the competences of the Commission and Council (which would have been a static approach based on the Treaties as they then stood), but rather to the *balance* of their powers, which has a more dynamic ring to it.

In 1985 the Court ruled that the "balance of powers between the institutions provided for by the Treaties" disallowed Parliament to "deprive the other institutions of a prerogative granted to them by the Treaties themselves".[5] In brief, in these judgments the Court accepted that the institutional balance doctrine

---

3 Case 14/59, *Société des fonderies de Pont-à-Mousson v. High Authority*, EU:C:1959:31.
4 Case 23/75, *Rey Soda v. Cassa Conguaglio Zucchero*, EU:C:1975:142, para. 9.
5 Case 149/85, *Wybot v. Faure a.o.*, EU:C:1986:310, para. 23.

limits an institution in the exercise of its competencies where these deprive another institution from using theirs. Three years later the Court implicitly rejected Parliament's suggestion that the "institutional balance" implied a "principle of equality".[6]

The most pertinent judgment came two years later, when the Court in *Chernobyl* described in more detail what the *institutional balance* implied. The Court found that each institution has a role assigned to it in the institutional structure created by the Treaties. That structure comprises a "system for distributing powers". The Court held that "observance of the institutional balance means that each of the institutions must exercise its powers with due regard for the powers of the other institutions". It also requires "that it should be possible to penalize any breach of that rule which may occur". It followed that the Court "which under the Treaties has the task of ensuring that in the interpretation and application of the Treaties the law is observed, must therefore be able to maintain the institutional balance".[7]

By 1996, the Court firmly placed the doctrine in the centre of the EU's institutional structure: "the institutional rules governing the allocation of powers between the various Community institutions occupy an essential place in the Community legal order".[8] Subsequently, the Member States referred to the "institutional balance" in Article 2 of the *Protocol on the application of the principles of subsidiarity and proportionality* adopted together with the Treaty of Amsterdam.

The institutional balance, then, underpins interinstitutional relations and, with that, also the processes that implement the CCP. It is to those processes that we must now turn.

3   The Council and the Member States

Many of the issues in the relations between the Union and the Member States in the field of the CCP pertain to the consequences of mixed agreements.

Mixed agreements have been around in the EU's external relations toolbox for a long time and have been recognised by the Court of Justice[9] as a valid

---

6   Case 302/87, *Parliament v. Council (comitology)*, EU:C:1988:461, para. 19 and 21.

7   Case C-70/88, *European Parliament v. Council (Chernobyl)*, EU:C:1990:217, para. 21–23.

8   Joined cases C-239/96R and C-240/96R, *United Kingdom v. Commission*, EU:C:1996:347, para. 69.

9   Ruling 1/78, EU:C:1978:202, points 34–36. See also Opinion 2/91, *ILO Convention 170*, EU:C:1993:106, para. 34–35 and Opinion 1/94, *WTO Agreement*, EU:C:1994:384, para. 108.

response to the often-occurring problem that an envisaged agreement strad-
dles the competence of the Union and that of the Member States. It is true
that mixity renders the procedure for the adoption of trade agreements more
difficult than that for negotiations of an agreement falling entirely within the
EU's competence. The saga surrounding the signature of the CETA, when the
Commission and even the Canadian government were reduced to negotiate
directly with the government of a Belgian region provides a vivid (and, one
hopes, sole) example of how difficult this can get. However, in the view of the
Court of Justice, "whatever their scale, the practical difficulties associated with
the implementation of mixed agreements ... cannot be accepted as relevant
when selecting the legal basis for a [Union] measure".[10]

Such mixity[11] has several consequences for the practice of the Council. I would
note the following points.

First, the situation must generally be avoided where an agreement is in force
for the Union but not as far as one or more Member States is concerned. Such
cases cannot always be prevented; for example, they occurred when the Union
started to join certain international agreements in the field of commodities trade
(to which typically some, but never all, EU Member States were Parties).[12]

This case aside, situations in which not all Member States participate in a
mixed agreement are not ideal since they can lead to difficulties of interpretation and uncertainty for operators and to difficulties of international representation vis-à-vis the international partner(s) concerned. In the past this
problem was resolved at the stage of the adoption of the *negotiating directives*
by resorting to *hybrid decisions* which constituted, at the same time, the Council decision on signature as well as the decision by the representatives of the
Member States. That practice was disallowed by the Court,[13] which accepted
that the decision of the Member States entails consensus whereas the Council
decision does not.[14] The current practice in the case of mixed agreements is
therefore normally to adopt a Council decision adopting the negotiating directives simultaneously with a decision of the representatives of the Member

---

10   Opinion 2/00, *Cartagena Protocol*, EU:C:2001:664, para. 41. See also Opinion 1/08, GATS
        Schedule, EU:C:2009:739, para. 127.

11   Other forms of mixity (notably combining TFEU and TEU legal bases) can be imagined,
        but fall outside the scope of the present paper.

12   Examples are the International Coffee Agreement (OJ 2008, L186/13) and the International
        Rubber Study Group Constitution (OJ 2011, L264/14). The EU Member States are no longer
        party to these agreements.

13   Case C-28/12, *Commission v. Council (Transport)*, EU:C:2015:282, para. 44, 47–55.

14   *Ibid*, para. 52.

States.[15] Later on in the procedure the Council adopts the decision to *sign* the agreement only when all Member States have indicated that they are in a position to sign. This is not an additional voting rule replacing the qualified majority voting rule that normally applies to trade agreements[16] but is intended to ensure the coherence and consistency of international representation required by the Court[17] and to avoid complications with the international representation of the Union.

Secondly, the principle of unity of external representation implies that the Council will not normally *conclude* a mixed agreement until all Member States have ratified it. Since Member States in practice generally need some three to six years for ratifying mixed agreements, the normal practice is for the Council to decide on *provisional application* in such cases.[18] The reasons for doing so lie in the necessity to keep the political momentum: trade partners can hardly be expected to sign major agreements that subsequently remain in abeyance for years pending Member State ratifications.

Thirdly, the principle of unity of external representation has a further incidence on such provisional application. Most trade agreements concluded thus far by the Union are mixed, because they straddle the competence of the Union and of the Member States. It is not possible to apply such agreements provisionally in their entirety, since this would require all the Member States to do the same (or to ratify them in advance as far as matters falling within their competence are concerned). Since the constitutional laws of a number of Member States make no provision for provisional application, or make this very difficult, the solution chosen in practice is to apply only those parts of the agreement provisionally that fall within the Union's competence. This explains, for example, why parts of the investment chapter as well as the investment court system provisions of the CETA are excluded from provisional application,[19] a choice that proved to be not incorrect in the light of the subsequent *Singapore FTA* Opinion of the Court of Justice.[20]

---

15 Such decisions of the Member States are, in principle, not actionable in Court: Joined cases C-181/91 and C-248/91, *Parliament v. Council and Commission (Emergency aid)*, EU:C:1993:271, para. 12.

16 Under Art. 207(4), first sub-paragraph TFEU. The cases in the other sub-paragraphs of Art. 207(4) TFEU requiring unanimity are quite rare in practice.

17 Case C-246/07, *Commission v. Sweden*, EU:C:2010:203, para. 75.

18 On provisional application of EU FTAs, see the contribution by J. Heliskoski in this volume.

19 Council Decision (EU) 2017/38 of 28 October 2016 on the provisional application of the Comprehensive Economic and Trade Agreement (CETA) between Canada, of the one part, and the European Union and its Member States, of the other part (OJ 2017, L11/1080).

20 Opinion 2/15, *Singapore FTA*, EU:C:2017:376, para. 292–293.

Last, the consequence of mixity on the *implementation* of international agreements must be mentioned. At the time of the signature of the CETA, the German *Bundesverfassungsgericht* (Federal Constitutional Court) was seized with a request for an injunction to block the German government from signing and provisional application of the CETA on the grounds that the agreement is incompatible with German constitutional law. One of the issues to which the applicants in that case had taken offence was the Joint Committee set up by Article 26.1 of the CETA. Such joint committees are a mechanism common in trade agreements concluded by the EU and have been around for decades. The Joint Committee consists of representatives of the parties and is authorised to take legally binding decisions as specified in the agreement. Within the Union, the adoption of such a decision requires a preceding Article 218(9) TFEU decision.

The *Bundesverfassungsgericht* declined the application, but did note that the CETA does not provide for any guaranteed participation of Germany within the Joint Committee.[21] Moreover, it reasoned that there is no possibility for Germany to influence the decision (*Einwirkungsmöglichkeit*); the same applies for the special committees under the CETA.[22] Lastly, whilst it is true that the decisions of the Joint Committee are prepared in the Council, that institution votes with qualified majority. In the German court's view, this also limits Germany's influence.[23] The court did not exclude that the prerogatives of the Bundestag could be violated by this.[24]

The *Bundesverfassungsgericht* suggested that the matter concerning the Joint Committee could – at least as far as provisional application is concerned – be solved through an interinstitutional agreement in which it would be agreed that Article 218(9) TFEU decisions be adopted with unanimity. The Court noted that this would be in line with the practice of adopting Decisions of the Representatives of the Member States.

Instead, the Council adopted, on the context of the CETA's signature, Statement No 19 from the Council and the Member States, which reads as follows:

> The Council and the Member States recall that where a decision of the CETA Joint Committee falls within the competence of the Member States

---

21   Joined cases 2 BvR 1368/16, 2 BvR 1444/16, 2 BvR 1482/16, 2 BvR 1823/16 and 2 BvE 3/16, *CETA*, Judgment of 13 October 2016, point 62.

22   *Ibid*, point 63.

23   *Ibid*, point 64.

24   *Ibid*, point 65.

the position to be taken by the Union and its Member States within the CETA Joint Committee shall be adopted by common accord.[25]

This (legally not binding) statement is to be interpreted and applied in line with the *Hybrid decisions* case.[26] In other words, the voting rule of Article 218(8) TFEU remains unaffected but, if the Joint Committee is to adopt decisions that concern the Member States' competence, it will only do so if it is established that all Member States can accede to them *qua* contracting parties.

As a separate point, it is now clear that, for Article 218(9) TFEU to apply, it is in fact not necessary that the EU is a party to the agreement. It may well be that some, or all, of the Member States are party to the agreement but the EU is not. In many cases, the organisation created by the agreement may not allow for the participation of entities such as the Union. The Court has clarified that, also in such situations, when the organisation deals with matters that involve the Union's competence, the Union's position vis-à-vis the adoption by the organisation of decisions with legal effects is to be established in accordance with Article 218(9) TFEU.[27] This interpretation is logical when viewed against the need to ensure the consistency of action vis-à-vis third partners. This matter is becoming less pronounced now that many international organisations – especially many organisations dealing with commodities – have adapted their founding instruments to provide for a role for *regional economic integration organisations* such as the Union.

Before the Court two final issues in relation to Article 218(9) TFEU have come up. That provision speaks of "positions to be adopted on the Union's behalf in a body set up by an agreement, when that body is called upon to adopt acts having legal effects". The Court's Grand Chamber has clarified that this covers more than decisions that have legal force under the agreement itself. In *OIV*[28] the question arose whether recommendations by the International Organisation of Vine and Wine (known by its French acronym OIV) had legal effects. Under the OIV agreement they did not; but EU law turned the recommendations into binding EU law as far as the Union's legal order is concerned. The Court clarified that, in such cases, it is necessary to have recourse to Article 218(9) TFEU for the establishment of the Union's position and that therefore a Commission proposal for a Council decision is required. A similar *cas de figure*

---

25 For the text, see: OJ 2017, L11/15.
26 Case C-28/12, *Commission v. Council (Transport)* (Grand Chamber), EU:C:2015:282, para. 44, 47–55.
27 Case C-399/12, *Germany v. Council (OIV)*, EU:C:2014:2258 (Grand Chamber), para. 49–55.
28 *Ibid,* para. 56–65.

presents itself with the OECD Arrangement on Export Credits which, as a result of Regulation 1233/2011,[29] is transposed into (binding) Union law.

In another case the Court clarified that the voting rule for an Article 218(9) TFEU decision is found in Article 218(8) TFEU.[30] Therefore, in the cases that fall within the second sub-paragraph of that provision the Council needs to vote with unanimity.

4   Relation with the Commission

Most of the interaction between the Commission and Council in the field of trade takes place within the Trade Policy Committee (TPC). In several respects this is not a typical Council preparatory body. To begin with, it is one of the Treaty-based committees, finding its own legal basis in the third sub-paragraph of Article 207(3) TFEU. In practice it is a body in which the Commission traditionally tends to wield more influence than in most other preparatory bodies of the Council. For most trade agreements the TPC acts as Article 218(4) TFEU committees "in consultation with which the negotiations must be conducted". In this sense, the Treaty of Lisbon has not changed the practice very much.

Since the entry into force of the Lisbon Treaty, the Council's relations with the Commission in the context of the CCP have changed in several respects. I first note the following developments on *procedural* issues, in increasing order of relevance to the institutional balance.

First, in the WTO context it is established practice that the Commission represents the Union in litigation before the WTO's Dispute Settlement Body. In Opinion 2/15 (*Singapore FTA*) the Court's Grand Chamber held that the WTO Dispute Settlement Body, "whilst not formally a court, essentially performs judicial functions".[31] The Commission does not consult the TPC on the briefs it submits to WTO panels. It is true that Article 218(9) TFEU does not apply to such briefs.[32] However, arguably the Council could insist on such consultation since the Court has held in *ITLOS* that "the principle of sincere cooperation requires the Commission to consult the Council beforehand if it intends to

---

29   Regulation (EU) No 1233/2011 of the European Parliament and of the Council of 16 November 2011 on the application of certain guidelines in the field of officially supported export credits and repealing Council Decisions 2001/76/EC and 2001/77/EC (OJ 2011, L326/45).

30   Case C-244/17, *Commission v. Council (Kazakhstan agreement)*, EU:C:2018:662, para. 27–28.

31   Opinion 2/15 (n. 20), para. 299.

32   Case C-73/14, *Council v. Commission (ITLOS)*, EU:C:2015:663, para. 63–71.

express positions on behalf of the European Union before an international court".[33] In practice this does not happen, mostly for reasons relating to deadlines and lack of capacity in the Member States.

Secondly, generally speaking the TPC's ability to keep oversight over on-going negotiations has changed somewhat, as result of a court challenge outside the trade sphere. In *Gas emissions*, the Court's Grand Chamber considered the rights and obligations of an Article 218(4) TFEU committee and found, on the one hand, that such a committee has no right to establish detailed negotiating positions that bind the Commission; moreover, not even the Council can do this.[34] On the other hand, the Court ruled that the Commission is obliged to provide the Article 218(4) TFEU committee with

> [...] all the information necessary for it to monitor the progress of the negotiations, such as, in particular, the general aims announced and the positions taken by the other parties throughout the negotiations. It is only in this way that the special committee is in a position to formulate opinions and advice relating to the negotiations.[35]

The Commission can even be required to provide such information to the Council.[36] The Court even accepted that the Council can impose, in the negotiating directives, procedural arrangements governing the process for the provision of information, for communication and for consultation between the special committee and the Commission.[37]

This judgment makes sense when viewed against the background of the *Chernobyl* dictum quoted above that "[o]bservance of the institutional balance means that each of the institutions must exercise its powers with due regard for the powers of the other institutions". It does leave open the possibility for the Council to amend the negotiating directives but in practice this often is politically difficult.

Thirdly, a perhaps more pernicious assault on the institutional balance and the balance of power within the TPC comes from the Commission's strategy on transparency in trade. This started – at the height of popular discontent about TTIP – with the Commission's communication "Trade for All", in which

---

33   *Ibid*, para. 86.
34   Case C-425/13, *Commission v. Council (Gas emissions)* (Grand Chamber), EU:C:2015:483, para. 89–90.
35   *Ibid*, para. 66.
36   *Ibid*, para. 67.
37   *Ibid*, para. 78.

the Commission laid out a number of policy initiatives. Among these featured the commitment to "invite the Council to disclose all [free-trade agreement] negotiating directives immediately after their adoption". Moreover, the Commission committed to extend the TTIP practice of publishing EU negotiating texts online for all trade and investment negotiations and, after finalising negotiations, to publish the initialled text of the agreement immediately.[38] Things went a step further when Commission president Juncker announced, in his *State of the Union* speech of 13 September 2017, that "[f]rom now on, the Commission will publish in full all draft negotiating mandates we propose to the Council". Subsequently, the Commission applied this new policy not only to trade agreements, but to agreements across the board.

These unilateral policy initiatives seem to be at odds with the views of at least the General Court, which accepts that

> [...] the formulation of negotiating positions may involve a number of tactical considerations of the negotiators, including the European Union itself. In that context, it is possible that the disclosure by the European Union, to the public, of its own negotiating positions, even though the negotiating positions of the other parties remain secret, could, in practice, have a negative effect on the negotiating position of the European Union.[39]

Moreover, where negotiating directives betray, indirectly, the positions of other parties to the negotiations, there is all the more reason to be careful.[40] The General Court's 2018 Judgment in *AccessInfo*,[41] in which it confirmed its earlier case law, suggests it may not be persuaded by the Commission's practice in this regard.

Apart from the consequences for third parties and the negotiations at hand, the Commission's practice has an incidence on the balance of power within the TPC. The knowledge that recommendations for trade agreements are to be made public, and hence known to the party with whom negotiations are to be conducted, causes them to become ever more bland documents. This clearly was not the intention of the Treaty drafters, who considered negotiating

---

38   European Commission, 'Trade for All – Towards a more responsible trade and investment policy', COM(2015) 497 final, 14 October 2015.

39   Case T-301/10, *In 't Veld v. Commission*, EU:T:2013:135, para. 125. This was confirmed by Case T-331/11, *Besselink v. Council*, EU:T:2013:419, para. 71–72.

40   Case T-301/10, *In 't Veld v. Commission*, para. 124.

41   Case T-851/16, *AccessInfo Europe v. Commission*, EU:T:2018:69, para. 48.

directives sufficiently important to make a special mention of them in Article 218(4) TFEU. Even if the Council maintains a case-by-case policy for determining whether adopted negotiating directives public should be made public,[42] the possibility that this may happen militates against putting overly tactical or sensitive instructions in the document. Since the TPC cannot give further instructions to the Commission without an amendment of the negotiating directives[43] (not an easy process since it tends to reopen many carefully negotiated compromises), this effectively leaves the Commission with a larger discretion than it otherwise would have had – which is hard to reconcile with the *Chernobyl* dictum quoted above.

Some of the *substantive* changes to the CCP equally had an effect on the Council's relation with the Commission and, as a result, on the institutional balance. Before the Lisbon Treaty entered into force, trade agreements were typically mixed because they covered culture, transport services, sustainable development and intellectual property rights. Here the changes in the last ten years have been significant.

To begin with, unlike its preceding Article 133 TEC, Article 207 TFEU no longer declares *cultural and audiovisual services* to fall within the shared competence of the Union and the Member States,[44] thus removing a classical bone of contention dating from pre-Lisbon times.

Moreover, in Opinion 2/15 the Court severely restricted the Council's discretion in the field of *transport services*. Until that Opinion, the Council had taken the view that transport services were a shared competence within the meaning of Article 4(2) TFEU which had not been exercised by the Union. Therefore, in many matters of transport policy – and notably in the field of maritime transport, on which there is very little Union legislation – the Union was not competent to contract international obligations unless the Council decided to exercise its competence in the adoption of a particular trade agreement. Even if, in recent comprehensive FTAs, the Council decided that the EU should exercise its competence in the field of transport,[45] this matter had considerable

---

42 There have been a few cases where it decided to do so, such as the negotiating directives for TTIP (Council doc. st11103/13 dcl.1 of 9 October 2014, TISA (Council doc. st6828/15 of 5 March 2015 and CETA (st9036/09 ext.2, st12838/11 ext.2, both of 15 December 2015) and the association agreement with Chile (st9536/17 dcl.1 + add.1 of 20 February 2018).

43 Case C-425/13, *Commission v. Council (Gas emissions)*, EU:C:2015:483, para. 88.

44 Second sub-paragraph of Art. 133(6) TEC.

45 For the FTA with South Korea see Council Decision 2011/265/EU of 16 September 2010 on the signing, on behalf of the European Union, and provisional application of the Free Trade Agreement between the European Union and its Member States, of the one part, and the Republic of Korea, of the other part (OJ 2011, L127/1), for the CETA

importance as a safety valve for Member States to ensure that their dearly held interests were taken on board. However, in *Opinion 2/15* the Court found the transport services provisions in the agreement at issue to have succumbed to the *ERTA* effect[46] and have become an exclusive competence. The Court's reasoning is, on this point, quite surprising: for instance, it declared that the maritime services in the Singapore FTA had become an exclusive competence because of the adoption of a three-page regulation dating from 1986.[47] The same legislation seems to have escaped the Court's notice when, in Opinion 1/08, it discussed the question whether the EU had exclusive competence to conclude agreements to modify the EU's GATS Schedule.[48] The exclusive competence in the fields of rail and road transport rests on a similarly slender base in internal Union law.[49] As the result of this somewhat tenuous reasoning, in most cases transport services are likely to be an exclusive competence of the Union for the same reason. As a result, even though the Council will now look at these matters on a case by case basis, the room for a policy choice whether the Union should exercise its competence in the field of transport services has become quite limited.

As far as *trade-flanking policies* (for example competition law and trade and sustainable development) are concerned, in order to determine whether provisions of the agreement at issue fell within the scope of Article 207 TFEU, the Court assessed in Opinion 2/15 whether the clause in question relates to trade

---

Council Decision (EU) 2017/38 of 28 October 2016 on the provisional application of the Comprehensive Economic and Trade Agreement (CETA) between Canada, of the one part, and the European Union and its Member States, of the other part (OJ 2017, L11/1080), neither of which excludes transport.

46 Named after Case 22/70, *Commission v. Council (ERTA)*, EU:C:1971:32, para. 30–31; codified in Article 3(2) TFEU.

47 Council Regulation (EEC) No 4055/86 of 22 December 1986 applying the principle of freedom to provide services to maritime transport between Member States and between Member States and third countries (OJ 1986, L378/1).

48 Opinion 1/08, *GATS Schedule*, EU:C:2009:739.

49 Directive 2012/34/EU of 21 November 2012 establishing a single European railway area (OJ 2012, L343/32) for rail transport, and Regulations (EC) No 1071/2009 of 21 October 2009 establishing common rules concerning the conditions to be complied with to pursue the occupation of road transport operator and repealing Council Directive 96/26/EC (OJ 2009, L300/51), (EC) No 1072/2009 of 21 October 2009 on common rules for access to the international road haulage market (OJ 2009, L300/72) and (EC) No 1073/2009 of 21 October 2009 on common rules for access to the international market for coach and bus services, and amending Regulation (EC) No 561/2006, (OJ 2009, L300/88) for road transport.

and has direct and immediate effects on it.[50] This test essentially copies the test it developed in the *Daiichi* case.[51] On this basis, the Court ruled that such provisions fell within the scope of Article 207(1) TFEU, with only parts of investment and investment dispute settlement falling within shared competence.[52]

Whilst this reasoning is not objectionable as far as the competition law of the Singapore FTA clauses are concerned, the situation is more complicated in the field of *sustainable development*. Modern EU trade agreements typically comprise provisions covering, on the one hand, provisions related to the environment and climate change and, on the other hand, clauses pertaining to social standards. In the Court's logic, these provisions are covered by the Common Commercial Policy. The Court concludes that these provisions

> [...] are intended not to regulate the levels of social and environmental protection in the Parties' respective territory but to govern trade between the European Union and the Republic of Singapore by making liberalisation of that trade subject to the condition that the Parties comply with their international obligations concerning social protection of workers and environmental protection.[53]

However, the international obligations which the Parties agree to respect include, among other things, a series of ILO Conventions which, effectively, *do* set minimum standards to be respected by the EU and Singapore. Thus, logically, these matters cannot be brought under the sway of Article 207 TFEU; and since part of social standards are explicitly excluded from the competence of the Union,[54] a case can be made that the Singapore FTA should have been mixed for this reason too. In summary, it seems that the Court accepts that standards laid down in international agreements can be brought under the scope of Article 207 TFEU, but other standards cannot. It is respectfully submitted that this distinction seems artificial.

As used by the Court in *Singapore FTA* the *Daiichi* standard becomes very wide indeed. The Court indicates only two limitations. To begin with, provisions

---

50   Opinion 2/15, para. 36–37. On this point, see also the contributions by M. Cremona and A. Rosas in this Volume.

51   Case C-414/11, *Daiichi Sankyo and Sanofi-Aventis Deutschland*, EU:C:2013:520, para. 51–52. See also Case C-137/12, *Commission v. Council*, EU:C:2013:675, para. 57, and Opinion 3/15, *Marrakesh Treaty on access to published works*, EU:C:2017:114, para. 61.

52   Opinion 2/15, para. 134 and 136 (for the competition law clauses) and 157–161 (sustainable development).

53   *Ibid,* para. 166.

54   Art. 153(5) TFEU.

laying down environmental standards can fall under the environmental policy rather than trade. This fits the Court's older case law, such as *Energy Star*.[55] Moreover, the Court finds in a number of cases (intellectual property, competition law, sustainable development) that provisions in the Singapore FTA fall within the scope of Article 207 TFEU since they "in no way [fall] within the scope of harmonisation of the laws of the Member States of the European Union, but [are] intended to govern the liberalisation of trade".[56]

The Court has also transformed the trade-related aspects of *intellectual property rights* into an exclusive competence.[57] In Opinion 2/15 the Court accepted that the intellectual property provisions of a trade agreement may require the parties to adhere to "multilateral conventions which include a provision relating to moral rights" (i.e., copyrights) without straying outside the scope of Article 207(1) TFEU.[58]

In contrast to these tendencies towards exclusive competence, in Opinion 2/15 the Council had argued strongly that *non-direct investment* falls within the residual competence of the Member States. Article 64(2) TFEU provides for a legal basis for legislating on capital movements but this is limited to

> [...] measures on the movement of capital to or from third countries involving direct investment – including investment in real estate – establishment, the provision of financial services or the admission of securities to capital markets.

Other forms of investment are excluded from the scope of Article 64(2) TFEU and thus, logically, remain in the competence of the Member States.

However, the Court disagreed and found that the Union's competence is exclusive as far foreign direct investment standards are concerned, but *shared*, "pursuant to Article 4(1) and (2)(a) TFEU" for provisions pertaining to other investment.[59] It then – somewhat surprisingly – concluded that it follows that the provisions on investment standards in the agreement could not be approved by the Union alone.[60] This is odd since, if non-direct investment is shared

---

55   Case C-281/01, *Commission v. Council* (*Energy Star*), EU:C:2002:761, para. 41–43.
56   Opinion 2/15 (n. 20), para. 126. See for similar comments para. 135 and 165.
57   Case C-347/03, *Regione autonoma Friuli-Venezia Giulia and Agenzia regionale per lo sviluppo rurale*, EU:C:2005:285, para. 79–83, C-414/11, *Daiichi Sankyo and Sanofi-Aventis Deutschland*, EU:C:2013:520, para. 49–52 and Opinion 3/15, *Marrakesh Treaty on access to published works*, EU:C:2017:114, para. 78.
58   Opinion 2/15 (n. 20), para. 129.
59   *Ibid*, para. 243.
60   *Ibid*, para. 244.

pursuant to Article 4(1) and (2)(a) TFEU, the Council could logically always decide to exercise the competence. Perhaps the Court too had some misgivings about its dictum, since in *COTIF* it attempted to explain it by clarifying that

> [...] in making that finding, the Court did no more than acknowledge the fact that [...] there was no possibility of the required majority being obtained within the Council for the Union to be able to exercise alone the external competence that it shares with the Member States in this area.[61]

To say the least, this adds a different flavour to an important point in Opinion 2/15.[62]

Last, the Court finds that the *investor-to-state dispute settlement* (ISDS) regime "removes disputes from the jurisdiction of the courts of the Member States"; it "cannot, therefore, be established without the Member States' consent". It then reasons that the ISDS provisions of the Singapore FTA fall "not within the exclusive competence of the European Union, but within a competence shared between the European Union and the Member States".[63] Note that, in this case, there is no reference made to Article 4 TFEU.

However, it is respectfully submitted that the wording used is not quite logical. The competence for concluding agreements on the jurisdiction of the courts of the Member States lies with the Member States. The Court indicates no basis within the Treaties that provides for a legal basis for the Union to organise the Member States' court organisation. The important point to grasp is that shared competence in *this* context is very different from the shared competence of Article 4(1) and (2)(a) TFEU. In the latter case the Union can decide to exercise the competence; in the former, however, the Member States competence is residual; there just is no basis on which the Union can regulate the matter. Even if the Council had decided to exercise its competence as far as investment protection standards are concerned, the agreement should still have been mixed because of the ISDS provisions. Since, in practice, it is hard to imagine to have an agreement comprising only investment protection standards but no form of investment dispute settlement, the conclusion can remain that investment agreements concluded by the Union remain mixed.

---

61   Case C-600/14, *Germany v. Council* (*COTIF*), EU:C:2017:935, para. 68.
62   It is humbly submitted that this finding may not entirely clarify matters either since the Commission had not even submitted a proposal for a Council Decision to sign the agreement and the Council had, at that point, not even discussed the matter.
63   Opinion 2/15 (n. 20), para. 292–293.

These changes in competence, especially as far as the widened scope of Article 207 TFEU is concerned, imply that less matters are considered to trigger mixity. That, in turn, allows for the adoption of trade agreements (not covering investment dispute settlement) on the basis of Article 207(4), first paragraph TFEU. That implies a simple qualified majority vote in the Council. Even though the Court did not require any such change, the Commission now considers it useful to negotiate investment and investment protection provisions separately from other trade agreements. Thus, it issued recommendations for trade agreements with Australia and New Zealand that do not include investment and investment protection.[64] The Council accepted this new policy[65] and it will have several important effects. To begin with, the resulting free-trade agreements agreements will, in principle, not be mixed. This implies that they do not need to be ratified by the Member States since the consent of the European Parliament suffices. Moreover, since there is no ratification by Member States (a process that normally takes years), there is normally no need for provisional application of the agreements. More importantly, to the extent that future trade agreements fall entirely within the exclusive competence of the Union, they can normally[66] be adopted with only qualified majority. The first major free-trade agreement to be adopted on this basis is the Agreement between the EU and Japan for an Economic Partnership.[67] Even if there is a strong culture within the Council to attempt to achieve consensus (in order to provide for maximum political support) this will make it more difficult for any Member State to insist on matters that are close to its heart. For example, in 2019 one Member State was outvoted when it opposed the adoption of negotiating directives for a trade agreement to be negotiated with the United States.[68]

Of course, if the Council were to favour a broader agreement including investment, it can always amend the negotiating directives. Moreover, the

---

64 Recommendation for a Council Decision authorising the opening of negotiations for a Free Trade Agreement with Australia, COM(2017) 472 final and Recommendation for a Council Decision authorising the opening of negotiations for a Free Trade Agreement with New Zealand, COM(2017) 469 final, both of 13 July 2017.

65 Council conclusions on the negotiation and conclusion of EU trade agreements, Council doc. st9120/18 of 22 May 2018.

66 It is true that the second and following sub-paragraphs of Art. 207(4) TFEU foresee unanimity, but cases where these provisions come into play are actually quite rare.

67 For text, see OJ 2018, L330/3.

68 Council Decision authorising the opening of negotiations with the United States of America for an agreement on the elimination of tariffs for industrial goods (Council doc. st6052/19 of 9 April 2019 and ADD.1 + COR.1).

Commission would fail in its task if it was instructed to negotiate an agreement including investment and investment protection but failed to press for such an outcome.

5 Relations with the European Parliament

Before the entry into force of the Treaty of Lisbon, the European Parliament's rights in the field of the CCP were quite limited. Article 300(3) TEC gave the Parliament not even the right to be consulted on trade agreements. At the time this had not stopped the Council from agreeing with the Parliament the *Westerterp procedure*, which involved arrangements on informing the Parliament of the envisaged agreement and for the Council to participate in a debate in the relevant Parliamentary committee.[69]

The Treaty of Lisbon brought a Copernican revolution in the institutional balance as far as the CCP is concerned, on three points. First, under Article 218(6)(a)(v) TFEU the European Parliament obtained the right to give its consent to trade agreements. Secondly, under Article 218(10) TFEU, it obtained the right to be "immediately and fully informed at all stages of the procedure". Both of these rights affect the Parliament's relationship with the Council; hence they affect the way in which the Council deals with the CCP. Last, the Parliament became co-legislator on trade legislation. Let us briefly review these three rights separately.

In pre-Lisbon days, the Parliament did have a *right of consent* (and with that, a right of veto) over association agreements. It used its muscle for the first time on 9 March 1988, when the Parliament voted down three protocols amending the 1975 Agreement between the EEC and Israel. Since that occasion the Parliament has jealously protected its prerogative and, as for example the vetoing of the SWIFT and ACTA agreements illustrated, stands ready to use it.[70] Armed with this experience, the Parliament has attempted to use its right of consent as a crowbar to obtain more influence over international agreements. If the Parliament refuses to give its consent, then the Council has to repeal the decision signing the agreement (and, where relevant, providing for provisional application).[71]

---

69   Annex to Council doc. R/2641/73 of 5 November 1973 at 3–4.

70   See for example its Resolution on the Intergovernmental Conference (OJ 1997, C115/165).

71   For an example see Council Decision 2012/15/EU of 20 December 2011 repealing Council Decision 2011/491/EU on the signing, on behalf of the European Union, and the provisional application of the Protocol between the European Union and the Kingdom of Morocco setting out the fishing opportunities and financial compensation provided

The Parliament's *right to information* was considerably strengthened by Article 218(10) TFEU, which provides that "[t]he European Parliament shall be immediately and fully informed at all stages of the procedure" In the *Mauritius* case the Court's Grand Chamber ruled that the Council violated this provision by informing the Parliament of a decision on signature over three months after its publication in the Official Journal.[72] The Court considered the notification to Parliament an essential procedural requirement within the meaning of the second paragraph of Article 263 TFEU, the violation of which leads to nullity of the decision.[73]

In *Tanzania* the Court went a step further. It clarified that the obligation of Article 218(10) TFEU applies to any procedure for concluding an international agreement.[74] Although the Parliament claimed, among others, that the Council had breached Article 218(10) TFEU by not providing it with the negotiating directives,[75] the Court pointedly did not address this claim. It did, however, recall that

> [t]he aim of that information requirement [of Article 218(10) TFEU] is, inter alia, to ensure that the Parliament is in a position to exercise democratic control over the European Union's external action and, more specifically, to verify that the choice made of the legal basis for a decision on the conclusion of an agreement was made with due regard to the powers of the Parliament.[76]

The Court stressed in *Tanzania* that Article 218(10) TFEU also extends to the stages that precede the conclusion of such an agreement, and covers, in particular, the negotiation phase.[77] The Court then found that the obligation to inform the Parliament of the conduct of negotiations rests on the shoulders of the Council.[78] To the extent that this involves the transmission of Council decisions this is logical. However, one can seriously question how logical it is to make the Council responsible for informing the Parliament of the negotiations

---

for in the Fisheries Partnership Agreement between the European Community and the Kingdom of Morocco, (OJ 2012, L6/1).

72   Case C-658/11, *Parliament v. Council (Mauritius)*, EU:C:2014:2025, para. 77–78.
73   *Ibid.*, para. 80.
74   Case C-263/14, *Parliament v. Council (Tanzania Agreement)*, EU:C:2016:435, para. 68.
75   *Ibid*, para. 57.
76   *Ibid*, para. 71.
77   *Ibid*, para. 75.
78   *Ibid*, para. 73.

themselves: the Council is normally not represented at negotiation sessions. The Trade Policy Committee (and, for non-trade negotiations, other Council bodies) are themselves debriefed some time (often weeks) after negotiation rounds and are thus not in a position to debrief the Parliament "immediately". Last, it is peculiar that the Parliament should hear from the second hand what happened. In practice it is indeed the Commission rather than the Council that debriefs the Parliament.

In *Tanzania* the Council had been more diligent than in *Mauritius* in informing the Parliament of its decision on conclusion by sending this within nine days to the Parliament. However, the Court still considered this to fall short of the *immediately* standard of Article 218(10) TFEU.[79] The fact that the Council had published the decision in the Official Journal, where the Parliament could find it, did not alter that.[80]

In the meantime, the Parliament, Council and the Commission in 2016 concluded the Interinstitutional Agreement on better law-making. Whilst they did not manage to agree on arrangements concerning Article 218(10) TFEU in that context, paragraph 40 of the document foresees follow-up negotiations "in order to negotiate improved practical arrangements for cooperation and information-sharing within the framework of the Treaties, as interpreted by the Court of Justice of the European Union".[81] The Parliament has pulled out of these negotiations.

The Parliament obtained an important increase in its powers when it saw the *ordinary legislative procedure* (formerly co-decision) extended over the CCP. In practice this works generally well, although one cannot entirely escape the perception that the Parliament sometimes lacks the expertise to engage meaningfully in discussions on trade policy especially when these touch upon details of WTO law, a matter not always on the Parliament's radar screen.

Whilst the Parliament's role in the process leading to the adoption of international agreements certainly has improved, it does not imply equality with the Council. The Court has expressly rejected the notion that the institutional balance would imply parallelism between the Paliament and the Council.[82]

---

79   *Ibid*, para. 81.
80   *Ibid*, para. 80.
81   Interinstitutional agreement between the European Parliament, the Council of the European Union and the European Commission on better law-making (OJ 2016 L123/1), para. 40.
82   Case 302/87, *Parliament v. Council (comitology)*, EU:C:1988:461, para. 19 and 21.

6   Conclusion

This inquiry started with a brief overview of the concept of institutional balance, followed by a review of developments of the Council's practice in the CCP as it has affected its relations with Member States, the Commission and the European Parliament.

As far as the Council's relations with the Member States are concerned, the events of the last ten years do not seem to have greatly affected the institutional balance. However, one matter currently outstanding is the *Bundesverfassungsgericht*'s final ruling on the compatibility of the CETA with the German Constitution. One matter of particular interest will be the question whether the German court will follow the sweeping manner in which the European Court of Justice considered many trade-flanking provisions in the Singapore FTA to fall within the scope of Article 207 TFEU.

As far as the Council's relations with the Commission are concerned, the case law on procedural matters (*Gas Emissions*, *ITLOS*, *OIV*) has clarified the respective prerogatives without changing the balance between the institutions dramatically. The same cannot be said of the Commission's Trade for All policy, which will cause negotiating directives to become more and more trivial and a power shift to the benefit of the Commission. The changes in the scope of the CCP caused an even stronger shift in the institutional balance. The Court's expansive interpretation of Article 207(1) TFEU reduces the negotiating power of Member States within the Council and, as a result, shifts power towards the Commission.

The expansion of the Parliament's prerogatives was an obvious change in the institutional balance which – in this case – was desired by the Treaty drafters. However, the Parliament continues to attempt to increase its role in external relations by using the right to consent and to information as *crowbars* to obtain influence on the negotiating process and by interpreting its right to be *informed* as a right to provide its *opinion* at different stages of the process.[83]

Acknowledgement

This contribution represents only the views of its author. It does not bind, nor may it be attributed to, the Council or to its Legal Service.

---

83   See, for example, Rule 108(3) of its Rules of Procedure (January 2017 edition): "Parliament may, on a proposal from the committee responsible, a political group or Members reaching at least the low threshold, ask the Council not to authorise the opening of negotiations until Parliament has stated its position on the proposed negotiating mandate on the basis of a report from the committee responsible".

CHAPTER 24

The Role of the European Parliament in the Shaping of the Common Commercial Policy

Andrej Auersperger Matić

1 Introduction

The entry into force of the Treaty of Lisbon in 2009 marked a fundamental shift in the institutional architecture of the European Union in the area of international trade.[1] In the light of many concerns about the legitimacy and economic effects of trade policy, as well as persisting uncertainties about the division of powers in this domain, the new Treaty provisions enlarged and clarified the substantive scope of the Common Commercial Policy and reformed the decision-making procedures of the Union by effectively adding the European Parliament as a key policymaker to the previously existing bilateral relationship between the Commission and the Council. Under the new Article 207 TFEU, the European Parliament not only became a co-legislator on an equal footing with the Council,[2] but also obtained the power to give or deny consent to international trade agreements. Given that, taking into account the very slow progress of discussions within the World Trade Organisation (WTO), bilateral trade agreements have become the main legal instrument of the Common Commercial Policy, the importance of this change cannot be overestimated. Other institutional modifications that were introduced by the Treaty of Lisbon, such as the new framework of delegated and implementing acts, and the formal link between the Common Commercial Policy and the general principles of the Union's external action, further strengthened the means by which the exercise of that policy could be subject to democratic supervision and review. The European Parliament obviously welcomed the new scrutiny powers, but the new system also carried the risk that the new triangular architecture

---

1   M. Krajewski, 'New Functions and New Powers for the European Parliament: Assessing the Changes of the Common Commercial Policy from the Perspective of Democratic Legitimacy', in M. Bungenberg, C. Herrmann (eds.), *Common Commercial Policy after Lisbon* (Springer, 2013), p. 67–85.
2   On the relation between the Council and the European Parliament in the context of the CCP, see also the contribution by B. Driessen in this volume.

would hamper the effectiveness of trade policy and limit the Union's ability to act as a credible partner in international relations.[3]

After a decade of experience under two legislatures (2009–2014 and 2014–2019), it can be concluded that such concerns have proven to be unfounded. The reforms introduced by the Treaty of Lisbon significantly increased the transparency and accountability of the actions of the Commission and the Council in the domain of trade, without reducing their ability to act. Nevertheless, important modifications to the policymaking process and political strategies had to be adopted. Moreover, new mechanisms and institutional adaptations among and within Union institutions had to be put into place, both in terms of interinstitutional coordination and in terms of relations with trading partners. While this has made the policy process more complex and arguably more difficult, no fundamental break or reorientation of trade policy took place in the decade after Lisbon.[4] On the contrary, during this period the Union has negotiated a significant number of comprehensive bilateral trade agreements that are more ambitious in scope than any previous arrangements, and it has thereby reinforced its status as the largest trading area in the world with corresponding influence on trading rules. This happened despite the less-than-favourable economic climate in the aftermath of a severe economic crisis and in a less-than-friendly political environment characterised by unprecedented and vocal opposition to free trade in Europe, numerous obstacles to further progress of negotiations within the World Trade Organisation and, most recently, a more critical and assertive attitude of the United States administration toward its trading partners.

The present text examines the role that the European Parliament has played in this context and the impact that it has had on Union policies. This impact is analysed with reference to notable trade negotiations, important legislation and litigation in the European Court of Justice concerning important institutional issues, in particular the overarching theme of Union versus Member State competences in the area of trade.[5] The inflection point in this context was Opinion 2/15,[6] in which the Court of Justice provided a comprehensive

---

3   D. Kleimann, 'Taking Stock: EU Common Commercial Policy in the Lisbon Era', CEPS Working Document No. 345 (2011).

4   G. Siles-Brügge, *Constructing European Union Trade Policy* (Palgrave Macmillan, 2014), p. 187–201.

5   Case C-414/11, *Daichi Sankyo and Sanofi-Aventis Deutschland*, EU:C:2013:520; Case C-389/15, *Commission v Council*, EU:C:2017:79.

6   Opinion 2/15 *Free Trade Agreement between the European Union and the Republic of Singapore*, EU:C:2017:376.

interpretation of the scope of the Common Commercial Policy post-Lisbon in a number of areas, in particular transport services, intellectual property rights, investment protection and commitments on trade and sustainable development.[7] It is now clear that the vast majority of areas concerned by recent comprehensive bilateral free trade agreements fall under the Common Commercial Policy, and therefore under the EU's exclusive competences. On the other hand, the EU's competence for investment protection is limited to foreign direct investment, and, crucially, the issue of investor-state dispute settlement falls under shared competence. The overall result of Opinion 2/15 proceeding is thus favourable to Parliament, as it strengthens the role of Union institutions and in effect limits the requirement for obtaining Member State ratifications of trade agreements to the most controversial areas only. Moreover, it means that future free trade agreements of the Union – with the exception of investment protection arrangements – can be designed in a manner that will allow them to be adopted by the Union only pursuant to Article 218 TFEU, which grants the European Parliament the key legitimating power.[8] Thus, the Economic Partnership Agreement between the EU and Japan, one of the most significant trade deals negotiated with a major trading partner and signed on 17 July 2018, entered into force already on 1 February 2019, as no Member State ratifications were necessary because it does not include an investment protection chapter. By contrast, the recent trade agreements with Singapore and Vietnam, which both envisaged investment protection commitments, had to be split into two separate instruments – a free trade agreement and an investment protection agreement – that follow different ratification tracks.

By way of general assessment, it can be said that Parliament has succeeded in adapting to its newly acquired decisional prerogatives and that its work has resulted in a much higher visibility of controversies over international trade, both inside and outside the Union. It has also ensured an enviable and unprecedented degree of transparency and democratic accountability. The European Parliament also achieved some significant policy modifications, of which the most important is undoubtedly the Union proposal to replace the international regime of investor-state dispute settlement with a permanent investment court.[9] Nevertheless, as the political disputes surrounding the negotiation of transatlantic trade agreements and the legal battle over Union competences

---

7   M. Cremona, 'Shaping EU Trade Policy post-Lisbon: Opinion 2/15 of 16 May 2017', *European Constitutional Law Review* 14 (2018), p. 231. On this issue, see also the chapters by M. Cremona and A. Rosas in this volume.

8   M. Krajewski (n. 1), p. 80–83.

9   On this issue, see also the chapters by C. Brown; G. Van der Loo; and M. Hahn in this volume.

have plainly shown, Parliament has struggled to establish itself firmly as the premier forum of democratic control of trade policy in the EU.

2   Institutional Adaptation after Lisbon

The institutional architecture in the sphere of external relations of the Union under the Treaty of Lisbon has in principle brought about a balanced and transparent division of powers that to a considerable extent mirrors arrangements found in national democratic constitutions.[10] Under Article 17 TEU, the Commission ensures the Union's external representation and takes the relevant initiatives, while the supervisory role is split between Council and Parliament. Under Article 16 TEU, Council carries out policy-making and coordinating functions, and under Article 14 TEU, Parliament exercises functions of political control and consultation. Accordingly, an important supervisory and legitimating role is accorded to the European Parliament, with the latter now also having the right of democratic scrutiny of the Union's external action. Moreover, the principle of institutional balance laid down in Article 13(2) TEU underlines that each institution shall act within the limits of the powers conferred on it in the Treaties and in conformity with the procedures, conditions and objectives set out in them. Each institution must therefore exercise its powers with due regard for the powers of the other institutions. These general parameters are supplemented with the specific provisions in the TFEU. In the area of trade, Article 207 TFEU now provides that legislation to implement the Common Commercial Policy is adopted under the ordinary legislative procedure and that international trade agreements are adopted with the consent of the European Parliament.

With respect to Parliament's legislative powers, the new arrangements have not created any major difficulties, as they only extended the decision-making format hitherto used in other policy areas than trade. The Parliament obtained co-decision powers on par with those of the Council, which means that a more prominent role has been granted to its Committee on International Trade (INTA),[11] but as the institutional infrastructure was already in place, no major adaptation was necessary in institutional terms. The main practical consequence of the Treaty of Lisbon regime was therefore simply the introduction of the tripartite decision-making procedure, whose nerve centre are

---

10   On the institutional architecture in relation to the CCP, see also the contributions by D. Kleimann and B. Driessen in this volume.

11   S. Gstöhl, D. De Bièvre, *The Trade Policy of the European Union* (Palgrave, 2018), p. 51–52.

the *trilogue* negotiations between Parliament, Council and the Commission. The negotiations take place on the basis of positions formulated by Council working groups or COREPER and those taken by either the INTA Committee or the plenary. Internal proceedings within Parliament, though they have been streamlined over the years, for the most part follow the same route as before. Thus, for policy measures relating to the Common Commercial Policy, the deliberation of a position begins in the INTA Committee once a legislative proposal of the Commission has been transmitted to it from the plenary. Typical subsequent steps include the appointment of a rapporteur, several exchanges of views in committee, informal discussions among the political groups and finally the adoption of the position or a formal report in the committee. This is followed by interinstitutional negotiations, unless the matter is referred to the plenary for a vote on proposed amendments, in which case negotiations are based on the position adopted in plenary.

As is the case in other areas, the trilogue negotiations in principle require an in-depth examination of each legislative proposal. Parliament accordingly has to prepare well to make sure that it presents its views forcefully to its institutional counterparts. Significant differences can arise between the three institutions, in terms of overall approach to the matter at hand or policy nuances, but it should be noted that virtually all trilogues result in the adoption of a compromise text which forms the basis of the ultimately adopted legislative act. Negotiations tend to proceed reasonably quickly and are generally completed in several months, though there are exceptions. With a view to reforming the Anti-Dumping Regulation, for example, the Commission adopted its proposal in 2013 but protracted negotiations only allowed the final act to be adopted in 2018.[12] A file can also be blocked for a significant period of time if the Member States in the Council find it difficult to reach an agreement, so negotiations cannot even start. This happened, for instance, with the proposed International Procurement Instrument.[13] On the other hand, due to its different structure

---

12   European Commission, 'Proposal for a Regulation of the European Parliament and of the Council amending Council Regulation (EC) No 1225/2009 on protection against dumped imports from countries not members of the European Community and Council Regulation (EC) No 597/2009 on protection against subsidised imports from countries not members of the European Community', COM(2013) 192; Regulation (EU) 2018/825 of the European Parliament and of the Council of 30 May 2018 amending Regulation (EU) 2016/1036 on protection against dumped imports from countries not members of the European Union and Regulation (EU) 2016/1037 on protection against subsidised imports from countries not members of the European Union (OJ 2018, L 143). On this issue, see also the contributions by F. Hoffmeister, P. De Baere and E. Vermulst in this volume.

13   European Commission, 'Proposal for a Regulation of the European Parliament and of the Council on the access of third-country goods and services to the Union's internal market

and voting rules, Parliament has – with very few exceptions – no difficulties in reaching decisions or adopting positions, and its challenges are mainly practical and organisational. In the context of trilogue discussions, for example, Parliament's negotiating team is usually composed of a larger number of persons – members, officials, political advisers and assistants – than the teams of the Commission and Council, a fact that reflects the Parliament's more complex political structure. The established practice is that the Parliament's negotiation team is led by the INTA Chair in the presence of the rapporteur for the file in question, with the assistance of the Parliament secretariat and political group advisers. Depending on the sensitivity of the file, the trilogue negotiations can also take place on a technical level, following a mandate given by political authorities. One aspect of the trilogue negotiations that is often criticised is their lack of transparency to the outside world.[14] A recent development in this regard is the ruling of the General Court on the scope of public access to the key negotiating document, the multiple-column table in which the positions of the institutions and possible compromises are noted.[15] Consequently, this document is now more widely available to the public, which can request it on a case-by-case basis. Increased transparency is however a double-edged sword, and it remains to be seen whether it will in any way hamper the effectiveness of the trilogue process.

The implementation of the new institutional arrangements has created a more difficult situation with respect to the other main mechanism of policy-making, namely the conclusion of international agreements. Under the scheme laid down in the Treaty of Lisbon, Parliament and Council do not "co-decide" about proposed international agreements. Rather, the Council is the main policymaking body and Parliament is involved in the process of negotiation and conclusion of international agreements only at a relatively late stage, when it expresses its approval or rejection of an agreement and thereby provides democratic legitimacy.[16] It has therefore no formal possibility to modify agreements and can only influence their content through earlier contacts with the Commission. The Commission negotiates in accordance with the negotiating directives (or *mandate*) adopted by the Council, so the European Parliament

---

in public procurement and procedures supporting negotiations on access of Union goods and services to the public procurement markets of third countries', COM (2012) 124. On this issue, see also the contribution by S. Woolcock in this volume.

14   European Ombudsman, Case OI/8/2015/JAS, Decision setting out proposals following her strategic inquiry concerning the transparency of Trilogues.

15   Case T-540/15, *De Capitani v European Parliament*, EU:T:2018:167.

16   On this point, see also the contribution by D. Kleimann in this volume.

formally cannot influence decisions to launch negotiations or the content of negotiating directives. Article 218(10) TFEU nevertheless provides that "the European Parliament shall be immediately and fully informed at all stages of the procedure". The unequal positions of Council and Parliament within the structure of Article 218 TFEU has predictably created certain tensions and brought about a number of institutional innovations.[17]

To reflect the new system of powers in the Treaty of Lisbon, Parliament and the Commission concluded, shortly after the latter entered into force, a Framework Agreement that sought to provide basic principles regarding the conduct of negotiations of international agreements.[18] The Framework Agreement provided that the Commission shall inform the Parliament about its intention to propose the start of negotiations at the same time as it informs the Council,[19] to present draft negotiating directives to Parliament and to "take due account of Parliament's comments throughout the negotiations".[20] Moreover, the Commission committed itself to keeping Parliament regularly and promptly informed about the conduct of negotiations, and explain whether and how Parliament's comments were incorporated in the texts under negotiation. In the case of international agreements that required the Parliament's consent, the Commission also agreed to provide to Parliament during the negotiation process all relevant information that it also provides to the Council. Practice has shown that these obligations were implemented gradually and with varying degrees in different areas. The INTA committee nevertheless quickly established suitable institutional arrangements necessary to give full effect to the information requirements and the need to regularly exchange views with the Commission during trade negotiations. Exchanges of views and debriefings with Commissioners and the Commission Directorates-General have now become a generalised practice that allows committee members to follow trade negotiations and formulate their views. In order to explain the envisaged content of various agreements or their various aspects, Commission staff also frequently participate in special hearings or technical briefings that are frequently held on Parliament premises. Furthermore, at the end of 2011 the INTA committee appointed several standing rapporteurs in order to facilitate follow-up of trade negotiations or preparations for negotiations, mainly in the form of so-called *monitoring groups* that typically meet before and after negotiation

---

17 On this point, see also the contribution by B. Driessen in this volume.
18 Framework Agreement on relations between the European Parliament and the Commission (OJ 2010, L304/47).
19 *Ibid*, Annex III.
20 *Ibid*, Annex III.

sessions. This mechanism is now well established and the INTA committee now has nearly 40 standing rapporteurs and groups set-up for this purpose.

In addition to its standard methods of democratic scrutiny, such as holding debates and submitting oral questions to the Commission, the INTA committee has also regularly availed itself of the possibility to propose parliamentary resolutions to express members' views on the desired content of trade agreements.[21] Rule 114 of Parliament's Rules of Procedure provides for the possibility of drawing up reports when the Union intends to start negotiations on the conclusion, renewal or amendment of international agreements, as well as at any stage of the negotiations and even later, up to the point of the conclusion of the agreement. The Parliament may thus express its views regarding the various decisions and recommendations that concern the opening and conduct of negotiations, though neither the Commission nor Council are bound by the Parliament's views. Rather, the point is to ensure that Parliament's view is known in advance, so as to avoid surprise when an agreement must obtain its formal consent. With respect to the negotiation of the Free Trade Agreement between the European Union and Japan, for example, the Parliament in 2012 first adopted a short resolution in which it simply requested that the Council withhold approval to start the negotiations until Parliament had the opportunity to define its position on the proposed negotiating mandate.[22] The latter was then adopted a few months later, with a series of recommendations regarding sensitive issues like public procurement, market access in certain strategic sectors, the protection of geographical indications and a chapter on trade and sustainable development.[23]

The most elaborate scrutiny structure was established in relation to the landmark trade agreement that was envisaged to be negotiated with the United States, the Transatlantic Trade and Investment Partnership (TTIP), which took place from 2013 to 2016.[24] The wide scope of the agreement and its potentially far-reaching implications for the Union's internal market suggested that many areas of the Parliament's concern could be affected, which is why a number of committees were involved in the formulation of Parliament's positions.

21   S. Gstöhl, D. De Bièvre (n. 11), p. 51.

22   European Parliament resolution of 13 June 2012 on EU trade negotiations with Japan, P7_TA(2012)0246.

23   European Parliament resolution of 25 October 2012 on EU trade negotiations with Japan, P7_TA(2012)0398.

24   T. Takács, 'Situating the Transatlantic Trade and Investment Partnership (negotiations) in European Union Common Commercial Policy', *Legal Issues of Economic Integration* 43 (2016), p. 341.

The importance of TTIP discussions led to the establishment of a special coordination group of committee chairs headed by Parliament's President, and the close following of negotiations was given special emphasis by the INTA Committee and its monitoring group for the United States, which was also chaired by the INTA chairman. Among the more pressing issues in this context was the confidentiality of negotiation documents, and it is notable that due to significant public pressure, the Commission introduced a transparency initiative, which made an unprecedented number of negotiating documents (especially the Union position on different chapters of the agreement) available to the public. After several months of discussions, Parliament also obtained from the Commission the right for all its members to have access to the more sensitive categories of confidential documents relating to TTIP talks, in particular the so-called *consolidated texts* that also reflected the negotiating position of the United States. The Parliament was thus able to be closely involved in the conduct of TTIP trade talks, with intensive questioning of the Commission on many key issues and especially investment protection. Parliamentary scrutiny of TTIP discussions, which took many shapes, at the end resulted in a well-publicised resolution, adopted on 8 July 2015, containing an extensive list of recommendations to the Commission.[25]

Whereas it is understandable, given the nature of the political relationship between the institutions, that the Commission has undertaken important engagements in relation to the Parliament regarding the following of trade negotiations, it was more difficult to establish a *modus vivendi* in this respect between Council and Parliament.[26] The ambiguity inherent in Article 218(10) TFEU concerning the duty to inform led to a number of disputes, some of which ended up before the Court of Justice. The Parliament notably initiated – and ultimately prevailed – in two cases brought against the Council because of the failure of the latter to transmit relevant documents, concerning the agreements on the transfer of pirates with, respectively, Mauritius and Tanzania.[27] In the rulings, the Court of Justice emphasised that the Parliament's involvement in the decision-making process is the reflection, at Union level, of the fundamental democratic principle that the people should participate in the exercise of power through the intermediary of a representative

---

25   European Parliament Resolution of 8 July 2015 containing the European Parliament's recommendations to the European Commission on the negotiations for the Transatlantic Trade and Investment Partnership (TTIP), P8_TA(2015)0252.

26   On this issue, see also the contribution by B. Driessen in this volume.

27   Case C-658/11, *Parliament v Council*, EU:C:2014:2025; Case C-263/14, *Parliament v Council*, EU:C:2016:435.

assembly. In the view of the Court, the scope of the information obligation under Article 218(10) TFEU concerns a series of decisions and documents, in particular the authorisation to open negotiations, the definition of the negotiating directives, the completion of negotiations, the authorisation to sign the agreement, and where necessary, the decision on the provisional application of the agreement.[28] Following these cases, the three institutions agreed to search for solutions on a tripartite basis. In the Interinstitutional Agreement on Better Law-Making of 2016,[29] they acknowledged the importance of "ensuring that each institution can exercise its rights and fulfil its obligations enshrined in the Treaties as interpreted by the Court of Justice" regarding the negotiation and conclusion of international agreements. The Better Law-Making Agreement envisaged special negotiations on improved practical arrangements for cooperation and information sharing in the context of international agreements. The arrangements are intended to consolidate the information and scrutiny rights of Parliament, so as to allow it to ensure democratic legitimacy of the decisional process in the area of international agreements. However, the negotiations on this delicate issue have not yet been successfully completed.

The Better Law-Making Agreement also formalised and validated arrangements (in particular standard clauses) that had previously been agreed with respect to another important innovation of the Treaty of Lisbon, namely the new structure of delegated powers and in particular the new mechanism of *delegated acts* under Article 290 TFEU.[30] The latter places Parliament and Council on the same footing when it comes to the supervision of the Commission's delegated powers, unlike implementing acts where the Parliament may only object on narrow legal grounds while the Member States retain influence through committees of experts. Though perhaps not as critically as in certain other fields of Union action, the scope of application of the delegated acts procedure in the field of the CCP was from the outset an object of some controversy between Council and Parliament. Delegated acts play a prominent role in the operation of the Generalised Scheme of Preferences (GSP), the implementation of safeguard clauses in trade agreements, and, perhaps to a lesser extent, in a number of legislative acts containing import or export rules. It should not be a surprise that throughout the post-Lisbon period, the

---

28   Case C-263/14, *Ibid*, para. 76.
29   Interinstitutional Agreement between the European Parliament, the Council of the European Union and the European Commission on Better Law-Making (OJ 2016, L123/1).
30   On this issue, see also the contribution by J. Bourgeois and M. Chamon in this volume.

Parliament advocated, with mixed success, the use of delegated acts wherever an issue of policy might be at stake. A notable recent example is the Conflict Minerals Regulation, concerning the setting of relevant volume thresholds of minerals and metals.[31]

Finally, it should be emphasised that the newly acquired role of the Parliament has evolved generally in the context of the rather complex process of negotiating and concluding international agreements by the European Union, which gives rise to a number of structural peculiarities. One of these is the multiplicity of decisions relating to a single international agreement and the interaction between them. As a corollary of the practice of *mixity*, for instance, the Council for years formalised the need to associate Member States in key decisions with regard to several non-trade agreements in so-called *hybrid* decisions on the signature of these agreements, adopted by both the Council and the governments of the Member States. The Commission successfully challenged this practice in the Court of Justice with the support of Parliament as intervener, because the practice implies a conflation of voting rules and confusion about the legal nature of the decision.[32] Another dimension of decisional multiplicity is temporal and substantive, as the Commission adopts two or even three proposals for decisions – on signature, conclusion and, possibly, on provisional application of the agreement – to structure the conclusion process. Within this structure, the possibility of provisional application envisaged in Article 218(5) TFEU has presented a particularly intricate issue for the Parliament.[33] It is intuitively understandable that once an agreement is put into effect, political pressure to approve it increases and this may to some extent reduce the weight or authority of the Parliament's consent. For this reason, the Parliament insisted that provisional application should not take place before consent has been granted.[34] It seems that in recent years, the Commission and Council have taken note and now avoid adopting provisional application decisions before Parliament approves an international agreement.

---

31 Regulation (EU) 2017/821 of the European Parliament and of the Council of 17 May 2017 laying down supply chain due diligence obligations for Union importers of tin, tantalum and tungsten, their ores, and gold originating from conflict-affected and high-risk areas (OJ 2017, L130/1).

32 Case C-28/12, *Commission v Council*, EU:C:2015:282.

33 On the provisional application of EU FTAs, see the contribution by J. Heliskoski this volume.

34 European Parliament resolution of 5 July 2016 on a new forward-looking and innovative future strategy for trade and investment, P8_TA (2016) 0299, para.36.

3   Policy Formulation

For policy experts, accustomed for decades to the interplay between the Commission and Council and its Trade Policy Committee as the main policy fora of the Union in the area of trade, the most intriguing question that accompanied the inclusion of the European Parliament in the Union's decisional structure was whether this would significantly change the direction of the Union's approach to trade. A simple answer to this question would be a qualified "no", although one should note that the first decade of the Treaty of Lisbon has also marked important shifts in public perception of international trade and its regulation and that this circumstance very much influenced the positions that Parliament adopted throughout the first decade after Lisbon. More importantly, as a political body Parliament has itself provided a forum for a healthy public debate on many trade issues, and has, as is the case with Council, often been politically divided between *free-traders* and *protectionists*. An assessment of its role accordingly very much depends on one's political view and attitudes to free trade. As a general matter, it is nevertheless reasonably clear that for the most part, the Parliament's positions in the post-Lisbon period broadly followed the views espoused in key policy documents of the Commission such as the *Global Europe* communication of 2006, the *Europe 2020 Strategy* and, more recently, the *Trade for All* strategy of 2015.[35] In a nutshell, this involves supporting trade liberalisation discussions at multilateral level and in particular in the framework of the WTO, making a strengthened effort to conclude ambitious and comprehensive bilateral free trade agreements with trading partners while protecting key sectors, and insisting on viable trade defence mechanisms and import or export rules that seek to promote fair trade and human rights in third countries.

As far as trade legislation is concerned, the Parliament negotiated important pieces of trade law in the last decade and has proven to be a reliable partner to the Commission and Council. Its amendments to proposed trade acts have been somewhat more *protectionist* than those of Council, with Parliament notably emphasising the need to include provisions on human rights and fair trade, in particular regarding the respect of environmental and labour rights. Attitudes however varied somewhat in time. An early legislative file, concerning the Generalised Scheme of Preferences (GSP) Regulation, did not indicate

---

35   European Commission, 'Global Europe: competing in the World', COM (2006) 567 final, 4 October 2006; European Commission, 'Europe 2020: A strategy for smart, sustainable and inclusive growth', COM (2010) 2020 final, 3 March 2010; European Commission, 'Trade for All' (2015).

any major divergences between Council and Parliament. The latter had some-what different views on certain points – for instance, the precise contours of the scope of delegated acts, temporal validity of the act, the precise lists of beneficiary countries and sensitive products, as well as certain eligibility criteria – but negotiations proceeded smoothly and the act was adopted rather quickly.[36] A more visible difference appeared during the discussions of the proposal for a Conflict Minerals Regulation, an instrument intended to prevent the minerals trade from funding conflict and human rights violations.[37] Its aim is to oblige all but the smallest importers of tin, tungsten, tantalum and gold to do due diligence checks on their suppliers and by requiring big manufacturers to disclose how they plan to monitor their sources. In this case, Parliament succeeded in persuading the Council and the Commission, who initially proposed only voluntary due diligence checks, that the latter should be mandatory for importers. The Parliament also secured an undertaking that big firms that buy tin, tantalum, tungsten and gold to use in their products will be encouraged to report on their sourcing practices and will be able to join a special register.

Among other important pieces of legislation, it is important to mention the trade defence instruments and in particular the adaptation of the anti-dumping methodology in the light of China's accession to the WTO.[38] In May 2016 Parliament adopted a resolution on China's market economy status, expressing a strong opposition to granting this status to China as long as it did not meet the relevant criteria.[39] Parliament notably underlined that the Union should continue to use a non-standard methodology in anti-dumping investigations of Chinese imports in determining price comparability. The Commission subsequently tabled its proposal to reform the relevant sections of Union anti-dumping law, which envisaged that the analogue country methodology would cease to apply to WTO members that are non-market economies, but also allowed for the calculation of values based on costs of production and

---

36   Regulation (EU) No 978/2012 of the European Parliament and of the Council of 25 October 2012 applying a scheme of generalised tariff preferences and repealing Council Regulation (EC) No 732/2008 (OJ 2012, L303/1).

37   Regulation (EU) 2017/821 of the European Parliament and of the Council of 17 May 2017 laying down supply chain due diligence obligations for Union importers of tin, tantalum and tungsten, their ores, and gold originating from conflict-affected and high-risk areas (OJ 2017, L130/1).

38   On the EU's trade defence instruments, see also the contributions by F. Hoffmeister, P. De Baere and E. Vermulst in this volume.

39   European Parliament resolution of 12 May 2016 on China's market economy status, P8_TA(2016)0223.

sale reflecting undistorted international prices in case of substantial market distortions. In the legislative procedure, the Parliament defended a more robust approach to anti-dumping rules, which was partly incorporated in the final outcome.[40] This included in particular the addition of new criteria to the non-exhaustive list proposed by the Commission to determine significant distortions. Moreover, considerations about compliance with social and environmental standards in exporting countries were taken into account as regards the choice of the appropriate representative country to determine normal prices of imports.

Unsurprisingly, the more publicised and more controversial aspect of trade policy in the last decade was the process of negotiating and concluding trade agreements. The first test of the power shift under the Treaty of Lisbon was the process of the conclusion of the free trade agreement between the European Union and South Korea, which was the first of the comprehensive *new generation* trade agreements as well as the first trade agreement with an Asian country. It was devised as a mixed agreement, so the process of conclusion involved both the European Parliament and the parliaments of the Member States. After the initialling of the text in 2009, the Commission published, on 9 April 2010, the draft decision on its conclusion, in which it also acknowledged Parliament's contribution in the form a resolution that the latter had adopted already in 2007.[41] The conclusion procedure on the level of the Union proceeded quite swiftly despite the fact that the agreement posed some political problems.[42] After a positive appraisal in the INTA committee, the plenary gave its consent to the agreement on 17 February 2011 by 465 votes to 128, with 19 abstentions.[43] The agreement was provisionally applied from 1 July 2011, but only entered into force on 13 December 2015 after all Member States completed their ratifications. This process indicated a large degree of consensus among

---

40   Regulation (EU) 2017/2321 of the European Parliament and of the Council of 12 December 2017 amending Regulation (EU) 2016/1036 on protection against dumped imports from countries not members of the European Union and Regulation (EU) 2016/1037 on protection against subsidised imports from countries not members of the European Union (OJ 2017, L1338/1).

41   European Commission, 'Proposal for a Council Decision concluding the Free Trade Agreement between the European Union and its Member States and the Republic of Korea', COM (2010) 137.

42   G. Siles-Brügge (n. 4), p. 97–123.

43   European Parliament legislative resolution of 17 February 2011 on the draft Council decision on the conclusion of the Free Trade Agreement between the European Union and its Member States, of the one part, and the Republic of Korea, of the other part, P7_TA(2011)0063.

policymakers on both the Union and Member State levels about the future of trade policy. It however also demonstrated the cumbersome nature of mixity and the highly impractical divergence between the political and legal points of acceptance of an international agreement, a problem that has been tempered somewhat with the mechanism of provisional application.

Only shortly thereafter, both the European Parliament and national governments encountered a major political controversy in the shape of the Anti-Counterfeiting Trade Agreement (ACTA), which was supposed to establish international standards for intellectual property rights enforcement.[44] The agreement was signed in October 2011 by more than thirty countries, including the European Union and 22 of its Member States. Nevertheless, after an enormous pressure by civil society organisations, mainly on the grounds that ACTA would stifle free speech and endanger access to medicines in developing countries, political opposition gained traction and after a negative vote of five committees, Parliament on 4 July 2012 declined consent to the agreement with 478 votes against, 39 in favour and 165 abstentions.[45] This vote effectively ended the ratification in the European Union, and showed that the European Parliament was able to exercise its role as the premier forum of political debate about trade in the EU and enhance its visibility in this role. The ACTA episode was nevertheless an exception from a political standpoint, as Parliament was in subsequent years generally highly supportive of the Commission's efforts to proceed with negotiations of comprehensive bilateral trade agreements with a number of countries including Peru/Columbia, Singapore, Vietnam, Japan, Canada and others.

The special case in this respect were of course the (by now notorious) TTIP negotiations with the United States of America, which took place between 2013 and 2016. The negotiations were special not only because of the paramount importance of the United States as the biggest trading partner of the Union, but also due to the complex and multifaceted nature of the legal relationship that was to be established. Parliament devoted enormous attention to these

---

44   European Commission, Proposal for a Council Decision on the conclusion of the Anti-Counterfeiting Trade Agreement between the European Union and its Member States, Australia, Canada, Japan, the Republic of Korea, the United Mexican States, the Kingdom of Morocco, New Zealand, the Republic of Singapore, the Swiss Confederation and the United States of America, COM (2011) 380.

45   European Parliament legislative resolution of 4 July 2012 on the draft Council decision on the conclusion of the Anti-Counterfeiting Trade Agreement between the European Union and its Member States, Australia, Canada, Japan, the Republic of Korea, the United Mexican States, the Kingdom of Morocco, New Zealand, the Republic of Singapore, the Swiss Confederation and the United States of America, P7_TA(2012)0287.

negotiations and closely followed them at every step, with regular exchanges of views with Commission negotiators. As public protests and intense mobilisation of civil society organisations against TTIP took place, Parliament reflected the main concerns in its positions and its key resolution, especially as regards the most controversial topics, especially services of general interest, regulatory cooperation, food standards, geographical indications, data protection and the protection of the cultural sector.[46] The most controversial issue, investment protection, was the one where Parliament's influence had the most obvious repercussions. Faced with hostility among large segments of the public, and with Parliament's demand that the mechanism of investor-state dispute settlement be reformed, the Commission finally adjusted its investment protection policy. Only two months after Parliament's resolution, it proposed the "Investment Court System",[47] based on the idea of a permanent judicial body with permanent judges and an appellate panel.[48] The new system, which would be included in all new bilateral free trade agreements with investment chapters, was designed to allow adjudication of investment protection claims in an impartial and fully independent manner, by making more explicit the *right to regulate* of public authorities. Moreover, the Commission agreed to seek a comprehensive solution to the problem of legitimacy of investment protection mechanisms by negotiating an international agreement that would institute a multilateral investment court. The reform of the investor-state dispute settlement system and the modification of the Union's trade negotiation strategy in this domain is arguably Parliament's most significant success in the shaping of the Common Commercial Policy in the post-Lisbon period.

Given that the TTIP talks were suspended in the beginning of 2017, Parliament did not get an opportunity to formally take a position on its conclusion, and after this juncture, public controversy about TTIP in particular and the Union's trade policy in general also calmed down. Nevertheless, negotiations did continue with the other transatlantic partner. In late 2016 the Commission was thus able to propose the signature of the Comprehensive Economic and Trade Agreement between the European Union and Canada (CETA), in which the investment dispute resolution method was modified and replaced with the Investment Court System. The signature process however led to a severe

---

46   European Parliament Resolution of 8 July 2015 containing the European Parliament's recommendations to the European Commission on the negotiations for the Transatlantic Trade and Investment Partnership (TTIP), P8_TA(2015)0252.

47   European Commission, Commission draft text TTIP - investment, 16 September 2015.

48   On the Investment Court System, see also the contributions by C. Brown; and G. Van der Loo and M. Hahn in this volume.

political crisis because Belgium, alone among the Member States, could not agree to CETA and in particular to the Investment Court System as proposed, due to the misgivings expressed by its region of Wallonia. A difficult compromise was reached, including a demand to request an opinion from the Court of Justice, and the Council decision on signature was eventually adopted. Only a few months later, on 15 February 2017, the European Parliament was able to give its consent to the conclusion with broad support, which is perhaps somewhat surprising considering the many controversies that surrounded transatlantic trade negotiations.[49] At this time, CETA is provisionally applied and the Investment Court System is not yet operational, so the full implications of CETA are not yet known. What is clear from the CETA signature story is that the Parliament did not appear to have played a major role in the public debate in the crucial moments, and that it was not accepted as the key legitimating institution by the Member States. This is the unfortunate consequence of *mixity*, though the good news is that this problem at least should appear much less frequently after Opinion 2/15, given that trade agreements without an investment protection chapter will henceforth be approved by the European Parliament and not the parliaments of the Member States. Moreover, it must be noted that the crucial element of the CETA compromise, a request for an Opinion of the Court of Justice on the legality of the Investment Court System, has led to Opinion 1/17, in which the Court concluded that investment protection as designed in CETA was indeed legal from the point of view of the Treaties.[50] Interestingly, as the matter is very controversial politically among the political groups, Parliament decided not to submit observations in these proceedings.

In addition to its political role in the legislative process and in the scrutiny and conclusion of international trade agreements, Parliament has also used litigation as a means of reinforcing its views, in particular in the form of intervention in cases before the Court of Justice with important institutional implications. The most important in this regard was the question of Union competence for trade matters, which evolved over a long period and reached its culmination in Opinion 2/15, where the Parliament submitted observations in support of exclusive Union competence as the only actor supporting the Commission's claims.[51] This is significant because no less than 24 Member States supported

49 European Parliament legislative resolution of 15 February 2017 on the draft Council decision on the conclusion of the Comprehensive Economic and Trade Agreement (CETA) between Canada, of the one part, and the European Union and its Member States, of the other part, P8_TA(2017)0030.

50 On this issue, see the contribution by G. Van der Loo and M. Hahn in this volume.

51 On Opinion 2/15, see also the contributions by M. Cremona and A. Rosas in this volume.

the Council's opposing view that the competence for the conclusion of the Free Trade Agreement between the European Union and Singapore was shared, and that therefore the agreement was mixed.[52] Parliament's institutional position in this context was understandable for the simple reason that the weight of the consent procedure on the level of the Union is much greater if no further national ratifications are necessary. Parliament in fact intervened on several prior occasions in support of the Commission to assert exclusive Union competence, notably in the *Conditional Access Services* case and the *Lisbon Agreement* case.[53] The surprisingly high number of Member States that argued against exclusive competence in Opinion 2/15 however indicated that many governments of the Member States still do not see the European Parliament as the institution that expresses the viewpoints of European citizens, and accord that role to themselves.

Parliament also participated in a number of other proceedings raising important systemic issues for trade law. A case in point is the *Rusal Armenal* case against anti-dumping measures, which raised the question of the possibility to challenge the legality of norms of Union law in the light of the provisions of WTO agreements. In the appeal procedure against the judgment of the General Court,[54] Parliament intervened in support of the Commission to defend the view that under the circumstances of the case, the WTO Anti-Dumping Agreement could not be invoked against measures adopted by the Union institutions. It should be noted that this was a case where all three main Union institutions took the same view, so it is perhaps not surprising that the Court of Justice ultimately considered that it was not possible to invoke norms of WTO law in situations such as the one under review, because the relevant provisions of Union's anti-dumping law were not intended to ensure the implementation, in the Union legal order, of a particular obligation in WTO law. The Parliament's position here was motivated principally by the concern that extending the direct effect to WTO law provisions in such a way would render important parts of Union legislation on trade defence mechanism difficult or even impossible to apply.

4   Conclusion

The development of interinstitutional balance in the first decade after the entry into force of the Treaty of Lisbon reveals that both in procedural and

---

52   Opinion 2/15, *Free Trade Agreement between the European Union and the Republic of Singapore*, EU:C:2017:376.

53   Case C-137/12, *Commission v Council*, EU:C:2013:675; Case C-389/15, *Commission v Council*, EU:C:2017:79.

54   Case C-21/14 P, *Commission v Rusal Armenal ZAO*, EU:C:2015:494.

substantive terms, the European Parliament has adapted well to its new prerogatives, without placing a substantial burden on the decisional process or disrupting the operation of the Common Commercial Policy formulated by its institutional counterparts. It has also improved the visibility of policy issues and political controversies about international trade while ensuring a heightened degree of transparency. The Parliament has not diverted the main policy orientations expressed by the Commission and Council, and contributed to Union legislation and the shaping of trade agreements in a responsible fashion, by taking into account the lively public debate about the scope and possible effects of trade rules in the modern economy. The most important policy change achieved was the replacement of the investor-state dispute settlement mechanism hitherto advocated by the Commission by the Investment Court System. However, the political disputes surrounding the negotiation of transatlantic trade agreements and the structure of the legal dispute over Union competences have demonstrated that even after ten years of decision-making in the trade field, the Parliament is still not fully acknowledged as the legitimising institution. Moreover, in the light of the dramatically changing political landscape in many Member States, it remains to be seen whether in the future the Parliament's positions on trade will remain as constructive as they have been so far.

CHAPTER 25

Provisional Application of EU Free Trade Agreements

Joni Heliskoski

1 Introduction

Comprehensive free trade agreements (FTA s)[1] between the European Union (EU) and third countries are usually concluded as mixed agreements, that is, agreements the contracting parties to which include not only the EU in its own right but also the Member States in their individual capacity. This means that the definitive entry into force of such agreements requires, in addition to the completion of appropriate Union procedures, their ratification by the Member States in accordance with their respective constitutional procedures. As this usually takes several years from the signature of an agreement, the parties often have recourse to the technique of *provisional application of treaties*[2] in order to give immediate effect to all or some of the provisions of an agreement

---

[1] For purposes of the present analysis the notion of an FTA covers cooperation, partnership, trade or other such agreements concluded by EU on the basis of Art. 207 TFEU (alone or in conjunction with other legal bases) as well as association agreements concluded on the basis of Art. 217 TFEU. For the difficulties of adopting pre-conceived typologies of EU's external agreements, see M. Maresceau, 'A Typology of Mixed Bilateral Agreements', in C. Hillion, P. Koutrakos (eds.), *Mixed Agreements Revisited* (Hart, 2010), p. 11–17.

[2] See Art. 25 of the Vienna Convention on the Law of Treaties (VCLT) and Art. 25 of the Vienna Convention on the Law of Treaties between States and International Organizations or between International Organizations (VCLTIO). Since 2012, the provisional application of treaties has been included in the work programme of the International Law Commission (ILC). At its seventieth session in 2018, the ILC adopted, based on five reports of the Special Rapporteur Mr. Juan Manuel Gómez Robledo, draft guidelines on the provisional application of treaties with commentaries, as the draft *Guide to the Provisional Application of Treaties*, on first reading (see *Report of the International Law Commission*, Seventieth Session (30 April-1 June and 2 July-10 August 2018), Official Records of the General Assembly, Seventy-third Session, Supplement No. 10, UN doc A/73/10, para. 79–90). The EU has also contributed as an observer to the work of the Commission and the addendum to the *Fourth report* by the Special Rapporteur (UN doc A/CN.4//699/Add.1 (23 June 2016)) contains examples of recent EU practice on provisional application agreements with third States. An addendum to its *Fifth report* (UN doc A/CN.4/718/Add.1 (21 June 2018)) contains a selected bibliography on the topic.

prior to the completion of the constitutional requirements for its definitive entry into force. The technique has acquired considerable significance in practice: since the entry into force of the Treaty of Lisbon, *all* FTA s signed by the EU and its Member States have been applied provisionally, as a whole or in part, by the Union (and, in one case, Member States) pending their conclusion and ratification. At the time of writing, this practice consists of the following FTA s:

Agreement	EU legal basis of provisional application	Signature	Date of Provisional application EU and MS*	Entry into force
Framework Agreement between the EU and its Member States, on the one part, and the Republic of Korea, on the other part (Korea FA)[a]	207, 212 TFEU	10/05/2010	10/5/2010 03/02/2011 (ES)* 16/3/2011 (SK)* 05/03/ 2014 (FI)* DE declaration*	01/06/ 2014
Free Trade Agreement between the EU and its Member States, of the one part, and the Republic of Korea (Korea FTA)[b]	91, 100(2), 167(3), 207 TFEU	06/10/2010	01/07/2011	13/12/ 2015
Partnership and Cooperation Agreement between the EU and its Member States, of the one part, and the Republic of Iraq (Iraq PCA)[c]	79(3), 91 and 100, 192(1), 194, 207, 209 TFEU	11/05/2012	01/08/2012	-
Trade Agreement between the EU and its Member States, of the one part, and Colombia and Peru, of the other part (TA/ Colombia & Peru)[d]	91, 100(2), first subparagraph of 207(4) TFEU	26/06/2012	01/03/2013 (EU-Peru); 01/08/2013 (EU-Colombia)	-

Agreement	EU legal basis of provisional application	Signature	Date of Provisional application EU and MS*	Entry into force
Agreement establishing an Association between the EU and its Member States, on the one hand, and Central America on the other (Central America AA)[e]	217 TFEU	29/06/2012	01/08/2013 (Honduras, Nicaragua and Panama); 01/10/2013 (Costa Rica and El Salvador); 01/12/2013 (Guatemala)	-
Association Agreement between the EU and the EAEC and their Member States, of the one part, and Georgia, of the other part (Georgia AA)[f]	37, 31(1) TEU 217 TFEU	27/06/2014	01/09/2014	-
Association Agreement between the EU and the EAEC and their Member States, of the one part, and the Republic of Moldova, of the other part (Moldova AA)[g]	37, 31(1) TEU 217 TFEU	27/06/2014	01/09/2014	-
Association Agreement between the EU and the EAEC and their Member States, of the one part, and Ukraine, of the other part (Ukraine AA)[h]	37, 31(1) TEU, 217 TFEU 217, 79(2)(b) TFEU	21/03/2014, 27/06/2014	01/11/2014 01/01/2016	01/09/2017

Agreement	EU legal basis of provisional application	Signature	Date of Provisional application EU and MS*	Entry into force
Enhanced Partnership and Cooperation Agreement between the EU and its Member States, of the one part, and the Republic of Kazakhstan, of the other part (Kazakhstan EPCA)[i]	37, 31(1) TEU 91, 100(2), 207, 209 TFEU	21/12/2015	01/05/2016	-
Economic Partnership Agreement between the EU and its Member States, of the one part, and the SADC EPA States, of the other part (SADC EPA States EPA)[j]	207(3) and (4), 209(2) TFEU	10/06/2016	10/10/16 (Botswana, Lesotho, Namibia, Swaziland, South Africa); 04/02/2018 (Mozambique)	-
Framework Agreement between the EU and its Member States, of the one part, and Australia, of the other part (Australia FA)[k]	207, 212(1) TFEU	07/08/2017	-	-
Partnership Agreement on Relations and Cooperation between the EU and its Member States, of the one part, and New Zealand, of the other part (New Zealand PARC)[l]	207, 212(1) TFEU	05/10/2016	12/01/2017	-

Agreement	EU legal basis of provisional application	Signature	Date of Provisional application EU and MS*	Entry into force
Comprehensive Economic and Trade Agreement (CETA) between Canada, of the one part, and the EU and its Member States, of the other part (Canada CETA)[m]	43(2), 91, Article 100(2), 153(2), 192(1) and the first subparagraph of 207(4) TFEU	30/10/2016	21/09/2017	-
Political Dialogue and Cooperation Agreement between the EU and its Member States, of the one part, and the Republic of Cuba, of the other part (Cuba PDCA)[n]	37, 31(1) TEU 207, 209 TFEU	12/12/2016	01/11/2017	-
Cooperation Agreement on Partnership and Development between the EU and its Member States, of the one part, and the Islamic Republic of Afghanistan (Afghanistan CAPD)[o]	37 TEU 207, 209 TFEU	18/02/2017	01/12/2017	-
Comprehensive and Enhanced Partnership Agreement between the EU and the EAEC and their Member States, of the one part, and the Republic of Armenia, of the other part (Armenia CEPA)[p]	37 TEU 91, 100(2), 207, 209 TFEU	24/11/2017	-	-

[a] For text, see OJ 2013, L20/2.

[b] For text, see OJ 2011, L127/6.

[c] For text, see OJ 2012, L204/20.

[d] For text, see OJ 2012, L354/3.

[e] For text, see OJ 2012, L346/3.

[f] For text, see OJ 2014, L261/4.

[g] For text, see OJ 2014, L260/4.

[h] For text, see OJ 2014, L161/3.

[i] For text, see OJ 2016, L29/3.

[j] For text, see OJ 2016, L250/3.

[k] For text, see OJ 2017, L237/7.

[l] For text, see OJ 2016, L321/3.

[m] For text, see OJ 2017, L11/23.

[n] For text, see OJ 2016, L337 I/3.

[o] For text, see OJ 2017, L67/3.

[p] For text, see OJ 2018, L23/4.

The purpose of this chapter is to address some of the central legal issues related to provisional application of the EU's FTAs based on the actual practice relating to such agreements. The chapter opens with a brief account of EU law relating to the legal basis of provisional application of international agreements as well as the status of agreements provisionally applied by the EU (2). Next, the chapter explores the central issue of the defining of the scope of provisional application of FTAs in relation to both the question of the various legal techniques applied for this purpose in practice and the choice of the substantive fields that are either included in – or left outside of – the scope of provisional application (3). The chapter then discusses the question of the termination of provisional application, notably in the light of a refusal by a Member State to ratify an agreement that the EU applies provisionally (4). Finally, the chapter concludes by way of an overall assessment of the practice of provisional application of FTAs (5).

2 The Legal Basis and Effects of Provisional Application by the EU and the Member States

In its original form, the Treaty establishing the European Community did not contain any express provisions on the possibility of provisional application of international agreements between the Community and third countries. By virtue of the Treaty of Amsterdam, a specific legal basis providing for the authorisation of provisional application of such agreements was inserted in paragraph 2 of Article 228 TEC. The decision on provisional application was to

be taken by the Council, acting, as a rule, by a qualified majority[3] on a proposal
from the Commission. While no consultation or assent of the European Parliament was required, the Parliament was to be "immediately and fully" informed
on a decision concerning provisional application of an agreement by the Community. One purpose of this Treaty change was to remove the need to enter
into so-called "interim agreements" whereby the trade provisions of certain
association or cooperation agreements could be brought into force in advance
of their other provisions – the principal agreement having been concluded as a
mixed agreement, the entry into force of which required the ratification by the
Member States.[4] Because of the Treaty change, it became possible to decide by

---

3   The Council was to act unanimously when the agreement covered a field for which unanimi-
    ty is required for the adoption of internal rules and for association agreements referred to in
    Art. 310 TEC.
4   A. Dashwood, 'External Relations Provisions of the Amsterdam Treaty', *Common Market Law
    Review* 35 (1998), p. 1019–1024. Prior to the entry into force of the Amsterdam Treaty decisions
    on provisional application of trade agreements by the European Community were based on
    paragraph 2 of Art. 228 EC governing the conclusion of international agreements. In that
    regard, it may be noted that the first sentence of the first subparagraph of paragraph 3 of Art.
    228 TEC did not provide for the consultation of the European Parliament for trade agree-
    ments concluded on the basis of paragraph 3 of Article 113 TEC on the Common Commercial
    Policy. In trade policy, however, the technique of provisional application of international
    agreements was mainly used in relation to (bilateral) agreements on textile products or ag-
    ricultural products, or for the purposes of (multilateral) commodities agreements drawn up
    under the auspices of the United Nations Conference on Trade and Development (UNCTAD).
    With regard to bilaterally-structured cooperation or association agreements of a mixed na-
    ture, a more common technique for speeding up the entry into force of some their provisions
    was to conclude an "interim agreement" between the EC and the given third country covering
    those provisions of the cooperation or association agreement that were deemed to fall within
    the scope of application of Article 113 TEC. Such interim agreements preceded, for instance,
    the Europe Agreements concluded with countries of Central and Eastern Europe (for text,
    see OJ 1992, L114/2 (Poland), OJ 1992, L115/2 (the Czech and Slovak Federal Republic), OJ 1992,
    L116/2 (Hungary), OJ 1993, L81/2 (Romania), OJ 1993, L323/2 (Bulgaria) and OJ 1996, L344/3),
    the Agreement on Cooperation and Customs Union with the Republic of San Marino (OJ
    1992, L359/14), the Partnership and Cooperation Agreements with the Russian Federation
    (OJ 1995, L247/2), Ukraine (OJ 1995, L311/2), Moldova (OJ 1996, L40/11), Kazakhstan (OJ 1996,
    L147/2), Georgia (OJ 1997, L129/23), Armenia (OJ 1997, L129/3), the Kyrgyz Republic (OJ 1997,
    L235/3), Uzbekistan (OJ 1998, L43/2) and Azerbaijan (OJ 1998, L285/2), respectively, as well
    as the Euro-Mediterranean Agreement with Israel (OJ 1996, L71/2). While that practice was
    also followed after the entry into force the Amsterdam Treaty, the technique of provisional
    application of trade and trade related provisions of cooperation or association agreements
    also started to gain ground. See, e.g., Agreement in the form of an Exchange of Letters con-
    cerning the provisional application of the trade and trade-related provisions of the Euro-
    Mediterranean Agreement establishing an Association between the European Communities
    and their Member States, of the one part, and the Arab Republic of Egypt, of the other part
    (OJ 2003, L345/115) and Council Decision 2008/805/EC of 15 July 2008 on the signature and

means of a more simplified procedure on the provisional application of trade and other agreements on behalf of the Union pending their ratification by the Member States.

The provisions of Article 228 TEC are now included in paragraphs 5, 8 and 10 of Article 218 TFEU, with certain changes to the structure and drafting. The Council, acting by either a qualified majority or unanimity[5] on a proposal by the negotiator, shall take the decision on the provisional application. The European Parliament shall be *"immediately and fully informed at all stages of the procedure"*. As the only change to the substance in comparison with Article 228 TEC, paragraph 5 of Article 218 TFEU authorises the Council to decide on the provisional application *"if necessary"*. It is unclear what precisely constitutes the necessity required by the provision concerned, as there is no case law on the issue. In the case of FTAs to be concluded by both the EU and its Member States, however, it has become a common practice[6] to decide on the provisional application in order to enable their entry into force on a provisional basis pending the conclusion and ratification of the agreement by the Union and all of its Member States.[7] This should be considered a legitimate objective that may be served by a decision on the provisional application of an FTA.

An issue that has proven much more contentious in the practice of the institutions is the role of the European Parliament in the decision-making of the institutions on the provisional application of international agreements.[8] While

provisional application of the Economic Partnership Agreement between the CARIFORUM States, of the one part, and the European Community and its Member States, of the other part (OJ 2008, L 289/1). On the comparison between the technique provisional application of treaties and the conclusion of interim agreements, see I. Smyth, 'Mixity in Practice – A Member State Practitioner's Perspective', in C. Hillion, P. Koutrakos (eds.) (n. 1), p. 304 and 313–5.

5 According to Art. 218 (8), second subpara. TFEU the Council shall act unanimously, *inter alia*, when the agreement covers a field for which unanimity is required for the adoption of a Union act as well as for association agreements and the agreements referred to in Art. 212 TFEU with the States which are candidates for accession.

6 However, there are also recent bilateral mixed FTAs that do not provide for provisional application. See, e.g., the Framework Agreement on Comprehensive Partnership and Cooperation between the European Union and its Member States, of the one part, and the Socialist Republic of Vietnam, of the other part (for text, see OJ 2016, L 329/8); the Framework Agreement on Partnership and Cooperation between the European Union and its Member States, of the one part, and Mongolia, of the other part (OJ 2017, L 326/7) and the Framework Agreement on Partnership and Cooperation between the European Union and its Member States, of the one part, and the Republic of the Philippines, of the other part (OJ 2017, L 343/3).

7 In most cases, FTAs enter into force on the first day of the second month following the date of deposit of the *last* instrument of ratification or approval.

8 See D. Thym, 'Parliamentary Involvement in European International Relations', in M. Cremona, B. de Witte (eds.), *EU Foreign Relations Law* (Hart, 2008), p. 211–2.

paragraph 10 of Article 218 TFEU only requires the Parliament to be *"immediately and fully informed at all stages of the procedure"* other than the conclusion of an agreement, the Parliament has taken the view that, as a rule, the Council should not decide on the provisional application before the Parliament has given its consent to the conclusion of the agreement. The Council, on the other hand, is of the opinion that it has a broad discretion to decide on this matter in the light of the political context of a given agreement.[9] In the case of certain FTAs, the practice has been to postpone the start of the provisional application until the European Parliament has given its consent to the conclusion of the agreement.[10] The Council has however insisted that there is no obligation under Article 218 TFEU to do so, and the practice has been rather diverse.[11]

As regards the *status and legal effects* of international agreements in the EU legal order, paragraph 2 of Article 216 TFEU provides that agreements *concluded* by the Union are binding upon the institutions of the Union and on its Member States. According to the settled case law of the Court of Justice, such agreements become an integral part of the EU legal order from the date of their entry into force. They have primacy over secondary EU legislation, which must be interpreted as far as possible in accordance with those agreements.[12] However, the

---

9   See C. Kaddous, N. Piçarra, *General Report for Topic 3* (*'The External Dimension of the EU policies'*) for the XXVIII Fide Congress (2018), p. 18. The question of the involvement of the European Parliament in the decision-making on provisional application of international agreements is currently being discussed by the institutions in the context of the implementation of the Inter-institutional Agreement between the European Parliament, the Council of the European Union and the European Commission on Better Law-Making (OJ 2016, L 123/1).

10   See G. Van der Loo, 'Less is more? The role of national parliaments in the conclusion of mixed (trade) agreements', Asser Institute, Centre for the Law of EU External Relations (CLEER), CLEER Paper 1/2018, p. 27–8 and R. Passos 'Some Issues Related to the Provisional Application of International Agreements and the Institutional Balance', in J. Czuczai, F. Naert (eds.), *The EU as a Global Actor- Bridging Legal Theory and Practice. Liber Amicorum in Honour of Ricardo Gosalbo Bono* (Brill Nijhoff, 2017), p. 380–393.

11   The EU has started to apply an agreement provisionally *before* obtaining of the consent of the European Parliament to its conclusion in the case of the Korea FA (for the Council decision, see OJ 2013, L20/1), the Iraq PCA (OJ 2012, L204/18), the AAs with Georgia (OJ 2014, L261/1) and Moldova (OJ 2014, L260/1), the Kazakhstan EPCA (OJ 2016, L29/1), the New Zealand PARC (OJ 2016, L321/1), the Afghanistan CAPD (OJ 2017, L67/1) and the Armenia CEPA (OJ 2018, L23/1). However, the provisional application of the agreement began only *after* the Parliament gave its consent in the case of the Korea FTA (for the Council decision, see OJ 2011, L127/1), the Peru & Colombia TA (OJ 2012, L354/1), the Central America AA (OJ 2012, L346/1), the Ukraine AA (OJ 2014, L161/1 and L278/1), the SADC EPA States EPA (OJ 2016, L250/1), the Canada CETA (OJ 2017, L11/1080) and the Cuba PDCA (OJ 2016, L337I/1).

12   See, e.g. Case C-15/17, *Bosphorus Queen Shipping*, EU:C:2018:557, para. 44.

Treaties do not contain any provision governing the status and effects in EU law of an international agreement the Union has decided to apply provisionally pursuant to paragraph 5 of Article 218 TFEU, nor has the Court of Justice ever directly addressed the issue. It is however arguable that, in principle, the status and legal effects of an agreement applied provisionally by the Union are similar to those attributed by paragraph 2 of Article 216 TFEU to an agreement concluded by the Union. First, as a matter of international law, provisional application produces legal effects as if the treaty were actually in force and the obligations arising therefrom must be performed under the *pacta sunt servanda* principle.[13] Secondly, such an interpretation would seem to follow from the Court's judgment in *International Fruit Company* concerning the General Agreement on Tariffs and Trade (GATT). While the GATT never formally entered into force, but was applicable on a provisional basis by the contracting parties, including all the Member States of the European Community (without the Community), the Court held that the GATT was binding on the Community on a similar basis as agreements concluded by the Community.[14] The same should *a fortiori* be the case with agreements that the Union in its own right has decided to apply provisionally pursuant to paragraph Article 218(5) TFEU. On the above grounds, therefore, one may conclude that such agreements become an integral part of Union law and have similar legal effects as agreements concluded by the Union.

As regards the legal basis for provisional application of international agreements by *the Member States*, one must only acknowledge that any detailed analysis of the question would clearly exceed the scope of the present study. Suffice it to note that constitutions of Member States take different views as to provisional application of international agreements. There are Member States in which the constitution or the legal system prohibits provisional application (e.g. Cyprus, Italy, Luxembourg and Portugal). In some other Member States,

---

13   See *Fourth report on the provisional application of treaties* by Juan Manuel Gómez-Robledo, Special Rapporteur of the International Law Commission (UN doc A/CN.4/699 (23 June 2016)), para. 87 and Guideline 6 (Legal effect of provisional application) of the draft Guide to the Provisional Application of Treaties (n. 3) adopted by the ILC on first reading, providing that "[t]*he provisional application of a treaty or a part of a treaty produces a legally binding obligation to apply the treaty or a part thereof* as if the treaty were in force [...] *unless the treaty provides otherwise of it is otherwise agreed*" (emphasis added). However, as the commentary (para. 5) explains, provisional application of treaties remains different from their entry into force, insofar as it is not subject to all rules of the law treaties.

14   Joined Cases 21/72 to 24/72, *International Fruit Company and Others*, EU:C:1972:115, para. 18. See also Opinion of AG Darmon in Case C-241/07, *Maclaine Watson & Company Limited v Council and Commission*, EU:C:1989:229, where the AG treats the Sixth International Tin Agreement, provisionally applied by the European Community, as one "concluded" by the Community (para. 110).

provisional application is subject to the same procedure as is followed for the ratification of a treaty (e.g. Austria, the Czech Republic, Finland and Germany). There are also Member States that either permit provisional application in exceptional circumstances (e.g. Belgium, France and Greece) or allow it subject to certain conditions (e.g. Denmark, Lithuania, The Netherlands, Slovenia, Sweden and the United Kingdom). Finally, some Member States allow provisional application either generally (e.g. Spain) or as a matter of uncodified practice (e.g. Hungary and Romania).[15] At the same time, the question of provisional application of international agreements by Member States is not as important from the point of view of the practice concerning the provisional application of EU FTAs. In most cases, the agreement only provides for the provisional application thereof by *the European Union* (and the third State concerned)[16] and there has been only one post-Lisbon FTA that (some) EU Member States have actually applied provisionally alongside with the Union.[17]

3   The Definition of the Scope of Provisional Application of EU FTAS

3.1   *Preliminary Considerations*

A question that arises specifically in the context of provisional application of international agreements that are to be concluded by the EU and its Member States on the one hand and a third State (or States) on the other hand concerns the definition or identification of the provisions of the agreement that are subject to the provisional application. As a matter of *international law*, the parties to a treaty are, in principle, free to define the scope of the provisional application.[18] As a matter of *EU law*, however, the decision on the provisional

---

15 See *Third report on the provisional application of treaties* by Juan Manuel Gómez-Robledo, Special Rapporteur of the International Law Commission, UN doc A/CN.4/687 (5 June 2015), para. 19 and 25.

16 Some FTAs however provide for their provisional application by either *"the Parties"* (e.g. the Korea FA, the Peru & Colombia TA, Canada CETA) or *"the EU Party"* (and the third State concerned) (e.g. the Korea FTA). As regards agreements providing for provisional application by *"the Parties"*, it may be noted that this term is usually defined as meaning *"on the one hand, the European Union or its Member States or the European Union and its Member States within their respective areas of competence as derived from the [TEU] and the [TFEU] (the "EU Party"), and on the other hand, [the third State concerned]"*.

17 This was the case for the Korea FA, which the EU as well as Finland, Slovakia and Spain applied provisionally.

18 See Art. 25 of the VCLT and para. 3 of the commentary to Draft Art 22 on the Law of Treaties, *Yearbook of the International Law Commission* 1966, Vol II, UN doc A/CN.4/SER.A/1966/Add.l.

application of an international agreement on behalf of the EU must respect the principle of conferral articulated in Article 5(2) TEU. Under that principle, the Union shall act only within the limits of the competences conferred upon it by the Member States in the Treaties to attain the objectives set out therein. This means that the Union may only agree to provisional application of an international agreement to the extent that the provisions of the agreement subject to the provisional application on behalf of the Union fall within the Union's competence.[19] Indeed, the main rationale of provisional application of international agreements by the Union is to enable more timely application of those provisions of the agreement that are deemed not to fall within the competence of the Member States and that are, accordingly, not required to be ratified by the Member States.

The above considerations then give rise to two questions that are central for the analysis of the practice of provisional application of EU FTAs. The first concerns the *legal techniques* by means of which the scope of the provisional application of FTAs by the EU (and, as the case may be, Member States) is defined in practice (3.2). The second relates to the practice concerning the identification of the *substantive parts* of FTAs that are either included in or excluded from the scope of preliminary application (3.3).

3.2   The Techniques of Defining the Scope of Provisional Application

In the light of the actual practice concerning provisional application of EU FTAs, the following techniques for defining the scope of application of an agreement have been used:

3.2.1   Provisional Application of the Entire Agreement by the EU and Its Member States

Article 49(2) of the Korea FA provides as follows:

> *Notwithstanding paragraph 1, this Agreement shall be applied on a provisional basis pending its entry into force. The provisional application begins*

---

19   As the Court of Justice has explained in the context of a decision of the Council and the Representatives of the Governments of the Member States meeting within the Council on the provisional application of an international agreement, the Union and the Member States "[...] *must act within the framework of the competences which [they have] while respecting the competences of any other contracting party*" (Case C-28/12, *Commission v Council*, EU:C:2015:282, para. 47. See G. Van der Loo & R. Wessel, 'The Non-ratification of Mixed Agreements: Legal Consequences and Solutions', *Common Market Law Review 54* (2017), p. 754.

on the first day of the first month following the date on which the Parties
have notified each other of the completion of the necessary procedures.

Article 2 of Council Decision 2013/40/EU of 10 May 2010 on the signing, on
behalf of the European Union, and provisional application of the Agreement[20]
provides as follows: *"Pending the completion of the necessary procedures for its*
entry into force, the Agreement *shall be applied on a provisional basis [...]".*[21]
While the agreement was negotiated and concluded as a mixed agreement –
and, thus, on the assumption that it falls in part within the competence of the
Union and in part within that of the Member States – the Council Decision
appears to cover the entire agreement and to imply that the agreement in its
entirety is provisionally applied by *the Union*. This however does not seem to
have been the intention of the Union and its Member States. First, while Article 1 of the Decision refers to the approval of the signing of the Agreement
"on behalf of the Union", Article 2 thereof states that *"the Agreement shall be*
applied on a provisional basis", with no reference to the provisional application
being limited to the Union in its own right. Secondly, three Member States also
deposited notifications of their intention to apply the Agreement on a provisional basis.[22] Thirdly, one Member State (Germany) declared, with regard
to Article 47(2) of the Agreement, that *"[...] it can apply the Agreement on a*
provisional basis only in accordance with its national law"[23]. It therefore seems
that the intention of the Member States, articulated in Article 2 of the Council
Decision, was to apply the Agreement on a provisional basis by both the Union
and its Member States, without however spelling out which parts of the Agreement are be to applied by the Union and which parts by the Member States.
In that sense, the Decision could be regarded as an act of a *concealed hybrid*
character, adopted jointly by the Council exercising not only Union competence but also, and on the basis of an *authorisation* from the Representatives
of the Governments of the Member States meeting within the Council, that
of the Member States. If the construction of the Council exercising Member
State competence is not accepted, the only alternative would be to argue that
the exercise of Union competence covers the entire agreement. This would
however be at odds with both the mixed nature of the agreement as well as the

---

20   For the text of the Council decision, see OJ 2013, L 20/1.
21   Emphasis added.
22   Spain, Slovakia and Finland(see n. 17).
23   See Declaration/Statement by Germany with regard to the EU-Korea FA, to consult
      at: https://www.consilium.europa.eu/en/documents-publications/treaties-agreements/
      ratification/?id=2010020&partyid=D&doclanguage=en.

notifications concerning provisional applications submitted by certain Member States. Be that as it may, it now follows from the judgment in *Commission v Council*[24] that such a procedure merging of a Union act and an act of the Member States is contrary to Article 13(2) TEU and Article 218 TFEU, at least if no distinction is made between the elements falling within Union and Member State competence. This approach has not been applied in respect of the provisional application of any other post-Lisbon FTA.

3.2.2   Partial Provisional Application of the Agreement by the EU, with an Express Definition in the Agreement and in the Decision of the Council, Possibly Together with a Caveat on the Scope of the Union's Competence

The other post-Lisbon FTAs have been subject to provisional application only by *the Union* on the one hand and the third State (or States) concerned on the other hand, without the participation of the Member States. In that regard, the first principal variant has involved partial provisional application of the agreement by the EU, with an express definition of the parts of the agreement that are subject to the provisional application both in the agreement and in the decision of the Council on the provisional application of the agreement by the Union. As will be seen in the following, the decision of the Council (or, exceptionally, the agreement) may also have included a caveat purporting to limit the scope of the provisional application to those elements of the agreement that fall within the competence of the Union.

By means of this technique, the agreement may *positively enumerate* the provisions that are subject to the provisional application. For instance, Article 117(1) of the Iraq PCA provides that "[...] *the Union and Iraq agree to apply Article 2, and Titles II, III and V of this Agreement*". Article 3 of Council Decision 2012/418/EU on the signing and provisional application of certain provisions of the Agreement[25] then provides that "[...] *the Agreement shall be applied provisionally* [...] only in so far as it concerns matters falling within the Union's competence".[26] The Council decision on the provisional application may also authorise provisional application of a more limited scope than the agreement itself. For instance, Article 353(4) of the Central America AA enables the provisional application of Part IV (Trade) of the Agreement by the European Union and each of the Republics of the Central American Party. However, the first paragraph of Article 3 of Council Decision 2012/734/EU on

---

24   Case C-28/12, *Commission v Council* (n. 19).
25   For the text of the Council Decision, see OJ 2012, L 204/18.
26   Emphasis added.

the signing of the Agreement and provisional application of Part IV there-of[27] excludes Article 271 (criminal sanctions relating to the infringement of intellectual property rights) from the scope of the provisional application, presumably on the understanding that that provision does not fall within the EU's competence.[28]

By means of a slightly different variant, the agreement may also *exclude* certain provisions from the scope of the provisional application. Article 113 of the SADC EPA States, for instance, provides as follows (emphasis added):

> 3. *Pending entry into force of this Agreement, the EU and the SADC EPA States agree to apply the provisions of this Agreement* which fall within their respective competences
>
> [...]
>
> 5. *Provisional application of this Agreement between the EU and a Member of SACU shall* exclude *the agricultural market access concessions and the fisheries market access concessions referred to in Article 24(2) and Article 25(1), that are denoted by an asterisk (*) in the tariff schedules as set out in Annexes I and II, until such time as all members of SACU have ratified or provisionally applied this Agreement.*
>
> 6. *Provisional application or entry into force of this Agreement between the EU and a Member of SACU shall exclude the agricultural market access concessions referred to in Article 24(2) and Article 25(1), that are denoted by an asterisk (*) in the tariff schedules as set out in Annexes I and II, until such time as the conditions set out in Article 16 of Protocol 3 are met.*

Article 3 of Council Decision 2016/1623/EU on the signing and provisional application of the Agreement[29] then provides as follows (emphasis added):

> 1. As regards those elements falling within the competence of the Union, *the Agreement shall be applied by the Union on a provisional basis as provided for in Article 113(3) thereof, pending the completion of the procedures for its conclusion. This does not prejudge the allocation of competences between the Union and its Member States in accordance with the Treaties.*

---

27 For text, see OJ 2012, L 346.

28 Given that Council Decision 2012/734/EU does not contain a caveat limiting the scope of the provisional application to matters falling within the Union's competence, the provisional application covers the whole of the remainder of Part IV, that is, the trade provisions of the Agreement.

29 For text, see OJ 2016, L 250.

2. Article 12(4) of the Agreement shall not be provisionally applied *by the Union.*

While the Agreement does not exclude Article 12(4) from the scope of the provisional application, Article 3(2) of Council Decision (2016/1623/EU) appears to indicate that that provision, laying down an obligation of the Member States of the EU to collectively undertake to support certain development cooperation activities, does not fall within the competence of the EU.

3.2.3   Partial Provisional Application of the Agreement by the EU with No Definition in the Agreement but with an Express Definition in the Decision of the Council, Possibly Together with a Caveat on the Scope of the Union's Competence

As the second principal variant, the agreement itself may leave open the scope of the provisional application that is only defined by the Council decision on the provisional application of the agreement on behalf of the Union. Article 330(3) of the Colombia and Peru TA merely provides that *"the Parties may provisionally apply this Agreement fully or partially"*, while Article 3(1) of Council Decision 2012/735/EU on the signing and provisional application of the Agreement[30] then provides that "[t]*he Agreement, with the exception of Articles 2, 202(1), 291 and 292 thereof, shall be applied on a provisional basis by the Union* [...]". The Council Decision in question includes no caveat limiting the provisional application to matters falling within the Union's competence.

In some cases, there is an express provision laying down an obligation upon the Union to notify the other party the provisions that are subject to provisional application. Article 431 of Georgia AA, for instance, provides as follows (emphasis added):

3. *Notwithstanding paragraph 2 of this Article, the Union and Georgia agree to provisionally apply this Agreement in part, as specified by the Union, as set out in paragraph 4 of this Article, and in accordance with their respective internal procedures and legislation as applicable.*

4. *The provisional application shall be effective from the first day of the second month following the date of receipt by the depositary of this Agreement of the following:*

  (*a*) the Union's notification *on the completion of the procedures necessary for this purpose,* indicating the parts of this Agreement that shall be provisionally applied; *and*

  (*b*) *Georgia's deposit of the instrument of ratification in accordance with its procedures and applicable legislation.*

---

30   For text, see OJ 2012, L354/1.

Article 3(1) of Council Decision 2014/494/EU on the signing and provisional application of the Agreement[31] then specifies the provisions of the Agreement that are applied provisionally between the Union and Georgia. However, the provisional application would take effect "[...] *only to the extent that they cover matters falling within the Union's competence, including matters falling within the Union's competence to define and implement a common foreign and security policy*". An essentially similar technique has been used in respect of the Moldova AA, the Kazakhstan EPCA, the Ukraine AA, the Afghanistan CA as well as the Armenia PA.[32]

3.2.4   Partial Provisional Application of the Agreement by the EU (and the Member States) with a Procedure Set out in the Agreement to Define the Scope Thereof

Finally, in some cases, the agreement sets out a procedure the purpose of which is to determine, by a mutual agreement between the Union (and, as the case may be, the Member States) and the given third State, the scope of the provisional application.

In that regard, Article 15.10(5) of the Korea FTA provides as follows (the footnote and emphasis added):

(a)   This Agreement *shall be provisionally applied from the first day of the month following the date on which the EU Party and Korea have notified each other of the completion of their respective relevant procedures.*

(b)   *In the event that certain provisions of this Agreement cannot be provisionally applied,* the Party which cannot undertake such provisional application shall notify the other Party of the provisions which cannot be provisionally applied. *Notwithstanding subparagraph (a), provided the other Party has completed the necessary procedures* and does not object to provisional application within 10 days of the notification that certain provisions cannot be provisionally applied, the provisions of this Agreement which have not been notified shall be provisionally applied *the first day of the month following the notification.*

---

31   For text, see OJ 2014, L261/1.

32   The are some differences in drafting, however. As regards the scope of the provisional application, the Georgia AA, the Moldova AA, the Ukraine AA and the Afghanistan CA refer to "*this Agreement in part, as specified by the Union*" while the Kazakhstan EPCA and the Armenia AA use a more neutral reference to "*this Agreement in whole or in part*".

Article 3(1) of Council Decision 2011/265/EU on the signing and provisional application of the Agreement[33] then specifies the provisions that are not provisionally applied by the Union.[34] While the Member States may also apply the agreement provisionally,[35] this is not the case in practice. Nor does Council Decision 2011/265/EU limit the scope of the provisional application of the Agreement by the EU to matters falling within the Union's competence. An essentially similar procedure is provided for in Article 30(7)(3)(b) of the Canada CETA providing that:

> *If a Party intends not to provisionally apply a provision of this Agreement, it shall first notify the other Party of the provisions that it will not provisionally apply and shall offer to enter into consultations promptly. Within 30 days of the notification, the other Party may either object, in which case this Agreement shall not be provisionally applied, or provide its own notification of equivalent provisions of this Agreement, if any, that it does not intend to provisionally apply. If within 30 days of the second notification, an objection is made by the other Party, this Agreement shall not be provisionally applied.*

Article 1(1) Council Decision 2017/38/EU on the provisional application of the Agreement by the Union[36] then defines the scope provisional application by indicating the provisions that are not applied provisionally by the Union.[37] While the Council Decision does not limit the scope of the provisional application by a reference to the Union's competence, Article 1(1)(d) thereof provides that the provisional application of Chapters 22, 23 and 24 of the Agreement *"shall respect the allocation of competences between the Union and the Member States."*[38] The

---

33 For text, see OJ 2011, L 127/1.

34 It emerges from the notice published in OJ 2011, L 168 that Korea did not object to the provisional application as specified in Council Decision 2011/265/EU.

35 Art 15.10(5)(a) of the Agreement refers to provisional application of the Agreement by *"the EU Party and Korea"* and Art 1.2 defines *"the EU Party"* as *"the European Union or its Member States or the European Union and its Member States within their respective areas of competence as derived from the Treaty on European Union and the Treaty on the Functioning of the European Union"*.

36 For text, see OJ 2017, L 11/1080–1.

37 It emerges from the notice published in OJ 2017, L 238/9 that Canada did not object to the provisional application as specified in Council Decision 2017/38/EU.

38 Chapters 22, 23 and 24 of the Agreement cover trade and sustainable development, trade and labour and trade and environment, respectively.

Agreement is not applied provisionally by Member States even if they were entitled to do so.[39]

Some FTAs appear to contain a procedure for defining the scope of the provisional application by a mutual agreement between the European Union (without the Member States) and the third party concerned. After referring to the indication by the EU of the parts of the Agreement that shall be provisionally applied, Article 86(3), second subparagraph, of the Cuba CA provides for the "confirming", by Cuba, of its "agreement" to the parts of the Agreement thus indicated by the Union. Unlike in the case of the Korea FTA and the Canada CETA, the Agreement does notspell out the consequences of the absence of such a confirmation. Article 3 of Council Decision 2016/2232/EU on the signing and provisional application of the Agreement[40] also includes a caveat providing for the provisional application of certain provisions of the Agreement *"only to the extent that they cover matters falling within the Union's competence, including matters falling within the Union's competence to define and implement a common foreign and security policy"*. In that respect, the arrangement is very similar to that provided for in the Moldova AA, the Kazakhstan EPCA, the Ukraine AA, the Afghanistan CA and the Armenia PA (cf. supra).

Finally, both the Australia FA (Article 61(2)) and the New Zealand PARC (Article 58(2)) refer to the provisional application of *"mutually determined provisions of this Agreement"* by Australia and New Zealand, respectively, and the European Union, without however providing for the procedural steps through which the provisions concerned are defined. As in the case of the Cuba CA, the decisions of the Council on the signing and provisional application of the agreements[41] limit the provisional application to provisions covering matters falling within the Union's competence.

3.2.5   Assessment

An overview of the techniques of defining the scope of provisional application calls for the following observations from the point of view of legal certainty. While the agreement and/or the decision of the Council approving the provisional application on behalf of the Union may identify the parts of the

---

39   Art. 30(7)(3)(a) of the Agreement refers to provisional application of the Agreement by *"the Parties"* and Art. 1(1) defines *"the EU Party"* as *"the European Union or its Member States or the European Union and its Member States within their respective areas of competence as derived from the Treaty on European Union and the Treaty on the Functioning of the European Union"*.

40   For text, see OJ 2016, L 337.

41   Council Decision 2017/1546/EU (OJ, 2017, L 237/5–6) and Council Decision 2016/1970/EU (OJ 2016, L 304/1–2).

agreement that are provisionally applied, the provisional application by the EU is usually subject to a caveat limiting the provisional application to *"matters falling within the Union's competence"*. The only cases in which no such caveat is made by the Union concern either trade agreements (i.e. the Korea FTA, the Colombia and Peru TA and the Canada CETA) or an association agreement the provisional application of which is limited to the trade provisions of the agreement (i.e. the Central America AA). The absence of the caveat is natural, given that trade falls in any event within the Union's exclusive competence in the area of the Common Commercial Policy (Article 207 TFEU).[42] As regards, however, other FTAs, the scope of which extends beyond trade and the Union's CCP, the limitation of the scope of the provisional application in terms of the Union's competence might prove problematic under international law, at least if there is no agreement on such a limitation between the parties.[43] In the light of the actual practice, however, the practice of limiting the scope of the provisional application of FTAs to *"matters falling within the Union's competence"* does not seem to have become an issue. The other contracting parties generally seem to have accepted the practiceand there seems to be no evidence of instances where the EU would have sought to evade one of its treaty obligations by invoking limitations to its competence.[44] In that regard, it should also be remembered that the caveat made by the Union always refers to the EU's competence rather than the much narrower category of the Union's exclusive competence. Therefore, and given the broad character of the definition of the scope of the Union's external competence,[45] it seems plausible to assume that

---

42   See Opinion 2/15 (Free Trade Agreement between the European Union and the Republic of Singapore), EU:C:2017:376, para. 33–167.

43   Guideline 12 (Agreement to provisional application with limitations deriving from internal law of States and rules of international organizations) of the draft *Guide to the Provisional Application of Treaties* (n. 2) adopted by the ILC on first reading, refers to the right of a State or an international organization "[...] *to agree in the treaty or otherwise to the provisional application of the treaty or a part of the treaty with limitations deriving from the internal law of the State or from the rules of the organization.*" However, the commentary (para. 4) explains that "[*t*]*he existence of any such limitations* [...] *needs only to be sufficiently clear in the treaty itself, the separate treaty or in any other form of agreement to provisionally apply a treaty or a part of a treaty*".

44   Cf. the practice concerning mixed multilateral conventions in respect of which non-EU parties often insist on the EU to provide a declaration of competence specifying the division of competence between the Union and its Member States. On this practice, see J. Heliskoski, 'EU Declarations of Competence and International Responsibility', in M. Evans, P. Koutrakos (Eds.), *The International Responsibility of the European Union. European and International Perspectives* (Oxford, Hart Publishing, 2013), p. 189.

45   See Art. 216(1) TFEU.

those provisions of an FTA that are identified as being provisionally applied would fall, in any event, within the scope of the Union's competence. Therefore, rather than delimiting the scope of application of the agreement vis-à-vis the other contracting party, the standard caveat limiting the provisional application to "*matters falling within the Union's competence*" mainly seems to serve the purpose of accommodating the concerns of Member States over the scope of the provisional application by the EU touching upon areas of Member State competence.[46] On the other hand, the provisions that are *excluded* from the scope of the provisional application of an FTA by the Union should not necessarily be interpreted as falling outside the Union's competence.

3.3   *The Material Scope of Provisional Application of FTA s in Practice*

A question that is distinct from the *legal techniques* for defining the scope of provisional application concerns the identification, in the actual practice, of the *substantive policy areas* that are either included in or excluded from the scope of the provisional application of the EU's FTA s.

It may be only natural that the thrust of provisional application of FTA s has traditionally concerned areas falling within the Union's exclusive competence, covering, notably, *trade* under Article 207 TFEU on the Common Commercial Policy.[47] However, the scope of provisional application of FTA s has broadened over the years, often going beyond trade-related elements into areas ranging from economic cooperation to the Common Foreign and Security Policy (CFSP).[48] A recent example is the Cuba CA the provisional application of which covers,[49] inter alia, Political Dialogue (Part II), Cooperation

---

46   G. Van der Loo, R. Wessel (n. 19), p. 755–6. Another common device to alleviate the above concern is to include, in the Decision of the Council on the provisional application of an agreement by the Union, a statement that "the provisional application of parts of the Agreement by the Union does not prejudge the allocation of competences between the Union and Member States in accordance with the Treaties".

47   There may however be exceptional cases in which the provisional application of an FTA does not cover the trade provisions of an agreement, as was initially the case with the Ukraine AA. The provisional application that started on 21 March 2014 pursuant to Council Decision (2014/295/EU) of 17 March 2014 on the signing and provisional application of the Agreement (OJ 2014, L 161) only covered Title I, Articles 4, 5 and 6 of Title II and Title VII (with the exception of Article 479(1)) of the Agreement. Provisional application of, *inter alia*, Part IV (Trade and Trade-related Matters) was later covered by Council Decision (2014/668/EU) (OJ 2014, L 278).

48   See C. Kaddous & N. Piçarra (n. 9), p. 19, and G. Van der Loo &R. Wessel (n. 19), p. 755.

49   See Council Decision (EU) 2016/2232 on the signing and provisional application of the Agreement, OJ 2016, L 337.

and Sector-policy Dialogue (Part III)[50] and Trade and Trade Cooperation (Part IV).[51]

Apart from the broadening of the scope of provisional application of FTA s, the practice shows that the Council is somewhat *inconsistent* in the way it decides to either include a certain subject-area within the scope of provisional application or exclude it from that scope. While an exhaustive account of all post-Lisbon FTA s would not be possible for reasons of space, the following *examples* could serve to illustrate the inconsistent nature of the Council's practice:[52]

> First, *"political dialogue"* is *excluded* from the scope of provisional application of the Iraq PCA and the Central America AA but it is *included* therein in the case of the Korea FA, the Georgia AA, the Moldova AA, the Ukraine AA, the Kazakhstan EPCA, the Australia FA, the New Zealand PARC, the Cuba CA, the Afghanistan CA and the Armenia PA.

> Secondly, *"readmission of nationals"* is *excluded* from the scope of provisional application of the Central America AA, the Iraq PCA, the Kazakhstan EPCA, the Australia FA, the New Zealand PARC and but it is *included* therein in the case of the Korea FA, the Georgia AA, the Moldova AA, the Ukraine AA, the Cuba CA, the Afghanistan CA and the Armenia PA.

> Thirdly, *"portfolio investment"* is *excluded* from the scope of provisional application of the Canada CETA but it is *included* therein in the case of the Korea FTA.[53] Moreover, investment is wholly or partly excluded from the scope of provisional application of the Kazakhstan EPCA, the Australia FA, the New Zealand PARC and the Armenia PA while no

---

50 Covering democracy, human rights and good governance (Title II); promotion of justice, citizen security and migration (Title III) (with exception of money laundering (Art. 29) and consular protection (Art. 35)); social development and social cohesion (Title IV); environment, disaster risk management and climate change (Title V); economic development (Title VI) (with exception of transport (Art. 55) insofar as concerns cooperation on maritime transport as well as good governance in taxation (Art. 58); and regional integration and cooperation (Title VII).

51 With the exception of the provisions on customs (Art. 71) to the extent that they concern border security, and intellectual property (Art. 73) insofar as it concerns cooperation on non-agricultural geographical indications.

52 There may of course be differences in the nature of both the agreements themselves and their individual provisions that make it difficult to compare the scope of provisional application under the various FTA s.

53 This point has also been made in D. Kleimann, G. Kübek, 'The signing, provisional application, and conclusion of trade and investment agreements in the EU: the case of CETA and Opinion 2/15', (2016) *EUI Working Papers* 2016/58, p. 16.

limitations in that regard apply to the Korea FA, the Iraq PCA, the Peru & Colombia FTA, the Central America AA, the Georgia AA, the Ukraine AA, the EPA/SADC EPA States, the Cuba CA, the Afghanistan CA and the Armenia PA.[54]

Fourthly, "*criminal enforcement of intellectual property rights*" is *excluded* from the scope of provisional application of the Central America AA, the Korea FTA, the Georgia AA, the Moldova AA, the Ukraine AA, the Australia FA, the New Zealand PARC and the Kazakhstan EPCA but it is, in principle, *included* therein in the case of the Iraq PCA, the Peru & Colombia FTA, the EPA/SADC EPA States and the Cuba CA.

Fifthly, "*environment and/or climate change*" is *excluded* from the scope of provisional application of the Central America AA, the Georgia AA, Moldova AA, the Kazakhstan EPCA, the Australia FA, the New Zealand PARC, the Armenia PA, the Afghanistan CA but it is *included* therein in the case of the Korea FA, the Korea FTA, the Iraq PCA, the Peru & Colombia FTA, the Ukraine AA and the Cuba CA.

In addition, there are several areas or subjects that are typically (but not always) excluded from the scope of the provisional application of the EU's FTAs. They include *CFSP policies* such as disarmament and non-proliferation of weapons of mass destruction; serious crimes of international concern and the International Criminal Court; small arms and light weapons and fight against terrorism. In the field of the Freedom, Security and Justice, excluded from the scope of provisional application are typically the protection of personal data; migration, asylum and border management, fight against organised crime and corruption, combating illicit drugs; and money laundering and terrorism financing. In the area of trade, criminal enforcement of intellectual property rights stands out. Finally, certain *sectoral policies* such as transport policy; economic dialogue or cooperation; employment and social policy; public health; education, training and youth; tourism; research and technological development; and disaster risk management tend to be excluded from the scope of provisional application. Again, however, the picture is not entirely consistent as many of these areas or subjects have been subject to provisional application in the case of the Korea FA, the Iraq PCA and the Cuba CA, in particular. The existence of such exceptions shows that an exclusion of a particular provision from the scope of provisional application does not seem to be based on a

---

54   It has to be noted that the commitments in the field of investment differ greatly from one agreement to another.

perceived lack of the Union's competence. Rather, there may either be a desire of the Council not to exercise the Union's competence or a political decision that provisional application of a given provision is not, in a given case, appropriate or desirable.

4   Termination of Provisional Application

While provisional application of a treaty produces legal effects as if the treaty were actually in force, Article 25 of the VCLT[55] provides a more flexible way of terminating the provisional application. Under that provision, provisional application may be terminated if a State notifies the other States between which the treaty is being applied provisionally of its intention not to become a party to the treaty, unless the treaty otherwise provides or the negotiating States have otherwise agreed. In other words, unless the treaty provides otherwise, a State (or an international organisation) may unilaterally terminate provisional application at any time.[56] Some (but not all) of the EU's post-Lisbon FTAs contain express provisions on the termination of their provisional application by means of a written notification to the other party or the depositary of the agreement. The termination then takes effect after a period specified in the agreement has passed from the notification.[57] The remainder of the FTAs fall back upon the general rules of international law on the provisional application of treaties, enabling, as explained above, unilateral termination of the provisional application with an immediate effect.

Those FTAs containing provisions on the matter provide for the right to terminate provisional application by "a party". Given the standard definition of a

---

55   For a similar provision, see Art. 25 of the VCLTIO.

56   See *First report on the provisional application of treaties* by Juan Manuel Gómez-Robledo, Special Rapporteur of the International Law Commission, UN doc A/CN.4/633 (3 June 2013), para. 50, referring to Section 3.4 of the United Nation's *Treaty Handbook* (UN publications, Sales No. E.12.V.1, 2012). See also J. Czuczai, 'Mixity in Practice: Some Problems and Their (Real or Possible) Solutions', in C. Hillion, P. Koutrakos (n. 1), p. 243–4 and F. Hoffmeister, 'Curse of Blessing? Mixed Agreements in the Recent Practice of the European Union and its Member States', in C. Hillion, P. Koutrakos (n. 1), p. 258–9. For a more limitative reading of Art. 25 of the VCLT, see L. Bartels, 'Withdrawing Provisional Application of Treaties: Has the EU Made a Mistake?', *Cambridge Journal of International and Comparative Law*, vol. I (1) (2012), p. 118.

57   The termination takes effect "*on the first day of the month following notification*" (Korea FTA); "*on the first day of the second month following [the] notification*" (Canada CETA); or "*six months after the receipt of the notification by the depositary*" (Central America AA, Moldova AA, Ukraine AA, Kazakhstan AA, Armenia AA).

party in EU's FTA s,[58] that right is attributable to the European Union and, if an FTA is applied provisionally by Member States (as in the case of the FA Korea), to Member States, within their respective areas of competence. However, since the entry into force of an agreement requires the completion of ratification or other procedures by all the parties (including all of the Member States), the question arises as to whether a notification by a Member State of its intention not to ratify the agreement has any implications on the provisional application of an agreement by the EU. Could the provisional application of the agreement as between the EU and the third State continue in spite of the notification, or could the notification by a Member State also vitiate the basis of the provisional application between the EU and third State?

As a matter of international law, no obstacles to continued provisional application of the agreement appear to exist between the EU and the third State if neither the Union nor the third State wishes to terminate it in the light of the notification of by Member State. While Article 25 of the VCLT refers to the provisional application of a treaty *"pending its entry into force"*, paragraph 2 of the provision governs the termination of provisional application of a treaty or a part of a treaty *"with respect to a State [...]"* *if that State notifies [...] of its intention not to become a party to the treaty"* (emphasis added). In other words, a notification by a Member State of its intention not to ratify an agreement could only have implications on the possible provisional application of the agreement by that Member State, not by the EU. Moreover, a delay (even if that was significant) or reduced probability of ratification is not, as such, a ground for termination of provisional application.[59] Therefore, provisional application of an agreement between the EU and a third State would only be terminated if *those parties* agreed upon such termination or if one of *them* notified the other of its intention not to become a party to the agreement, in accordance with the principles set out in Article 25 of the VCLT.[60]

Insofar as EU law is concerned, it follows from Article 216(2) TFEU that the treaty-obligations covered by the decision of the Union to apply the agreement would continue to bind the Member State concerned *qua* Member State of the EU. Whether a notification by a Member State of its intention not to ratify a

---

58   As regards the definition of the term "the Parties", see n. 16.
59   See *Provisional Application of Treaties*, Memorandum by the Secretariat, a description of the procedural history of the consideration by the ILC of the negotiation, at the 1968–69 Vienna Conference on the Law of Treaties, of Art. 25 of the VCLT, UN doc A/CN.4/658 (1 March 2013), para. 101–8. It emerges from the Memorandum that provisions to this effect were discussed but not adopted by the Conference. See also Report on the work of the sixty-seventh session (2015) of the ILC, UN doc A/70/10 (14 August 2015), para. 282.
60   In a similar vein C. Kaddous, N. Piçarra (n. 9), p. 21.

mixed agreement would create an obligation (based, e.g. on Article 4(3) TEU) for the Union to terminate the provisional application on its behalf is an open question as there is no case law on the matter.[61] What seems to be clear is that a decision to terminate the provisional application by the EU should be taken in accordance with the applicable Union procedures as set out in Article 218 TFEU.[62] It could be argued that the institutions should apply the same procedure as for the decision to provisionally apply the agreement.[63]

One could also defend the view that a notification by a Member State of its intention not to ratify an FTA has no immediate implications for its provisional application between the EU and the third State concerned on practical grounds. There is namely always a possibility that the Member State in question might reconsider its position, and there are ways to entice it to do so.[64] First, the parties could amend the agreement in order to make the recalcitrant Member State to change its position. Secondly, a legal (or political) act other than an amendment to the agreement – for example, a declaration clarifying the interpretation of some of its provisions – might be sufficient in that regard, as demonstrated by the Decision of the Heads of State or Government of the 28 Member States designed to persuade The Netherlands to ratify Ukraine AA.[65]

---

61   For an incident of one Member State invoking Art. 25(2) of the VCLT in order to prevent the (partial) provisional application of the Agreement on Trade, Development and Cooperation between the European Community and its Member States, of the one part, and the Republic of South Africa, of the other part (OJ 1999, L 311/3), see A. Rosas, 'The Future of Mixity', in C. Hillion, P. Koutrakos (n. 1), p. 367–70.

62   See the statements entered into Council minutes upon signature of the Canada CETA on behalf of the Union (OJ 2017, L 11). The Council stated that "[i]f the ratification of CETA fails permanently and definitively because of a ruling of a constitutional court, or following the completion of other constitutional processes and formal notification by the government of the concerned state, provisional application must be and will be terminated. The necessary steps will be taken in accordance with EU procedures." The declarations of certain Member States imply that a Member State could invoke Art. 30.7(3)(c) of the Agreement concerning termination of provisional application and thereby trigger the relevant "EU procedures". See the declaration by Germany and Austria providing that "[...] as Parties to CETA they can exercise their rights which derive from Article 30.7(3)(c) of CETA. The necessary steps will be taken in accordance with EU procedures" and by Poland declaring that "[...] as a Party to CETA it can exercise its right which derives from Article 30.7.(3)(c) of CETA. All necessary steps will be taken in accordance with the EU procedures." Belgium (ibid, at 17) "[...] noted the right of each party to end the provisional application of CETA in accordance with Article 30.7 of the agreement." See Van der Loo (n. 19), p. 29–31 and, for an analysis of the German and Austrian statements, see D. Kleimann, G. Kübek (n. 55), p. 20–21.

63   G. Van der Loo, R. Wessel (n. 19), p. 761–2.

64   On various solutions, see G. Van der Loo, R. Wessel (n. 19), p. 762–8.

65   For the text of the Decision, see http://www.consilium.europa.eu/en/press/press-releases/2016/12/15-euco-conclusions-ukraine/.

5   Conclusions

If, as a matter of international law, flexibility and voluntary nature are conceived of as central attributes of the technique of provisional application of treaties,[66] the practice of provisional application of FTAs of the EU certainly lives up to those characteristics. In the period from the entry into force of the Treaty of Lisbon to the present day, the technique of provisional application has enabled to speed up considerably the entry into force of trade and, increasingly, other provisions of FTAs. While the ratification and definitive entry into force of FTAs easily takes several years from the signature of an agreement, it is usually possible to begin the provisional application within a few months after the signature. In this way, the technique considerably alleviates the inconveniences arising from the delayed entry into force of mixed agreements.

The flexibility of provisional application is also demonstrated by the practice of how the parties define the scope of provisional application. While areas such as trade are as a rule included, the technique enables the parties to select, on a case-by-case basis, the provisions that become subject to provisional application – a possibility that the parties clearly make use of in deciding the scope of provisional application of each new FTA. In that sense, the technique of provisional application is a device of choice à la carte, rather a set menu of the kitchen. The practice also shows that the scope of provisional application is expanding from the traditional pattern of confining it to trade towards the inclusion of other policy areas such as justice and home affairs and even the CFSP. However, a lot depends also on the nature of the provisions in question. In areas other than trade, provisions which *"are limited to declarations of the contracting parties on the aims that their cooperation must pursue and the subjects to which that cooperation will have to relate"*[67] – as the Court of Justice recently described the CFSP-related provisions on, inter alia, conflict prevention and crisis management as well as regional stability in the Kazakhstan EPCA, both covered by the provisional application – are perhaps more likely to become subject to provisional application than provisions that set out obligations determining in concrete terms the manner in which cooperation is to be implemented.

One important aspect of the practice concerning provisional application of the EU's FTAs relates to the way in which the Member State are willing to enable the Council to exercise not only exclusive but also non-exclusive (shared, complementary or CFSP) competences of the Union in the context of accepting

---

66   See paragraph 7 of the general commentary to the *Guide to the Provisional Application of Treaties* (n. 2).

67   Case C-244/17, *Commission v Council*, EU:C:2018:662, para. 45 (emphasis added).

the provisional application of an agreement by the Union. At the stage of conclusion of international agreements of a mixed character by the Union, the Member States are still much more reluctant to allow to the Council to exercise such potential competence, presumably out of the fear of pre-emption and supremacy that the exercise of shared competence may entail under Article 2(2) TFEU. Whether the exercise of shared competence in the context provisional application would give rise to pre-emption and supremacy – with implications on the stage of conclusion of an agreement – is an open question in the absence of case law. However, the willingness of the Member States to enable the Council to make use of the Union's non-exclusive competence for the purposes of accepting provisional application of FTAs is yet another illustration of the flexibility of the technique of provisional application of treaties.

The question as to the implications of a refusal by a Member State to ratify an FTA for the continuation of its provisional application is also one to which no definitive answers may be given in the absence of practice. In the case of the Ukraine AA, that question was avoided by a political solution enabling the Netherlands to go reconsider its position and go ahead with the ratification. The moment of truth may well come with the Canada CETA in respect of which there is political uncertainty surrounding national ratification procedures in certain Member States. A possible refusal by a Member State (or Member States) to ratify the Agreement may mark the ultimate test of the cherished flexibility of technique of provisional application for FTAs. However, over the years, the EU's institutions have shown a considerable ability to find their way out of various impasses and it is difficult to imagine that they could not work out a solution this time around, too.

Finally, it remains to be seen how the new practice – reflecting the definition of the Union's competence in external economic relations as laid down by the Court in Opinion 2/15 on the Singapore FTA – of "splitting" agreements into a free trade agreement to be concluded only by the Union in its own right and an agreement on the protection of investment to be concluded as a mixed agreement is going to affect the role of provisional application in the Union's external relations. So far, the technique has only been applied to the FTAs negotiated with Singapore[68] and Vietnam.[69] Obviously, there is no need for

---

68 See Council Decision 2018/1599 of 15 October 2018 on the signing, on behalf of the European Union, of the Free Trade Agreement between the European Union and the Republic of Singapore (OJ 2018, L267/1) and Council Decision 2018/1676 of 15 October 2018 on the signing, on behalf of the European Union, of the Investment Protection Agreement between the European Union and its Member States, of the one part, and the Republic of Singapore, of the other part (OJ 2018, L279/1).

69 See Council Decision 2019/1121 of 25 June 2019 on the signing, on behalf of the European Union, of the Free Trade Agreement between the European Union and the Socialist

provisional application of the part covered by the trade agreements in order to speed up their entry into force during the delay traditionally caused by ratifications of the Member States. As regards the part concerning the protection of investment, the Commission has not proposed provisional application of the investment protection agreements with Singapore and Vietnam.[70] Whether or not the technique of splitting of trade agreements will become the prevailing practice, is however unlikely to do away with the need for provisional application of the Union's FTAs. This is the case because the scope of many of the FTAs is much broader than that of the agreements concluded with Singapore and Vietnam, extending well beyond the confines of the Union's exclusive external competence.

Republic of Viet Nam (OJ 2019, L177/1) and Council Decision 2019/1096 of 25 June 2019 on the signing, on behalf of the Union, of the Investment Protection Agreement between the European Union and its Member States, of the one part, and the Socialist Republic of Viet Nam, of the other part (OJ 2019, L175/1).

70   In the proposals for Council decisions on the signing of the Investment Protection Agreements, the Commission explained that "[it] *is mindful of the balance to be struck between moving forward with the reformed EU investment policy and the sensitivities of EU Member States as regards the possible exercise of shared competence on these matters*" and, therefore, it had not had not made a proposal to provisionally apply the agreements. However, the Commission said it was ready to make such a proposal, should Member States wish the Commission to do so (see COM(2018) 195 final of 18 April 2018, p. 8, (Singapore) and COM(2018) 694 final of 17 October 2018, p. 8, (Vietnam)).

Index

Studies in EU External Relations

Edited by

Marc Maresceau (*Ghent University*)